Teach Your Child
to
Swim

Teach Your Child
to
Swim

Susan Meredith

with Carol Hicks
Swimming consultant and Amateur Swimming Association staff tutor,
Crystal Palace National Sports Centre

and Jackie Stephens
Amateur Swimming Association tutor,
Crystal Palace National Sports Centre

Designed by Joanne Kirkby

Illustrated by Roger Fereday

With advice from the Amateur Swimming Association:
Alison Bell, Mary Bainbridge, Jean Findlay, Jean Cook, Lorna Hunt

Edited by Robyn Gee
Revision editor: Kirsteen Rogers
Series editor: Felicity Brooks
Cover designer: Laura Hammonds
Cover illustrator: Shelagh McNicholas

With thanks to:
Little Dippers and Waterbaby
and
Amateur Swimming Association

Association for Spina Bifida and Hydrocephalus
The Royal Life Saving Society UK
Scope
Epilepsy Action
UK Deaf Sport
Down's Syndrome Association
The National Autistic Society
Diabetes UK
Asthma UK
RNIB

Contents

Teaching children to swim

Swimming is a very valuable skill to teach children. It helps them keep safe, it's an excellent all-round form of exercise they can do throughout their life, and it can be relaxing, exciting, therapeutic and, of course, fun.

One-to-one support

Research has shown that children make most progress in swimming when they're introduced to the water by a parent, carer or other adult they know well. The close one-to-one relationship makes it easier to build up their confidence, which is essential for learning to swim.

You don't have to be an expert swimmer yourself, or even to swim at all, to get children started, as long as you're confident walking in shallow water. All you should be aiming to do in the early stages is to enjoy being in the water together.

Using this book

The first part of this book has ideas for safe and gentle introductory activities. The emphasis is on allowing children to go at their own pace without putting them under pressure.

Once children are afloat, you can move on to the chapters that introduce swimming strokes and other water skills. You may be able to use these to improve your own swimming as well. As the children get older, you could work together to improve each other's performance. Older children might find it helpful to read the strokes and water skills sections for themselves, and you can encourage children of all ages to look at the pictures.

Close support from a trusted adult is very important for building up a small child's confidence in water.

When to start

Some people believe that after nine months in a fluid environment babies are born without fear of water and able to swim, so the sooner you introduce them to the water, the better. There are specific methods for helping very small babies learn to swim, and some of them have achieved spectacular results.

Current medical thinking is that you can take children into a well-ventilated swimming pool at any age (normally around four to five months), whether or not they've been immunized, as long as the water is warm enough. Psychologically, it's best if babies are used to going in the big bath at home before you take them to a pool.

Babies who are just learning to sit up often need extra encouragement to relax and lie flat in the water.

The ideal age

For many babies, four to five months can be the ideal age to start going to the pool. By about six months they're usually starting to sit up and will try to do this in the water as well as out of it. By eight to nine months they're often becoming more fearful both of water and strange environments. In general, the older children are when they first start going swimming, the more apprehensive they're likely to be. That said, there's no point in going swimming early if you don't feel you're both ready.

Tip...

Once you start, try to go swimming regularly. Children learn much more in short, frequent visits than in occasional long ones.

Keep it fun

The first step towards learning to swim is feeling at ease in the water, so it's well worth planning ahead to make sure a child's first experience of swimming is a happy one.

As children progress, remember that swimming should carry on being fun. Although the different strokes and skills are explained in some detail, don't become too concerned with achieving the perfect style. Many of the best swimmers swim at least partly by instinct and wouldn't be able to analyse what they do. Improvement often comes naturally with plenty of progressive practice and, above all, continued enjoyment of the water.

In the bath

Bathtime provides a great opportunity to prepare babies and young children for going swimming. Washing them gets them used to feeling water on their head, face and body, and play activities in the bath can help get them ready for future activities at the swimming pool.

Babies and water

Babies are used to moving their arms and legs about in a fluid environment before birth and will do the same when they're put in water soon after they're born, as long as they feel relaxed and safe.

As they develop, many babies and young children go through various phases in their attitude to water. Some babies feel insecure at first when their clothes are taken off, and many actively dislike bathtime at some stage. None of the bath play activities shown here should be forced on children who aren't enjoying them. If children who were previously happy in the water suddenly become unhappy, just revert to earlier, gentler activities until the phase passes.

Giving reassurance

Always reassure babies during bathtime by chatting, smiling and singing to them. Remember to praise them often and maintain eye contact as much as possible. Keep the emphasis on fun and helping them to feel happy and confident in the water. Bath play also gives you the chance to become more used to handling a baby in water. It's important that you're confident with the activities, as babies sense this and find it reassuring.

Bathtime provides an ideal opportunity for babies to get used to being in water.

8

Safety...

Timing

The most practical time for bath play is at a baby's usual bathtime. Do it before you wash them, as soapy water can make them slippery to hold. Keep bathtime short to start with, then gradually lengthen it, taking your cue from the child. To start with, very young babies may stay in water of a suitable temperature for about five minutes. You can build this up little by little to 10–15 minutes by the age of three months.

Warm air and water

Bathtime provides children's first experiences of water so try to keep them as relaxed as possible, making sure they aren't put off by feeling cold.

For young babies the water temperature needs to be between 29°C (84°F) and 32°C (90°F). The water should feel warm to your elbow or the inside of your wrist. If you want to measure the temperature more accurately, you could use a thermometer. The bathroom needs to be warm too, with the temperature as high as 24°C (75°F) if you can manage it.

Bathtime activities

The next few pages suggest activities that can be used in the bath. Many of them can be used in the baby bath, in the big bath and eventually in the swimming pool. By repeating activities at each stage, you can help children progress confidently to each environment in turn. Always build up the activities gradually, and make sure children are happy with one activity before moving on to the next.

In the baby bath

To support a baby in the bath, slip your hand behind their neck so their head is supported by your forearm and hold the top of the arm furthest away from you. Put your other hand under their bottom and lower them gently into the bath, keeping their head clear of the water. You can then take your hand from under their bottom and use it for some of the water activities described over the page and, later, for washing them.

Maintain eye contact and keep smiling and talking reassuringly.

If the baby is happy in the bath, slip your free hand under their bottom again and then slowly lower their head until the ears are just submerged for a short time. Avoid this activity if the baby has sensitive ears or is suffering from an ear infection.

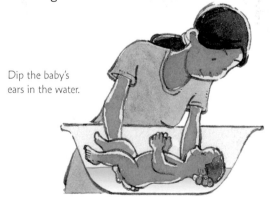

Dip the baby's ears in the water.

You may be able to take your hand from under their bottom and use it to attract their attention from above. This gives the baby something to look at and helps them to adopt a flatter body position in the water.

Swishing to and fro

Gently swish the baby backwards and forwards in the bath, with one hand under their head and the other under their bottom. Avoid letting water splash their face at this stage. Once babies have learned to sit up, at around six to nine months, they may show signs of distress when put on their back in the bath, and prefer to sit up.

Encouraging breath control

It's worth trying to get babies used to water on their head and face right from the start. Let them know that something is going to happen by saying something like, "Ready, go!" before you start. Babies learn to recognize this as a cue to hold their breath and not to suck in water. Without this cue, they might try to snatch a quick breath and start to cough or choke.

Use your fingers to sprinkle a little water over the baby. Start with their body and shoulders then progress to the back of their head. If they enjoy it, gradually sprinkle water further forwards on their head and let a little trickle over their face. Use the warning cue, "Ready, go!".

Tip...

Singing nursery rhymes or action songs to accompany activities such as sprinkling water, floating and swishing can help make the experience fun. Songs can also provide continuity if you repeat them when your baby transfers to a swimming pool.

Sponges, bottles and beakers

Use the "Ready, go!" cue and gently squeeze a sponge near the baby, to show what happens. Then squeeze it over their body, shoulders and the back of their head, repeating the cue with each squeeze. As they get more comfortable with the sensation, let a little water trickle over their face. Let them play with the sponge too.

Repeat the activity using plastic containers, such as bottles and beakers. Remember to give your cue before you start. Babies often enjoy playing with the containers too, and with other bath toys that squirt, sprinkle and pour.

Use sponges, cups and sprinkle toys to introduce babies to different sensations during their bathtime.

Preparing for the big bath

At two or three months old, some babies are ready to go in the big bath. This may seem vast to them, compared with the baby bath, so a good intermediate step is to put the baby bath inside the big bath. This allows them to get used to the larger area gradually.

A non-slip mat on the bottom of the big bath gives extra security and protection, but it is still never safe to leave babies or young children unsupervised in the bath.

In the big bath

Once they are in the big bath, repeat the activities they've done in the baby bath. Keep using your cue and reassure the baby constantly by maintaining eye contact, smiling and talking.

Babies under about six months may float happily on their back with just a hand under their head.

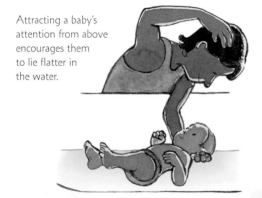

Attracting a baby's attention from above encourages them to lie flatter in the water.

As they get older, gradually encourage them to lie flat in the bath without support. The water must be shallow enough to come only half-way up their head, so their face is well clear of the water. Encourage them to kick by gently holding their legs below the knee and moving them up and down, keeping them as straight as possible and repeating the cue, "Kick, kick!".

On their front

From about three to four months, babies may also like lying on their front in shallow water. Support them from behind under their shoulders, with your fingers across their chest and your thumbs uppermost. Then move them gently to and fro.

If the baby is too young to support their head, stretch your fingers under their chin to prevent their face going in the water. Babies might curl their legs up under them to start with, but they'll gradually learn to relax and straighten out.

You can't maintain eye contact in this activity, so reassure the baby by talking.

Older babies or young children may enjoy walking their hands or forearms along the bottom of the bath while kicking their legs gently. They can do this on their back as well as on their front.

Sitting babies in the middle of the bath leaves room for you to support them from behind and keeps them at a safe distance from the taps.

Water play

Once babies are able to sit up in the bath, give them a selection of toys, such as sponges and plastic watering cans or other sprinkle toys, to play with. Containers are good because they give babies the opportunity to pour water over themselves. Besides bath toys, you could give them plastic containers, spoons, ladles, strainers and funnels from the kitchen.

Encourage babies to splash with their hands by putting floating toys such as ducks in front of them and showing them how to push them along. Reaching out to play with toys helps develop their arm movements too. It's better to let them do the splashing, although they may enjoy you gently splashing their tummy or back.

Ears under

At each bathtime, encourage older babies or children to lie flat on their backs with their shoulders or, even better, their ears, under water. Afterwards, let the water drain from their ears by tilting their head to each side for a few seconds, and dry them with a towel. Avoid the activity if they have sensitive ears or an ear infection.

Blowing bubbles

Blowing bubbles in the water is an important skill as it's the first stage in learning to breathe correctly when swimming. This can be started in the bath from the age of 12 months.

Start by blowing bubbles across the surface of the water.

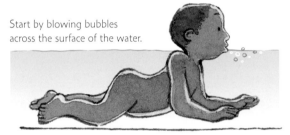

Once they can blow bubbles across the surface, get them to blow with their mouth under water, progressing to submerging their nose, eyes then face as they blow. Encourage them to keep their eyes open under water, by getting them to pick up small objects from the bottom of the bath.

In the bath together

Sharing a bath with your child, from the age of about two months, does a lot to build their confidence, especially if they're nervous of water. It's easier if a second person lifts the baby in and out of the bath. Start with familiar activities you've done in the baby bath and big bath then move on to the ones suggested here.

Young children can be encouraged in their bath play by sharing a bath with an older child. You'll need to supervise even more closely than usual, and it may be safer to avoid a shared bath at the stage when a baby is learning to stand up.

Supported floating

Sit behind the baby and hold them with your hands under their shoulders and thumbs over the top. Press your wrists and forearms together to support their head, and see if the baby is happy to float in this way. Small babies often float easily like this, but they stop floating so well once they can sit up because they try to sit up in the water. When they are comfortable in this position, slowly swish them to and fro, avoiding water flowing over their face.

Gliding and kicking

From the age of three to four months, you can lie babies on their front, face to face with you. Hold them under their arms with your wrists together to support their chin and keep their face out of the water, then gently glide them back and forth. Don't insist on doing this activity if they dislike going on their front. Next, let the baby lie in your lap on their back, hold their legs below the knees and move them to simulate kicking, repeating the cue, "Kick, kick!".

You may like to prepare babies for their first visit to a pool by putting a swim nappy on them, and wearing your swimsuit.

Babies may rest on your legs to start with: they'll probably stretch out into a floating position as they relax.

Tip...

If you are intending to put armbands on your child at the swimming pool, it's a good idea to let them try them on and play with them in the bath before they wear them at the pool.

Sharing a bath with your children is an ideal way to get them used to being in the water with you.

Finding a suitable pool

Swimming pool facilities vary considerably and it may be worth travelling a little further afield than you otherwise would to find one with specially good facilities for babies and young children.

Access to the pool

Find out how easy it is to get to the swimming pool. Are there access ramps for pushchairs and wheelchairs? Check the public transport service to the pool or, if you are going by car, find out how easy it is to get from the car park to the pool.

Teaching pools

Is there a separate pool for small children? These are often called teaching pools and are usually about 1m (3ft) deep throughout or graduated from 0.5m (1ft 6in) to 1m (3ft). The water is warmer than the main pools, and the atmosphere is usually more relaxed and inviting. Check when the pool is open, and find out when it is quietest. Babies and toddlers are likely to be upset or distracted by a lot of noise and activity. Before you go, it's also a good idea to find out whether swimming hats are required.

All non-swimmers need warm water, and it's essential for babies. They lose heat quickly, but don't have a shiver reflex, so they can get extremely cold very quickly, with no apparent symptoms until they start to turn blue. For babies and toddlers the water needs to be at least 29°C (84°F) to be safe, and is better between 30°C (86°F) and 31°C (88°F). By the time a child is three, 28°C (82°F) is enough. It is recommended that the air temperature is one or two degrees higher than the water temperature.

Tip...

Some swimming pools have information about temperatures on display to the public; if not, you could ask a staff member.

The warm air and water in teaching pools provide a relaxing and comfortable environment for adults and children.

Changing facilities

Are the changing facilities suitable for babies and young children and accessible by male and female carers? There should be changing mats or changing tables, bins for nappies, playpens or special chairs to put babies in while you get changed and non-slip matting on the floor. You may need to check whether the changing facilities are suitable for people with disabilities, with extra space, grab rails, a changing bed and a shower chair available.

Find out where the lockers are, and what (if any) the charge is for using them. If you plan to bring a pushchair, wheelchair or car seat, check out storage facilities for these too.

Ideally, the toilets should be fairly near the pool, especially for newly potty-trained toddlers or children for whom continence management is an ongoing issue.

Water depth

If the water is shallow, between 0.3m and 0.5m (1ft and 1ft 6in), it's easy to get in and out. Some children find shallow water less intimidating as they can stand without using flotation aids and they're likely to be able to lie horizontally in the water without aids at an earlier stage. If there is an area of very shallow water, young children can sit, crawl or splash about. However, children may become too used to having their feet on the floor, and the constant bending down may cause back problems for some adults.

In deeper water, between 1m and 1.3m (3ft and 4ft), adults can usually hold children more comfortably and maintain eye contact easily. Children can try a wider variety of entries, such as jumping in, with and without adult support, and they may learn to swim earlier, as their feet can't touch the bottom. It may be more difficult to get into and out of the pool, though. Adults who are nervous of water may feel less secure and the water may be cooler, which can be off-putting. Children may need to use flotation aids for more of the time, and they may find themselves out of their depth more quickly.

Getting in and out

How do you get into and out of the pool? Some toddlers prefer to walk into the water rather than being carried. A gentle slope or wide, shallow steps are best for this. Wheelchair users may prefer a sloped entry, or need a hoist, which some pools have available on request.

This teaching pool is shallow enough for toddlers to walk confidently, and deep enough for them to try getting afloat.

What to take

A visit to the swimming pool will be a much more enjoyable experience for you and the child if you come well prepared. Here are a few suggestions of things you might need to consider.

Swim nappies or pants

Children who aren't yet potty trained will need to wear a swim nappy. These can be disposable or reusable, and come in various sizes and designs, from nappies with Velcro® or tie fastenings to pull-on pants. Most can be worn on their own or underneath swimming costumes.

For a snug leak-free fit, look for styles with adjustable waists and elasticated legs. Babies are likely to be most comfortable in nappies made from breathable waterproof material.

Tip...

Try a new swim nappy on your child before you go to the pool to make sure it's comfortable and fits well.

The other thing to bear in mind when opting for a particular style of swim nappy is how easily you can remove it if the child does a poo.

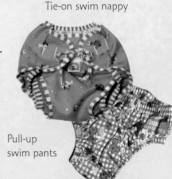

Tie-on swim nappy

Pull-up swim pants

Swimsuits

Choose something that fits well and is easy to get on and off. Look for styles that don't impede movement – swimming trunks, rather than shorts, are better for boys. Make sure your own swimsuit is comfortable and practical, too, and can't be tugged down too easily.

Towels and bath robes

Wrapping children in a big, soft towel or bath robe after they come out of the pool can help them feel warm and secure after their adventures in the water. It will also absorb any leaks while they're not wearing a nappy. A hooded towel has the added advantage that it keeps their head warm while you dry them. An extra towel can be useful, too.

Remember to pack towels for you and the child. The bigger, the better.

Bath toys

Bringing a couple of favourite bath toys to the pool can make children feel more at home. Toys can help them explore the properties of water by watching what floats and what sinks, or by enjoying splashing and pouring. They can also be used in activities that will help build up their confidence in water.

Encouraging children to reach out for toys is a great way to get them to stretch their arms.

Swimming hats

Some swimming pools require users to wear swimming hats. There are two main types. Rubbery ones (made of latex or silicone) are more waterproof, and stretchy cloth ones are more comfortable, and easier to get on and off.

Tip...

Children and adults with long hair should wear it tied back, to keep it out of the way, and to help keep the pool clean.

Goggles

It's best to avoid goggles for babies and young children as they aren't made small enough to get a proper fit. It can also be dangerous if children try to pull them off, as they can bounce back and hit the eyes. Goggles can be useful for contact lens wearers, and older children who spend more time in the water. Some people who wear glasses buy prescription goggles for swimming.

Sun protection

If you're taking children to an outdoor pool, make sure you're both adequately protected from the sun. Use waterproof sunscreen, sunshades and protective clothing as appropriate.

Checklist...

✔ Swim nappy and/or swimsuit
✔ Spare swim nappy
✔ Your swimsuit and towel
✔ Child's towel and hooded bath robe
✔ Swimming hat (if needed)
✔ Flotation aid (if needed)
✔ Tissues for wiping noses
✔ Sun protection, as appropriate
✔ Nappy bag (if needed)
✔ Money for locker
✔ Bath toys
✔ Shampoo and shower kit
✔ Spare socks/pants for child as these often get dropped
✔ Plastic bags for soggy stuff
✔ Bottle of milk for afterwards if child is bottle-fed
✔ Drink for older child
✔ Healthy snacks to nourish and distract afterwards
✔ Toy or bath book to amuse your child while you dress and undress

Flotation aids

There are several types of flotation aid for helping learner swimmers, from simple foam boards to complete buoyancy vests. It's a good idea to see how children get on in the water during early pool visits before deciding what, if any, flotation aid to use.

Safety...

Always remember that flotation aids are NEVER a substitute for close supervision. They will not stop children from drowning.

With and without

It's important that children get used to being in and around water both with and without flotation aids. This means they can experience the support and buoyancy the aids offer, while avoiding becoming overdependent on them and still recognizing that they may not yet be able to swim without support.

Choosing an aid

Whatever type of flotation aid you choose, make sure it meets the national safety standards and bears appropriate safety warnings*. Talk to other adults about their children's experiences with flotation aids, and, if appropriate, borrow one to try it out.

Look for aids that give support and allow children to lie as flat as possible in the water, but don't restrict movement too much. Babies and young children need to get used to the look and feel of an aid before they can use it effectively. These pages contain information about the most common aids.

Flotation aids such as this buoyancy vest can help children gain confidence in the water.

Flotation aids: pros

✓ Build up children's confidence in the water

✓ Can give children stability while they learn swimming postures and actions

✓ Offer variety and relaxation

Flotation aids: cons

✗ Some children become reliant on them and find it difficult to make the transition to unaided swimming

✗ Can foster a false sense of security in some children

✗ Can foster a false sense of security in adults – a flotation aid isn't a life jacket, and children must still be supervised at all times

* In the UK, flotation aids should carry the British Standard number BS EN 13138:2003 and the following warnings: "Use only under competent supervision", "Will not protect against drowning", "To be worn on upper arm only" (for armbands).

Armbands

✓ Encourage independence in water

✗ May restrict arm movement

✗ Not suitable for babies under 12 months

These inflatable plastic cuffs keep the arms afloat while allowing the rest of the body to move freely. Make sure the armbands are small enough to stay on, and choose a style with a flat strip that sits where the arm rests against the upper body, to allow as much arm movement as possible. Styles with two inflatable chambers and safety valves are safest and have the benefit that the amount of air in the lower chamber can be reduced as children gain confidence.

Squeeze the safety valve while inflating or deflating the chamber.

Press the valve down into the inflated chamber.

Tip...

Partially inflate armbands before putting them on children's arms, then finish inflating them once they are in position. Release some of the air before you pull them off.

One advantage of double-chamber armbands like these is that if one part is punctured, the other will still offer children some support.

Armdiscs

✓ Easy to fit

✓ Versatile

✓ Less restrictive than armbands

✗ Not suitable for babies under 12 months

Armdiscs are foam discs that clip together to give variable buoyancy. Most children use three discs on each arm to start with, then gradually reduce the number as they become more confident in the water.

Flexible foam cuffs hold arm discs in place.

Inflatable rings

✗ Unsuitable for non-swimmers

Inflatable rings (rubber rings) are not recommended as flotation aids for non-swimmers. Babies and very young children can fall out of them and, when used with armbands, they can lift a child's body so high out of the water that they lose the ability to balance. Inflatable rings can be fun to play with for older children who can swim.

Baby seats

✓ Allow babies to kick freely

✗ Weight restrictions apply (refer to manufacturers' guidelines)

✗ Can tip up easily

Baby seats like this are safer than rubber rings, but you must still stay close at hand as they can easily topple over.

Floating baby seats are inflatable cushions with a sunken seating pouch that has holes for babies' legs to dangle through. They are suitable for babies who can sit, but who are no more than a certain weight (for example 11.5kg (25lbs)) for each size of seat. They allow babies to splash and kick freely, but they should only be used for a short time, as babies soon get chilly with their shoulders out of the water.

Buoyancy clothing

✓ Many styles to choose from

✓ Some styles allow independence to be built up gradually

✗ Not suitable for babies under 12 months

Buoyancy clothing includes belts, backpack-style harnesses, vests, jackets and bathing suits with built-in or removable foam floats. Styles with removable floats allow children to gain independence gradually.

Buoyancy belt

Floats

✓ Can be used from 12 months

✓ Useful for leg and arm action practice

✗ It is easy for children to let go of them inadvertently

Polystyrene floats are useful for encouraging a horizontal position in the water. There are various types: the most common are flat floats sometimes known as kickboards. You may be able to start using floats with children from as young as one year old, unless they are teething, when they tend to bite pieces out of them, which could cause them to choke.

Pull-buoys are shaped floats, usually used by advanced swimmers, that are held between the legs or ankles for support.

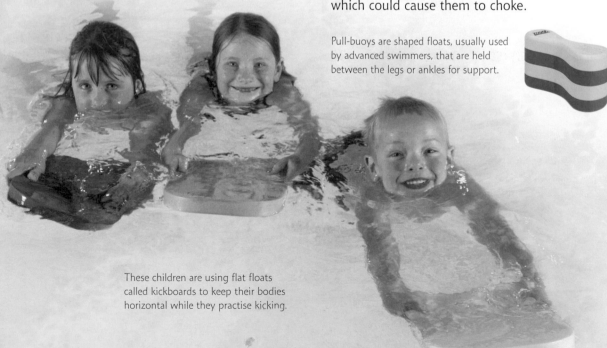

These children are using flat floats called kickboards to keep their bodies horizontal while they practise kicking.

Woggles

✓ Versatile

✓ Allow children to experiment with balance in the water

✓ Allow arms and legs to move freely

✗ Not suitable for babies who are teething

Children can use woggles to support them while they are on their front, as shown here, or on their back.

These long, flexible foam tubes can be used from an early age to support the upper body, tummy, back or legs. As with flat floats, close supervision is needed because children can let go of woggles and may sink. They can also be used in conjunction with other aids, such as armbands or armdiscs.

Specialized supports

Various specialized supports are available for swimmers with particular physical needs. A mobility specialist or physiotherapist should be able to advise you.

Comparison of flotation aids...

	Suitable for babies under 1 year?	Easy to reduce dependency?	Suitable for stroke practice?
Armbands	✗	✓	✓ *leg action
Armdiscs	✗	✓	✓ *leg action
Baby seats	✓ *with supervision	n/a	✗
Buoyancy clothing	✗	✓	✗
Floats	✗	✓	✓
Inflatable rings	✗	✗	✗
Woggles	✓ *with supervision	✓	✓

Going to the swimming pool

Once children are confident playing, swishing and splashing in the bath, they should be ready for you to take them to a swimming pool.

Early visits to the pool

The first time you take children to a pool it's a good idea just to look around and watch from the viewing area, so they can get used to the atmosphere. On your next visit you may want to get changed and go to the poolside. If they seem keen, you may decide to get in the water. Don't worry if you have to repeat this a few times.

Non-swimming adults

You don't need to be able to swim to take babies or young children swimming: you'll be in shallow water and they won't be ready to learn strokes for a while. It's important not to appear nervous of the water, though, as your fear may be transmitted to the child. If you are nervous, go with another adult who is confident, join an adult and child class, or even consider taking swimming lessons yourself.

Adult and child classes

These are usually for babies up to the age of about three to four, with an adult. They are a great way of getting you started with teaching children to swim and encouraging you to go to the pool regularly. You can find out what classes are available from pools, libraries or the local council.

Before you enrol, you might want to visit a class and check on the pool's facilities. Classes should be small enough for the teacher to be able to give individual advice, and must have no more than 12 babies, each with an adult. Look for classes with a relaxed, happy atmosphere, and make sure the teacher has a recognized qualification*. The atmosphere will be quieter and the water smoother if the class has exclusive use of a pool, not just one area roped off from other swimmers.

Classes like this one give adults and children the chance to learn new skills in a relaxed, informal environment, under the supervision of a qualified teacher.

*In the UK this will be the "Adult and Child Water Activities" qualification from the Amateur Swimming Association.

Swimming pool safety

Following these guidelines will help you keep children safe at the swimming pool:

- Never leave babies or young children unattended at the pool, even for a moment, in or out of the water. Don't even turn your back on them.

- Children who can't swim should be watched closely in the water and on the poolside and even those who can swim need close supervision.

- Teach children from the start that they must never:
  - run along the poolside
  - push people
  - jump in too close to them
  - splash people
  - grab hold of them
  - try to duck them

Children who are just learning to walk need very close supervision in and around the pool.

First time in the pool

Your first time in the pool is likely to be most enjoyable if you go on a day when you have plenty of time and both you and the child are on good form. Don't go when a child is tired or hungry, or for an hour after a meal or feed. The main aim is for them to enjoy themselves, so don't try to do too much or stay in the pool too long. Make a mental list of the things you want to do so you don't end up just standing around.

When not to swim

It's unwise to take babies or young children swimming if they seem even slightly unwell. They shouldn't swim if they have a cold, or any nose, throat, chest, ear or eye infection; if they have diarrhoea or a stomach upset; or if they have athlete's foot, which is highly contagious. Many pools allow people with verrucas to swim if these are covered with water-resistant gel or a rubber sock (both available from a pharmacy).

If children have additional medical needs, such as asthma, diabetes or epilepsy, it's a good idea to talk to their doctor or health visitor before taking them swimming for the first time.

Before...

Make sure that costumes and trunks are clean before you go swimming. Clean babies' bottoms before putting swim nappies on them and wipe their noses if you need to. Check that children's hands, faces and knees are clean, and give them a shower if necessary. Get children to blow their noses and go to the toilet. Make sure they (and you) aren't eating sweets or gum – besides being unhygienic, these can be a choking hazard. Once you're in the water, respond quickly to requests to go to the toilet. If babies show signs of doing a poo, get out of the pool right away.

...and after

After swimming, everyone should go in the shower to rinse off the chemicals in the water as these can irritate the skin. You don't need to use soap, though. It's important to dry children's ears, particularly after swimming. Tilt their head first to one side for a few seconds, then to the other, to let the water drain out. Then dry them with a towel. Bring a towel or bath robe to wrap around yourself while you are getting children dressed. By the time you've finished dressing them, you'll almost be dry yourself.

How long to stay in

Remember to note the time you get in, and don't extend the maximum times given here. If the water is too warm or too cold, then these times should be reduced.

Age of child	0–6 months	6–18 months	18 months –3 years	3 years and older
Maximum on 1st visit	10 minutes	15 minutes	20 minutes	30 minutes
Maximum after several visits	30 minutes	30 minutes	40 minutes	45 minutes (no more than 30 to be spent working hard)

Length of time in the pool

This depends on the water temperature, the age of the children, and how much fun they're having. The chart above shows the maximum time children should spend in the pool. It's important to build up to these times slowly. Even if children are happy, they may get chilled or overtired. If they're cold and shivering, get them out straight away. Wrap them in a towel at once, then dry and dress them before you get changed yourself. Dress them extra warmly to go out in cool weather, and make sure they wear a hat.

Using flotation aids

The advantages and disadvantages of using flotation aids are discussed in detail on pages 18–21. Whatever you decide, it's important to use aids as and when appropriate and to avoid overusing them. It's much better for children's confidence if they get used to entering and leaving the water without them.

You can often help put nervous children at ease by holding them close and establishing eye contact as soon as you can.

Nervous children

Some children may refuse to get into the pool at first. This is quite a common response, as to a child, this water can be more frightening than the bath at home. Avoid forcing them in; just let them watch from the poolside or walk around pointing out how much fun other children are having. Encourage them to sit on the edge and dangle their feet in the water with you.

If this happens for several visits, it may be worth trying to get in the water anyway. If children are still very scared, it may be better to give up the idea of swimming for a few months, then try again.

Getting into the water

The ideal way to get into the pool with a baby is to give the baby to someone else to hold while you get in, then have them pass the baby to you. If there's no one else available, you can try these ways, depending on the age of the baby.

Poolside entry

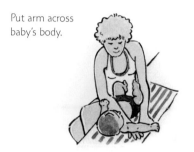

Put arm across baby's body.

Slide in backwards.

Lift baby in.

Lay the baby on a towel or mat by the pool. Sit down, keeping hold of the baby with one hand.

With one arm across the baby's body to stop them from rolling, turn and slide into the water.

When your feet are firmly on the bottom of the pool, lift the baby in to join you.

Protect child with arm as you slide in.

Climb down with your back to the water.

Child turns backwards and slides in.

Be careful not to bang chin on poolside.

With babies who can sit up or young children, slide in as shown here, putting one arm across the child.

With young children who can manage the ladder, go down first, then help them down the same way.

From the age of about 18 months, you can encourage children to turn and slide backwards into the water.

Get in yourself first, so you can help them, especially if they're too small to touch the bottom.

Shallow steps or a slope

With babies, just walk straight into the pool, holding them securely. You will be top-heavy carrying a child, so slide your feet along the bottom to avoid slipping.

Let toddlers and older children walk in, holding your hand and sliding their feet along the bottom. As they gain confidence over the sessions you can encourage them to walk in without holding hands.

Hold baby securely.

Slide feet along bottom.

Jumping in

This is a great confidence-builder, which you can start teaching even young babies, once they've been to the pool a few times and are happy in the water.

Start by sitting babies on the edge of the pool. From about a year you can stand them on the edge, but continue to hold them under their shoulders, not by the hands, or there'll be too much pressure on their shoulder joints.

Holding the child under their shoulders, lift them into the water, so that it comes up to their shoulders. To make it more fun, you can sing *Humpty Dumpty* while you do this.

As soon as they are in the water, turn them onto their front and glide them back to the side of the pool, showing them how to hold on to the rail or trough.

When they're used to being lifted in and provided they know how to blow out in the water, you can start momentarily submerging them after lifting them in.

Jumping in alone

Gradually, you'll be able to encourage children to jump in to you on their own. The water needs to be at least 0.9m (3ft) deep for this to be safe. To begin with, catch them under their arms before they go under.

Teach them to position their toes over the edge before jumping, and to jump well out from the wall to avoid hitting it; never let them run and jump into the water as they may slip and hurt themselves. Encourage them to bend their knees after entering the water. Always glide them back to the rail after they jump, until they can swim back on their own.

It's important that you're ready to catch children when they first start to jump in like this. Give them a cue such as "One, two, three, jump!", get them to join in and later give the cue themselves.

Holding children

There are various ways to support children in the water. What you choose will depend on the amount of independent control they have of their head and posture, and how much support they need for an activity. Here are some of the commonly used holds. Positions for particular activities are described later with the activities.

Cradle hold

This hold is particularly suitable for babies who can't yet support their head. It allows you to talk to them easily and to maintain eye contact. Being held close will help them to feel safe.

Keep a baby's ears out of the water to start with.

Protective hold

With the baby's back to your chest, hold them with one hand across the chest, and the thumb supporting the chin. Use your other hand to support their thighs until you're deep enough for the water's buoyancy to hold them up. This hold is useful for moving babies through the water or passing them to another adult.

You can use this hold with babies from the age of two months.

Hold children gently and confidently, but also allow them to experience the support offered by the water.

Carry hold

With the baby in a seated position, bring one arm around their back and hold the leg furthest away from you. Use your other hand to support their back and shoulder. Their near arm should be over your shoulder and their head close to yours, so you can make good eye contact, smile and talk to them.

Use this hold with children who can control their head but can't yet sit.

Hip hold

As children grow and their posture control develops, you'll be able to sit them on your hip, with one leg either side of you. Like the carry hold, this position is useful for entering the water where the pool has a sloping entry, and for moving around in it.

Put one arm around the child's back and the other hand underneath for support.

First activities

First activities in the water should aim to get children to relax, enjoy themselves and so build their confidence. Here are some ideas for things you could try at the start of each session. Singing songs and nursery rhymes can be useful for helping children relax too.

Face to face

It helps give children confidence if you always keep your face on a level with theirs. With a baby or toddler, this may mean kneeling on the pool bottom, if it's shallow enough. In deeper water, you'll probably feel more stable and comfortable standing with your legs wide apart and knees slightly bent.

How much to do

The activities on these two pages may be enough for a baby or nervous child's first visit. With an older toddler or child who takes to the water easily, you may want to go on to the activities described on the following pages.

Standing on the bottom

Depending on the depth of the water, children may not be tall enough to stand on the bottom of the pool straight away. This means that unless there's a gently sloping entrance they can't do the walking, running and jumping activities described opposite to begin with. If children can touch the bottom on their first visit, encourage them to stand from the start.

Sprinkling toys like this one can help babies become more familiar with the feeling of water trickling onto their skin.

Sinking and bobbing

Do this on the spot to start with, then walking slowly around the pool.

Hold the child close. (Hold a child who is standing by the hands.)

Gently sink down until your shoulders are in the water.

Rise and sink again, so the child gets used to the lapping water.

Bouncing

If children are happy, start bouncing gently up and down, holding them close to you, then further away as their confidence increases. Try singing action songs such as *Pop! goes the weasel* as you bounce.

Hold the child in front of you.

Lift them up gently.

Lower them with a gentle splash.

Trickling water

When children are used to water on their body, gently trickle some over the back of their head, then, if they like it, try a few drops over their face. You could sing one of the trickling water songs shown on page 31.

Blowing bubbles

If they are happy putting their mouths in the water, encourage children to blow bubbles. This is the first stage of learning to breathe correctly when swimming so it's a useful skill as well as being fun.

Water play

Take along one or two favourite bath toys and see if the baby will pat them along. Older babies and toddlers might like to "wash" themselves with a sponge or pour water over themselves from a container.

Walk, run and jump

If children are tall enough to stand, get them to walk across the pool holding your hand, or slide their feet along the bottom. They could then try running across, or pretending to be a kangaroo and jumping across.

Action songs

Action songs are great for encouraging children to do things in the water that they might otherwise be reluctant to do, such as getting their face wet. They often play a large part in adult and child swimming classes, too.

Some action songs, such as the *Hokey cokey*, work particularly well with mixed-age groups like this one.

Using action songs

On these pages the actions are shown in italic type and ideas for extra verses are marked with asterisks (*). Unless you're carrying the child, stay where the water is shallow enough for them to stand on the bottom of the pool.

Ring-a-ring o' roses

(Hold hands and walk around in a circle.)
 Ring-a-ring o' roses,
 A pocket full of posies,
 A-tishoo! A-tishoo!
 We all fall down!
(Crouch down or briefly duck under water.)

(Circle again, crouching low in the water.)
 The cows are in the meadow,
 Eating buttercups,
(Blow bubbles into the water.)
 A-tishoo! A-tishoo!
 We all jump up!
(Jump high out of the water.)

Oh, the grand old Duke of York

(March on the spot, or dandle baby gently up and down in time. Hold the baby facing you to start with, then later with their back towards you.)
 Oh, the grand old Duke of York,
 He had ten thousand men:
 He marched them up to the top of the hill,
(Walk forwards or lift baby up.)
 And he marched them down again.
(Walk backwards or bring baby down.)
 And when they were up they were up,
(Walk forwards or lift baby up.)
 And when they were down they were down,
(Walk backwards or bring baby down.)
 And when they were only half-way up,
(One step forwards or lift baby up a little.)
 They were neither up nor down.
(One step backwards or lift baby right up then down.)

This one is also good for exercising adults' arms.

Round the mulberry bush

(Hold hands and walk around in a circle.)
 Here we go round the mulberry bush,
 The mulberry bush, the mulberry bush,
 Here we go round the mulberry bush
 On a cold and frosty morning.
 This is the way we *jump up and down**,
 Jump up and down, jump up and down,
 This is the way we *jump up and down,*
 On a cold and frosty morning.

*Kick our legs, turn around, wash our face, have a shower, wash our hair, blow bubbles

Hokey cokey

(Stand in a circle.)
 You put your *right hand** in.
 You pull your *right hand out.*
 In, out, in, out,
 And *splash it all about.*
 You do the hokey cokey,
 And you *turn around.*
 That's what it's all about!
(Hold hands, walk to middle of circle and back.)
 Oh, the hokey cokey
 Oh, the hokey cokey *(To middle and back.)*
 Oh, the hokey cokey *(To middle and back.)*
 Knees bend, arms stretch
 Hurrah, hurrah, hurrah!

*Left hand, right leg, left leg, whole face, whole self

If you're happy and you know it

 If you're happy and you know it,
 Splash your hands*;
 If you're happy and you know it,
 Splash your hands;
 If you're happy and you know it,
 And you really want to show it;
 If you're happy and you know it,
 Splash your hands.

*Kick your legs, turn around, wash your face, have a shower, wash your hair, blow bubbles

Trickling water songs

Sprinkle water with your fingers at first. As children gain confidence, you can use your hands, then toys or cups to sprinkle and pour. The carry hold is described on page 27.

Mary, Mary, quite contrary

(Carry hold, sprinkle water over child.)
 Mary, Mary, quite contrary,
 How does your garden grow?
 With silver bells and cockle shells,
 And pretty maids all in a row.

Doctor Foster

(Carry hold, sprinkle water over child.)
 Doctor Foster went to Gloucester
 In a shower of rain.
 He stepped in a puddle
(Sink lower in water.)
 Right up to his middle
 And never went there again.

Incy, wincy spider

(Carry hold, with your shoulders in the water, and gradually stand up.)
 Incy, wincy spider climbed up the spout;
 Down came the rain
(Trickle water on baby.)
 And washed the spider out.
(Swish baby from side to side.)
 Out came the sunshine
 And dried up all the rain,
(Blow on baby's face.)
 So incy, wincy spider
 Climbed up the spout again.
(Sink down and gradually stand up again.)

Repeat the song and actions in different styles, for example as a slow or tiny spider.

Bouncing and jumping songs

Bounce children up and down in time with the rhyme of these songs. Start with gentle splashes and make bigger lifts and splashes where indicated.

Humpty Dumpty

> Humpty Dumpty sat on a wall,
> Humpty Dumpty had a great fall;
> *(Lift up and splash down.)*
> All the King's horses, and all the King's men
> Couldn't put Humpty together again.
> *(Lift up and splash down.)*

(To use this song to get children into the pool, start with them sitting on the poolside and lift them in at "had a great fall".)

Hickory, dickory, dock

> Hickory, dickory, dock!
> *(Lift up and splash down.)*
> The mouse ran up the clock;
> *(Lift and hold.)*
> The clock struck one,
> *(Say "Bong!".)*
> The mouse ran down,
> *(Splash down.)*
> Hickory, dickory, dock!

Tip...

Older children can have fun adapting the rhymes and making up actions of their own.

Pop! goes the weasel

> Half a pound of tuppenny rice,
> Half a pound of treacle.
> That's the way the money goes,
> Pop! goes the weasel.
> *(Lift up and splash down.)*
> Up and down the City Road,
> In and out The Eagle,
> That's the way the money goes,
> Pop! goes the weasel.
> *(Lift up and splash down.)*

Floating songs

Children can float with or without a flotation aid or adult support, lying on their front or their back.

Twinkle, twinkle

Twinkle, twinkle, little star,
How I wonder what you are.
Up above the world so high,
Like a diamond in the sky;
Twinkle, twinkle, little star,
How I wonder what you are.

It's important to maintain good eye contact with children during action songs, and encourage them with lots of smiles and hugs.

Rocking and swishing songs

You can use these gentle songs with young babies from the beginning. Older children can use them to practise floating on their front and back, spreading their arms and legs out into star shapes, or curling up into a tuck position, then stretching straight again in time to the music.

Rock-a-bye baby

(Cradle hold (see page 27), rock baby from side to side.)
  Rock-a-bye baby, on the tree top,
  When the wind blows, the cradle will rock;
  When the bough breaks, the cradle will fall,
  And down will come baby, cradle and all.

Bring back my bonnie

(Hold child on their front and swish them gently from side to side.)
  My bonnie lies over the ocean,
  My bonnie lies over the sea;
  My bonnie lies over the ocean,
  Oh, bring back my bonnie to me.

(Hold child out in front and whoosh towards you on each "bring back".)
  Bring back, bring back,
  Bring back my bonnie to me, to me;
  Bring back, bring back,
  Bring back my bonnie to me.
(End with a big hug.)

Rolling and turning over songs

Young children will need you to roll and turn them over (see page 37) but older children will be able to practise rolling over and turning themselves.

There were ten in the bed

  There were ten* in the bed
  And the little one said,
  "*Roll over, roll over*";
  So they all *rolled over*
  And one fell out.

*Nine, eight, seven ... one
("And the little one said "Good night!")

Teddy Bear, Teddy Bear

  Teddy Bear, Teddy Bear, *turn around*,
  Teddy Bear, Teddy Bear, *touch the ground*,
  Teddy Bear, Teddy Bear, *reach up high*,
  Teddy Bear, Teddy Bear, *wink one eye*,
  Teddy Bear, Teddy Bear, *slap your knees*,
  Teddy Bear, Teddy Bear, *sit down please*.

I'm a little pancake

Sing to the tune of I'm a little teapot.

(Start with child floating on back, swish them gently from side to side.)
  I'm a little pancake on my back.
  I'm a little pancake, nice and flat.
  When I'm nearly ready, cooked and browned,
  Flip me over. *(Turn child onto front.)*
  Turn me round.

  I'm a little pancake, upside down.
  I'm a little pancake, golden brown.
  When I smell delicious, nearly done,
  Flip me over, *(Turn child over.)*
  Yum, yum, yum!

Hold the child under the arms to turn them over.

Getting afloat

As soon as children are happy in the water you can start thinking about getting them afloat. Some children are confident enough to get into a horizontal position on their very first visit to the pool, but most prefer to remain upright for the first few sessions.

Planning a session

Start each session with introductory activities from the previous section, then progress to the activities described here. Avoid rushing through activities, and remember that children feel more confident if you keep down to their level, maintain eye contact, smile and talk reassuringly.

Supporting children in water

There are various ways of supporting children in the water, that are appropriate at different stages of their development. All the positions shown on these pages can also be used to encourage a kicking action. With babies and young children, remember to use the "Kick, kick!" cue.

Supporting young babies

Young babies without much control of their head need help to keep their face out of the water. Hold them under their arms, with your wrists together to support their chin, then move backwards, telling them to kick.

Put your thumbs over the child's shoulders.

As they gain strength in their neck, support them under their arms only. Keep them low in the water so they can feel its buoyancy, not just your support. Their chin should rest on the surface of the water.

Some children may dislike water on their upper body early on, but you can gradually lower them and yourself into the water as they get more used to the sensation.

Supporting from the side

As children gain confidence in the water, you can support them from the side, with your hands around their upper chest, and your thumbs around their shoulders. Hold them gently and firmly to start with, and relax your grip a little when they're ready.

It's difficult to maintain eye contact in this position, so keep talking to reassure the child.

Supporting toddlers

From about two years old, as children gain strength and confidence, you can reduce your support and hold them gently by their upper arms, then their forearms and then their hands.

Hold children's arms and hands down in the water.

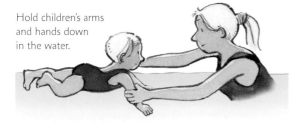

Using the side

Encourage children to hold the trough or rail at the pool edge while lifting their legs up. You may need to put your hand under their tummy at first. Encourage them to relax.

Children will stretch out in a flatter position as they gain confidence.

Using floats

From about eighteen months, you can give children a float to hold under each arm. Be prepared to give extra support by holding their floats and walking backwards. Make sure they don't let go.

Float under each arm, legs apart in relaxed position

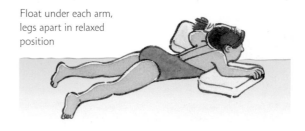

Using a woggle

Give children a woggle to hold in front of them with both hands, while resting their chin on the foam bar and lifting their legs. To start with, some children may need support under their armpits as you walk backwards through the water.

Chin resting on woggle

When they have gained confidence, get them to lean forwards onto a woggle and tuck it under their arms, lifting their legs and letting the woggle and the water take their weight. Again, you may need to give extra support under the armpits initially, or to hold their hands to encourage them to lean forwards.

Woggle supporting child under armpits

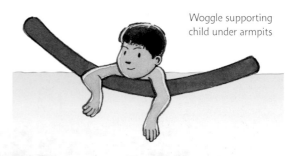

Support on the back

Most young babies respond best to being put on their back in the water. Support them under their head and bottom then, once they seem secure, gently take your hand from under their bottom. They will probably float quite happily. Some young babies can even float for a few moments without any support at all, but have your hands ready to take over again. Gently move the child sideways, supporting them with one or both hands.

Help babies lie flat in the water by waving, or holding a toy above them.

Supporting an older baby

Babies who can sit up often object to being put on their back in the water. To help them feel more secure, let them rest their head on your shoulder, with their face against your cheeks and their ears out of the water. Hold them under their arms or, for greater security, stretch your arms out underneath their body and hold their legs.

Rest the child's head on your shoulder and hold their arms or legs.

If you want to initiate a kick, hold a baby's legs below the knee, and gently move their legs in a kicking action, as you walk backwards through the water, repeating the cue, "Kick, kick!".

Supporting older children

Get toddlers or older children to lie back in the water while you stand behind them and support them under their arms. Encourage them to relax and enjoy the floating sensation.

Make a game of looking at each other upside down.

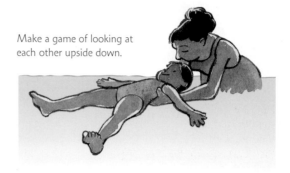

Using floats

From about 18 months, see if children will lie back and float, holding a float under each arm. Give them extra support under their shoulders at first, if they want it, and make sure they hold the floats firmly.

Head back and eyes looking up at the ceiling

Using a woggle

Give children a woggle and let them tuck it under their arms and lean backwards onto it, lifting their legs and feeling the buoyancy offered by the woggle and the water. They may need you to support under their back to start with.

Legs relaxed in a comfortable position

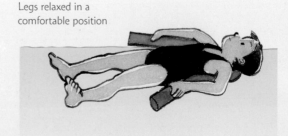

Turning over in the water

This is a good confidence-building skill and can be useful if children are not especially happy in a certain position. To turn the child over again, roll them back the way they came.

Keep young babies' mouths clear of the water.

Hold the child under their arms, standing at the side if they're on their front, or behind if they're on their back. Gently roll them over.

They may like to pretend to be a pancake in a pan and sing *I'm a little pancake*. Roll them over at the words "flip me over".

You could also sing *There were ten in the bed*, rolling them over on "roll over". Eventually, they'll learn to turn themselves over.

Kicking

Most babies and young children kick spontaneously in the water but if they don't, try making their legs kick to give them the idea. Rest the top of their body against your chest and shoulder, then stretch your arms under their tummy if they're on their front, or their bottom if they're on their back. Hold their legs below the knee and move them up and down, repeating the kicking cue as you walk backwards across the pool.

Hold children's legs below the knee, keeping the kick under the water.

Encourage children to keep their legs straight as they lie back in the water and kick.

Kicking using a float

From about eighteen months, children can practise kicking while lying on their front or back, with a float under each arm. Give them extra support by holding them under the shoulders

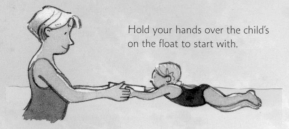

Hold your hands over the child's on the float to start with.

The next stage is to hold a single float between you and the child, and walk backwards, guiding them as they kick.

until you feel they're completely comfortable. Alternatively you may have to hold their hands on the floats so they keep a good grip. Let them hold the floats on their own when they're ready.

Be ready to support their shoulders or head if needed.

Give children a single float to hug to their chest as they lie on their back and kick. Walk backwards as they move.

Putting their feet back down

To help them stay safe, children need to learn to regain a standing position, both in shallow water (to stand up) and in deep water (to change from their front to their back, change direction or

perform another skill such as treading water). Some children can do this naturally, others may need to be taught it. This skill should be practised using flotation aids at first.

 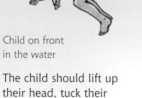   

Child on front in the water

Stand in front of the child, ready to hold their hands if they need you to.

The child should lift up their head, tuck their knees up and press down with their hands.

This will gradually bring them into an upright position in the water.

They can then put their feet down, using their arms to help them balance.

Child on back in the water

The child should press down with their hands, lift up their head and tuck their knees up.

Their hands sweep forwards and up, palms facing up, as they become upright.

They can then put their feet down, using their arms to help them balance.

Stand behind the child, ready to support their shoulders if needed.

Encouraging arm movement

The best way to encourage babies to move their arms is to put a toy in front of them and get them to stretch out for it. Hold them under their arms, with your fingers stretched out to support their chin if they need help supporting their head. Hold them close to you, cheek to cheek, until they gain confidence.

Keep babies low in the water so they can feel its buoyancy.

Encourage children to use their arms and legs while you continue supporting them. When you feel they are ready, gently let go, but be prepared to take hold again quickly and calmly if needed.

If children are using a flotation aid that leaves their arms free to move (for example a buoyancy vest), suggest that they use a paddling action to pull themselves towards the toy.

Early arm actions

From about nine months old, you can sit the baby on a shallow pool step or on your knee with their back to your chest, and move their hands in a "dog paddle" action so they get the idea of stretching and pulling. Remember to keep their hands in the water.

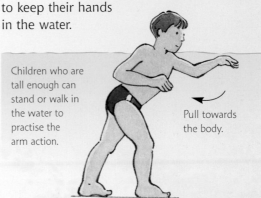

Children who are tall enough can stand or walk in the water to practise the arm action.

Pull towards the body.

You could also demonstrate other types of arm actions too, for example breast stroke arm action, and get children to copy. They can do this with and without a flotation aid or support from an adult.

Throw a bath toy a little way ahead of a child then encourage them to use their arms and legs to move through the water to fetch it.

Pushing and gliding

Pushing and gliding through the water is a useful skill as it encourages the horizontal, streamlined body position which is needed for swimming efficient strokes. It also allows even quite young children the freedom of moving through the water unaided for a few seconds.

Keep low down, with child's chin on water.

Between two people

You can push and glide babies and children of all ages from the time they can hold their head up. Avoid forcing them to do it if they aren't enjoying it. Remember to keep down to their level, smile and let them know that something is about to happen, by giving a cue such as "Ready, steady, go!".

Supporting the baby or child under the arms, one person glides them smoothly to another, who is standing a few paces away ready to take them gently again under the arms. Keep low down, with the child's chin on the water, and don't actually let go at this stage.

Keep hold of the child during glide to begin with.

Once children have grasped the idea of blowing out into the water, encourage them to put their faces in the water during the glide, if they're not doing it already.

The next stage is to let go of them for a moment just before the change-over. As they get older and their leg and arm movements get stronger, you can gradually increase the length of time you let go for and the distance between the two adults, so that the child "swims" between you.

From the side

Children may be able to start pushing and gliding from the side from about the age of two. They should hold the trough or rail with both hands, put their feet on the wall and then push off and glide towards you.

Children will probably want you to catch them straightaway to begin with. As they gain confidence, you can gradually increase the distance you stand from the side.

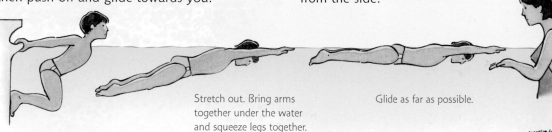

Get ready to push off with feet.

Stretch out. Bring arms together under the water and squeeze legs together.

Glide as far as possible.

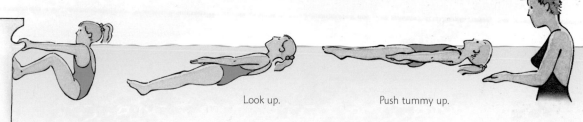

Get ready to push off with feet.

Look up.

Push tummy up.

Pushing and gliding children between two people like this can give them an early experience of "swimming" through the water.

To the side

Gently glide older babies or young children to the side from about 0.5m (2ft) away, encouraging them to take hold of the trough or rail. Keep hold of them until you know they understand how to grasp the rail or side of the pool.

When children are tall enough, they can push off from the pool bottom and glide to the side. Encourage them to stretch out like arrows, put their face in the water and increase the distance they glide. As they push off from further away, get them to kick their legs.

Breathing

Learning how to breathe (that is, breathing out when the face is in the water, and breathing in when the face is out of the water) is an essential part of learning to swim. Don't press children to put their face in the water in the early sessions; just encourage them if they do so spontaneously.

Blowing bubbles

The best way of learning how to breathe out is by blowing bubbles. Children learn quickly by copying, so to get started, first blow gently in the child's face to show them what to do. Get them to copy you, perhaps by pretending to blow out birthday candles. Then blow again, with your mouth on the surface of the water.

As children gain confidence, you can have fun experimenting. Vary the speed with which you blow out, to create streams of small popping bubbles, or big, loud ones. Try humming while you blow bubbles, or pretending to be speedboats or engines. If children are reluctant to blow bubbles in the pool, cup a little water in your hand and show them how to blow bubbles into it, or try blowing through a drinking straw.

Lower your hand to the water's surface as you blow.

Aim for long streams of bubbles as you blow through straws.

Get children to copy you blowing bubbles in the water.

Blowing plastic toys along the surface can help children control their breathing. Teaching aids called "egg-flips" are often used in lessons. As children blow on the "eggs", they flip over to reveal a contrasting colour.

Blowing bubbles under water

Once children can blow bubbles on the surface, get them to go under doing the same thing. Gently sink down together just under the surface, then come straight up again. If they splutter, reassure them and tell them how well they've done.

Don't insist on submerging if they really hate it. It's best to do it only once or twice each session in any case. Older children who are apprehensive about putting their face in the water may be willing to do it little by little, mouth first, then nose, and so on.

Head-butt float

Older children could try moving through the water blowing bubbles while pushing a float or ball along with their nose or head. Remind them to come up to take a breath when they need to.

Blow out steadily and aim to increase the length of time a breath lasts.

Motor boats

Encourage children to blow bubbles with their face in the water by getting them to push and glide and make engine noises. They can do this between two adults, or on their own with a float.

Encourage children to kick to travel further.

Shallow water method

Learning to swim in shallow water can give children a lot of confidence. The water needs to be no deeper than 30–45cm (12–18in), so they can support themselves in a horizontal position with their hands on the bottom of the pool and their head out of the water. The sea can be an ideal place to learn to swim in this way.

Lying on front, hands on bottom of sea or pool, head out of water

Lying on back, hands on bottom of sea or pool, face out of water

The idea is that children walk their hands along the bottom while kicking their legs. As they become more confident, they can begin to take their hands off the bottom too and add an arm action, but with the knowledge that they can quickly put their hands back down if they need to.

Deep water method

Another approach is to teach children to swim while they're out of their depth, first with close fitting flotation aids, such as armbands, then gradually without. This method, which needs particularly close supervision, may help them gain confidence in deep water, but you need to make sure they don't become either more fearful, or overconfident.

Playing underwater games such as tag, and catching sinking objects like this dive stick are fun ways to encourage children to open their eyes under water.

Submerging together

Hold the child close, facing you. Give the cue "Ready, go!" or "1, 2, 3" then blow on their face and bend your knees so you're both submerged briefly. By blowing on them you'll encourage them to hold their breath. It's important that you smile, and remember to praise them when you come up. If they splutter, reassure them. Only do this once or twice in any session, and only repeat it if the child seems happy.

Going under

Children should be introduced gradually to submersion, starting by trickling water over their body, head then face. Routinely submerging young babies is not recommended (see "Submerging young babies", opposite) and it isn't necessary as humans don't normally swim under water but along the surface. For toddlers and young children, brief submersion after jumping in, or to pick up objects from the bottom of the pool is acceptable. Avoid forcing children to submerge if they don't like it, and always be ready to help them to the surface if needed.

Here are some ideas for activities to build up children's confidence under water.

Blow on child's face then submerge together.

Sinking action songs

There are several action songs that provide contexts for brief submersions. With young children you could try singing *Ring-a-ring o' roses*, briefly submerging them at the words "We all fall down." *Oranges and lemons* gives a good opportunity for older children to duck briefly under the water as they go under the arch, and *See-saw, Margery Daw* is an ideal accompaniment for them to bob in and out of the water.

Two adults or older children hold hands to make an arch for *Oranges and lemons.*

Encourage children to open their eyes under water by asking if they can see you when you submerge together.

Sunken toys

Sit babies or toddlers on a step or in a very shallow part of the pool next to a sunken toy and get them to reach and pick it up. Support them in a sitting position and don't let them swallow the water.

Hold a toy or ring under water for older children to retrieve, gradually holding it lower in the water as they become more confident. In shallow water, you can allow the toy to sink to the bottom of the pool. Sports shops sell weighted rings and sticks that are designed to sink slowly. Children can either wait until these have sunk to the bottom of the pool, or try to intercept them before they reach there.

Submerging young babies

A few methods of teaching advocate frequent or deep submersion. Opinion is divided, but some experts say these are best avoided for various reasons.

- Going too deep in the water can put a dangerous amount of pressure on a young child's ears. The pressure on a baby's ears at a depth of 1m (3ft) is equivalent to that of an adult at 5m (16ft) – a deep diving pit.

- Frequent submerging may increase the risk of ear infections.

- It can be dangerous for children to swallow a very large amount of water.

- Frequent submerging may have long-term psychological effects that are not immediately apparent.

Children who swim under water

Children who swim unaided before the age of about three will do so just under the surface. Don't discourage them, but watch them very closely and help them to come to the surface for air. Signs of needing to take a breath include shaking their heads or moving their arms and legs faster. Guide them to the surface straight away, holding them under their arms or chin. Eventually they'll learn to surface on their own.

Some babies naturally swim under water like this, but you need to make sure they come up for a breath.

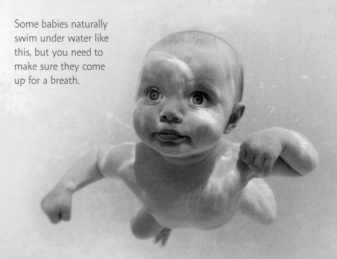

Progressing to strokes

It is important not to try to rush children through the stages of learning to swim or to start teaching them to do the proper strokes (front crawl, back crawl and breast stroke) too soon. Always remember that your main aim is for children to enjoy the water.

Children don't have the strength to swim on the surface of the water until they're about three. Then, they may be able to do a dog paddle type of stroke on their front, and swim on their back with their arms by their sides.

Remember...

Children's progress in swimming may vary considerably. Although you may feel a child is learning slowly, providing they continue to enjoy their experiences in the water, they too will swim competently in time.

When to start

Before children start to learn the major strokes, they should be able to swim at least 10m (about 11yds) on their own and be happy doing all the activities described so far in the book. Some children may be able to start the strokes as early as aged four or five, though it's unusual for children to have the strength or understanding to do them properly before they're six or seven. At the same time as children start learning the strokes, they can be introduced to other water skills as well.

Children need to have the strokes and skills demonstrated to them. If you aren't a good swimmer yourself, find someone else they can watch, and go through the pictures in this book with them. You may also want to start thinking about classes. Many pools hold classes for children without their carers from the age of three, though some children may prefer to stay in adult and child classes until they are four. You can find out what classes are available from the pools, the library or local council.

The building blocks

To swim successfully, children need to combine the ability to float with a means of propelling themselves through the water. It's important to build up each stroke gradually and systematically, first teaching the body position, then the legs, arms, breathing and finally the timing and coordination.

Planning a session

Once you start teaching children the strokes, remember that swimming should always be fun. Continue to start the session with introductory activities of the type shown earlier in the book. Spend about a third of the session on a stroke and, following that, add a contrasting skill. Make sure you leave enough time for them to play in the water at the end of the session.

Here is one possible way of breaking up the time in a 30-minute session:

- 1 minute
  Discuss with the child what you are going to do in the session.

- 4 minutes
  Do some introductory activities and/or swim a stroke the child already knows, say front crawl.

- 12 minutes
  Learn a new stroke, say back crawl.

- 8 minutes
  Introduce a contrasting water skill, say treading water, and practise previously learnt strokes and skills.

- 5 minutes
  Play time. Let children do what they like but remember to watch them closely and give help when it's needed.

Specific needs

All children develop confidence and skill in water at different rates, so it's important always to allow children to learn at their own pace. In addition, some children may have other specific needs to consider when you're planning a session at the swimming pool.

Getting advice

There are relatively few long-term medical conditions that make it inadvisable to take children to a swimming pool, and there are many benefits to be gained from taking part in appropriate activity in the water. These range from physical benefits such as toned muscles, increased stamina and improved coordination, to opportunities for developing social skills and self-confidence as well as having lots of fun.

If you're thinking about taking a child with specific needs to the swimming pool, it's a good idea to gather as much information as you can. Consult your family doctor or other members of your child's healthcare team and, if you can, learn from the experiences of other parents and carers, through support groups or national organizations. Their advice, combined with your own knowledge of the child, will enable you to decide how best the child's needs can be met.

Learning together

Some pools offer separate sessions for people with specific needs in addition to regular pool access. As with other aspects of children's development, it's important to emphasize the similarities with other children, rather than the differences. Your positive approach will help them to achieve their potential, and you'll both learn along the way when adjustments need to be made, and what these should be. Set realistic goals and be proud of their achievements.

The information on the following pages addresses some of the practical issues you may need to consider. You can also visit the Usborne Quicklinks website at **www.usborne-quicklinks.com** for links to organizations which may give you further guidance.

With appropriate support, children with additional needs can benefit greatly from experiences at the swimming pool, from water play to learning to float and swim.

Asthma

Swimming is usually an excellent form of exercise for children and young people with asthma. The warm humid air in the pool is less likely to trigger symptoms of asthma. However, this is not the case for everyone and swimming in cold or chlorinated water can trigger some people's asthma. If swimming does make a child's asthma worse, always ensure they use their reliever inhaler immediately before they swim, and have it close by when they swim, in case they need it.

Autistic spectrum disorders

Take children to the pool at a time when it's quiet, and there are as few distractions as possible. Wearing ear plugs and plastic sunglasses can help to reduce the amount of aural and visual stimulation at the pool. Alternatively, playing gentle music can help to camouflage sounds too.

Highly structured sessions can give children a reassuring routine and then you can introduce new skills gradually within a familiar framework. Children might find it reassuring if you identify a spot at the side of the pool that they can return to after each activity. You may find it effective to use equipment of the same type, texture and colour to work on the same skills, for example always to practise front-crawl leg action with a blue, smooth float. Using laminated task cards to introduce particular activities, such as having a shower, can also help to relay information and reinforce ideas.

Babies with Down's syndrome often take very well to the water and go on to become confident swimmers.

Continence management

A child's care team will be able to advise on how best to manage continence in the pool. Successful control can often be achieved by combining specialized swimwear or appliances with their usual continence management techniques.

Diabetes

If children have Type 1 diabetes, it is important to check their blood glucose levels before and after exercise. Swimming can use a lot of energy so make sure they eat extra carbohydrate (such as a biscuit or fruit) before going in the pool, and after the session too. Take along a plastic container of dilute sugary drink, in case their blood glucose levels drop too low during the session. If they start to show symptoms of a hypo, get them out of the pool and give them a sugary drink followed by a carbohydrate snack.

Down's syndrome

It's especially important to maintain good eye contact while giving instructions. Repetition and review will help reinforce activities and skills you have practised together, and it's important to set clear expectations and limits. Some activities, such as diving, may be unsuitable for children who have cervical spine instability, so check with the child's specialist.

Epilepsy

Children with epilepsy should never swim alone or take unnecessary risks. If there is a lifeguard present, make them aware of the child's epilepsy. A "buddy system" is a discreet way of supervising swimmers, especially as they get older. The buddy will swim with them and be able to offer help. If no qualified lifeguard is present, the child should not swim deeper than the buddy's shoulder height. If a buddy system can't be used, it may be better for a "supervisor" to watch from the waterside. Avoid overcrowded situations, as it might be difficult to notice if a child needs help.

If a child has a seizure, stay calm. From behind, keep their head and face out of the water. If possible, move them to a shallow area, while holding their head above water. Do not restrict movement or place anything in their mouth. Once jerking has stopped, move the child onto dry land. Place them on their side to recover and stay with them until they feel better.

Gross motor delay

Children may need extra support getting to the poolside and into the water and they may need an adult in the water with them. Wheelchair users might consider using sticks or walking frames if appropriate, and hoists are available at many pools. Young children can usually be carried. It's a good idea to inform the lifeguards, so they can give children appropriate supervision and freedom in the pool, as children often develop swimming styles which appear uncoordinated, even when they have become competent swimmers. A child's physiotherapist will be able to advise on the use of floats, and provide specialized ones if needed.

If children use a wheelchair, it's a good idea to cover the seat with a plastic sheet and a towel, ready for when they get out. Wrap the child in another towel before they sit down to keep them warm and avoid their muscles going into spasm.

Stretchy waterproof bands can help keep the ears dry, as well as holding ear plugs in place.

Hearing impairment / Deaf

Remove hearing aids before entering the water, unless they are waterproof. It's usually safe for children to swim with cochlear implants, as long as the external part of the aid has been removed, but be sure to check with their specialist first. Silicone ear plugs can help keep water out of the ears, and waterproof headbands can help hold them in place, as well as helping to keep the ears dry. Some doctors may advise against swimming if children have had an operation to insert grommets. Unless a doctor or ENT specialist advises otherwise, children should avoid diving or swimming deep under water, because of the risk of the increased pressure damaging the remaining hearing.

Visual impairment

The echoing sounds within a pool can be very disorientating, so choose a quiet session within a small group. Let children experiment with the water, allowing it to splash on and around them. Before they start learning to swim, make sure they can walk across the pool to understand its width and depth. Encourage them to use rope or lane markings to help them swim in a straight line and check their progress. Use your voice to help them come towards you and use descriptive verbal instructions as well as appropriate touch to guide the children on the correct strokes as they progress.

Front crawl

Front crawl is the fastest and most efficient swimming stroke. It's a good stroke to start with as it follows easily from the dog paddle that children use when they first start swimming and is the most natural to teach and learn.

First things first

It's important to build up the stroke gradually, making sure children master each stage before going on to the next. Firstly concentrate on the body position, next practise the leg kick, then add the arm action and finally the breathing. To keep it interesting, always let children try the whole stroke at the start and end of the practice.

If you can't demonstrate the stroke yourself, find someone who can and get children to look at the pictures in this book. Remember not to spend more than a third of a session on a particular stroke.

Body position

The body should be streamlined and stretched, and as flat as possible, with a slight slope down to the hips and the shoulders resting on the surface of the water. The legs and arms should be stretched, with the toes and fingers relaxed but pointed. The arm action and breathing will cause a certain amount of body roll, but this shouldn't be too exaggerated.

The head should be in a natural position, not lifted or too deep in the water. If it's lifted, the hips and legs will drop too low; if it's buried, they'll be raised too high. The water line should be between the nose and hairline, while the eyes, which should be open, look down and forwards.

Body position practices

1. Push and glide from the pool bottom holding a float under each arm or with a woggle under the armpits.

2. Push and glide from the pool bottom holding a float out in front, with the face in the water.

3. Push and glide from the pool bottom without a float, with the face in the water, the arms extended and one hand on top of the other.

How smooth and fast a child's front crawl is depends as much on their body position as on their stroke action. Here are some points to remember:

Foot only just breaks surface.

Feet extended but relaxed

Legs stabilize body.

Foot shouldn't go much lower than body depth.

Tip...

If a child is still not keen on putting their face in the water, get them to repeat some of the activities from page 43. Playing some of the games from pages 84–85 might help build up their confidence too.

Leg action

The legs should stabilize the body and provide some forward movement, though most of this comes from the arms.

The legs should kick up and down, alternately and continuously, keeping close together. The movement should start at the hips and end with a whip-like action of the feet. The legs should be kept straight with the feet extended but relaxed. The feet shouldn't go much deeper than the depth of the body on the down-kick and should only just break the surface of the water on the up-kick, making a small splash.

Children usually do six leg kicks per arm cycle, but this isn't important and they will not be able to count them anyway. The opposite leg kicks down at the start of the arm pull, as this helps to balance the body.

Leg action practices

1. Kick, holding on to the rail.

2. Kick, holding a float under each arm, or with a woggle tucked under the armpits.

3. Kick, holding a float out in front, with the chin on the water.

4. Kick, holding a float out in front, with the face in the water.

5. Kick, with arms outstretched, with the face in the water, the arms extended and one hand on top of the other.

Shoulders rest on the surface.

Water line between nose and hairline

Head in natural position, eyes looking forwards and down

Legs kick starting at hip.

Body streamlined and stretched

Most of forward movement created by arms.

Arm action

Most of the forward movement in front crawl comes from the arm action. This is continuous and alternating, one arm sweeping through the water while the other recovers.

Elbow bent

Palm faces outwards.

Hand enters water between shoulder and centre-line of body.

The arm enters the water thumb first, with the elbow bent, fingers together and the palm of the hand turned to face diagonally outwards.

The hand should enter the water between the shoulder and the centre-line of the body.

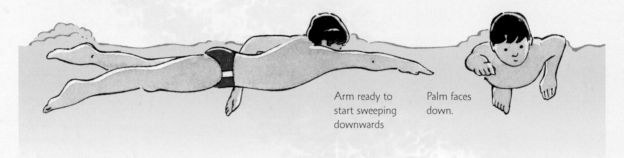

Arm ready to start sweeping downwards

Palm faces down.

The wrist and forearm follow the hand into the water and completely submerge then the elbow starts to straighten.

At the same time, the forearm rotates so that the palm is facing down and slightly backwards, ready to sweep towards the feet.

Palm faces feet.

Hand close to centre-line of body

The arm sweeps downwards and backwards, with the hand keeping close to the centre-line of the body, the palm facing the feet.

The elbow bends again. It must be kept high to ensure that the water is swept backwards and not downwards.

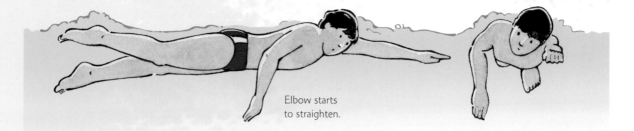

Elbow starts
to straighten.

The hand continues under the body, palm still facing the feet, and sweeps back towards the thigh, with the elbow gradually straightening.

By the time the thumb reaches the thigh, the elbow should be almost completely straight, ready for the last part of the stroke.

Elbow leaves
water first.

Hand leaves water,
little finger first.

The elbow bends again and is the first part of the arm to leave the water. The arm then swings forwards quickly but in a relaxed way.

This part of the stroke doesn't propel the body forward, so as little time and energy as possible should be used on it.

Arm action practices

1. Practise the action standing on the poolside, leaning forwards slightly.

2. Practise the action standing in shallow water.

4. Push and glide from the side or the pool bottom, start to kick with the legs, then introduce one or two arm cycles. Increase the number of arm cycles as the stroke improves.

3. Practise the action walking in shallow water.

Push and glide.

Breathing

Breathing should be blended into the stroke with as little interference as possible. The action should be smooth and unhurried.

Action

Breathing out takes place gradually through the nose and mouth, while the face is submerged. The head should turn like a door knob, keeping the body position as streamlined as possible. It doesn't need to be lifted out of the water because the forward motion of the body creates a trough in which to breathe.

Timing

Once the stroke is mastered, children may choose to breathe on both sides, every third arm pull. This method is likely to produce a balanced action. Breathing on both sides also has the advantage of letting swimmers see what is happening on either side of them.

As the hand sweeps back to the thigh, the head turns, ready to breathe in when the elbow comes out of the water.

As the arm swings forward, the breath is taken underneath it.

The head should be back in its normal position before the hand enters the water.

Breathing practices

1. With one hand on the rail, the other low down on the wall, practise turning the head while kicking.

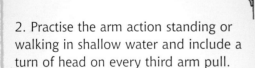

2. Practise the arm action standing or walking in shallow water and include a turn of head on every third arm pull.

3. Kick, while holding a float and practise turning the head to breathe.

4. Practise the full stroke, first holding the breath, then breathing occasionally, then increasing the number of breaths taken.

Tip...

The breath can be let out gradually, forced out in one go just before the next breath in, or released mainly as a trickle and forcing out the last bit of air before taking another breath.

Common faults

Most of the common faults in front crawl come from trying to build up the stroke too quickly, without mastering each stage in turn. Always make sure children can watch the correct action being demonstrated and show them the pictures in the book.

The checklist opposite lists the most common faults and their corrections. When you're correcting a child's stroke, keep your instructions as simple and short as possible. The corrections sometimes need to be exaggerated until they become a habit.

Front crawl checklist

Fault

✗ Kicking too deep. This is caused either by the head being held too high or by a weak kick.

Legs too low   Head too high

✗ Feet come out of the water on the up-kick. The head may be buried too deep or the kick may be coming from the knees.

Kicking from knee

✗ Feet point to the bottom of the pool. This is caused by keeping the ankles rigid and it results in lack of forward movement when kicking.

✗ Kicking with the legs apart.

✗ The hand enters the water across the centre-line of the body, so the swimmer "snakes" up the pool.

✗ Slapping the water with the hand.

✗ Pulling too deeply with a straight arm, resulting in lack of power in the arm action.

✗ Not sweeping back with the arm, only down and in, resulting in lack of power.

✗ Not keeping the palm facing the feet, or forgetting to keep the fingers together, resulting in lack of power.

✗ Recovering with the hand too high.

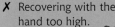

✗ Lifting the head to breathe.

Correction

✓ Practise pushing and gliding with the face in the water.

✓ Practise kicking, holding a float out in front, with the face in the water.

✓ Push and glide. Adjust the position of the head.

✓ Kick, holding a float out in front. Make sure the head is in the correct position. Then practise kicking from the hips with "long legs" and without making a splash.

✓ Kick at the rail or with a float, keeping the ankles floppy and the toes pointed.

✓ Kick with a float, trying to brush the legs together.

✓ Repeat the arm action practices, aiming to enter the water with the hand wide of the shoulder.

✓ Repeat the arm action practices, with the emphasis on "spearing" the water with the hand and putting the thumb in the water first.

✓ Repeat the arm action practices, concentrating on keeping the elbow high and gradually bending it.

✓ Repeat the arm action practices, concentrating on sweeping right through to the thigh.

✓ Repeat the arm action practices, emphasizing "catching" or "fastening onto" the water with the palm and fingers before the start of each sweep.

✓ Repeat the arm action practices, emphasizing that the elbow leaves the water first and remains higher than the hand as the arm swings forward.

✓ Repeat the breathing practices, emphasizing that the head should turn like a door knob and one ear should stay in the water.

Back crawl

Back crawl is a useful stroke for anyone who doesn't like putting their face in the water, or finds the front crawl breathing technique tricky, though some people are put off it because they can't see where they're going.

One thing at a time

The action for back crawl is basically an upside-down front crawl. It's an easy stroke to teach and learn once the body position has been mastered. Remember that it is important for children to see the correct stroke demonstrated. If you can't do this yourself, enlist the help of someone who can, and show the child the pictures in this book.

Be sure that they build up the stroke gradually, mastering the body position first, then the leg action, arm action and finally the breathing. Spend about a third of a session practising the stroke, and let children start and end the practice by swimming the whole stroke, to keep their interest.

Body position

The body should be streamlined and stretched, and as flat as possible. Beginners sometimes tend to try sitting up in the water, but this should be avoided. The head should be held still and in line with the body throughout the stroke. The position of the head should be lifted slightly as if supported by a pillow. The ears should be submerged and the eyes should look up and slightly forward towards the feet.

The top part of the body will roll to the side of the pulling arm and this is a natural part of the stroke. The arm action will also make the hips sway from side to side, though this movement should be kept to a minimum by the regular up-and-down action of the legs.

Body position practices

1. Push and glide from the pool bottom, holding one float under each arm.

2. Push and glide from the pool bottom, holding a float on the tummy.

3. Push and glide from the poolside without a float, and arms by the sides.

4. Push and glide from the poolside with arms extended beyond the head.

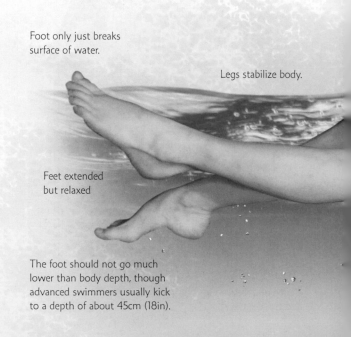

Foot only just breaks surface of water.

Legs stabilize body.

Feet extended but relaxed

The foot should not go much lower than body depth, though advanced swimmers usually kick to a depth of about 45cm (18in).

Leg action

As in front crawl, the main function of the legs is to stabilize the body rather than to provide movement.

The legs kick up and down, alternately and continuously, keeping close together. The movement starts at the hips and ends with a whip-like action of the feet. The legs should be kept straight with the feet extended but relaxed. The feet should not go much deeper than the depth of the body on the down-kick and should only just break the surface of the water on the up-kick, making a small splash.

As in front crawl, there are usually six leg kicks to each arm cycle, with the opposite leg kicking down at the start of each arm pull to balance the body. There's no need to worry about timing particularly at this stage though, as this usually comes naturally as the stroke improves. However, it is important to encourage a good kicking action in back crawl, otherwise the body will perform a "snaking" action.

Tip...

If a child is nervous about lying back in the water, encourage them to push and glide, resting their head on a float or woggle and then practise kicking with the float or woggle in the same position.

Leg action practices

1. Kick, holding a float under each arm, or with a woggle tucked under the armpits.

2. Kick, holding a float over the tummy.

3. Kick, holding a float over the tops of the knees to stop them from bending.

4. Kick, while sculling with the hands (see page 70 for how to scull).

5. Kick, with the hands on the tops of the thighs.

This photograph illustrates the main features of back crawl.

Leg kick starts at hip.

Ears in water

As a swimmer becomes more confident, the head will lift slightly so the eyes look upwards and forwards towards the feet.

Body streamlined and stretched

Most of movement comes from arms.

Arm action

As in front crawl, most of the propulsion comes from the arms, and the action is continuous and alternating, one arm sweeping through the water while the other recovers. There are two types of arm action.

The straight arm action is often used by beginners and people who swim just for fun. The bent arm action is faster and more powerful. It's used by competitive swimmers, and beginners to whom it comes naturally. Both actions start in the same way.

Start of arm actions

Palm faces outwards.   Hand directly behind shoulder

With the arm and hand in a straight line, the arm enters the water directly in line with the shoulder. The little finger enters first, palm facing outwards and fingers together. There should be little or no splash. The hand "fastens onto" the water, ready to start the sweep.

Straight arm action

Arm sweeps out to side.   Arm straight

The arm remains straight and starts to sweep.

It sweeps outwards and slightly downwards.

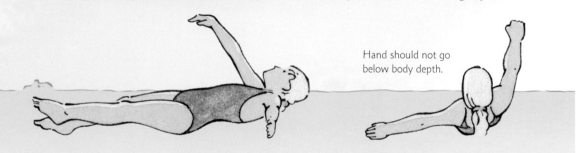

Hand should not go below body depth.

The hand reaches its lowest point at the end of the sweep, when it is level with the shoulder.

It should not go below body depth. (The other arm starts to lift at this stage.)

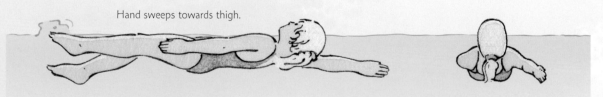

Hand sweeps towards thigh.

The hand continues its semi-circular pathway, sweeping inwards towards the hips.

The arm remains straight as the hand comes out of the water, back of hand or thumb first.

Bent arm action

Elbow bent

The hand starts to sweep towards the feet. As it does so, the elbow bends and the palm

starts to come into position facing the feet. (The other arm starts to lift out of the water.)

Fingers point upwards.

Bend at elbow about 90°.

By the end of the sweep, when the shoulder, elbow and hand are level, the bend at the elbow is about 90°.

At this stage, the other arm is sweeping through the air, over the shoulder, and the palm is turning outwards ready to enter.

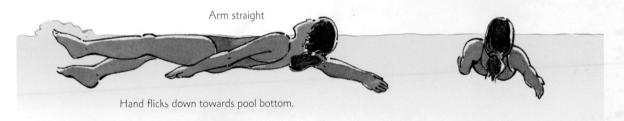

Arm straight

Hand flicks down towards pool bottom.

The hand now sweeps towards the feet and the elbow gradually straightens. The movement ends with a flick of the hand

down towards the pool bottom. This has the effect of raising the shoulder in preparation for the arm leaving the water.

End of arm actions

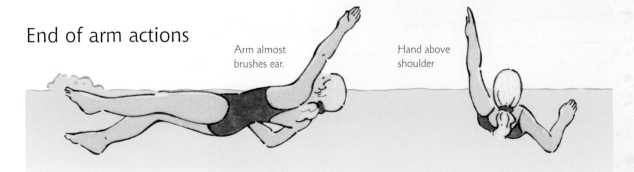

Arm almost brushes ear.

Hand above shoulder

Both actions end in the same way. The arm is lifted smoothly out of the water, straight, with wrist relaxed and the palm facing the thigh.

The arm swings back over the head, almost brushing the ear, the wrist turns so the palm is facing outwards ready to re-enter the water.

Choosing an arm action style

The action you demonstrate might depend on which one you do yourself. If children are over the age of about six, it may be worth showing them the stronger, bent arm action from the start. If one arm action comes more easily to a child than the other, let them concentrate on that.

Breathing

Breathing in back crawl is fairly relaxed but beginners sometimes tend to hold their breath, so you may need to remind children to breathe normally and regularly. As the stroke improves, encourage them to take a complete breath every stroke cycle.

Arm action practices

1. Practise the arm action standing on the poolside.

2. Practise the arm action with the feet hooked under the rail, if there is one.

3. Push and glide from the side or pool bottom, kick the legs then try one or two arm cycles. Increase the number of arm cycles as the stroke improves.

4. Practise the arm action with one arm, holding a float on the tummy.

5. Practise swimming the whole stroke with a smooth, continuous arm action.

Breathing practices

Do the full stroke, breathing in on one arm pull and out on the other. Concentrate on smooth, rhythmic breathing and avoid holding the breath.

Breathe in.

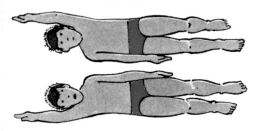

Breathe out.

Common faults

The best way to avoid faults creeping in is always to master the stroke in stages. Keep any corrections clear and simple, and let children see the correct stroke demonstrated.

Back crawl checklist

Fault

Legs too low

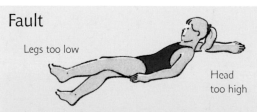

Head too high

✗ Sitting up in the water is caused by fear of putting the head back. It results in the head being too high and the legs too low.

Correction

✓ Get them to practise pushing and gliding with a woggle under the shoulders, concentrating on putting their head back and their ears in the water. Get them to look up and push their tummy up.

✓ Kick, holding a float behind the head. (Only use this practice with timid swimmers.)

Back crawl checklist (continued)

Fault

Correction

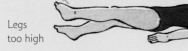

Legs too high

✗ Putting the head too far back. This is usually caused by trying to look ahead and results in the legs being too high in the water.

✓ Kick, holding a float on the tummy. Put the chin on the chest and look at a fixed point on the poolside.

✗ Kicking from the knees.

✓ Kick, holding a float over the thighs. Concentrate on kicking from the hips with "long legs". The knees should not press against the float.

✗ Kicking with stiff ankles.

✓ Kick, holding a float over the tummy, keeping the ankles floppy and the toes pointed.

✗ Kicking with a lot of splash.

✓ Kick with a float over the tummy. Concentrate on stretching out, putting the head back and keeping the legs under the surface.

✓ Practise the arm action standing on the poolside.

✗ Putting the back of the hand, instead of the little finger, into the water first.

✓ For a short distance, try doing the arm action with one arm only, holding a float under the other arm and kicking with the legs.

✗ Hand enters the water too wide of the shoulder.

✓ Practise the arm action standing on the poolside.

✓ Do a few strokes, aiming to enter the water with the hand across the centre of the head.

✗ Hand enters the water across the centre-line of the body.

✓ Practise the arm action standing on the poolside.

✓ Do a few strokes, aiming to enter the water with the hand wide of the shoulder.

✗ Sweeping too deeply, causing bobbing up and down.

✓ Do a few strokes, concentrating hard on not letting the arm go below body depth.

✗ Arm not leaving the water thumb first and bending during recovery.

✓ Practise the arm action on the poolside.

✓ Practise with one arm only for a short distance, holding a float under the other arm.

Breast stroke

This is a popular stroke with people who swim just for fun. It is essential for survival swimming because it's less tiring to swim over long distances than other strokes, and it is used for life saving.

Build up slowly

Remember that it's important for children to see the stroke demonstrated correctly. Be sure that they build up the stroke gradually, starting with the body position, then mastering the leg action, the arm action and finally the breathing. Breathing need not be a problem for beginners, as it's possible to swim the stroke keeping the face out of the water all the time.

Tip...

It's fine for children to swim with their face in the water if it's comfortable. If their legs come out of the water, they can lift their head slightly, which will lower the legs.

One advantage of breast stroke is that swimmers can see where they are going.

Body position

To swim a good breast stroke, the body should be as flat and streamlined as possible. The two sides of the body should be kept symmetrical through the stroke, with the shoulders parallel to the surface of the water. The head should be kept steady and the eyes should look along or just under the surface of the water.

It's harder to achieve this position in breast stroke than in front crawl because the head has to be lifted to breathe and the heels should not break the surface of the water during the leg kick. This means the body is at more of an angle, sloping down from head to feet. The aim is to keep the angle as slight as possible to keep water resistance to a minimum.

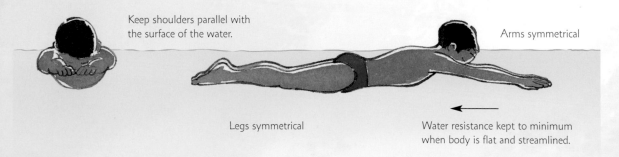

Keep shoulders parallel with the surface of the water.

Arms symmetrical

Legs symmetrical

Water resistance kept to minimum when body is flat and streamlined.

Body position practices

1. Push and glide with a float under each arm or a woggle under the armpits.

2. Push and glide with a float held in front.

3. Push and glide without a float.

4. Once leg and arm actions have been added, improve the body position by stretching out between each stroke, keeping the arms close to each other and the legs together.

5. Stretch out, putting the face in the water.

Advanced body position

Breast stroke is the slowest of the strokes, so competitive swimmers are always looking for new ways to make it quicker and more efficient. Advanced swimmers learn to undulate like dolphins as they move through the water. To do this, they lift their chest and shoulders out of the water during the arm action, then they dive forwards, and glide like a torpedo under water in an outstretched streamlined position for a moment before starting the next stroke.

Keeping the shoulders square throughout the stroke and avoiding moving the head more than needed will help children develop a good technique.

Tip...

Doing the body position practices with a woggle under the armpits will help keep the shoulders and hips level.

Leg action

Much of the forward movement in breast stroke comes from a strong leg kick. There are two types of leg action: the wedge kick and the whip kick. The kick you show to a child might depend on which one you do yourself.

The whip is a faster, more powerful kick. It is used by competitive swimmers but is also suitable for beginners, if it comes naturally to them. The wedge is a slow, relaxed kick used by people who swim just for fun. It is generally a wider kick than the whip and looks more "frog-like".

The whip kick is the easier kick to learn. It can be taught from the start and is the action usually taught to children in classes. If the wedge kick leg action comes more easily to them though, let them concentrate on that at this stage. Gently guiding a child's legs through the kicking motion can help them get used to the correct action, but avoid forcing the action.

Tip...

Aim to have both legs doing the same thing at the same time to achieve a smoother stroke.

Whip kick

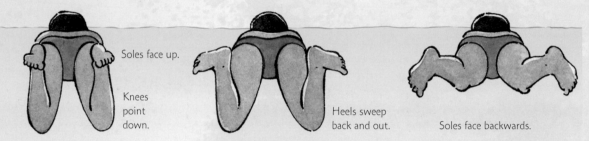

Soles face up.

Knees point down.

Heels sweep back and out.

Soles face backwards.

The feet are drawn up to the bottom about hip width apart, with the knees pointing downwards to the pool bottom and the soles facing upwards.

With the feet turned out, and toes turned towards the shins, the heels sweep mainly backwards and slightly outwards in a whip-like action.

As the legs straighten, the soles of the feet come into a backward-facing position. The legs are brought together again behind the body.

Wedge kick

Knees point forward and outwards.

Soles sweep back and out.

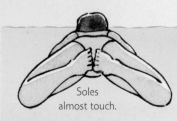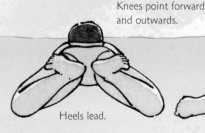

Soles almost touch.

Heels lead.

Heels lead.

The feet are drawn up towards the bottom, with the knees pointing forwards and outwards and the soles of the feet almost touching.

With the toes turned towards the shins and the heels leading, the soles of the feet then sweep outwards and backwards.

The legs are straight by the end of the kick. The heels continue to lead as the legs sweep back together again behind the body.

Feet position

The important factor in both types of kick is the position of the feet. They should be turned outwards, with the toes turned up towards the shins.

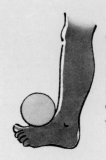

Get children to imagine they are holding a ball between the top of their feet and their shins.

Both kicks start and end with the legs straight out behind the body, feet together and extended but relaxed.

Leg action practices

1. Practise the leg action sitting on the edge of the pool. Start with the legs outstretched, then draw them up towards the bottom. Turn the feet out and the toes towards the shins. Push out to the side, with the heels leading in a circular motion as if around the edges of a hoop, then bring the legs back together again.

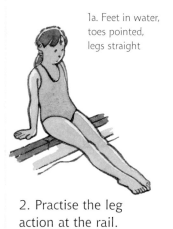

1a. Feet in water, toes pointed, legs straight

1b. Feet move towards bottom, then turn out.

1c. Push heels out in a circle then squeeze legs together again, toes pointed (a).

2. Practise the leg action at the rail.

4. Practise the leg action lying on the back, with a float under each arm, or using a woggle.

3. Practise the leg action, holding a float under each arm, or with a woggle.

Child watching the feet to make sure they are turned out

6. Practise the leg action holding a float out in front, with the face in the water.

7. Practise the leg action with the arms outstretched and the face in the water.

5. Practise the leg action, holding a float out in front, with the chin on the water.

Arm action

The breast stroke arm action is a continuous circling movement with a short glide. There are two types of action: the bent arm action, done with the whip kick (see page 64) and the straight arm action, which is done with the wedge kick.

Tip...

Encourage children to look forwards as they practise and use the arm action, and to make sure they can see their arms throughout the stroke.

Starting arm actions

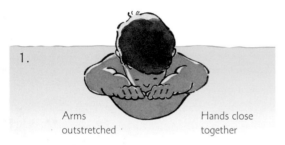

1.

Arms outstretched   Hands close together

Both arm actions start and end in the glide position, with the arms outstretched and the hands close together. As the arms stretch forwards, they should be angled slightly down, to about 15cm (6in) below the water's surface.

2.

Arm sweep begins.

The palms then turn outwards and the arms start to sweep outwards, downwards and backwards until they are just beyond shoulder width apart.

Bent arm action

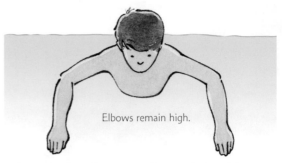

Elbows remain high.

When the hands are just beyond shoulder width apart (see illustration 2, left), the elbows bend but remain high while the hands sweep backwards and downwards, palms facing the feet and fingers pointing to the pool bottom.

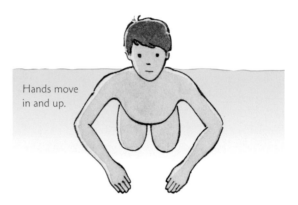

Hands move in and up.

When the hands are underneath the elbows, they start to move together again in a swirling, inwards and upwards movement. The elbows follow the hands in to the sides of the body.

Hands in prayer position

The palms will probably be in a prayer position or facing upwards at the end of this movement. They should be turned downwards at the start of the glide.

Straight arm action

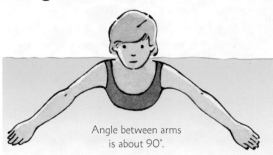

Angle between arms is about 90°.

When the hands are just beyond shoulder width apart (see illustration 2 on the page opposite) the arms remain almost straight and continue the sweep until they're almost level with the shoulders and wide of them, and the fingertips are about 30cm (12in) below the surface.

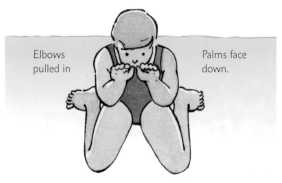

Elbows pulled in

Palms face down.

The elbows now bend and drop, the hands are brought together with the palms facing downwards and the elbows are pulled in to the sides of the body. The arms then stretch forwards smoothly and quickly.

Hands and fingers

Whether children are using the straight arm or bent arm action, encourage them to keep their fingers together and palms slightly cupped as they sweep out to the side. This will help them to pull through the water.

Aim to create "spoons" – hands slightly cupped, fingers together.

Avoid "forks" – flat hands with splayed-out fingers.

Arm action practices

1. Practise the arm action standing on the poolside, leaning forwards. The fingers should be cupped not splayed.

1a. Arms outstretched and hands together

Bend at the hips.

1b. Keep elbows high.

1c. Prayer position

2. Practise the arm action standing in shallow water.

3. Push and glide with the chin on the water and a woggle under the armpits, then make an arm stroke. Gradually increase the number of strokes.

4. Remove the woggle and repeat practice 3 holding a pull-buoy between the legs.

Pull-buoy

5. Push and glide from the side with a woggle under the armpits and with the chin on the water. Make an arm stroke and then a leg kick and glide, gradually increasing the number of strokes.

Breathing and coordination

Once their arms and legs are working well together, children will swim the stroke more efficiently if they put their face in the water for part of the stroke and so reduce the angle of their body.

Breathing and coordination practices

1. Standing in the water, do the arm action and breathe to the front.

2. Practise the leg action, holding a float in front with the face in the water. Every few strokes, raise the head minimally to breathe just as the legs are starting to be drawn up to the bottom.

3. Push and glide from the side of the pool and add one full stroke.

4. Practise the full stroke with the face in the water, increasing the number of breaths taken across the width of the pool.

5. Do the full stroke, breathing every stroke.

6. Count the number of strokes it takes to swim a width, then try to reduce it.

7. Do two arm strokes to one leg kick.

8. Do two leg kicks to one arm stroke.

Remember...

Pull, breathe, kick then glide. While the arms are moving, the legs are streamlined and vice versa.

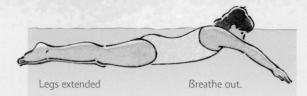

Legs extended   Breathe out.

Breathing out should take place into the water through the mouth and nose during the glide and first part of the arm pull. When the arm action begins, the legs are fully extended.

Legs start to be drawn up.   Breathe in.

A breath is taken at the end of the final sweep of the arm pull and the legs start to be drawn up to the bottom. The head should be raised to breathe by pushing the chin forward the minimum amount needed for the mouth to clear the water.

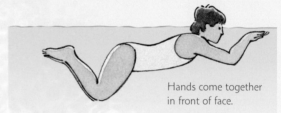

Hands come together in front of face.

The legs continue to be drawn up as the hands come together in front of the face.

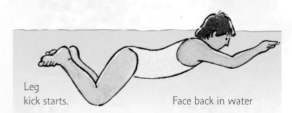

Leg kick starts.   Face back in water

As the arms stretch forwards, the leg kick starts. The face should be back in the water.

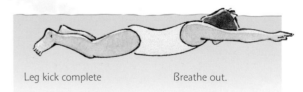

Leg kick complete   Breathe out.

By the time the arms are fully extended, the leg kick is complete.

Common faults

The best way to avoid faults creeping in is to master the stroke in stages. Keep any corrections you have to make clear and simple. Let children see the correct action demonstrated.

Breast stroke checklist

Fault	Correction

✗ The head is held too high out of the water so the hips and legs are too low and the body meets a lot of water resistance.

Water resistance

✓ Do breathing practices.

✓ Push and glide with the chin on the water.

✗ Not kicking symmetrically is caused either by moving the head about or not keeping the shoulders or hips level.

✓ Practise the leg action, first holding a woggle under the armpits or a float under each arm, then holding a float out in front, with the chin on the water. Concentrate on looking ahead, keeping the head steady and the shoulders level. This should keep the hips level. Make sure the knees bend the same amount and in the same direction.

✗ Pointing the feet, instead of turning them out and up.

✓ Push and glide from the rail with the feet placed on the wall like a frog's feet.

✓ Pretend to be a frog and jump into the water (at a safe depth) with the feet turned out.

✓ Practise the leg action lying on the back, watching the feet to make sure the heels are pushing back.

✓ Practise the leg action holding a woggle under the armpits, a float under each arm or one float out in front. Focus on pushing back hard with the heels.

✗ Pulling too far back.

✓ Practise the arm action standing up. Make sure the movement takes place in front of the shoulders and that the hands are always in sight.

✗ Bobbing up and down is caused either by bringing the knees too far under the body or by lifting the head too high to breathe.

✓ Practise the leg action with one or two floats or a woggle, ensuring the heels come up to the bottom.

✓ Do the breathing practices, keeping the head and shoulders steady and just pushing the chin forward until it is on the surface of the water.

More water skills

Children can start learning the skills described on these pages at the same time as starting to learn the major strokes. They will add variety and most of them are very useful survival skills.

Tip...

Remember to introduce new water skills one at a time so that children don't get confused.

Sculling

This is an arm action that children can use either to keep afloat in one place or to move gently through the water.

Children should lie flat on their back with their arms by their sides. The arms should be straight but relaxed, with the hands in line with the forearms. The arms then move sideways away from the body with the little fingers raised slightly so that the palms are facing outwards and downwards. The angle of tilt should be no more than 30°.

The hands shouldn't move more than about 30cm (12in) away from the body before turning to come in again. On the inward movement the thumbs should be raised so that the palms face inwards and downwards.

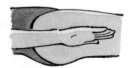 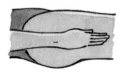

Palms push away from body.   Palms pull towards body.

This action should be repeated continuously. There should be equal pressure on both outward and inward movements and the movement should start at the shoulders.

Sculling on the spot

To scull on the spot, the action should be made with the palms facing downwards.

Palms face down.

Sculling head first

To travel head first, the sculling action should be made with the wrists bent upwards.

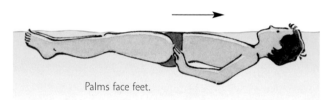

Palms face feet.

Sculling feet first

To travel feet first, the sculling action should be made with the wrists bent downwards.

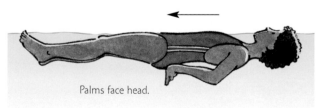

Palms face head.

Tip...

Children may find it helpful to practise with a pull-buoy between their ankles to start with, to keep them afloat.

Sculling practices

1. Practise the arm action standing on the side of the pool.

2. Practise the arm action standing in the pool, with the arms resting on the poolside at shoulder height. Imagine scooping out a hole in sand, using the thumbs on the outward movement and the little fingers on the inward movement.

3. Practise the arm action standing in shoulder depth water with the arms outstretched to the front and submerged. Start off slowly and build up speed.

4. Start the previous practice, then tilt the fingers upwards, lie back in the water and continue sculling. Move the hands so that they are alongside the hips. This should produce a head-first scull.

5. Begin as in practice 3, then tilt the fingers downwards, lie back and continue sculling to produce a feet-first scull.

6. Begin as in practice 3, then, keeping the palms flat, lie back and continue sculling to produce an on-the-spot scull.

Treading water

A good way of staying in one place in an upright position while using as little energy as possible is to tread water. This is useful if children are in difficulty and need to attract attention by waving.

The aim is to keep the mouth and nose above the water by making slow movements. It's a waste of energy to try to hold the body high out of the water. The arms should make gentle sculling actions at chest level, palms facing downwards, while the legs do either a breast stroke kick, or a cycling or scissor action.

Treading water practices

1. Practise the leg action with a woggle under the armpits or a float under each arm.

2. Practise, holding on to the rail or trough first with both hands, then with just one hand while the other sculls out to the side.

3. Practise treading water astride a woggle.

4. Practise treading water using the various leg actions, aiming to stay afloat for longer each time.

Mouth and nose above surface

Arms make sculling movements.

Breast stroke kick

Cycling action

Scissor kick leg action

Floating

Floating is a vital survival skill that helps children conserve energy if they are in trouble in the water. The floats are shown in what is generally considered to be their order of difficulty. How well each child floats in a particular position depends partly on how they're built, so it's worth them trying all the floats to see which suits best.

The key to successful floating is feeling confident enough to relax completely. Start in shallow water so children can put their feet down quickly if needed. They can move to deeper water as their confidence increases.

Tip...

Encourage children to count during a float and aim to float for a little longer each time. They shouldn't hold face-down floats longer than a count of ten before coming up to breathe.

Floating on the back

Children should lie flat on their back with their arms by their sides. They may need to make gentle sculling movements to begin with until they get their balance and feel buoyant in the water. Floating in the star shape shown below will make them even more buoyant.

Children will find floating easier if they keep their head back like this and look up at the ceiling or sky.

Floating on the front

Children should breathe in and lie with their face in the water, either with their arms and legs outstretched or in a star shape. They should lift their head to breathe when they need to.

Lie horizontally.

Mushroom float

Children should lie on their front, take a deep breath in and then tuck up into a ball, hugging their legs with their arms. Their back should be as rounded as possible.

Pull the nose towards the knees.

Floating upright

This needs to be practised in fairly deep water from the start. After getting into an upright position, the arms should be outstretched, and the head tilted back, so the mouth and nose are just above the surface of the water.

Floating practices

Encourage children to try all the different ways of floating, supported by a woggle, or holding two floats, either at arms' length or under their arms, depending on the float they are doing.

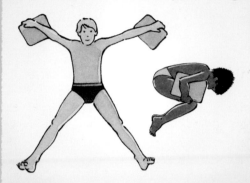

Get them to practise floating with your hand under their back, shoulders or head, gradually reducing the amount of support you give them, and finally removing it, as they gain confidence.

Floating alphabet

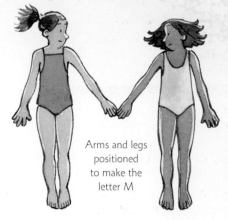

Arms and legs positioned to make the letter M

Once children feel confident floating on their back or front, they could try making different letter shapes, such as a T or Y. This activity can be done in pairs too, to make letters such as A, M or V.

Heat Escape Lessening Position (HELP)

If children get into difficulty in cold water, they can improve their chances of survival by keeping their internal organs warm while keeping their head above water (the body loses most heat through the head). They can practise the HELP position by hugging a thick float (or piece of floating debris such as a plastic bottle) with their legs pressed close together and their body suspended straight down, or leaning slightly backwards.

In an emergency, a child's clothes can help them conserve body heat, so once children are confident, it can be useful for them to practise this skill wearing a T-shirt and light-weight trousers or a skirt.

This girl is in the HELP position with her head above water, legs close together and arms hugging a float to her chest. This would help her survive if she were in trouble in cold water.

Jumping

Once children are confident about jumping into shallow water (of minimum depth 1m (3ft) or level with the child's armpit when standing on the bottom of the pool) they can start jumping in out of their depth (as long as they know how to come to the surface again). The straddle and tuck jumps described on these pages can be useful if children need to jump into water in an emergency without knowing its depth.

Straight jump

Children should jump up and out from the edge of the pool and enter the water with their body upright, toes pointed and their eyes looking forwards. After entering the water, it's important to bend the knees to avoid injuring the spine if they happen to touch the bottom.

When they are doing a straight jump, remind children to point their toes, and make their bodies tall and thin like a pencil.

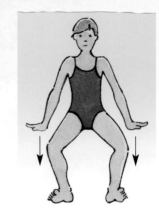

Press down with the palms of the hands.

To surface, children should do a strong breast stroke leg kick and pull their arms down strongly from above their head to their sides, pressing downwards with the palms of their hands.

Straddle or step jump

Children should not make this jump from a height of more than 1m (3ft) above the water or it will be painful. Although it is a shallow jump, to begin with it should be practised in water that is at least 0.5m (1.5ft) deeper than the height of the child with their arms stretched above their head, to be sure they avoid hitting the pool floor.

Children should step out from the edge of the pool, rather than jump, and enter the water with one foot forward, the other back. The arms should be in front of the body at shoulder level with the elbows bent. The top part of their body should be leaning forwards slightly. This position increases the area of their body that hits the water and so prevents them sinking very far.

As they enter the water, children should keep their legs apart and press the palms of their hands down towards the bottom of the pool. This will also help stop them from sinking.

One foot forward, one foot back

74

Tuck jump

A tuck jump will make a slightly deeper entry into the water but can be made from a greater height than a straddle step. It should be practised in deep water. As children jump or step off the edge, they should tuck the knees up to the chest, clasping the arms round the legs, so that their bottom hits the water first. Surfacing is the same as for a straight jump.

Tuck to stretch jump

Children should jump up and out with their arms by their sides. At the top of the jump they should tuck their knees up and clasp them with their hands. They should then lift their arms above their head and straighten their body to as near vertical as possible before hitting the water.

Star jump

Children should jump up and out, making a star shape with their arms and legs. Before hitting the water, they should bring their legs together and raise their arms above their head, so their body is as straight and vertical as possible. The star, tuck and stretch jumps will help prepare children for diving head first into the pool.

Climbing out

There might not always be steps around when children need to get out of water, so for safety reasons, they should practise climbing out of the water without a ladder.

As their arms get stronger they can practise pulling themselves up from deeper water, where they won't have the help of a push-off from the bottom.

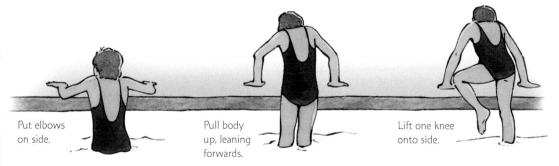

Put elbows on side.

Pull body up, leaning forwards.

Lift one knee onto side.

Start off in shallow water, reach up and put the elbows onto the poolside.

Push off from the pool bottom, lean forwards and pull the body up until the arms are straight and supporting the body.

Lift one knee onto the poolside, then bring up the other and stand up.

Surface diving

It can be useful to be able to dive from the surface in an emergency, but children are more likely to use surface dives at the swimming pool for the fun of picking things up from the pool bottom or swimming through someone's legs.

Head-first surface dive

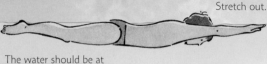

Stretch out.

The water should be at least shoulder depth.

Head between arms

1. Children should take a deep breath and stretch out on their front.

Bend at hips.

Breast stroke arm pull

2. They should make a quick breast stroke arm pull and bend sharply at the hips, forcing the head and shoulders down into the water.

Straighten at hips.

Push arms forward.

3. As the legs start to come out of the water, the hips should straighten so the legs are raised into the air. At the same time, the arms should be pushed forwards again until they are outstretched in line with the body.

Weight of legs drives body down.

Arms in line with body

4. Children can go deeper by making another breast stroke pull, but no leg action should be made until the legs and feet are totally submerged.

5. To get into a more horizontal position for swimming under water, the fingers should be turned upwards and the head lifted.

Submerging practices

1. Blow bubbles in the water.

2. Swim through someone's legs.

3. Go down to touch the pool floor.

4. Count how many fingers someone is holding up under the water.

Feet-first surface dive

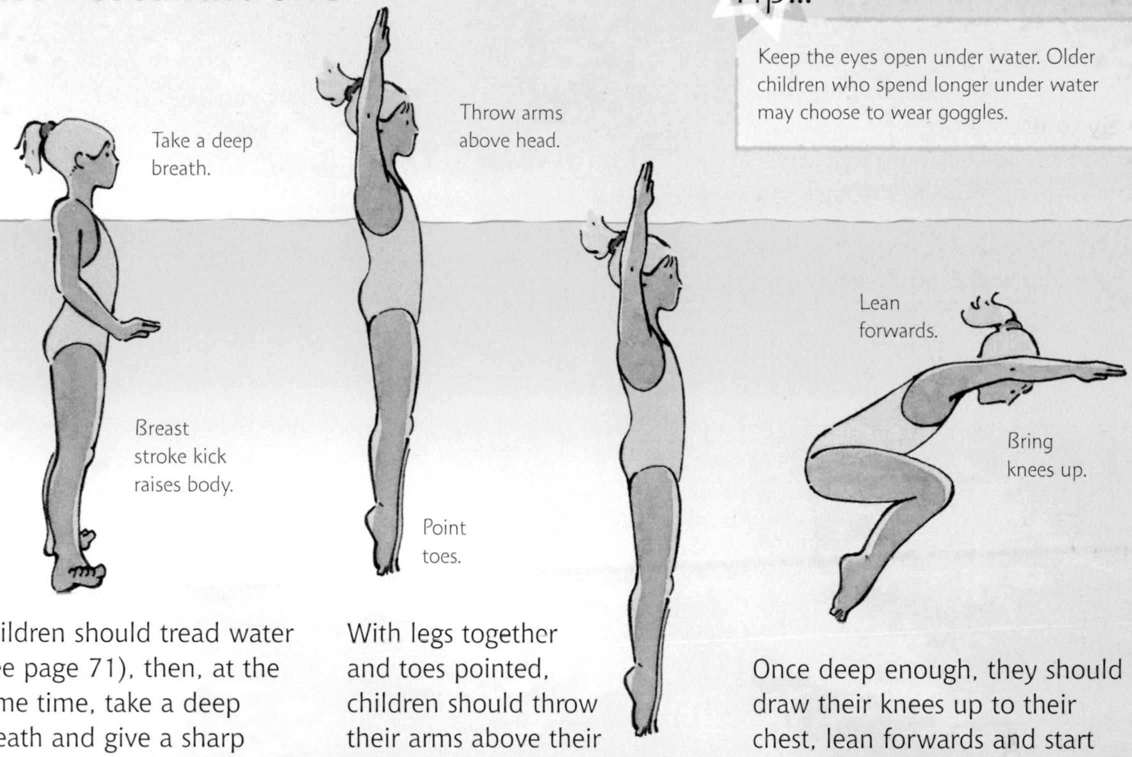
Take a deep breath.
Breast stroke kick raises body.
Throw arms above head.
Point toes.
Lean forwards.
Bring knees up.

Children should tread water (see page 71), then, at the same time, take a deep breath and give a sharp kick to raise their body high out of the water.

With legs together and toes pointed, children should throw their arms above their head, and let their body sink under the water.

Once deep enough, they should draw their knees up to their chest, lean forwards and start swimming, keeping their head down to stay under water.

Tip...

Keep the eyes open under water. Older children who spend longer under water may choose to wear goggles.

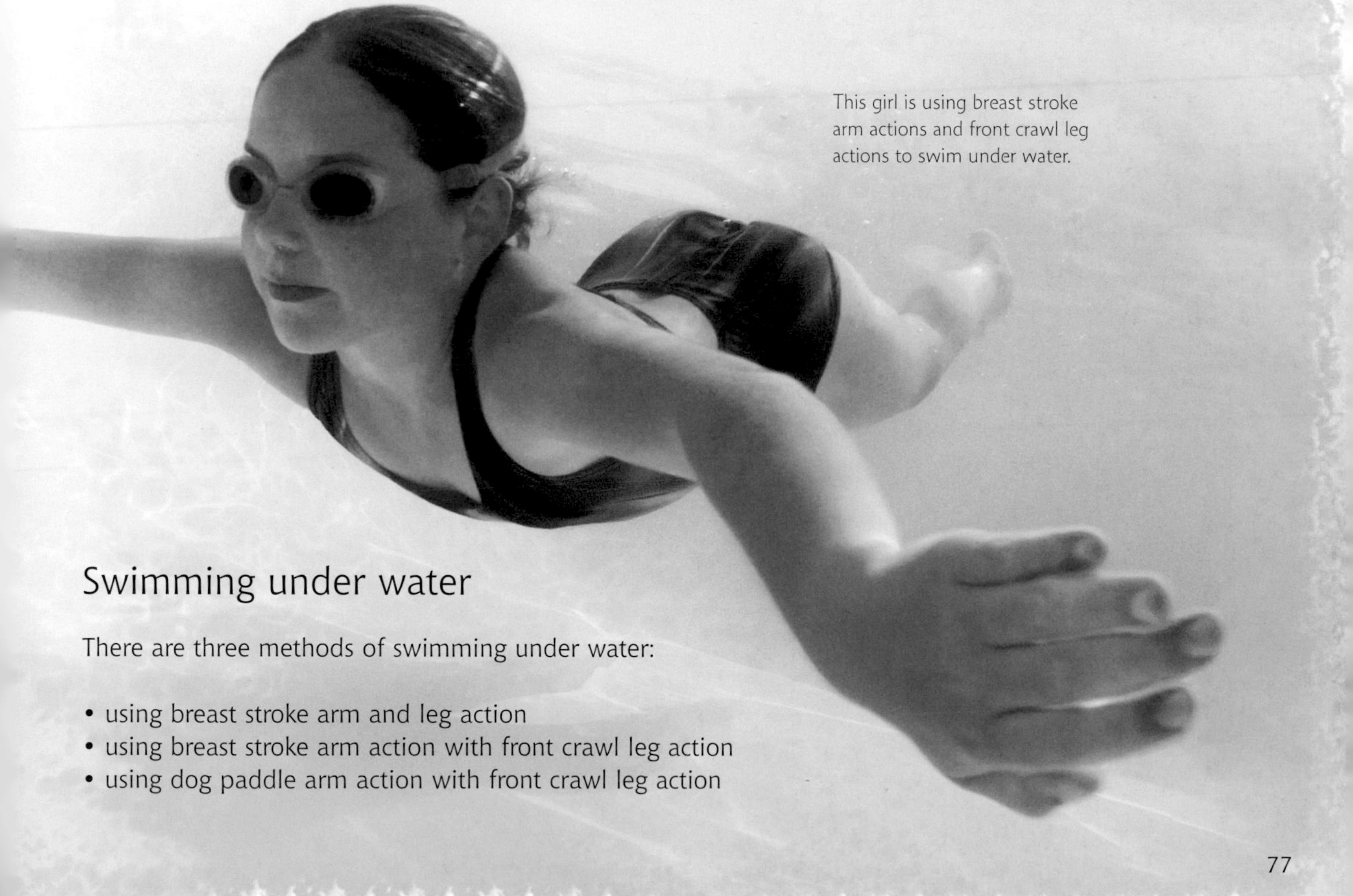

This girl is using breast stroke arm actions and front crawl leg actions to swim under water.

Swimming under water

There are three methods of swimming under water:

- using breast stroke arm and leg action
- using breast stroke arm action with front crawl leg action
- using dog paddle arm action with front crawl leg action

Somersaults

Turning somersaults
in the water is fun and
helps children to develop
confidence. It's also very
good preparation for
diving and learning
to do flip turns.

*During a somersault,
keep in a tucked
position with the
back rounded and
the toes pointed.*

Forward somersault

Children should start by lying on their front,
doing an on-the-spot scull with their arms,
before raising the head to breathe in.

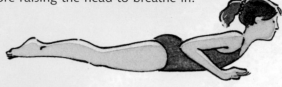

They should bring their knees up
to their chest and, tucking their
chin down to the knees, press
down with their palms and
start to somersault forwards.

Making backward
scooping movements
with their hands will
help children rotate
their body. Encourage
them to imagine they
are turning a skipping
rope backwards.

Their body should be kept
in a tight tucked position
throughout the somersault,
with the back rounded
and toes pointed.

When the head reaches the surface,
children should start to straighten
out and scull on the spot again,
then raise their head.

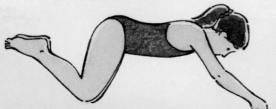

Tip...

Hum to prevent
water from going
up the nose.

Backward somersault

Children should start on their back, doing an on-the-spot scull with their arms, then breathe in.

Tip...

The tighter the tuck, the faster the somersault will be, so practise getting the knees to touch the chest.

Lifting their bottom and pulling their knees towards their eyes, they should press down with their palms and start to somersault backwards.

Somersault practices

1. Practise the tucked position without somersaulting.

2. Push and glide from the side then somersault, on the back or front.

Making forward scooping movements with their hands will help children rotate their body. Encourage them to imagine they are turning a skipping rope forwards.

3. Swim breast stroke then somersault forwards.

They should keep their body in a tight tucked position throughout the somersault, with their back rounded and toes pointed.

4. Spring off the pool bottom into a somersault.

When their lower legs reach the surface, they should start to straighten out and scull on the spot again.

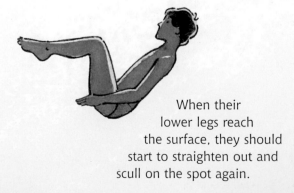

79

Diving

Diving can add a completely new dimension to a swimming session and offers children a lot of fun and a sense of achievement. Some children take to diving more naturally than others, though, and you should avoid forcing children to dive, as some may find it frightening.

Before you start

Children need to be thoroughly confident about swimming in deep water, jumping into deep water and swimming under water with their eyes open before they start diving. They also need to have good breath control.

Before they start diving properly, they should try the submerging practices described on page 76 and the preliminary practices described on these pages. The submerging, stretching and jumping practices can all be done in the shallow end. The getting into the water practices need to be done in deeper water.

Always make sure the water is deep enough for diving. It needs to be at least 1.8m (5ft 10in) for children attempting the dives described on pages 82–83. Instil into children that their hands must always enter the water first when they dive and that they should keep their heads firmly between their arms, to avoid any risk of head or spine injuries.

Tip...

Encourage children to keep their arms against the ears and to look at their tummy to protect their head and spine.

Jumping practices

1. Jump as high as possible out of the water, keeping the body streamlined and stretched.

2. Jump and dive over a partner's arms, held on the surface of the water.

3. Jump into a handstand in shoulder depth water.

4. Jump as high as possible and turn in the air, keeping the body streamlined and stretched.

5. Jump as high as possible and make different shapes in the air.

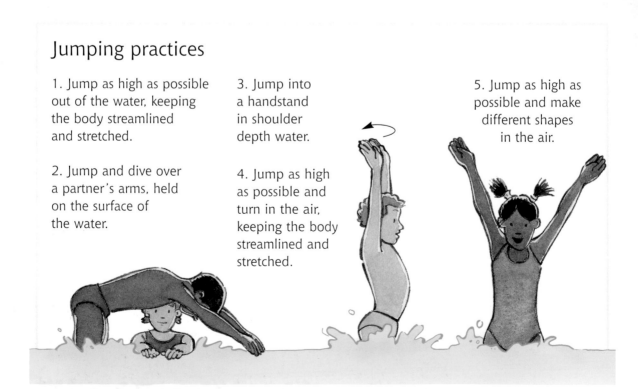

Pushing, gliding and stretching under water help children get ready for learning to dive in.

Stretching practices

1. Standing on the poolside, stretch up as tall as possible.

2. Push and glide from the side, turn the head to one side and roll in that direction. Roll from the front to the back and vice versa.

3. Do a mushroom float (see page 72), then stretch out horizontally.

4. Push and glide from the side to the pool bottom, then surface, either by turning the fingers up or lifting the head.

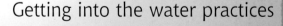

5. Do several surface dives (see page 76) one after the other like a leaping dolphin.

6. Do a handstand in shoulder depth water, concentrating on getting a good stretch.

7. Push and glide from the side into a forward or backward somersault.

Getting into the water practices

Jump into the water from the side of the pool, forwards and backwards, making different shapes in the air. (See pages 74–75 for jumps and how to surface.) Remember to bend the knees after entering the water, to avoid injuring the spine on landing.

Sitting dive

Children may prefer to dive in from a sitting position to begin with.

One hand clasps the fingers of the other.

Sitting with their feet on the rail or trough, children should extend their arms above their head, clasp one hand with the other and put their chin down to their chest.

Keep arms pressed against ears.

Taking care to keep the arms and head in this position, children should bend forwards until they overbalance, lift their hips up and then push off from the rail and stretch forwards and down.

Kneeling dive

Children may like to start diving with one foot in front of the other. In this case, they should make sure their front foot grips the edge of the pool firmly to avoid slipping. They should progress to a two-footed take-off as soon as possible to avoid dives becoming lop-sided.

Children should go down on one knee at the pool edge with the toes of their front foot gripping the edge, and the toes of their back foot resting on the floor. Their arms, head and hands should be positioned as for the sitting dive.

One hand over the other

They should lean forwards until they overbalance, then push off with their front foot and stretch forwards and down, taking special care to keep their head down because of the greater height involved.

Eyes looking at tummy

A diver can achieve a streamlined shape like this by keeping their legs together and toes pointed, their head tucked between the arms, and one hand on top of the other.

Crouch dive

Children should crouch on the poolside, with their toes gripping the edge and their arms and head and hands in the same position as before.

This time, when they overbalance and push off, they should try to get their legs straighter and aim for a less flat entry into the water.

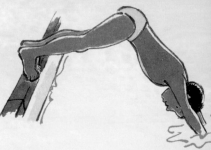

Lunge dive

This is a progression from a kneeling dive.

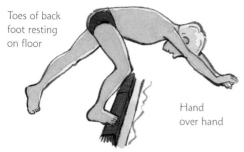

Toes of back foot resting on floor

Hand over hand

For this dive, children should stand on the edge of the pool, with their front leg well bent and their back leg straighter. Their toes should grip the edge firmly. The arms, head and hands should be in the same position as before.

Aim to enter the water well away from the side.

They should overbalance and push off with their front leg, at the same time lifting their back leg into the air, then bring both legs together during flight.

Tip...

Head down, hips up: remind children to squeeze their arms onto their ears and look at their tummy as they dive, pushing their hips up as they launch from the side.

Plunge dive

This is a progression from a crouch dive and forms the basis for racing dives.

Look at a point to aim for.

Children should crouch on the edge, looking at the point where they aim to enter the water.

Keep head down and hips up.

They should overbalance forwards, swing their arms into position, lower their head and push off vigorously with their feet.

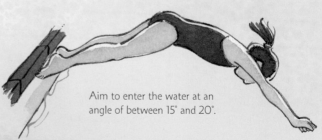

Aim to enter the water at an angle of between 15° and 20°.

Children should stretch as fully as they can during flight and keep this streamlined position until their body is totally submerged. To surface, they should tilt their fingers upwards and raise their head. Encourage children to glide as far as possible before starting to swim.

Games

Playing games in the water is not only fun and relaxing, but can also encourage children to be more versatile in their movement in water. Here are a few ideas for games to play at the swimming pool.

Playing games

The type of games that can be played in a public pool will depend on its rules and regulations and on how crowded it is. Most of the games described here don't need balls or other equipment as many pools do not allow these except in organized classes.

You will need to supervise all games especially closely; accidents are more likely to happen if children are excited and playing in a group. Children who aren't totally competent when out of their depth should wear armbands.

Most of these games will probably work best with more than the minimum number of players. You may be able to adapt the games, or invent others, to suit the age, ability level and number of children involved. Don't forget the value of action songs and rhymes, especially for younger children (see pages 30–33).

On-the-spot games

These can be played in a small area of the pool.

Simon says (3+ players)

One person is "Simon", who gives instructions such as, "Simon says, 'Blow bubbles!'". Everyone must obey, unless the words "Simon says" are missed out, when they must not. Keep everyone in the game, even if they make a mistake.

Electricity (3+ players)

Players stand in a circle holding hands. One player "switches on" the current by squeezing the hand of the person next to them, who then squeezes the hand of the next person and ducks under the water. This continues around the circle.

These children are playing "kick-of-war", and strengthening their front crawl leg action at the same time.

Safety...

Avoid playing games with balls in the sea. These can be dangerous, as balls tend to float or blow away from the shore and children are tempted to follow them.

Still pond (3+ players)

Everyone floats as still as possible while one person watches. The last one to move wins.

Kick-of-war (2+ players)

Players lie on their front, holding a float between them, then kick to move themselves forwards and push their opponent backwards.

Races

Children can race individually or in teams. Make sure the teams are evenly matched in terms of ability, and keep the emphasis on having fun.

Skill races (2+ players)

Besides ordinary swimming races and relay races, players can run, jump, hop, side-step or walk on their hands through the water.

Bubble-blowing (2+ players)

Players walk or run, stopping to put their face in the water and blow bubbles every time they have gone an agreed number of paces.

Canoe race (2+ pairs)

Players in each pair stand one behind the other, facing in the same direction, with one woggle tucked under their right arms and another tucked under their left arms. (Small diving rings can be used to pull the ends of the two woggles together into a canoe shape.) Pairs race using front or back crawl leg kick.

Treasure hunt (2+ players)

Individuals, pairs or larger teams race to collect objects such as floats, balls and sinkable toys, and place them in a container or hoop on the side of the pool. This can be played as a race or by allocating points for different objects.

Tunnel swim (2+ players)

Players divide into two teams. Each team stands in line, one player in front of the other, legs apart. The person at the back of each team swims through the team's legs and stands up at the front. The next person then sets off, and so on until each player has swum through the tunnel.

This game is good practice for underwater swimming.

Pair swim (2+ pairs)

Each pair holds hands, then pushes off from the side and swims an agreed distance together, one-handed. Children can play this game with or without floats or woggles.

Shadow swim (2+ pairs)

One partner swims under water, while the other shadows them at the surface.

Try to match speed and stroke style.

Chain scull (2+ pairs)

Players in each pair lie on their back, one behind the other, with the feet of the back player gently resting on the shoulders of the front player. The pairs then scull an agreed distance head first or feet first.

Chasing games

Crows and cranes (3+ players)

Players line up on opposite sides of the pool. One person stands in the middle with a float and calls out the names of two people, one from each side. They have to race to the middle, take the float and try to get it back to their side without their opposite number touching them. A player who is touched gets a penalty point or takes over as the person with the float.

Statues (4+ players)

One player is "it" and the others have to stand still when "it" touches their arm (or other part of their bodies, agreed beforehand). Players can be "unfrozen" by another player touching them or swimming through their legs. The last one caught becomes "it".

Log roll tag (3+ players)

"It" floats or sculls on their back, surrounded by the others who must try to get as close to "it" as possible. "It" suddenly rolls over and tries to catch someone. Whoever is caught becomes "it".

Sharks and minnows (3+ players)

One person is the shark and stands in the middle of the pool. The others are minnows and line up at one side. When the shark shouts "sharks and minnows", they have to try to reach the other side without being caught. Anyone who is caught changes into a shark and helps catch the remaining minnows. The last player to be caught becomes the shark in the next game.

Red letter (3+ players)

"It" stands at one side of the pool, with their eyes shut, and facing away from the rest of the players, who line up on the opposite (home) side. "It" calls out letters of the alphabet; whenever a letter is called out that is in a player's name, that player can take a step forward. The aim is to reach and touch the other side, but when they are getting close, "it" suddenly shouts, "red letter!", turns round and chases them. Anyone who is caught before getting back to the home side becomes "it".

Playing games such as "sharks and minnows" can help children gain confidence in the water.

Swimming in the sea

The sea can be an excellent place to learn to swim, provided you are extremely careful about safety. Salt water is particularly buoyant, and there is often a large area of shallow water.

Safety...

Tides and currents can make the sea a dangerous place, so watch children carefully at all times.

Young children and the sea

Some young children are very frightened of the sea and need the same sort of handling as timid children at the pool. Avoid forcing them into the sea. Just let them play on the beach, encouraging them gradually to get nearer to the water until they're ready to venture in.

Water temperature

Children get cold more quickly than adults because they have less body fat, so they shouldn't stay in the sea when they're cold. It's not a good idea to put babies in any but the very warmest sea because they have no shiver reflex and can get dangerously cold with no apparent symptoms. (The sea in Britain is unlikely ever to be warm enough for babies.) The temperature of toddlers and young children also needs to be monitored very carefully.

If children are shivering, get them out of the water straight away and wrap them in towels, but don't rub them. It's most important to keep the body's internal organs warm, and rubbing only takes the blood away from them to bring it to the body surface.

Seaside safety

It is vitally important to take special care about safety in the sea. Follow the rules below and instil them into children. Some of the pool safety precautions also apply to the seaside.

- Never swim where a warning, for example a red flag, is displayed.

- Don't swim in places without information about the state of tides and currents.

- Never swim unless a competent adult is watching all the time. Young children should have an adult in the water with them.

- Only go out a short way, then swim parallel to the shore. This is especially important if the tide is going out, as it'll be harder to swim back than it was to swim out.

- Don't swim near boats, jet skiers, windsurfers or surfers.

- It's safest not to play on air-beds or in inflatable toy boats. Tides, winds and currents can quickly whip them out to sea.

Coping with emergencies

Routine safety precautions that you should take at swimming pools and in the sea are described earlier in the book. On these pages are a few more things to instil into children in case they are ever in trouble. The rest of the section gives some basic advice on how you can help a child in difficulty.

Life saving courses

You are most likely to help others successfully, without putting yourself in unnecessary danger, if you have followed a recognized life saving course. These are available for competent swimmers of all ages and you can find out more information at your local pool, library or council, or on the Internet.

If you are in difficulty

Try to keep calm. If you are near the edge of the water, try to reach it and get out. If you cannot, see if there is anything you can hold on to while you shout for help and wave one arm to attract attention.

Hold on to anything suitable, shout and wave.

If you fall into water with your clothes on, take off anything heavy that will drag you down, such as a jacket, coat or shoes. Light clothes help the body to retain heat, so you should leave those on.

Try to keep afloat with the minimum of exertion, treading water or adopting the HELP position (see page 73). Treading water can be especially useful because you can wave one arm as you do it to attract attention, as shown here.

If you are in difficulty, tread water and wave to attract attention.

Exerting yourself as little as possible is important, not only to prevent you getting tired, but also to help keep you warm if you are in cold water, that is, water of less than 25°C (77°F). (In Britain, the temperature of unheated water seldom reaches 15°C (59°F).) Any movement will lead to a drop in body temperature by increasing the blood flow to your body surface; this blood is cooled by the water and then circulates around your body, lowering its temperature.

If possible, avoid getting your head wet, too. Unlike most of the rest of your body, your head doesn't have an insulating layer, which means you lose heat from it very quickly.

Tip...

If several people are involved in an emergency, huddle together as closely as possible, depending on the type of floating support available. For example, if you're wearing life jackets, huddle together in a ring, or hold on to a life raft or boat.

If someone else is in difficulty

Shout for help or send someone to fetch help. Don't get into the water yourself if you can possibly rescue the person without doing so. They may be panicking and drag you down with them. Speak to them calmly and keep any instructions clear and simple.

Near the edge

If the person is near the edge of the water, lie down flat, hold on to something secure if possible, and try to grab their wrist (don't let them grab you). Getting down low and grabbing the wrist, rather than the hand, reduces the risk of being dragged in yourself. If anyone else is with you, they should kneel down and hold your legs.

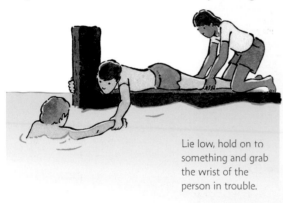

Lie low, hold on to something and grab the wrist of the person in trouble.

If the person is too far out to reach with your hand, quickly look for something to extend your reach: a stick or branch, rope, scarf, towels or clothes, knotted together if necessary. Lie down as you pull the person in.

Hold on to something, lie down and reach out with a branch, rope or clothes.

Further out

If the person is too far out to reach, throw something that will float, such as a beach ball, rubber ring, or plank of wood for them to hold on to. Don't aim it directly at them but try to make sure it lands within easy reach. Once they are holding the object, tell them either to stay where they are or to try to reach safety by kicking with their legs.

Throw a buoyant object, such as a ball, to a person too far out to reach.

If you're alone, you may be able to wade in until you're close enough to throw or hold something out to the person. If you hold something out, first lean backwards and get a firm foothold to avoid being pulled over.

Rescue key points

- **Summon help.**
  Shout or send for help.

- **Reach.**
  Lie down flat and hold on to something. Reach out to grab the person's wrist. Extend your reach if necessary, for example by using a branch, stick, clothing or rope.

- **Throw.**
  Throw a floating object such as a lifebelt, ball, or piece of wood.

- **Go for help.**
  If help has not already been summoned, go for help. Then come back and reassess the situation.

- **Avoid getting into the water unless you absolutely have to.**

Quite far out in deep water

If you're a very good swimmer, you could swim out to the casualty with a floating object. Take off any bulky clothes and your shoes first. Be sure to push the object towards them so that they grab it, not you. Now you can either wait with them until help arrives, go back on your own to fetch help, or encourage them to swim back with you as they hold on to the object and kick with their legs.

Sculling backwards using an upside-down breast stroke leg action will help you supervise and encourage a person in trouble.

As a last resort, it may be possible to give the casualty some clothing to hang on to so you can tow them, swimming on your side or your back.

Use side stroke with a scissor kick as you tow the person to safety.

Getting a casualty out of water

If the person can't get out of the water on their own, help them by pushing them out. If they can't manage, tell them to hold on to something and get out yourself. Then, holding their wrist and bending your knees, count to three and pull them out. You may need a second person to help you lift someone who is the same weight as you, or heavier.

Now lift them up over the edge, letting them rest first of all on your extended straight leg before you lower their body gently to the ground. Take care to protect their head as you do this. Now lift their legs over the edge.

Helping a choking baby

If you can, use a finger to remove an obvious obstruction from a baby's mouth (be careful not to push it down). If they are still choking, lay them face down with their head lower than the rest of their body, and give them up to five sharp slaps on the back, with a flat hand. After each slap, check the mouth to see if the obstruction has cleared.

If this is unsuccessful, lie the baby on their back and place two fingertips on their breast bone, a finger's width below the nipples. Give up to five sharp thrusts into the chest. Check the mouth each time. Send for an ambulance and repeat the cycle of slaps and thrusts until the baby recovers or help arrives. If the baby becomes unconscious, start CPR immediately (see page 91) and send for an ambulance if one isn't already on its way.

Helping a choking child

If a child can't clear the obstruction by coughing, lean them forwards and give up to five sharp slaps between the shoulders. Check the mouth after each slap and remove any obvious obstruction (be careful not to push it down).

If this is unsuccessful, stand or kneel behind them, place your fist in their upper abdomen and press sharply into the body and upwards up to five times. Check the mouth each time. Give up to another five back slaps. Send for an ambulance and repeat the cycle of slaps and upper abdomen presses until the child recovers or help arrives. If the child becomes unconscious, start CPR straight away (see page 91) and send for an ambulance if one isn't already on its way.

Resuscitation

If a person is unconscious, it's possible that they're not breathing. Their heart may also have stopped beating. In either case, it is vital you start resuscitation immediately, to get oxygen into their lungs and get the heart pumping the oxygenated blood round their body. The brain suffers particularly quickly from lack of oxygen.

Check for signs of consciousness by gently shaking and shouting at the casualty. If they don't respond, check the mouth and clear it of any obstruction, such as seaweed or vomit, if necessary. Use two fingers to tilt the head back with the chin lifted up. (For a baby, use only one finger, making sure you don't tilt the head back too far.) This straightens out the airways and removes the tongue from the back of the throat so they can breathe. Spend up to 10 seconds checking for signs of breathing. If they are breathing, put them in the recovery position (see page 93).

If you can't see, hear or feel them breathing, send for medical help straight away and prepare to start CPR.

Tilt the head back and lift the chin.

CPR

CPR (cardiopulmonary resuscitation) combines external chest compressions (see page 92) and rescue breathing. You should never perform CPR on a healthy person or a conscious casualty.

If the casualty is a baby or child, give five rescue breaths, then give them 30 chest compressions alternating with two rescue breaths. If the casualty is an adult and help is not already on the way, go for help, then come back and give CPR, starting with chest compressions, and following every 30 compressions with two rescue breaths. Keep going with CPR until help arrives, you are exhausted or the casualty recovers. If normal breathing returns, put them in the recovery position (see page 93).

Performing rescue breathing

If the casualty is **a baby or a small child**, keep the head tilted back, open the mouth, then seal your lips around the mouth and nose, and breathe into their lungs gently and steadily, watching their chest rise as the lungs are filled with air. (Blow from your cheeks rather than breathing deeply from your lungs.)

Mouth covers baby's mouth and nose.

If the casualty is **a larger child or an adult**, keep the head tilted back, open the mouth with one hand and with your other hand pinch the nostrils firmly together. Seal your lips around the mouth and breathe into the lungs slowly and steadily, watching the chest rise as the lungs are filled with air.

When the chest falls, put in the next breath.

Mouth covers mouth only.

Rescue breathing in water

You may need to start rescue breathing while you're still in the water. If you're within your depth, try to support the casualty's body with one arm, use two fingers to hold their chin shut, closing the mouth, and blow into the nose.

Mouth covers casualty's nose.

Remember...

You may need to adjust your technique depending on the size of the casualty. For example, rescue breaths should preferably be given to a child through the mouth, but if your mouth covers the mouth and nose of a small child, then this method would be most appropriate.

Performing chest compressions

Lie the casualty on their back on a firm surface while you kneel alongside, facing their chest and in line with the heart. Pressure needs to be applied to the breastbone. Performed incorrectly, chest compressions can injure the casualty further, so it is important to press in the centre of the casualty's chest.

Babies

Use very gentle pressure with two fingers. Press at a rate of 100 times per minute to a depth of 1/3 of the chest cavity.

Children

Use light pressure with the heel of one hand. Press at a rate of 100 times per minute to a depth of 1/3 of the chest cavity.

Adults

Place the heel of one hand in the centre of the chest. Place the heel of the other hand on top and interlock your fingers to hold them away from the casualty's body. Push straight down 4 to 5cm (about 2in). Bend your elbows slightly to release the pressure (don't rock) between compressions, keeping your hands on their chest. Aim for 100 compressions per minute.

Remember...

You may need to adjust your technique depending on the size of the casualty. For example you may find you need to use two hands, rather than one, to give chest compressions to an older child, making this method most appropriate.

Resuscitation key points

- **Remove casualty from danger.**

- **Check response.**
  Does casualty respond to speech and touch?

- **Summon help.**
  If casualty responds, put them in the recovery position and go for help.
  If there is no response, shout for help.

- **Open the airway.**
  Tilt the head, clear obstructions, lift the chin.

- **Check breathing** (for up to 10 seconds).
  Look, listen and feel for signs.

- **No breathing – give rescue breaths.**
  Give **5 breaths** to babies and children.
  (If an adult is not breathing and help is not on its way, go for help now. Then return and start CPR with 30 chest compressions. If help is on its way, go straight into CPR with 30 chest compressions.)

- **Still no breathing – start CPR.**
  Perform chest compressions in the centre of the chest.

- **Babies and children**
  Use two or three fingers for **babies.**
  Use the heel of the hand for **children.**
  30 compressions: 2 breaths
  100 compressions per minute
  Depth: 1/3 chest cavity

  Give CPR for 1 minute then, if help is not already on its way, go for help (you can take a baby or small child with you). If you have to leave a child to go for help, continue CPR as soon as you return.

- **Adults**
  Use clasped hands.
  30 compressions: 2 breaths
  100 compressions per minute
  Depth: 4–5cm (about 2in)

- **Stop CPR when:**
  Help arrives.
  You are exhausted.
  Casualty recovers.

The recovery position

An unconscious person who is breathing and whose heart is beating should be put in the recovery position. By doing this, you will help to keep their airways clear so they can breathe easily and will not choke. (People often vomit before they lapse into, or as they come round from, unconsciousness.)

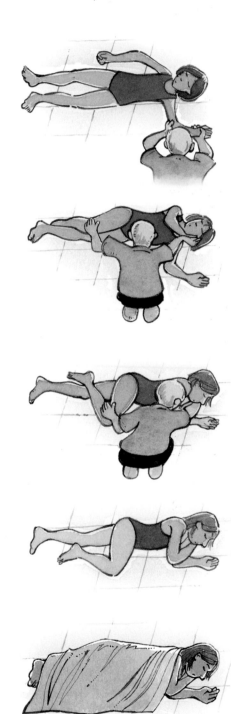

1. Straighten the legs and place the arm nearest to you at right angles to the body, with the palm upwards.

2. Bring their other arm across the chest and hold the palm against the cheek to support the casualty's head while you turn them. (Turn scratchy rings away from their face.) Hold the leg furthest away from you above the knee and lift it towards you. The leg will bend while the foot stays on the floor.

3. Keeping hold of the casualty's knee and supporting the head, use the leg as a lever to help roll them over towards you. Adjust the casualty's upper leg if necessary, so the hip and knee are both bent at right angles.

4. Tilt the chin forwards to keep the tongue clear of the airways. Adjust the position of the hand under the cheek if you need to.

5. Cover the casualty with a coat or towel to keep them warm.

Going further

Swimming classes are an excellent way to help children become more confident in the water and improve their skills. There are classes for children of different ages and levels of ability.

Classes and clubs

Going to classes and clubs can improve children's swimming and fitness and give them the chance to meet other swimmers. They can provide information about the many nationally recognized awards that children can take at different levels and in different types of swimming. Classes and clubs can also help children follow up or develop an interest in a particular aspect of swimming – perhaps learning life saving or diving, or taking up synchronized swimming, water polo, or open water swimming.

Finding information

The best place to find out about classes and clubs in your area is from the notice board at your local swimming pool. The local council (recreation and amenities department) should also have lists on their websites, and libraries may have information too. Remember to make sure that any class or club is run by people with a recognized qualification*.

Joining a swimming class or club can help children develop their swimming skills, make new friends and form part of a healthy lifestyle.

Internet links

The Internet is a good source of information about local swimming pools and teaching your child to swim. At the Usborne Quicklinks Website we have created links to websites you may find useful.

To visit the sites, go to **www.usborne-quicklinks.com** and type the keyword "swim". Here are some of the things you can do on the Internet:

• Look for baby-friendly swimming pools in your area.

• Watch animated demonstrations of strokes.

• Brush up on the words and tunes to action songs and nursery rhymes.

Internet safety

The websites recommended in Usborne Quicklinks are regularly reviewed. However, the content of a website may change at any time and Usborne Publishing is not responsible for the content of websites other than its own. We recommend that children are supervised while on the Internet.

*In the UK, this will be from the Amateur Swimming Association or the Swimming Teachers' Association.

Index

Photography credits

Every effort has been made to trace the copyright holders of the material in this book.
If any rights have been omitted, the publishers offer to rectify this in any future edition,
following notification. The publishers are grateful to the following organizations and
individuals for their contribution and permission to reproduce this material.

Usborne Publishing is particularly grateful to:
Amateur Swimming Association
Delphin Swim Discs
Down's Syndrome Association
Floaties (www.qpie.co.uk)
Jaco Enterprises, Inc.
Kushies®
Swimshop®
Zoggs International Ltd

(t = top, m = middle, b = bottom, l = left, r = right)
4 © Daniella Boutin; 6b © Daniella Boutin; 7t Profimedia.CZ s.r.o/Alamy; 8b LWA-Dann Tardif/CORBIS;
10b David Oliver/Stone/Getty Images; 11b © Usborne Publishing Ltd; 12t © Usborne Publishing Ltd;
13b Taxi/Getty Images; 14t Creatas/Oxford Scientific; 15b Profimedia.CZ s.r.o./Alamy; 16b Stockbyte Gold/Getty
Images; 16mrt Kushies Swim Nappy © Kushies®; 16mrb Floaties Standard Aquanappy © Incy Wincy, info@
incywincy.net, Tel. 0118 3773 581, www.incywincy.net; 17t © Daniella Boutin;
18b RubberBall/Imagestate; 19bl © Usborne Publishing Ltd, courtesy of Delphin Swim Discs www.
schwimmscheiben.de; 19br © Early Learning Centre; 19m © Usborne Publishing Ltd;
19t Vstock/Alamy; 20b © Daniella Boutin; 20mr Zoggs Pull Buoy, courtesy of Zoggs International Ltd, www.
zoggs.com; 20tl photograph included by kind permission of the ASA; 20tr Win Swim Belt courtesy
of Swimshop® www.swimshop.co.uk; 21t © Daniella Boutin; 22b Profimedia.CZ s.r.o./Alamy;
23tr RubberBall/Alamy; 24b ACE STOCK LIMITED/Alamy; 26b Roy Ooms/Masterfile www.masterfile.com;
28 © Daniella Boutin; 30t © Daniella Boutin; 32b Profimedia.CZ s.r.o./Alamy; 34b Tim Kiusalaas/Masterfile
www.masterfile.com; 37 © Daniella Boutin; 39b Profimedia.CZ s.r.o./Alamy; 40b © Daniella Boutin;
42b © Daniella Boutin; 44t © Daniella Boutin; 45b Zac Macaulay/The Image Bank/Getty Images;
47b Profimedia.CZ s.r.o./Alamy; 48b © Down's Syndrome Association; 49t Ear Band-It® headband
photo courtesy of Jaco Enterprises, Inc., Phoenix, AZ, www.earbandit.com; 50&51b © Daniella Boutin;
56&57b © Daniella Boutin; 62m © Daniella Boutin; 63b © Daniella Boutin; 72b photograph included by
kind permission of the ASA; 73b © Daniella Boutin; 74 © Daniella Boutin; 77b David Nardini/Masterfile www.
masterfile.com; 78 © Daniella Boutin; 81t David Nardini/Masterfile www.masterfile.com;
82&83 © Daniella Boutin; 84b © Daniella Boutin; 86b © Daniella Boutin;
94b Candice Farmer/Taxi/Getty Images

Usborne Publishing is not responsible and does not accept liability for the availability or content of any website
other than its own, or for any exposure to harmful, offensive, or inaccurate material which may appear
on the Web. Usborne Publishing will have no liability for any damage or loss caused by viruses that
may be downloaded as a result of browsing the sites it recommends.

This revised edition first published in 2006 by Usborne Publishing Ltd,
Usborne House, 83-85 Saffron Hill, London EC1N 8RT, England.
www.usborne.com

Christine McMillan-Bodell

HAIRDRESSING & BARBERING

3rd edition

www.heinemann.co.uk

✓ Free online support
✓ Useful weblinks
✓ 24 hour online ordering

0845 630 4444

Heinemann is an imprint of Pearson Education Limited, a company incorporated in England and Wales, having its registered office at Edinburgh Gate, Harlow, Essex, CM20 2JE. Registered company number: 872828

www.heinemann.co.uk

Heinemann is a registered trademark of Pearson Education Limited

Text © Christine McMillan-Bodell, 2009

First published 2009

12 11 10 09
10 9 8 7 6 5 4 3 2

British Library Cataloguing in Publication Data
A catalogue record for this book is available from the British Library.

ISBN 978 0 435468 30 9

Edited by Rachael Williams
Designed by Wooden Ark
Typeset by Tek-Art
Original illustrations © Pearson Education Ltd, 2009
Illustrated by Mark Watkinson
Cover design by Wooden Ark
Picture research by Caitlin Swain
Cover photo/illustration © Anne Veck Salon, photographer Marco Loumiet
Printed in Spain by Graficas Estella

Websites
The websites used in this book were correct and up-to-date at the time of publication. It is essential for tutors to preview each website before using it in class so as to ensure that the URL is still accurate, relevant and appropriate. We suggest that tutors bookmark useful websites and consider enabling students to access them through the school/college intranet.

Contents

Acknowledgements

The author and publisher would like to thank the following individuals and organisations for permission to reproduce photographs: Anne Veck/Marco Loumiet p**6**; Masterfile/Robert Karpa p**8**; Alamy Images/PlainPicture GMBH&co.KG p**19**(bottom left [BL]); Science Photo Library/Cordelia Molloy p**19**(bottom right); Carlton Professional p**29**(BL), **173**(BL); iStockPhoto/Greg Nicholas p**34**; Image by TONI&GUY p**38**, **84**, **104**; Anne Veck/Clark Wiseman p**54**, **72**, **158**; Image Source p**68**, **144**; Goldwell p**69**; Science Photo Library p**88**, **89**; Denman p**109**(combs); HairTools p**109**(crimping irons); Anne Veck/Julian Knight p**118**, **132**; GettyImages/Giulio Marcocchi p**155**(bottom), **160**; Anne Veck p**166**(image I), **168**; JG photography/Alamy p**171**; Biophoto Associates/Science Photo Library p**172**(bottom). **All other photos:** Pearson Education Ltd/Mind Studio; Pearson Education Ltd/Gareth Boden/Chris Honeywell/Jules Selmes/Tudor Photography.

For their invaluable help and expertise at the Level I photoshoot the author and publisher wish to thank Anne Veck of Anne Veck Salons and the staff at her Bicester location. Thanks are also due to our models, Alice Carter and Catherine Lewis.

Every effort has been made to contact copyright holders of material reproduced in this book. Any omissions will be rectified in subsequent printings if notice is given to the publishers.

Author acknowledgements

Updating this book has enabled me to meet some truly professional people who are committed to hairdressing and care about it deeply as a vocation. When faced with challenges in life, it can be easy to put things off. But with planning and a positive attitude it is surprising what can be achieved. So often I use the words, 'I can, I am and I have.' Hard work and a lot of give and take is what you need to put in as you approach a long and rewarding career in hairdressing. Good luck to each of you!

Without the never-ending love, support and commitment of my family and friends, this book certainly would never have been written. I would like to dedicate this book to my partner Neil who has recently been diagnosed with head and neck cancer – he has always given 110% support.

Thank you to Banbury Postiche of Oxfordshire for their help, Anne Veck Hair Design, Bicester for her expertise and thank you to our models. Finally, to all at Heinemann (publishers, editors, artists, researchers): thank you.

Foreword by Andrew Barton

For a working class lad from a small town in Yorkshire, I've not done too badly. I've recently been named the most expensive and sought after hairdresser in the UK – pretty impressive to think that I started in a village salon! For me, there is no such thing as a typical day. One day I'm working with celebrities on a glamorous photo shoot, the next I could be travelling the world flying the British hairdressing flag with Saks at glitzy hair shows and educational seminars. I'm also recognised as TV's favourite hair expert and love spending time making clients happy at the Saks flagship salon in London. So how did all this come about?

I started a very traditional hairdressing apprenticeship in my home town of Barnsley in Yorkshire, which was tough and very disciplined, but years later I'm forever grateful for it. Along with attending college to study for my hairdressing qualifications, it was the best possible start. Learning all the key skills to the best standard has undoubtedly helped me further down the line in my career at Saks. Whether it's been working on everyday clients, supermodels, superstars or creating hair for super designers at the catwalk shows, it's always important to have a good foundation of knowledge.

When I was at the first stages of my career, I had to remind myself constantly to be patient and know that I could not learn everything at once. Keeping a diary of what I learned really helped me to see just how far I had come.

I think I have the best job in the world and I'm amazed by just how much excitement I get from my work every day. Working with a great team is possibly the best advice I can offer anyone. Never accept an OK standard and push your own creativity through experimentation and trial and error.

Hairdressing is competitive, it's fast, ever-changing and of course it's about providing a service, and the service of making someone feel great about themselves through their hair is wonderful. I swear, the smile a client shows you on her face when you've done her hair is magical and addictive!

Because hairdressing is always changing, there's always something to learn and discover, whether new products or techniques. You'll never be bored and as British hairdressing and training are widely acknowledged as the best in the world you're guaranteed to have the best start for the career of your dreams!

Andrew Barton x

Andrew Barton
Saks International Creative Director
www.saks.co.uk

Saks
HAIR & BEAUTY
www.saks.co.uk

Introduction

Why choose a career in hairdressing?

Hairdressing is a multi-billion pound industry and employs approximately 200,000 people in the UK. As hairdressing is constantly evolving, creative people are always needed to meet the demands of an ever-changing industry.

Today's hairdressers cater for the needs of a multi-ethnic society: from European to Asian and African type hair, there is a growing demand for skilled hairdressers. A vast range of products and resources, including the latest organic treatments, are available to you as a hairdresser and to your clients, helping you make an informed choice of the most appropriate treatment for your client.

Combining realistic work experience with developing your knowledge and understanding makes for a level-headed approach to achieving a professional qualification. Once you are a hairdresser, there is an exciting future waiting for you in a high-tech industry, with the chance for you to become your own boss or consider other routes such as image consultant, sales representative, teaching, wig-making, salon manager, freelance hairdresser, specialist hairdresser, colour technician, perm technician – whatever you choose to do. Wherever you go, people will always need their hair to be styled, so enjoy your job security and travel the world!

About this book

This book will take you through the basics of hairdressing and barbering. It covers all of the relevant performance criteria and range statements linked to the latest National Occupational Standards required to complete the Level I qualification in Hairdressing and Barbering.

European and Asian hairdressing is the main focus of the book. It includes the latest units in barbering, blow-drying, plaits and twists and hair extensions, with illustrated step by step guides to help you learn a variety of practical hairdressing procedures. The introductory unit, All about hair, covers what you will need to know about the basic structure of hair and the different hair types.

The book is divided into two sections.

- In the workplace contains all the units which relate to your work with clients and colleagues, as well as your responsibilities in the salon.
- Practical skills deals with the practical hairdressing procedures you need to learn.

To help you achieve each unit of work, the book contains:

>> Get up and go! features designed to involve you in an active role in your learning and development

✂ Sharpen up! features that will help you think about the practicalities of hairdressing and the type of situations you will have to deal with every day

? Memory jogger features for you to test your knowledge so you know what you might have to brush up on

⬆ Get ahead features designed to help you make the step from Level I through to Level 2, preparing you for the world of work which lies ahead.

What is an NVQ/SVQ?

A National Vocational Qualification (NVQ) or in Scotland a Scottish Vocational Qualification (SVQ) is made up of separate units that set out exactly what you must be able to do, and to what standard. The diagram below shows how the qualification is structured. If you are doing this qualification with City & Guilds it is called a Level I Diploma.

The practical work you carry out will be linked to the performance criteria in each unit, and the assessor will mark you against the standards set by the awarding body. This means you must carry out certain practical activities to the standard set out by the awarding body, and your assessor will help you with this.

Level I Hairdressing and Barbering consists of **four** mandatory units plus **two** optional units. To achieve the full qualification you need to achieve **six** units in total.

The following units are **mandatory** and must be completed:

- G20 Make sure your own actions reduce risks to health and safety
- G3 Contribute to the development of effective working relationships
- GH3 Prepare for hair services and maintain work areas
- GHI Shampoo and condition hair

You must also complete **two** of the following optional units:

- G2 Assist with salon reception duties
- GH2 Blow-dry hair
- GH4 Assist with hair colouring services
- GH5 Assist with perming hair services
- GH6 Plait and twist hair using basic techniques
- GH7 Remove hair extensions
- GBI Assist with shaving services

All about hair

What is hair?

Hair is made up of a protein called keratin. Your skin and nails are made from the same protein. A strand of hair is called a hair shaft, and it is made up of three layers: the cuticle, cortex and medulla.

Hair structure

The hair shaft is covered in overlapping cuticles, which can be thought of as being like fish scales or the tiles on a roof. When the hair is in good condition, the cuticles lie flat and when the hair is in bad condition the cuticles may be lifted or even torn away, exposing the cortex layer of the hair shaft.

Hair in good condition

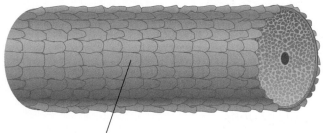

Cuticle scales lying close together

Hair in bad condition

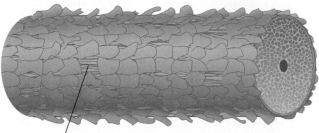

Cuticle scales open and misshapen. Some scale may have been completely destroyed, exposing the cortex

> Hair in good and bad condition

The effect of humidity on the hair is dependent on how well conditioned the hair shaft is and how flat, smooth and even the cuticle scales are. Hair is 'hygroscopic', which means that it absorbs moisture from the atmosphere. Hair that is porous will absorb moisture from the atmosphere more readily than hair that is non-porous. You should take great care when working on porous hair so as not to over-dry it. Directing airflow down the length of the hair shafts can help protect the cuticles.

» Get up and go!

Look at some different types of blow-drying products and consider their purposes. Think about products which can be used before and after the blow-dry. Create a chart of styling products and list the most suitable types of hair to use them on and what effects they will have. Show this information to your stylist or assessor and discuss the benefits of each product.

Cuticle

The outer layer is known as the cuticle layer of the hair shaft. The cuticle has overlapping scales wrapped around the centre of the hair known as the cortex. The hair when in good condition reflects the light and is smooth and shiny. The cuticle scales will also be tightly compacted giving a non-porous outer layer.

Cortex

The cortex layer of the hair shaft is made up of bundles of fibrils. Imagine a bundle of dried spaghetti or a bundle of pencils in your hand and this will reasonably reflect the structure of the cortex layer of the hair shaft. In the cortex we can see chemical changes altering the basic structure of the hair shaft. For example, when we perm the client's hair or apply a permanent colour we alter the basic structure of the hair. All chemical changes take place in the cortex. This includes bleaching, relaxing, permanent colouring and perming.

Medulla

The central layer of the hair is known as the medulla. It has no part to play in hairdressing treatments; it is simply made up of air spaces along the length of the hair shaft. The medulla may be present in some hairs but not in others, and may not be present for the full length of the hair.

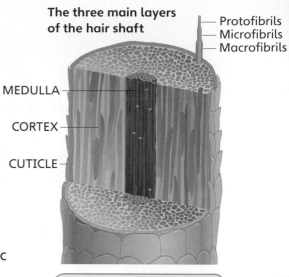

The three main layers of the hair shaft

- Protofibrils
- Microfibrils
- Macrofibrils

MEDULLA
CORTEX
CUTICLE

The hair shaft

Why do we have hair?

Protection

Hair has a protective function. If an object were to fall on your head the hair on your scalp would offer some, although limited, protection. The hair inside your nose acts as a filter when breathing, helping prevent dust and debris from entering your nasal passages, and your eyelashes offer some protection against dust entering your eyes.

Warmth

Hair acts as an insulator by helping keep the surface of the skin warm. You may notice when you are cold that hairs will stand up. This is the body's attempt to keep warm, by trapping a layer of warm air between the surface of the skin and the hair, which is standing up.

Looking good

How does your hair make you feel? Mostly when our hair looks good, we feel good! Hair offers a different dimension to how we feel about ourselves and how we can express ourselves. A freshly shampooed and well conditioned head of hair will give us an added confidence when compared with a head of hair which is greasy and in need of some tender loving care. Growth patterns of the hair may affect our choices of style, and you will need to consider the root direction of a client's hair when helping them select a style.

Different face shapes

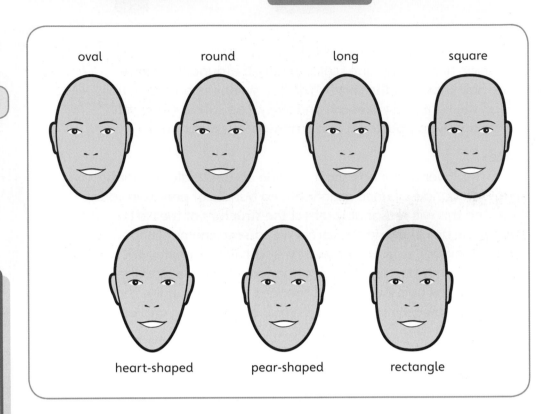

oval   round   long   square

heart-shaped   pear-shaped   rectangle

>> **Get up and go!**

You are what you eat! As you have learned, hair is made up of a protein called keratin, and the basic building blocks of proteins are amino acids. We get these amino acids from the foods we eat, so you really can affect the condition of your hair with the types of food you eat. Think about the food you eat and the effect it might have on your hair. Hair loss and scalp problems can be caused by a poor diet and if our diet is poor, the likelihood is our hair will suffer.

Keep a food diary for one week, keeping a note of the food you eat and its nutritional value. Do you think you are getting enough protein, carbohydrates, vitamins and minerals to feed your body and your hair?

Your hair acts as frame around your face, rather like a frame around a painting. And your hair can be styled to complement your face shape and to disguise less attractive features. Think about a client who may have a very wide forehead; would you give them a fringe?

Hair condition and hair types

Hair and scalp conditions can be divided into dry, normal, greasy and dandruff-affected.

Hair in good condition is soft to touch and hair in bad condition feels rough, dry and brittle. Hair can also be one of the following different types:

- Caucasian/European
- Asian/Oriental
- African type.

You will notice the hair is either straight or has an amount of natural wave or curl present.

- The Caucasian/European hair shaft can be straight, wavy or curly and its cross-section is oval shaped.
- The Asian/Oriental hair shaft can be straight and/or coarse and its cross-section is round.
- The African type hair shaft can be tightly or loosely curled and its cross-section is kidney shaped.

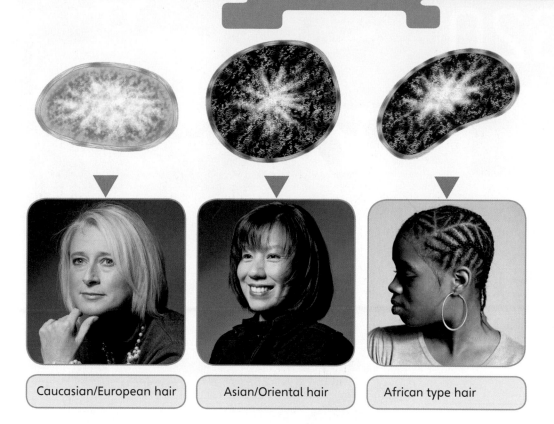

| Caucasian/European hair | Asian/Oriental hair | African type hair |

The texture of hair will vary from client to client and may also vary within the same head of hair. Texture can be fine, medium or coarse and is determined by touch.

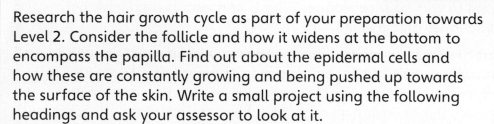

Get ahead

Research the hair growth cycle as part of your preparation towards Level 2. Consider the follicle and how it widens at the bottom to encompass the papilla. Find out about the epidermal cells and how these are constantly growing and being pushed up towards the surface of the skin. Write a small project using the following headings and ask your assessor to look at it.

- Alpha and beta keratin
- How the cells change shape as they move along the hair follicle
- The cuticle, cortex and medulla
- Colour producing cells (melanocytes)
- The three stages of the hair growth cycle: anagen, catagen and telogen

Include photos and sketches to help the reader understand what you are explaining.

? Memory jogger

What protein is hair made of?

Name the three layers of the hair shaft.

What happens to the cuticles when hair is in either good or bad condition?

Where in the hair does chemical change take place during certain hairdressing services?

Why do we have hair?

Name the three different hair types and describe how they differ.

UNIT G20

Make sure your own actions reduce risks to health and safety

Anne Veck, photographer: Marco Loumiet

Hairdressing is a fun-loving, people-oriented industry, but to stay safe you need to follow certain procedures when you are using electrical equipment and chemicals and when working with the public. Continual training is essential to reduce accidents and the occurrence of poor health and environmental damage in the salon. With the necessary training, you will be a more effective and successful hairdresser – would you go back to a stylist who used dirty brushes in an untidy and neglected salon, no matter how brilliant the cut and colour?

Health and safety covers three key areas: your responsibility to your clients; your employer's responsibilities to you, your colleagues, clients and visitors; and your responsibility to your colleagues and yourself.

You need to be aware of the risks in your workplace and how to deal with them. This will help you ensure that your actions do not create any health and safety hazards and that you do not ignore hazards that present risks in your workplace. You must take responsible action to resolve things, including reporting situations which may present a danger to people in your workplace, and seeking advice.

In this unit you will learn about:

- Identifying the hazards and evaluating the risks in your workplace
- Health and safety laws
- Workplace policies
- Personal presentation and behaviour
- Safe working practices.

Here are some key words you will meet in this unit:

Job description – a detailed description of the specific duties you must carry out

Workplace responsibilities – rules and regulations you must abide by

Equipment – items such as hairdryers, steamers, ultraviolet cabinet, scissors

Precautions – a preventative measure to safeguard your health and safety

Alert – to be watchful for anything that needs to be attended to

Reporting – a system for alerting other people to a situation

Personal presentation – how you present yourself for your day to day work

Products – the products you use on an everyday basis, e.g. shampoos, colours, perm lotion

Professional image – the high standards of a professional place of work, e.g. current and relevant salon equipment with well trained staff

Cross-infection – an infection which can transfer from one person to another

Environment – the working environment must be a healthy and safe place to be

Instructions – a detailed list of how to carry out a treatment or how to use a particular product

Controlling risks – measures which are put into place to prevent a risk escalating

Safe working practices – working practices which show your method of work is safe and without risk of harm

Additional assistance – help from a colleague or other resource

Identifying the hazards and evaluating the risks in your workplace (I)

This unit covers the health and safety duties for everyone in the hairdressing industry. Every employee and employer is required to behave safely and professionally. You must always be responsible for your own behaviour and make sure your actions do not create a health and safety risk. For example, if you see something in the salon which is potentially dangerous you must take sensible action towards putting things right. This may involve writing the risk down and/or reporting it to a more senior member of staff.

Hazards, risks and control

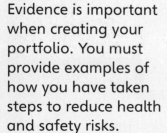

The salon is a great place to work. However, you must be aware of risks and hazards

It is extremely important you understand the terms 'hazard', 'risk' and 'control'. The Health & Safety Executive (HSE) is the body appointed to support and enforce health and safety laws. They have defined the terms listed above in the following ways:

- hazard – something with potential to cause harm
- risk – the likelihood of the hazard's potential being realised
- control – the means by which risks identified are eliminated or reduced to acceptable levels.

Sharpen up! ✂

Evidence is important when creating your portfolio. You must provide examples of how you have taken steps to reduce health and safety risks.

Almost anything may be a hazard, but may or may not become a risk. You need to demonstrate you understand the health and safety requirements and policies in the salon. You should be constantly improving your own working practices and work areas, preventing any risk of you or others being harmed. You must be able to identify risks arising from any hazards you have identified. You must know which hazards you can deal with safely in accordance with workplace instructions and legal requirements. Work within the limits of your own authority and report any situation you feel needs the attention of a more senior member of staff.

A trailing electrical cable is a hazard. If it is laying across a walkway there is a high risk of someone tripping over it, but if it lies flat to the floor alongside the wall out of the way, the risk is much less.

Poisonous or flammable chemicals are hazards and may present a high risk. However, if they are kept in a properly designed secure store and handled by professionally trained people, the risk is much less than if they are left out in the salon for anyone to use – or misuse.

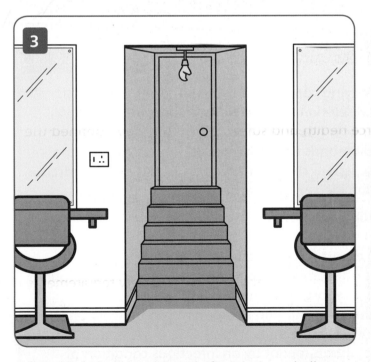

A failed light bulb is a hazard. If it is just one bulb out of many in a room, it presents very little risk, but if it is the only light on a staircase, it is a very high risk. Changing the bulb may be a high risk if it is high up, or if the power has been left on, or low risk if it is in a table lamp which has been unplugged.

A heavy box is a hazard. It can present a high risk to someone who lifts it incorrectly, rather than someone who uses the correct manual handling techniques.

Identifying the hazards and evaluating the risks in your workplace (2)

'Get smart, get trained and get it right, first time, every time'

The Health and Safety at Work Act 1974, (see page 14 for more information) covers everyone in the salon – employees, self-employed people and visitors, such as technical reps and clients. You must be trained before you carry out any job within the salon, no matter how small or quick the task is. Failing to comply with correct working practices within the salon could harm you or your colleagues. Professional hairdressers are legally bound to abide by manufacturers' instructions, the salon policy and local bylaws.

Failure to follow the act can result in heavy penalties. Criminal proceedings, heavy fines and/or imprisonment do happen, not just to salon owners but also to the individual responsible for failing to comply. If you have any issues about health and safety, discuss them with a member of staff. Make sure the discussion is recorded, and any action required is followed up. In this unit you will learn about a variety of policies and regulations you must follow during your working life.

Get up and go!

Correctly name the people responsible for health and safety in your workplace. Create a flow chart detailing their name and position within the salon along with their responsibilities, e.g. Salon Manager Emma is responsible for risk assessment. Identify the person who is responsible for reporting any accidents to the Health and Safety Executive. Present this to your assessor when you have completed it.

Get ahead

Design a pack of playing cards to be used in the salon as a memory jogger and revision tool. Perhaps you could code the cards using the symbols hearts, spades, clubs and diamonds. For example, use diamonds as 'doing' cards, hearts as 'thinking' cards, clubs as 'discussion' cards and spades as 'dig and research' cards. Here are some ideas for the different kinds of activities.

- Diamonds: demonstrate how you would lift a product from a high shelf.
- Hearts: thinking about the psychology of colour and how different colours affect mood, why do salons choose the colours they do for their interiors, uniforms, etc.?
- Clubs: discuss which fire-fighting equipment can be used on electrical and non-electrical fires.
- Spades: find out what is meant by an infectious condition of the body, and why potentially infectious conditions should be reported.

Sharpen up!

Neil had been working in the salon for three months. The salon owner was keen to advance Neil's knowledge and often demonstrated hairdressing techniques to him. This included removing colours, shampooing and rinsing perms. Neil was responsible for the usual day-to-day duties, such as client care and general salon organisation.

One evening near Christmas, Neil had a lot of clients to deal with. He was asked to place a plastic cap over a client's bleached hair and place her under a dryer. Neil had been keen to learn the correct way to apply and process bleach and always read the manufacturer's instructions. He discovered dry heat was not recommended for this type of bleach and quietly explained this to the stylist. At this time the client started to complain she was uncomfortable under the hood dryer. Neil went to investigate and discovered the bleach had run down the client's neck and back, bleaching her clothes and burning her skin. Neil was then instructed to rinse the client's hair and deal with her clothes as best as he could. The client was angry that no apology was offered by the salon owner and claimed she would sue.

Who was negligent? Can the client sue both Neil and the salon owner? Discuss this situation with your colleagues.

Get up and go!

Draw a simple plan of the hairdressing salon where you work. Walk round the salon and identify where the following are located: fire exits, specified assembly points, fire extinguishers and first aid equipment. Use a key to help explain your sketch.

Identify the hazards in the salon above and make a list of them. Give the same exercise to another member of staff and compare your results.

Identifying the hazards and evaluating the risks in your workplace (3)

Slippery surfaces present a risk to you and your clients and can be caused by water and hair on the floor

Wearing long, loose clothes in the salon is a hazard. It may only be a low risk if the work area is clean, tidy and quiet. However, when you are expected to move quickly from one area to another, it presents a high risk as your clothing could get caught on the worktops, door handles, or perhaps on the heel of your shoe as you climb a flight of stairs.

If you find faulty equipment, pass on suggestions for reducing risks, report it to a senior colleague and make a note of the discussion.

Look at the table below and describe your responsibilities for health and safety in the salon as an employee. Discuss the completed table with a colleague. Part of the table has been completed for you.

Verbally and non-verbally report any hazard to a senior member of staff, and provide evidence you have dealt with hazards which present a risk

Hazard	Risk?	Sort it?	Report it?	Control measures
Trailing flexes	Yes	Yes	Yes	Run the flex alongside the wall
Broken bulb				Check all electrics daily
Loose hair on the floor		Yes		
Broken edge on worktop				Make good until permanently repaired
Spillage on the floor			Yes	
Perm lotion running into your client's eyes	Yes			
Saturated cotton wool around the hairline			Yes	
Colour stain around the hairline				
Broken vent on hairdryer				

Within the salon you must identify working practices which could harm you or other people. Remaining alert to potential hazards will help protect everyone in the salon at any time. Remember: you need to concentrate and keep alert when dealing with products, tools and equipment.

Your physical wellbeing is essential not only to you but also to others within the salon. Too many late nights, over indulgence in food or alcohol or additional stress with personal issues will have a bearing on how you carry out your day-to-day duties. You are part of a team – if one person does not give 100% it will have a serious impact on the health and safety of the team and your clients. Make sure your behaviour does not put the health and safety of you or others in your salon at risk.

⟫ Get up and go!

After reading the left-hand paragraphs, make a list of the potentially harmful working practices you come into contact with on a daily basis.

Cut hair lying on the salon floor is a hazard. If it is not swept up, it may cause an accident

⟫ Get up and go!

Have a look at the following documentation and complete it with the help of a colleague. Report those hazards which present the highest risks to the people responsible for health and safety in your salon. When complete, check the details with a senior member of staff.

HAZARD CHECKLIST
Which hazards are present in my workplace?

Date .... Checked by ....

	Relevant to my workplace?	Risk assessment complete?
Fire		
Electric shock		
Posture		
Workplace environmental conditions		
Use of mains gas appliances		
Use and storage of chemical substances		
Hazardous substances		
Slips and trips		
Falls		
Falling objects		
Stress		
Work equipment		
Maintenance		
Infection control		
Other (list)		

? Memory jogger

Explain what the following terms mean: 'hazard'; 'risk'; 'control'.

What does the word 'alert' mean?

How does stress present itself as a hazard?

What may happen if there was a trailing wire across the salon floor?

What can you do to reduce the risk on a slippery floor?

Health and safety laws (1)

We are now going to look at the key factors within each of the health and safety laws which affect your day-to-day work. You are working with many different aspects of health and safety every day and in many cases this can be a natural process. The laws which relate to you and others in the workplace are there to protect everyone, whether they are a member of staff or a visitor to the salon. The acts you should be aware of are listed below.

- The Health and Safety at Work Act 1974
- The Fire Precautions Act 1971
- The Electricity at Work Regulations 1989
- The Workplace (Health, Safety and Welfare) Regulations 1992
- The Manual Handling Operations Regulations 1992
- The Personal Protective Equipment (PPE) at Work Regulations 1992
- The Reporting of Injuries, Diseases and Dangerous Occurrences Regulations (RIDDOR) 1995
- The Provision and Use of Work Equipment Regulations (PUWER) 1998
- The Control of Substances Hazardous to Health Regulations (COSHH) 2002

>> **Get up and go!**

Think about your responsibilities in your job. Read the list of workplace regulations above and write a simple statement about how each affects your day-to-day work in the salon. Use the diagram on page 20 to help you. This information may then be presented as part of your communications key skills short talk.

The Health and Safety at Work Act 1974

The Health and Safety at Work Act 1974 covers everyone: employees, self-employed people and visitors, such as technical reps and clients. The act covers a variety of working practices and is linked to many associated pieces of legislation covering any specific job role within any industry. The act informs both employer and employee with respect to many aspects of health and safety within the workplace and outlines everybody's duties and responsibilities.

Employers have slightly different obligations from employees. Employers are bound by a duty of care to each of their employees. This means everything an employer does when setting up and running a business will be done with the safety of all who come into contact with the business in mind. In order for this to be effective, the following must be adhered to by all employers.

- A workplace and systems of work must be provided and maintained.
- The use, handling, storage and transport of articles and substances must be accounted for.
- Information, instruction, training and supervision must be provided.
- Access and exits must be clear and free from hazard.
- The working environment, facilities and welfare arrangements must comply with the act.

The act's key message

It is your duty to maintain the health and safety of yourself and others who may be affected by your actions.

The Fire Precautions Act 1971

If you discover a fire you must raise the alarm calmly and safely. Staff, clients and visitors must be notified and escorted from the building using the nearest fire exit. Dial 999 and ask the operator for the fire service. Give the operator your name and the address of the salon, as well as brief details of the situation.

If you have been trained in fire fighting (and if the fire is small) use the most appropriate fire extinguisher to tackle the fire, but only if it is safe for you to do so.

Under the Fire Precautions Act 1971 all premises are required to have fire-fighting equipment, which must be maintained in good working order.

> **? Memory jogger**
>
> Who is the person responsible for reporting health and safety matters in the salon?
>
> How would you deal with the following?
>
> - Slippery surfaces.
> - Spillages.
> - Obstructions to doorways.
> - Hydrogen peroxide spillage on the floor.

> **» Get up and go!**
>
> Evidence is important when creating your portfolio and within your own work role. Provide some examples of how you have taken steps to reduce health and safety risks in the salon. Take photographs and use them as evidence. Think about before and after shots.

Fire is dangerous. If you discover a fire you should treat it with caution. Breathing in hot air from a fire can damage your airways and lungs. Burning chemicals can give off toxic fumes; if you breathe in these fumes they can cause asphyxiation. Smoke-filled buildings are a health hazard because you cannot see or breathe.

Fire can damage the salon by causing decorations to smoulder, ceilings to collapse, fixtures and fittings to burn and damage to walls. Fire damage to the salon can lead to blocked passageways, which could cause a lethal hazard – someone could suffocate due to a lack of oxygen.

Health and safety laws (2)

Fire prevention and fire-fighting equipment

To put out a fire you need to be trained in dealing with a variety of different fires. You can be trained to use a fire extinguisher in order to put out small fires. To extinguish a fire you need to remove one of its three components – oxygen, heat or fuel.

>> **Get up and go!**

- Find out where your fire-fighting equipment is in the salon and how often you have a fire drill.

- What types of fire extinguisher do you have? Take photographs of each type of fire extinguisher and explain the difference to your assessor.

Types of fire extinguisher

There are many ways in which to put fires out safely and we must remember the fire extinguishers provided in the salon are there for a professional purpose. All fire extinguishers are colour coded to indicate the type of fire it can be used for.

Class A A water extinguisher can be used to put out fires involving paper, coal, textiles and wood

Class B A foam extinguisher can be used to put out fires involving flammable liquids such as grease, oil, petrol and paints (but not cooking oil or grease)

Class C A carbon dioxide extinguisher can be used to put out fires involving flammable gases

Class Electrical A dry powder extinguisher can be used to put out electrical fires

Class F A blanket can be used to put out fires involving cooking oils and fats

✂ Sharpen up!

Knowing which types of extinguisher should *never* be used on which types of fire is as important as knowing which types of extinguisher *should* be used on which types of fire!

⏩ Get up and go!

- Which types of extinguisher can be used on more than one type of fire?
- Which types of extinguisher should never be used on which types of fire?

Fire extinguishers should be easily accessible

⏩ Get up and go!

Discuss the value of inviting a member of the Fire Brigade into your salon and asking them to talk about the different types of fire extinguisher available to you and your colleagues. Use the evidence they bring for your Health and Safety project. They may offer to give a small controlled demonstration of how to use a fire extinguisher.

❓ Memory jogger

What would you do if you found that a fire extinguisher in your salon was damaged?

What three things are required for a fire to start?

What is the most appropriate fire extinguisher for dealing with an electrical fire?

What could be the possible consequences of using incorrect fire equipment?

List three precautions you could take to eliminate the possibility of fire.

Many fires could be avoided if simple house-keeping rules were applied in the workplace.

- Fire doors must be kept closed and unlocked to prevent a fire from spreading and to enable staff and visitors to leave the buildings safely.
- Keep fire exits free from rubbish at all times.
- All electrical equipment must be used in accordance with manufacturers' instructions and must be regularly inspected by a qualified electrician. Correct fuses must be fitted and sockets must not be overloaded.
- Keep aerosols away from any heat source, including the sun and radiators.
- Carelessness causes fires – look out for your own and others' safety.

Health and safety laws (3)

The Electricity at Work Regulations 1989

A qualified electrician must test every electrical appliance in the salon once a year. This includes 'domestic' equipment, such as the washing machine, the fridge, the cooker and the kettle, as well as all hairdressing equipment. A written record must be kept of these tests and shown to the health and safety authorities upon inspection.

The act's key message

All electrical equipment must be used appropriately and with precaution, checked and tested. The position of plugs and sockets must be safe and the space you are working in must have adequate lighting. Any faulty or damaged equipment must be removed from use, labelled and reported to a responsible person.

Safe use and storage of electrical equipment

All salons depend on electrical equipment such as handheld hairdryers and steamers, so it is important to handle and store this equipment safely. Below are some guidelines on the safe use and storage of electrical equipment.

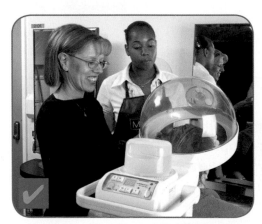

Know how to use the equipment

Be trained in the equipment's use

Use the equipment only for the purpose intended

Visually check the equipment prior to use

Switch off the equipment and remove from the power supply when finished

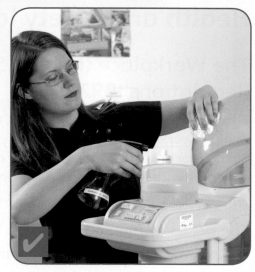

Be trained in the equipment's use

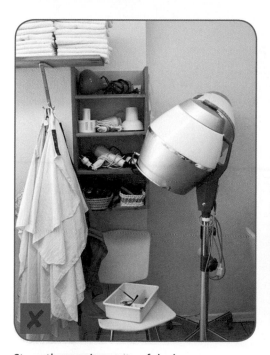

Store the equipment safely, in an allocated area

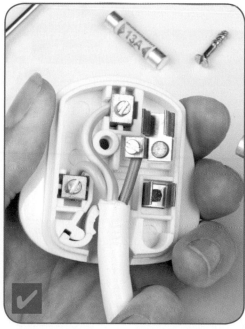

Test the equipment regularly – this should be carried out by a qualified electrician

❓ Memory jogger

What responsibilities do you have under the Electricity at Work Regulations?

How often should equipment be checked for damage?

Describe how you would deal with the following:

- no power to an appliance
- knotted electrical cables
- cable trapped under a heavy styling unit
- having wet hands when working with clippers
- wet salon floor
- faulty electrical equipment.

≫ Get up and go!

Look at each piece of electrical equipment in your salon and find out when they were recently PAT tested. (This means a qualified electrician tests your hairdryers, clippers, tongs, etc. every twelve months, labels it with a 'Portable Appliance Test' or PAT sticker, and dates it when the test was completed.) Bring this information to your assessor and discuss your findings.

Health and safety laws (4)

The Workplace (Health, Safety and Welfare) Regulations 1992

This regulation requires all at work to help maintain a safe and healthy working environment. Every employer is required to provide a safe working environment for all at work. Make sure you follow environmentally friendly working practices. Consider the risks to the environment which may be present in your salon and in your own job.

The act's key message

When working in the salon you must maintain a safe and healthy environment.

The Workplace (Health, Safety and Welfare) Regulations 1992 cover all these things

- Maintenance of workplace and equipment
- Indoor temperatures
- Ventilation
- Cleanliness and the handling of waste materials
- Room dimensions
- Conditions of floor and traffic routes
- Falls or falling objects
- Window, gates, doors and walls
- Moving walkways and escalators
- Sanitary conveniences
- Washing facilities
- Drinking water
- Accommodation for clothing
- Facilities for changing clothing
- Facilities for staff to rest and eat meals
- Lighting

» **Get up and go!**

Write a simple list of the health and safety practices you come across at work. Discuss your findings with your colleagues. You may find that some tasks are performed differently in some salons. Ask your colleagues the reasons why they have chosen to work this way and what the benefits are for them and their clients. Do they vary their working practices according to the client they are working on?

The Personal Protective Equipment (PPE) at Work Regulations 1992

These regulations state you must wear suitable protective gloves and an apron when dealing with any chemical or harmful substance. Clients must also be suitably protected during any chemical treatments. By making sure you use PPE you will meet the health and safety regulations and workplace policies. Remember, PPE includes preparing your clients' hair and protecting their skin where necessary prior to any chemical treatment.

The act's key message

Your employer must provide appropriate personal protective equipment for working with chemical treatments and you must always use it when applicable.

? Memory jogger

How does your salon dispose of salon waste?

How does your salon dispose of sharps?

Why are you encouraged to wear PPE?

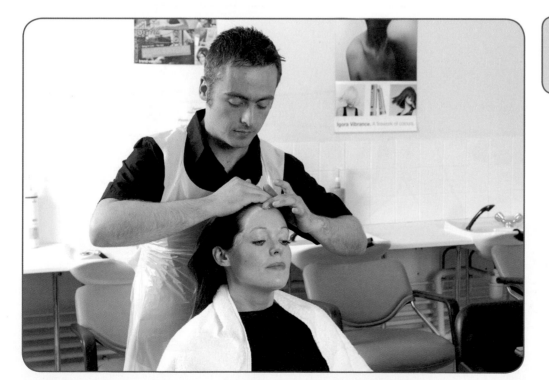

Personal protective equipment must be worn when carrying out chemical treatments

Health and safety laws (5)

The Manual Handling Operations Regulations 1992

This act requires measures such as following a set procedure when dealing with heavy or awkwardly shaped objects. The act deals with lifting items, pushing or pulling hairdressing trolleys, carrying loads and stacking shelves. All people at work must minimise the risks from lifting and handling objects.

The act's key message

This act provides guidelines for protecting yourself and others and minimising risks when lifting heavy objects.

Safe handling practices when dealing with hazards and risks

A box of heavy stock is an example of a hazard – it presents a risk to someone who needs to lift it manually, so safe handling practices must be used. The most common types of injury from lifting incorrectly are back strain and pulled muscles.

Assess the risk

Assess the box before you attempt to move it. Is it too heavy or bulky to move safely? If so, you could take out some of the items in the box before lifting or ask another member of staff for help.

If something is too heavy for you to lift on your own, ask a colleague for help

You must be trained in correct lifting practice, as with all aspects of your day-to-day work. Plan your route and remove any obstructions. Do you have a safe passageway to carry this load? Where are you going to put it down? Think about the lift you are going to carry out. Is the load to be lifted of a regular shape? Does it have sharp edges? Do you need to wear protective gloves? Are you wearing suitable clothes which will allow you to bend and move freely?

Safe lifting practices

Think about the lift. Where is the load to be placed? Do you need help? Are handling aids available?

With your feet close to the load, bend your knees and keep your back straight. Tuck in your chin. Lean slightly forward over the load to get a good grip

When you are sure of your grip on the load, straighten your legs and lift smoothly. Remember to keep your back straight

Carry the load close to your body

Health and safety laws (6)

The Reporting of Injuries, Diseases and Dangerous Occurrences Regulations (RIDDOR) 1995

All injuries must be reported to the member of staff responsible for health and safety. The salon accident book must be completed with basic personal details of the person (or people) involved and a detailed description of the incident. Because there might be legal consequences due to the injury, all witnesses must provide clear and accurate details of what happened.

The act's key message

You must report:

- fatal accidents
- any major injury sustained at work
- work-related diseases
- any potentially dangerous event which takes place at work
- accidents causing more than three days' absence from work.

A page from an accident book

ACCIDENT REPORT FORM

SECTION 1 PERSONAL DETAILS

Full name of first aider/staff member _____

Position held in salon: _____

Date: _____

Accident (injury) ☐   Incident (illness) ☐

Time and date of accident/incident: _____

Full name of injured/ill person: _____

Staff member ☐   Client ☐   Other ☐

Address: _____

Tel. no: _____

SECTION 2 ACCIDENT/INCIDENT DETAILS

Describe what happened. In the case of an accident, state clearly what the injured person was doing. _____

_____

Name and address/tel. no. of witness(es), if any: _____

_____

Action taken

Ambulance called ☐   Taken to hospital ☐   Sent to hospital ☐   First aid given ☐

Taken home ☐   Sent home ☐   Returned to work ☐

SECTION 3 PREVENTATIVE ACTION

Preventative action implemented ☐

Describe action taken: _____

_____

Date implemented: _____

Signature of first aider/staff member: _____

Signature salon manager/owner: _____

Date: _____

Get up and go!

Locate your salon's accident book. Look at the information contained within the book.

- Does it break the Data Protection Act?
- Can you identify the person/people who have had an accident in the salon?
- How available and visible should the accident book be?
- Where should it be stored?
- Where are the personal details related to those persons who have had an accident kept?

Discuss your findings with a colleague and then with your assessor.

The Provision and Use of Work Equipment Regulations (PUWER) 1998

These regulations lay down important health and safety controls on the provision and use of work equipment. Employers must provide equipment for use which is properly constructed, suitable for its purpose and kept in good working order. Training on how to use each piece of equipment must be provided by the employer. Staff who use the salon equipment must be competent in its use.

The act's key message

You must be competent when using tools and equipment in the salon.

Get up and go!

Walk around your salon and look at some of the tools and equipment. If it is helpful, take a photo of each piece of equipment. Look at the equipment objectively and make a note of the state of repair of each piece.

- Is it in good working order?
- Does it need to be thrown away?
- Can it be repaired?

Let your assessor know your conclusions.

Health and safety laws (7)

The Control of Substances Hazardous to Health (COSHH) Regulations 2002

Chemicals, including perm lotions, neutralisers and hydrogen peroxide, are hazardous and present a high risk. They must be handled, stored, used and disposed of correctly in accordance with COSHH 2002. This means every chemical and product used within the salon must be assessed for risk.

Find out about the working practices within your salon and those which are relevant to your job description. It's easy to forget the risks involved in using shampoos and conditioners – remember, the ingredients can sometimes cause skin and scalp irritation. All manufacturers are duty-bound to inform you of the ingredients in each hairdressing product stored in your salon. Each item must be catalogued in a register for staff to access so all staff who are trained can deal with the possible dangers of the products they use.

Many products, such as hairspray, mousse, perm lotion and hydrogen peroxide, are potentially hazardous and should be stored in a cool, dark, locked fire-proof cabinet, preferably on a low shelf.

Potentially hazardous products should be stored correctly

Always read and follow salon instructions, suppliers' or manufacturers' instructions and follow legal requirements as appropriate. This is very important when working with products, equipment and materials. Should you find a difference between salon, suppliers' or manufacturers' instructions you must report this to a senior member of staff. This will help you make the correct decision when using products and equipment on your clients. You must use products for their intended professional purpose only.

> An example of a manufacturer's product instructions

HYDROGEN PEROXIDE SOLUTION

Composition
Stabilised acidic aqueous solutions or emulsions containing hydrogen peroxide of various strengths for use with:

Permanent Colorants
Bleach powder
Permanent waves as neutralisers

Ingredients
Hydrogen peroxide
Hair tighteners Colorant remover up to 40 vol or 12%
Preparations containing higher concentrations of hydrogen peroxide are outside the scope of the Cosmetics Directive. In such cases, seek the advice of the supplier regarding COSHH assessments.

Hazards identification
Irritant to eyes and skin.

First-aid measures
Eyes: Rinse eyes immediately with plenty of water. If irritation persists seek medical advice.
Skin: Wash skin immediately with water. If irritation persists seek medical advice.
Ingestion: Seek medical advice immediately.

Accidental release measures
Always use water to dilute and mop up spillages.

Handling and storage
Always use non-metallic utensils to avoid rapid decomposition of the product. Do not allow contact with easily combustible materials such as paper. Store in cool, dry place away from sunlight and other sources of heat. Always store hydrogen peroxide in the container supplied. It is particularly important that no contamination enters the containers as this could lead to decomposition resulting in the liberation of heat and oxygen. Therefore, replace cap immediately after use.

Exposure controls/personal protection
Always wear suitable protective gloves. Avoid contact with eyes and face. Do not use on abraded or sensitive skin.

Stability and reactivity
Hydrogen peroxide may react with other chemicals to form dangerous materials (e.g. explosive). Therefore, avoid mixtures other than recognised formulations. Combustion may occur if hydrogen peroxide is allowed to dry out on materials such as paper, hair, wood, etc.

Disposal
Wash down the drain with plenty of water. Do not incinerate.

The act's key message

Any substances used in your salon could be hazardous to health and should be stored, handled, used and disposed of according to legislation, manufacturers' instructions and local bylaws.

Sharpen up!

Remember: good ventilation is important when mixing colours and bleaches and when using colouring preparations. Windows and/or an air vent must be opened, as chemicals can be dangerous if inhaled.

? Memory jogger

Why should infectious conditions be reported to your salon manager?

Give an example of what might be an infectious condition.

What does COSHH stand for?

For what reason do you store harmful substances in a locked cupboard?

Why do salons have accident books?

What would you do next if you accidently cut a client's ear?

Briefly describe your duties for health and safety relating to the following regulations:

- RIDDOR
- PUWER
- COSHH

Workplace policies (I)

If there are more than five people employed in your salon, a workplace policy is required. The policy is written to clarify what the risks are at work on a day-to-day basis, to bring to your attention any precautions which may be necessary and to clarify who is responsible.

All members of staff must cooperate with the workplace policy to make sure the salon is a safe and healthy place to work. This should include checking that work areas are kept clean, fire exits are not blocked and you have enough space to work comfortably without bumping into work stations or other salon staff.

>> **Get up and go!**

Find out if the salon where you work has a workplace policy.

- Do you have a member of staff who is qualified in first aid?
- How would you contact the first aider?
- What happens in the salon when the first aider is absent?

>> **Get up and go!**

Complete the missing word(s) from each of the following health and safety laws:

- Fire P_____ Act (1971)
- Health and S_____ Act (1974)
- Electricity at W_____ Regulations (1989)
- Workplace _____Regulations (1992)
- Manual H_____ Operations Regulations (1992)
- Personal Protective E_____ at Work Regulations (1992)
- Reporting of Injuries, D_____, and Dangerous Occurrences Regulations (1995)
- Provision and U____ of Work Equipment Regulations (1998)
- Control of S_____ Hazardous to Health Regulations (2002)

Sterilising equipment

Sterilising equipment will ensure a hygienic working environment, preventing the risk of cross-infection and infestation. It also promotes a high standard of cleanliness to your clients. Equipment must be cleaned thoroughly before using any sterilising method. The methods of sterilisation available in the salon may include:

- barbicide
- ultraviolet
- autoclave.

You must use tools and equipment which are clean, safe and fit for their purpose – tools and equipment identified at the time of consultation must be readily available to use for professional purposes. This might include pintail combs to weave sections of hair, highlighting hooks to pull strands of hair through a highlighting cap, or professional foil strips to assist colouring. Equipment should be cleaned and sterilised as soon as possible after use to ensure it is ready for the next treatment.

Barbicide

The most popular method of sterilising is barbicide. Barbicide is quick and easy to use, but will only inhibit the growth of bacteria. You must read and follow the manufacturer's instructions when making up the solution and you must remember to change it daily.

Ultraviolet

Placing tools which are clean and dry in an ultraviolet cabinet will prevent the growth of bacteria. You must remember to turn your tools every 15 minutes to sterilise them all over.

Autoclave

The most effective method of sterilising is the autoclave, which will completely destroy all living bacteria on the surface of your tools. However, not all equipment can withstand the heat of an autoclave – temperatures reach up to 125°C!

Barbicide

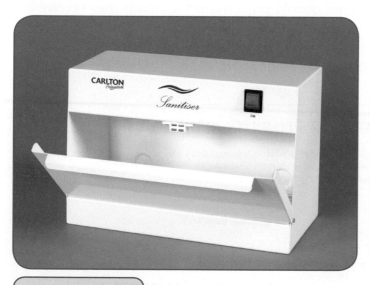

Ultraviolet cabinet

Autoclave

❓ Memory jogger

Which is the most effective method of sterilising salon equipment?

Describe the method for using an ultraviolet cabinet.

» Get up and go!

Are your salon's practices safe? Find out if there are any differences between your salon's workplace policies and suppliers' or manufacturers' instructions in relation to day-to-day practical jobs. Think about neutralising, rinsing off a colour and blow-drying a client's hair. These are practical activities, which are carried out every day in every salon, and you will find that practices vary.

Workplace policies (2)

Public- and treatment-liability insurance

Did you know all salons are duty-bound to take out public- and treatment-liability insurance? If a member of staff were to injure one of your clients in the salon as a result of negligence, the client would have grounds to sue the member of staff and the salon.

The employer's insurance certificate must cover all staff, clients and visitors to the salon and must be displayed for all to read, should they wish. The name of the insurance company, the salon name and address, the nature of the business and the start date and renewal date will be included. The salon will have to renew this certificate of insurance every year.

The insurance company requires evidence if a claim is made. They must be certain all reasonable steps were taken to prevent the situation occurring. Were all tests carried out correctly and recorded? Were the manufacturer's instructions read, understood and followed?

Insurance companies do not always pay out on the claims they receive if they are suspicious of negligent practices. Should this be the case, where is the money going to come from? Will the salon owner have to sell the salon? Will you have to find the money yourself if you were responsible?

> An employer's liability insurance certificate

CERTIFICATE OF EMPLOYER'S LIABILITY INSURANCE (A)

(Where required by regulation 5 of the Employer's Liability (Compulsory Insurance) Regulations 1998 (the Regulations), one or more copies of this certificate must be displayed in each place of business at which the policy holder employs persons covered by the policy.)

Policy No	R3/21LG52123
Reference No	92L31
1. Name of policy holder	Mrs Tiffany Tsang trading as Top Tips
2. Date of commencement of insurance policy	31 July 2004
3. Date of expiry of insurance	31 July 2005

We hereby certify that subject to paragraph 2:-
1. The policy to which this certificate relates satisfies the requirements of the relevant law applicable in Great Britain, Northern Ireland, the Isle of Man, the Island of Jersey, the Island of Guernsey and the Island of Alderney (b); and
2 (a) the minimum amount of cover provided by this policy is no less than £5 million (c). Signed on behalf of EverSure plc (Authorised Insurer)
R J Stanley
CHIEF EXECUTIVE OFFICER UK

Notes
(a) Where the employer is a company to which regulation 3(2) of the Regulations applies, the certificate shall state in a prominent place, either that the policy covers the holding company and all its subsidiaries, or that the policy covers the holding company and all its subsidiaries except any specially excluded by name, or that the policy covers the holding company and only the name subsidiaries.
(b) Specify applicable law as provided for in regulation 4(5) of the Regulations.
(c) See regulation 3(1) of the Regulations and delete whichever of paragraphs 2(a) or 2(b) does not apply. Where 2(b) is applicable, specify the amount of cover provided by the relevant policy. paragraph 2(b) does not apply and is deleted.

YOUR CERTIFICATE OF EMPLOYER'S LIABILITY INSURANCE IS ATTACHED ABOVE.
THE EMPLOYER'S LIABILITY (COMPULSORY INSURANCE) REGULATIONS 1998 REQUIRE YOU TO KEEP THIS CERTIFICATE OR A COPY FOR 40 YEARS.

Please fold as shown and insert the certificate in the protective cover provided. A copy of the certificate must be displayed at all places where you employ persons covered by the policy. Extra copies of the certificate are available on request.

Situation vacant

Specific duties related to health and safety should be stated in your job description and made clear to you at interview. Below is an example of a job description for you and your colleagues to discuss.

Job Description   **Post Holder Junior**
Job Title   Junior
Place of Work   Cutting Creations, Aylesbury

Candidate Specification

The successful candidate will

- Have good interpersonal skills; demonstrate a professional level of client care
- Be flexible and willing to work as a team member
- Work Saturdays and at least one late evening each week
- Take responsibility for securing models for practice and assessment purposes
- Update practical skills regularly at training sessions
- Take an active interest in all aspects of work within the salon
- Attend hairdressing seminars and professional courses in order to keep abreast of current and emerging techniques
- Demonstrate appropriate health and safety practices when working in the salon
- Complete the appropriate hairdressing qualification within the specified timeframe
- Undertake other reasonable duties as required by senior staff

Specific duties
Undertake day-to-day duties such as

- Shampoo and condition hair and scalp
- Assist with perming, relaxing, neutralising, and colouring for both European and African type hair
- Assist with salon reception duties
- Sell retail products
- Make refreshments
- Reduce the risks to general health and safety by taking reasonable care, co-operating with requests made by senior staff and not interfering with or misusing any piece of equipment, tools or products
- Sterilise equipment
- Continuous preparation for hairdressing treatments and maintain the salon work areas
- Wash and dry towels and gowns
- Stock checking

About the salon and our staff
We are a friendly team who enjoy busy professional lives. We strive for perfection, sincerity and honesty in everything we do.

Our skills are updated on a regular basis by attending regular seminars and holding regular teach-in evenings. We look forward to working with you and wish you an enjoyable and rewarding time with us.

The candidate will enjoy

- Two weeks' paid holiday each year
- The national minimum wage
- A 40-hour working week
- 9am – 6pm (1 hour for lunch every day)

Dear Dana,

I have recently seen an advertisement in the Hairdressers Journal and I am interested in applying for the job. My hair is mousy brown and I thought it could do with spicing up a bit. I know it is important to look my best when I attend interviews. I really am worried about my appearance. Can you help?

Yours sincerely,

Lisa

> A job description

Dana says:

It would be a good idea to go to the salon and ask for their advice and guidance about different types of colour, but say you do not want to commit to a colour. Ask about suitable temporary products and listen to what they say. Do they have coloured hair mascara, temporary colours or perhaps semi-permanent colours? Look around the salon and decide if you would like to come back for an interview or if would rather look elsewhere.

The opportunity this experience presents will stand you in good stead when dealing with prospective employers. Remember, all job interviews are different and the experience is invaluable. By taking this approach you will have obtained some sound advice about how to colour your hair and, because you have visited the salon, you will be able to make an informed decision about your job application. If you like what the salon suggested, book an appointment and view the salon from a client's perspective.

Good luck!

Dana

? Memory jogger

Think of three safe practices when using colouring and bleaching products.

What effect could unprofessional behaviour have on your colleagues and clients?

High standards of personal presentation and professional dress create a good first impression for clients

Get up and go!

Carry out a small survey of various salons in your area and find out what their staff wear. Bring your findings back to your salon and discuss them with your colleagues. For safe working practices within the salon, you need to think about the most appropriate materials to wear. Write down the most suitable types of materials your tops, skirts and trousers must be made from.

Personal presentation and behaviour (I)

First impressions are very important. People can form an opinion of you within a few seconds of meeting you. They will judge you on the way you look and the way you behave. Imagine how clients would feel if you arrived at your salon looking as if you had just fallen out of bed! Do you think they would want you to do their hair if you looked like you could not take care of your own appearance? The way you look really matters. However good your hairdressing skills may be, if you look untidy and unwashed, the image you present will give clients a bad impression.

One of the most important things to remember is the appearance of any salon must be one of cleanliness, tidiness and good organisation. Your first impression when you go into a salon will help you to make your mind up whether or not you would want to be a client or member of staff there. If the salon appears to be clean, tidy and run efficiently you are more likely to think it is a nicer place to be than somewhere dirty or untidy.

First impressions count

Many rules and regulations will form a part of your everyday life in the salon. Equally important to your day-to-day work is your personal presentation. Your personal presentation should be a total image, from head to foot, of safety and professionalism.

Dressed for success!

Clothes must be neat and streamlined, so no flowing skirts, trousers or loose baggy tops. Black tends to be the industry's preferred colour, although this varies from salon to salon. Make sure your personal presentation and behaviour in the salon:

- protects the health and safety of you and other people
- meets legal responsibilities
- complies with salon instructions.

Sometimes fashion shoes look great but are not always good for your feet. You will spend a lot of time on your feet when you are working in the salon and it is important to choose shoes which fit properly and meet certain health and safety requirements. Choose full-covered leather shoes with closed-in toes and low heels. Leather allows the feet to breathe and will help prevent unpleasant foot odour. Full-covered shoes are worn in the salon for health and safety reasons – they will protect your feet if you drop something sharp on them. Sensible shoes will also stop hairs from becoming stuck in the soles of your feet!

Get up and go!

Think of the reasons behind the following statements about salon dress.

- Your clothes must be streamlined and not baggy.
- You must always wear full-covered shoes or boots with a low heel and sole.

Personal hygiene

Hairdressers are constantly on their feet and work in close proximity to their clients and colleagues. Your clothes must be clean and pressed on a daily basis. You must shower daily and use a suitable deodorant. Tops must meet the waistband of your trousers or skirt – your client does not necessarily want to see your pierced navel or recent tattoo. Tops must also have sleeves, short or long. When you lift your arms up to work on your client's hair, they do not want to see your underarm hair or smell an unwashed armpit! Smells can linger, so try to avoid spicy meals during the week. Remember too that the smell of cigarette smoke can linger on your clothing and breath.

 Get up and go!

Think about the causes of bad breath. How can you avoid these? Discuss with a colleague various ways in which to prevent bad breath.

Conversation topics to avoid

Conduct also falls within your personal presentation. All you say and do is part and parcel of you as a professional person. It is pointless being correctly dressed only to follow it through with inappropriate conversation and conduct. Topics of conversation to stay away from are personal issues such as sex, drugs, religion and politics. These topics of conversation can cause friction within the salon and are best avoided. Remember: the client is your primary concern so you must demonstrate a professional, business-like approach to all aspects of the client's visit.

Personal presentation and behaviour (2)

Efficient working practices

By positioning your tools within easy reach and keeping them well organised you will make efficient use of your time and working area. Being well prepared and organised will also present a professional image to your clients. Remove waste at the end of all perming, colouring and lightening treatments and dispose of it in line with local bylaws. This will leave your work surfaces free from any risk or hazard and will present a tidy working area.

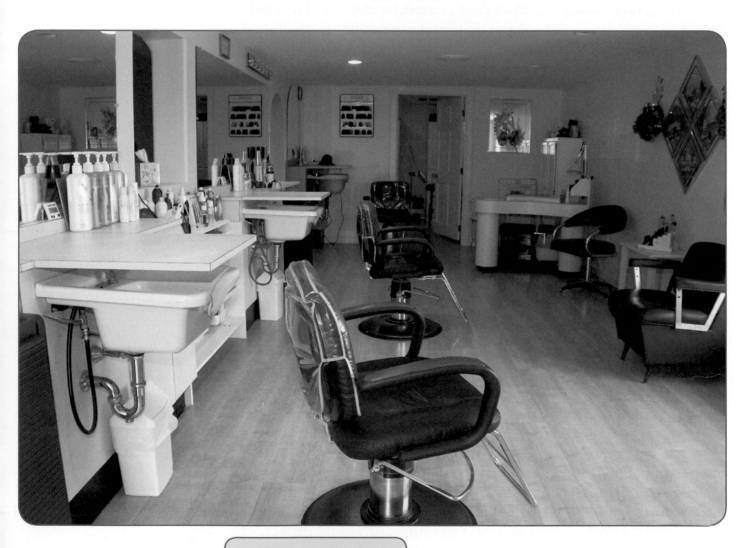

A well-organised working area will give your clients a good first impression

Personal conduct

Personal conduct covers all areas of your working life, from dealing with clients and other members of staff to eating and drinking. What kind of an impression would you create if you ate in your work area?

Are you an extrovert who likes to show everyone how happy you are? What kind of an impression does your behaviour create? Be happy and remember, good personal conduct demonstrates to your clients how professional you are. Sensible behaviour means potential accidents are prevented, you promote a healthy and safe place to work and the Health and Safety Act is respected.

General behaviour in the salon includes body language. If you do not agree with something, does it show in your body language? Consider whether taking drugs (either obtained legally by a doctor or illegally) affects your colleagues and clients, as well as your standard of work. Always remember to check out the salon's policy for smoking and alcohol.

Finally, conduct also includes reporting staff absence and punctual timekeeping. This means you must inform your employer of any absence and indicate your expected return date. This will enable your manager to reorganise your work schedule and allocate jobs to other members of staff.

» Get up and go!

Think about how you would hand over to a member of staff at the end of a day.

What about the appointments for tomorrow? Have they all been accounted for in terms of resources? This needs to be done on a nightly basis just like your cashing up procedures in reception.

Suggest a handover process to your line manager and trial it for a period of time, refine it and put it into place as a standard practice.

? Memory jogger

How does personal presentation affect health and safety in the salon?

List three ways you can keep your breath fresh.

How can you make sure you do not have body odour?

Your colleague has long hair. How might this affect health and safety in the salon? What can she do to minimise risk?

Describe positive body language in the salon.

You can avoid damaging your hands with these simple steps:

- Avoid exposure to chemicals and excess wet work.
- Wear single-use gloves when using hairdressing products such as shampoo, dyes and bleaches and for work with hands in water.
- Apply hand cream before starting work and each time you wash your hands.
- Dry your hands thoroughly after washing.
- Throw away single-use gloves every time you take them off and change between clients.

Safe working practices

In this unit you have covered the many different aspects of health and safety. You have learned that to work in the hairdressing industry, you will always need to demonstrate you understand the health and safety requirements and policies in the salon. This knowledge will provide present and future employers with a professional employee who can demonstrate an approved code of practice for maintaining a safe and healthy working environment.

Health and safety at work

Health means being well, both physically and mentally. Safety means being free from risk of danger and injury. In order to stay well in everyday life, we need:

- shelter, food and drink
- clean air
- space to work and move around
- an ambient temperature
- freedom of movement with no risk of harm.

Safety and comfort for you and your client

We have looked at the reasons why everyone is required to behave safely and professionally. You must take reasonable care for the health and safety of yourself and others who may be affected by what you do. You must also cooperate with your employer, salon owner or manager to ensure health and safety procedures are followed.

Further information

Use the following sources to further develop your knowledge and understanding of this unit.

Websites

You can find useful information on the websites for the following organisations:

- Health and Safety Executive
- COSHH Essentials
- UK Fire Service
- NHS Plus

Books and leaflets

- Health and Safety Executive: priced and free publications are available from HSE Books. Tel: 01787 881165 or visit their website.

Organisations

- Contact the British Occupational Hygiene Society (BOHS) on 01332 298101 or visit their website to find out more about occupational hygiene.
- Look in the Yellow Pages under 'Health and safety consultants', 'Health authorities and services' or 'Occupational health'.

Look at the list of employment-related acts and regulations in the left-hand column of the table, most of which you have learned about in this unit. Match them with the appropriate statement in the right-hand column, for example: **N** Equal Opportunities Legislation (Amended 2003) is matched with **4** Everyone should be treated equally as an individual, regardless of their race, religion or disability.

Act or regulation	Statement
A Health and Safety at Work Act (1974)	**1** Accidents must be written in the salon accident book and serious injuries must be reported to the local enforcement officer.
B Electricity at Work Regulations (1989)	**2** Salons that hold client information on a computer must register with the Data Protection Register, and all information must be kept confidential and available to the client if they wish to see it. The salon must not threaten to or misuse information.
C Control of Substances Hazardous to Health (COSSHH) Regulations (2002)	**3** Employers must provide free of charge all necessary personal protective equipment for employees.
D Personal Protective Equipment (PPE) at Work Regulations (1992)	**4** Everyone should be treated equally as an individual, regardless of their race, religion or disability.
E The Provision and Use of Work Equipment Regulations (PUWER) (1998)	**5** The salon must be kept safe and clean, and employees must obey salon rules.
F Employer's Liability Act (1998)	**6** All people at work must know how to minimise their risk of injury from lifting and handling objects.
G Fire Precautions Act (1971)	**7** This law applies to the storage, use and disposal of all hairdressing products and chemicals.
H The Cosmetic Products Regulations (2004)	**8** Hairdressing chemicals and waste must be disposed of safely.
I Environmental Protection Act (2005)	**9** This is an insurance cover for employers and employees in the event of accidents to themselves and their clients.
J Workplace Regulation (1992)	**10** This law covers the rules which recommend the different volumes and strengths of hydroxide-based products, i.e. hydrogen peroxide.
K Manual Handling Operations Regulations (2002)	**11** This act is designed to protect everyone involved in working situations. It states the responsibilities of both employers and employees regarding health and safety in the workplace.
L Reporting of Injuries, Diseases and Dangerous Occurrences Regulations (RIDDOR) (1995)	**12** All fire-fighting equipment must be in good working order, be suitable for the types of fire likely to occur and be readily available.
M Data Protection Act (2003)	**13** This law states that a qualified electrician must check every electrical appliance every 12 months.
N Equal Opportunities Legislation (Amended 2003)	**14** The employer has a duty to select equipment for use at work which is properly constructed and kept in good repair.

Note: the content of this table was correct at time of printing.

Remember – it is good practice to check regularly for amendments to keep yourself up to date.

UNIT G2

Assist with salon reception duties

First impressions count to a lot of people. Whether about you as an individual or the salon as a whole, the overall impression the client receives when they enter your place of work is very important. Within the first few seconds, your client is making a judgement about everything they see and hear. Look at your reception area. Is it clean, tidy, welcoming and professional?

This unit is about assisting with salon reception duties. You will have to demonstrate that you can keep the reception area neat and tidy, welcome people entering the salon, deal with their questions and make straightforward appointments. Using good communication skills when people come into the salon, or when they telephone the salon, is an important part of this unit.

In this unit you will learn how to:

Maintain the reception area

Attend to clients and enquiries

Help to make appointments for salon services.

Here are some key words you will meet in this unit:

Communication – can be verbal (words) or non-verbal (body language, etc.)

Clients – the people who come into the salon and pay for a treatment

Enquiry – a request for information

Stationery – note paper, letter headed paper, envelopes, compliment slips, etc.

Hospitality – a gesture of giving, e.g. hot or cold drinks, magazines, looking after the client

Recording – taking a note of information, usually an appointment time and service in the appointment book

Confidentiality – respect and privacy of an individual's information

DPA – the Data Protection Act

Body language – communicating using your body, e.g. facial expressions, body movements, how you sit or stand

Retail – selling products such as shampoo and conditioner to your clients

Policy – the terms and conditions laid down by a business; course of action followed when faced with a particular situation

Maintain the reception area (I)

The reception area is the first part of the salon visitors see. You may be the first person in the salon your clients come into contact with. First impressions are important. The way in which people are dealt with will affect whether they want to come back. How you conduct yourself and treat clients can affect your salon's existing and future success.

The reception area – is it clean and tidy?

Is your salon reception area clean, tidy and welcoming? Put yourself in the place of a client and look at your reception critically. Would you feel as if you were in a professional salon? Not all salons have a separate reception area, but even so, the area in which the client is welcomed must be professionally presented. It is your duty to make sure the reception area is clean and tidy at all times.

The reception area is the 'shop window' of the salon – it needs to give clients a good impression

Retail products

Your salon may sell a range of retail products. It is your job to display these neatly and to make sure the display is kept fully stocked, clean, dust-free and tidy at all times. This will encourage clients to look at the products and will also help them to decide whether they want to pick one up and buy it. This type of work is best done when the salon is quiet. It may be first thing in the morning or there may be quiet times during the day when you could dust and rearrange the products on display.

Remember, all staff must be fully aware of products stocked by the salon and how to use them. When discussing the benefits of the products with clients, you must only state what the product itself says. If you give misleading or incorrect information you may have to deal with an angry client, which could be difficult. The knowledge and understanding you learn from your technical reps will prove invaluable when you discuss products with your clients.

Retail product displays should look good so clients are tempted to buy!

>> Get up and go!

Make suitable suggestions to your assessor about how you would like to display products and stock in the reception area of your salon. Where products are on display, think about using empty boxes or bottles. This will help to prevent theft. If stock losses can be kept to a minimum, this will directly affect your salon's final profit. Make a simple list of the most popular salon retail products and list the cost of each product. You may find this information useful when dealing with enquiries.

Sharpen up!

Who should you report low levels of stationery and products to in your salon? Did you know women spend more on retail products than men?

Maintain the reception area (2)

Security of stock

It is vital to keep the salon's stock secure. Small items can be removed easily without anyone noticing. The thief may be a visitor to the salon or even a member of staff. Stock should be regularly checked against actual sales to show whether anything is missing.

Make it difficult for thieves to take your salon's stock

Low levels of stock

As well as hair styling and treatment products and equipment, you will need a variety of other resources to help you do your job, such as stationery. Take a regular stock check of pencils, erasers, pencil sharpeners, rulers, appointment pages/books, calculators and message pads, as well as salon products. You will also need to regularly check you have enough change in the till. Promptly reporting stock shortages can make the difference between offering a professional service and making an appointment, closing a sale, or irritating the client by making him or her wait.

WELLA HAIR PRODUCTS	
Wella Lifetex Shampoo	£4.50
Wella Lifetex Mousse Conditioners	£4.80
Wella Lifetex Intensive Conditioners	£4.60
Wella High Hair Product Samples	£1.99 each or 3 for £5.00
Wella Hair Mascara	£3.50

A retail products list

Faulty products

Sometimes accidents happen and stock may become damaged. Remove all faulty products from the reception area as soon as you can and report them to the person who controls the stock. Look for faulty stock as you prepare it for sale, for example, damaged or loose packaging, cracks or splits in bottles, leaks, and so on. Removing faulty products is essential to the smooth running of the reception area and can mean the difference between a client buying a product or not.

Many salons operate commission on all retail products sold, so it pays to be alert when dealing with stock.

Looking after your clients

Clients like to be looked after. Be friendly and polite, and remember to offer them a drink and something to read. Make sure the newspapers and magazines you offer are suitable for a general age range and are up to date. Your salon may have a client care policy of offering both non-alcoholic and alcoholic drinks. This is sometimes free to the client as part of the salon's hospitality.

It is good practice to offer refreshments when clients are waiting for the stylist to attend to them. It gives the client a feeling that something is happening.

Some salons have a video playing showing the different types of work the salon offers. This can reassure the client as they see the level of care and professionalism taken to produce the video.

» Get up and go!

Find out where the following items are kept in your salon:

- Cups and saucers.
- Glasses.
- Plastic cups for children.
- Soft drinks for children.

Where do you get more stock of coffee, tea, sugar and milk?

? Memory jogger

What does the word 'professional' mean to you?

What are the advantages of selling retail products (see the list on page 42)?

How does your salon keep its stock secure?

Who do you report low stock levels to?

What incentive would you offer staff for selling retail products?

What is the total cost, without using a calculator, for two shampoos and three intensive conditioners?

Attend to clients and enquiries (I)

Imagine you have walked into your salon for the first time and you want to find out how much a haircut is. How would it feel to be a client? The salon reception area is often a busy place, and it needs to look inviting, so when carrying out reception duties you will need to maintain a professional area of work and behave professionally at all times.

Welcoming people is what your job is all about. Make them feel special and let them know you are pleased to see them. Be knowledgeable about your area of work and speak with confidence and pride about the services your salon offers. You will need to discuss the range of treatments and their timings with a range of clients and will therefore need to learn about them.

Always stay calm and in control of any situation which arises and, if necessary, contact a senior member of staff if you find the situation becomes too difficult to deal with.

Personal appearance

When working in the reception area, your personal appearance is paramount to the success of attracting and maintaining clients. Your clothing should be neat, clean and professional at all times. Choose a suitable hairstyle to reflect your salon's standards. If you are male, are you clean shaven or growing a beard? First thing in the morning you need to shave if you are usually clean shaven. If you wear a beard, then keep it clean and well trimmed. Some make-up may help to give you a professional look and simple jewellery is better for working during the day. How about your shoes? Will they support your feet during the day without too much discomfort? Adopting these simple practices will help to give your clients confidence, paving the way to an enjoyable salon visit.

A positive and polite manner

Communication is a vital part of reception work. It is important to the success of the business. Your salon will probably have a precise greeting they will want you to use such as 'Good morning/afternoon. My name is Adrienne. May I help you?' Get into the habit of using standard professional statements and they will become second nature to you.

Smile when dealing with people who are making enquiries, be attentive and help them in a positive and polite manner. This will help the person to decide if he or she wants to return to your salon. Always show positive body language – clients may pick up on negative body language and decide to leave and not return.

There are two types of communication:

- Verbal communication uses the spoken word, either face to face or over the telephone.
- Non-verbal communication, for example, is when you write down a message or an appointment for a client. It can also mean reading, listening, or the body language you use such as nodding, smiling, frowning, and sign language. Written messages must be clear. It is often a good idea to take the message to the person concerned for his or her immediate attention.

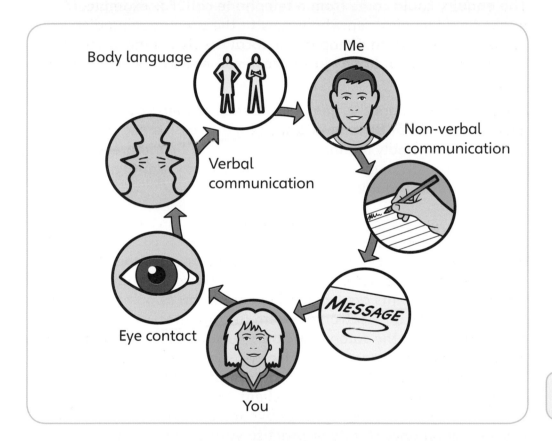

Verbal and non-verbal communication

Communication needs to be effective and clear to everyone involved. Speak at a suitable pace and use everyday business-like language, i.e. avoid using technical jargon or slang. Use an interesting and pleasant tone of voice and use appropriate open and closed questions for the client you are attending to. When a client makes an appointment, you will need to repeat the information back to him or her to make sure both you and the client understand it. Smile, look attentive and interested, and show positive body language by facing the client and not hopping about on one foot ready to take off for an early lunch!

>> **Get up and go!**

Discuss with a colleague the effects of positive and negative body language when dealing with clients.

Attend to clients and enquiries (2)

Identifying the purpose of an enquiry

Not all visitors to the salon will be clients wanting to make an appointment. They may have come to make a delivery or to read the water meter. Whatever the nature of the enquiry, find out what the purpose is as soon as possible. If you are busy, acknowledge the person and indicate you will be with him or her shortly.

The enquiry could come from a telephone call. For example, it might be a technical rep who is new to the area needing directions to your salon. Locate a map of the local area showing where the salon is and keep it handy just in case you need to help someone find their way.

Should you need another member of staff to help you, inform the visitor you will not be long and seek further assistance promptly. An efficient, friendly manner will give a good first impression of how the salon deals with visitors by correctly identifying the purpose of the enquiry.

Confirming appointments

The salon's business is driven by those who operate the appointments system. Perhaps your salon has a manual system, where appointments are written in pencil in an appointments book, or there may be an electronic system (a computer). As soon as the client comes into the salon, ask how you can help and identify the client's appointment as efficiently as you can. Once you have confirmed their appointment, promptly inform the relevant member of staff. Suggest to your client, he or she might like to take a seat if they are early or if they have to wait for the stylist. This is also a good opportunity to practise your client-care policy by offering refreshments and magazines.

Some salons have a self-service touch-screen appointments system whereby clients can check themselves in on arrival. What advantages might a system like this have? Of course, there will be no crowding around the reception desk as clients who have booked appointments can use the screen and then make their own way to the waiting area where you can greet them personally and offer refreshments as usual. More and more businesses are realising the benefits of IT, and salons have reaped the rewards of using automated tills, appointment and stock systems for many years.

►► Get up and go!

Find out the costs of different treatments and services offered by your salon. Clients may ask you for this information when they make an appointment. Find out how long each treatment or service takes. What is your salon's procedure for making and recording appointments? Discuss your findings with your assessor.

? Memory jogger

Why is it important to make client appointments correctly?

The telephone is ringing and a client is also waiting at reception. In which order do you deal with the enquiries?

List four different enquiries a salon receptionist might deal with during a normal day.

A client would like an appointment with Sheila at 10.30 am but she is busy then. What could you do?

What items of stationery should be available at reception at all times?

Attend to clients and enquiries (3)

Recording messages

The importance of passing on messages to the right person at the right time often requires diplomacy and tact. You must be able to read the situation in the salon before rushing in to pass on a message. You will need to learn how and when to ask questions and to say things that suit the purpose of the call.

Below are some typical situations you may have to deal with.

- *The senior stylist is busy with a client. Her mum rings with an important message.* It is often best to check if the stylist is able to come to the telephone to take the call and, if not, write the message down.

- *A client has phoned to complain about a service she has received and has asked to speak to the manager.* In situations such as this, you will need to be calm, responsible and tactful. If the manager is not there or busy, tell the client the manager will call them back. Speak clearly to avoid any confusion and write down as much information as the client can give you, not forgetting their telephone number.

Telephone Message

FOR	Ian
FROM	Mrs Price
TEL. NO.	020 870181

TELEPHONED ✔   PLEASE RING ✔

CALLED TO SEE YOU ☐   WILL CALL AGAIN ☐

WANTS TO SEE YOU ☐   URGENT ☐

MESSAGE: *Needs to speak to you asap – call on the above number up to 5.30pm*

DATE: 29.09.09   TIME: 11.15am

RECEIVED BY: Robert

Use the salon's message pad to take down messages

Show the client you have listened by recapping the information. This will also ensure you have all the correct information and there is no misunderstanding. Keep your tone of voice objective (i.e. don't take sides). Politely ask the client to hold, then take the message to a senior member of staff and await instructions.

When writing down a message, use your salon's message pad. Listen carefully to the caller before writing down the message. Always read it back to confirm accuracy. Take the message to the stylist or the person concerned and pass any reply back to the caller. Give all information clearly and accurately and make sure all confidential information is given only to authorised people.

» Get up and go!

What is your salon's policy for taking and recording messages? Discuss with a colleague what to do in each of the following situations:

- A client rings for a treatment list and tariff.
- The wholesaler rings to confirm the salon's order.
- A future bride is enquiring about the cost of three hair-up styles.

Confidential information

What is confidential information? In the salon, this will include:

- the contents of client records
- client and staff personal details such as name, address and telephone number
- financial matters relating to the business.

Sometimes personal conversations with colleagues may be confidential. Confidential information should only be given to authorised people.

The Data Protection Act (1998)

Under this act, you must not pass on any personal information to another person without the permission of the person involved. Your salon may obtain, hold and use personal data which is relevant for its own use. The consequences of dealing with confidential information inappropriately may lead to a disciplinary procedure. Take care only to use business information for the purposes of the business and keep the information within the walls of the salon.

» Get up and go!

Find out what your salon's procedures are for maintaining confidentiality. What might be the consequences if you break the salon's confidentiality policy?

Write down the differences between using an appointment book and a computer when making clients' appointments in relation to confidentiality.

? Memory jogger

A client is early for their appointment – what needs to be done?

A client is extremely annoyed because she has lost her earring at the salon. What can you do about it?

What is the main purpose of the Data Protection Act?

Why is it important to pass on messages at the time of receiving them?

Why is it important to have good communication between salon staff?

What type of answer can you expect from a closed question?

Help to make appointments for salon services (I)

People contact the salon in a variety of ways. It could be that clients telephone, visit the salon, a friend may make an appointment on their behalf, or they may send an email or text message to enquire about an appointment. You will need to know about the services the salon offers together with the products and available times you can offer an appointment.

Information such as each stylist's lunch hour, start and finish times, day off and late nights worked is all part of how your salon operates, and it will help you to know this when making appointments. Services such as cuts, blow-dries, sets, conditioning treatments and hair-up styles are non-chemical treatments. Colours, perms, relaxers, bleach, highlights and lowlights are chemical treatments. The salon will set aside a specific amount of time for each service. For example, it may take a few hours to complete a chemical service, while a cut or set may take less than an hour. You must make sure you leave enough time for each service to be finished professionally.

When making an appointment always make sure you deal with the request politely and promptly.

Page from an electronic appointments book

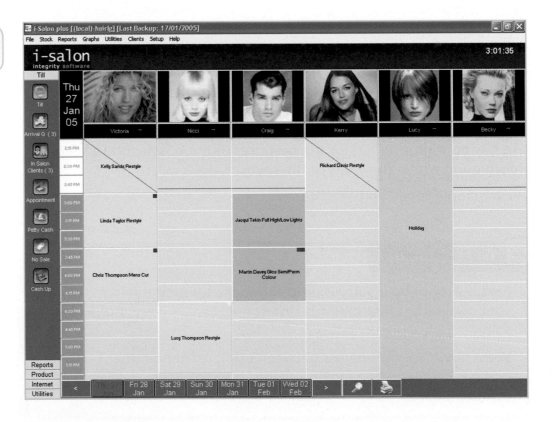

Identifying the client's requirements

Your client's request may take a few minutes to deal with and may cover a range of services offered by the salon. It's also possible the client may be making an appointment for several people and this will need your patience and knowledge of how the salon operates. Look at the appointment page and find out who is free and who will be able to offer each of the services requested. Ask for the client's name and the treatment they are interested in, enquire about the timeframe most suitable to your client and ask which member of staff they would like to carry out the treatment. Record their telephone number alongside their name in case there is a need to change the appointment. If you are not sure how to deal with a particular appointment request, then you should ask a senior member of staff for assistance.

Confirming appointment details

Your client's name, telephone number, service requested, date, time and member of staff booked for the service must always be discussed and confirmed with the client when he or she makes an appointment. Repeat the information for the appointment to the client and ask if it is acceptable. Always make sure the client is aware of the length of time anticipated for their particular treatment. If the client is in the salon, ask whether he or she would like an appointment card with the details written down.

On the appointment page or computer screen, make sure all of the information is recorded accurately, in the right place, at the right time and you have left the stylist sufficient time to complete the service. This means, for example, not booking a chemical treatment too late in the afternoon, as this would mean both stylist and junior stylist leaving the salon later than usual at the end of the day.

If using a manual appointment system, make sure your writing is neat and easy to read. Use a pencil to make appointments so that mistakes or cancellations can be easily changed. This helps to make good use of the available space on the page and keeps the information clear and easy to follow.

» Get up and go!

With a colleague, practise making appointments for the following clients:

- Mrs McMillan would like a blow-dry. She has long hair.
- Mrs Gilchrist would like a perm and cut.
- Mr Griffen would like a dry cut.
- Miss Nicol would like highlights on medium-length hair.
- Mr Schneider would like a beard trim.

Help to make appointments for salon services (2)

Telephone appointments

Many appointments are made by telephone. When answering the phone, remember to smile – the client can hear the difference in your tone of voice! Listen carefully to what the client is saying and make each appointment as promptly as you can. Using the phone properly and efficiently is important to the smooth running of the salon business. It can be the first point of contact between you and the client.

On answering the phone, remember to tell the caller the name of the salon and who you are, for example 'Good morning, Head Start, Laura speaking. How can I help you?' As soon as the caller tells you his or her name, start to use it. It gives the call a personal touch and lets them know you have listened to basic information and as such, you have already begun to develop a professional relationship.

If you need to discuss appointment details with a colleague, it is a good idea not to leave the client holding on listening to salon background noise. Most phones have a mute button which will allow you to talk to your colleague without the caller hearing. Remember to press the mute button again when you return to speak to the client, otherwise he or she will not hear you! Repeat the information back to the client and check he or she is happy with the appointment time, date and stylist.

If you are making an appointment for a client who would like a permanent colour which touches the skin, you must remember to offer a skin test. Skin tests are recommended by the manufacturer and should be carried out 24–48 hours before the permanent colour application. Complete the appointment booking by saying something like, 'Thank you. We look forward to seeing you soon. Goodbye.'

This section is designed to further develop your skills and knowledge whilst working on reception. It will help familiarise you with how payments are handled. The most popular type of payment is cash, closely followed by credit or debit cards. Other types of payment include:

- cheques
- gift vouchers
- account.

There are many different methods of payment

Get ahead

What do you need to be aware of when a client hands over money at reception? There are lots of forged notes and coins in circulation and you need to know how to deal with a situation where you think a client is trying to pay with forged money, should it arise. Talk to your assessor about the advantages and disadvantages of handling cash as opposed to credit and debit cards.

Draw up a simple SWOT chart and list the Strengths, Weaknesses, Opportunities and Threats of using cash and credit/debit cards. Compare these methods of payment with cheques, gift vouchers and payment by account.

Things for you to think about:

- Does your salon still accept cheques? Is a cheque guarantee card needed?
- Are credit/debit cards still valid? Check the expiry date.
- The cost to the salon of using credit/debit cards – banks charge businesses for this service.
- Are gift vouchers still valid? Always check the use-by date.
- Are accounts paid on time?

? Memory jogger

List the information needed when making an appointment.

When the phone rings, how soon should you answer it?

When answering the phone, what should you say?

Give two reasons why appointments need to be made correctly.

What types of payment method does your salon accept?

UNIT G3

Contribute to the development of effective working relationships

Anne Veck, photographer: Clark Wiseman

A happy salon is a pleasant place to work and visit. Good working relationships with clients and colleagues are essential to the smooth running of the salon. A client's trust and goodwill must be earned. Showing you can do your job well will give clients confidence in your ability. If you upset a client or behave in an unprofessional way, the client may not come back to the salon. On the other hand, if the client is happy with your work, he or she is likely to return. You are very much a part of a team when you work in the salon.

This unit is about forming good relationships with clients in a way that promotes goodwill and trust, being able to work effectively when supporting your colleagues and using opportunities for learning within your job role.

In this unit you will learn how to:

- Develop effective working relationships with clients
- Develop effective working relationships with colleagues
- Develop yourself within the job role
- Understand employment policies and procedures.

This unit will also give you the chance to find out the best ways to develop your skills within your job role. You will then be ready to move on in your chosen career.

Here are some key words you will meet in this unit:

Communication – verbal and non-verbal ways in which to transfer information

Appeals procedure – a procedure you can follow should you have a grievance

Confidential – respect and privacy of an individual's information

Hospitality – offering refreshments, making the client comfortable

Courteous – polite and with good manners

Professional development – training activities to improve your skills/knowledge

Relevant person – responsible person

Technical activities – cutting, perming, colouring and straightening treatments

SWOT – Strengths, Weaknesses, Opportunities, Threats

TEAM – Together Everyone Achieves More

Goodwill – professional bond brought about by trust and respect

Trust – professional confidence

Develop effective working relationships with clients (I)

Clients are the most important part of your work. You will need to treat them with respect, which will help them to trust you and make them want to keep coming back. Welcome your client with a smile and by offering refreshments and magazines, making sure they are comfortable.

Listen carefully to what the client is saying

Communicating with clients

When communicating with your clients, try to remember the following.

- Use a friendly, calm, confident and polite manner.
- Try to attract and keep eye contact.
- Listen, and focus on what the client is saying.
- Use good questioning skills in order to find out information.
- Maintain client confidentiality by respecting them as people who trust you enough to carry out a professional treatment.
- Keep all you hear from your clients to yourself. Do not gossip, either about clients or to clients.
- Use positive body language. Stand up straight and use your eyes to express yourself when talking, remembering to smile. This will put the client at ease, especially if they are shy and timid.

Handling clients' personal items

Often clients will trust you to take care of their belongings while they visit the salon. Look in your reception area to see if there is a sign which makes it clear that the salon does not take responsibility for personal belongings, even if there is somewhere to hang coats and bags. Whatever your salon's policy for clients' belongings, it must be communicated clearly to them. Nevertheless, you should handle clients' belongings with reasonable care.

Dealing with client concerns

There are many mirrors in a salon and you will need to learn to use them for different purposes. Think about using the mirror to hold a conversation, or to look at the hairstyle as it is developing. You can also use the mirror to check for signs of unhappiness, or if the client is confused or angry. How would you recognise when a client is angry or confused?

To be an effective team member, you must make sure the client's comfort and needs are dealt with confidentially and professionally. It may be that the client's concern is within your job responsibilities, and you can deal with it in a professional way. Should you ever need to discuss a client's concern, you should know who to report the matter to. The salon manager is usually the person to report difficult situations to. Always work within your salon's client-care policy and deal with the concern promptly and efficiently. This will encourage the client's trust and goodwill.

>> **Get up and go!**

Clients who have cause to complain may do so quite loudly. This could lead to an embarrassing situation for all staff and clients in the salon. Remember to let the client know how their complaint is being dealt with and by whom. No one likes to be kept waiting, so deal with queries and concerns promptly. Does your salon have a complaints procedure? Is there a process to follow for client complaints? Research your salon for a policy on how to deal with a client complaint, finding out who deals with these issues. Consider how best to deal with a complaining client and make appropriate suggestions to your assessor.

Develop effective working relationships with clients (2)

Client comfort

Look after your clients. Offer them a drink and a magazine, and perhaps discuss other treatments or services the salon offers. Always offer them the same level of professionalism on each and every visit. Ask simple questions to make sure they are comfortable and to let them know you have thought about their comfort and care. Ask at regular intervals if they feel satisfied with the level of treatment they have received. You must strive to satisfy your client on every visit to ensure their return.

Your appearance and behaviour

Your standard of behaviour must be professional at all times. The way staff behave, either when dealing with clients or with each other, will be noticed by everyone in the salon. Remember, your behaviour contributes greatly to your professional image and this includes being punctual and having a good record of attendance.

The client's comfort is very important

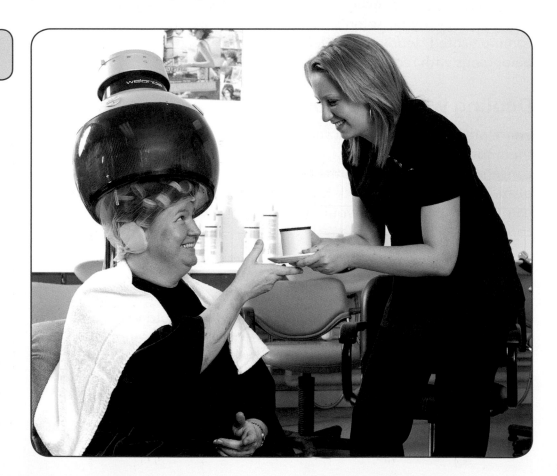

>> Get up and go!

Manners cost nothing and yet they are one of the most important attibutes and will help you develop a good relationship with your clients and colleagues.

Try this: set yourself a target of giving and receiving at least ten 'thank yous' during your working day. Each time you do something for someone and they say thank you, jot it down and work towards your target of ten. How many times do you thank people? Now work towards your own target of giving ten.

This is a nice exercise and one which should be fun and easy to do. What's more, it should help you to realise how many times people recognise what you have done for them and, of course, remember that it is a two-way street.

Could you display this information discreetly on the salon wall, just to let people know you are developing your working relationships?

Know your salon's standards for appearance and meet them by wearing the appropriate uniform, make-up and jewellery. You will also need a suitable professional hairstyle. This must reflect your salon's standards and image, and will show clients you take pride in your own hair and appearance, helping you build a professional relationship with them.

✂ Sharpen up!

Think about the different standards of dress within your salon and other places of work you have had contact with (e.g. shops, banks, other salons).

What did you think when you saw the staff? Were they suitably dressed? Did they look professional?

Consider these points and think about how your clients may view the staff who are attending to them, based on their appearance.

? Memory jogger

Who is responsible for your clients' belongings?

Think of three reasons why you should look after your client when they visit the salon.

How would you recognise that your client is angry or confused?

Why are attendance and punctuality important from a client perspective?

Develop effective working relationships with colleagues (I)

Teamwork is vital to the smooth running of the salon. You will need to be sure the people you work with are happy about how you are carrying out your job role. Unless you ask how well you are performing your role, possibly you will not find out until there is something to discuss, and then it may be from your line manager's point of view. Make general enquiries about how you are performing and whether you have done what has been asked of you on a regular basis.

You are an important member of staff who is central to the success of all treatments taking place within your salon. Your role is to help your team as much as you can, all day and every day. Your colleagues are relying on you to carry out your job in a professional way. Do not let them or your clients down by failing to turn up at work.

All staff need to be motivated and should aim to offer their clients a professional service. Good working relationships are important to the smooth running of the salon and all staff must be happy to take part in whatever job needs doing. Below is a simple acronym which will help you to remember what teamwork is all about:

Together
Everyone
Achieves
More

Being courteous

A happy salon environment makes a good impression on clients. Staff working well together – being friendly, helping each other and behaving like a team – will help to create a good atmosphere. As well as being friendly and respectful to clients, you must also be friendly and respectful to colleagues.

Asking for and giving help

When asking colleagues for help and information, you should be polite and courteous. Sometimes it is not what you ask for, but the way in which you ask for it that counts. If a colleague asks for your help, always give it willingly and with a smile.

Making efficient use of your time

Stylists and managers expect to receive a speedy and efficient service from their staff, which is you! You will need to manage your time well, which in turn will help the salon to run smoothly. In a salon, time is money so it is essential your time and your colleagues' time is used effectively. In practice, this means making sure everything is prepared ready for the stylist to move on to the next client.

Your line manager

There may be times when you need to speak to your line manager, either about work-related issues (e.g. treatments, procedures, policies) or other things, such as training, holiday or time off. Always treat a manager with the respect their position deserves. Managers have worked hard to achieve their job role and are in a good position to help you if you show them you are serious about your career. If you need time off, make sure you have a genuine reason and ask politely for their agreement, giving as much notice as possible.

If you need time off, you will need to agree it with your line manager

>> **Get up and go!**

Look at the list of appointments below.

- Mrs Kraft – perm and set at 9.30 am
- Miss Wyatt – highlights and a cut at 10 am
- Mr Rossetti – beard trim at 11.30 am
- Miss Zhang – cut and blow-dry at 2.30 pm
- Mrs Morris – dry trim at 4 pm
- Mrs Cooper – hair up at 5 pm

Sue is a stylist who works from 9 am through to 6 pm. Create a stylist's column for Sue's day, blocking out the time needed to work on each client. For example, Sue will need 30 minutes to wind Mrs Kraft's perm, 15 minutes to set it and a further 15 minutes to dress out. Can Sue have lunch and, if so, when?

>> **Get up and go!**

With a colleague, take on the roles of line manager and salon junior and role play asking for an early lunch hour. The junior should use negative types of communication in the first instance and then try again using positive types of communication. How did the person playing the manager respond in both instances? Which approach do you think is best? Discuss the results of your scenario with your assessor.

Develop effective working relationships with colleagues (2)

Assisting colleagues

Your job includes passing tools and equipment such as rollers, pins, perm papers and perm rods to the stylist. You should pass these in such a way as to enable the stylist to progress more quickly with the treatment. This will help the stylist to make efficient use of their time.

Making drinks for clients, cleaning the backwash basins, sweeping the floor, maintaining record cards, carrying out skin tests, flushing the hot water through first thing in the morning, and replacing the barbicide are all part of your daily responsibilities. You can also assist colleagues by ensuring the reception area is clean and tidy and all retail shelves are neatly displayed and fully stocked. Keep the salon tidy by clearing away used towels, used cups and saucers, and tinting bowls, which will need to be rinsed out.

 Sharpen up!

Why not create a checklist to include your main tasks during the day? This checklist could include a column for tasks, a column for each hour of the day and a column for your initials. This way both you and your line manager will be able to keep an eye on when the tasks were last completed.

Some of the hands-on hair treatments you will be asked to do will include:

- shampooing
- colour removal
- neutralising
- conditioning treatments
- removing rollers and perm rods
- preparing clients' hair for further treatments, such as sectioning the hair so the stylist can apply colour.

Always give assistance to your colleagues which matches your job responsibilities.

≫ Get up and go!

Running out of products or other resources may seriously affect salon services. Always report any problems such as this to the relevant person. Who is this person in your salon?

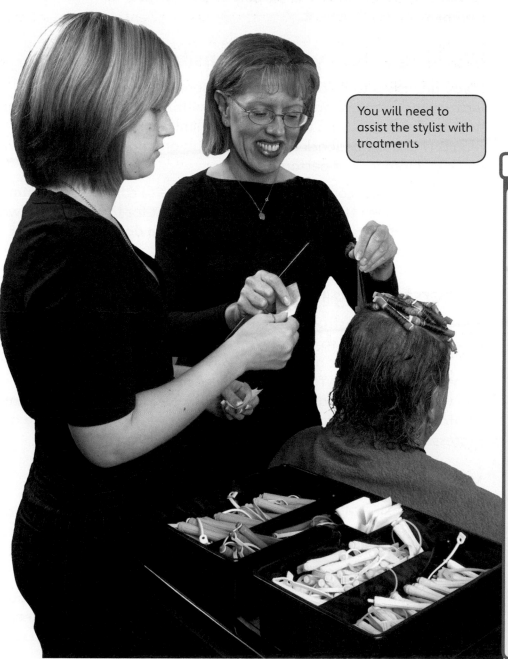

You will need to assist the stylist with treatments

? Memory jogger

How can you contribute to effective working relationships?

What teams are you part of? How do you feel when people do not play their part?

Discuss with a colleague how you would fit into an existing team.

How would you feel if you were trying to speak to someone and the person appeared bored or did not bother to look at you?

If you need time off, how do you ask your line manager's permission?

With a colleague, write a list of genuine reasons for taking time off from work.

Develop yourself within the job role (I)

Try to get into the habit of identifying your own strengths and areas for further improvement. On a regular basis you will have the opportunity to sit down with your line manager, or another person who is responsible for staff development, to agree an appropriate way forward for you to develop further in your job role. Use this opportunity positively, keep a record of what was discussed and consider any training you undertake as part of your continuous professional development.

Working within your responsibilities

If you are asked to do a task but are unsure how to do it or the instructions you have are unclear, check with your line manager about how to proceed. Always work within the limits of your job role and regularly ask for feedback on how well you are progressing and how you can improve your performance.

The consequences could be serious if you were to carry out a treatment you had not been trained to do. Use equipment for the purpose it was intended and check it is safe to use. If you are in doubt, ask a senior member of staff.

Understanding instructions

You may find the instructions you have been given to carry out a task are not clear. If so, discuss the appropriate course of action with a senior member of staff. This will ensure you know exactly what you have to do. The task can then be carried out correctly, you will avoid misusing a product or piece of equipment, and client comfort and satisfaction will be maintained, helping to promote a professional image.

Your professional development

How you develop in your job role is important to your own professional progression and to the success of the salon. By working with the person who is responsible for providing staff training in your salon, you will be able to develop your own personal training plan for success.

Using the existing framework of qualifications as a guide, make your plan. When you have developed your own professional record, keep it up to date. Many of your senior colleagues will be able to help with this as it is also part of their job to keep themselves up to date.

Discuss your personal training plan with your supervisor and plan how you are going to achieve areas for further development. Remember to include a review date when you can sit down together to review your progress.

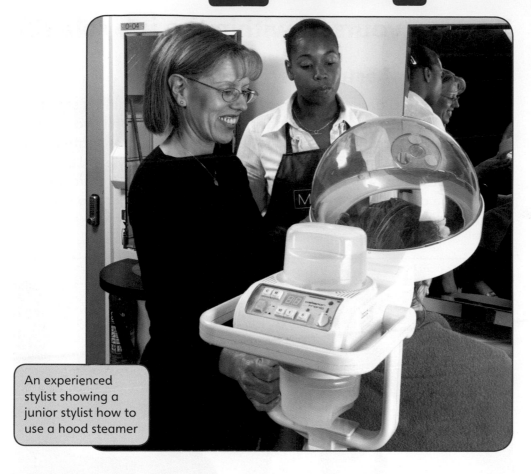

An experienced stylist showing a junior stylist how to use a hood steamer

Carrying out your action plan will help you to:

- develop your strengths
- focus on areas for further development
- promote good working relationships within the salon
- become more efficient at your job in the salon.

It is a good idea to keep a daily record of the type of work you do, so you and your manager can reflect on what you have been doing. It is best to have a weekly review so your memory is clear and a positive discussion can take place.

» Get up and go!

Good staff are hard to find. What do you think are the qualities that make a good salon staff member? Make a list. Now list the types of things you want to improve, for example, your shampooing or communication skills. Think about the future. What do you want to achieve? Where do you want to be in five years' time? How are you going to get there? Discuss these questions with a colleague and develop a SWOT chart, listing your Strengths, Weaknesses, Opportunities and Threats.

Develop yourself within the job role (2)

Learning opportunities

Everyone learns differently. You may learn best by watching a stylist at work, or by listening to instructions either before or while you are doing a task. Take advantage of all the skills being demonstrated every day by senior staff. You can also learn when assisting stylists. Look at how they stand or hold their hands when carrying out a treatment. Look at the client's hair before, during and after the service so you can see how the style develops.

A junior stylist being trained to apply a conditioning treatment

There are many opportunities to learn and develop your professional skills. Try visiting some of the shows and exhibitions held every year to see top stylists demonstrate hair-up styles, cuts, colours and other new and exciting aspects of the hairdressing industry. Ask your colleagues to help you learn if you find tasks difficult and take advantage of opportunities to learn when they are available, e.g. late-night training sessions, guest stylists, trade reps, etc.

Watch some of the many TV channels showing hairdressing salons and the many and varied types of work they are involved in. Keep up to date with techniques and products by reading the weekly *Hairdressers Journal*. Look at pop stars, movie stars and so on to find out what the latest fashions and trends are. Hairdressing is all about fashion and you must be up to date. Attend each and every staff training session and take part in the salon's training and development plan. Watch technical services and ask questions about what you see and why it is happening.

Magazines can help you keep up to date with trends and fashions in hairdressing

>> Get up and go!

With a partner, role play an experienced stylist instructing a junior stylist on how to blow-dry using a handheld hairdryer. The junior can practise sectioning the hair and holding the hairdryer correctly. Think of the stages involved in training someone: planning, preparation, locating suitable resources, choosing an appropriate time to demonstrate, etc. Also consider the health and safety aspects.

Now write up an activity plan where the points mentioned above have been addressed. Enlist the help of a couple of colleagues and put your plan into action. Reflect on the practicalities of the before, during and after stages of the demonstration and write up your thoughts on improvements for a future training event. This exercise should help you develop an understanding of the amount of time, effort and work that goes into giving a demonstration. Did you use your people skills to best effect?

Develop yourself within the job role (3)

Setting self-development targets and reviewing progress

Many salons will expect you to achieve Level 1 within one year. It is possible to achieve this qualification within this time, which would then mean you could be considered for a Level 2 training programme. You and your salon should set realistic targets through which to achieve units of work. Agree realistic development targets for yourself with your line manager or the person responsible for staff development. You must take personal responsibility for your own targets and understand the importance of meeting them. The salon owner may be unhappy if you fail to do so! Your personal development plan must be used continuously for the rest of your life.

Professional development includes keeping up to date with the latest styles, techniques and products

A calendar showing progression and achievement would be a useful piece of evidence to develop. This should show clearly what you need to do and by what date. It could also set out the salon's commitment to you as a staff member in terms of training. Review your progress regularly with your manager and use this to develop any further action you may need in working towards your agreed targets.

Meeting your self-development targets should lead to increased job satisfaction, and the opportunity to progress to other areas within hairdressing and attract a higher financial reward.

>> **Get up and go!**

How can you identify your own strengths and areas for further development? Pair up with a colleague and jot down a few notes on how you are going to best identify these. How about a client questionnaire to provide you with feedback? Similarly, how about a simple feedback sheet to circulate amongst your colleagues at work? The questionnaire could be made anonymous so no-one feels uncomfortable about completing it. The findings from this exercise should be viewed positively, whatever they may be, and could form part of the review process.

? **Memory jogger**

How do you keep up to date with the latest styles, techniques and products?

How often does your salon hold team meetings to discuss general issues?

Why should you work positively within a team?

What might happen if you ignore manufacturers' or stylist's instructions?

Explain the benefits of continued professional development.

Why should you respond positively to reviews from staff?

Goldwell

Employment policies and procedures

Procedures

Your job description and contract of employment

When you attend an interview, the job description (a list of the specific and general duties you will be expected to do) should be discussed. Once you start work at the salon, a copy of the job description will be placed in your records. Make sure you read it carefully and do what it says. You should be given a contract of employment within three months of starting your job.

Salon meetings

Most salons hold regular meetings and this is the time to discuss general issues which may concern you. Anything of a private nature must be kept confidential, such as staff details, client details, salon details and any disciplinary proceedings. Remember, if you breach the salon's policy for confidentiality, you could be disciplined.

The salon's appeals and grievance procedure

The salon will have copies of its appeals and grievance (complaints) procedure, which all members of staff should have access to. If you have a grievance, deal with the problem sensibly, calmly and professionally, and seek independent advice on how to deal with the situation. Find out who to report to when you have difficulties in working with a team member.

JOB DESCRIPTION – JUNIOR

Job title: Junior
Place of work: Styles 4 You, Paisley

Candidate specification

About the candidate
The candidate should:

- have good interpersonal skills and demonstrate a professional level of client care
- have the flexibility and willingness to work as a team member
- be able to work on Saturday and at least one late evening each week
- take responsibility for securing models for practise and assessment purposes
- update practical skills regularly at training sessions
- take an active interest in all aspects of work within the salon
- attend hairdressing seminars and professional courses in order to keep up to date with current and emerging techniques
- complete the appropriate hairdressing qualification within the specified time frame
- undertake other reasonable duties, from time to time, as required by senior staff.

Specific duties
Undertake day-to-day duties such as:

- shampoo and condition hair and scalp
- assist with perming, neutralising and colouring
- assist with salon reception duties
- sell retail products
- make refreshments
- reduce the risks to general health and safety
- sterilise equipment
- prepare hairdressing treatments and maintain the salon work areas (continuous)
- wash and dry towels and gowns
- check stock.

About the salon and our team
We are a friendly team who enjoy busy professional lives. We strive for perfection, sincerity and honesty in everything we do. Our skills are updated regularly by attending seminars and holding teach-in evenings. We look forward to working with you and wish you an enjoyable and rewarding time with us.

The successful candidate will enjoy: two weeks' paid holiday each year, the national minimum wage, a 37-hour working week, 9 am starts and one hour for lunch every day.

A job description for a salon junior

? Memory jogger

What may happen if you break rules of confidentiality?

Who would you report any problems in the salon to?

How can you identify your own strengths and areas for improvement?

Why should your salon have an appeals procedure?

UNIT GH3

Prepare for hair services and maintain work areas

Anne Veck, photographer: Clark Wiseman

When working in the salon, one of your main duties will be preparing clients for services and setting up products, tools and equipment for stylists. Regularly checking what services and treatments are booked, knowing what is needed for each of them and being able to tidy away and clean up properly afterwards are essential skills.

You will need to demonstrate that you can meet the standards for preparing and maintaining hairdressing work areas. Following certain health, safety and hygiene procedures will become a normal part of your day-to-day duties. Everything you have learned so far about health and safety and COSHH needs to be brought together in this unit. Go back to Unit G20 to remind yourself of the health and safety aspects of working in a salon. Your assessor will observe your performance, which must include preparation for different hairdressing treatments, such as ladies' or gents' hairdressing services.

In this unit you will learn how to:

- Prepare for hair services
- Maintain the work area for hair services.

Here are some key words you will meet in this unit:

Materials – resources you will need to carry out a client's treatment

Consultation – a meeting with a client to talk about and decide with them what they want from a treatment

Dispose – the correct removal of unwanted materials, products and other salon waste

Stock – products, materials and resources needed for clients' treatments

Service – what you have given your client by way of your help, time and expertise, e.g. cut, blow dry, colour, perm, etc.

Records – client details held either manually (on paper) or electronically (on computer)

Prepare for hair services (I)

Start as you mean to go on

Preparing for hair services isn't just about getting tools and equipment ready. Think about the type of people who may come through your salon door. Are they busy working people with little time on their hands? Are they parents with young children? Are they able-bodied or disabled? Notice your clients' body language as they enter the salon. Do they look rushed, frustrated, or perhaps calm?

You can begin to prepare for a client's hair service as soon as they enter the salon. If you notice a client has difficulty walking or moving around, or has a pushchair or shopping bags, find out if they need help coming into the salon. You may be able to hold the door for them, move things out of their way, or help them to a chair. Try to remember what help your client needed so you can be ready to offer it again next time they visit. Demonstrate a patient, positive attitude and make sure your body language is always professional.

>> **Get up and go!**

Here are a few different services and treatments your salon may have booked on a regular basis:

Service/treatment	Products, tools and equipment needed
Setting	
Blow-drying	
Perming	
Colouring	
Cutting	
Straightening	
Hair-up	
Plaiting	
Hair extensions	
Shaving	
Beard trimming	

Copy out the table and for each service list in the right-hand column the products, tools and equipment that will be required. Don't forget things like cotton wool, disposable gloves and barrier cream, and whether or not you will need to set up a trolley.

Now practise setting up trays with a colleague. Check each other's trays and find out if you have both included everything you need.

Setting up materials, tools and equipment

Think about the most sensible way in which to set up materials, tools and equipment for the hair services offered by your salon. What clients do you have booked in today? You will need to check the appointment book, see what stock is required for each service and check you have the necessary items in the stock room. Discuss each client's requirements with your stylist.

Gowns and towels, and tools and equipment required for popular hairdressing treatments, must always be readily available. This will present a professional image and help save time for you and the stylist. The client will also be able to have their treatment completed in good time, making the visit a cost-effective one for the salon and an enjoyable one for the client.

As each of the services your salon offers has its own particular requirements in terms of resources, you need to be thorough in your preparation. It is particularly important to check all electrical equipment is in good working order, clean and fit for its purpose. Similarly, are products good to use? Check for any punctures or leaks in tubes and containers, and whether lids have been replaced properly. For example, the stylist will need the following if a perm is booked:

- disposable gloves
- plastic apron
- combs
- section clips
- different sized rods
- end papers
- cotton wool
- tension strips
- plastic cap
- barrier cream
- the appropriate perming lotion and neutraliser
- manufacturer's instructions.

Preparing products and equipment for stylists is one of your most important responsibilities

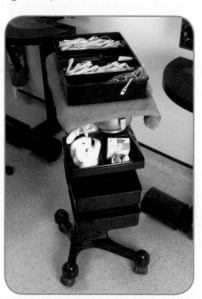

Perming trolley set up ready for stylist

? Memory jogger

What types of people may come through your salon door?

How do you know what to set up for each treatment your salon offers?

Prepare for hair services (2)

Preparing in good time

The tools, equipment and work area that stylists use need to be ready in time for the required treatment. Constantly think ahead and prepare the area as necessary for your stylist and, ultimately, your client. Be alert for signs that your team may need something, such as a comb or pair of clippers. Watch what each staff member uses – he or she may have a favourite comb or brush. Does this need to be sterilised before the next client?

Look at the appointment book on a regular basis so that you know what work is planned for the day. Bear in mind appointments might change during the day and you need to know the status of the appointment book at any one time. This means you need to liaise constantly with the receptionist to make sure changes are being passed on to you.

Now think about the type of work that has been booked in for the day. There may be several perms, some colours, a relaxer and a conditioning treatment. You will need to prepare for each treatment separately. Sometimes it is a good idea to check the appointments the day before, especially with chemical treatments. Check you have the necessary perms, relaxers and colours required for each of the clients.

Observe and anticipate

As you become more knowledgeable about hairdressing skills and get to know your colleagues, you will be able to observe what is happening in the salon and anticipate when your help is needed. Observation plays a major part in many hairdressing salons. Staff can 'speak' to each other using eye contact rather than words. Be alert to the signs that you may be needed and learn to identify your team's body language. This will help you anticipate the needs of other people, which in turn will benefit both clients and colleagues. Remember though to observe, not stare! Make sure that when you watch someone it is for a professional purpose.

At the end of a treatment

Timing in the salon is everything – sometimes things can happen too soon or not soon enough. Think about the products that may be needed at the end of a treatment. It could be serum, hairspray, wax, or a mixture of different products. Be on the look out for opportunities to assist your team as they are finishing off their clients.

Client records

Record cards are a professional record of what has been applied to your clients' hair. They are also a useful tool for recording positive comments and suggestions for any future treatment the client may request. The personal and professional information held on the record

Be ready to hand tools, equipment or materials to the stylist when they need them

card is protected by the Data Protection Act. It is very important for record cards to be stored correctly in a lockable cabinet.

When obtaining records for your stylist's client, always remember to check the name, address and telephone number. Clients may share the same surname and even the same first name, and you don't want to give the stylist the wrong information.

Clients' record cards must be stored properly in a locked cabinet

Sharpen up!

Client record cards hold detailed information from past treatments. This information is crucial to the success of any hairdressing treatment. Imagine a situation where a stylist is off sick. Would another stylist know what was previously used on the client? Do you remember all of the products, mixes, timings and results from past clients?

Records are important, to both your salon and your clients. They inform you of the products used previously, the timing and what the client's thoughts were regarding the result. Always have the client's record card ready in time for the consultation by the stylist. Clear away and file record cards as soon as they have been finished with. Your next client does not want the previous client's colour applied to his or her hair.

Get up and go!

Think of a retail incentive scheme where all staff are encouraged to sell retail products and more chemical and non-chemical treatments. This could lead to greater income for the salon and perhaps a higher return for all staff in terms of an increased salary.

Look at the retail chart below and think of a way in which all staff could benefit, from the junior to the senior manager.

Staff name	Week 1	Week 2	Week 3	Week 4
Sylvia				Straighteners
Sue	Conditioning mousse	Moisturising shampoo	Scrunchie	
Jane		Brush	Serum	
Charmaine	Hair shine		Chemical treatment	

At the end of week 4, the salon could simply total the cost of sales and reward the member of staff who sold the most. Some hairdressing companies donate gifts as retail incentives. Discuss this system with a senior member of staff at your next staff meeting.

Memory jogger

Why is timing important when setting out materials and products for your stylist?

What could you check against to find out what stock is needed for the day ahead?

Where should record cards be kept?

What does 'confidential' mean?

For whose benefit are record cards kept?

Prepare for hair services (3)

Cleaning the work area and sterilising tools and equipment

Remember to clear away all materials, tools and equipment when the stylist has finished with them. Wipe down the styling area with a suitable cleansing liquid at the most appropriate time and make sure the area is hair-free. Think about how you would feel if a stylist used a comb on your hair that had been used on clients all day without being cleaned and sterilised.

Salons are breeding grounds for bacteria. Make sure all equipment is clean for every client. Combs, brushes and all tools and equipment that have come into contact with the client's hair and scalp must be cleaned and sterilised ready for the next client. Sterilising destroys all living organisms. You may also use disinfectants in the salon to clean work areas. Disinfecting slows down the growth of bacteria.

Methods of sterilisation

Different tools and equipment need to be sterilised using different methods. For example, soft plastics cannot withstand the heat of an autoclave (which reaches 125°C) and will change shape or simply melt – a plastic roller will come out looking like a chewed piece of gum! Be careful to choose the right method for each piece of equipment. Take advice and guidance from the stylist or senior manager on how to sterilise correctly.

The three most commonly used methods of sterilising salon tools and equipment are:

- barbicide
- ultraviolet cabinet
- autoclave.

Barbicide is often used for sterilising combs and scissors and should be changed daily. An ultraviolet cabinet can sterilise small pieces of equipment made of plastic, such as brushes, combs and section clips. Autoclaves will sterilise objects made of rubber and metals, such as good quality combs and scissors.

>> Get up and go!

Make a list of the different types of sterilisation methods available in your salon.

Find out how each one works and what tools they are used to sterilise.

✂ Sharpen up!

What happens during a day in the life of a hairdresser? Think about your working day from start to finish and all the things you do. Many of them you probably do automatically and don't even think about. Maybe some of your colleagues aren't aware of all the things you do and how varied they are.

Make a list of all the tasks you do on an average day. Look at the list and think about how important each task is to the smooth running of the salon. Some of the things you do may be mundane, but if you didn't do them, life in the salon for your colleagues would soon become difficult.

Why not discuss your list at your next review or staff meeting? You may enlighten some people about what you do and ultimately surprise them!

? Memory jogger

What is the difference between disinfecting and sterilising?

Name three methods of sterilisation used in a salon.

What temperature does an autoclave reach?

Maintain the work area for hair services (I)

Disposing of hair and waste materials safely

The correct disposal of hair and waste materials is vital to the success of your salon. This isn't just to keep the salon looking clean and tidy – an Environmental Health Officer can, and often does, close down salons where staff have failed to deal with salon waste correctly.

Removing hair and waste from the salon means following health and safety procedures and using controlled and environmentally friendly methods. Here are some aspects of waste management you should be aware of.

- Loose hair should be cleared from basins to prevent blockages.

- Empty conditioner or shampoo bottles should be put in a plastics bin.

- Any left-over tint, bleach or perm lotion should be poured down the basin.

- Cut hair from the salon floor should be incinerated (burned) and disposed of by the local authority.

- Sharp items such as razor blades should be stored in a sharps box, which is then disposed of by a specialist company.

- Hairspray and mousse containers must be disposed of by a recognised company.

Removing waste quickly and correctly will give clients a professional image of the salon. It also reduces the risk of injury and cross-infection by keeping your work area clean and tidy during the service.

The Control of Substances Hazardous to Health (COSHH) Regulations (2002)

The COSHH Regulations greatly affect the way in which salons dispose of their waste by setting out basic measures employers and employees must take. In addition, each local authority has its own policy on how to deal with salon waste and this may mean that some salons have different procedures to others. However, in general, hair should be incinerated, aerosols should be disposed of separately from the general salon waste and sharps should be collected by a specialist refuse company.

A sharps bin is the only way to dispose of items like razor blades

» **Get up and go!**

Look at the methods of waste disposal your salon adopts. How do they dispose of hair, plastics, aerosols, chemical products and sharps? Contact your Environmental Health Services department via your local authority to find out how to dispose of salon waste in the correct way. You can also ask your assessor about the different strategies in place that aim to minimise the effects on the environment of salon waste disposal. Have there been any changes or updates to best practice? Present your findings to your assessor.

Checking and cleaning equipment

All salon equipment must be checked visually before each use and cleaned after each use in readiness for the next client. Make sure equipment is cleaned thoroughly following the manufacturer's instructions. Remember to wear suitable personal protective equipment (PPE) if using chemicals or cleaning fluid. Electrical equipment should be checked by a qualified electrician and PAT (Portable Appliance Test) tested each year. This will satisfy any health and safety checks your salon has.

Floors, seating, working surfaces, mirrors and basins must also be cleaned on a daily basis using appropriate cleaning equipment. Depending on how big your salon is, you may have independent cleaners who clean on a regular basis.

Towels and gowns

To avoid cross-infection, it is very important that clean towels and gowns are used for each client. Cross-infection is when an infection (such as a cold) or an infestation (such as head lice) is passed from one person to another. Make sure you have clean gowns and towels for every treatment.

As mentioned earlier in the unit, regular checking of the day's appointments will help you plan ahead. You will need to find out how many chemical and non-chemical treatments are booked in for the day so you can ensure you have the appropriate number and colour of clean towels for each client. At the start of each day, make sure there are enough clean towels and gowns to last. This part of your work is very important – if there are not enough clean towels and gowns, your salon cannot carry out services and treatments!

? Memory jogger

Why is it important to dispose of salon waste safely and correctly?

What are your salon's waste management procedures?

What are sharps?

What does PAT stand for?

What needs to be cleaned in the salon every day?

Maintain the work area for hair services (2)

Stock

Stock is all the products, such as shampoo, conditioner, hairspray, colour, perm lotion, etc., and consumable equipment, such as hair grips, end papers, etc., that your salon needs to run smoothly. Stock-taking systems vary from salon to salon. It is your responsibility to make sure that no product falls below the minimum stock level and these levels will need to be monitored on a regular basis. The stylist or senior manager will advise you on how much stock needs to be kept for each item.

> ## » Get up and go!
>
> Think about how it might be possible to improve the stock system at your salon. You could suggest a computerised system if the salon currently uses a manual one. If this isn't possible, why not come up with some improvements for the current system, such as using differently coloured pieces of paper to indicate how urgently ordering is needed or to list items that need ordering from different suppliers? Is this something you could discuss at one of your staff meetings?

Computerised stock systems

Your salon might have a computer system which updates stock levels as you enter sales. The system may also contain other information about the salon such as clients' records and details of each stylist's income and retail sales.

Storing stock

Make sure you know how and where to store materials, tools and equipment within your salon. Your responsibilities under the current COSHH Regulations are important when handling hair products and cleaning and disinfecting/sterilising chemicals. Some items of stock will need to be stored in a locked cabinet at ground level because of the chemicals they contain, including hydrogen peroxide, straightening products, bleaching, perming and neutralising products, and certain cleaning and disinfecting materials.

Consider your salon stock room and how the stock is stored. Ideally, nothing should be stored above head height, and all heavy items, such as large containers of shampoo and conditioner, should always be stored on the floor. Everything should be tidy and easy to find. Stock rotation should be practised so that older items are used before new ones.

Be knowledgeable about the stock your salon uses. Know what each product and item is for and how it should be used properly. Use personal protective equipment as appropriate when handling, storing or disposing of certain items.

Floors will need to be swept throughout the day

Cleaning work surfaces

Cleaning work surfaces effectively and leaving them ready for further treatments should include not just the parts of the salon used by clients, but the areas where you mix and prepare chemicals and make drinks. The floor, reception seating area, all working surfaces and mirrors must be kept hygienically clean. Any spillages on the floor must be cleared away immediately. Remember to wear personal protective equipment if necessary.

Floors will need to be swept throughout the day and mopped at the end of each day with a suitable disinfectant. Mirrors should be wiped with a suitable glass cleaner to avoid smearing and all working surfaces must be cleaned with a bactericide. To minimise cross-infection, it is essential to follow good housekeeping practices at all times.

Health and safety laws require salons to keep their refreshments area separate from areas where chemicals are mixed or disposed of. This is essential to good hygiene and a professional standard of working.

? Memory jogger

What types of item need to be stored in a locked cabinet?

Why is it important to regularly check stock levels?

Why should you not make a client's drink in the same area you use for mixing hair products?

UNIT GH1

Shampoo and condition hair

Image by TONI&GUY

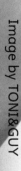

The word 'shampoo' is a Hindustani word meaning 'to press or rub'. Shampooing and conditioning hair is one of the most important treatments in hairdressing. It prepares the hair for any treatments or services and can be the start of a pleasurable hairdressing experience for the client – or a complete disaster if carried out incorrectly!

This unit is about the skill of shampooing and conditioning the hair and scalp. You will learn about different massage techniques and some of the products available for different hair types. This unit applies to both ladies' and gents' hairdressing salons.

In this unit you will learn how to:

- Maintain effective and safe methods of working when shampooing and conditioning hair
- Shampoo hair
- Apply and remove conditioners.

Here are some key words you will meet in this unit:

Minimise – reduce the effect of something

Friction – fast rubbing technique with a light plucking action

Products – shampoos, conditioners, styling sprays, creams and gels, etc.

Massage – manipulating the skin either manually or mechanically

Temperature – how hot or cold something is

Relevant person – assessor, stylist or line manager

Effleurage – slow, stroking, superficial movement, using the length of the hand

Rotary – penetrating, circular movement using the fingertips

Petrissage – slow, deep, penetrating circular movement using the fingertips

Surface – conditioner which lies on the outer layer of the hair shaft

Penetrating conditioner – conditioner which penetrates into the cortex layer of the hair shaft

Steamer – equipment providing moist heat, used during conditioning

Dermatitis – inflammation of the skin caused by an irritant

Maintain effective and safe methods of working when shampooing and conditioning hair (I)

Most people can shampoo their own hair at home and are likely to have done so many times. As a practising hairdresser, you will need to make sure your shampooing technique is of a high professional standard, and this will probably be a little different from how most people shampoo their own hair at home. The physical action of massaging a person's head can be invigorating, stimulating and relaxing. Be conscious of the person at your fingertips. Ask them how they like their hair and scalp to be shampooed.

Why shampoo hair?

We shampoo hair for three reasons.

- To remove excess natural oil, skin cells, dust and dirt.
- To remove the build-up of hair-care products.
- To prepare the hair for further treatments.

The success of the shampoo is important to the success of the following treatment, for example, the client's cut, perm or colour.

≫ Get up and go!

Look at the various shampoos and conditioners in your salon. Now complete the table below matching the products in your salon with the hair types. This information will be useful when offering clients professional advice about their hair and scalp condition.

Hair/scalp type	Shampoo	Conditioner
Coloured	Colour preserver	Colour preserver
Fine		
Permed		
Normal		
Dry/damaged		
Dandruff-affected		
Oily		

Preparation

Your salon's requirements for client preparation should include a thorough hair and scalp analysis by an experienced stylist who will confirm whether it is safe for you to carry out the treatment.

Protecting the client

The client's clothing must be protected at all times. Always use a clean gown and towel. If the client is not gowned properly, their clothing may get wet, or even damaged if they are having a chemical treatment.

Positioning the client and checking your posture

Position the client correctly at either the backwash or front-wash basin and check your client is comfortable. The client's position will affect how you stand at the basin and how tired you will feel at the end of the shampoo. Poor posture may have a long-term effect on your wellbeing, so make sure your position and posture during the shampoo minimises the risk of tiredness and injury to yourself.

>> **Get up and go!**

Practise preparing a colleague for a shampoo with a gown, towel and a waterproof cape. Consider how claustrophobic it may make you feel if everything is too tight. Remember to allow some room for your client to breathe – it can get warm under those protective layers. Always ask the client if they are comfortable.

Now find out how to prepare a client for the following services and practise on your colleague: perming; relaxing; colouring; cutting; setting.

? Memory jogger

Why do we shampoo hair?

What are the effects of having poor posture whilst shampooing your clients?

What products would you recommend for a client who has oily hair?

Why should you always gown a client correctly before carrying out any treatment?

What should be carried out before any hairdressing treatment begins?

What products would you recommend for a client with dry hair?

Position the client comfortably at a backwash basin

Maintain effective and safe methods of working when shampooing and conditioning hair (2)

Working methods

Using resources efficiently

Resources such as hairdressing products are expensive and it is important to use them cost effectively. Some shampoos have pump dispensers and these may help to reduce unnecessary waste by dispensing just the right amount of product. By minimising waste you save money, therefore making the salon a more profitable business.

Reducing the risk of cross-infection

Any tools or equipment that come into contact with clients' hair and skin must be completely clean. This will help to maintain a safe and hygienic working environment. As well as keeping the salon clean, you must always remember your personal cleanliness. Make sure your own standards of health and hygiene help to reduce the risk of cross-infection. For example, do not come into the salon if you have a cold or contagious disease, or an infestation such as head lice. Stay at home and minimise the risk of cross-infection; when the condition has cleared, it is then safe to return to work. By ensuring your personal standards of health and hygiene you minimise the risk of cross-infection, infestation and offence to your clients and colleagues.

Reducing the risk of injury

Your hands are essential to carrying out everyday tasks both in the workplace and at home. As your hands will often be in water, always dry them thoroughly and use a barrier cream and protective gloves. This will help to reduce the risk of contact dermatitis, a skin condition which often affects hairdressers. It is caused by constant contact with products, such as shampoos and chemicals. Should the condition worsen, you should seek medical advice.

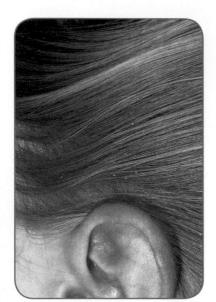

Head lice hatch from eggs called nits. They can be found on the hair shaft close to the scalp

>> Get up and go!

Next time you are in the salon, discreetly observe how many staff are wearing jewellery on their hands. It is best to leave your rings at home. This will make it easier for you to clean your hands properly and help prevent dermatitis. Ask your colleagues if they have ever suffered from dry, itchy hands or dermatitis.

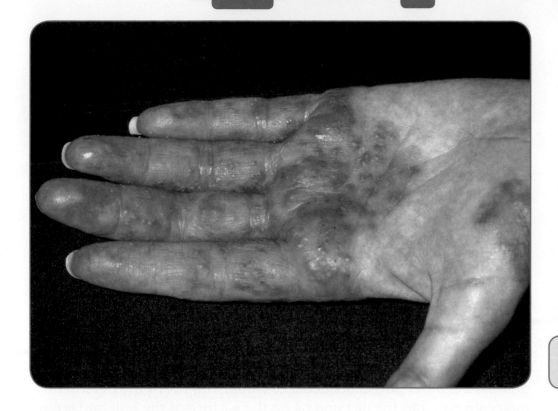

Protect your hands against dermatitis

It is essential to store, use, handle and dispose of products in accordance with manufacturers' instructions, salon policy and local bylaws. When dealing with resources in the salon, you will be expected to have a good working knowledge of the Control of Substances Hazardous to Health (COSHH) Regulations, therefore minimising the risk of harm or injury to yourself and others.

Re-filling and re-ordering products

Shampoos, conditioners and chemical products are in constant use in the salon.

Keep a look out for opportunities to replenish low levels of resources, when required, to minimise disruption to your own work and to clients. Should you notice that the stock level of any product is running low and needs re-ordering, report it to the relevant person.

? Memory jogger

What are the appropriate measures for disposing of chemicals in the salon?

Why should you re-fill products on a regular basis?

What does COSHH stand for?

Describe how dermatitis can be prevented.

How can you use resources cost-effectively?

» Get up and go!

With a colleague, think of reasons why shampoo and conditioner dispensers need to be regularly filled up and why stock levels of products need to be checked regularly. What might the effects be if the salon runs out of something? Who should stock shortages be reported to in your salon?

Shampooing hair (I)

How long should a shampooing and conditioning treatment take?

Depending on the length and thickness of the client's hair, a basic shampoo and surface condition should take 3–5 minutes. You might find it helpful to watch your colleagues and time them, making sure they make effective use of their working time. You must practise with:

- above shoulder-length hair
- below shoulder-length hair.

How shampoo works

Shampoo comes in many types, consistencies, colours and aromas. It mixes easily with water allowing grease, dirt and oil to be rinsed out of the hair. It works because it contains detergent molecules. Each detergent molecule consists of two parts – one part is attracted to dirt and oil, the other part is attracted to water. The tail of the detergent molecule digs into the dirt and oil on the surface of the hair and scalp. The head of the detergent molecule has a negative electric charge. As a result of massage movements, dirt and oil is repelled from the hair and rinsed away in the water.

How detergent molecules in shampoo cleanse the hair

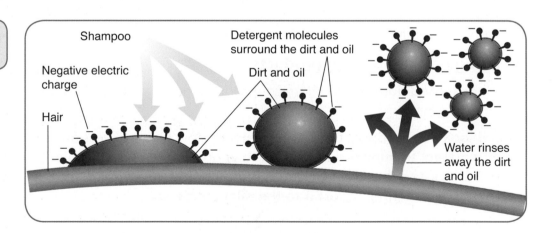

Shampoo flattens the surface tension of the water

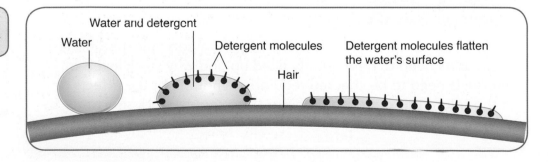

Water also has a high surface tension, which has the effect of producing a 'skin' on the surface of the water. Shampoos flatten the surface tension of water making it easier to shampoo the client's hair.

How conditioner works

Hair is made of a protein called keratin. The same protein is found in skin and nails.

Hair in poor condition may have been damaged by overuse of heated styling equipment, incorrect brushing or too many chemical treatments. Conditioners strengthen and moisturise the hair.

There are many types of conditioner. They include the following:

- Surface conditioner coats the hair shaft and smoothes down the cuticle scales leaving the hair tangle-free.

- Anti-oxidant conditioner prevents any further oxidation to the hair shaft after chemical treatments.

- Specialist treatment conditioners strengthen the hair shaft internally by filling the air spaces caused by damage with liquid protein. This gives the hair added elasticity, sheen and manageability.

- Almond or olive oils are used mainly for dry scalps.

A range of conditioning shampoos

? Memory jogger

How long should a shampoo and conditioning treatment take to complete?

Briefly explain how shampoo works.

What protein is hair made from?

What might cause hair to become damaged?

Why might you use an almond or olive oil to treat hair?

Shampooing hair (2)

Working with the stylist

There are many different levels of staff within a salon, including:

- staff who shampoo and carry out basic skills
- staff who practise technical skills like perming, relaxing, cutting and colouring
- senior staff who may manage the salon.

An experienced stylist instructs a junior member of staff

Part of your job role will involve learning to work with people and take instructions from senior colleagues. They may ask you to use a product in a particular way, or to change your massage movements to suit a different hair type and length. Following their advice and listening to the information they give will help you develop within your job role.

Using products and tools

Acid and alkali products

Acid and alkali products are regularly used in the salon. Acid products include perms, colours, shampoos, conditioners, bleach and peroxide. Acid-based conditioners are considered to be kinder to the hair because they close down the cuticle scales and return the pH of hair to pH 4.5–5.5. They also help maintain moisture within the hair shaft and give a smooth, shiny, tangle-free finish to the hair.

Alkali products include bleach, colours, perms, relaxers and some shampoos. These products lift the cuticle scales and give a roughened feel and appearance to the outer layer of the hair shaft. The pH of most hair when chemically treated is often more than pH 7, which is why the hair must be returned to its natural acid state of pH 4.5–5.5.

Steamers

A steamer produces a constant amount of steam contained within a hood. The hood is similar to that of a hood hairdryer. It works rather like a kettle. You will use a steamer to help:

- the penetration of conditioner
- replace lost moisture
- strengthen the internal and external layer of the hair shaft.

You should only use a steamer if you have been trained in how to do so and, as with all salon products, you should always follow the stylist's instructions in accordance with the manufacturer's instructions. The Electricity at Work Regulations cover the safe use of electrical equipment in the salon, including steamers (see Unit G20 for more information on these regulations).

First, fill the reservoir with distilled (not tap) water. This is to make sure no impurities coat the element and block the tiny water valves. With dry hands, plug in and switch on the steamer. While you massage the client's hair and scalp, the water will heat up and release steam into the hood. Place the client under the hood for 5–10 minutes. Remember to offer the client a drink or a magazine to read. When the time is up, take the client out from under the steamer. Switch off and unplug the steamer. Clean the steamer as soon as you have finished with it, leaving it ready for the next client.

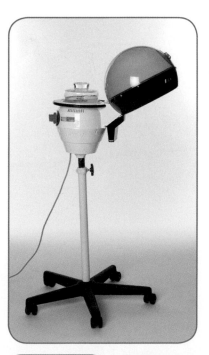

A steamer

Shampooing hair (3)

Water temperature and flow

The temperature of the water plays an important part in cleansing the hair and scalp. The flow of water is important too. Both the temperature and flow you use will depend on the amount of hair the client has and the sensitivity of their scalp. Very hot water will burn the client's scalp, but if the water is not hot enough, the hair will not be fully cleansed. There are times when you may need to use tepid (warm) water. For example, if the client's hair and scalp are oily, tepid water will help the sebaceous glands to produce less sebum (oil) when carrying out a light massage during the shampoo.

Test the temperature and flow of the water before you apply it to your client

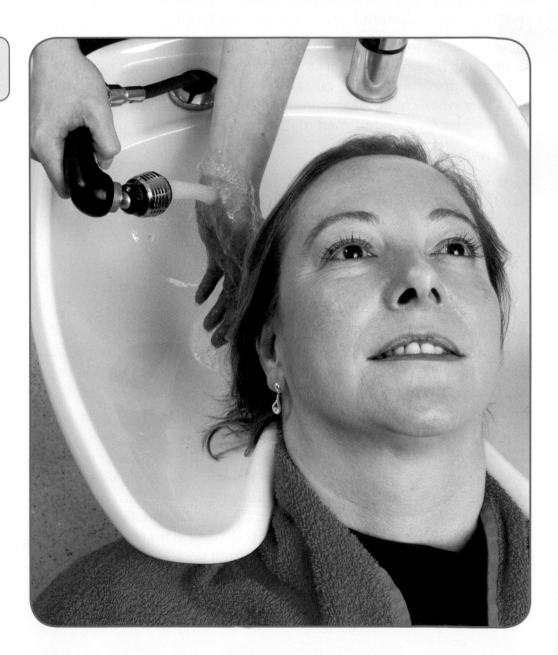

Before and during each shampoo, it is essential to test the temperature of the water, either on the back of your hand or on the inside of your wrist. Remember to check the temperature of the water is comfortable for your client regularly. Adapt the water temperature, flow and direction to suit the needs of your client's hair and the next part of the service. Always turn the tap off between shampoos. Hot water is too expensive to simply let run down the plughole!

Choosing shampoo

You will need to choose the most appropriate shampoo for the client's hair and scalp condition. Some treatments that follow a shampoo may not need a conditioner. For example, when perming a client's hair, conditioner will coat the cuticle and act as a barrier, giving an unsatisfactory result. Make sure you know which shampoo to use (go back to the table you completed on page 86 to remind yourself).

Be careful not to spill shampoo, but if you do, you will need to clear up any spillages straight away for the safety of your client, colleagues and yourself.

» Get up and go!

Take a look at the different hairstyles worn by colleagues at your salon. Some styles work better if the hair is not shampooed very often. Other styles need a regular shampoo. Create a simple list of hairstyles which require less frequent shampooing and hairstyles that require more frequent shampooing.

? Memory jogger

What is the natural pH of hair?

Why is a steamer used?

What type of water would you use in a steamer?

What massage movements are commonly used when conditioning?

Which massage movements are used mainly when shampooing?

When might you use tepid water to shampoo and condition a client's hair? Why?

Shampooing hair (4)

Massage techniques

During the shampoo and application of conditioner, you will need to use certain massage movements. The most popular movements used within the salon are:

- effleurage
- rotary
- petrissage.

The amount of shampoo you use for each client will be different depending on the length and thickness of their hair. A small amount of shampoo, no bigger than the size of a ten pence piece, is usually sufficient. Dispense the shampoo into the palm of your hand. Rub both palms together and then place the palms of your hands on the client's hair, smoothing the shampoo on to the scalp and down the hair length.

You can now use the massage movements. For a thorough shampoo and conditioning treatment, make sure your massage techniques achieve an even distribution of product over the hair and scalp. Take care not to pull your client's hair or scratch their scalp. This will cause irritation and discomfort to your client and may prevent the next part of the hair service from being carried out.

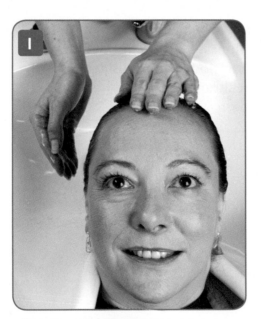

Effleurage movement

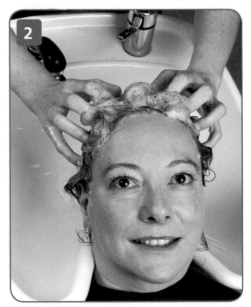

Rotary massage

Effleurage is used to spread the shampoo throughout the hair at the start of the shampoo and each time you repeat the application of shampoo. Effleurage is a light, slow and superficial movement used as a linking movement to rotary massage.

Rotary massage is used during the shampoo. It is much deeper and faster than effleurage. Your hands should be claw-like when positioned on the client's scalp and should move in small, fast, circular movements with a firm pressure.

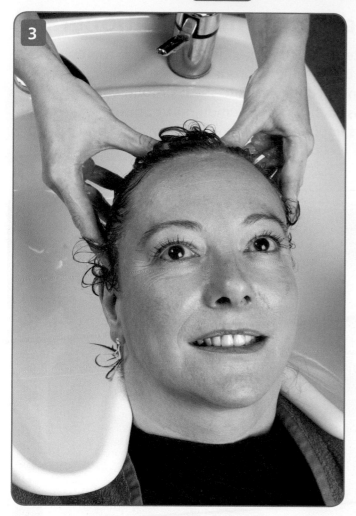

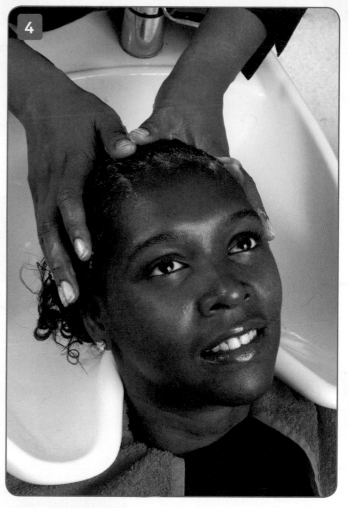

Petrissage movement

Petrissage is a slower version of the rotary movement and is used when carrying out a conditioning treatment. It should totally relax the client, assist penetration of the conditioner and promote blood circulation. Petrissage helps to make the hair smooth, shiny and manageable.

Friction massage

Friction is a massage movement that involves a fast rubbing technique and has a light, gentle plucking action. It is sometimes used when shampooing or when applying lotions such as astringents.

» Get up and go!

Find out from a colleague at your salon what an astringent is and what it is used for.

Applying and removing conditioners (I)

When you have completed the shampoo, you may have to apply conditioning products using the effleurage and petrissage massage movements. Always apply conditioners to the hair following the stylist's and manufacturer's instructions. A conditioning treatment will smooth down the cuticle scales, maintain moisture levels, protect and promote shine and improve the feel of the hair.

Surface conditioner is applied to protect and promote shine

When removing conditioning products it is important to:

- avoid disturbing the direction of the cuticle
- comb through your client's hair without causing damage to the hair and scalp
- leave your client's hair free of excess water and product.

Should any problems occur, speak promptly to the relevant person in your salon.

After you have finished shampooing and conditioning, rinse the hair thoroughly. This is important to the success of the following treatment. Stylists do not want to ask their client to return to the basin to have excess product removed from the hair. Towel-dry the hair and wrap it in a towel, using a turban style. If you have used a steamer, rinse the client's hair with cooler water than you shampooed with. This will help to smooth down the cuticle scales of the hair ready for styling.

Using effleurage massage when applying conditioner

Using petrissage massage when applying conditioner

Applying and removing conditioners (2)

Completing the shampooing and conditioning treatment

The stylist will need you to leave the client's hair free of excess moisture and tangle-free. You will need to comb through from the points to the roots of the hair, without causing any damage to the hair and scalp in preparation for the next treatment.

The client will welcome any advice or guidance you can offer about how to maintain their newly conditioned hair at home. Always be knowledgeable about the products your salon sells. Discuss with your client, at the consultation stage and at the basin, the suitability of professional shampoo and conditioning products. This will help maintain the moisture level of your client's hair and offer protection in between salon visits, particularly if they are having a chemical treatment such as a colour or a perm.

If a client tells you they are shortly going on a beach holiday, advise them to pack hair-care products such as sunscreen, leave-in conditioner and moisturising shampoo. In addition, they can help protect their hair by covering it with a sun hat and removing all traces of chlorine and sea water as soon as possible after swimming.

Make sure that you rinse the client's hair free of conditioner

Wrap the client's hair in a towel using a turban style

3

Comb through the client's hair, leaving it ready for the next service

Get ahead

Now you know how shampoos and conditioners can affect the hair, you might want to learn a little about how water affects hair. Did you know there are two different types of water: hard and soft? Each can affect hairdressing considerably. One can be more damaging than the other, particularly to the electrical equipment that steams or heats the water.

Find out which type of water area you work in and how this type of water can affect hairdressing. If you are in a hard water area, what measures can you take to prevent the build up of limescale? Write up your findings and present them to your colleagues. Can you make it into a mini-teaching session?

Step-by-step shampoo and conditioning

Gown up the client and analyse her hair and scalp before shampooing

Ensure the client is positioned comfortably before shampooing

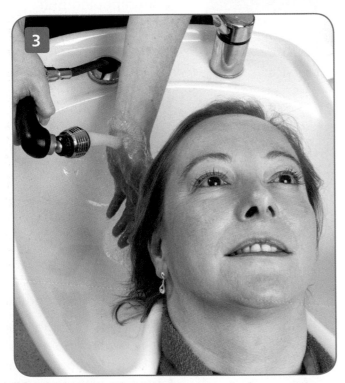

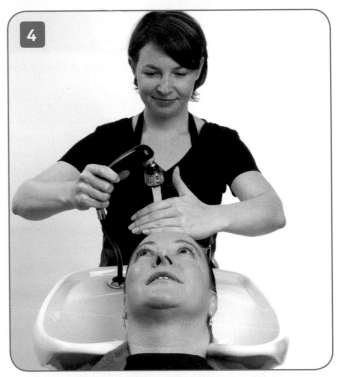

Test the temperature of the water before wetting the client's hair

Apply the water to the client's hair, taking care not to wet her face

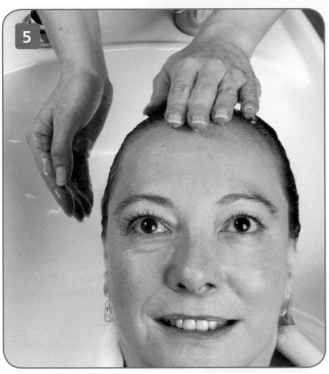

Using effleurage massage, apply the shampoo

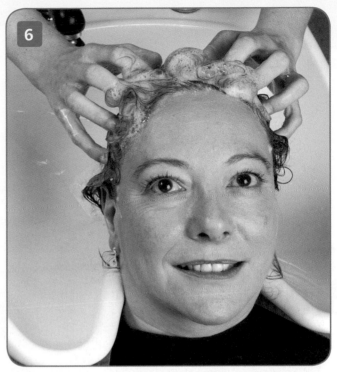

Use rotary massage over the whole head until the shampoo lathers and then rinse the hair free from shampoo

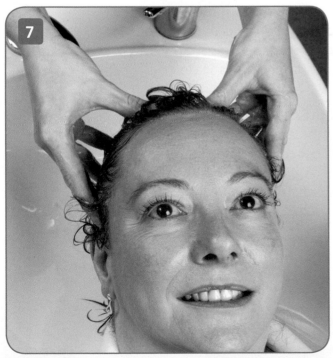

Apply the conditioner using both effleurage and petrissage movements. Rinse the conditioner from the hair and turn off the water. Wrap the client's hair in a towel

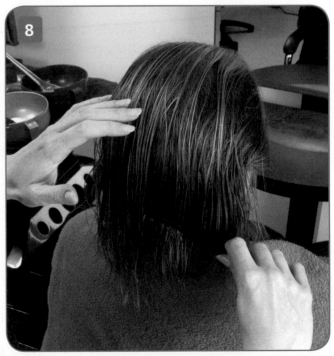

Squeeze the hair to remove excess water. Place a towel around the client's shoulders to prevent any drips and comb through the client's hair ready for further treatment

UNIT GH2

Blow-dry hair

Image by TONI&GUY

The cut and colour of a hairstyle are of course important, but blow-drying finishes the look. A hairstyle is an expression of a person and their personality – a statement of how they feel. Your client may wear their hair simply and understated at work during the day, but then require a sophisticated or fashionable look for the evening.

A hairstyle needs to complete the overall look the client is after and a professional blow-dry can help them achieve this. It is as important as wearing the right shoes to go with an outfit! Most clients will feel more confident after having a professional blow-dry as part of their treatment, and some will come to your salon for this service alone.

This unit is about carrying out basic blow-drying techniques following the instructions of your stylist, and applies to both hairdressing and barbering salons.

In this unit you will learn how to:

- Maintain effective and safe methods of working when drying hair
- Blow-dry hair.

Here are some key words you will meet in this unit:

Humidity – the amount of moisture in the atmosphere

Cross-infection – an infection that can be passed from one person to another

Infestation – a large number of parasites, e.g. an infestation of the hair and scalp with head lice

Commercially viable time – this basically means good value for money, i.e. hair cut = 30 mins

Disinfection – using chemicals and other methods to reduce the probability of infection

Texture – the way hair feels, determined by touch and helps you decide if hair is porous or non-porous

Cuticle – outside layer of the hair shaft

Cortex – where chemical changes take place in the hair shaft

Medulla – the part of the hair shaft that is full of air spaces and which plays no part when treating hair

Sterilisation – complete destruction of all living organisms

Autoclave – sterilisation system which works under pressure using water

Ultraviolet cabinet – sterilisation system that uses an ultraviolet light to kill bacteria

Maintain effective and safe methods of working when drying hair (I)

Protecting the client

As a first step when working in the salon, you must always protect your client and their clothing when preparing them for their service or treatment. The service could be a non-chemical treatment such as a blow-dry, set, hair cut or conditioning treatment, or perhaps a chemical treatment, such as a colour, bleach or perm. Make sure your client's clothing is effectively protected throughout the service and check with your stylist the most appropriate way to protect them. Many salons use the following items to protect clients:

- towels
- gowns
- waterproof capes.

Of course, all protective equipment should be clean. No one wants to smell the odour of the previous client or a previous treatment on the gown they are wearing. Clean resources also reduce the risk of cross-infection and infestation. Protective equipment should always be in plentiful supply and good condition.

» Get up and go!

Start to buy the *Hairdressers Journal* and use it to put together your own style book. You can then use your style book when you are consulting with clients about how they want their hair to be styled. Remember to consider the different types of clients who may visit your salon and include styles that will appeal to them. Remember to use gents' and children's hairstyles.

Look at your family's and friends' current styles – could you suggest something a little different to complement their features? Think about the practicalities of using your style book. It needs to be durable and waterproof and possibly sectioned into short, medium and long hairstyles.

Positioning your client

You will need to position your client in order to carry out the service, but you should do so without making them uncomfortable. You should also be aware of your own positioning and posture while you are working, ensuring you are minimising the risk of injury to yourself, and others. Having a good posture throughout the working day will help prevent you from feeling physically tired and, as a result, you should be able to work more efficiently.

For the blow-dry service, the client needs to be encouraged to sit square in the chair (not to one side) with their legs uncrossed. Sitting with crossed legs will lead to an unbalanced hairstyle. As the stylist, you need to stand with your feet hip-width apart and distribute your weight evenly over both legs (don't put all your weight onto one leg). Keep your head up and try to avoid stretching over the client or work area. Following these simple steps will minimise the risk of injury and fatigue.

Keeping a safe and clean work area

By keeping your work area clean and tidy throughout the service you will be able to make the best use of your time. If you regularly clear away used resources and things you no longer need, you will be able to access the things you do need easily and without delay. Making effective use of your time also means being organised and planning ahead so you're not constantly going back and forth across the salon to get equipment and products. Remember to prepare items like styling mousse, hairspray and a back mirror for finishing the service. Your client will be impressed at your professionalism and will be happy they are not kept waiting unnecessarily.

To ensure a safe working environment, all tools and equipment must be cleaned and sterilised in the correct way before being used. These measures will minimise the risk of cross-infection and infestation. Use appropriate cleaning materials to clean the areas you are working in and make sure you clean them regularly.

> **? Memory jogger**
>
> What items can be used to protect your clients?
>
> For what reasons should clean protective equipment be used for each new client?
>
> Why should a client be encouraged to sit with their legs uncrossed?
>
> How should you position yourself when working on a seated client?
>
> Why should all tools be cleaned and sterilised prior to each client?
>
> How can you make effective use of your time?

Maintain effective and safe methods of working when drying hair (2)

Sterilisation methods

Moist heat

Moist heat is used in an autoclave, which works rather like a pressure cooker. The distilled water inside the autoclave is heated to a temperature of approximately 125°C and must only be used for small pieces of equipment which have been cleaned using hot soapy water before being put into the autoclave. The autoclave will sterilise hard rubber, such as vulcanized rubber combs, and small metal pieces of equipment such as scissors. This method will make your tools sterile which means they are completely free from all bacteria.

Liquid chemicals (barbicide)

This can be an effective method of sterilising tools, provided the tools have been cleaned with warm soapy water first. The tools must then be immersed in the liquid and left for at least one hour.

Ultraviolet light

An ultraviolet (UV) cabinet uses UV light rays to kill bacteria. Again it is only effective when the tools are cleaned beforehand with warm soapy water. The UV light must reach all surfaces and this means you must turn your equipment in order to sterilise all sides.

Always remember to read and follow the manufacturers' instructions when using your salon's preferred method(s) of sterilisation.

Personal hygiene

As you are working in very close contact with clients and colleagues, you must make sure you smell clean and fresh every day. Personal clothing comes into contact with the skin and must be changed daily. You should also bathe or shower every day to remove body odour. Always use an effective deodorant on clean skin and practise good dental hygiene. Brush your teeth at least twice a day and consider using a mouth freshener such as a mouthwash. Regularly check your breath for stale smells of last night's dinner and perhaps cigarette smoke.

Your hands are in constant use and will carry bacteria from one place to another. Wash them regularly and keep your fingernails clean and free from sharp or broken edges. Cover any cuts in the skin on your hands with a suitable dressing. By having good personal standards of health and hygiene you will be minimising the risk of cross-infection, as well as giving a professional image and not offending your clients!

» Get up and go!

Take photographs in your salon or cut pictures from trade magazines of each of the following pieces of equipment: back mirror, combs, crimpers, flat brushes, handheld dryer, heated rollers, hood dryer, hot brushes, rollers, round brushes, section clips, straighteners, tongs.

Make a collage of the tools and equipment you are likely to work with every day. Perhaps you could involve a few colleagues and develop this as a small project.

? Memory jogger

Name three methods of sterilising tools and equipment in the salon.

What is the most effective method of sterilising small pieces of equipment in the salon?

Before using your chosen method of sterilisation, what must you do to your tools and equipment?

State the common name of one infestation you are most likely to find in a hairdressing salon.

How can you prevent body odour and bad breath?

Blow-dry hair (I)

In order to complete this unit successfully, you must carry out blow-dry services on two different hair lengths: above and below the shoulders, creating volume and movement. Pages 114–117 show step-by-step procedures for these.

Before you carry out a blow-dry service, you should always:

- work closely with the stylist and follow their instructions
- ask questions to check you understand
- be sure there is agreement between you, the stylist and the client regarding the desired style
- check what type of products you will be using, if required at all.

If you are unsure or do not understand, always double check with your stylist or a senior member of staff.

Observation

Watch your stylist as part of your professional development and take note of how they control their styling tools and equipment to minimise the risk of damaging the hair or causing the client discomfort. These skills must be practised many times before becoming perfect. The direction of airflow is important to achieving the desired look and avoiding damage to the hair cuticle.

Tools and products

The tools and products you use must be safe and fit for the purpose of hairdressing. The risk of damage to tools and equipment must be kept to an absolute minimum as they are expensive and may be made dangerous as a result. Always store your salon's equipment safely and in the correct place – this will give good value for money and ensure equipment remains in good working order.

- Make sure there are no kinks or knots in the cables of your dryer or other pieces of equipment.

- Never turn electrical equipment on or off with wet hands.

- When choosing brushes to blow-dry with, consider the texture, natural movement, density and length of the client's hair.

- Radial brushes create a soft rounded movement through the hair. The diameter of a radial brush will determine the size of the curl achieved on your client's hair.

- Using straighteners requires a steady hand and careful handling. Straighteners reach very high temperatures in a matter of seconds and you must know how to use them before attempting to use them on clients. They must always be used on dry hair and you should check the client's hair is in good enough condition to cope with the high temperature. For the time being, you may be able to use them on a client only under close supervision. For best results, take small sections, comb through and place the hair between the two plates. Gently close the plates and take the straighteners through the length of hair, allowing the section to drop. This will smooth the cuticle layer of the hair shaft and give a very professional finish to the style.

- Since working in a salon, you have probably noticed the tools of the trade are often personal to the stylist. Many stylists have favourite brushes, combs and scissors and are not always happy to share their equipment. Should you ever need to borrow a piece of equipment, be respectful by looking after it and returning it as soon as possible, clean and sterilised.

» Get up and go!

Draw up a list of the different styles which are achieved through blow-drying in your salon. Consider hair lengths and hair types.

Ask each stylist how long it would take to complete each blow-dry style, including any additional straightening or tonging. Compare these findings with what is considered to be an acceptable commercial timeframe.

Discuss your findings with each of the stylists. Remember, though: it is not a race, and sometimes hair density can play an important part in the length of time it takes to blow-dry a client's hair.

? Memory jogger

Explain why it is important to direct the airflow from a handheld dryer correctly.

What factors influence the choice of style you will create?

What should you think about when choosing a brush?

Why is it important to know how to use straighteners correctly?

List the tools you need to carry out a blow-dry.

Blow-dry hair (2)

The blow-dry service

Once your client's hair has been shampooed, the style discussed and chosen, and any application of products has been agreed by both your client and stylist, you can then start to blow-dry the client's hair.

The client

Your client must always be looked after throughout the service.

- Regularly check they are comfortable.
- Make sure there isn't any water or product running down the client's face.

Technique

- The blow-dry service must be completed within a commercially viable time and this is usually 30–45 minutes, depending on the length, type, density and texture of the client's hair. Make sure your client knows how long the service will take before you start.

- Work on towel-dried hair, not dripping wet hair.

- Don't drop wet hair onto dry hair as this will make the sections you have dried flop and lose shape.

- Wet hair is more delicate than dry. Any tugging may cause hairs to break, as well as causing your client discomfort and annoyance.

- In order to prevent burning your client's skin and hair, causing hair damage or discolouring the hair, keep your dryer moving and always follow the direction of the hair shaft. This will smooth the cuticle layer, giving a sleek, shiny finish.

- When your client's hair is delicate, keep the dryer on a cool setting and at least 1.25 centimetres away from the hair and scalp.

- Show the client the style as you build, develop and work towards the finished look. Use the back mirror and double-check the style is going according to your client's wishes.

- Allow the hair to cool after blow-drying. Doing this fixes the style in place and prolongs the length of time the style will keep its shape. Separate the hair using your fingers or use a tail comb if needed.

- Once you have completed the blow-dry, check with your client and stylist that the style meets both their requirements.

- Apply finishing products such as serum or hairspray if required.

Get up and go!

A good hairdresser will always advise their client on ways of maintaining their hairstyle at home. What aftercare advice can you give to your clients? Think about making an 'aftercare card', perhaps the size of a credit card, which you can give to clients after a blow-dry. Make sure the tips are easy to read and keep the information brief. You could include something like:

- Towel dry hair before blow-drying.
- Comb hair from the ends.
- Keep the hairdryer moving all the time.
- Avoid excessive heat.
- Minimise the use of straighteners.
- Remember to protect your hair from the sun.
- Avoid using rubber bands to hold your hair up.
- Use serum on dry hair to protect it.

Get ahead

Look back at the different face shapes on page 4. What styles would you suggest for each?

? Memory jogger

Why should you always advise the client how long a blow-dry will take?

Why should you take care to keep wet hair away from pre-dried hair?

Why should sections of hair be kept damp before blow-drying?

When giving a blow-drying service, when should you show the client their hair in the back mirror?

What are the benefits of allowing hair to cool before dressing out?

Why is it important to give your client aftercare advice?

Blow-dry hair (3)

Blow-drying using a radial brush

1

Correctly gown the client and, after your consultation, take them to the basin for shampooing and conditioning

2

After rinsing, towel dry the client's hair and comb through before you begin to section

3

Place the brush horizontally into the section of hair and take through to the ends, wrapping the ends around the brush. Follow through with the dryer and dry from the roots to points

4

To encourage root lift, lift sections straight up from the crown. Check with your client if the style is developing as required

Position yourself parallel to the section you are working on and complete the front section

Apply products such as spray or serum to complete the look as required

Blow-dry hair (4)

Blow-drying using a flat-backed brush

1

Correctly gown the client and, after your consultation, take them to the basin for shampooing and conditioning

2

After rinsing, towel dry the client's hair and comb through before you begin to section

3

Place the flat brush under the roots of the hair and blow dry, encouraging root lift and volume. Keep the dry hair from falling onto wet hair

4

Continue to move through the blow dry from the nape to the occipital bone, remembering to incorporate the sides of the client's head

To encourage a smooth and shiny look, direct the dryer down the hairshaft

You should stand parallel to the section you are blow drying when incorporating the sides. Check with the client if they are happy with the style as it develops

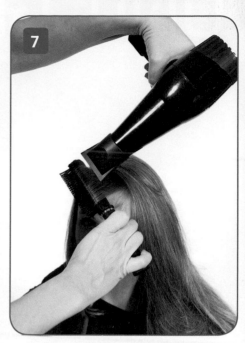

Angle the dryer and brush to finish the fringe area

Use straighteners and a comb for a polished finish

The finished look – apply products such as spray or serum to complete the look as required

UNIT GH4

Assist with hair colouring services

Anne Veck, photographer: Julian Knight

Not everyone is happy with their natural hair colour. Some of your clients may feel that their natural colour doesn't suit them, they have too much grey or that their style may look more up to date with a colour change. With the help of their salon, it is now possible for clients to achieve a natural looking hair colour change – or not so natural, if they want an unusual colour! Colouring hair can also add depth and shine, as well as lift the natural hair colour and leave it in better condition than before. Your clients do not even have to commit to a permanent colour, so can change their mind later and try something completely different.

This unit is about the basic skills of removing colouring and lightening products. The work involved will be carried out under the direction of the relevant person such as the stylist or assessor. This unit will apply for hairdressing students working in hairdressing and barbering salons.

In this unit you will learn about:

- Hair colour
- Maintaining effective and safe methods of working when assisting with colouring services
- Removing colouring and lightening products.

Here are some key words you will meet in this unit:

Dermis – the inner layer of the skin

Pigment – a substance that colours something

Emulsify – using the colouring product to help remove itself by moving the finger pads around the client's hairline

Eumelanin – brown/black pigment in the hair

Pheomelanin – red/yellow pigment in the hair

Cortex – layer of the hair where chemical changes take place

Cuticle – outer layer of the hair shaft

Surface conditioner – conditioner which coats the outer layer of the hair shaft

Antioxidant conditioner – conditioner which penetrates into the cortex layer of the hair shaft

Tangle-free – hair which has been combed smooth and is free from knots or tugs

Minimise – reduce the effect of something

Fatigued – weary; exhausted from over work or adopting a poor posture

Hair colour

What gives hair its natural colour?

Hair colour is genetic, which means the natural colour of your hair is a result of the mixture of both your mum's and your dad's genes. You do, however, usually receive a predominant gene for hair colour from either your mum or your dad, e.g. your mum/dad might have a strong red pigment as their natural colour. This colour may then dominate your natural colouring.

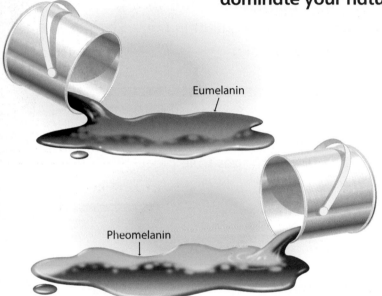

Eumelanin

Pheomelanin

When we look more closely at the process of how hair develops beneath the skin, we can see how hair colour cells produce colour. Cells called melanocytes in the cortex of the hair shaft produce two colour pigments called:

- eumelanin
- pheomelanin.

Everyone has varying proportions of eumelanin and pheomelanin. People who have naturally brown or black hair will have lots of the pigment eumelanin. People who have red or blonde hair will have more of the pigment pheomelanin.

> Which pigment have you got more of: eumelanin or pheomelanin?

» Get up and go!

Gather together some paints in primary colours (red, yellow and blue). Mix together in equal quantities:

- red and blue
- red and yellow
- yellow and blue.

What new colours did you create? You should have created purple, orange and green. These are secondary colours. By changing the amounts of each primary colour you mix together, you can create your very own colour. Which colours complement each other and go together well? Which ones don't go so well together? Be creative and make decisions about the colours you are making and mixing. Colouring hair can be creative and fun, and you can apply some of the skills you have just learned when in the salon.

Shades of hair colour

Colours come in different shades, which is how light or dark they are. When you look at a hair shade chart you will notice there is a numbering system. Hair shades are numbered between one and ten, with ten being the lightest (blonde) and one being the darkest (black).

Black, brown, red or blonde?

As we have already learned, hair colour comes from the pigments produced in the hair shaft. Different combinations of these pigments produce the many different natural colours and shades of hair. If a person has no pigments in the hair shaft, he or she will have white hair – this is due to the melanocytes no longer producing colour pigment. Reasons for white hair include ageing, heredity, trauma, shock, stress or childbirth. Interestingly, redheads have more hair than brunettes, and brunettes have more hair than blondes.

A range of colouring products

Colouring hair in the salon

Chemical treatments such as hair colouring and lightening may be offered in your salon. A new hair colour can completely change a client's look. Some of your clients may have experimented with colouring at home, which can be fun and done in no time at all. However, a professional colouring service carried out at a salon can give a much better result, with the added benefit of an expert opinion on what colour to go for.

Your salon may stock the following colouring products:

- temporary colours
- semi-permanent colours
- quasi-colours
- permanent colours
- lightening products
- vegetable colours.

The rest of this unit will deal with working effectively and safely when assisting with colouring services. You will also learn about removing colouring and lightening products from the hair, and materials such as foils, Easi Meche and the highlighting cap.

> ### ? Memory jogger
>
> Name the two pigments found in hair colour. Which gives black/brown hair? Which gives blonde/red hair?
>
> What happens if a hair contains no pigment?
>
> How do hair shade charts work?

> ### >> Get up and go!
>
> Test some hair samples with different types of colour. Note down the differences in hair condition and the colour result achieved. Perhaps you can make up your own shade chart.

Maintain effective and safe methods of working when assisting with colouring services (I)

Protecting the client

When preparing a client for a colouring service, or any other service, you must make sure they are properly protected. Use clean towels, gowns and waterproof capes. Follow the instructions of the stylist; they will tell you how best to protect the client, and may ask you to use specific towels for chemical treatments such as colouring.

Don't forget to take care of the client by offering them a drink and a magazine. The best time to do this is probably when the chemical treatment is processing.

Preparing the client for shampooing

Before shampooing, you will need to comb through the client's hair. Remove tangles carefully to avoid causing the client any discomfort. Check the client's scalp with the stylist, looking for any cuts or areas of irritation that may need special attention. You will also need to discuss with the stylist the correct shampoo to use.

>> **Get up and go!**

Does your salon have a towel system? Find out if they do and, if so, what colour towels are used for different treatments. For example, what towel would you use for a permanent colour? What colour towel you would use for a bleach treatment?

Salons use a lot of towels each day. Encourage your salon to go green, if it isn't already. This means washing towels on a cool or warm water programme. The electricity bill will be lower and the salon's energy usage will be more efficient, which is better for the environment.

Personal protective equipment (PPE)

You must always remember to wear personal protective equipment (PPE) when working with clients who are receiving a chemical treatment. Your hands and clothing must be protected at all times. Dermatitis is caused by an irritant coming into contact with the skin and can make skin dry, itchy and sore. Use barrier cream or a good quality hand cream when working in the salon to help prevent your skin from drying out. Protect your skin completely by wearing gloves when applying colouring products, rinsing colours and using hydrogen peroxide or bleaching products.

Positioning the client and checking your own posture

As you are preparing the client for shampooing, ask whether they would prefer a front-wash or backwash basin if a choice is available. Position the client at the basin and make sure they are comfortable. Make sure the client's neck is positioned correctly in the curve of the basin, otherwise the nape area may not be shampooed properly. By thinking about your own posture and standing correctly while shampooing you can reduce the risk of injury and fatigue. It is also a good idea to offer the client a towel to safeguard against unavoidable splashes.

Always wear personal protective equipment when carrying out a chemical treatment

Keeping your work area clean and tidy

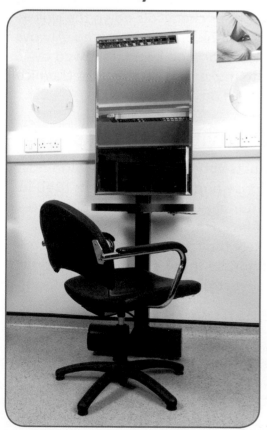

It is essential to keep your work area clean and tidy during chemical treatments. Think about the tools, equipment and products you are going to need and make sure you have them to hand. Clear away anything that has been used and won't be needed again. This will ensure you don't waste time or keep your client waiting while you go back and forth getting things, or look for the things you need in a messy work area. Keeping your work area clean and tidy will enable you to work more effectively and it also helps keep your workplace safe.

The work area should be kept clean and tidy

? Memory jogger

What should always be done before shampooing the client?

What does PPE stand for? Give some examples of PPE, along with when and why they should be used.

What is dermatitis and what causes it? How can you prevent it?

Why might you use a front-wash basin?

How would a dirty and untidy work area affect your work?

Maintain effective and safe methods of working when assisting with colouring services (2)

Reducing product wastage

Before using chemicals, always read the manufacturer's instructions and discuss them with the stylist. If you are asked to mix a chemical product, remember to mix only the amount you need just before it is to be used. Some manufacturers advise using scales to weigh the product, or you may use a measuring beaker instead in order to achieve an accurate mixture. Taking these steps will help to reduce product wastage. If extra product is required, it is more cost-effective to make it freshly as it is needed.

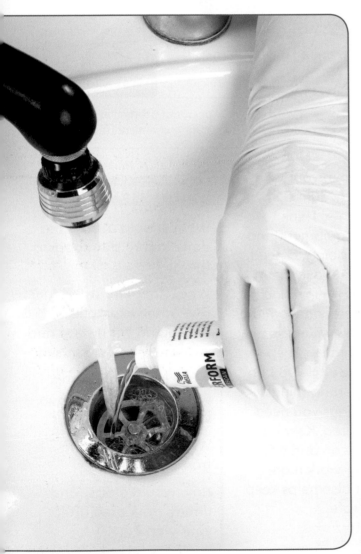

Disposal of chemicals

It is very important that you dispose of chemicals in the proper manner. Your salon must follow the Control of Substances Hazardous to Health (COSHH) Regulations (see page 26) and ensure products are disposed of in a safe and environmentally friendly way. Some salons have a specific basin for disposing of chemicals. Never pour chemicals down the sink in the salon's food and drink preparation area. Always flush them down the shampoo basin, followed by lots of cool water to make sure no smells or chemical waste linger round the basin.

Working safely with chemicals

Some of the products you will use in the salon have the potential to cause harm. The chemicals used in colouring and lightening treatments can damage clothing, skin and hair. However, if they are used correctly it is unlikely that anything will go wrong. You must always handle these chemicals with great care and follow all instructions given to you about their use.

Chemical waste should be flushed down the shampoo basin

You can reduce the amount of contact a chemical has with the client's skin by using barrier cream around the hairline. You should also always check you are using the right type of heat with each product or you could cause the client to suffer from chemical burns. If you ever have any concerns or problems, it is best to check with the stylist or assessor promptly and find out the correct course of action to take.

Re-ordering products

If the stock levels of a product are running low, remember to follow your salon's policy for re-ordering, which will probably involve telling the appropriate member of staff or writing it down. This will ensure you have sufficient products available, and also avoid having too much stock.

> **» Get up and go!**
>
> With a colleague, find out:
>
> - the different types of colouring and lightening products available in your salon
> - how they are applied
> - how long they last on the hair.

Reducing the risk of harm or injury to yourself, your colleagues and clients

Always keep a look out for hazards or risks which may arise during the course of the day. Clear away used product bottles and used materials such as bowls and cotton wool. Keep the floor clear from trailing cables, towels, gowns and cut hair, as well as items belonging to clients such as handbags, shopping bags, walking sticks and pushchairs. This will help to minimise the risk of any accidents occurring.

> **? Memory jogger**
>
> Why wouldn't you mix up all the chemicals you need for the day's appointments at the start of the day?
>
> What might happen as a result of pouring chemicals down the basin used for washing up and preparing drinks?
>
> How would you use barrier cream to protect your client?
>
> How can you reduce the risks of accidents in your salon?

Maintain effective and safe methods of working when assisting with colouring services (3)

Reducing the risk of cross-infection

Cross-infection is when an infection is passed from one person to another. You can take some very simple steps as you work to reduce the risk of this happening. Remember to always practise good personal hygiene and wear clean, well-pressed clothes. If you or any of your clients are showing signs of infection or infestation, you must report it straight away to a senior member of staff. They can then advise you what to do. You should also make sure you know how to use your salon's methods of sterilisation properly and ensure you always use clean tools and equipment on each new client.

It is not just for reasons of hygiene that tools and equipment should be properly cleaned. Cleanliness can also make the difference between achieving a professional result and a poor result from colouring and lightening. Make sure brushes and mixing bowls are always washed free of product so as not to contaminate the next product they will be used with. You should also have a different brush for each product you are applying. For example, do not mix bleach with a tint brush that has been used for applying a raspberry grape tint!

 Sharpen up!

In error, you use a tint brush for bleaching which was used previously to apply a rich red colour, but had not been washed out properly. What would happen to the client's hair colour?

Skin tests

Client preparation for colouring and lightening treatments varies from salon to salon, but it is very likely a skin test will need to be carried out 24–48 hours before the service can take place. This will ensure it is safe for the treatment to go ahead and the client won't suffer from any reaction to the product when it is applied. Skin tests will almost certainly be required for most semi-permanent colours, quasi-colours and permanent colours, but may also be needed for vegetable colours too. You must follow the instructions you are given for skin tests very carefully or the consequences could be serious. The results must be recorded on the client's record card.

If your client has sensitive skin or has reacted to other products, natural products such as vegetable colours can sometimes be safer alternatives. They are unlikely to cause dermatitis and do not usually require a skin test. Remember, though, not all clients can use natural products on their skin, so it is still worth checking the suitability first. The processing of vegetable colours may require exposure to oxygen in the atmosphere, which means the final colour result will not be achieved until the day after the treatment.

Incompatibility tests

Another type of test that may be carried out is an incompatibility test. This is where the stylist makes sure the client's hair is able to be coloured or lightened. Previous treatments or hair in poor condition can cause undesirable results. For example, metallic salts which are found in hair colour restorers and compound henna may cause the hair to boil, bubble and break during lightening treatments. If metallic salts are suspected, the stylist will not proceed. As with skin tests, the results should always be noted on the client's record card.

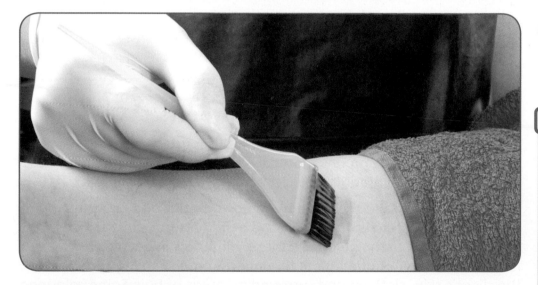

Carrying out a skin test

? Memory jogger

What can you do to reduce the risk of cross-infection?

How soon before a colouring or lightening treatment should a skin test be carried out?

Are vegetable colours always safe to use on everyone?

Why is an incompatibility test carried out?

Where should the results of any test be recorded?

» Get up and go!

With the help of a stylist, carry out an incompatibility test. You will need:

- a sample of hair
- a non-metallic bowl
- hydrogen peroxide
- perm lotion.

Ask your stylist about other types of hair and scalp tests, such as porosity tests and elasticity tests.

Removing colouring and lightening products (I)

Resources for colouring and lightening

You will need to prepare a trolley for the stylist with the following items:

- client record card
- clean towels (of the appropriate colours)
- barrier cream
- cotton wool
- shade chart
- foils or Easi Meche
- highlighting cap and hook
- tinting bowl and brush
- hydrogen peroxide (sometimes).

> **» Get up and go!**
>
> With a colleague, practise setting up a trolley for a colour or lightening treatment. Check each other's trolleys for any missing items. Now set up a trolley for each other, but deliberately forget one item. See if you can spot what is missing.

Assisting with the colouring process

Your role in the colouring process includes preparing the client for the treatment and removing any materials (such as foils, a highlighting cap or Easi Meche) and products from the hair after the treatment.

Always check with the stylist before removing colouring or lightening products and materials and follow the manufacturer's instructions. You must learn to remove products and materials in a way which minimises the risk of damage to the hair and colour being spread to the client's skin, clothing and surrounding areas of hair. Some colouring and lightening products require you to emulsify them before water is applied to the hair and scalp. This is important as the colour will not come off the skin if you miss this simple step.

Should there be any problems, refer them to the relevant person, usually the stylist, who will advise you what to do. The types of problems you may come across include the following.

- Colour bleeding onto an area of hair that has not been coloured.
- Bleach splashing into a client's eyes.
- Ripped hair, caused by the highlighting cap being removed roughly.
- An unsatisfactory result, which can be caused by Easi Meche or foils being removed before the end of the processing time.

The table below shows some common colouring problems and how to deal with them.

Fault	By whom	Correction	How to avoid
Colour seepage	Stylist	Recolour areas as necessary	Apply barrier cream to the areas not being coloured
Bleach in client's eyes	Stylist	Rinse with cool water immediately	Careful removal of colouring materials and products
Vigorous removal of the highlighting cap	Junior	Condition hair and massage scalp	Apply conditioner to the top of the cap before removing
Hair colour too warm	Stylist	Apply toner	Check base shade and use correct strength of products

Protect the client with a towel, gown and waterproof cape

Prepare the client for colouring with the stylist. This involves hair and scalp analysis, and combing and sectioning dry hair

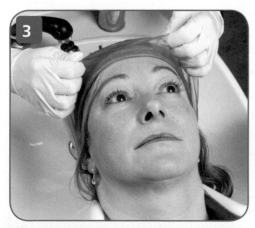

After the stylist has applied the colour and it has been allowed to process, remove the colouring products

Rinse the hair

Removing colouring and lightening products (2)

Applying conditioner

Once you have removed all of the colouring or lightening product, you may have to use a colour removal shampoo. Following this, squeeze out excess moisture from the hair then apply a suitable antioxidant conditioner or surface conditioner. Antioxidant conditioners will need to be left on the hair for at least three minutes. Antioxidant conditioners will:

- replace lost moisture
- help prevent further oxidation of the hair
- return the pH of the hair to its normal acid value.

Ask your stylist which conditioner to use.

Preparing the client for the next treatment

After rinsing the conditioner from the client's hair, towel-dry the hair and scalp and make sure they are free from excess products and moisture. Help the client to the styling area and comb the hair through, leaving it tangle-free without damaging the hair or scalp. Both the stylist and client need to be satisfied that you have removed all traces of product from the client's hair. Should you have any concerns about the products or how to use them, promptly refer any problems to your stylist or assessor for the appropriate course of action.

Remember to clean and tidy the basin area after you have prepared the client for the next treatment. Make sure all used products are disposed of correctly and leave the area free from risks of hazard, cross-infection or infestation, ready to be used by the next client.

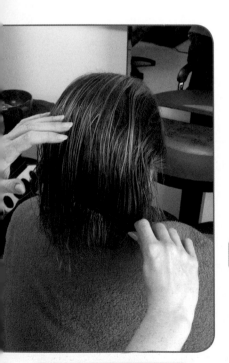

Comb through the client's hair leaving it ready for further treatment

✂ Sharpen up!

You could try to interest clients in temporary colours by wearing a suitable colour in your own hair at the salon. Try different coloured hair mascaras, sprays, mousses, setting lotions, glitters and gels. This will allow clients to see how they look and you can then talk about how you applied them and how you shampoo them out. Talk about the advantages and disadvantages of doing this with a senior stylist or your manager before you go ahead. If you can do this, remember not everyone will want pink highlights!

After-colour care

It is important to explain to clients how they should look after their hair at home. After-colour care involves helping the client to maintain the colour of his or her hair at home using the most appropriate shampoo and conditioner for colour-treated hair. This is part of professional client care, and by selling the client the correct products, you will be giving him or her expert advice and guidance which completes the colouring treatment.

Get up and go!

Find out how to prepare a bleaching product your salon uses by reading the manufacturer's instructions. Discuss the result, and how you found following the instructions, with a senior colleague.

Get ahead

This book contains a number of step by steps, which show how some practical hairdressing tasks are carried out (see page 129 for an example). Have a go at creating your own step by step showing how to apply semi-permanent colour. Take photographs in your salon and then arrange the photos in order so someone could follow the process. You might want to use the following steps as a guide to taking your photos.

- Step 1: The equipment you will need.
- Step 2: Shampooing the client.
- Step 3: Sectioning the hair into four.
- Step 4: Applying the product to the back of the head using either a tint brush and bowl or applicator bottle.
- Step 5: Applying the product to the side of the head.
- Step 6: Applying the product to the top of the head.
- Step 7: Working the product into the hair shaft.
- Step 8: Leaving the colour to process as per the manufacturer's instructions.
- Step 9: Shampooing and rinsing the product off.
- Step 10: The finished dried and styled result.

Perhaps you could display your step by step photos in your salon to help your junior colleagues. You could even create step by steps for other treatments.

Memory jogger

Colour has run into your client's eyes. What course of action would you take?

Name three things antioxidant conditioner does.

What are the benefits of offering clients aftercare?

UNIT GH5

Assist with perming hair services

Anne Veck photographer: Julian Knight

The reason some people have straight hair and others have curly hair is down to the shape of the hair shaft. A naturally straight hair has a circular cross-section, whilst a naturally curly hair has an oval cross-section. It is now understood that the hair follicle also has a big part to play in determining the curliness of hair as it affects the shape of the hair shaft, as well as the angle it grows at. In order to make straight hair curly, as happens during a perm, hairdressers have to change the structure of the hair using chemicals. This is now a safe process and can achieve incredible results.

The work involved in this unit should be carried out under the direction of the relevant person, such as the stylist or assessor. This unit will apply to hairdressing students working in both hairdressing and barbering salons, and is suitable for those working with Caucasian and Asian hair types.

In this unit you will learn about:

- What perming is
- Maintaining effective and safe methods of working when assisting with perming services
- Neutralising hair as part of the perming process.

Here are some key words you will meet in this unit:

Cortex – layer of the hair where chemical changes take place

Cuticle – outer layer of the hair shaft

Disulphide bonds – keratin bonds which are linked together in the cortex

Surface conditioner – conditioner which coats the outer layer of the hair shaft

Anit-Oxy conditioner – conditioner which penetrates into the cortex layer of the hair shaft

Tangle-free – hair which has been combed smooth and is free from knots or tugs

Texture – the way hair feels, determined by touch during the consultation

Fatigue – weary; exhausted from over work or adopting a poor posture

Perming – curling hair by using a chemical product

Neutralising – the process that fixes hair into its new shape

Asian hair – the hair shaft is round in shape, straight and/or coarse

Caucasian hair – the hair shaft is oval in shape and can be straight, wavy or curly

What is perming?

The desire to have curly hair is an old one and throughout history women, in particular, have tried various methods to transform their limp, straight hair into a bouncing head of curls. Hair can be made curly by simply wetting it and winding it, as well as through the use of heated styling equipment. These results are only temporary though and often don't achieve the desired look. With a permanent wave (or perm) curls can be chemically added to straight hair, although straight hair will grow back from the roots.

> **» Get up and go!**
>
> List the different ways in which curls or waves can be added to hair without the use of a perm. Discuss these with your stylist, considering the pros and cons of each.

Perms work by using chemicals to cause a permanent change in the structure of keratin, the protein found in hair. There are two main stages to perming hair.

- Stage I: A chemical is added to the hair that breaks open the disulphide bonds, which give hair its elasticity, in the cortex layer of the hair. This stage must be carefully timed to ensure the correct amount of bonds are broken.

The two stages of perming

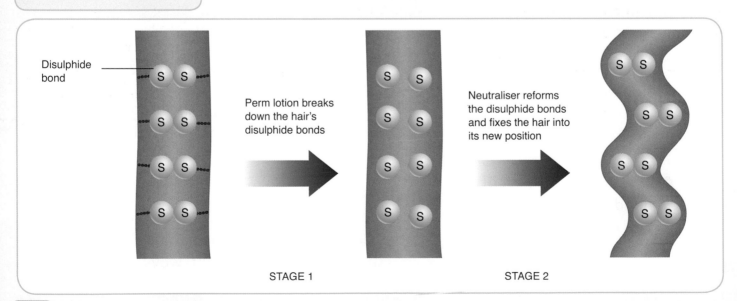

Disulphide bond

Perm lotion breaks down the hair's disulphide bonds

Neutraliser reforms the disulphide bonds and fixes the hair into its new position

STAGE 1   STAGE 2

- Stage 2: A second chemical containing hydrogen peroxide or sodium bromate is used to close the bonds, which causes the hair to take on the shape of the rods. This is called neutralising. Again, timing is essential when completing this stage in order to achieve the desired result and not damage the hair.

Because the change caused by perming is permanent, it can only be removed by cutting or growing the hair out, or reversing the treatment chemically.

Acid and alkaline perms

Perms can be of the acid or alkaline variety. Alkaline perms contain ammonia and have a pH of between 8.2 and 9.6. Acid perms have a pH of between 4.5 and 6.5 (remember, hair is acidic with a pH of between 4.5 and 5.5). Alkaline perms work more quickly than acid perms and usually hold their shape for longer. Acid perms act more slowly and are gentler on the hair. A stylist will choose either an acid or alkaline perm depending on the result required and the client's hair type and condition. Hair which is dry, damaged or porous will be better suited to an acid perm, which is less likely to cause damage.

Considering hair types when perming

Chemical treatments for Caucasian and Asian hair types are slightly different and you will need to be able to work with both. The differences between Caucasian/European and Asian/Oriental hair are important when choosing the most appropriate product. The Caucasian/European hair shaft can be straight, wavy or curly and has an oval cross-section. The Asian hair shaft can be straight and/or coarse and is round in shape.

The texture of hair will vary from client to client and may also vary within the same head of hair. Texture can be fine, medium or coarse, with fine hair having a small circumference and coarse hair a large circumference. To determine the texture, run your fingers along the length of a single hair. This information will be useful when you are choosing products.

» Get up and go!

What types of perm lotion are used in your salon for different hair types and conditions? Discuss them with your senior stylist.

? Memory jogger

Describe the two stages in perming hair.

Why might an acid perm be more suitable for some clients' hair?

Explain the difference between Caucasian/ European hair and Asian/ Oriental hair.

How can you determine the texture of hair?

Maintain effective and safe methods of working when assisting with perming services (I)

Protecting the client

Make sure your client is suitably protected for the perming service. Use clean gowns, towels and waterproof capes. Your salon may use specific towels for chemical treatments and different ones for non-chemical treatments.

Personal protective equipment (PPE)

Remember to wear personal protective equipment (PPE) when working with clients who are receiving a chemical treatment. Your hands and clothing must be protected at all times. Wear gloves when rinsing perm lotion and neutralising products from the hair. This is to protect yourself from the damage that perming chemicals can potentially cause.

Preparing the client for shampooing

Before shampooing, you will need to comb through the client's hair. Remove tangles carefully to avoid causing the client any discomfort and check the client's scalp with the stylist for any cuts or irritated areas. You will also need to discuss with the stylist the correct shampoo to use.

The pre-perm shampoo

The pre-perm shampoo will remove any build-up of hair-care products, open the cuticles and leave the hair at a neutral pH of 7 ready for either an acid or alkaline perm lotion.

Positioning the client and checking your own posture

Ask the client if they would prefer a backwash or a front-wash basin if available and position them carefully, checking they are comfortable. Remember to think about your own posture during the shampoo so as to reduce the risk of injury or fatigue.

Preparing the resources for perming

You will need to prepare a trolley for the stylist with the following items:

- client record card
- clean towels (of the appropriate colours)
- barrier cream
- cotton wool
- gloves
- apron
- a selection of combs
- a plastic bowl
- plastic cap*
- rods

Sharpen up!

Why might a salon use different coloured towels for perming and neutralising?

- end papers
- section clips
- tension strips
- Climazone or other heat source*

- gown
- waterproof cape.

* These items may be needed

All resources must be cleaned or sterilised after every use. This will help to minimise the risk of cross-infection.

Familiarising yourself with manufacturers' instructions

Here is a typical list of manufacturer's perming instructions.

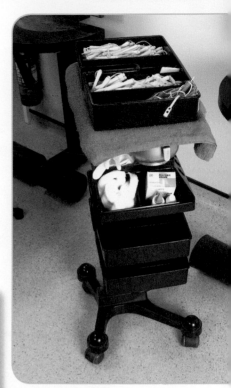

A trolley prepared for perming

Vitality
Vita Perm
Permanent wave
Instructions for use (read thoroughly).

1 Preparation:
- Check the condition and porosity of the hair then select the correct lotion.
- Shampoo the hair using a mild shampoo. Rinse thoroughly and towel-dry.
- To equalise hair porosity for an even curl result, a pre-perm treatment is recommended.
- Section the hair and select appropriate curler size for the chosen technique, then wind without lotion. Vitality End Papers make winding easier.

2 Application:
- Wear protective gloves.
- Carefully apply the perm lotion onto each curler, using the applicator nozzle.
- Repeat if necessary to ensure thorough penetration, but do not over-saturate.
- Allow to develop.

3 Development guidelines:
The suggested development times in the guidelines overleaf have been tested thoroughly and produce optimum results. However, if you are unsure about the overall condition and porosity of the hair, we recommend test curls should be taken to determine the final development time. Development times can be increased as required but care should be taken to avoid over-processing. When correct curl strength is achieved, rinse hair thoroughly for five minutes.

4 Rinsing and neutralising:
After completion of development time rinse all curlers thoroughly (2–3 minutes). Thoroughly blot the curlers to remove excess moisture.

Foam neutraliser:

- Pour 50ml of the neutraliser into a non-metallic bowl.
- Add an equal amount of warm water. The neutraliser is now ready to use.
- For maximum neutralisation, use a neutraliser sponge and apply two thirds of the neutraliser evenly to all the curlers, foam up thoroughly (do not foam up in the bowl).
- Leave to develop for five minutes.
- Gently unwind all the curlers and apply the remaining one third of the neutraliser through the hair.
- Distribute evenly and allow to develop for a further five minutes.
- Rinse thoroughly.
- Blot out excess moisture with a clean towel.

5 After care:
After rinsing out we recommend the use of a suitable after-care treatment.

Vitality UK Ltd. Newtown NW1 1AB

? **Memory jogger**

Why is it important to wear the correct PPE when assisting with perming services?

Name the three reasons why pre-perm shampoo is used.

List as many of the resources needed for perming as you can.

Maintain effective and safe methods of working when assisting with perming services (2)

Assisting with the perming service

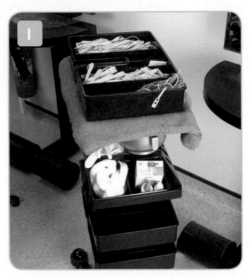

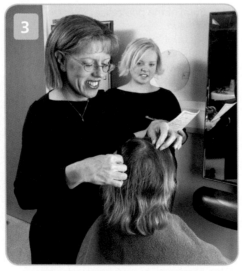

Ensure the trolley is prepared prior to perming

Protect the client with towels, a gown and a cape

Carry out a hair, skin and scalp analysis by dividing the hair into sections

Pass rods and papers to the stylist as they need them

Keeping your work area clean and tidy

Look at page 123 in Unit GH4 to find out how you can keep your work area clean and tidy, and why this is important.

>> **Get up and go!**

You could try to interest clients in perming services by wearing your own hair curly. Try curling your hair a couple of times during the week and take notice of the comments your clients make. Talk to them about the advantages of curling their hair and show them suitable styles.

Reducing product wastage

Look at page 124 in Unit GH4 to find out how you can limit the amount of products your salon wastes.

> ## » Get up and go!
>
> Find out how to prepare a neutraliser your salon uses by reading the manufacturer's instructions. Discuss the result, and how you found following the instructions, with a senior colleague.

Disposal of chemicals

Look at page 124 in Unit GH4 to find out how to properly dispose of chemicals in the salon.

Reducing the risk of harm or injury to yourself, your colleagues and clients

Look at page 125 in Unit GH4 to find out how you can reduce the risk of harm or injury to yourself, your colleagues and clients.

Reducing the risk of cross-infection

Look at page 126 in Unit GH4 to find out what cross-infection is and how you can take some simple measures to reduce the risk of it happening.

Skin and incompatibility tests

Skin tests involve applying a small amount of a product to the client's skin in order to ensure it is safe for a chemical treatment such as perming to go ahead. The test usually needs to be carried out 24–48 hours before the service can take place. You must follow the instructions you are given for skin tests very carefully or the consequences could be serious.

An incompatibility test involves taking a sample of the client's hair and applying the product to it. This is to make sure the client's hair is in a suitable condition to cope with the chemical treatment. The result of any test must be recorded on the client's record card.

> ## » Get up and go!
>
> Ask your stylist about other types of hair and scalp tests that are carried out, such as pre-perm test curl, development tests, porosity tests and elasticity tests.

> ## » Get up and go!
>
> With a colleague, find out:
>
> - the different types of perming products available in your salon
> - how they are applied
> - how long they last on the hair.

> ## ? Memory jogger
>
> How would a dirty and untidy work area affect your work?
>
> Why wouldn't you mix up all the chemicals you need for the day's appointments at the start of the day?
>
> How can you reduce the risks of accidents in your salon?
>
> What might happen as a result of pouring chemicals down the basin used for washing up and preparing drinks?
>
> What can you do to reduce the risk of cross-infection?
>
> Where should the results of any test be recorded?

Neutralising hair as part of the perming process (I)

Position the client at the basin and rinse hair thoroughly

Towel-blot the hair to remove excess water

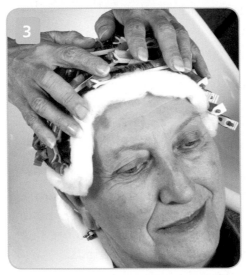

Check there is no excess water by pressing your hands over the rods

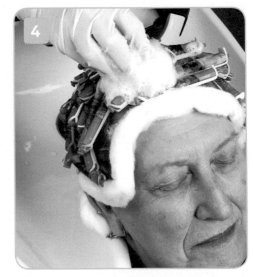

Apply the neutraliser to each rod and allow it to process according to the manufacturer's instructions

Rinsing out the perm lotion

You will need to follow both the stylist's and the manufacturer's instructions when rinsing the client's hair free of perm lotion. At the end of the processing time, the hair should be rinsed for a minimum of five minutes to thoroughly remove all traces of perm lotion. It is best to use warm water, which will leave the cuticles of the hair open, enabling the neutraliser to penetrate more effectively.

» Get up and go!

Discuss with your assessor the reasons why you would not massage or rub the scalp vigorously when rinsing out chemical products.

Towel-blotting the hair

The hair must be free from excess water before the neutraliser is applied. To remove excess moisture, you will need to towel-blot the hair. It is worth taking time to do this properly as too much water in the hair will dilute the neutraliser and ruin the perm. Check how wet the hair is by placing your hands over the rods – if you find lots of water on your hands, you must continue with towel-blotting. Some salons may use tissue or cotton wool to remove excess water from the client's hair.

Applying the neutraliser

As you have already learned, neutraliser closes the bonds that were broken by the perming lotion and fixes the hair into the shape of the rod being used. There are two main types of neutraliser used in the salon:

- hydrogen peroxide neutralisers
- sodium bromate neutralisers.

Correct timing of the neutralising process is crucial to the finished result. Over-processing can leave the hair frizzy, and under-processing will give a weak curl result. Make sure the client's skin is well protected before applying the neutraliser. Use barrier cream and damp cotton wool around the hairline.

You must match the neutraliser with the perm lotion being used. For example, an alkaline perm must be followed through with a hydrogen peroxide neutraliser. Some neutralising products can be used straight from the bottle, whilst others will need foaming up in a bowl first. The stylist will instruct you on how to use a particular product. You should also read the manufacturer's instructions, which will explain how to use the neutraliser safely and effectively.

Make sure you apply the neutraliser evenly throughout the client's wound hair, taking care to avoid any area which has not been permed. Unpermed hair can be protected by applying gel or conditioner. Leave the neutraliser on the client's hair for the recommended length of time. This will ensure the disulphide bonds are fixed into their new position. You may find it helpful to use a timer to accurately time the processing. Some types and lengths of hair may need a longer time to develop depending on the amount of hair wound around the rod.

An example of a neutralising product

? Memory jogger

How long do you rinse the client's hair prior to applying neutraliser?

Why towel-blot the hair before applying neutraliser?

Name the two types of neutraliser.

Why is timing the neutralising process correctly so important?

Neutralising hair as part of the perming process (2)

Removing the rods

With some neutralisers you will need to leave the rods in place during processing. Others require you to remove the rods after five minutes before continuing with the second part of the process. Always check the instructions to make sure you are using the product correctly. When you do remove the rods, you will have to do so very carefully so as not to disturb the curl and cause the hair to become straight. The hair is also in a very delicate state at this time and any rough handling can cause irritation to the client's scalp. Check with your stylist whether or not you should apply more neutraliser.

Removing the neutraliser

After the neutraliser has been left to process for the appropriate time, rinse it off thoroughly so that no traces are left in the hair. This will prevent chemical damage to the hair and makes sure the new shape is fixed.

Applying conditioner

Remove excess moisture from the client's hair by squeezing out the water by hand. Then apply a suitable antioxidant conditioner to the client's hair. Leave the conditioner on the hair for at least three minutes and then remove it, rinsing thoroughly. Towel-dry the client's hair and wrap it in a turban style before showing the client to the styling area. Comb through the hair, leaving it tangle-free for the next treatment. Make sure you leave the basin area clean and tidy ready for the next client.

Perming and neutralising problems

Perming and neutralising problems might include the hair returning to its natural straight look if the neutraliser is left in too long, frizziness, uneven curls along the hair length, straight hair at the sides or nape, or an irritable scalp. Mistakes can and do happen in the salon. When they do, stay calm and refer to the senior stylist immediately. To minimise the risk of a problem occurring, make sure you listen to all instructions given to you and check the manufacturer's instructions for each product.

The table opposite shows some common perming problems and how to deal with them.

Fault	By whom	Correction	How to avoid
Fish hooks	Stylist	Remove by cutting	Cover points of hair with end papers
Over-processing	Stylist/Junior	Cut and condition	Carefully time the process using the salon clock or a timer. Record the processing time on the record card
Neutraliser applied unevenly	Stylist/Junior	Re-perm if the condition of hair allows	Check the stylist's/manufacturer's instructions. Monitor application of neutraliser
Skin and scalp irritation	Junior	Rinse immediately with cool water	Carry out appropriate test before chemical treatment
Hair breakage	Stylist	Cut to disguise and use restructurant to strengthen hair	Carry out incompatibility test and pre-perm treatment

» Get up and go!

Not all product manufacturers produce a post-perm treatment. Some offer a product which can be used across a range of perms. Find out what products you can safely use for which perms. Discuss this with your assessor.

After-perm care

It is important to explain to clients how they should look after their hair at home. After-perm care involves helping the client to maintain their perm at home using the most appropriate shampoo, conditioner and styling products for permed hair. This is part of professional client care, and by selling the client the correct products, you will be giving him or her expert advice and guidance which completes the perming treatment.

Get ahead ⬆

Working either with a colleague or a training head, practise winding a spiral perm. This method of perming is time-consuming and needs you to be confident during the winding process as the sections of hair must be evenly wound around the bendy spiral rod. The hair you work on should be medium to long, towel-dried and in neat workable sections secured with butterfly clips. Start by taking sections of hair from the nape area, working from left to right on section one, alternating each section as you work up the client's head. This method of winding will give a degree of width on one-length hair cuts and a softer look on layered hair. Spiral perms do not promote root lift so be sure to discuss this with your client. You should aim to complete a medium-length spiral wind in one hour.

❓ Memory jogger

Why do you need to remove rods very carefully?

Why does neutraliser need to be removed completely from the hair?

What are fish hooks and how are they avoided?

What does after-perm care mean?

UNIT GH6

Plait and twist hair using basic techniques

Image Source

Plaiting and twisting hair is a very skillful technique and requires a high degree of manual dexterity (being good at using your hands). A single plait can give either an innocent or sophisticated look, depending on the style, whilst twists can be edgy and dramatic, completely changing the client's look. Both plaiting and twisting techniques can offer your clients something a little different, whether for everyday wear or a glamorous evening look. The techniques require patience and practice to perfect but you will then be able to offer them in addition to classic salon services, such as chemical treatments, cutting and styling.

This unit is about using basic plaiting and twisting techniques following the instructions of the stylist and is suitable for those working with Caucasian and Asian hair types. This unit applies for hairdressing students working in hairdressing and barbering salons.

In this unit you will learn about:

- Types of plaiting and twisting
- Maintaining effective and safe methods of working when plaiting and twisting
- Plaiting and twisting hair.

Here are some key words you will meet in this unit:

Sprays – used to hold a style

Serums – oil-based products used to smooth the cuticle

Gels – used to keep hair in place and add shine

Multiple corn rows – lots of tiny scalp plaits

French plait – usually one main plait secured to the scalp

Two strand twists – tiny twists involving two strands of hair

Traction alopecia – excessive tension applied to the hair and scalp causing baldness

Asian hair – the hair shaft is round in shape, straight and/or coarse

Caucasian hair – the hair shaft is oval in shape and can be straight, wavy or curly

Tangle-free – hair which has been combed smooth and is free from knots or tugs

Texture – the way hair feels, determined by touch during the consultation

Types of plaiting and twisting

Plaits are formed by intertwining (weaving together) strands of hair to create patterns or even structures. Material other than hair, such as ribbons or hair extensions, can be incorporated into the plait to give a more interesting finished look. Twists are formed by twisting sections of hair around each other. Both plaiting and twisting can create very artistic, intricate and ornate hairstyles, involving techniques that are very specialised and take time to master.

Plaits and twists can be created on short, medium and long hair, on any hair type or texture and on both males and females. They can be small or large and formed either close to the scalp or in loose hanging sections, giving the hair movement.

Looks that can be achieved by plaiting and twisting

Before you can proceed with a plaiting or twisting service you will need to be sure the client's hair can cope with the tension (pulling) that will be applied. You will also need to consider what styles are likely to suit them by looking at their hair and facial characteristics. You will therefore need to think about the following:

- hair type
- hair length
- hair density
- hair elasticity
- head and face shape.

Always follow the instructions of your stylist.

>> **Get up and go!**

Get together with a colleague and think about how each other's hair type, length, density and elasticity, as well as face and head shape, will affect a plaiting or twisiting service. What style would each of you recommend to the other?

Considering hair types when plaiting and twisting

You will need to think about the type of hair your client has when carrying out plaiting and twisting techniques. Caucasian/European and Asian/Oriental hair types have important differences and you will need to be able to work with both. One of the major differences is texture, which will vary from client to client and may also vary within the same head of hair. Texture can be fine, medium or coarse, with fine hair having a small circumference and coarse hair having a large circumference. To determine the texture, run your fingers along the length of a single hair.

You also need to know about the dangers of applying too much pressure on the hair when plaiting and twisting. Hair that is excessively pulled can lead to a painful and irritable scalp, as well as hair breakage. If this pulling, or tension, continues the client may suffer from what is known as 'traction alopecia', where the hair is pulled from the scalp due to excessive tension, leaving a bald area. This area will remain bald until new hair grows back through – it can be a month before you see only 1.25cm of new hair.

? **Memory jogger**

What types of things should you consider before carrying out a plaiting or twisting service?

How can Caucasian/European and Asian/Oriental hair differ?

What are the potential consequences of excessive tension on the hair and scalp?

>> **Get up and go!**

Find out about the different types of equipment that are used to create plaited and twisted styles. Don't forget about things like coloured hair pieces and hair ornaments that can be added.

Maintaining effective and safe methods of working when plaiting and twisting (I)

Protecting the client

Your client must be protected with clean towels, gown and waterproof cape. If your client is having colour added to their hair as part of the plaiting or twisting service, you may need to use particular towels intended for colouring. Remember that it is very important your client's clothes are adequately covered and protected during a colouring service.

Personal protective equipment (PPE)

Remember to wear suitable PPE when carrying out a plaiting or twisting service, particularly if you are using coloured sprays or gels. Gloves will protect your hands from these irritants, which can cause dermatitis.

Preparing the client for shampooing

Your client may need to have their hair shampooed before the plaiting or twisting service can be carried out. This may be due to a build up of styling products or perhaps the client's hair is excessively oily. Before shampooing, you will need to comb through the client's hair. Remove tangles carefully to avoid causing the client any discomfort. Check the client's scalp with the stylist, looking for any cuts or irritated areas which may need special attention. You will also need to discuss with the stylist the correct shampoo to use, which may be a clarifying shampoo that removes all previous products and leaves the hair in its most natural state.

Positioning the client and checking your own posture

As you prepare the client for the plaiting or twisting service, ask them whether or not they will need to move from the chair for any reason. The service may take an hour or two and so it is a good idea to find out if they have any physical needs you should be aware of. If they do need to get up and stretch or walk about during the service, you may like to offer them the opportunity to do so before you start any particularly tricky parts. Remember also to offer the client refreshments or a magazine before and regularly during the service.

As you will be working on the client for a long time, it is important to be aware of your own comfort. You should stand with straight legs and your feet slightly apart to maintain your balance. Keep your shoulders relaxed too. Taking these simple steps will help minimise your risk of developing injury and fatigue.

> **» Get up and go!**
>
> What products does your salon offer that can be used to add colour to your client's hair as part of a plaited or twisted style? Should they be used on wet hair or dry hair? Do they require any processing time? Discuss your findings with your assessor.

Get up and go!

Think about the concerns usually experienced by clients when they have their hair plaited or twisted. What might they be worried about? How can you reassure them? Talk through your thoughts with your assessor.

Keeping your work area clean and tidy

It is essential that you keep your work area clean and tidy during the service. This will ensure the service runs smoothly and also gives a professional image to the client. Position tools and equipment for ease of use and prepare the trolley with all of the resources you will need for plaiting or twisting, ensuring they are clean and in good condition.

Preparing the resources for plaiting and twisting

You will need to prepare a trolley with the following items:

- client record card
- clean towels (of the appropriate colours)
- gloves
- apron
- selection of combs
- old hairdressing scissors
- extension hair (if required)
- soft bristled brush
- section clips
- aftercare products
- aftercare sheet/card.

All resources must be cleaned or sterilised after every use. This will help to minimise the risk of cross-infection.

A trolley containing some equipment for plaiting and twisting

? Memory jogger

What type of personal protective equipment is available for you and your clients?

Why might a client need a shampoo before a plaiting or twisting service?

How can your posture reduce fatigue and the risk of injury?

 Get up and go!

You could try to interest clients in plaiting or twisting services by trying them out on your own hair. Try wearing a couple of different plaits and twists in your hair for a few weeks and take notice of the comments your clients make. Talk to them about the advantages of wearing plaits and twists in their hair and show them some suitable styles.

Maintaining effective and safe methods of working when plaiting and twisting (2)

Minimise the risk of damage to tools

The hairdressing profession relies on good quality, safe tools and equipment in good working order. Always do your best to look after your own tools and equipment and the salon's property. Before using, make sure items are safe and fit for their purpose, reporting any faults to the appropriate person.

Reducing product wastage

Before using any product, always read the manufacturer's instructions and discuss the instructions with the stylist. If you need to prepare a product, remember to prepare only the amount you need just before it is to be used. This will help to reduce wastage. If extra product is required, it is more cost-effective to make it freshly as you need it.

Reducing the risk of cross-infection

Reduce the risk of cross-infection by being alert to any signs of infection and covering any open wounds or cuts with a suitable waterproof dressing. Report any personal infection or infestation to the appropriate member of staff. Always practise good standards of personal hygiene and wear clean, well-pressed clothes every day. Clients who have an open cut or wound must be treated with particular care. Seek advice from the stylist or your assessor and find out if barrier cream would be appropriate on this occasion. The situation may require your client to return for the service once the open wound has healed.

All tools and equipment used during the service must be cleaned in the appropriate way. Make sure you are familiar with how to clean or sterilise everything you have used, including brushes, combs, section clips, gowns and towels. This will reduce the risk of cross-infection and ensure tools and equipment are kept in good condition.

Get up and go!

Discuss with a colleague what a commercially acceptable timeframe for plaiting and twisting hair is. Are these services listed on your salon price list? How much do they cost? Does your salon sell any products associated with plaiting and twisting? If so, what are they, how are they applied and how long do they last?

Reducing the risk of harm or injury to yourself, your colleagues and clients

Always keep a look out for hazards or risks which may arise during the course of the day. Clear away used product bottles and used materials such as bowls and cotton wool. Keep the floor clear from trailing cables, towels, gowns and cut hair, as well as items belonging to clients such as handbags, shopping bags, walking sticks and pushchairs. This will help to minimise the risk of any accidents occurring.

Removing plaits or twists

Depending on what style your client has gone for, they may need to come back to the salon to have their plaits or twists professionally removed. They may want to do it themselves, but inform them that it can be very time-consuming. You should discuss with the client a suitable timeframe to come back to the salon for a check-up appointment, which could be, say, two months after the plaits or twists were put in. Remember, the removal process must be costed as part of the salon's services and should appear on the price list. You should aim to remove a complete set of plaits or twists from short to medium-length hair in less than one hour.

 Memory jogger

What should you do if you find that a tool or piece of equipment is broken?

Why is it more cost-effective to make up products as you need them?

What might happen if the salon is left to become cluttered with used resources and items belonging to clients?

Plaiting and twisting hair (1)

Plaiting techniques – French plait

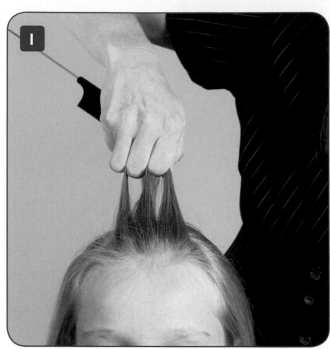

Correctly gown the client. Take the first section across the front hairline and divide into three strands

Cross the right hand section over into the centre, then cross the left hand section into the centre

Pick up more hair from the sides as you work along the top of the head, keeping the hair taut. Smooth each section as you work from the front hairline section

Keep the hair close to the client's scalp and the tension even as you continue to work towards the crown

Continue to plait down the hair length and secure the free ends with a covered band or ribbon

The completed scalp plait secured to the head

Best practice for plaiting and twisting

- Always think about your client's comfort. Are they coping with any discomfort? Do you need to stop and reduce the tension?

- Neat sections and partings are crucial to the success of a style created by plaiting and twisting. They will also increase the lifespan of the hairstyle.

- Another important factor is even tension. You will have to reach a balance between applying enough tension to create the style and not causing your client too much discomfort or even hair breakage. You will soon learn to adjust the tension of plaits or twists to suit both the style and the client.

- Sections of hair not being worked on need to be held out of the way. Use section clips or butterfly clips and bring down only the amount of hair you need to work on.

- Apply suitable products as necessary during the service, taking care to follow manufacturers' and the stylist's instructions. The types of product you may need include sprays, serums and gels, which will help maintain the life of the hairstyle and give a professional finish.

Plaiting and twisting hair (2)

Plaiting techniques – Multiple corn rows

1. Correctly gown your client and, after your consultation, begin to section the hair

2. Begin sectioning at the sides

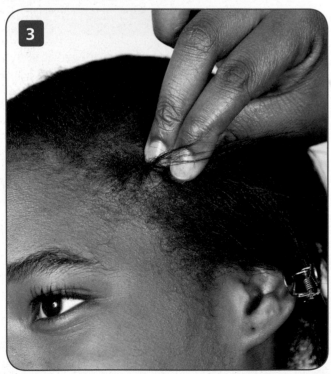

3. Form a small plait at the sides of the head

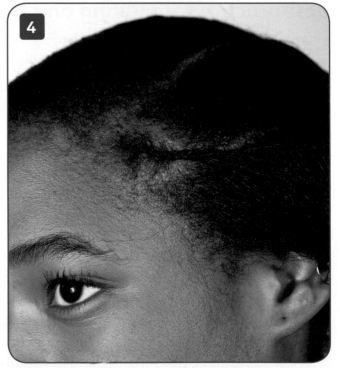

4. Work from the front hairline towards the nape area forming small neat plaits

Plait the longer lengths together, working from the front through to the napes

The completed corn rows seen from the side

The finished look

Traction alopecia

Excessive tension (pulling) on the hair may lead to traction alopecia where the hair comes away from the scalp leaving bald areas. You will need to be alert for signs of this during a plaiting or twisting service. Look for:

- a sore/sensitive scalp
- weeping/pus at the roots
- a reduced amount of hair in an area.

Should traction alopecia occur, the area should be looked after with great care as any open sores may lead to an infection. Wearing plaits and twists continuously or regularly can lead to traction alopecia and so is not recommended. If your client becomes concerned, they should return to the salon for professional removal of the plaits or twists.

Any sign of alopecia needs to be recorded on your client's record card, noting the location of affected areas. Talk to your client about why this has happened and speak to your stylist about advice you can give to help improve the condition of their scalp.

Traction alopecia

Plaiting and twisting hair (3)

Twisting techniques

Prepare the client for the twisting service and begin to section the hair

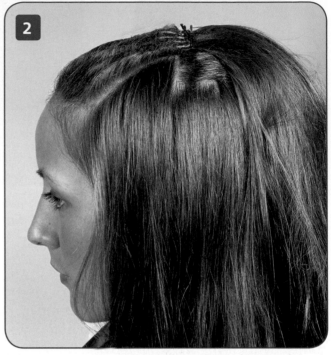

Take fine sections and twist the hair from the front hairline working back towards the crown

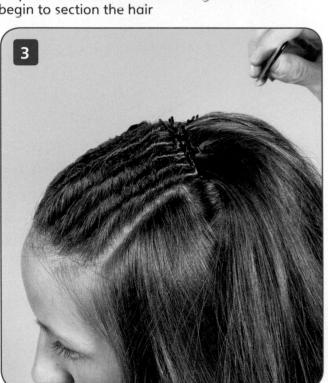

Secure the sections with hair grips as you work

Work down either side starting at the top of the client's head each time

5

The completed look

Aftercare

You can start to advise your client on how to look after their plaits or twists as soon as you start the service. If it is a style that is meant to be worn for more than a day or two, you should advise your client how to keep their hair clean. Shampooing is still possible but they should not rub their hair vigorously, and plaits should be washed in the direction of the plait. Suitable oils and moisturisers can also be applied to the hair in order to protect it and add shine. These measures should minimise tangles and prolong the style.

You will need to advise the client how long they can wear their hair in plaits or twists before they should have them removed so as to prevent traction alopecia. Finally, be knowledgeable about the retail products in your salon and give the client helpful advice about the most appropriate products for their hair and style. Aftercare is part of professional client care and completes the plaiting or twisting service.

❓ Memory jogger

How often should the client return for a consultation?

How soon do you start to advise your client on how to care for their new hairstyle?

Is it possible to shampoo hair with hair extensions?

UNIT GH7

Remove hair extensions

Anne Veck, photographer: Clark Wiseman

Hair extensions can completely transform a client's look: short hair can be replaced by long flowing locks, and volume, texture, colour and curls can be added in no time at all. Hair extensions can be funky and wild or serious and sophisticated. They can be added for fun and fashion or to help a client regain their hairstyle because of thinning hair. With an increasing demand for hair extensions it is very beneficial to be able to offer your clients this service in your salon.

In this unit, you will learn how to remove hair extensions following the instructions of a stylist. You will need to be able to use a number of tools and products in order to do this effectively and safely. The work involved will be carried out under the supervision of the relevant person, such as the stylist or assessor. This unit applies to hairdressing students working in hairdressing and barbering salons and is suitable for those working with Caucasian and Asian hair types.

In this unit you will learn about:

- Maintaining effective and safe methods of working when removing hair extensions
- Removing hair extensions.

Here are some key words you will meet in this unit:

Tension – pressure applied to the hair and scalp by excessive pulling

Traction alopecia – excessive tension applied to the hair and scalp causing baldness

Seal breaker – implement used to assist with removal of hair extensions

Extensions – additional hair applied to natural hair to offer length, texture, volume and colour

Asian hair – the hair shaft is round in shape, straight and/ or coarse

Caucasian hair – the hair shaft is oval in shape and can be straight, wavy or curly

Cuticle – outer layer of the hair shaft

Surface conditioner – conditioner which coats the outer layer of the hair shaft

Texture – the way hair feels, determined by touch during the consultation

Tangle-free – hair which has been combed smooth and is free from knots or tugs

Fatigue – weary; exhausted from over work or adopting a poor posture

Maintaining effective and safe methods of working when using hair extensions (I)

Why have hair extensions?

Hair extensions are either natural human hair or man-made synthetic hair fibres. They can be applied either by using heated equipment to seal the extensions to hair (hot hair extension systems) or by using other methods to seal the extensions (cold hair extensions). Cold systems can be less damaging to the hair than hot systems. A client may consider asking for hair extensions for the following reasons.

- If their hair is thin or thinning.
- To increase the length of their hair.
- To add volume.
- To add different colours without committing.
- To add curls or straightness.

> **» Get up and go!**
>
> You could try to interest clients in hair extensions by wearing them in your own hair. Try wearing some different textures, lengths and colours in your hair and take notice of the comments your clients make. Talk to them about the advantages of wearing extensions and show them some suitable styles.

Considering hair types when adding extensions

As you have learned, Caucasian/European and Asian/Oriental hair does differ due to the shape of the hair shaft, with Caucasian hair having an oval cross-section and Asian hair having a round cross-section. Hair can also be coarse, medium or fine. You will need to find out what type of hair your client has for the hair extension service to be successful.

You also need to be aware of the dangers of applying too much pressure on the hair when placing hair extensions. Hair that is excessively pulled can lead to a painful and irritable scalp, as well as hair breakage. If this pulling, or tension, continues the client may suffer from what is known as 'traction alopecia', where the hair is pulled from the scalp due to excessive tension, leaving a bald area. This area will remain bald until new hair grows back through – it can be a month before you see only 1.25cm of new hair.

Traction alopecia

Protecting the client and yourself

Protect the client's clothing with the appropriate towel, gown and waterproof cape. For your own protection, remember to wear personal protective equipment (PPE) when working with clients who are receiving a hair extension service. Your hands and clothing must be protected at all times. Wear the right type of gloves and apron when using hair extension removal products as they can burn through certain types of plastic.

Preparing the client for shampooing

You will need to comb through the client's hair to remove any tangles before shampooing. Use this time to check the client's scalp for cuts or irritated areas with the stylist. You will also need to discuss with the stylist the correct shampoo to use, which will probably be a clarifying shampoo that will remove all traces of product and leave the hair in its most natural state. Now might be a good time to advise the client not to shampoo their hair again for at least two days after the service. This is to give the hair extensions time to fully adhere to the hair shafts, allowing them to set properly.

Positioning the client and checking your own posture

As you prepare the client for the hair extension removal service, ask them whether or not they will need to move from the chair for any reason. The service may take several hours and so it is a good idea to find out if they have any physical needs you should be aware of. If they do need to get up and stretch or walk about during the service, you may like to offer them the opportunity to do so before you start any particularly tricky parts. Remember also to offer the client refreshments or a magazine before and regularly during the service.

As you will be working on the client for a long time, it is important to be aware of your own comfort. You should stand with straight legs and your feet slightly apart to maintain your balance. Keep your shoulders relaxed too. Taking these simple steps will help minimise your risk of developing injury and fatigue.

> **» Get up and go!**
>
> Because hair extension removal products 'melt' the bonds that hold the extensions in place, they can also melt other plastics that they come into contact with. Think about the materials and tools you use on a daily basis in the salon that are made from plastic. How can they be protected from unnecessary damage? Discuss your thoughts with your assessor.

> **? Memory jogger**
>
> Why might a client request hair extensions?
>
> What causes traction alopecia?
>
> Why must you make sure you are wearing the correct type of PPE when handling hair extension removal products?

> **» Get up and go!**
>
> Think about the concerns usually experienced by clients when they have their hair extensions removed. What might they be worried about? How can you reassure them? Talk through your thoughts with your assessor.

Maintaining effective and safe methods of working when removing hair extensions (2)

Keeping your work area clean and tidy

It is essential to keep your work area clean and tidy during the service. This will ensure the service runs smoothly and also presents a professional image to the client. Position tools and equipment for ease of use and prepare the trolley with all the resources you will need for removing hair extensions, ensuring they are clean and in good condition.

Working safely with hair extension products and tools

As with any product you use in the salon, always read the manufacturer's instructions and check with the stylist before using. Only make up the amount you need just before you need to use it. Some of the tools used when working with hair extensions, such as straighteners and the hot-bond hair extension system, often reach very high temperatures. Take great care when using these items to minimise the risk of accidents or injury.

Reducing the risk of cross-infection

Reduce the risk of cross-infection by being alert to any signs of infection and covering any open wounds or cuts with a suitable waterproof dressing. Report any personal infection or infestation to the appropriate member of staff. Always practise good standards of personal hygiene and wear clean, well-pressed clothes every day. Clients who have an open cut or wound must be treated with particular care. Seek advice from the stylist or your assessor and find out if barrier cream would be appropriate on this occasion. The situation may require your client to return for the service once the open wound has healed.

All tools and equipment used during the service must be cleaned in the appropriate way. Make sure you are familiar with how to clean or sterilise everything you have used, including brushes, combs, section clips, gowns and towels. You will also need to clean the applicator gun with the recommended cleaning product. This will reduce the risk of cross-infection and ensure tools and equipment are kept in good condition.

Reducing the risk of harm or injury to yourself, your colleagues and clients

Always keep a look out for hazards or risks which may arise during the course of the day. Clear away used product bottles and used materials

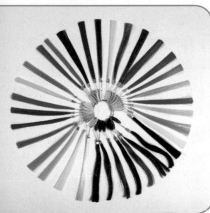

Hair extensions are available in different lengths and colours

such as bowls and cotton wool. Keep the floor clear from trailing cables, towels, gowns and cut hair, as well as items belonging to clients such as handbags, shopping bags, walking sticks and pushchairs. This will help to minimise the risk of any accidents occurring.

Skin and suitability tests

A skin test should be carried out before the hair extension service is carried out. The gum-based products used in a cold hair extension system come into contact with the client's scalp, so sensitivity and allergy to these products must be tested. The test is carried out by applying a small amount of the product to the client's skin or by applying a hair extension using the product.

A suitability test allows the stylist to make sure the client's hair is suitable for the hair extension service. The stylist will also tell the client what is involved with looking after extensions and ask whether they can do this. Between three and five extensions my be placed in the hair, for an agreed fee, and then the client will return to the salon for a check-up, which will determine suitability in terms of:

- Is the hair strong enough to hold extensions for three months?
- Has there been any hair breakage?
- Are there are signs of scalp irritation?
- Does the client fully understand how to care for their extensions?

The results of any test must always be recorded on the client's record card.

Preparing the resources for applying or removing hair extensions

You will need to prepare a trolley for the stylist with the following items:

- client record card
- clean towels
- barrier cream
- gloves
- apron
- selection of combs
- old hairdressing scissors
- mixing mat[1]
- extension hair[1]
- bonding gun[1]
- resin sticks[1]
- heatproof drip mat[1]
- soft-bristled brush
- section clips
- removal tools[2]
- scalp protectors
- aftercare products and advice card/sheet
- cotton wool
- removal solutions
- hair dryer.

[1] For extension application
[2] For extension removal

All resources must be cleaned or sterilised after every use. This will help to minimise the risk of cross-infection.

▶▶ Get up and go!

Find out how to prepare the hair extensions used in your salon by reading the manufacturer's instructions. Discuss the result, and how you found following the instructions, with a senior colleague.

A trolley prepared for applying or removing hair extensions

? Memory jogger

Why is it important to work in a clean and tidy salon?

What does a suitability test involve and why is it carried out?

Name as many items as you can that are needed for a hair extension application service.

Removing hair extensions (I)

Before the appointment

When you have a client booked in to have their hair extensions removed, you will have to think about how long the extensions have been in the hair. It is recommended that hair extensions remain in place for no more than three months, but your client could be having them removed before or after this time. Hair grows about 1.25cm each month and the amount of growth since having the extensions applied can affect the removal service – extensions that have been in place for more than three months can be uncomfortable to remove. You might want to ask the client to apply conditioner to the bonds the night before their appointment, which will help break down the plastic resin, making the removal a little easier.

Preparing for the service

When your client is being prepared for the removal service, let them know it may feel like they are losing a lot of their hair as the extensions are removed. However, this hair loss will just be the hair they would have naturally shed over the time period they had the extensions. The client should also be made aware how long the service will take. Depending on the type of hair extensions they have, it may take between 30 minutes and three hours.

You will need to prepare a trolley for the extension removal service. Items you will need in addition to those listed on page 163 are:

- seal breakers
- removal products
- cotton wool pads
- hairdryer
- seam releasers.

Make sure you wear suitable personal protective equipment throughout the service, to include gloves and an apron. Remember: hair extension removal products can be dangerous if you are not properly protected.

Removing hair extensions as instructed by your stylist

First, you will need to separate the bonds one by one to make sure they have not become tangled together. You can then brush through the client's hair with a soft-bristled brush, working from the points of the hair through to the roots, being careful not to damage the natural hair.

Take care not to apply too much tension whilst brushing through the roots as this may irritate the scalp.

The removal process for most extension systems will be similar to the ones described below but you should always check the manufacturer's instructions.

Removing hot hair extension systems

Section the client's hair and start the removal process on the hairline around the nape. Place a cotton wool pad underneath the hair extension bond and apply the removal solution, allowing it to penetrate the bond completely for the recommended time. This will soften the plastic bond, allowing the extension to be gently pulled away from the client's hair. Seal breakers may be needed before or after applying the removal solution, but this is dependent on the manufacturer's instructions.

Removing cold hair extension systems

Removing cold hair extensions follows a similar process to that described for hot hair extensions, except that the heat from a handheld hairdryer is used to activate the removal solution.

Using a hairdryer to speed up the removal of cold hair extensions

---

» Get up and go!

Why do you think a cotton wool pad is placed underneath the bond before applying the removal solution? Think about what the chemical does. Discuss your thoughts with your assessor.

? Memory jogger

What is the recommended maximum time for wearing hair extensions?

Why might some of the client's hair come away with the hair extensions?

Why is a hairdryer used when removing some cold hair extensions?

Why is it important to check the client's hair for any stray hair extensions?

Check all hair extensions have been removed

Check each section as you work through your client's hair, making sure you have removed all of the hair extensions. Extensions can be quite small and easily missed when working amongst a mass of hair. When all the extensions have been removed, comb through each section gently, working from point to root. The stylist will need to check all the extensions have been removed, and when they are satisfied, your client is ready for the next part of the service.

Removing hair extensions (2)

1 Prepare the trolley containing the tools and equipment needed for removing hair extensions

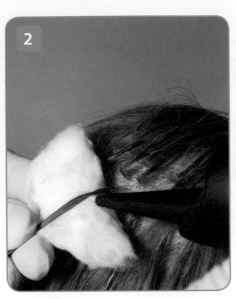

2 Wearing gloves to avoid any irritation, apply removal solution to soften the bond

3 Break the bond with the seal breakers

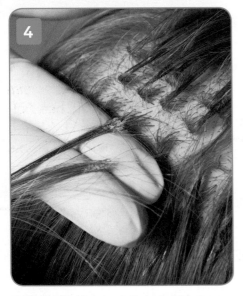

4 Pull the hair extension gently away from the scalp

5 Use a fine tooth comb to remove excess softened glue

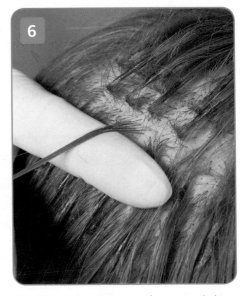

6 Continue to remove the remaining extensions

Best practice for removing hair extensions

- Always use products and equipment in line with the manufacturer's and stylist's instructions. Make sure you have understood any instructions given to you. If you are ever unsure, double check.

- Always use tools and equipment for their intended purpose and make sure you know how to use them properly. You will then be able to use them effectively and minimise any damage to your client's hair.

- Keep in mind the client's comfort throughout the service. Regularly check their position and ask them if they need to move or stand up.
- Gel or conditioner can be used to protect the client's own hair when applying removal solution to the extensions.
- Make sure the removal solution doesn't run onto your client's face or clothes.

>> **Get up and go!**

Discuss with a colleague what a commercially acceptable timeframe is for removing hair extensions. Does this service appear on your salon price list?

Removing hair extensions can be very uncomfortable or even painful for the client if it is not done correctly. The removal solution can irritate and damage skin and clothes so be especially careful when applying it. Take particular care around the eyes and consider using barrier cream around the hairline to prevent any solution running into the client's eyes. Always work in a well ventilated area as the removal solution can be very strong smelling. If you have any concerns at all during the service, always refer to your stylist for advice.

Shampooing the client's hair

The next part of the service, after the extensions have been removed, is a shampoo. This will remove all traces of the removal solution and bonding product, as well as any conditioner or gel you used to protect the client's hair. After shampooing, towel-dry the client's hair and scalp and make sure they are clean and free from products and excess moisture. Take the client to the styling area and comb through their hair, leaving it tangle-free without damaging the hair or scalp. Your client's hair is now ready for the next service, which may be more hair extensions!

Aftercare

You will need to advise your client how best to look after their new hair extensions at home. Tell them about any suitable products your salon sells and give them advice on appropriate hair care. The client should not rub their hair when shampooing and conditioning as this will cause the extensions to tangle with the client's own hair. Good aftercare advice will help the client maintain their extensions, make them want to return to your salon next time, and completes the hair extension service.

 Get ahead

Practise placing hair extensions on a male client. Applying a full head of hair extensions is time-consuming and requires neat and skilful work. You will need to think about a suitable colour, length, texture and style that are flattering to the client. Show your client some before and after photos and talk them through the process so they understand what will happen. Take some before and after photos of your client, as well as some photos of the process. You can use them to develop your portfolio, which can be used in your salon and at future interviews. You should aim to complete a full head of hair extensions on short to medium-length hair in less than four hours.

? Memory jogger

Why might you use gel or conditioner during the extension removal service?

Why shampoo the client's hair after removing extensions?

What aftercare advice could you give someone who has just had extensions applied?

UNIT GB1

Assist with shaving services

Anne Veck, photographer: David Howard

Barbering is one of the oldest hairdressing services. It is thought that the Egyptians were one of the first civilizations to develop barbering services, such as cutting hair and shaving. Many combs and cutting tools have been found during digs in various parts of Egypt. The cutting tools were sharpened flints, and the barbers would have met their clients in the street and carried out barbering services outside.

The word 'barber' is Latin and simply means 'beard'. Barbers used to carry out surgery as well as shaving services. Bandages stained with blood would be hung up to dry outside the barber's shop, and this is why barbers today sometimes have a red and white pole outside their business. The beard has long been a way of non-verbally communicating information such as the status and style of the wearer. A beard may tell you that the wearer is religious, wise or important, or it can simply be a way of saying, 'I am a man'. Facial hair styles change along with other fashions and trends but shaving services are always popular and in demand.

This unit is about the basic skills of shaving. The work involved will be carried out under the direction of the relevant person, such as the barber or assessor. This unit will apply for hairdressing students working in hairdressing and barbering salons.

In this unit you will learn about:

- Maintaining effective and safe methods of working when assisting with shaving services
- Preparing facial hair and skin for shaving services.

Here are some key words you will meet in this unit:

Lathering products – shaving creams and foams that are used as lubricants

Lubricant – a product which makes the surface of the skin slippery

Sharps – razors, scissors, needles, etc.

Astringents – products which have a stimulating effect on the skin

Contra-indication – an indication of the skin which would mean an alternative course of action

Barber – literally means 'beard'

Autoclave – sterilising system using moist heat

Barbicide – method of disinfecting tools in solution

Dermatitis – dry, itchy skin caused by an irritant

Effleurage – a stroking massage movement

Petrissage – a circular massage movement

Shaving brush – a small bristle brush used to apply lathering products

Maintaining effective and safe methods of working when assisting with shaving services (I)

Protecting the client

Your client must be protected with suitable and clean towels, gown and cape throughout the service. You will also need to have small pieces of cotton wool to hand to cover your client's eyes at certain times during the service. This is to protect the client's eyes from any product you may use or stray hair clippings when shaping the outline of the client's facial hair. It is important to regularly check your client's clothes are adequately covered and protected during shaving.

Personal protective equipment (PPE)

Remember to wear personal protective equipment (PPE) when assisting with shaving services. Your hands and clothing must be protected at all times. Dermatitis is a skin condition that makes your skin dry, sore and itchy. It is caused by irritants, such as chemicals in products, coming into contact with the skin. Use barrier cream or a good quality hand cream when working in the salon to help prevent your skin from drying out and to protect yourself from irritants. Gloves will prevent irritants from coming into contact with the skin. Gloves should also be worn when dealing with sharps and you will need to make sure the barber has a pair of gloves ready for their use. You will be working with sharp cutting and shaving tools and it is important to protect yourself properly.

 Sharpen up!

Does your salon or barber's have a towel colour system? If so, find out what colour towel you would use for a shave.

Positioning the client and checking your own posture

The client will sit in an adjustable barber's chair for the shaving service and you will need to adjust the elevation of the back of the chair to suit the barber who will be carrying out the service. Once you have

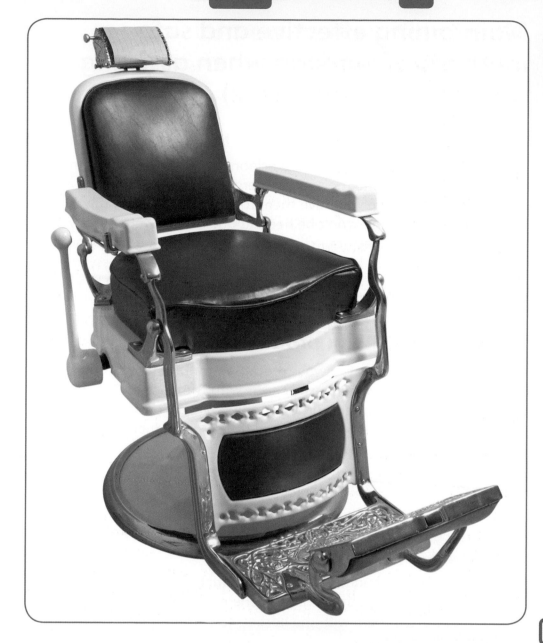

An adjustable barbering chair

adjusted the chair, make sure it is locked into position. Check your client's neck is positioned correctly in the curve of the neck rest and make sure they are comfortable. Ask if there are any areas they find easier or more difficult to shave. This information will help the barber and make the experience more comfortable for the client.

» Get up and go!

Ask your barber if you can practise using the barbering chair. You need to be knowledgeable about how it operates and the benefits of using such a chair. Practise with a colleague.

? Memory jogger

What items can you use to protect your client during a shave?

Why should you wear suitable PPE when assisting with shaving services?

Why is the client's position and comfort important?

Maintaining effective and safe methods of working when assisting with shaving services (2)

Keeping your work area clean and tidy

It is essential to keep your work area clean and tidy during shaving services. Think about the tools, equipment and products you are going to need and make sure you have them to hand. Clear away anything that has been used and won't be needed again. This will ensure you don't waste time or keep your client waiting while you go back and forth getting things, or look for the things you need in a messy work area. Keeping your work area clean and tidy will enable you to work more effectively and it also helps keep your workplace safe.

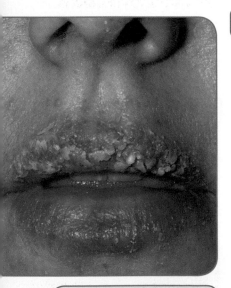

You must keep the work area clean and tidy

Working safely with products

Before using any product, always read the manufacturer's instructions and discuss the instructions with the barber. Only use products for their intended purpose and wear appropriate PPE when handling if necessary. If you are asked to use a product, only prepare the amount you need just before it is to be used. This will help to reduce wastage. If extra product is required, it is more cost-effective to prepare the product as you need it.

>> **Get up and go!**

Find out how to prepare the various products used in your salon or barber's for lathering the skin. Read the manufacturer's instructions and then discuss them with the barber. Talk about your findings with a junior colleague.

Reducing the risk of cross-infection

Cross-infection is when an infection is passed from one person to another. You can take some very simple steps as you work to reduce the risk of this happening. Remember to always practise good personal hygiene and wear clean, well-pressed clothes. If you or any of your clients are showing signs of infection or infestation, you must report it straight away to a senior member of staff. They can then advise you what to do. If you have an open cut or wound, cover it with a suitable waterproof dressing. Clients with open cuts or wounds must be treated with particular care. Seek advice from the

Impetigo is a bacterial skin infection

barber and ask if barrier cream would be appropriate at this stage. The situation may require your client to return once their wound has healed.

The two main infections you need to be aware of when assisting with shaving services are impetigo and barber's rash. Impetigo is a bacterial infection and can be recognised by yellow, crusty spots on the skin. Barber's rash is inflammation of the hair follicle, usually caused by unsterilised razors and shaving brushes. If you think the client has any kind of infection, promptly inform the barber.

You should also make sure you know how to use your salon's methods of sterilisation properly and ensure you always use clean tools and equipment on each new client. The main methods of sterilisation used in salons and barber's are:

- barbicide jars
- ultraviolet cabinets
- autoclaves.

All tools must be thoroughly cleaned with hot soapy water before being placed in any sterilisation equipment. Barbicide solution must be made up to the correct strength by reading the manufacturer's instructions and should be changed every day.

Ultraviolet cabinets use ultraviolet light to destroy bacteria, but as light is used, tools must be turned over so all sides are sterilised.

Autoclaves work like a pressure cooker and sterilise tools by heating them to high temperatures.

A jar of barbicide

An ultraviolet cabinet

An autoclave

? Memory jogger

Why is it important to prepare for a shaving service by getting ready all the tools and products you will need?

What are the advantages of only making up products as you need them?

Describe what impetigo and barber's rash are.

What must you do to each piece of equipment before you use any method of sterilisation?

Maintaining effective and safe methods of working when assisting with shaving services (3)

Reducing the risk of harm or injury to yourself, your colleagues and clients

Always keep a look out for hazards or risks which may arise during the course of the day. Clear away used product bottles and used materials such as bowls, cotton wool and razors. Keep the floor clear from trailing cables, towels, gowns and cut hair, as well as items belonging to clients such as shopping bags, walking sticks and pushchairs. This will help to minimise the risk of any accidents occurring.

> **» Get up and go!**
>
> Look at the different types of lighting in your salon or barber's. Do you have fluorescent tubes, spotlights or incandescent lights? Try to encourage your manager to go green and install energy-saving bulbs. They use up to 75% less electricity and last nearly ten times as long. Create a chart comparing the costs of each type of light along with their advantages and disadvantages. Show it to your manager and discuss how it might be more cost-effective and environmentally friendly to change the current lighting. Why might changing the lighting be costly at first but a good investment in the long run?

Re-ordering products

If the stock levels of a product are running low, remember to follow your salon's policy for re-ordering, which will probably involve telling the appropriate member of staff or writing it down. This will ensure you have sufficient products available, and also avoid having too much stock.

Used razor blades must be disposed of in a sharps bin

Disposal of waste

It is very important that you dispose of chemicals in the proper manner. Your salon or barber's must follow the Control of Substances Hazardous to Health (COSHH) Regulations and ensure products are disposed of in a safe and environmentally friendly way. Some salons have a specific basin for disposing of chemicals. Never pour chemicals down the sink in the salon's food and drink preparation area. Always flush them down the shampoo basin, followed by lots of cool water to make sure no smells or chemical waste linger round the basin.

Used razors must be placed in a sharps bin, which is then collected by a specialist refuse company. Waste also includes hair clippings, used cotton wool pads, disposable gowns and tissues. Make sure you dispose of these in line with COSHH and salon policy.

Preparing facial hair and skin for shaving services (I)

Preparing the client for shaving

Shaving is the art of removing facial hair entirely or creating shapes in it using either a manual razor or an electric razor. The overall purpose of shaving is to remove the unwanted hair from the client's face, leaving it in a desired style such as a beard or moustache, whilst also outlining neck hair and sideburns. The client needs to be consulted prior to the shave to find out what style they want.

Assessing the client's skin

Before carrying out a shaving service, the barber will assess the suitability of the client's skin, taking into consideration:

- existing skin conditions
- any cuts or abrasions
- facial skin features such as moles, scars or abnormalities of the surface of the skin
- facial piercings
- existing facial hair and its growth pattern
- shape and length of sideburns
- whether or not hot towels will be needed to soften the beard area prior to the shave.

A client prepared for a shaving service

Resources for shaving

You will need to prepare a trolley for the barber with the following items:

- client record card
- clean towels (of the appropriate colours)
- apron
- gloves
- barrier cream
- cotton wool pads
- tissues
- plastic bowl
- pre-packed towels ready for steaming
- powder
- shaving foam/cream/gel/oils
- disposable styptic pencil
- shaving brushes
- barbicide jar
- cooling products
- aftershave
- moisturiser
- disposable razors.

>> Get up and go!

With a colleague, practise setting up a trolley for a shaving service. Check each other's trolleys for any missing items. Now set up a trolley for each other, but deliberately forget one item. See if you can spot what is missing.

Sharpen up!

A lot of equipment is needed to carry out a professional shaving service. Do you know what each item is used for, for example, do you know why a styptic pencil might be used?

Disposable razors are commonly used for shaving, but some barbers will use a traditional fixed blade razor (also know as a straight razor or 'cut-throat' razor). Fixed blade razors are sometimes not allowed to be used in salons and barber's because they can be dangerous and must be handled with extreme care. Find out if your local council permits their use and what regulations are in place regarding the use of sharps for professional barbering services. Present this information to your colleagues as part of your communication skills.

Preparing facial hair and skin for shaving services (2)

1

Correctly gown the client and carry out your consultation

2

Place a hot towel around your client's face

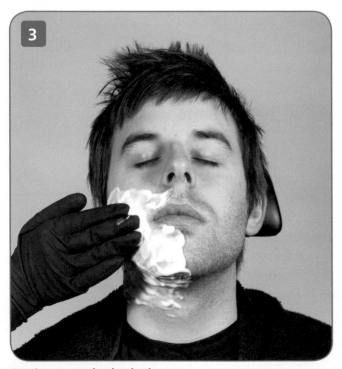

3

Begin to apply the lather

4

When your client is fully lathered the shave can begin

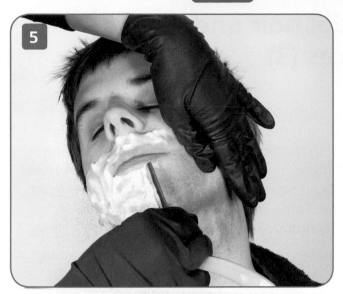

The barber will now carry out the shave

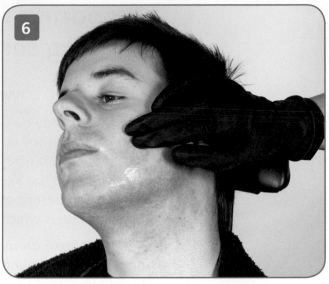

When the shave is complete, apply moisturisers to soothe and cool the skin

The finished look

✂ Sharpen up!

If you are male, you could try to interest clients in shaving services by wearing a moustache or beard at the salon/barber's. If you are female, you could enlist the help of a male colleague and help them try out different facial hair styles. Try this for a few weeks and take notice of comments clients make. Show them some of the different styles available and offer to assist them in trying a new look.

Preparing facial hair and skin for shaving services (3)

Using hot towels

Hot towels may be used during the shaving service to open up the pores on the face and soften the facial hair. This can make shaving easier for the barber and more comfortable for the client. A hot towel also cleanses the skin and can be relaxing for the client. Towels must be cleaned before each use. Some salons and barbers will use pre-packed towels which simply require steaming.

You must take great care when using hot towels as they can be hot enough to burn when freshly steamed. It is a good idea to practise handling a cold towel first to get your technique right before moving on to a hot towel. Wring out the towel until it is nearly dry, using a dry towel to help prevent burning yourself. Fold the towel to retain the heat and test its temperature on the back of the client's hand. Wrap the towel carefully around the client's face, leaving a space for his nose so he can breathe. Repeat this process two or three times and as you take the last towel off, begin immediately to lather the client's face.

A hot towel ready for the client

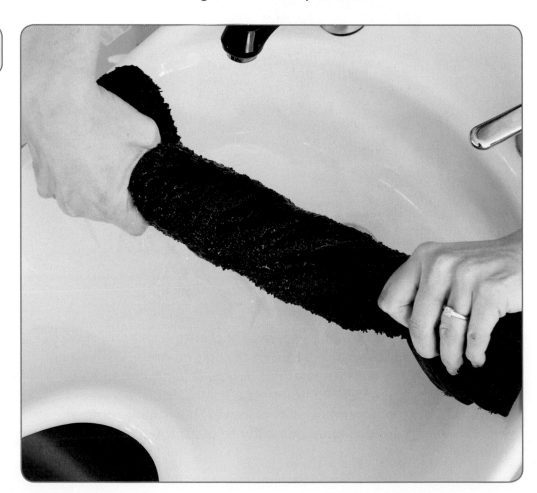

Lathering the client

Protect the client's eyes with cotton wool pads and ensure their neckline is protected with towels and tissues. Start applying lather under the chin, working in small circular movements moving upwards towards the left side of the face and then over to the right. Spread the bristles of the shaving brush out as you lather the top lip, being careful not to push the bristles inside the client's nose.

Work quickly and efficiently when lathering, making sure you cover only those parts of the face that are to be shaved. Lather must be applied evenly – not too thick or too thin. The purpose of lathering is to soften the hair and make the shave more comfortable for the client. If the hair is especially dense or strong, you may need to massage it into the facial hair with your hands, which will soften the hair further.

A hot towel will open the pores and soften the facial hair

Lather being applied to the client

Preparing facial hair and skin for shaving services (4)

Facial massage movements

You have learned about three massage movements that are carried out during shampooing and conditioning hair (look back at pages 96–97 to remind yourself):

- effleurage
- rotary
- petrissage.

You can use effleurage and petrissage movements on the face during shaving services. The light, slow, stroking movement of effleurage will help distribute the lather, whilst the circular movement of petrissage will help soften the cuticles of the hair shafts.

Facial massage can help distribute the lather and soften the hair

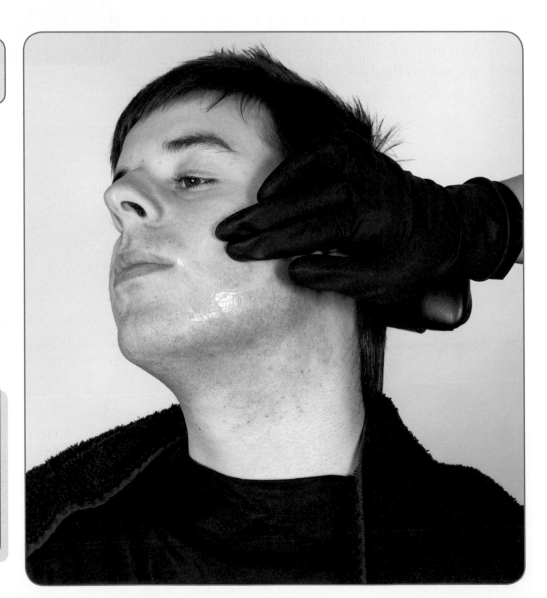

» Get up and go!

Practise using facial massage movements on a colleague and ask for feedback regarding the pressure and timeliness of the massage.

Assisting further with the shave

After completing the application of the lather, you should inform the barber who will then start the shave. Be on hand during the shave as you may be needed to supply additional products or materials, or to apply more lather if it begins to dry out.

When the barber has finished the shave, you will need to apply hot or cold towels as required. Your client may have opted for hot towels, which can be relaxing and calming or, alternatively, they may enjoy the invigorating effects of a cold towel to give them a fresh, lively feeling. Leave the skin free from all products and excessive moisture by towel blotting. You can now analyse the skin with the barber to determine whether it is suitable to apply further products or give a face massage, checking with your client if they would like this. Shaving balms, which cool and moisturise the skin, and aftershaves, which stimulate the skin, are popular choices following a shave.

Should there be any problems during the service, report them immediately to the barber, who will advise you what to do. Common problems include bleeding after the shave, which can be controlled by applying pressure to the site of the blood with cotton wool. Make sure you are wearing gloves whilst doing this. A disposable styptic pencil or a little powder can also help with the bleeding.

Aftercare

Aftercare is an important part of the shaving service and could mean the difference between the client choosing to return or not. Give your client advice on when next to return for a shaving service and also when and how to use suitable exfoliating products. These will help remove dead skin cells from the surface layer of the skin and prevent hairs from growing into the skin.

Get ahead

Practise using a stencil, and design different styles into your client's hair. Use a training head in the early stages of your development, then progress to a client who you have consulted with, to create your own signature styles. Take photographs of your styles and build up a style book for use in the salon.

? Memory jogger

List three resources needed for shaving.

What are the steps taken before the blade touches the client's skin?

Why are hot towels used?

Would preparation of an open razor include sterilising or lubricating?

›› Get up and go!

Using paper and pencil, create some facial hair styles of your own. Think about styles that will suit different types of people. Now attempt to recreate your styles on a training head, progressing to a client. Take photographs of the results and build up a style book for use in your salon or barber's.

Index

BTEC
Entry 3/Level 1

edexcel
advancing learning, changing lives

BUSINESS ADMINISTRATION
ENTRY LEVEL 3/1

Conrad Tetley

Student Book

Published by Pearson Education Limited, a company incorporated in England and Wales, having its registered office at Edinburgh Gate, Harlow, Essex, CM20 2JE. Registered company number: 872828

www.pearsonschoolsandfecolleges.co.uk

Edexcel is a registered trademark of Edexcel Limited

Text © Pearson Education Limited 2010

First published 2010

13 12 11 10
10 9 8 7 6 5 4 3 2 1

British Library Cataloguing in Publication Data
A catalogue record for this book is available from the British Library

ISBN 978 1 846 90921 4

Edited by Liz Cartmell and Janine de Smet
Designed by Pearson Education Limited
Typeset by Tek-Art
Cover design by Pearson Education Limited
Cover photo/illustration © Getty Images/Digital Vision Thomas Barwick
Back cover photos © Shutterstock/Yuri Arcurs and Masterfile/George Remington
Printed in the UK by Scotprint

Disclaimer

This material has been published on behalf of Edexcel and offers high-quality support for the delivery of Edexcel qualifications.

This does not mean that the material is essential to achieve any Edexcel qualification, nor does it mean that it is the only suitable material available to support any Edexcel qualification. Edexcel material will not be used verbatim in setting any Edexcel examination or assessment. Any resource lists produced by Edexcel shall include this and other appropriate resources.

Copies of official specifications for all Edexcel qualifications may be found on the Edexcel website: www.edexcel.com

Contents

About your BTEC E3/L1 Business Administration Student Book v

About the author

Conrad Tetley has ten years teaching experience working at a large specialist business and enterprise college in Bradford. During that time he has taught a range of academic and vocational courses from BTEC Entry Level to Level 3. Conrad is a Member of the Chartered Institute of Assessors and an accredited Teacher Learning Academy Verifier. He has been involved in developing qualifications at national and regional levels for a number of years and has recently contributed to Edexcel's Level 2 Higher Business, Administration and Finance Diploma textbook.

Credits

The authors and publisher would like to thank the following individuals and organisations for permission to reproduce photographs:

Getty Images/Iconica p. **1**; Shutterstock/Yegorius p. **2**; iStockPhoto/Chris Schmidt p. **7**; iStockPhoto/Roland Frommknecht p. **8**; iStockPhoto/Marcus Clackson p. **13**; Shutterstock/Monkey Business Images p. **17**; Shutterstock/Pavol Kmeto p. **20**; Photolibrary/Novastock p. **23**; Alamy Images/fStop p. **24**; Shutterstock/Robert Milek p. **24**; Shutterstock/Theodore Scott p. **24**; Shutterstock/oksana2010 p. **24**; Shutterstock/blueking p. **25**; Shutterstock/MAFord p. **25**; Pearson Education Ltd/Devon Olugbenga Shaw p. **27**; Shutterstock/dani3315 p. **28**; Shutterstock/Eray Haciosmanoglu p. **28**; Getty Images/Stockdisc p. **31**; Alamy Images/Edwin Remsberg p. **32**; Pearson Education Ltd/Lord & Leverett p. **38**; Photolibrary/Flirt Collection p. **45**; Alamy Images/Moodboard p. **44**; Masterfile/George Remington p. **57**; Shutterstock/Andrey Arkusha p. **58**; Getty Images/Taxi p. **60**; Alamy Images/Michael Pearcy p. **67**; Shutterstock/James Peragine p. **68**; Shutterstock/2happy p. **79**; Shutterstock/Peter Elvidge p. **80**; Shutterstock/Elena Elisseeva p. **91**; Getty Images/Iconica p. **92**; Shutterstock/Yuri Arcurs p. **101**; Shutterstock/Ioana Drutu p. **102**; Masterfile p. **113**; Shutterstock / Marcel Mooij p. **114**; Shutterstock/StockLite p. **116**; Shutterstock/StockLite p. **121**; Shutterstock/3divan p. **129**; Rex Features/Geoffrey Robinson p. **131**; Shutterstock/ifong p. **134**; Shutterstock/macigoven p. **134**; Shutterstock/Stephen Van Horn p. **134**; Shutterstock/Mickolay Khoroshkov p. **135**; Shutterstock/Haywire Media p.**135**; Shutterstock/Paul Paladin p.**141**

Every effort has been made to contact copyright holders of material reproduced in this book. Any omissions will be rectified in subsequent printings if notice is given to the publishers.

About your BTEC Entry 3/Level 1 Business Administration

Choosing to study for a BTEC Entry 3 or Level 1 Business Administration qualification is a great decision to make for lots of reasons. Many businesses need administrators in order to run smoothly. Behind every successful company there are many administrators, helping to make the organisation focused and effective. As businesses grow they need more skilled administrators who have good communication skills and are well organised. This qualification will help you to develop these skills.

Your BTEC Entry 3/Level 1 Business Administration is a **vocational** or **work-related** qualification. It will give you the chance to gain knowledge, understanding and skills that are important in the subject or area of work you have chosen.

What will you be doing?

This book covers enough units for you to gain any of the following qualifications:

- BTEC Entry 3/Level 1 **Award** in Business Administration

- BTEC Level 1 **Certificate** in Business Administration

In order to complete a BTEC Level 1 **Diploma** in Business Administration you will need to complete another unit from the specification. Our BTEC Entry 3/Level 1 Business Administration Teaching Book and Resource Disk contains Unit 6 in addition to the units covered in this Student Book.

If you are unsure your tutor will let you know what level of qualification you are aiming for.

How to use this book

This book is designed to help you through your BTEC Entry 3/Level 1 Business Administration course. It is divided into 13 units to match the units in the specification. Each unit is broken down into smaller topics.

This book contains many features that will help you get the most from your course.

Introduction

Each chapter starts with a page that gives you a snapshot of what you will be learning from that unit.

MANAGING YOUR HEALTH AT WORK

UNIT 2

When you enter the world of work, you will soon discover that what you do at work and how you complete it can affect your life outside work. Therefore, it is really important to look after yourself so that your body can fight everyday illnesses such as cold, flu, backaches and stress.

Through this unit you will investigate why staying healthy is important and learn how to keep well so that you can stay fit and healthy while working.

In this unit you will:

• Know why it is important to be healthy at work

• Know how to keep healthy at work

What do you think is meant by the term 'work-related illness'?

Activities

You will find activities throughout the book. These will help you understand the information in the unit and give you a chance to try things for yourself.

Activity: Marketing tools

In pairs, create one piece of marketing information, for example, a leaflet, poster or maybe a website to advertise Waite's Weights to both adults and children.

Put some thought into whether the same marketing material will be suitable for both sets of people.

Case studies

Case studies show you how what you are learning about applies in the real world of work.

Case study:
Waite's Weights

Waite's Weights is a gym and health spa business owned and managed by Peter Waite. It is located in Bradford. Throughout the last ten years, Waite's Weights has grown steadily and now employs 25 staff including gym instructors, pool attendants and administrators on a full- or part-time basis.

Before opening his gym, Peter Waite realised that the market for gym and spa memberships was going to grow. The media had repeatedly highlighted that, as a nation, children were taking less exercise. Adults were working longer hours and this was stopping them from taking regular exercise.

So, when the time came to raise funds from banks to open his business, Peter decided to use the examples of school children and working adults as major marketing factors in his business plan.

As time would tell, this was a very good idea which has allowed Waite's Weights to expand. In order to get more customers, Peter Waite advertised a number of gym packages aimed at school children and working adults.

Functional skills

Useful pointers showing you where you can improve your skills in English, Mathematics and ICT.

Functional skills

This activity will help you develop your **English** speaking and listening skills.

Key terms

The words you need to understand are easy to spot, and their meanings are clearly explained.

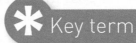

Key term

Sport
An activity that involves physical exertion and competition.

Remember!

Look out for these boxes. They point out really important information.

Remember

When receiving instructions, try the technique below to make sure you understand what you're being asked to do.

1. Listen to the instructions.
2. If you are uncertain of anything, ask.
3. Repeat the instructions back to the person who gave them.
4. Ask them to **confirm** your understanding by asking 'Is there anything else?'

Check

You'll find a reminder of key information at the end of each topic.

 Check

*   It is important to manage your health at work so that you remain fit and able to do your duties.
*   Keeping fit will also help with your enjoyment of work.

Assessment page

This page will help you check what you have done so far and give you tips for getting the best mark you can for each task.

Assessment overview

This table shows you what assessment criteria you need to meet to pass the unit and on which pages you will find activities and information to help you prepare for your assignments.

Edexcel's assignment tips

At the end of each chapter, you'll find hints and tips that will help you get the best mark you can.

Your book is just part of the exciting resources from Edexcel to help you succeed in your BTEC course. Visit www.edexcel.com/BTEC or www.pearsonfe.co.uk/BTEC2010 for more details.

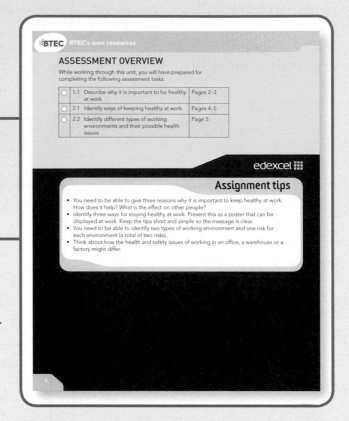

BTEC BTEC's own resources

ASSESSMENT OVERVIEW

While working through this unit, you will have prepared for completing the following assessment tasks:

○	1.1 Describe why it is important to be healthy at work	Pages 2–3
○	2.1 Identify ways of keeping healthy at work	Pages 4–5
○	2.2 Identify different types of working environments and their possible health issues	Page 5

edexcel

Assignment tips

- You need to be able to give three reasons why it is important to keep healthy at work. How does it help? What is the effect on other people?
- Identify three ways for staying healthy at work. Present this as a poster that can be displayed at work. Keep the tips short and simple so the message is clear.
- You need to be able to identify two types of working environment and one risk for each environment (a total of two risks).
- Think about how the health and safety issues of working in an office, a warehouse or a factory might differ.

MANAGING YOUR HEALTH AT WORK

When you enter the world of work, you will soon discover that what you do at work and how you complete it can affect your life outside work. Therefore, it is really important to look after yourself so that your body can fight everyday illnesses such as cold, flu, backaches and stress.

Through this unit you will investigate why staying healthy is important and learn how to keep well so that you can stay fit and healthy while working.

In this unit you will:

- Know why it is important to be healthy at work

- Know how to keep healthy at work

What do you think is meant by the term 'work-related illness'?

L01 The importance of being healthy at work

While at work it is important to take your health seriously so that you stay healthy and avoid any problems with illness. This will also help to make sure that the work you produce is free from mistakes which you might make if you felt unwell.

Also, if you are free from illness and managing to keep on top of your work, it normally leads to more enjoyment at work. Enjoying work is an important factor in how well you do your job. If you are successful you may get recognised for this and may be offered promotion or possibly a wage rise. For most people this would increase their levels of self-confidence and self-esteem.

Effects of unemployment

Sometimes people have to face spells of unemployment in their working lives. However, it is often the approach a person takes after they have been made unemployed which shows how successful they will be in the future.

Unemployment not only means someone earns less or no money, it can also be costly in other ways, including affecting their physical and mental health. If people are unemployed for long periods of time, confidence and self-esteem can be affected. This can make someone fearful of applying to organisations for work.

 Key term

Promotion
When your employer rewards you by giving you a more important job. It often means earning more money.

 Case study:
Waite's Weights

Waite's Weights is a gym and health spa business owned and managed by Peter Waite. It is located in Bradford. Throughout the last ten years, Waite's Weights has grown steadily and now employs 25 staff including gym instructors, pool attendants and administrators on a full- or part-time basis.

Before opening his gym, Peter Waite realised that the market for gym and spa memberships was going to grow. The media had repeatedly highlighted that, as a nation, children were taking less exercise. Adults were working longer hours and this was stopping them from taking regular exercise.

So, when the time came to raise funds from banks to open his business, Peter decided to use the examples of school children and working adults as major marketing factors in his business plan.

As time would tell, this was a very good idea which has allowed Waite's Weights to expand. In order to get more customers, Peter Waite advertised a number of gym packages aimed at school children and working adults.

Activity: Group discussion

Why do you think Peter Waite thought it was important for school children and working adults to be healthy at school and work?

Which other target groups might Peter Waite want to attract in the future?

Activity: Marketing tools

In pairs, create one piece of marketing information, for example, a leaflet, poster or maybe a website to advertise Waite's Weights to both adults and children.

Put some thought into whether the same marketing material will be suitable for both sets of people.

Check

- It is important to manage your health at work so that you remain fit and able to do your duties.

- Keeping fit will also help with your enjoyment of work.

L02 How to keep healthy at work

Below are some of the most common **health issues** found in the workplace.

Health issue	How it is caused
Backache	Poor posture or unsuitable chair
Aching wrists and fingers	Poor wrist and hand positioning when typing
Weight gain	Eating too much and not exercising enough
Eye strain	Working in poorly lit conditions
Viruses, e.g. cold/sore throat	Sometimes caused by sharing equipment, e.g. telephones
Aching legs	Caused by poor seating position

As an employee of a business you should think about how you can stay healthy for work. After all, you are not much use to an employer if you keep having time off because you are sick. It is therefore important to know a few simple ways in which you can try to keep yourself healthy. Below are a few ideas that may help:

✳ Key terms

Health issue
A potential problem in the workplace that may affect a person's health.

Poor posture
Positioning of the body which could cause long-term damage while working. Always try to adopt the correct posture.

Make sure the temperature of your working environment is comfortable

Avoid poor posture by using a suitable chair

Manage your workload to avoid stressful situations

Make sure you get enough sleep

Ideas for keeping healthy

Avoid arm/wrist strain by using a wrist support

Eat a healthy diet in and out of work

When lifting heavy objects use lifting equipment

Exercise outside work to stay fit

Take regular breaks to avoid wrist/eye strain

When dealing with hazardous materials wear protective clothing

Below are some health factors to consider when working in different environments.

Health factor	Type of environment	Problems caused by health factor at work
Sickness	Hospital	Could pass on virus to patients which could be dangerous
Dizziness	Driving environment	Could cause an accident injuring self and others
Epilepsy	Nightclub	Flashing lights could potentially cause an epileptic seizure
Back strain	Warehouse	Lifting could cause back problems to get worse which may result in a long-term injury
Serious viral throat infection	Call centre/office	Could pass on illness through use of shared equipment, e.g. telephones

 Case study:
Waite's Weights services

Waite's Weights offers the following gym and spa services:

- Health spa (including swimming pool, sauna, steam room)
- Beauty services (including nails, facials, etc.)
- Gym (including rowing machines, spinning bikes, weight machines, weights).

Activity: Advertising Waite's Weights

Look at the table on page 4 which explores health issues at work and at the table above which lists five factors that should be considered when working in different environments.

Create one brochure for Waite's Weights which advertises how the business could help people to avoid these problems. Your brochure needs to tie together how the services offered by Waite's Weights can help people to avoid suffering from health issues such as these.

When you have completed your brochure, present your ideas to the rest of your group.

Check

- Make sure you know how to adapt your environment so that you stay healthy at work
- Be aware of how different working environments present a range of potentially different health issues.

ASSESSMENT OVERVIEW

While working through this unit, you will have prepared for completing the following assessment tasks:

○	1.1 Describe why it is important to be healthy at work	Pages 2–3
○	2.1 Identify ways of keeping healthy at work	Pages 4–5
○	2.2 Identify different types of working environments and their possible health issues	Page 5

Assignment tips

- You need to be able to give three reasons why it is important to keep healthy at work. How does it help? What is the effect on other people?

- Identify three ways for staying healthy at work. Present this as a poster that can be displayed at work. Keep the tips short and simple so the message is clear.

- You need to be able to identify two types of working environment and one risk for each environment (a total of two risks).

- Think about how the health and safety issues of working in an office, a warehouse or a factory might differ.

WORKING IN BUSINESS & ADMINISTRATION | UNIT 5

The term administration covers a very broad area. If on completion of this course you obtain a job or go on to study this aspect of business in more detail, you may specialise in one particular area. Within administration there are many exciting and varied jobs such as working in a marketing department or maybe in IT support. However, all of these jobs will require a core set of skills which you will learn about in this unit.

This unit will give you an introduction to what it's like working in this important area.

In this unit you will:

- Know what activities are routinely undertaken by administrators
- Be able to follow instructions to carry out administrative tasks

Why do you think a big business needs administrators?

LO1 The role of an administrator

In business, administration is a range of tasks that need to be completed for the organisation to work effectively. This means that administrators perform an important function, helping managers, sales people, etc. to focus on making the organisation successful.

📁 Case study:
Malek's Motors

Malek's Motors is a car dealership in Bristol, run by Azeem Malek. The business employs two sales people, Carlos and Sharon, and Azeem deals with the business management.

Customers looking for cars make appointments with Malek's Motors to organise test drives. In order to book a test drive, the customer must show their driving licence and proof of identity to one of the sales staff. The business needs to keep a copy of these documents to cover their customers on their insurance.

Malek's Motors is getting more and more customers. Azeem is very pleased – this means more money! However, he, Carlos and Sharon are finding it difficult to keep track of the different test drive bookings, meetings and documents that they have to deal with each day.

Activity: Group discussion

You think Azeem should employ an administrator. As a group, identify the different tasks you think an administrator would do if they worked at Malek's Motors.

How would this help Azeem to make his business more successful?

How do administrators help a business?

A business will have a number of different **functional areas**. These may include some of the following:

Business function	Purpose
Sales	Selling products or services to customers. The sales department is important because it brings money into the business.
Marketing	The marketing department will advertise the business's products or services. They often work very closely with the sales department.
Finance	The finance department will manage the business's money. It will make sure that the customers pay for the products or services they receive. It will also make sure that the business pays any money it owes.
Production	Not all businesses have a production department. Businesses that make and sell products will probably have one. This department will make the products the business sells.

All the departments in a business will have their own administrative tasks. These may involve keeping copies of financial documents, sending out letters, sending invoices to customers, and many more tasks.

As a business becomes more successful, so the amount of administration each department needs to keep on top of grows. One or more administrators can help the business department to focus on their individual functions by completing the department's administrative tasks.

Key term

Functional areas
Different parts or departments of a business that focus on a limited range of important tasks.

Activity: Group discussion

Working in small groups, choose one business function and identify three different administrative tasks that the function might need help with.

How could this help a business be more effective?

Check

- Administrators help businesses to run smoothly by providing support to business functions.

- Businesses have a range of different functions. They may share an administrator between different functional areas, or each functional area may have its own administrator.

LO1
LO2
Administrative tasks

Below and opposite are some of the tasks that administrators commonly perform.

Task	How this helps the organisation	Skills needed
Answering the telephone	The administrator is the first point of contact for customers or suppliers. The administrator can direct callers to the people within the organisation that they need to talk to.	Good verbal communication
Filing and retrieving documents	Organisations need to keep a lot of information. This information may be about customers, suppliers, products, etc. and may need to be accessed at any time. The administrator will use good filing techniques to make it easy to access this information.	Good organisational skills The administrator may also need good IT skills as the filing may be electronic as well as paper-based
Producing documents using IT	Different types of documents need to be produced quickly and effectively. The administrator may also use tools such as mail merge to send the same information to many different people or organisations.	Good IT skills

Activity: How am I doing?

Look at the skills administrators need. How do you think you rate for each skill?

Give yourself a score for each from 1 to 5, with 1 being an area for improvement and 5 being excellent.

Key term

Verbal communication
Talking to someone – or a group of people – to give them information.

Task	How this helps the organisation	Skills needed
Photocopying and collating documents	A manager may need many copies of the same document to hand out at a presentation, for example. The administrator would save the manager time by photocopying and collating the documents.	Good IT skills
Collecting, sorting and distributing mail	A big organisation will receive a lot of mail each day. The administrator will make sure the mail gets to the right people.	Good organisational skills Good communication skills – it's important to know who everyone is
Receiving visitors	Organisations have a lot of different visitors, from customers to suppliers. The administrator will help organise meetings and will make sure the visitors see the right people.	Good verbal communication skills Professional behaviour

Activity: Routine tasks

Now look at the tasks you identified for an administrator working for Malek's Motors (page 8). Can you identify any other tasks that an administrator would need to perform?

What skills do you think an administrator working for Malek's Motors would need? Working in pairs, use the tables to suggest the skills the administrator would need.

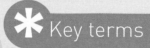

Key terms

Collate
To mix copies of different documents together to give information in a specific order.

Professional behaviour
Acting in a business-like manner. When receiving visitors, answering the phone, etc., you are the public face of your employer. First impressions of an organisation are as important as first impressions of a person.

Check

- Administrators need good IT skills, strong verbal communication skills and have to be well organised.

- Administration involves a range of different tasks.

L01 Understanding and following instructions

As an administrator you need to be able to follow instructions accurately (i.e. without mistakes). This is because you will often be completing a task for someone else – on their behalf – and they may need the task completed in a specific way.

For example, when receiving a visitor for a meeting you might be given specific instructions. These could include:

- Contacting the other meeting attendees so they are aware that the visitor has arrived
- Getting the visitor to sign the visitors' book
- Taking the visitor to the meeting room
- Arranging for a drink for the visitor.

! Remember

When receiving instructions, try the technique below to make sure you understand what you're being asked to do.

1. Listen to the instructions.

2. If you are uncertain of anything, ask.

3. Repeat the instructions back to the person who gave them.

4. Ask them to confirm your understanding by asking 'Is there anything else?'

◎ Activity: Instruction ladder

1. One person should think of some instructions for a skill they use either in the workplace or in a hobby. This shouldn't be anything too complicated, so it may only be part of a task.

2. They explain the steps that need to be completed to a partner who uses the listening technique above to check their understanding.

3. The partner then gives the instructions to the next person, and so on, until everyone in the class has been given the instructions.

Case study:
Malek's Motors

Malek's Motors has employed you as an administrator. Azeem is presenting a range of cars to a local business that is looking into leasing a fleet of cars.

This is an important presentation because the deal would earn Malek's Motors a lot of money. Azeem needs to look professional and well organised in order to give the business confidence in him.

Azeem has produced a PowerPoint presentation and a spreadsheet. The presentation contains photos and basic information about the cars. The spreadsheet includes information about how much each type of car would cost the business.

Activity: Paired discussion

Why do you think it would be important for you to follow Azeem's instructions carefully?

What should you do if you are uncertain of what Azeem is asking you to do?

Check

- Always make a note of the important information in any instructions you receive.
- Check you understand the instructions and ask questions if you need to. This will help you do a better job.

L01 Carrying out a task

Case study:
Malek's Motors

Malek's Motors has a new customer. Azeem's presentation to the business interested in a fleet of cars went very well. They have asked for a **formal quote**. Azeem has written a letter to the manager of the business, Derek Smith.

He has asked you to type the letter and check it for spelling errors. The letter is on the opposite page. He would like it to be printed and addressed to Derek's business: Smith's Taxis, The Square, Cranbrook Road, Bristol.

Azeem would like a copy of the letter to be filed in case he needs to check the quote at a later date.

Activity: Individual activity

On a piece of paper, produce a **flow chart** to show the steps you need to go through in order to complete this activity.

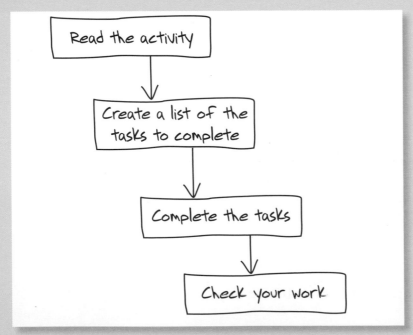

Functional skills

By presenting information, you will be demonstrating your **English** speaking skills.

Your flow chart may need more or fewer steps than the example shown here.

14

Activity: You are the administrator

Follow Azeem Malek's instructions in the case study on the opposite page. Check your work against your flow chart to make sure you complete all the steps you need to.

Dear Derek,

Following on from our meeting last Tuesday, I am pleased to enclose a quote for the lease of eight people carriers from Malek's Motors. These vehicles will be brand new, and as we discussed, we will service them at 12 months or 12,000 miles, whichever is sooner.

The lease of the eight vehicles for a period of 36 months will cost £23,000 per annum. Over the three-year period, this will be £69,000 including VAT at 17.5%.

If you would like any further details, please don't hesitate to get in touch. I look forward to working with you.

Yours sincerely,

Azeem Malik

Now check your work to make sure it's accurate and correct.

Key terms

Formal quote
This is when a business puts together a set of costs for a customer. For example, if you wanted to buy a computer, you might ask for a quote for a particular model. This would tell you how much you would pay if you decided to buy the computer.

Flow chart
A list of tasks or stages that need to be completed, linked together in a specific order. Some tasks will need to be completed before others can be started. For example, you would need to type the letter in word-processing software before spell checking it.

Functional skills

This activity will help you to practise your **ICT** skills.

Check

- Work out what you need to do to complete a task.
- Complete the task.
- Check that you have done everything you have been asked to.

ASSESSMENT OVERVIEW

While working through this unit, you will have prepared for completing the following assessment tasks:

○	1.1	Identify routine administrative tasks	Pages 8–11
○	2.1	Check understanding of instructions and ask for clarification where necessary	Pages 12–13
○	2.2	Follow instructions to complete a limited range of administrative tasks accurately	Pages 14–15

Assignment tips

- Ask someone who works in an administrative role to tell you about their day-to-day work.

- From what they tell you, you should be able to identify four routine office tasks.

- When listening to instructions remember to repeat the tasks back to the person.

- Remember, never be afraid to ask if you are not clear what you are being asked to do.

WORKING IN BUSINESS & ADMINISTRATION

When working in business administration it is important to be flexible and comfortable with learning new skills. As an administrator, you may be expected at times to complete several jobs at once. It is therefore very important to be able to adapt to learning new and quicker ways of completing tasks.

While you are working you will also be expected to present yourself and the business you work for in a positive manner. One way of doing this is to complete your work to deadline and to handle sensitive information professionally.

In this unit you will:

- Understand the role of an administrator within an office
- Be able to carry out routine administrative tasks
- Be able to present yourself positively
- Be able to organise your work effectively
- Know the importance of confidentiality of information

What tasks do you think an administrator will do as part of their job?

L01 Understand the role of an administrator

Administrators play a very important role in the smooth running of an organisation. They are responsible for many different tasks which, if not completed successfully, could cause major problems for a business.

Different activities carried out by administrators are shown in the table below.

Task	Why it is carried out	What could happen if task is incorrectly completed
Producing documents using IT	For example, writing letters to tell customers, suppliers or other organisations about something that is happening that may affect them.	A problem may occur such as a customer receiving an order late. This may affect the customer's business, for example if they will not have products to sell as a result.
Checking, collating and providing information	Businesses receive a lot of information each day. This could include post, invoices and catalogues. An administrator will collect mail and make sure it gets to the right person, file important documents, and obtain information when it is needed.	Important information and notices might not get through to the correct person. This could result in late deliveries, or late payments of invoices, or lost orders. This could cost the business money.
Coordinating arrangements for meetings	A business meeting may involve several people from different organisations. For example, a meeting could be between a sales representative, a marketing executive and a supplier. The meeting could be held at the supplier's office. An administrator would send information to the meeting attendees beforehand, book a meeting room, make sure the meeting was in everyone's calendar and arrange any necessary travel.	If all delegates do not have the correct information in advance of the meeting, including travel details, it might not happen. This can result in the supplier having a poor impression of the business, and possibly taking their trade elsewhere.
Receiving visitors	Companies often have a member of staff working on reception as it presents a professional image to customers or visitors. It also makes sure that people are directed to where they need to go so security is improved.	If a receptionist is rude to a visitor or customer this will give them a bad impression of the company which could result in them going elsewhere. Also, if visitors are not signed in properly, there is no accurate record of who is in the building in the event of a fire.

Task	Why it is carried out	What could happen if task is incorrectly completed
Answering the telephone and making phone calls	Companies use the telephone to communicate with each other as it is quick and effective. Often callers like to talk to someone as it gives them confidence that their request will be carried out. Also, it is seen by some businesses as good customer service to encourage person-to-person communication.	If an employee cannot answer the caller's query, or does not know who to transfer the person to, this will give an unprofessional image of the business and the caller may decide to go elsewhere in the future. Also, if the person who answers the call is not polite, customers may be put off dealing with the business.
Preparing outgoing mail	To make sure that mail is sent to the right place it is important that it is prepared correctly. In preparing mail, the sender must check that the mail is securely packaged, addressed and the correct amount of postal fees paid. Many businesses these days rely on the Internet to sell by mail order only. These businesses will send out a lot of mail, and it is important for their customers that products are delivered effectively. Also, other businesses often rely on the efficient delivery of mail so they can meet the needs of their customers.	If an employee accidentally uses the wrong address or doesn't pay the right postage the customer may not receive their mail. This will annoy customers. If this situation happens often, customers will lose trust in the business and go elsewhere. The business will also develop a reputation for bad customer service.

Activity: Administrator – job description

Imagine you work in the human resources department of a business. You have been asked to write a job description for the new position of sales administrator.

Use the tasks listed in the table to write a description of what you think the job would involve. Then try to identify the skills a sales administrator might need.

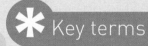

Key terms

Invoice
A document sent to customers requesting payment for the supply of goods or services.

Delegate
Someone attending a meeting. This person may represent another business, and so will want to give a positive impression of their organisation.

Check

- Administrators need to be well organised, especially if they are filing important documents that will be needed at a later date.

- It is important for an administrator to know a lot of different people within the organisation to make sure visitors, telephone calls and mail go to the right people.

L01 Achieving team goals

Case study:

Sinfield's Supplies

Sinfield's Supplies sells catering supplies to hotels, cafés and restaurants. The business is run by Jack Sinfield and employs four staff. They are his two sons, Ryan and Keith, who look after orders and sending goods, Alfie who is the company accountant and Lucy who takes care of all administration tasks within the business.

Recently, Jack has noticed that the business is receiving more complaints from customers than ever before. Few customers are receiving orders on time. He decides to look into the reasons why.

After a short time it becomes clear to Jack that a number of his staff are either:

- Starting work late in the morning

- Leaving early before the end of the working day or

- Taking longer lunch breaks than they are meant to.

In the light of these problems Jack calls a staff meeting to discuss the matter. At the meeting Jack starts by saying that his team of staff is not meeting the goals of the business.

Activity: Group discussion

What do you think Jack meant by 'goals' of the business?

Why do you think Jack told his staff they were not meeting the goals of the business?

How could Jack solve this problem?

Can you think of any other issues that might be causing Sinfield's Supplies problems?

Team communication

It is important in business to work as a team. By doing so, **business goals** can be achieved more easily. However, it is important to understand how to **prioritise** work in order to set team goals. As with any team (a good example being a premier league football team) all members must work towards achieving the same end result. If this is not the case, the team will not succeed.

It is also important when working as a team to communicate very clearly. If this does not happen other team members may not understand instructions and tasks may be carried out incorrectly. Clear communication also covers the use of written, **graphical** and electronic communication methods – again there could be problems if communication is confusing.

Team support

When working as a team member it is very important that you support one another. As with any successful sports team, each member must play their part. In the case of working as an administrator this may involve listening to others to try to resolve a problem or helping another person if they are getting behind with their work.

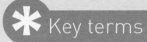
✳ Key terms

Business goal
A business goal is what the business is aiming to do – this might be as simple as make a profit.

Prioritise
Decide on the order for dealing with a number of tasks according to their relative importance.

Graphical communication
The use of visual images such as diagrams, illustrations or designs to convey meaning.

Activity: What does Jack have to do?

Read the Sinfield's Supplies case study to the left again.

Before Jack can take any action he must prioritise which issues are causing him the most problems.

Individually, you need to prioritise Jack's three top issues that he must deal with first. Give reasons for your choices.

Check

- To achieve team goals each group member must be clear what his or her role is and how it helps the team to achieve its overall goal.

- To be an effective team member you must listen and help others.

**HH LEARNING CENTRE
HARROW COLLEGE**

L02 Carry out routine administrative tasks

From the case study on page 20 it is clear that some of Jack's staff are not carrying out routine tasks as they should be. It is important that, when you work as an administrator, you are able to carry out routine tasks effectively so mistakes do not happen.

Activity: What routine tasks do administrators carry out?

On a plain piece of paper, draw and complete the mind map below showing as many routine administration tasks as you can think of. You might also want to include the skills needed to complete the work correctly.

One example has been completed and a second has been started. Try to add at least eight tasks and as many skills needed as you can think of.

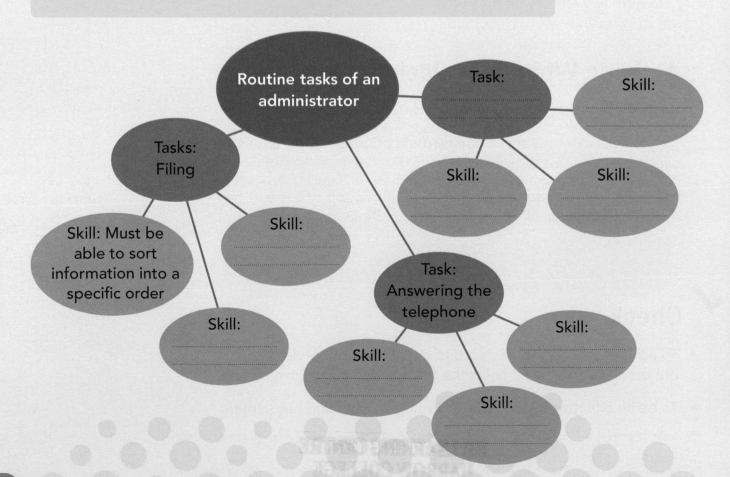

Case study:

Sinfield's Supplies

You have been employed as a general administrator at Sinfield's Supplies. You are expected to provide support where needed. The nature of the job makes it very interesting as you will be able to see how all parts of the business work.

However, as with most jobs, this post does have a number of routine tasks that have to be completed.

Activity: List the tasks

Make a list of the routine administrator tasks you think you will have to carry out.

Why is successful completion of these tasks important to the business?

Which tasks could be completed using ICT?

Following instructions

Administrators need to make sure they follow instructions accurately in order to do their jobs. (For some guidance on following instructions, see *Unit 5 Understanding and following instructions*, page 12.)

Activity: Telephone conversation

In pairs, role play a telephone conversation. One person plays the role of a customer service adviser while the other takes on the role of a customer.

Before you have the conversation the 'customer' needs to write down what they are going to talk about. During the conversation the 'customer service adviser' should write down what they think the customer wants.

At the end of the conversation, compare notes and then swap roles.

Remember

When receiving instructions, try the technique below to make sure you understand what you are being asked to do.

1. Listen to the instructions.

2. If you are unsure of anything, ask.

3. Repeat the instructions back to the person who gave them.

4. Ask them to confirm you have understood correctly by asking 'Is there anything else?'

Check

- Routine administration tasks are the ones that are completed daily or often.

- Following instructions involves listening carefully and asking questions if you are not sure.

L02 Using office equipment and office etiquette

Office equipment

When working in administration you will need to use many different types of office equipment. Some of these are shown in the table below. It is important that you read the manufacturer's instructions before starting to use them. This is very important for three reasons:

- So you do not damage the equipment

- So you do not injure yourself

- So your work is of a high quality.

Piece of office equipment	What is it used for?
Franking machine 	Franking machines are used to automatically stamp letters. Companies use them as it would be too time-consuming to put individual stamps on the hundreds of letters they normally send out every day. Franking machines also have the advantage that the business does not have to go out to buy stamps. Instead it pays the postal company direct.
Printer 	
Shredder 	
Telephone 	

Piece of office equipment	What is it used for?
Fax machine	
Photocopier	

Office etiquette

It is really important to think of others when you are working in an office environment. You will soon become unpopular if you can't be bothered to complete tasks and other people have to do them. However, it is not difficult to keep **colleagues** happy – it is simply a matter of good manners.

So what can be done to make sure that you play your part and the office you work in runs smoothly? Below are some ideas:

- Make sure that you keep equipment clean and hygienic
- Make sure that you refill printers and photocopiers when you have used them and paper levels are low
- Report any problems to your supervisor – this avoids slowing down the workflow and makes sure others do not get into trouble for damaging machinery
- Keep waste to a minimum by spell checking, reusing scrap paper for notes and double-sided copying
- Separate different types of waste so that it can be recycled
- Be helpful to others who you work with.

 **Key terms**

Colleague
Someone from the same organisation as you. They could be more junior than you, someone at the same level as you (sometimes called a 'peer'), or someone at a more senior level than you.

Etiquette
Good manners and thinking about other people. It is good etiquette to refill the photocopier because it would be irritating to have to fill it with paper before you wanted to use it each time.

 ## Activity: Office etiquette

Carry out research into office **etiquette**. Prepare a poster that could be pinned up in an office reminding people how to behave professionally.

Check

- Instructions for using office equipment are there to protect the user from harm, save the company money and make sure that machinery is used properly.
- Office etiquette is important as you will be expected to behave in a professional manner when working as an administrator.

L03 Health and safety and positive presentation

Health and safety

All employers have a **legal duty** to make sure that employees work in an environment that is safe and free from **risks**. The Act of Parliament which covers this is called the Health and Safety at Work Act.

If a business does not work within the Health and Safety at Work Act, then it can be taken to court and sued if it is found to be at fault. Most businesses take health and safety very seriously and employ staff whose job it is to check health and safety in the workplace.

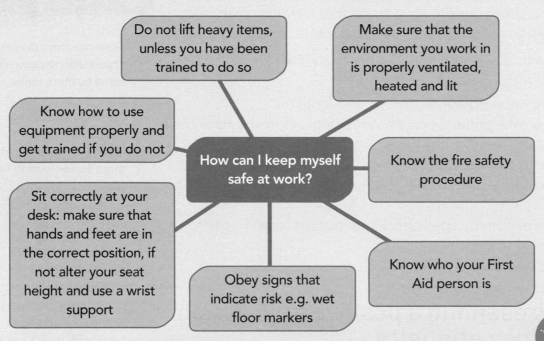

Do not lift heavy items, unless you have been trained to do so

Make sure that the environment you work in is properly ventilated, heated and lit

Know how to use equipment properly and get trained if you do not

How can I keep myself safe at work?

Know the fire safety procedure

Sit correctly at your desk: make sure that hands and feet are in the correct position, if not alter your seat height and use a wrist support

Obey signs that indicate risk e.g. wet floor markers

Know who your First Aid person is

✱ Key terms

Legal duty
Something a business has got to do. If a business does not do their legal duty, they could be acting illegally.

Risk
A risk is the chance that something might happen. For example, if wires are trailing across a corridor there is a risk someone could trip over them.

Acronym
Shortening a long name by using the initial letters of each word. For example, the BBC is an acronym for the British Broadcasting Corporation.

Functional skills

If you use the Internet to research for this activity, you will be practising your ICT skills.

Activity: What do the following mean?

Individually, research the following **acronyms** and create a poster which tells other group members what they mean:

- COSHH
- PPE
- RIDDOR
- HSE.
- PUWER

Present yourself positively

When working in administration it is important to present yourself in a positive manner so that your colleagues know that you are working towards the same goal as them.

There are many ways in which you can present yourself positively including:

- Dressing professionally for work
- Arriving at work and appointments/meetings on time
- Being constructive towards colleagues and not criticising
- Asking questions so you do not make mistakes
- Making sure you do what you have said you are going to do.

Activity: Role play – dealing with a negative worker

For this role play you will need to work in pairs:

- One person needs to be an employee who is very negative towards their work
- The other person plays the role of the employee's manager in an interview situation. During the role play the manager needs to pay close attention to the manner of the employee and to find out why he or she is negative towards work and discuss possible solutions.

As a starting point, both people need to work together and make a list of reasons why the person is negative towards work. They then need to make another list of possible solutions.

The role play may be scripted or non-scripted.

Activity: Presenting a positive impression

As a group make a list of the top ten tips for making a good impression on others. After you have made your list, discuss it to make sure you have put the tips in the correct order. You may need to change the order of your initial list.

 ## Check

- It is important to follow health and safety legislation so that you do not injure yourself or harm others through your actions.

- When working in business, employers like to see employees presenting themselves in a positive manner.

L05 Organise your work effectively and understand confidentiality

Effective organisation

When working in administration it is very important to organise your work and manage your time effectively, otherwise jobs may get forgotten or not completed.

The good news is that modern technology has made this task very easy and is quite affordable. Devices such as Personal Digital Assistants (PDAs) and mobile phones have changed the way workers organise their workload.

Activity: Comparing PDAs and Smartphones

For this task you need to research at least ten PDAs including Smartphones. You are to compare the features of the devices and then work out which ones would be most suitable for the people below:

- A sales representative
- A middle manager in a bank
- A managing director of a large steel production company.

Prioritising tasks through discussion

Often in business you will be in a situation where two important jobs need to be completed at the same time. However, you only have one set of hands!

In this situation you will need to negotiate with your supervisor which job you are going to complete first. In doing this, you will need to give good reasons why you have chosen to prioritise one job over another.

Activity: Making a 'to do' list

Working individually, think about your next week at your centre and at home. Make a list of all the things you have to do. Then put your list in order of priority. It is often surprising how many things you can fit into one week.

The importance of confidentiality of information

When working for a company it is important that information is kept **confidential**. Reasons for this include:

- Personal details cannot be made available to the public
- Company documents will not get into the wrong hands
- To make sure that the business is working within the Data Protection Act. If a company is found not to be **complying** with the law it can face legal action which usually results in large fines.

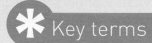

✱ Key terms

Confidential
Information that should not be shared, such as salary details, company strategies, customer contact details, etc.

Comply
To act by the guidelines or rules set out in a law, such as the Data Protection Act. It is a business's legal duty to comply with these laws.

! Remember

When storing and using information:

- Never leave confidential information unattended – lock away paper copies and lock your screen when you leave your computer
- Make sure that if you are using a computer with confidential information that your screen is positioned in such a way to stop other people looking at it
- When giving someone else information, be careful – make sure that you know who you are talking to and the amount of information you can tell them
- Set passwords on sensitive files to help keep them secure
- Come up with a list of questions to ask the person that you are shadowing.

Activity: How long should information be stored on file?

For this task, you need to research the different types of information that might be stored on file by businesses. Think about the kind of details you have had to give when buying something over the Internet.

When you have researched this, find out for how long that information can be legally stored – this is called a 'retention period'.

Present your work to your group.

✓ Check

- It is important to organise your work so that tasks get completed on time. Employees will then know they can rely on you and you will soon become a trusted member of staff.

- It is important to know when to share information and when not to. Letting information get into the wrong hands could be costly to you and your business.

ASSESSMENT OVERVIEW

While working through this unit, you will have prepared for completing the following assessment tasks:

○	1.1 Describe different activities carried out by administrators	Pages 18–19
○	1.2 State how the work of an administrator helps a team achieve its goals	Pages 20–21
○	2.1 Follow instructions to complete routine administrative tasks	Pages 22–23
○	2.2 Use key equipment according to organisational procedures	Pages 24–25
○	3.1 Dress appropriately	Page 27
○	3.2 Adopt a positive manner in dealings with colleagues and/or customers	Page 27
○	4.1 Use simple tools to organise your time	Page 28
○	4.2 Prioritise tasks in discussion with your supervisor or manager	Page 28
○	5.1 State the reasons why it is important to keep some information confidential	Page 29
○	5.2 Give examples of information that should be kept confidential	Page 29

edexcel

Assignment tips

- You need to describe four activities carried out by administrators.

- You also need to state two ways in which administrators help achieve team goals.

- Your tutor will need to observe you completing three administrative tasks. They will also need to observe you using at least two types of key equipment.

- You will need to give three reasons why it is important to keep some information confidential. You will also need to give examples of three different types of confidential information. Try to think about the kind of information that might be stored in different systems, and what this might mean for confidentiality.

- You may be able to combine two assessment tasks in one activity if you pick your tasks carefully.

COMMUNICATING ELECTRONICALLY

All administrators need to be able to communicate effectively – both face to face and electronically. As an administrator you will be expected to deal with problems and queries effectively by yourself.

In today's business world much of the work you deal with will be sent to you electronically, as emails and text messages, etc. You will be expected to deal with these in a similar way.

In this unit you will learn about different electronic communication methods and the most suitable methods to use in certain situations.

In this unit you will:

- Be able to communicate electronically

- Be able to use the Internet securely

When do you think it would be appropriate to use text messages to communicate in business? When might it not be appropriate?

L01 Effective communication

Case study:
Mulkern's Foods

Mulkern's Foods is an organic food production and farming company based in Shrewsbury. The business is owned by Jack Mulkern and employs three staff – Simon, Geoff and Bridget. Simon and Geoff are involved with the production and packaging of the food. Bridget is in charge of dealing with all the administration. Jack is responsible for overall management of the business.

Mulkern's Foods mainly sells its goods direct to specialist shops and upmarket pubs and restaurants. However, the business also runs a small shop from its factory. All the staff help to run this shop, taking turns alongside their main roles.

Even though there has been a recession, and customers have been spending less, the shop has been very successful. However, Jack has noticed that while turnover – money coming into the shop – has increased by 50 per cent over the last two years, his profit has only increased by 11 per cent. This is worrying him.

He has asked all staff to check their work processes to find out where they might be spending more money than they need to. After a month, Jack realises that much of this spending is linked to sending correspondence, including letters and invoices, to customers.

Business communication methods

In business you will be expected to communicate with people who work at different levels in the organisation. This may range from an office junior to a director. It is therefore important to know which electronic communication methods are suitable for employees at different levels within the business.

Opposite is a table which shows the suitability of the four main methods you will be investigating.

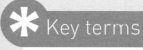

Key terms

Turnover
Money coming into a business from customers. For example, if a customer buys a pie from Mulkern's shop for £2, this money counts towards the business's turnover.

Profit
Money left over when all costs have been taken out of the turnover. In order to make the pie, Mulkern's Foods needs to spend a total of £1.50 on ingredients, making the pie and cooking the pie. The difference between what Mulkern's Foods spends to make the pie, and the amount the customer pays for the pie, is its profit.

Correspondence
A broad term for any form of written communication. This could include letters, emails, faxes, text messages, etc.

Type of electronic communication method	Where is it appropriate to use it?
Email	Email is probably the communication method used most often in business today. Email has many benefits over 'snail' mail (posted mail) because it is cheap, quick, and different types of documents can be attached.
	Email is appropriate for most office communications. However, some legal communications still have to be written in the traditional way.
Fax	Until email became popular, faxing was a favoured method of communication. This is because you can send an exact copy of a document. Faxing is a quick method of communication unless the telephone line is busy.
	Faxing is appropriate in situations where a person needs to see exactly what another person has sent. It is useful for sending documents such as plans, contracts or orders.
SMS (short message service) text messaging	Texting is now used in business quite often by employees. However, SMS messages cannot contain as much information as emails. They are useful if a person is based in the 'field', i.e. not working in an office, as they can be quickly and cheaply contacted.
	Useful for non-sensitive information or colleague-to-colleague communication.
Internet	The Internet is a very popular method of communication. Companies often use the Internet for marketing and advertising purposes. However, most sites will have a 'Contact' page where you can write to the business if you need to.

Activity: Group discussion

From the case study it would seem that Mulkern's Foods is quite a traditional company which does not use modern communication technology as well as it could.

1. Identify the different types of communication technology Mulkern's Foods could use to reduce its costs.

2. Why do you think Mulkern's Foods has not used modern technology?

3. Do you think SMS text messaging would be an a suitable method to help reduce Mulkern's Foods' costs?

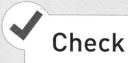

Check

- The four methods of electronic communication you will need to investigate include emails, faxes, text messages and the Internet.

- It is important that you choose the correct communication method for the type of message you are trying to send.

L01 Communicating with different people

Working as an administrator in the business, you will need to communicate effectively with a range of different people. These may be people within the same business as you (sometimes called 'internal customers') or someone from outside the business (an 'external customer').

The word '**customer**' is very important in both these cases. This is because you should always remember that you are providing a service to these people.

Internal customers

Internal customers are people from the same business as you, i.e. your **colleagues**. They may work in the same department, a different part of the business, or could even be your boss.

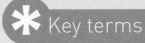

Key terms

Customer
Someone to whom you provide a service. This might be someone from a different organisation, or it could be someone who works for the same business as you.

Colleague
Someone from the same organisation as you. They could be more junior than you, someone at the same level as you (sometimes called a 'peer'), or someone at a more senior level than you.

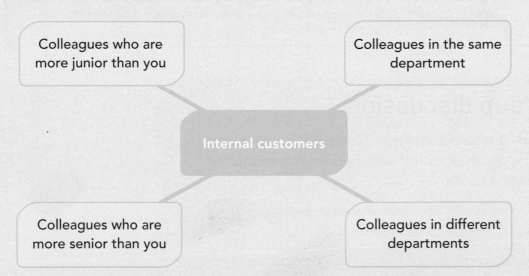

For example, in the case of Mulkern's Foods (see page 32), Jack might be meeting with an important client to discuss a large order. This would be very important for the business as it could bring in a lot of money. For the meeting, Jack might need the sales history of the client. He would ask Bridget, the administrator, to find the information he needs before the meeting.

It is important that Bridget gets the information to Jack by the time he has asked for it as it could affect the business.

External customers

An external customer is someone from a different organisation from the one you work for. This could be someone buying something from your business, or it could be a supplier. An external customer may be a private individual (a member of the public, not representing anyone else) or representing another business.

When dealing with external customers you must keep the following in mind:

- You are representing your business so make sure you give a good impression

- Everyone is different – some people may not know your business as well as you, or may not be communicating in their first language, so be patient and understanding

- If you can't answer a question, ask someone who can.

Activity: Internal or external?

Read the case study on page 32 again. In pairs, discuss whether the following are examples of internal customers or external customers.

1. Jack asks Simon to pack a selection of Mulkern's Foods' samples for a meeting he will have with a potential customer.

2. Bridget receives a telephone call from a customer who needs to know what time the shop closes.

3. Jacinta is a local cake baker and is meeting Jack to see whether he would be interested in selling her cakes in the shop.

✔ Check

- An internal customer is someone from the same organisation as you.

- An external customer is someone from a different organisation, or a private individual.

(L01) Email

Email is electronic mail and in many cases it has taken the place of letters in business communication. Email is fast and – most importantly – cheap, meaning that businesses can cut down on the amount of money it costs to send information to customers and suppliers.

Email basics

You can do a lot of things with email. Some of the basics are explained in the table below.

Term	What this means
cc	This stands for 'carbon copy', which refers to the old way in which businesses made copies of important documents. You cc someone into an email if they need to be aware of the email, but not necessarily do anything about it.
bcc	This stands for 'blind carbon copy'. The person who receives the email will not know that someone has been copied (cc'd) into the communication.
Attachment	Email is often used to send electronic documents. This could include a word-processed file, a digital photograph, a digital video, or even a computer program. You need to be careful when opening attachments as they could contain a nasty surprise, such as a computer virus. Only open attachments from people you know and trust.
Forward	You may have received a question by email that you cannot answer. You can send the email to someone else who would be able to answer the question. This is known as forwarding an email. It is usually polite to add an explanation to the message you are forwarding so the recipient knows what to do with it.

Email etiquette

When using email, it is important to use an appropriate **tone**. This means that you need to check your work for the following points before sending an email.

- Is your message clear? Will the **recipient** easily understand the information you are trying to get across? If not, how could you explain it more clearly?

- Is your language appropriate? Try not to be too familiar, but at the same time not too abrupt.

- Are you being polite? Remember to thank someone for their email, or add 'please' to anything you are asking your recipient to do. You will be amazed by how much it helps!

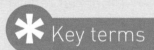

Key terms

Email etiquette
Good practice guidelines. These are things to consider when sending emails, and can help avoid embarrassing cases of misunderstanding.

Tone
The way in which one person speaks to another person.

Recipient
Someone who receives something. In this case, someone who receives an email.

Activity: A catalogue of errors

Geoff from Mulkern's Foods emailed a supplier with a question about a product that he was thinking about ordering for the business. However, when he got the email below in reply, he decided to take his business to another organisation.

From: Jackie Shields
To: Geoff Banks
50.
Thanks,
Jackie

From: Steve Bachmann
To: Jackie Shields
Hey Jackie, how's your head this morning? Ha! That was some night out!
Can you reply to this customer? He obviously hasn't read the catalogue.
S

From: Geoff Banks
To: Steve Bachmann
Dear Steve,
I am considering ordering several packs of silver foil trays
(catalogue no. 145). Please could you tell me the number of trays
in each pack?
Yours sincerely,
Geoff

What is wrong with the email…? What would you suggest Jackie and Steve should do differently?

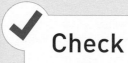

Check

- Always think about your recipient when sending an email. What tone of language is appropriate? What do they need to know?

- Always think twice before opening an attachment – it could cause your computer some harm. Do you know the sender? Are you expecting someone to send you an attachment?

L01 More on emails and faxes

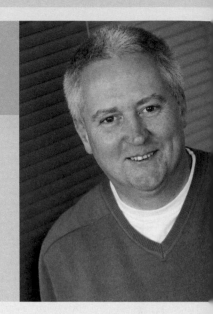

Case study:
Mulkern's Foods

After much discussion and research, Jack Mulkern has decided to spend a lot of money on communication technology and training for his business. However, Jack and his staff know very little about modern communication technology and even less about the correct way to use it.

Jack decides that he needs to call in outside help. He has heard of a company called 'Super Communication Solutions' which provides training on how to use communication technology.

Activity: Presentation

As an employee for Super Communication Solutions, you are going to give a presentation to explain what the following mean – and how to carry out each task – when emailing:

- How to send, forward and reply to an email
- Sending and receiving attachments
- Using cc and bcc
- The type of language that should be used
- What you should do if you receive an email from an unknown user
- Risks of downloading files and software
- Risks of sharing information such as chain emails and personal details.

Prepare and send a fax

Until recently a very common method of communication in business was the use of facsimile, or fax for short. Faxes are useful because the recipient receives an exact copy of what a person is sending.

Even though email can do a similar task, businesses still use faxes as they are the easiest way of quickly sending documents with signatures between people. For example, this might be used for contracts.

When you send a fax, it goes directly to the recipient's fax machine. If you are sending a fax to someone in a large business, the fax machine is unlikely to be at their desk. In order to avoid confusion, you need to include the following information on a cover sheet:

- To: where you print the recipient's name

- From: where you print your name, and the name of your business

- Date: the date on which you are sending the fax

- Pages: the total number of pages faxed, including the cover sheet.

Fax machines

As with most types of electronic equipment, fax machines come in various types, ranging from very simple ones to complex multi-function machines. It is no use having a fax machine if you do not know how to operate it efficiently.

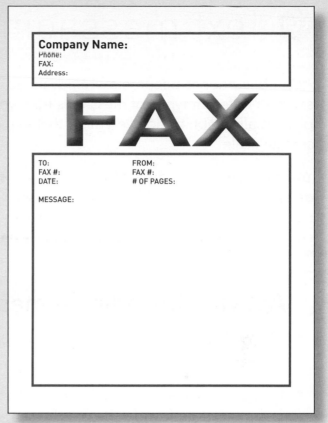

Activity: Create a fax cover sheet for your own business

For this individual activity you need to create a fax header sheet for a business of your choice. You must make sure that all the correct information is contained on the fax cover sheet, including a logo for your business.

Functional skills

If you use word-processing software to create a fax cover sheet, you may be showing you can use a number of ICT skills.

✔ Check

- Faxes can be used to send a copy of something for which you don't have an exact electronic copy. For example, a signed contract, or an order form sent to you by another business.

- When sending a fax, you need to make sure you include a summary of the number of pages, the sender, the recipient and the date on a cover sheet.

L01 # Text messaging

As mobile phones become more advanced, the opportunities for sending different types of messages from your mobile increase. The latest phones allow you to do everything that you can do on a laptop only on a smaller scale.

You can now send emails, **Multimedia Message Service (MMS)** messages and **Instant Messaging (IM)** messages from your phone. However, one basic requirement still exists – the need to make sure what you are sending makes sense and can be understood.

Activity: Encoding a message

For this activity you will work on your own initially and then as part of a group.

1. Think up a complex sentence which relates to business administration and write out the sentence using Standard English (i.e. full words).

2. Convert the message as best you can into text message language. If you are struggling for an **abbreviation** use the Internet for research – there are plenty of text message dictionaries online.

3. Stand up in front of your group and read out your text message. See how many group members can decode the message correctly.

SMS text messaging

Short Message Service (SMS) text messaging has become very popular over the last 20 years. This is because it has become more affordable and easy to do. Nearly all mobile phones have a text message facility.

However, in business, texting has its limitations:

- Only a small amount of information can be sent in a text message

- 'Text' language is often not appropriate in a professional situation.

Communications need to be clear and accurate. Uncertainty about the meaning of a message can be very costly to business.

Multimedia Message Service (MMS)
Allows you to send and receive not only text but also sound, images and video.

Instant Messaging (IM)
An instant text messaging service that happens in 'real time'.

Abbreviate
To make a word shorter, either by taking out letters (e.g. 'tomorrow' becomes 'tmro') or by cutting the word short (e.g. 'Saturday' becomes 'Sat').

Short Message Service (SMS)
Allows you to send or receive text messages only up to 160 characters in length.

Activity: When to text

Draw and complete the mind map by stating when text messaging is appropriate in business and when it is not, and why.

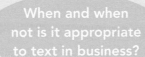

When and when not is it appropriate to text in business?

! Remember

- It may be acceptable to use a text message to communicate with a colleague who is out of the office...

- but you need to make sure your message is clear and accurate...

- and fits into 160 or fewer characters.

Activity: Appropriate?

Why would this style of text message not be appropriate for business?

In pairs, make a list of reasons and present what you have found to your group.

Hi Mr Brwn Soz, will be a bit l8 4 meeting. Stk in traffic. Will be thr as soon as! ☹

✓ Check

- Before you send a text message for business purposes, ask yourself if this is the most appropriate way to communicate.

- It is important that any business communication you send from your mobile phone is clear and accurate.

L02 Using the Internet securely

The Internet is a great source of information. With a few clicks of the mouse it is possible to find answers to a huge number of questions. Search engines like Google, Ask or Bing can help you find any information you want.

However, it is important that you use the Internet securely (safely). There are many reasons for this including the security of personal data and avoiding the potential for **cybercrime** to happen.

To increase Internet safety and security, Internet service providers have developed very advanced systems and software to reduce the risk of problems. However, very often the most basic security measures can have the most effect. For example, always use passwords that are difficult to work out. It is recommended that passwords should be no less than eight characters in length (ideally 12) and contain letters, numbers and characters.

Key term

Cybercrime
A type of crime that uses computers. This can include identity theft, stealing from online bank accounts, stealing information, etc. You have to be very careful with information you give away online to avoid cybercrime.

! Remember

- Information on the Internet is more reliable from some sources than others. Services like Wikipedia can be edited by anyone (but is checked by Wikipedia staff), so might not be 100 per cent accurate. The BBC website is edited and checked on a regular basis.

- Secure websites start their address with https:// (the 's' means 'secure'), and your web browser will show a padlock icon. This means that it is safe to enter personal details. If the website does not display a padlock icon, think carefully before you give any personal information.

◎ Activity: How can I keep my information secure and free from viruses?

In pairs, make an Internet security poster. Discuss the bullet points below in your poster. Explain how they can improve or reduce levels of Internet security.

- Need to keep passwords secure
- Viruses and virus protection
- Firewalls
- Security updates

- Dangers of file sharing
- Letting other people know your personal details
- Giving unauthorised people access to data.

When you have completed your poster, pass it to another group for them to mark out of ten.

When marking another group's work you must provide supportive comments on what is good about their poster and what could be done to improve it.

Using the Internet effectively

As well as using the Internet securely it is important to know how it works. For example, do you know how a search engine works? Do you know how to save results so they can be found and used again in the future?

In simple terms, the Internet is a huge database of information arranged into websites. When you type in what you are looking for in a search engine, all you are doing is instructing the computer to search and find websites that contain the words you have typed in.

Sometimes you may find the search engine will return strange results. Remember a computer is only a machine and the Internet is only a piece of software – they cannot think for themselves. Change your search terms, and see if you can get a better result.

Activity: A day in the life of an administrator

Bridget from Mulkern's Foods is on holiday and has left you a list of things to do. You need to choose the most appropriate electronic communication method to use for each one. Give reasons for your answer.

- Send a completed order form to a supplier for four packs of foil trays.

- Remind Geoff while he is out of the office that he needs to phone The Old Boot in Whittington.

- Find a list of pubs within 50 miles of Shrewsbury for Jack to target with a marketing campaign.

✔ Check

- When finding information on the Internet, make sure you can trust the source. If you are not sure of something, check it with another website.

- Always check whether a web page is secure before entering personal details.

ASSESSMENT OVERVIEW

While working through this unit, you will have prepared for completing the following assessment tasks:

○	1.1 Send, receive and forward emails	Pages 36–37
○	1.2 Prepare and send a fax	Pages 38–39
○	1.3 Prepare and send a clear and accurate text message	Pages 40–41
○	2.1 Log on to the Internet	Pages 42–43
○	2.2 Access an appropriate website showing awareness of security	Pages 42–43

Assignment tips

- You need to think about how you will produce your assessment work for this unit. You can use saved files and printouts. However, your tutor will need to witness you preparing and sending a clear and accurate text message.

- You need to be aware of – and be able to talk through – the security issues around accessing websites. You may need to record conversations with your tutor for this. You could also add notes to screenshots to show your awareness of security issues when using the Internet.

MAKING & RECEIVING CALLS

When working as an administrator, one of the most common tasks you will carry out will be to make and receive telephone calls. It is therefore very important that you learn how to use telephones in line with company rules. A key skill you will need to learn is how to present a positive image to anyone who contacts the company you work for.

In this unit you will:

- Be able to make telephone calls correctly

- Be able to receive telephone calls correctly

- Know why it is important to an organisation that calls are handled appropriately

What do you think are the most important skills for using the telephone effectively?

L01 Making calls

Case study:
Smith's Motorcycles

Andrew Smith decided to open his own motorcycle sales and repairs shop. The business expanded and within three years of opening it employed 20 people. Five worked on the sale and repair of motorcycles and the remaining 15 dealt with customer orders over the telephone and online, as well as carrying out day-to-day administration duties.

However, Andrew's business started losing sales. It was noticeable that there were fewer telephone enquiries than the year before and this worried Andrew.

Karen, the administration manager, had a meeting with Andrew to discuss the situation. She suggested that staff were not dealing appropriately with customers over the telephone.

Identify the purpose of a call

It is important to think carefully about a call before you make it. By understanding clearly the purpose of your call, you can plan what you are going to say to the other person and how you are going to say it. It is important to choose the right words and tone for the situation.

Check the name and number of the person to be called

Have you ever received a telephone call from a person who has got some of your personal details (i.e. name, address, etc.) wrong? If you have an unusual name, this can happen regularly.

While this can be annoying on a personal level, in a business situation it can be costly. After all, if a person is calling from a business that you deal with regularly and cannot get your details correct, what sort of image does that present? Businesses must act professionally at all times if they are to keep a good reputation. This includes knowing the correct name and number of the person being telephoned.

Communicating clearly and accurately

It is important to communicate basic information clearly and in a way that the listener can understand. The checklist below gives some ideas to help you make sure your call is clear and well structured:

- Write down what you are going to say and check it carefully

- Re-write it in a logical sequence (so it is easy to follow what you are saying)

- Write down questions that you want to ask

- Think about how you will answer any questions

- Think about the language and tone of voice you are going to use

- Think about how familiar you are with the person you are calling. This will affect the style of your telephone call.

Remember to summarise the key points at the end of the call so that you are both clear what has been said or agreed.

Activity: Group discussion

Think of a time when you have received poor service over the telephone.

Using this experience, create a telephone script that the administrators at Smith's could use to make sure that customers get the same level of service every time. Think about the following:

- Why is it important for administrators to identify the purpose of a call?

- Why it is important to speak to customers correctly?

- Why are administrators often known as the 'face of the company'?

Check

- Clear communication is important when making a telephone call. To avoid any embarrassing problems, plan what you are going to say before you pick up the telephone.

- Make sure that you have the correct number for the person you are calling as this will save time.

L02 Receiving calls

Answering a call promptly and politely observing any organisational procedures

Most organisations will have certain expectations of staff when their job involves answering telephone calls from customers. Many businesses have strict **policies** that must be followed when staff answer the telephone. For example the phone should be answered in three rings.

If you ever get the chance to visit a call centre, ask one of the call centre telephonists if you can look at their telephone script. A telephone script tells the operator exactly what he or she has to say and the questions to ask a customer.

Policy
A principle or course of action adopted by an organisation or individual.

Activity: Sitting next to Nelly

Ask if your tutor can arrange for you to visit a company where you can spend a short period of time in the office sitting next to a member of staff who is answering telephone calls.

Listen to the language the person uses along with the different ways in which he or she uses the tone of their voice when dealing with different callers. (In the past, it used to be called learning by 'Sitting next to Nelly' if you learned by sitting next to another person!)

Functional skills

When listening to the way someone uses language, you will find you can improve your **English** learning.

Identifying a caller, where they are calling from and the purpose of their call

It is important to identify correctly where a caller is calling from and the purpose of their call so that you have some idea of what they are calling about. Also, if you are transferring a person to another member of staff, you will need to pass this information on. Identifying callers is all part of presenting a professional image of the business.

The diagram opposite gives you some good pointers when dealing with calls.

1. Ask politely who is calling

5. Always end a phone call by asking if you can help the caller further

2. Find out if the person wishes to speak to you or be transferred to someone else

4. Take notes so you do not forget why the person has called. Note their phone number as you may need to phone them back later

3. If the person wishes to speak to you – listen carefully and use clear, accurate language

Case study:
Smith's Motorcycles

During his meeting with Karen, Andrew discovered that a number of his staff were not taking notes when customers were ringing the business. Karen felt sales were being affected because staff did not always call customers back if they could not answer their questions straightaway. This alarmed Andrew and so he decided to do something about it.

Activity: Providing an efficient service

1. Why might staff not take notes when customers called the business?

2. Suggest how Andrew could improve this situation.

3. How might customers feel about the business if, after being promised, they were not rung back?

Check

- It is important to identify the purpose of a call so that you know how to deal with the caller.

- Answer telephone calls quickly and politely so that you don't keep a customer waiting.

L02 Confidentiality and security

Organisational procedures

When dealing with telephone calls, it is important that you do not discuss certain things with callers. For example, you are not allowed to discuss another person's personal details without their permission. If you do, you will be breaking the Data Protection Act. This is a complex law and it is designed to protect the use of an individual's information.

If this law is broken you can be held personally liable for prosecution, meaning you could be taken to court and fined.

The key points of the Data Protection Act are outlined below.

Data should not be transferred to other countries without adequate protection

Data should be obtained and processed fairly and lawfully – meaning that the owner normally needs to consent to the information being used

Data should be accurate and up to date

Key points of the Data Protection Act

Data should only be processed for limited purposes

Data, including personal data, should be kept for no longer than necessary

Data must be stored securely

Data which is kept should be adequate and relevant but not excessive

Activity: Data Protection booklet

Individually, prepare a booklet outlining the key points of the Data Protection Act. Use any websites recommended by your tutor to help with your research.

When you have completed your booklet, swap your work with a friend and make suggestions as to how their booklet can be improved.

Dealing with sensitive information

It is important to make sure that sensitive information is kept confidential and private. This also applies to the information that is given to customers over the telephone.

While uncommon, people do make 'bogus' calls. These types of calls are usually meant to gain information from a person or organisation. In a business setting, such calls are made to get hold of information which could be of use to a competitor, for example in knowing a business's profit margin on items.

To avoid information getting into the wrong hands, companies have policies and systems in place. One of the main methods is to limit the amount of information a person can access. Normally a junior member of staff has access to less information than a more senior member of the company.

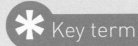

Key term

Profit margin
The amount of profit expressed as a proportion of the turnover. So if a customer buys an item for £2, which costs £1.50 to produce, the profit margin is $33\frac{1}{3}$ per cent.

Activity: Call centre

Imagine you work in a call centre. Prepare a telephone script which makes sure that you cover all data protection requirements.

Now get into pairs. Your partner should 'call' you and try to trick you into giving away sensitive information. Swap roles.

Check

- The Data Protection Act is a law which makes sure that data is stored and processed fairly and lawfully.

- Protect yourself by always following your company's procedures for dealing with sensitive or confidential information.

L02 Taking short messages

Sometimes you will need to answer a telephone call and write down a short message which needs to be passed to another member of staff. This will happen normally when the other person is on the telephone dealing with another caller or when they are out at lunch.

In order to give your colleague as much information as possible, it is important to note down:

- the date and time of the call

- the caller's name and number

- the purpose of their call, as accurately as possible.

It is also helpful to give an idea of how urgent the message is and whether or not the recipient needs to take any action.

Normally, a business will have a specially formatted note-taking pad which will look like the one below:

Phone

☎ messages

Caller's name: _____

Call taken by: _____

For the attention of: _____

Time of call: _____

Reason for call: _____

_____

_____

_____

_____

_____

_____

_____

_____

Functional skills

You will be practising your writing skills in **English** by taking messages carefully and accurately.

Activity: Heard it on the grapevine

1. As a group arrange yourselves in a circle. One person needs to write down a short message on a piece of paper, typically three to four lines.

2. The person must then whisper that message to the first person in the circle.

3. The last person who receives the message should then write down what they have been told on a piece of paper.

4. The two messages should then be looked at side by side to compare the spoken and written messages. Think about the questions below when comparing the messages.

- What has happened?

- Why has this happened?

- What might happen in the workplace if the same thing happened?

Activity: Taking messages

You are to role play in pairs a telephone conversation in which one of you is phoning a business to leave a short message. The other is the administrator taking the message. On an A5 piece of paper prepare a message pad like the one on page 52.

When the administrator has taken the message and completed all the points on the message pad, he or she should repeat the message back to the caller. The caller then scores the administrator marks out of 10 for the accuracy of the message. Then reverse roles.

Check

- Use short messages to make sure you have captured what a person is saying in a telephone conversation.

- If you are in any doubt, ask the caller to repeat what they have said so that you can pass on an accurate message.

L03 Well-handled calls and the benefits to business

Making a good impression

The first impression you give a person can often be the lasting one they will have of you. The same is true when working in business administration. The difference is that you are representing the company you work for and, therefore, the impression you give represents both you and the business. The key is to know how to make a good impression.

Some of the ways this can be achieved are outlined below:

- Your tone of voice – if you are aggressive or miserable, the person you are talking to will get a negative impression of you and your company.

- Clarity – it is important to be clear when speaking to people on the telephone so that you do not have to repeat yourself too much, and a person fully understands what you are saying. To avoid being misunderstood, try not to use business jargon (unless you know the person you are talking to understands what you are saying). Use simple and short sentences. You may need to repeat yourself if you are clarifying instructions as this will help to avoid mistakes.

- Listening – this is a skill we take for granted. However, it takes practice to be a good or active listener. Active listening involves fully understanding the conversation while adding to what has been said. You do this by asking questions or asking for points to be repeated if they are not clear. Part of active listening is the skill of making notes while staying focused on what has been said.

- Questioning – it is said in business that it is better to not say anything than ask a 'bad' question. As with listening, asking questions is a skill that is developed with practice. It is important to understand the purpose of a telephone call and the way the conversation is going to make sure that any questions you ask add to it and do not distract from the discussion.

- Checking information when taking a message – this is a very important skill that must be used whenever you take a telephone message. You must write down exactly what the caller is saying. The message may need to be passed on and, if it is incorrect, the person will follow the instructions and end up with the wrong result.

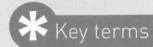

Key terms

Impression
The image of a person that someone is left with after talking to or dealing with another person.

Tone
The way in which one person speaks to another person.

- Giving accurate and up-to-date information – when people call a company for advice or help, they expect to be given information which is both accurate and up to date. For example, in the past customers might be told that an item was in stock while in reality none was available. The customer therefore faced disappointment when they arrived to collect their goods. While this still happens, technology has improved the efficiency of tracking items and so the chances of being let down by a business have been reduced.

The benefits a good impression can bring

By presenting a good impression of an organisation, customers feel positive about dealing with the business in the future. If customers are satisfied with the service they receive, they might tell others about it and so new customers are attracted to the business.

However, if people receive a negative impression of a business, they will also pass this experience on to others and this may negatively affect the business.

Functional skills

Practising telephone conversations will help to improve your speaking and listening skills in **English**.

Activity: Role play

In pairs, think up five different role play telephone situations which involve a conversation with each other.

Try to choose a variety of callers and practise using different tones and language.

Check

- Practise your listening and questioning skills in order to improve.

- Only ask questions that are relevant and add to the conversation.

ASSESSMENT OVERVIEW

While working through this unit, you will have prepared for completing the following assessment tasks:

○	1.1	Identify the purpose of the call	Pages 46–47
○	1.2	Confirm the name and number of the person to be contacted before making the call	Page 46
○	1.3	Make a call communicating basic information clearly and accurately	Page 47
○	2.1	Answer the call promptly and politely, observing any organisational procedures	Page 48
○	2.2	Identify the caller, where they are calling from and the reason for their call	Pages 48–49
○	2.3	Follow any organisational procedures relating to confidentiality and security	Pages 50–51
○	2.4	Take short messages	Pages 52–53
○	3.1	State how appropriate tone and language create a positive impression	Pages 54–55
○	3.2	State how creating a positive impression during a call benefits the organisation	Pages 54–55

Assignment tips

- Your tutor may set you a role play of a telephone call for this unit. For this you will need to take on a particular role and think about how you should prepare for the call. You will also need to follow a clear process when answering a call to achieve all the grading criteria.

- In preparation for making and receiving a call, you might find it useful to draw a flow chart. This will help you to identify the different steps you need to go through and will help you pass this unit.

- You will need to state two benefits of creating a positive impression for the organisation. You may do this through a recorded conversation with your tutor.

WELCOMING VISITORS

Businesses receive all sorts of visitors – from suppliers and customers to potential employees. For many visitors, the first impression they will have of the business is the receptionist.

First impressions are important, so through this unit you will learn how to welcome visitors and create a positive impression. You will also learn why organisations feel this is such an important skill.

In this unit you will:

- Be able to welcome visitors in a positive way

- Know why it is important to an organisation that visitors are made welcome

Why do you think first impressions are so important for businesses?

L01 Visitors

An organisation will receive any number of visitors over the course of a day. These may include:

- members of the public
- people from the same organisation
- people from other organisations, such as suppliers, customers or clients.

Each of these will be visiting your organisation for a different reason.

Case study:
Chalky College

Chalky College has around 1000 students aged between 14 and 19 studying at its two campuses. The college regularly receives 20 or more visitors a day. All visitors need to sign into the visitors' book, be given a visitor badge and be met at reception by a member of staff.

Colm works on reception. He has had a long week, and is distracted by some issues outside work. A visitor comes to the reception desk and asks to speak to Amy Smyth. Colm says: 'Sorry mate, don't know her. Can't help you.'

He thinks Amy probably works at the other campus, but it would take a few minutes to find out.

Activity: First impressions count

What kind of impression would Colm have made? What if the visitor's meeting with Amy Smyth was important? What do you think Colm should have done differently?

Why do visitors come?

- To visit an individual employee – depending on the type of organisation, this may be for a sales meeting, to discuss a new product, to agree on some details of a decision.

These visitors will probably need to be met at reception by the employee they are visiting. So the receptionist will need to contact the employee, tell them who has arrived, and arrange for them to meet the visitor.

- For large meetings, or conferences – these may involve people from the same organisation (perhaps from different offices) and people from outside organisations (sometimes called 'delegates').

  If a meeting is particularly large, it would not be practical to have all the delegates met by individual employees. It is likely that there would be a list of people attending, and the receptionist would direct the delegates to make their own way to the meeting.

- Businesses receive a range of different deliveries – from products that have been ordered by an individual member of staff to regular postal deliveries. If an organisation is large enough to have a post room, the receptionist would probably direct most deliveries to it.

  However, if the organisation does not have a post room, the receptionist may sign for deliveries. (This is important for some deliveries as it can be used as evidence that the goods were delivered.)

  If a delivery is addressed to an individual employee, the receptionist would need to contact the employee to arrange for the delivery to be collected.

What do visitors want?

Visitors may request information. For example, a visitor may ask for a catalogue, or a contact telephone number. It is important that receptionists handle these requests effectively as these visitors may become customers or suppliers for the organisation.

If the receptionist cannot provide the information, he or she should contact someone within the organisation who is able to.

Activity: Handling visitors

As a small group, think about one organisation you all know. Try to identify all the different reasons why visitors might be calling at the organisation. What skills do you think would be important when welcoming all these different visitors? What sorts of information might the visitors need?

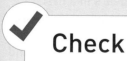

Check

- An organisation may receive visitors for a wide range of reasons.

- It is important that the receptionist is able to direct visitors to the right person within the organisation.

L02 The importance of making a good impression

A first impression can be a lasting one. Working in reception, you are often the first person that a potential customer, supplier or employee sees from the organisation. That means that they may form an opinion of your organisation based entirely on their first impressions of you!

Does the person in the photo make a good impression? If you had to judge the organisation they worked for by looking at this photograph, what would you say?

What makes a good impression?

Many different things can work together to make a good first impression. However, a lot of it comes down to customer service, that is the level of service and care that the visitor feels they received from the organisation.

Things that visitors may remember include:

- Polite and friendly service – did they feel welcome, or were they treated as if they were getting in the way?

- Helpful service – did the organisation go that extra mile to answer their questions, or to make their visit pleasant?

- Professional demeanour – was the receptionist professional and effective?

A good impression can help the organisation gain more business. It is worth remembering that customers will tell *one* of their friends about *good* customer service, but will tell *ten* of their friends if they have *bad* customer service.

✳ Key term

Professional demeanour
This is how someone appears in a first impression. If you are dressed smartly, are polite and helpful, and address the visitor's needs effectively, you are likely to be thought of as having a professional demeanour.

Who are you welcoming?

You are likely to welcome a wide range of different people into your organisation. These will probably include at least some of the different groups in the diagram below:

Potential employees, who may be visiting for a job interview – if your organisation is to attract the best people, it needs to give a good first impression

Clients – your customers, without them you wouldn't have a job

Different types of visitors

Suppliers who work with your organisation on a regular basis. The better service you provide them, the better service they will provide you

Members of the public, who may be clients or service users for your organisation

Activity: What if...?

In pairs, suggest what might happen if each of the different visitor groups above has a good first impression of the organisation.

Then suggest what might happen if they have a bad first impression.

How would this affect the organisation?

Check

- Working on reception, you will be responsible for giving a good first impression of the organisation.

- A good first impression can help the organisation win new customers. A bad first impression can mean the organisation loses customers.

L01 How to welcome visitors

Your organisation is likely to have **procedures** for welcoming visitors. These should be followed closely as they can be very important – both for the security of your organisation, and for keeping an accurate list of visitors in case there is an emergency.

1. Greet visitor

When working on reception, you will be responsible for answering telephone calls, answering or forwarding emails, as well as welcoming visitors.

You should acknowledge all visitors, even if you are on the telephone. Making eye contact and showing the visitor you know they are there will create a good impression.

2. Identify reason for visit

You need to identify the reason for the visit in order to help the visitor. 'Hello, how can I help you?' is probably the most friendly and open way you could do this.

Before you can help the visitor you need to find out:

- Who they are, and what organisation they come from

- The purpose of their visit

  o If they are visiting someone from your organisation, you need to find out who they are visiting

  o If they are visiting for a large meeting or a conference, you need to identify which meeting they are attending in case there is more than one being held at the same time.

3. Contact appropriate person

If the visitor is there to see a particular person, you will need to contact that person to let them know their visitor is in reception.

4. Ask visitor to sign in

All visitors will need to sign a visitors' book. This will help to keep a record of who is visiting the organisation, and may also act as their **visitor's badge**. Most visitors' books record the following information:

- Name
- Organisation
- Person they are visiting
- Car registration
- Time in
- Time out.

5. Waiting

The visitor may need to wait to be met, either because they are early or because it will take a little while for the employee to get to reception. Once the visitor has signed in, you should ask them to take a seat.

If you know how long the visitor is likely to be waiting, you should tell them. They may be able to get on with some work, if they have enough time, so it's not time wasted.

Depending on the likely length of their wait, and the equipment available in reception, you might ask them if they would like a drink.

 Key term

Visitor's badge
A badge or security pass, identifying the visitor.

 Functional skills

Through the activity below you will practise your **English** speaking and listening skills.

Activity: Role play

In pairs, work through the sequence of welcoming a visitor. One of you should take Role A and the other Role B.

Role A: You are from Onyx, a local business, and visiting Bob Jenkins in marketing. Your car registration is H48 0BCZ.

Role B: You are the receptionist. Bob Jenkins is going to be in a meeting for another 15 minutes, so won't be able to collect his visitor for a little while.

Once you have worked through the role play, discuss what you thought went well. What would the visitor's first impression of the organisation be?

Check

- Remember to acknowledge every visitor – even if you are very busy.
- You need to make sure all visitors going into the organisation sign the visitors' book.

L01 Communicating with visitors

To work on reception, you need to have good communication skills. You also need to understand the organisation you work for, because you are likely to be asked a wide range of questions.

Routine questions

The types of question you will be asked in reception will vary depending on the kind of organisation you work for. See the list on the right.

Finding answers

If you are asked questions that you don't know the answer to, don't worry, be honest and say so. It is very rare for anyone to be able to answer every question. One of the most important skills is being able to identify someone who could.

This will mean working out the best person to ask in the organisation. To do this you will need to:

- Work out which department the question relates to

- Identify the person in that department who will either be able to provide an answer, or be able to find someone who can answer the question

- Contact them, and explain the question clearly and politely

- Either tell the visitor the answer to the question, or how long an answer is likely to take.

Routine questions receptionists are asked

↓

Directions – to facilities, a particular building or entrance

↓

Contacts – a person who the visitor needs to speak to about a specific issue or is meeting at a particular time

↓

Sales information – such as a request for a catalogue or order form

↓

Very specific questions that you might not know the answer to – you should know who in the business will know the answer

📁 Case study:
Chalky College

Colm is having a better day. He is working on reception and is on the telephone to his girlfriend. He notices a visitor come in and head towards him. He makes eye contact with the visitor to acknowledge their presence. 'I've got to go, so I'll call you later,' he says to his girlfriend.

'Hello, how can I help you?' Colm says to the visitor.

'Hello, I'm from Smith's Office Supplies. Would you be able to tell me who is in charge of purchasing printer ink?'

Colm thinks hard. 'No, sorry, I don't know. However, I know someone who will know. Take a seat. This should take about five minutes.' He picks up the telephone and calls someone in another department.

Activity: A good impression

What kind of an impression would Colm have made? What do you think Colm did well?

Tone, language and manner

When working in reception, making a good first impression of the organisation is important. Here are some things to consider:

- Speak clearly – make sure the meaning of what you are saying is easy to understand. This is even more important if you are giving someone directions, as they may not know the office as well as you

- Be polite. Thank visitors for completing the visitors' book or handing back their visitor's pass

- Use a warm and friendly tone. Open questions like 'How can I help you?' go a long way in helping you to appear welcoming

- Remember your body language. Make eye contact with visitors. This will show that you have acknowledged them, and that you are dealing with them personally. Don't fold your arms when speaking to someone – this is called 'closed' body language and may give a negative impression

- Smile!

Activity: Design a poster

Working in small groups, produce an A3 poster giving instructions for good practice for someone working in reception. This should cover:

- How to greet a visitor and answer their questions

- What to do if you are unable to answer their questions

- Top tips for giving a good impression.

Check

- If you don't know the answer to a visitor's question, ask someone who does.

- Remember to be polite, friendly and helpful – this will give a good impression of your organisation.

ASSESSMENT OVERVIEW

While working through this unit, you will have prepared for completing the following assessment tasks:

○	1.1 Welcome visitors and establish the purpose for their visit	Pages 58–59
○	1.2 Follow organisational procedures for receiving visitors	Pages 62–63
○	1.3 Answer routine questions	Page 64
○	1.4 Make visitors feel welcome during any period of waiting	Page 65
○	1.5 Use appropriate tone and language, including body language, when dealing with visitors	Page 65
○	2.1 State how treating visitors politely and in a positive way benefits the organisation	Pages 60–61

edexcel ▦

Assignment tips

- Quite a lot of the assessment for this unit will be through practical tasks that your tutor will witness. You will need to know the agreed procedure for greeting visitors (i.e. signing the visitors' book, etc.). You will also need to be aware of your body language. Try to think about the way you sit or stand, and what it might be saying about you.

- You will need to follow two types of organisational procedure when welcoming visitors. You will also need to answer two routine questions correctly and clearly.

- You will need to identify one benefit to the organisation of treating visitors politely and in a positive way. You should try to give the reason a context. For example, you could say why the visitor might be visiting, and the effect this may have on their long-term dealings with the organisation.

HANDLING MAIL | UNIT 18

When employed by a company as an administrator, you will often need to handle mail. Dealing with incoming and outgoing mail is a very important task to make sure that information is kept flowing within the business. If there are problems with the distribution of mail, then the impact on the business can be dramatic, including the possibility of losing customers.

In this unit you will:

- Know why it is important for a business to handle mail efficiently and securely

- Be able to deal with incoming mail

- Be able to deal with outgoing mail

Every day it is thought that between 60 and 80 million items of mail are sent or received. How many different reasons can you think of why a business would need to send mail?

L01 The importance of handling mail efficiently

How efficient distribution of mail benefits a business

Mail can be seen as the lifeblood of the world economy as businesses depend on information to work effectively. If there is a hiccup in the system, and mail does not get to where it is supposed to be going on time, then this can cause big problems for a company.

An efficient mail distribution system can benefit a business in many ways. First, it is important that mail is received in a timely manner. A customer would not be pleased if their order arrived at a supplier six weeks after they had placed it just because it became caught up in the internal mail system.

Second, an efficient mail system presents a professional image to customers. If a customer rings up with a query and their order can be found quickly then they will think that the company you work for is on the ball.

Case study:
Pattison and Sons Builders

Pattison and Sons is a building business run by a father and his sons. Jim Pattison is the Managing Director of the business and his sons, Russell and Richard, specialise in bricklaying and joinery. The business, which has been successful for many years, is run on a very traditional basis with very little use of modern ICT.

Due to a large increase in their workload, the father and sons team can no longer manage all the administration and building work, so they decide to employ an administrator.

After interviewing a number of candidates, Barbara is chosen. The three family members of the business are very happy with their choice of administrator and feel she will do a good job. However, Barbara has mainly dealt with email and the occasional letter at her previous employers.

It is soon clear that Barbara is starting to have problems dealing with the mail. Sometimes she forgets to invoice customers or she invoices customers incorrectly, often sending letters to the wrong address. She is also forgetting to respond to requests for payment from suppliers. Jim notices that his cash flow is not as healthy as it used to be and this concerns him greatly.

✳ Key terms

Invoice
An invoice is a document sent to customers requesting payment for the supply of goods or services.

Cash flow
Money flowing in and out of a business in the form of payments and receipts.

Activity: Group activity

As a group, consider how Barbara's mistakes are affecting the cash flow of the business. What sort of impression do you think both suppliers and customers of Pattison and Sons are getting of the business?

What could Pattison and Sons have done when Barbara started to work for the business that might have helped to avoid these problems?

Why mistakes or delays can have a negative effect

If you look back to the Pattison and Sons case study, it gives some idea of the type of problems that can happen if a person is not dealing with mail correctly. Businesses rely on getting paid for the goods or services they provide. If they do not have any money coming into the business then they cannot pay suppliers or employees' wages. It is often said in business that a company can operate while in debt but it cannot continue to trade if it has no cash flow. Also, if a business is not dealing with mail quickly, delays will give customers a **negative impression** as their queries may not be getting dealt with quickly. This could even lead to a customer taking their business elsewhere.

Key term

Negative impression
When a customer receives poor service and bases their future opinions of the business on that view.

Activity: Mail handling problems and their impact

Create a table which follows the same layout as the one below.
An example of how the table needs to be filled in has been given.

Problem	Potential effect on business
Information not received by correct person	Information not processed on time or incorrectly processed. For example, a customer may suffer delay or receive the wrong goods.
Information is received late	
Invoices received late	
Payments to customers sent late	

✔ Check

- Efficient mail distribution is important as it saves a company time and money.

- Internal mail is the term given to mail that is sent internally within a business.

L01 The importance of handling mail securely

Dealing with confidential information

When **dealing with mail** in a business environment you will often be handling mail that is confidential. The information could be confidential for many reasons. For example, it could contain personal details or information that is sensitive to the business which, if it falls into the wrong hands, could give competitors an advantage.

It is important to handle mail securely for a number of reasons:

1. It does not look good if an organisation keeps losing mail and customer or personal details 'leak' out. This can be very damaging to an organisation, as the general public may lose trust in them and decide to take their business elsewhere. (Over the last few years there have been several high profile cases of private data being lost or stolen.)

2. Businesses have to operate efficiently to remain competitive. If important information is slow to arrive, or gets lost, it will take longer for a job to be completed and the hold-up may cause customers concern. In the long term the company might lose customers.

The Data Protection Act

The **Data Protection Act**, 1988, is a law that was passed to control the means by which data can be stored, processed and used by businesses. The Act covers both paper-based information and information stored on a computer. Importantly, the responsibility of making sure that a person follows the Act lies with the person using the computer. This means that, if a piece of information is passed to the wrong hands, the person who gets hold of the information and passes it on could be liable if the case goes to court. The following highlight some of the key parts of the Data Protection Act:

- Data should be obtained fairly and lawfully

- Data held should not be excessive

- Data must be kept up to date

- Data must not be kept longer than needed

- An individual has the right to see any data stored about them.

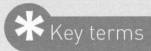

Key terms

Dealing with mail
A very important operation within a business as many customers still use mail as a way of doing business. Efficient mail delivery ensures that mail does not go missing and customers receive good levels of customer service.

Data Protection Act
A law which protects the general public from having their personal data misused.

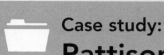

Case study:
Pattison and Sons Builders

After a couple of months it soon becomes clear that Barbara is doing more than just handling mail incorrectly. It seems that not only is the business's cash flow in trouble due to Barbara's mistakes, Pattison and Sons is also struggling to win new business.

Every time the company gives a quote for a new building job the price seems to be always mysteriously beaten. This worries Jim greatly – his company has always won business because it offers competitive quotes and work is carried out to a high standard. The next day Jim decides to investigate why his company cannot secure new business and what he finds alarms him immensely.

Follow correct procedures for delivering confidential mail

Use of appropriate postal service recorded delivery or special delivery

Ways of keeping mail confidential

Labelling post 'Confidential' or 'Confidential, not to be opened before delivery'

Use of special envelopes or postage bags

Activity: Group discussion

What do you think Barbara could be doing which is costing Pattison and Sons business? Which law is in place to protect the private information of businesses and individuals? What can Jim do now to improve the situation?

Check

- Confidential information is data that is sensitive to a business or individual.

- The Data Protection Act is a law which is designed to protect individuals and businesses from improper use of data.

L02 Dealing with incoming mail

Sorting post appropriately

The Royal Mail estimates that on average 84 million items of post are sent every day. Making sure that all the mail is delivered to the correct place is a massive job. However, that is not where it stops.

When mail is delivered to a business it must be **sorted** into the correct order so it can be sent to the correct department within the business. That may seem a simple task but a large business can receive several thousand items of post a day and so the scale of the job is very large. Despite the popularity of email, many businesses still employ staff to sort and deliver mail to the correct departments. A popular name for the area within the business in which these employees work is the 'Mail Room'. The diagram below shows the **flow of mail** through a business.

✳ Key terms

Sorting
The process of putting mail into different piles so it can be distributed to the correct department.

Flow of mail
The process which mail goes through from when it is sent until it arrives at its destination.

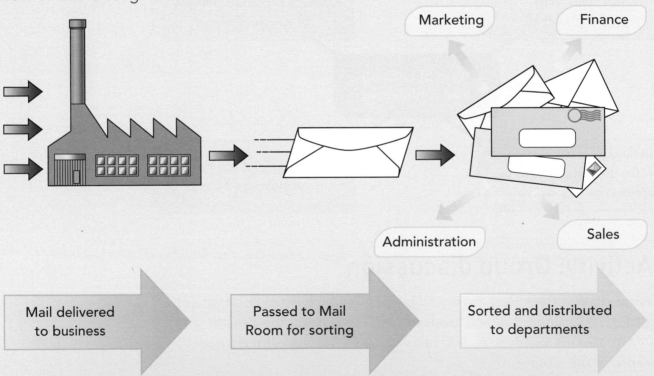

Activity: Wrongly delivered mail

Look at the diagram above and make a list of problems that might result in mail not being distributed to the correct department.

Where do you think the problems are most likely to occur and why? Can you think of a simpler, more efficient system?

Suspicious or damaged items

When working in a mail sorting room, it is really important that you know how to look for suspicious items of post. Over the years there have been a number of times where the postal system has been used to cause harm to others. In 2001, a number of people were killed when a letter containing the bacterium Anthrax was sent through the post. Thankfully, however, such incidents are very rare indeed.

As well as suspicious items, mail room operatives must be watchful in dealing with damaged items of post. When dealing with damaged items there are a number of things you need to know.

1. You must know the procedure for dealing with damaged items.

2. Who you need to report the problem to.

3. You would normally be required to contact the sender to inform them that the item was damaged upon receipt.

4. They may need to send out a replacement or be advised that their despatch team are not sending out mail securely.

5. You would need to know the reporting/recording procedure for the receipt of damaged items.

Activity: Procedures for dealing with suspicious or damaged items

For this task you are to work in pairs. You are to imagine you work for a large organisation and have been asked to develop a new procedure for dealing with suspicious or damaged items of mail.

You need to draw up a written procedure and a flow chart of your new idea.

After you have finished developing your idea you need to present your work to your group.

✔ Check

- Incoming mail is post that has been sent to the business and is 'incoming'.

- Suspicious or damaged items must be recorded and reported using the correct procedure so that the problem can be corrected.

L02 Distributing incoming mail

Distribute incoming mail accurately and to a deadline

Earlier we discussed the need to distribute mail efficiently and accurately. This is because, very often, a person will be expecting to receive an item of mail and they cannot make progress until this item is received.

Companies will often have in place what are known as 'service level agreements'. These documents are simply an agreement between two companies explaining what level of service they can expect to receive.

One of the standards will relate to the time allowed to deal with mail. The agreement may say for example 'all mail will be dealt with and replied to within 48 hours of receipt'. If this is the case, all mail must be processed within two working days, otherwise your employer will be breaking their agreement. This would not help your relations with a valued customer.

Making sure post is delivered to the correct person

If you work in a large organisation then it is likely that you will receive hundreds, if not thousands, of items of mail each day. Imagine also that your company employs a couple of thousand people in the office where you work. This should now give you some idea of the scale of operations that are needed to make sure post is delivered to its correct destination. Often companies follow a similar procedure to make sure that mail is sent to the correct person. This would normally work in the following way:

1. Sacks of inbound mail are dropped off at the company's mail room for sorting.

2. The mail is sorted into departmental piles (this can be done by putting the letters into named pigeon holes to keep them separate).

3. The mail may then be sorted into named employee piles.

4. The mail is delivered to the correct person by hand.

Delivering post at set times of day

Most businesses will have written policies for the handling of mail. These policies will clearly set out the time by which employees should receive mail. They usually describe the way in which post is to be delivered and precisely where in the department post is received.

Activity: Policy for dealing with incoming mail

Work individually to create a new policy for dealing with incoming mail. Your policy must include your procedures, along with timescales and actions you could take if those timescales are not met.

How could this help a business be more effective?

Activity: Service standards

Ask your tutor to arrange a visit to the administration office of your centre.

While visiting the administration office try to interview one of the administration staff about the expected service level they have to provide in dealing with post.

After you have had your visit, you need to create a poster which highlights what you have discovered.

Functional skills

If you use design or word-processing software to produce the poster, you will be practising your ICT skills.

Check

- If mail gets lost, or is not processed quickly, then customers may start to lose faith in the business.

- Dealing with mail at set times is important so that staff have a deadline to work to and customer promises can be met.

L03 Dealing with outgoing mail

Collecting post at set times

The latest time in the day that mail can be sent should be set out in the policy for handling mail.

It is important to remember that outgoing post must be collected from departments in time. It can then be collected by whichever postal service is used and delivered to its recipient in an acceptable timescale.

It is difficult otherwise for businesses to make promises to customers if employees are sending out mail at different times.

All large businesses have postal deadlines which mean that if an item of post is not ready for posting at a certain time, it will have to wait until the next day. It is not simply a case of putting all of the mail in the local postbox – in business, companies tend to use a variety of different postal services. You are going to explore these later in this unit. There may be additional tasks to do. For example, you may be required to frank mail so it can be posted. If there are hundreds of items this will take a long time. So you have to remember that the last postal collection is likely to be early in the evening and you cannot afford to miss it.

Despatching

Despatching is the term given to sending mail out by a postal service. When despatching mail there are a number of important things you have to remember. All postal services have a set way in which they like post to be addressed. They may provide labels for you to write and stick on, or even plastic postal bags in which to put your mail. However, whichever method the business uses, there are basic requirements which must be met including:

- Checking if the mail is urgent

- Identifying the type of postal service needed and arranging this through an appropriate delivery company

- Knowing the weight and size of the package (this will affect how much it will cost to deliver)

- Making sure that the package is sealed and securely packaged

- Making sure that the package is clearly and accurately addressed

- Checking that all appropriate delivery documentation is completed.

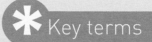
Key terms

Postal services
The term given to a range of different mail delivery companies.

Franking
The process of passing mail through a machine which franks a stamp on to it. The purpose of franking is to save time.

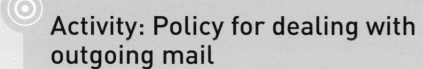

Activity: Policy for dealing with outgoing mail

Work individually to create a new policy for dealing with outgoing mail. Your policy must include your procedures, along with timescales and actions you could take if those timescales are not met.

Activity: Costing up the price of a delivery

Contact a range of delivery companies by telephone or via the Internet and find out which is the cheapest for delivery of the following package:

- Package size: 50 cm long × 30 cm wide × 15 cm deep

- Weighs 1.2 kg

- From the postcode of your centre to SW1A 1AA (find out who lives here!).

When carrying out your research complete the table below.

Name of delivery company	Name of service/features of service	Cost
Parcelforce	Express 9 - guaranteed by 9 a.m. next working day	£29.50

Check

- Accurate despatching of mail is important otherwise it may get sent to the wrong person. This would cause delay and possibly some embarrassment to the business.

- It is important to use the right delivery service for the needs of the business. When thinking about a courier, cost and delivery times must be considered.

ASSESSMENT OVERVIEW

While working through this unit, you will have prepared for completing the following assessment tasks:

○	1.1	State how efficient distribution of mail benefits a business	Pages 68–69
○	1.2	State why inaccuracies or delays can have a negative impact	Pages 68–69
○	1.3	Identify procedures to protect confidential information	Pages 70–71
○	2.1	Sort incoming mail appropriately	Page 72
○	2.2	State how to deal with suspicious or damaged items	Page 73
○	2.3	Distribute incoming mail accurately and to a given deadline	Pages 74–75
○	3.1	Collect and sort outgoing mail accurately and on time	Pages 76–77
○	3.2	Despatch outgoing mail on time	Pages 76–77

edexcel :::

Assignment tips

- Remember that 'efficient' means that mail is delivered on time and to the correct person. You need to state two ways in which this benefits the business.

- You need to provide two examples to show why inaccuracies or delays can have a negative impact.

- You need to provide two examples to identify procedures to protect confidential information.

- A number of the assessment tasks for this unit will be practical. When you are being observed for assessment, it is very important that you can be seen to go through all the checks that you need to complete. It might be a good idea to talk through the task you are completing as you are observed so your tutor can understand your thought processes.

CREATING BUSINESS DOCUMENTS

When working in administration you will be faced with a wide variety of business documents. As part of your role, you need to both create and handle many different types of business documents accurately and efficiently. This means you need to know when it is appropriate to use a template and house style, as well as understanding what communication style you should use.

In this unit you will:

- Know that there are different types of business document

- Know why it is important to use the right communication style in business documents

- Be able to produce routine business documents

Why do you think it is important to understand the different types of documents you will use as an administrator?

L01 Different types of business documentation

Effective communication is important for the smooth running of a business. People within the organisation need to be able to choose and use appropriate **business documents** to communicate information internally and to those outside.

They can also be used to give instructions, attract potential customers and confirm agreements. You will learn about the different documents used for these purposes later in the unit.

 ### Case study:

The Moorcroft Hotel

The Moorcroft is an exclusive 5-star hotel in Leeds that boasts an 18-hole championship golf course and a luxury health spa. It opened in 1990. In late 2009 it became clear that membership numbers had almost halved and hotel room bookings had reduced by 35 per cent.

Director of Operations Charlie Statham took on the task of uncovering the reasons for the decline. She found that instead of membership subscription reminders being sent out by letter, they were using email to save postage costs. However, many of the customers' email addresses were wrong or out of date, and the reminders were getting caught in customers' junk mail filters.

 ## Activity: Group discussion

As a group, discuss what you think Charlie Statham should do to solve the problems at The Moorcroft Hotel. Think about how long-standing members may have felt if they believed the business had just ignored them. How might this have affected the business? How could Charlie ensure this could never happen again?

Sending documents

As shown in the case study about The Moorcroft Hotel, businesses need to choose carefully how to communicate information through business documents. Choosing how to send a business document is important in order to make sure the information gets to the right person in an effective format. Some of the most common delivery options for communicating business information and the **purpose of each document** are in the table below.

Document type	Purpose of document
Letter	• Letters can be formal. • Letters are used to communicate with people and organisations outside your business. • Letters come in many forms. Their main purpose is normally to advise a business, customer, supplier or business contact that an event has happened or is about to happen or to confirm agreements and contracts.
Memo	• A memo (full name *memorandum*) is a document used within a business to inform employees that an event is about to happen. • Memos are not usually written in the same formal manner as letters.
Emails	• Email is a now very popular as it is quicker and cheaper to send complicated documents than traditional 'snail' mail (i.e. letters). It is now one of the most common methods of business communication. • Email can be used for many purposes including communicating with customers, suppliers, colleagues and other business contacts.
Faxes	• Faxes were a popular method of communication before email became widely used. • Faxes are still in use today and have the benefit of letting exact copies of documents (handwritten) be sent to another person in a different place.

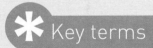

Key terms

Business documents
Documents either in paper or electronic form which are used in business for a number of different purposes. For the document to be useful, it must be completed with accuracy.

Purpose of document
Each type of document performs a specific function. It is important that the correct document is used for the correct process if an administrative system is to work efficiently.

Activity: Sending documents

Imagine you are applying for a job at The Moorcroft Hotel. For this activity you are to apply in writing for the post of 'Hotel Receptionist'. Your letter of application must be professional in terms of content and the way it looks. You then have to create an address for The Moorcroft Hotel and finally prepare an envelope for the letter.

Check

- It is important to think about how business documents will be sent. How can you make sure the information gets to the right person?

- Some business documents are only used within an organisation, while others can be used for colleagues, customers, suppliers, etc.

L01 Uses of business documents

Businesses use a variety of types of document, each of which has a very specific purpose. The following two tables describe the most common types of document you are likely to come across while working as an administrator and also the purpose of each document.

The first table (below) describes business documents used in meetings and to advertise a company. The second table (on the right) describes documents used by businesses to order, pay for and deliver items.

Document type	Purpose of document
Agenda	An agenda is a document that is used to advise workers what is going to be discussed at a meeting. Agendas are always written in the same format and include the following: • Name of person who called meeting • Type of meeting • Time, date and venue of meeting • List of attendees • Apologies for absence (list of people who cannot attend) • Matters arising from previous meeting • Items to be discussed • Any other business (AOB) • Date and time of next meeting. An agenda should be sent out in good time before a meeting so that if attendees need to carry out research for the meeting they have time to do so.
Minutes	Minutes are a formal record of what has been discussed at a meeting. Normally a secretary or nominated person will be asked to attend and write up the minutes of a meeting.
Reports	Reports are formal documents which bring together and summarise the findings of research or information that is important for a business. Reports are often used to present information on sales figures.
Promotional flyers	Promotional flyers are used to advertise a product, service or event. Flyers come in many designs and sizes but are usually bold and colourfully designed. A flyer will contain logos and images of what is being advertised.

Document type	Purpose of document
Order forms	An order form is a document that is used to order items from a business or supplier. Order forms are laid out in a very clear manner and will include sections to enter the following information: • Address of supplier • Date of order • Order number • Description of item • Item code • Quantity of item needed • Cost(s) of items ordered • Total cost of order • VAT • Total cost of order including VAT. It is common for order forms to be transmitted electronically by Electronic Data Interchange (EDI) or more often by email. Both the purchaser and supplier will keep records of orders sent so they can make sure they send and receive the correct items.
Delivery notes	A delivery note is a document that is usually attached to an item when it is in the process of being delivered. The delivery note contains information about what the package contains. It is useful for warehouse workers so they can check off the items that have been sent against what is in the package.
Invoices	An invoice is a request for payment that is usually sent out between 30 and 90 days after an order has been sent. Invoices contain the following information: • Invoice number • Name and address of customer • Description and quantity of items being invoiced for • Total invoice amount • VAT • Total invoice amount including VAT • Payment terms.

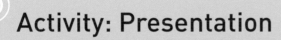

Activity: Presentation

For this task you will work in pairs to create a presentation that highlights different business document types and their purposes.

You may choose to base your presentation on one of the following:

• Documents used in meetings (e.g. to present sales briefings or research findings)

• Documents used when ordering items (e.g. to order paper and stationery or other products).

Functional skills

By presenting information, you will be demonstrating your English speaking skills.

Check

• Business documents help businesses operate efficiently as they each have a specific purpose. Using the correct type of document avoids confusion.

• Business documentation must have a clear and appropriate layout, otherwise it is easy for the user to make mistakes.

L01 Document templates and **L02** language

Templates

Business templates are used for many reasons including speed (i.e. making it possible to create documents quickly), accuracy and efficiency. Templates allow a business to create a set of documents that can be edited as necessary.

Templates are ready-made documents that are saved on a business's computer network. Each document has areas that are protected. This means that there are sections which cannot be changed and so they stay accurate and **consistent** every time the document is printed out. However, the document also includes areas that can be edited so it can fit with the needs of the user.

Key term

Consistent
If something is consistent, it remains the same or largely unchanged.

> Consistency – using templates means documents all look similar, making them more professional

> The benefits of using templates

> Time-saving – templates help employees create business documents

> Clarity – templates help make sure all important information is included

Activity: Use a template

Using the Internet (or a document that your tutor has provided) find an example of a template for one of the business documents listed on pages 82–83. Print the document and make notes on it to identify the areas where an employee would need to input information.

Try to identify which information would be the same each time the document was created and which information would need to be updated each time.

Using the correct communication style in business documentation

It Is important to understand when it is appropriate to use **informal** and **formal communication** style. Different **stakeholders** will expect to be addressed in different ways. For example, an employee would use formal language when writing a letter to a senior manager in another business, but may use informal language when communicating with a colleague.

It is usual practice to use formal language when communicating with people outside your company. This is because formal language presents a professional image of the business you work for. You should use formal language when communicating with a senior manager from your organisation, because they will expect you to be precise and clear.

Formal communication
  - Contacting external customers
  - Confirming payment
  - Contacting senior managers
  - Dealing with customer queries

When should you use formal or informal communication?

Talking to your peers in the same department

Informal communication
  - Talking to team members for social purposes

Activity: Formal and informal language

Imagine you are an administrator for a busy company. Draft a 200-word memo asking the staff for their comments on the postal distribution service. In pairs share your memos and try to distinguish between formal and informal language.

Key terms

Informal communication
Communication which uses 'everyday' language and is not kept on record for future reference.

Formal communication
Communication which uses professional language and where a record is kept for future reference.

Stakeholder
Anybody with some form of interest in a business who stands to lose if it is run badly.

✔ Check

- Document templates save you time and help present a more consistent image.
- Generally, formal language is best used when communicating with external customers and senior staff.

L02 House style

A house style is a set of guidelines produced by a business for the appearance of its documents. It might include the following:

- Rules for how the company should use its logos
- Guidelines on which fonts should be used in documents
- Notes on how employees should spell certain words.

The house style helps keep the style of an organisation's documents consistent (even though employees will be creating many different documents) and presents a more consistent, professional image.

A good house style should be well thought out and will reflect the type of organisation it is being used for. For example, many water utility companies use the colour blue in their logos and communications.

Activity: What does the logo say?

Research a number of well-known company logos. Draw and complete a table like the example below explaining the design of each logo.

Business logo	Explain why you think the logo has been designed in the way it has and what the impact of the design will be on the company's house style
E.g. **SPANDAS**	The logo for the supermarket SPANDAS has been designed so that the name of the business is the first thing you see. The colours have been chosen because they provide a clear contrast which is readable to people who may have sight difficulties: white writing on a red background. The logo is clear and simple. The supermarket aims for the image to reflect the way they want customers to feel about shopping with them (that they provide a simple and easy way to shop).

Writing appropriate routine documents

When working in business administration you will be expected to produce documents that will be sent to people outside your organisation. Accurate spelling, punctuation and grammar are very important, as is the correct opening and complimentary close. Also, select the correct type of communication for the message you are trying to get across.

Things to avoid when writing business communications

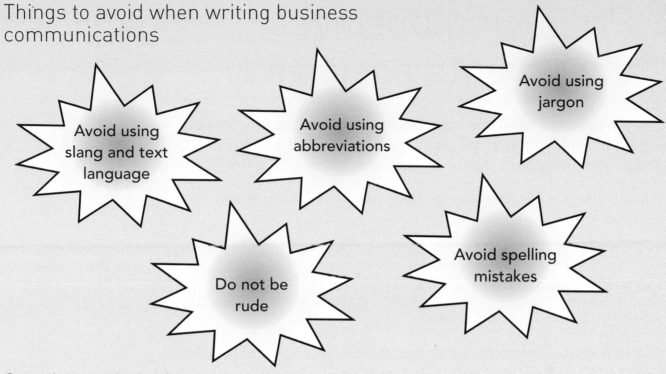

Opening and closing

When writing a letter or email to an individual, there may be times when you know the name and title of the individual and other times when you do not. There are some rules you need to remember when writing formal letters or emails.

	Appropriate greeting	Complimentary close
If you know the individual's name and/or title	Dear Jane OR Dear Mrs Smith	Yours sincerely
If you do not know the individual's name	Dear Sir/Madam	Yours faithfully

Activity: Writing a house style guide

Draw up a house style guide for openings and closings to be used in different circumstances for an organisation that you know.

✔ Check

- A house style can be used to present information consistently and make decisions about fonts, colours, logos, etc.

L03 Producing business documents accurately

It is very important that all business documents are prepared accurately. There are a number of simple ways in which you can make sure your business documents are accurate and professional, including the following:

- Get a colleague or supervisor to check your work for clarity and accuracy

- Make sure that your spell checker is set up correctly on your computer

- Use a dictionary

- Keep sentences short and simple

- Use templates where possible as they reduce the chance of mistakes.

Activity: The Moorcroft Hotel

After Charlie Statham carried out her investigation into why golf and leisure membership numbers had gone down, she found out that much of the documentation used by the business was not fit for purpose. She has decided to review and change the format and content of the documents currently being used.

For this task you are going to:

1. Look again at the different business documents in the tables on pages 82–83 and make sure you understand their purpose.

2. Research the designs and formats of other companies' documents, including their letter headings and logos, to give you some ideas.

3. Produce new designs for all the documents you think The Moorcroft uses.

4. Make sure you think about what kind of business it is and the image it wants to create.

5. Design a new company logo.

Activity: Proofreading

Charlie Statham has drafted a letter to her customers to apologise for the lack of communication from The Moorcroft over the last year and to invite them all to a free health spa event. She has used Miss J. Jonas as the example in her letter. It is important that Charlie's letter is accurate so that the company maintains a professional image.

Read through the letter and proofread it for accuracy and spelling.

Misses J. Jonas
32 Acacia Avenue
Middlesburn
West Yorkshire
WY25 5RF

The Moorcroft
Morcroft Hall
Middlesburn
West Yorkshire
WY12 8DR
T: 0113 8941414

2/5/2011

Der Mrs. Jona

RE: Free health spa event

I am writing to apologse for our lack of comunication with you over the last 12 months. To rward you as l loyal customer I would like to ivite you to attend our free health spa event on the 22nd May 2011. If you would like to attend ring the phone number above and simply book your plce. I hope you can atend the event and I look forward to meeting you.

Yours faithfully,

Charlie Statham
Director of Operations.

Check

- Remember that all business documents give people an impression of the business that sent them.

- You need to check your work to make sure it is accurate and professional.

ASSESSMENT OVERVIEW

While working through this unit, you will have prepared for completing the following assessment tasks:

○	1.1 Identify different types of business document and when they might be used	Pages 80–83
○	1.2 State why templates are used for some business documents	Page 84
○	2.1 Give examples of when to use a formal or informal communication style	Page 85
○	2.2 State why some businesses adopt a 'house style' for certain documents	Page 86
○	3.1 Produce routine business documents using the appropriate communication style	Pages 86–87
○	3.2 Check documents for accuracy	Pages 88–89

Assignment tips

- Identify four different documents. You might find it useful to explain what they would be used for in business by 'telling a story' through the documents. For example, if a business sends a document to a customer, what do they get back and what happens next?

- Give two examples of when to use a formal communication style and two examples of when to use an informal communication style. Try to explain why this communication style is suitable for each example.

- Produce three routine documents, which should include two different types of document. You can produce two versions of the same type of document, but you need to produce a different type of document for your third example.

RECORDING BUSINESS TRANSACTIONS

As an administrator you may be working in a job where you have responsibility for recording the flow of money in and out of a business. In this unit you will learn about the most frequently used financial recording documents. In order for a business to operate successfully these documents should be completed accurately and in a timely fashion.

In this unit you will:

- Know the documents used to record business transactions

- Be able to complete an order form for office supplies

Why do you think it is important to complete financial documents accurately?

L01 # Documents used to record business transactions

It is important you understand that each **financial document** mentioned in this unit has a very specific purpose. The first set of documents we are going to look at are used when a company buys and sells items.

The recording of these **transactions** helps the business to keep track of its cash flow. Imagine cash flow being like the blood supply in a person's body – cash flow keeps a business alive. If a business has more money going out than coming in, it will not be able to survive for very long.

Case study:
Williamson's Music

Williamson's Music is a music production company based on the outskirts of Preston, Lancashire. The business is owned and run by Mark Williamson.

The business has been running for eight years. In that time it has not made huge profits but just enough for Mark to get by on.

The business specialises in creating and remixing music for the underground club scene. While the business is Mark's only source of income, he has treated it more like a hobby than his only source of a wage.

In common with the philosophy of this type of music industry, Mark will produce work for artists and either not charge them for it or forget to do so. His accounts are out of date and in an awful mess. Recently, times have been hard for Mark so he has decided that he must formalise the way he runs his business if it is to survive.

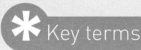 **Key terms**

Financial documents
Specific documents that are used to record the buying and selling of goods.

Transaction
The process of paying or receiving money for goods that have been bought or sold.

Activity: Group discussion

What financial problems might Mark be facing by running the business in the way he currently does? What sort of advice do you think an accountant might give Mark about organising his finances better? How would this advice help Mark in the future?

Activity: Williamson's Music

Mark Williamson has asked for your help. He realises that if he is going to make money from his business he will need a professional set of financial documents.

You will have to produce, individually, each of the documents mentioned in the table on the following pages. You will design a logo and make sure that the layout and content of each document is accurate.

To complete this task you will have to do some research on the Internet to get a feel for each document. You can also refer back to *Unit 19 Creating business documents* (pages 86–89) for help with this activity.

Functional skills

Through finding information on the Internet for this activity you will be practising your **ICT** skills.

Petty cash

Petty cash is the term given to the small amount of money a business may keep in its office to buy small items. It is very important for a business to keep a small sum of petty cash (normally no more than £100) as certain items need to be bought to keep the business running efficiently. Such items include stationery, stamps and refreshments. However, even though the amounts spent may only be small, it is still very important that it is accounted for. For this reason, most businesses will have petty cash receipts and a recording procedure.

Item is bought from a shop. A receipt is issued for the value of the item.

Recording petty cash purchases

The flow diagram on the right gives an example of how a business may record its purchases from petty cash.

Receipt is passed to person in charge of petty cash. They will complete a petty cash voucher for that receipt.

Activity: Recording petty cash

The flow diagram shows a very simple petty cash recording procedure. You now need to create a new petty cash procedure for Williamson's Music.

Petty cash voucher and receipt should be kept together and will then be entered in the accounts of the company.

Check

- Each financial document mentioned in this unit has a very specific purpose.
- It is very important to account for the spending of petty cash.

The main financial documents used for buying and selling goods are shown in the following table. Use the information to help you with the case study and activities on the previous pages.

Name of document	Purpose of document
Purchase order	Purchase orders are used when a business wants to buy goods or services. Purchase orders are usually completed by a person with some authority and contain the following details: • Company name • Company address • Contact numbers/email address • VAT registration number (if VAT registered) • Order number • Supplier reference • Order date • Quantity/ description/item code number/unit price of goods • Signature and date of person in authority.
Delivery note	A delivery note comes with a delivery when it is received by a business. Two copies of a delivery note are usually sent and one copy is kept by the customer while the other is sent back to the supplier. The delivery note lists what has been delivered. This allows the receiving company to check if the correct items have been received, the correct quantity has been sent and if they were received on time and in good condition. The delivery note will contain the following information: • Supplier name and address • Customer name and address • VAT registration number (if VAT registered) • Contact numbers/email address/website address • Despatch date • Order number • Customer account number • Invoice number • Quantity/description/item code number/unit price of goods • Delivery date • Signature and date.
Goods received note (GRN)	A goods received note is a document which is completed internally within a business. It is usually completed by the person or department (usually the warehouse) who received the goods. The GRN provides a double check that the goods have been received on time and in good condition. The GRN will also indicate the supplier name and details. After completion a copy is sent to the accounts department and this will trigger off payment for the goods. A GRN will contain the following information: • Supplier name and address • Name of haulage/courier company • Date the GRN was written out • Name of person who checked stock • Order number • Quantity ordered/quantity delivered/description of goods • Indication of whether or not goods were received in an acceptable condition.

Name of document	Purpose of document
Invoice	An invoice is a document that is used to request payment from a customer for goods or services that have been supplied. It is important that invoices are prepared correctly otherwise a customer may become upset if they are charged too much or, alternatively, your business will lose out on profit if goods are not invoiced for correctly. An invoice will contain the following information: • Name and address of company sending invoice • Name and address of company being invoiced • Contact details/email address/website address • VAT number (if VAT registered) • Order number • Customer account number • Date and tax point • Invoice number • Item codes/quantities being invoiced for/description of items/unit price/ total unit price/invoice total/VAT element/total amount due • Payment terms.
Credit note	A credit note is used when a business has been overcharged for goods and services. In effect, a credit note is like a refund for being overcharged. There are a number of reasons why a credit note might be issued including: • Wrong prices quoted by supplier • Invoice incorrectly sent out • Wrong or damaged goods sent and customer returning goods ordered. A credit note will contain the following information: • Name and contact details of supplier • Contact details/email address/website address • VAT number (if VAT registered) • Name and address of customer • Invoice number • Credit note number • Item code of product being overcharged for • Quantity of items • Description of items • Unit price/net value/total cost/VAT/total amount being refunded • Reason for return.
Remittance advice slip	A remittance advice slip is usually attached to the invoice and makes payment easier for the customer and supplier. Traditionally, a remittance advice slip accompanies the payment which is sent by the customer to the supplier. However, technology has now made it more straightforward for payments to be made electronically straight into a supplier's bank account. In some ways this has reduced the use of a remittance advice slip.
Cheque	A cheque is a form of payment which is sent from the customer to the supplier. In completing a cheque a customer writes the following on it: • Amount in words • Date of cheque • Amount in figures • Signature (usually someone in authority). The cheque will contain additional printed details such as cheque number, branch sort code and account number and the address of the business's bank branch. Cheques are likely to be phased out by 2018 and will cease to be legal tender.
Receipt	A receipt is a document which advises the customer that their payment has been received and processed. Businesses keep receipts so they can check them against their bank statements to ensure they tally. Businesses also need them for tax purposes when filling in their end of year accounts.

L02 Complete an order form for office supplies

It is important to remember that a business must keep a close eye on its finances. Even small items which cost very little start to add up if bought on a regular basis. For this reason most companies have a procedure which must be followed before an order is placed. This allows the business to control its spending by carefully planning what it needs to spend its money on. However, a business cannot operate without supplies and therefore, at some stage, orders have to be placed.

Planning to place an order

The flowchart below provides an idea of the process a business goes through when it is planning to place an order.

Complete a purchase order form accurately

It is very important that purchase order forms are filled out accurately. It may be that a customer is waiting for the goods that you are ordering and, if they do not arrive on time or as requested, the customer will feel let down and possibly not buy from you again. There are a number of common mistakes that occur on purchase order forms including:

- Ordering the wrong item
- Entering the wrong product code
- Ordering the wrong quantity
- Describing the product incorrectly
- Inserting an incorrect unit price
- Calculating unit and total costs incorrectly.

There is an example of a purchase order form on the page opposite.

Stock checking

Check how much stock the business currently has

⬇

To buy or not to buy?

Decide if an order needs placing
If, yes then

⬇

Obtaining stock details

Find out the stock code, description and price details of items required
Complete a purchase order or pass to a staff member who has the authority to do so

⬇

Sending purchase order

Send a copy of the purchase order to the customer and another copy to the accounts department of your employer

Williamson's Music
22 Acacia Avenue
Fulbrook Preston
PR6 9JR
(T) 01924 666555 (M) 09876 767123 (E) wm@anymail.com

PURCHASE ORDER

Order Date: _____   Order Number: _____

Shipping Method (tick)		Payment Method (tick)	
Post	Courier	Cash	Other

Qty	Item Code	Item Description	Unit Price	Unit Cost
			Sub Total	
			VAT	
Supplier Name and Address Details			Total Cost	
			VAT	
			Total Cost	

Functional skills

This activity will help you practise your **Mathematics** skills.

Activity: Williamson's Music order

For this task you need to complete an order for the following items for Williamson's Music. Mark requires the following items:

- 3 x 50 pack of recordable CDs = £4.99 each
- 20 x pack of CD labels = £1.99 each
- 6 x pack of CD boxes = £2.65 each
- 1 x microphone = £109.99

You need to work out VAT at 17.5 per cent and the order is to be sent to:

J & S Music Supplies
Pendle Street, Settle
North Yorkshire BD25 8ES

Check

- Always be 100 per cent accurate when completing purchase orders as mistakes can be very costly.

- Always check that you definitely need items before ordering them to avoid wasting company money.

L02 Delivery notes, invoices, cheques and receipts

Delivery notes

As mentioned earlier, delivery notes are completed by the seller and tell the buyer what is being delivered. An example of a basic delivery note is shown here.

Williamson's Music
22 Acacia Avenue
Fulbrook Preston
PR6 9JR
(T) 01924 666555 (M) 09876 767123 (E) wm@anymail.com

DELIVERY NOTE

Delivered To:
SR Music
Smith Street
Cardiff
CF12 7ER

Delivery note no: 765
Delivery methord: Courier
Your order: SR234
Order Date: 19/4/2011

Stock code	Quantity supplied	Item Description
4312	14 sets	Earphones

Received by: _____ Date: _____

Invoices

An invoice is a request from a seller for money that is owed. It is important that it is accurate as a mistake could lead to the seller paying the wrong amount. This may lead to the company going elsewhere for goods in the future. An example of a basic invoice is shown here.

Williamson's Music
22 Acacia Avenue
Fulbrook Preston
PR6 9JR
(T) 01924 666555 (M) 09876 767123 (E) wm@anymail.com

INVOICE

Invoice To:
SR Music
Smith Street
Cardiff
CF12 7ER

Invoice Number: 001345
Order Number: SR234
Order Date: 19/4/2011

Payment Terms = 60 Days

Qty	Product Code	Description	Price	Total Price	Discount	Net Price
14	MP68	Microphone	109.99	1539.86	15%	1308.88

Order Value	1308.88
VAT 17.5%	229.05
Total Cost	1537.93

Cheques

A cheque is a legal document which, when completed by a person or business, forms an instruction to make payment for goods or services. In recent years, personal cheques have become less popular due to safer and more efficient electronic banking card services.

However, in business cheques are still a popular method of payment. This is because, unlike other methods, the money does not leave a bank account straightaway. It normally takes five days for a cheque to clear which means extra interest on the money the business has deposited with a bank. An example of a cheque is shown here.

Supplier receipts

The receipt is probably the most familiar document of all when looking at financial documents. A receipt provides proof of purchase and can be used for returning items or obtaining refunds if they are faulty. Businesses use receipts in much the same way as consumers do – the only difference is they will retain them for tax purposes to calculate VAT.

Activity: Analysing receipts

Collect as many receipts as you can over the period of a week and bring them into your centre. Compare the different layouts. Now make a collage out of the receipts. Make sure you label the different parts of the receipt.

Check

- It is important that invoices are paid on time otherwise this may affect the cash flow of the business that has supplied you. Companies can also charge extra for overdue invoices.

- Despite cheques being a very old payment method they are still popular because they are easy to write and secure, which means they can be sent through the post without risk. However, cheques are expected to be phased out in 2018.

ASSESSMENT OVERVIEW

While working through this unit, you will have prepared for completing the following assessment tasks:

○	1.1	Identify the types and purpose of documents used to record business transactions	Pages 92–95
○	2.1	Make plans to order appropriate supplies for a given situation	Page 96
○	2.2	Complete a purchase order form accurately	Pages 96–97
○	2.3	Receive the supplies and the delivery notes	Page 98
○	2.4	Receive the invoice from the suppliers	Page 98
○	2.5	Make out the cheque to pay the invoice	Page 99
○	2.6	Receive the supplier's receipt for payment of the invoice	Page 99

Assignment tips

- Try to include an example of when each document might be used to help show what it is used for.

- It is likely that you will complete the documents used to order office supplies. You will then be asked questions about what you have done, so it is important to know the purpose and features of each transaction.

- Try to get into the habit of giving reasons for answers, so every statement (for example, 'I used a cheque') is followed with the word 'because'.

SUPPORTING BUSINESS MEETINGS

When working in administration you will often need to organise and support business meetings. The task of arranging meetings has to be undertaken professionally and requires many skills. If a meeting is badly organised it can give a poor impression of an organisation and for that reason is a very important job. This unit will give you an introduction to the skills you need to arrange successful business meetings.

In this unit you will:

- Know what is required to hold a business meeting

- Be able to set up a room for a meeting

- Be able to support a meeting

- Be able to complete follow-up activities after a meeting

Why do you think it is important for businesses to have well-organised meetings?

L01 What is required to hold a successful business meeting?

Across the world, throughout every minute of the day, meetings at businesses will be taking place. Meetings form an important part of a business's success. Without them, important plans would not get discussed and employers would not have a clear picture of how to improve and move their businesses forward. However, a meeting is only as good as the planning that has gone into it. There is a famous saying you might want to keep in mind when organising meetings: 'fail to prepare – prepare to fail'.

Successful meetings do not just happen – they are planned for. Throughout this unit you will learn the skills needed to host successful meetings.

Case study:
Sprite & Co

Sprite & Co is a small manufacturing company based in North Yorkshire. The business is owned and run by Louise Sprite and her two children, Mary and Charlie. The company also employs 15 other staff in a range of production and administration roles.

The business specialises in making expensive equipment for the medical industry. The products have to be made to very high standards in a very clean environment. The company is a leader in its field and has been for the last ten years.

However, due to tightening budgets and cheaper imports from Asia, the business is starting to struggle. Recently a series of very important meetings has been arranged with a number of NHS trusts who are interested in buying a new piece of equipment. If Sprite & Co could secure the contracts, then the future of the business would be safe for the next five years. Louise has asked her Head of Administration, Jane Tapp, to take responsibility for organising the meetings.

Activity: Group discussion

Discuss the things Jane Tapp must think about before arranging the NHS meetings.

Why is it important for Jane to think about the factors you have identified? What might be the consequences of overlooking these factors?

Requirements of hosting a meeting

The table below shows a number of points that have to be considered before arranging a meeting. A few examples have been given:

Requirement to be considered	Reason for considering	Consequence of not considering
Number of participants	So that all the arrangements will be suitable, e.g. enough chairs, delegate packs, refreshments, etc.	There may not be enough space/resources for all the participants
Informing attendees of the date of meeting	So attendees know when the meeting is going to happen	Nobody will arrive for the meeting
Advising time and venue of meeting	So attendees arrive on time and know where to go	Late arrivals will interrupt the meeting
Providing pre-meeting reading	So attendees know what the meeting is about and what they are expected to say	The meeting will take longer and will not be as informative
Arranging refreshments	To make attendees feel comfortable in the meeting	Attendees will get restless and the meeting may become disrupted

Activity: Group discussion

Some meetings need to be held in-house while it might be better to hold others off-site. Can you think of the advantages and disadvantages for either location for different types of meeting?

Check

- Meetings are important for businesses so that they can plan for the future and staff are informed of jobs that need to be completed.

- People who attend meetings are known as **delegates** or attendees.

Key term

Delegate
Someone attending a meeting. This person may represent another business.

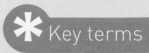

L01 Types of meeting

Not all meetings are the same. For example, a meeting that is being held to arrange a staff social event will be much less formal than a meeting which is attended by the board of directors of a business.

An easy way to remember the difference between a **formal meeting** and an **informal meeting** is that records are always kept of a formal meeting. This is because they may contain important information that needs to be referred back to at a later date. Also, whenever a meeting takes place between the company you work for and an outside person or business, this is usually a formal meeting.

However, meetings do not always happen at the place where you work – they may take place at another venue and this is known as an off-site meeting. If a meeting does go ahead at the place where you work, and only involves employees from your company, this is known as an in-house meeting.

Other types of informal meetings might include:

- Team briefings
- Staff training.

Documentation required for meetings

As mentioned earlier, meetings must be well planned if they are to run successfully. Part of the planning involves making sure that the correct business documentation is in place for the meeting. Examples of the types of documentation that need to be considered when planning and hosting a meeting are shown here and on the opposite page.

An **agenda** is a document which lists the items to be discussed at a meeting.

✳ Key terms

Formal meetings
A meeting between senior staff or a business and their suppliers or customers. Records are always kept.

Informal meetings
Often a meeting between colleagues. Records are rarely kept.

Agenda
An agenda is a document that is sent to attendees before a meeting to let them know what is going to be discussed.

AGENDA
Sprite & Co

New Technology Group meeting
Room 1 at 10 a.m. – 18 April 2011

---

1. Apologies for absence
2. Minutes of previous meeting
3. Matters arising
4. New technology
5. New technology training
6. Any other business (AOB)
7. Date and time of next meeting

Called by: Jane Tapp
30 March 2011

Here are some sample **minutes** from a meeting. These are a record of what has been agreed at a meeting and by whom.

Other documentation that may be used

As well as the agenda and minutes, and depending on the location and type of meeting, it would normally be appropriate to send a notification of the date and time of the meeting to attendees along with any presentation or notes required to support the meeting.

Sprite & Co.

Minutes of meeting – New Technology Group – 18 April 2011

Present: Jane Tapp (JT), Rob Jones (RJ), James Pratt (JP), Bob Johns (BJ), Nusrat Khan (NK)

1. **Apologies for absence:** Jenny Smith, Andrew Taylor.
2. **Minutes of previous meeting:** Accepted as correct and true.
3. **Matters arising:** Cost of new technology higher than costed for.
4. **New technology:** RJ discussed project managing the new technology – his suggestion was accepted by JP, BJ and NK.
5. **New technology training**: BJ and NK suggested off-site training, although it was agreed by all that in-house training would be better.
6. **Any other business:** BJ agreed to research suitable training providers for the new technology training.
7. **Date and time of next meeting:** 18 October 2011, 10 a.m.

Activity: Typing up an agenda

Jane Tapp from Sprite & Co has delegated to you the task of typing up an agenda for one of the forthcoming NHS meetings, so it must be complete and accurate.

The agenda has to include the following information:

- Keeping costs manageable
- New reporting structures
- The proposed structure of NHS contracts
- Service level the NHS can expect from Sprite & Co.

Key term

Minutes
Minutes are a formal record of a meeting which highlight what has been agreed and who is taking responsibility for completing a particular task.

Check

- Meetings can be formal or informal, depending on their purpose. Records must always be kept of a formal meeting.

- Documentation for a formal meeting should include an agenda and the minutes, along with any supporting information such as notification of the date and time of the meeting and presentation notes.

LO2 Set up a room for a meeting

For meetings to be successful and worthwhile, delegates must have all the required documents and paperwork for the meeting. When a person attends a meeting they will receive a pack which contains items such as an agenda, copies of electronic presentation slides and booklets, etc.

If the meeting is going to be a large conference-style one, hosting hundreds of delegates, then the creation of **delegate packs** can be a massive job and cannot be left to the last minute. The table below highlights a number of other key considerations when **setting up a room**.

Key terms

Delegate pack
Information given to delegates which is designed to support the meeting.

Setting up a room
The process of making sure that rooms are set up and fit for the purpose of the meeting.

Consideration	Why is this consideration important?
Confirming refreshments for meeting	Meetings can last for a long time. It is usual practice to place bottles of water at the very least on delegate tables. Sometimes, the bottled water will be accompanied by mints or boiled sweets. Providing this type of refreshment allows delegates to concentrate, particularly if it is a long meeting.
Confirming consumables, for example, cups/pens, etc.	Make sure that enough items have been provided for the number of delegates attending. If delegates have bottled water on their tables, then you need to supply them with enough cups or glasses. Similarly, it is usual to provide delegates with pens when they attend meetings. Therefore, you must ensure there are enough available for each person.
Timing of refreshments	The timing of refreshments is important because delegates may become restless if they have to wait too long for a drink or something to eat. If refreshments are given too early, the flow of the meeting may be disrupted.
Equipment	It is important to check that all necessary equipment is available and working for presenters. It is very unprofessional to begin a meeting and then start setting up your equipment halfway through. A presenter nowadays would expect the following to be available in a meeting room: data projector, flip chart, pens, adequate power supplies and a means to adjust the lighting in the room.
Room temperature	This is often forgotten but the temperature of a room can affect the success of a meeting. You must remember that the temperature of a room will increase with the number of delegates attending. It is important that the room is not too hot or delegates will start to feel uncomfortable and begin to doze. If a room is too cold it will also limit the amount of useful work that can be completed as delegates will not be able to concentrate on what is being discussed.

Order of performing tasks

It is important that you follow a procedure when setting up a room for a meeting, otherwise problems may occur. The chart below shows a basic procedure that could be followed to make sure the meeting is successful.

> **Follow instructions**

> **Put tasks in the order in which they need to be completed**

> **Make sure tasks are completed on time**

Functional skills

If you use word-processing software to produce the documentation for a meeting, you will be practising your ICT skills.

Activity: Planning a meeting

Imagine you are holding a meeting to discuss this unit of work with your class group. For the meeting you must create a plan, as well as an agenda, and any other accompanying documents.

Check

- Always make sure that you know how many people are attending the meeting. This will help you plan all the other arrangements.

- Always follow a logical sequence when planning a meeting so you do not forget any important details.

L03 Support a meeting

Your work in supporting a meeting could affect whether or not it is likely to be a success. As a host you will have to carry out a number of administration tasks including welcoming delegates and serving refreshments. Other tasks you may need to carry out are shown in the diagram opposite.

Taking notes

Taking notes at a meeting is an essential task and it is important that the notes follow a logical sequence. The normal way of taking notes is to have a piece of paper which includes the agenda items as headings, with space to write in between the headings. Using this method helps the notes tie up with what has been said at the meeting.

The notes should be laid out in such a way that there is space both to record any decisions that have been taken and to show who is to carry out any actions. This is important. Often meetings can take a long time and people may forget what they have agreed to do unless it has been noted down.

Case study:
Sprite & Co

It soon becomes clear that the meetings arranged at Sprite & Co are not going as well as planned. The company was expecting to win the NHS contracts quite easily – after all Sprite & Co is a leading supplier which has supplied the NHS for a number of years – but this is not happening.

Something is not right so, in an attempt to find out what the problem is, Jane Tapp has decided to review the way meetings are planned. It quickly becomes clear what the problems are:

1. The rooms being used to host the meetings have no natural light and are quite dismal. On average the contract meetings last between three and four hours and this is a long time to sit in miserable surroundings.

2. The meeting rooms are not tidied between meetings and empty cups and half eaten biscuits are left lying around.

3. It seems that visitors are left waiting in the reception area for a long time before meetings take place.

Activity: Group discussion

Why do you think all the factors in the case study might affect the decision making process in the contract meetings?

What can be done in the future to improve the situation?

Taking simple notes

Signing delegates in and issuing name badges

Other tasks undertaken to support meeting

Recording non-attendance

Recording attendance

Activity: More documents!

This activity follows on from the activity on page 107: Planning a meeting.

You have now arranged your meeting and the last thing you need to do is organise name badges and attendance documentation. Create a name badge for each delegate attending your meeting and a register that can be used for recording attendance and non-attendance.

Check

- Supporting a meeting means providing administrative support to make sure it runs smoothly.

109

L04 Complete follow-up activities after a meeting

It is very important when a meeting draws to an end that a number of essential tasks are completed. These tasks range from making sure that the meeting room is tidied up to making sure that documents are distributed after the meeting to relevant colleagues. The table below includes some of the key follow-up activities that must be undertaken after a meeting has finished.

Follow-up activity	Why that activity is important
Clearing the room for the next meeting	It is important to carry out this task so that there is no hold-up between meetings. It would be very unprofessional to keep colleagues waiting while a room is being tidied.
Helping colleagues	Provide support to colleagues. For example, give directions to where they want to go if they do not work at your company. Other support would include practical things such as helping a colleague carry paperwork and equipment back to an office.
Understanding the need for privacy	Very often senior managers have private matters to discuss after the meeting has finished. It is therefore important to respect this by not moving in and out of a room where they are discussing private matters.
Tidying up	Tidying up is very important and this includes both confidential and non-confidential information. Confidential information may need to be securely taken to a specific place or possibly shredded after the meeting.
Have notes checked for accuracy	Any notes taken in the meeting must be accurate. It is always wise to get a colleague who attended the meeting with you to check that what you have written is accurate.
Distribution of documents	You may need to send documents such as minutes, presentation slides and other paperwork to colleagues at a later date. This must be done promptly and all data must be accurate and understandable.

Activity: Follow-up tasks

For this task you need to contact the Administration Manager at your centre and ask if you can help to undertake some of the follow-up activities after a meeting has taken place.

Activity: Preparing minutes

Minutes are a record of a meeting. In pairs discuss what they might record.

Look at the Sprite & Co minutes of a meeting on page 105. Consider whether this record would be better described as decision notes and write down your ideas. Share your ideas as a group and go on to discuss the following questions:

Who should decide on the format of the minutes?

In what circumstances would you consider recording the discussion that led up to a decision?

Who are the minutes prepared for?

Are the minutes used as a form of communication between those present at the meeting and other staff in the business? If so, what does this say about the best format for them?

Check

- Always make sure that delegates are signed in and out of meetings. This is not only for the benefit of the business that is hosting the meeting but also for fire safety reasons.
- Follow-up activities are as important as the meeting itself. If you promise to do something, make sure that is exactly what you do.

ASSESSMENT OVERVIEW

While working through this unit, you will have prepared for completing the following assessment tasks:

○	1.1 List the requirements for holding a formal meeting	Pages 102–104
○	1.2 Identify the types of documents which support business meetings	Pages 104–105
○	2.1 Present a plan for setting up a room for a meeting	Pages 106–107
○	2.2 Set up a room for a meeting	Pages 106–107
○	3.1 Provide support at a meeting	Pages 108–109
○	3.2 Take notes at a meeting showing the key action points agreed	Page 108
○	4.1 Clear a room after a meeting	Pages 110–111
○	4.2 Complete follow-up activities after a meeting	Pages 110–111

edexcel

Assignment tips

- You might find it useful to create a table listing the different types of business documents used to support business meetings, and then identify what they do. This will help you establish what you are trying to achieve with each document when you come to set up a meeting.

- When you take notes at a meeting make a list of who was present and whether anyone sent their apologies for being unable to attend. Keep a list of action points identified at the meeting. Remember to list who needs to do what by when, as these are really important bits of information that people will need.

- You need to produce all the documents that attendees would expect to receive after a meeting. You may not need to send these to the attendees, but you will need to submit them to your tutor.

BUSINESS ADMINISTRATION GROUP PROJECT

When working as an administrator in business you will often need to work with other people. In many situations, a group of people can be more productive than one person working on their own. Throughout this unit you will get the chance to develop many key skills including communication, working as a team member, self-management and problem solving.

In this unit you will:

- Find out about an aspect of local business administration
- Demonstrate work-related skills in presenting information as a team member
- Assess own work-related skills in finding out about an aspect of business administration

Why do you think businesses want people to work together well?

L01 Explore an aspect of local business administration

The job of an administrator is varied. This means that people working in the role must be flexible and willing to take on many different roles and tasks. As a result, working in administration can be worthwhile and rewarding.

Below are some of the tasks you may need to complete when working as an administrator:

- Supporting a meeting
- Working on reception
- Dealing with communications including letters, emails, telephone calls and SMS messages
- Organising security
- Dealing with health and safety issues
- Managing recycling and other environmental procedures (for example, minimising waste)
- Dealing with administration systems, i.e. entering data into a computer or creating reports
- Communicating with staff from different parts of the organisational structure.

For more details about the different tasks you might be involved with, see *Unit 14 Working in business and administration*, pages 18–19.

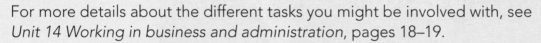

Activity: Create a mind map

Create a mind map of the eight administrative tasks listed above. On your mind map show all the activities you can think of that are involved for each task. For example, show what an administrator would have to do in order to support a meeting.

Aspects of business administration

To complete this unit you will need to make contact with a business and discuss the role of business administration within the organisation. A visit to the business would provide you with the best research opportunities, although you could also contact the company by telephone.

Whichever method you choose to make contact, it is important you research the administrative roles above.

Activity: Group task

Functional skills

You will be practising your **English** and **ICT** skills by researching different businesses.

1. In small groups, and using the list on page 114, choose five aspects of business administration that you would like to learn more about. In discussion with your tutor, select one of your five choices to explore further.

2. You should now carry out some research to find a suitable company for your task. A suitable company is one that often uses this aspect of business administration. Use the Internet, local newspapers or a telephone directory to identify different businesses that could help you with your research.

3. As a group you need to decide what tasks should be completed for your research. You then need to decide who is doing what. Prepare an action plan, so that everyone in your group is clear about what they need to do. An example of an action plan is given below.

4. After carrying out your research into different businesses, you might find it useful to read through the guidance for using different communication technologies (see *Unit 15 Communicating electronically*, page 33).

Business Administration Group Project Action Plan Name of Company: XYZ Industries			
Action	**To be carried out by who**	**Date to be completed by**	**Outcome**
Draw up questionnaire	Andy	27/9/2010	To have drawn up a questionnaire
Telephone company	James	28/9/2010	Obtain a name of contact
Internet research	Sabia	28/9/2010	Find out more about business
Write up questions to ask at visit	Mandy	29/9/2010	Know who is asking what when visiting company

Check

- Carry out research into one administrative aspect of a business.

- Choose which aspect of business administration to focus on by looking at the list on page 114.

(L01) Teamwork

To complete this unit successfully, you must work as part of a team. It is important to develop team working skills as most employers will expect you to be able to work with your colleagues with little or no support.

Team working is an essential skill to learn. It is very difficult for one person to attempt a large project or task by themselves. It is much easier to break the task down and get team members to take **responsibility** for an aspect of work and complete it. Working as a team means you can produce lots of ideas. This can be useful when trying to solve a problem.

The mind map below shows six ways in which you can be more effective as a team member:

✱ Key term

Responsibility
When you are responsible for a task, it is your duty to complete the task on time and follow any instructions you have been given.

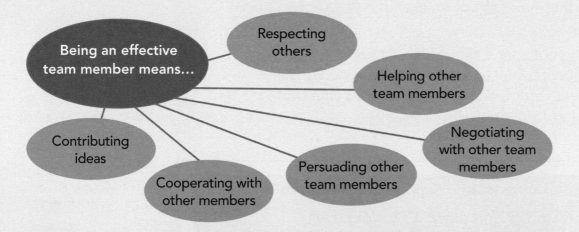

Activity: Team working

Work in pairs or small groups to build a bridge which spans a metre gap and can carry the weight of a small object. The bridge must be no lower than 30 cm from the floor. You are to make the bridge out of everyday materials (for example, newspaper, sticky tape, paper clips, etc.). The winning team is the one which constructs the bridge that holds the most weight and looks the best.

Sources of information

When carrying out the research for this unit it is important to use both primary and secondary research.

Primary research is the type that you carry out yourself, for example by drawing up a questionnaire or interviewing a member of staff on a visit to a company. Primary research is also known as field or original research.

Secondary research is information you get from other sources (it is not research you have carried out yourself). For example, reading an article on the Internet or in a newspaper is secondary research.

In general terms, primary research is often thought to be more reliable and accurate than secondary research.

 Key terms

Primary research
Original research carried out by you, for example a questionnaire.

Secondary research
Research carried out by another person which you have used in your work, for example a quotation from a book.

Activity: Research task

Working on your own, you are going to research four theorists who specialise in motivation. Use textbooks and the Internet to prepare a short presentation for your group.

The theorists you need to research are:

- Elton Mayo
- Frederick Herzberg
- Douglas McGregor
- Frederick Winslow Taylor

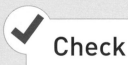

Check

- You will need to understand the benefits of teamwork to an individual and a business.

- You will need to complete primary and secondary research for the group project.

L01 The Internet

The Internet is a fantastic source of information which has made the process of information gathering far easier than it was ten years ago. However, as with most readily available resources, it must be used with some caution. Due to the 'open' nature of the Internet, it is very easy for people to 'post' information on websites, and sometimes it is not necessarily 100 per cent correct. For this reason you must not rely solely upon the Internet – instead, use the Internet and compare it to another reliable source.

Internet search engines

The Internet is a massive database of information and for this reason it can be impossible to find quickly the piece of information that you are looking for. 'Search engines' help you search for information.

A search engine, in simple terms, searches for information that matches what you have written in the text input screen. You may notice on occasions that you search for one thing and something completely unrelated is found. If this happens, you may need to change the text you are searching for to get a better match.

Activity: Using Internet search engines

First of all, choose a partner. Then, on your own, write down 15 questions that you think your partner will not know the answer to. Your partner will do the same for you.

Swap questions. Individually you are to research the answers to the questions on the Internet and then come together as a pair to check that your answers are correct.

Confidentiality

It is important to keep data confidential, and simple steps need to be taken, for example locking drawers and filing cabinets. If data gets into the wrong hands it could be potentially damaging in a personal sense to the general public. It could also be commercially damaging to a business if the information gets into the hands of a competitor.

You need to be careful with the information you gather in your research. The businesses you talk to might tell you sensitive information that they would not want everyone to know.

If information that is confidential 'gets out' and becomes public, it is known as leaked data.

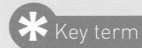 **Key term**

Leaked data
Information that is made available to the public when a business or individual wants to keep the information to themselves.

 Activity: Leaked data

Use the Internet to research one incident of data being leaked to the general public. Over the last few years there have been several high profile cases.

Report back to your tutor using a presentation to explain what you have found and what it might have meant for the person that the leaked data related to.

 Check

• It is your responsibility as a data user to make sure that you follow the Data Protection Act at all times, otherwise you may be personally liable for any problems caused.

• Remember that confidentiality applies to written information as well as digital data.

LO2 Work-related skills

Communication skills

A key skill that you will need to develop throughout this piece of research is communication. It is very important that when you are communicating with a person, a group or an organisation, you clearly get across what you need to say. Communication comes in many forms including spoken, written or visual (for example, diagrams). Whichever method is being used it must be suitable and clear.

Communication methods	Advantages	Disadvantages
Written	Permanent record Easy to understand Can be confidential	Takes time to prepare Can be confusing if poorly written
Spoken	Instant feedback Quick Cheap	'Chinese whisper' effect can distort the message Can be misunderstood easily if not clearly presented
Visual	Difficult concepts can be easily demonstrated May appeal to some people more than written or spoken methods	Usually needs to be accompanied by a written or spoken explanation leading to more work Can be expensive if high-quality colour images are being used

Activity: Contacting the business you are researching

In your group, write a letter to the organisation you are researching. You need to tell the organisation about your BTEC Entry 3/Level 1 Business Administration course, what you would like its help with, and include your contact details for it to reply.

It is important that your letter is professionally written and accurate. You might want to check the guidance given in *Unit 19 Creating business documents*, page 87–89.

Listening and questioning skills

To make your research effective you need to develop good listening and questioning skills. There are certain things you can do to make sure that you actively listen and ask questions:

- If possible, make eye contact with the person who is speaking
- Make notes of what is being said
- Do not interrupt
- Ask **open questions**
- Do not be critical or negative.

Open questions

Open questions require a longer answer than 'yes' or 'no'.

'What kind of meetings do you organise?' is an open question. Compare that to 'Do you organise scheduled meetings?'

Think about how an interviewee's answer might be different for each question. How much information are you likely to get from their answer?

Team member

Working effectively as part of a team is important for your future career. There are ways that you can improve your personal effectiveness as a team member. Look back to the mind map on page 116 which shows how you can make an effective contribution as a team member.

Activity: Practice interview

Working as a group, assume you have arranged a visit to interview an employee at the business you are researching. Role play typical questions (including open ones) and scenarios you may come across on your visit, so that you are confident when carrying out the interview. For example, you could ask a question like: 'In what ways do you feel you contribute to the team you work in?'

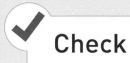

Check

- When contacting businesses, it is important that your message is clear and easy to understand.

- Being an effective team member is important for your future career, and for this unit.

L02 Self-management

Self-management is the skill of being able to complete tasks on time through good time management. Effective self-management means that you will be a more effective team member.

Good self-managers will understand their limitations in terms of how much work they can complete in a given amount of time. Also, good self-managers are flexible – they can change their plans quickly to take on board new ideas or suggestions.

When working on the research project, there will be times when you will have to work as a self-manager to complete the tasks you have been set. The table below shows the key requirements of a good self-manager.

✳ Key term

Self-management
The process of organising your time and your work in order to successfully complete tasks.

Prioritising

When you are managing a number of different tasks, you may need to prioritise your work. This is when you decide which task is most urgent. Sometimes the easiest way to set priorities is by working out when each task needs to be completed by – the one that needs to be completed soonest is your top priority.

Self-management skill	Why is this skill important?
Flexibility	This is an important skill because, for this project, you may have to change your original plans and ideas. On a wider scale, employers need employees that are flexible and willing to change, otherwise they will get left behind as technology and procedures move on.
Organising self	It is impossible to be a successful self-manager if you cannot organise yourself. Organising yourself involves getting all the materials together that you need for your job and making sure you know what is expected of you.
Accepting responsibility	Accepting responsibility is important because colleagues need to know that they can trust you to get things done. After all, their job might depend on you doing something first. It is also important to accept responsibility if you make a mistake, otherwise someone else may be blamed unfairly. This will also damage trust within your team and affect the way the team works.
Completing all tasks set and on time	It is important that you complete all the tasks you have agreed to do so that the team is not held up. Also, on many occasions in business, tasks have to be completed by a certain time otherwise this could cause problems and delays. It is also important that you complete all tasks for this piece of research work as your fellow team members will be relying on you to do so.

Remember

- If you are flexible and change your plans to fit in with other people, there may come a time when they can do the same for you.

Activity: Prioritising your work

This task requires you to work individually. Imagine that you work in an office. Below are a range of everyday tasks that you must complete. Place them in order of priority giving reasons for your choice:

- Support a meeting to discuss an event tomorrow evening

- Deal with communications including letters, emails, telephone calls and SMS messages from attenders and non-attenders at the event tomorrow evening

- Organise security for an event tomorrow evening

- Deal with health and safety issues relating to an event tomorrow evening

- Deal with administration systems – for example, entering data or creating reports – this is part of your normal daily routine

- Liaise with staff from different parts of the organisation to make sure everyone is informed about tomorrow evening's event.

Check

- To complete this unit successfully, you will need to manage your work effectively.

L02 Problem solving

A key skill in being an effective group worker is the ability to solve problems. Often when carrying out research things do not go to plan. There are many types of problems, some of which are small and others that are slightly larger.

However, one of the most important skills you can have is the ability to overcome problems. The diagram below shows some of the potential problems you could face while working as an administrator.

Key term

Problem solving
The process of developing creative and flexible solutions to problems that may arise.

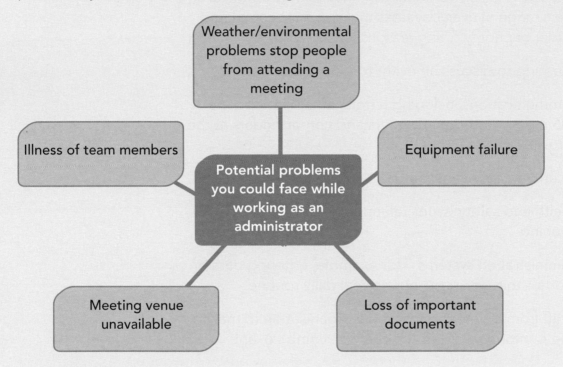

Some of these problems could be avoided through planning. For example, book a venue for a meeting well in advance of the date of the meeting. If you leave it too late, you might find that the venue you want will not be available.

However, some problems such as weather or illness may be unavoidable. It is best to think about and plan what could be done to reduce the effect these things may have on your plans.

Activity: Problems

In your group make a list of the problems you might face while carrying out this piece of research. Suggest at least one way you could get round each problem.

Presentation skills

When you are giving a presentation, you should consider the following guidelines:

- Try to keep the amount of text on a slide to a minimum – the slides should support what you are saying rather than be a script

- If you have handouts, make sure you have enough copies for all the attendees

- Remember to leave time for any questions at the end of the presentation

- Make sure you have all the equipment you need for the presentation, including a venue

- Speak slowly and clearly.

Activity: Present your findings

As a group, you will need to present the findings of your research back to your tutor and the rest of the group. In order to do this, each member of the group will need to contribute to the planning and the presentation.

Check

- Planning can help you to solve problems before they happen.

- Some problems cannot be avoided, but there are usually things you can do to reduce their effect.

- You need to plan your work as a team in order to make the most of your presentation.

L03 Assess own work

The process of receiving **feedback** and setting **targets** helps you to improve your skills. When you receive feedback from your tutor, your work will improve if you are able to take their comments on board. In the workplace you will receive feedback from your manager, and if you take in their comments, your work will improve and so will your chances of promotion and better pay.

In order to complete this unit, you need to receive feedback and set targets for improvement. Feedback may come from your tutor or from your peers (that is, other learners on your course).

Providing feedback

If you are going to give feedback on someone's performance, you need to remember that people can be sensitive. While feedback should be honest, it should always be constructive (that is, helpful). If you feel that someone needs to improve something, you could try:

- Identifying something that they did really well, and then

- Identifying the area you think they need to improve, giving examples and suggestions if you can.

For example:

> **Feedback:**
>
> I thought your contribution to the team was really good - you were enthusiastic and came up with some very good ideas. If you were to look for an area for improvement, I think it would be your time management. There were a couple of times when you didn't meet a deadline, which meant someone else wasn't able to start work when they thought they needed to.

Activity: How good is your work?

When you have completed your research, your tutor will assess what you have done. After you have made any changes it would be a good idea to send a copy to the business you have researched. They will be pleased that you have shown an interest in the business and they might even use some of your suggestions.

After you have shown the business your work, ask them if they will provide feedback on it.

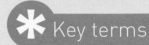
Key terms

Feedback
Constructive and helpful comments that will help you to identify what you have done well and what you can improve.

Targets
Things you want to achieve, also known as objectives. These are usually goals you want to complete in the next 6 or 12 months in order to improve your performance at work.

Setting targets

Once you have received some feedback, think about how you will address any issues that have been raised. First, you should write down your strengths and areas for improvement. You might want to draw up a table like the one below.

Strengths	Areas for improvement
Enthusiastic	Time management
Came up with some good ideas	

Now work out how you can improve the areas identified. For example, if you need to improve your time management skills, you could keep a diary of all the tasks you have to complete. This will help you manage your priorities and keep track of when you have a deadline coming up.

Targets should be reviewed regularly to make sure you are working towards them effectively. The best way to judge a target is to make it as specific as possible. For example, a target of 'improve my time keeping' is not very helpful as it is impossible to measure.

Try to set dates and include quantities, to make sure your targets are measurable. So, for example, the target could be 'to submit all my coursework on or before the deadline for the rest of the year'.

Activity: Setting targets

With your tutor, agree on what targets you will set, and how you will measure them. You will need to review your progress towards these targets regularly, so make sure you keep them safe.

Check

- It is important that feedback is constructive – this has to be something that someone can work with.

- Targets should be measurable and practical in order to be effective.

ASSESSMENT OVERVIEW

While working through this unit, you will have prepared for completing the following assessment tasks:

○	1.1	Identify an aspect of local business administration	Pages 114–115
○	1.2	Work as a team member, in finding relevant information	Pages 116–117
○	2.1	Use communication skills to present information clearly and accurately	Pages 120–121
○	2.2	Make a positive contribution as a team member in presenting the information	Page 125
○	2.3	Use self-management skills to meet deadlines and solve problems	Pages 122–124
○	3.1	Receive feedback	Page 126
○	3.2	Set targets	Page 127

Assignment tips

- As a team, one of your first tasks should be to work out what tasks need to be completed as part of the group project. This will help give roles for different team members and prevent anyone doing the same tasks as someone else. It will also avoid anything being forgotten.

- When you receive feedback, remember that no one is perfect. There are always things that people can do to improve their work, and some things will be harder work and take longer than other things. Be realistic about what you expect from yourself and make sure your targets are practical and manageable.

IDEAS FOR SMALL BUSINESSES

By completing this course you will have developed a good level of skill in many business areas. This unit gives you the chance to apply what you have learned by developing your own business idea. You will learn important business skills, including how to carry out market research and you will look into production and selling costs. At the end of the unit you will bring together all that you have learned by producing a business plan.

In this unit you will:

- Be able to select an idea for a small business using work-based skills

- Be able to carry out market research for your small business idea

- Be able to produce a simple business plan

Have you got the right skills to be successful in business?

L01 Select an idea for a business

Business ideas

Some of the most successful business people in the world started out by coming up with a simple business idea. Very often the simplest ideas are the best. This is because customers can understand them easily and they are simple to bring into reality.

Over the last 100 years, industry has changed. Fifty years ago the manufacturing sector (businesses that focus on producing a product) made up the largest part of the UK's economy.

However, more recently industries such as banking and insurance (sometimes called the service sector) now create more wealth for the UK than factories. Therefore, when you are considering possible ideas, try to think about services you could offer as well as products you could sell.

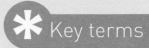

Key terms

Manufacturing sector
This includes businesses that focus on making a product.

Service sector
The service sector includes industries that provide a service such as banking and insurance.

Customer needs
The needs of customers that a business must consider when developing a product.

Activity: Business pioneers

Use the Internet to find out who are the top ten most successful business people in the world.

Create a table that includes their name, the name of their business and what their business does.

Customer needs

A business can only survive if there is demand for its products or services. Over the years there have been many companies and people spending large amounts of money on developing products only to find later that very few people want to buy them.

Nowadays, businesses spend a lot of money and time researching the market to check that a market exists for their products when they are launched. However, there are no guarantees and even the biggest companies have launched products that have been unsuccessful.

Activity: Success or flop

Below is an example of a bad invention.

Individually, use the Internet to carry out research to find five successful products and five products that have been unsuccessful.

While carrying out your research, try to identify which company was behind each product.

Check

- A business idea will only be successful if customers want what the company is making. This is known as meeting customer needs.

- Businesses carry out extensive market research before launching a product. This way they have a better chance of making sure that the item meets the customers' needs.

L01 Costs

Production costs

Many products have been launched and have been successful. However, in the long run, the costs of production have far outweighed the selling costs. The luxury car market is a good example. If a manufacturer cannot sell enough luxury cars to cover the costs of production, then the production and selling of the cars must stop. If not, the business could end up losing a lot of money.

It is important that you think very carefully about how much an item will cost to make and sell when you are considering the product or service you are going to launch.

Selling costs

Selling costs can be the forgotten cost in business. Often a person or business will launch a potentially successful idea but will forget to think about the costs of selling that item. Each of these individual costs can be quite small. However, there are often a lot of them and, when put together, they can mount up. If cash has not been set aside, a good idea can fail through poor planning and a lack of cash flow.

Examples of selling costs include:

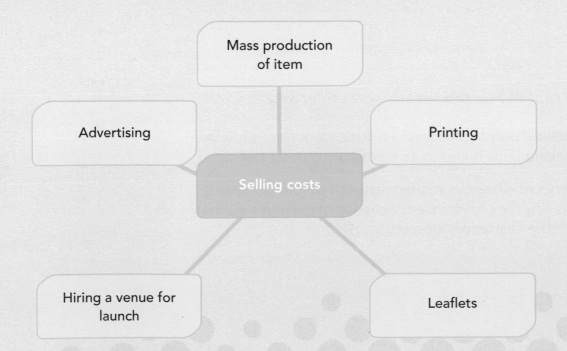

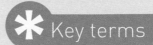

✳ Key terms

Production costs
Any costs that are involved in the production of a product or the provision of a service.

Selling costs
All the costs that are involved in selling a product.

Activity: Different types of cost

1. Individually, create a presentation that explains:

- production costs

- selling costs

- fixed costs

- variable costs

- start-up costs

- running costs.

Use the Internet to help with your research.

2. You need to provide three examples of each type of cost.

3. Now try to work out which costs would be most relevant to your business idea. Give an explanation of this in your presentation.

Activity: What is the cost?

As a group you are going to start up a small social enterprise company that makes biscuits and muffins. You then have to sell the products you have made. During the production process keep a close eye on your costs and make a note of how much you spend.

After you have sold all your products, create a spreadsheet which allows you to work out the production costs, selling costs, fixed costs, variable costs, start-up costs and running costs. You will need help from your tutor to complete this task successfully.

Functional skills

By completing the 'What is the cost?' task you will be developing your Mathematics and ICT skills.

Check

- A business can only survive if the money coming in from the sale of its goods and services is greater than the production costs of those goods.

L01 Research and sources of information

Businesses carry out research using a lot of different sources. Companies exist whose only purpose is to carry out research on behalf of other businesses. This can be expensive!

You will not need to carry out research that is as in-depth as that produced by a market research business. However, you must do some research to make sure your idea is **feasible** (that is, that there is likely to be a market for it). The table below gives some ideas about where you can find market research information.

Research source	What will the source tell me?
Internet	Contains information on almost any product that is available on the market. The Internet also has many review sites where users can provide feedback on products and ideas.
	If you wish to pay, you can also get current in-depth market research data from market research businesses.
Newspapers	Provide information on new companies opening up or businesses closing down. This will give you an idea of the levels of competition and demand.
	Newspapers also contain lots of advertising so you can get an idea of how others are trying to sell their products.
Business directory, e.g. Yellow Pages	Provides contact details of businesses selling the same or similar products or services to your idea. Again, you can assess the competition.

Research source	What will the source tell me?
Magazines	Provide information on competitors, often in the form of product reviews. Magazines also include glossy pictures which show you what competitor products look like.
Market research reports	These reports are available online (although very expensive) or at any major local library. They are very detailed and contain lots of facts and figures about the state of a specific market and how well different products are selling. These documents would be one of the most useful sources of information for a major business.

Activity: Which are the most useful research resources?

For this task you are to work individually.

Carry out a small piece of research to find out which are the top ten selling cars of the year. Use as many of the sources from the table as you can to do this.

Write down which were the most helpful sources and explain why.

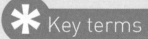
Key terms

Feasible
Possible and practical to do. If a business idea is feasible, research will show that there are enough people who will want to buy the service or product.

Sources of information
Places where information can be found, to provide a realistic idea of the potential success of a business idea.

Check

- 'Sources of information' relates to where information can be found to help solve a problem or provide research to support your work.

- Research is only of any use if it is reliable and accurate.

L01 Communication and other skills

Good **communication skills** are vital in business. This is particularly true when you are trying to gain interest in, or sell, your product. It is important that you speak clearly when you are discussing your idea so that people can get a good idea of what you are describing.

Again, as mentioned earlier in this book, you must apply good listening skills. You need to appear professional when dealing with important people. The same is true for written communication. It must be **accurate** in every way including spelling, punctuation, layout and choice of images, and so on.

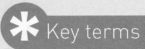

Key terms

Communication skills
The ability to talk and listen to others with a high degree of accuracy.

Accurate
Free from errors. To make sure documents are accurate, you need to check them carefully.

Activity: Sales presentation

For this task you are to work individually.

Imagine you work in sales and must choose a product you would like to sell. Prepare a convincing sales presentation for the item you have chosen and deliver it to your tutor or group.

Team member

As mentioned in *Unit 22 Business administration group project* (starting on page 113), it is important to work as part of a team so that jobs can be completed in less time. Working as a team is also vital if a problem crops up – many people can make suggestions to try to solve it.

Self-management

As mentioned in *Unit 22*, self-management is a large part of the success of any business venture. As a team member, you must be reliable so that others can trust you to carry out the tasks that you have agreed to do. Being a good self-manager means that you must be flexible and willing to work with new ideas or suggestions.

Problem solving

As mentioned in *Unit 22*, good business people tend to be skilled at solving problems. It is unlikely that everything will go to plan. There are often parts of a plan that you might not have thought about, or something might have changed. If this happens you must be open to suggestions and flexible when solving the problems that may crop up.

Activity: Personal skills

Think of times in your life when you have had to:

- be part of a team

- be a self-manager

- solve problems.

Create a collage with images that represent these three situations.

For each situation, write brief notes to explain how you handled it.

Check

- Communication skills are essential skills to make sure that spoken, written and visual messages are clearly transmitted and received.

- Self-management is the process of managing your time so that you can successfully complete all tasks to a deadline.

LO2 Market research techniques and LO3 producing a simple business plan

The table on pages 134–135 provides some suggestions of published or secondary sources of information. However, in business, information is no good if it is out of date. Therefore, companies often carry out primary market research. They do this in many different ways including:

! Remember

Primary research is the type that you carry out yourself, for example, by drawing up a questionnaire or interviewing a member of staff on a visit to a company.

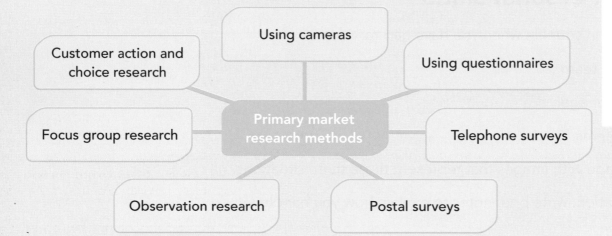

- Using cameras
- Customer action and choice research
- Using questionnaires
- Focus group research
- Primary market research methods
- Telephone surveys
- Observation research
- Postal surveys

◎ Activity: Benefits and drawbacks of research methods

In pairs, research the benefits and drawbacks of each of the methods highlighted above. Put your findings into a briefing paper which will be given to all other group members.

◎ Activity: Research task for business idea

On your own, carry out some market research to work out how successful your business idea might be. Use at least three different research methods (including primary and secondary) so that you can build a more complete picture of your market.

Refer to the previous activity above when choosing the most suitable research methods.

Produce a simple business plan reflecting market research

For any start-up business, the business plan is the most important document that needs to be prepared. The reason for this is that a good business plan may encourage **investors** to take a **risk** and invest in your idea. Importantly, for the business owners, a business plan gives a clear view of what the business is aiming to do in the short, medium and long term. Business plans tend to focus on three main areas:

- An outline of your business idea

- An outline of the market you are trying to launch into

- An outline of your financial structure.

On the right is an example of the information that needs to be included in a business plan.

Business Plan for XYZ Company

- ↘ Outline of business idea
    - o Description of product service
    - o Reason for designing product/ starting business?
    - o Anyone else involved with you in this venture?
- ↘ Outline of the market
    - o Who are you aiming the product or service at?
    - o Competitors?
    - o Customers?
- ↘ An outline of yourself and your background in business including experience
- ↘ An outline of how you intend to market and sell your idea
- ↘ An outline of how you are going to price your product or service, and an indication of how you arrived at this price
- ↘ An outline of technical resources and skills needed to produce or provide product or service.

Activity: Business plan for your idea

For this unit you need to produce a business plan for your business idea. Have a look at the example above or carry out some Internet research into other layouts. Often banks will provide business plan templates on their websites. This might be a good place to look in order to get you started.

Using the headings and information you need to include in a business plan, create your plan using a word-processing program.

 ## Key terms

Investors
People or businesses that give a business money. They invest in the business because they expect to receive some of the profits.

Investment risk
A risk in business is often based on how likely it is that a business or investors will lose money.

 # Check

- A product or service idea needs to be researched in depth.

- For a business idea to be successful, it must be designed with a target market in mind.

 Functional skills

By producing a structured document clearly explaining your business idea, you will be practising your **English** skills.

ASSESSMENT OVERVIEW

While working through this unit, you will have prepared for completing the following assessment tasks:

◯	1.1 Select a small business idea to research	Pages 130–133
◯	1.2 Demonstrate work-based skills by: • Communicating clearly • Working as a team member • Demonstrating self-management skills • Problem solving	Pages 136–137
◯	2.1 Plan simple market research	Pages 134–135
◯	2.2 Carry out simple market research	Pages 134–135
◯	3.1 Produce a simple business plan reflecting the market research	Pages 138–139

Assignment tips

- You need to show that you have chosen a business idea from a range of possible ideas. Once you have identified a range of different ideas, you might want to write a list of the pros and cons for each idea in order to choose the best one. Keep this list so you can use it for your assessment for this unit.

- When you produce your business plan, you need to include the following information:

  o What the product or service is

  o When and where the product or service is to be sold, and at what price

  o The target market for the product or service

  o The human, physical and financial resources you need to offer the product or service

  o How you plan to pay for the set-up costs

  o How you will advertise and sell the product or service to customers.

JOB OPPORTUNITIES IN BUSINESS ADMINISTRATION

Once you have completed your BTEC course in Business Administration you can start to apply for jobs in administration. Through this unit you will explore job opportunities that are available across different areas of business.

You will also investigate conditions of employment including contracts of employment, qualifications and skills needed for different administration roles. Finally, you will start making plans for your future after you successfully complete this course.

In this unit you will:

- Know about job opportunities in business administration

- Know about terms and conditions of employment within business administration

- Know about the qualifications and skills needed for jobs in administration

- Be able to plan how to start work within business administration

What does your future hold for you?

L01 Job opportunities

Through studying Business Administration and successfully completing this course, a whole new world of job opportunities will open up for you.

It is important to research job opportunities (for example, what the job involves, what the company is like) as understanding the job can help you find something you enjoy and will be successful at. Often people see a job advertised that they like the sound of but they do not really know what the job will involve or the qualifications and skills needed to get that job.

This can cause problems because, if they are constantly being turned down for jobs, it will affect their self-esteem and confidence in applying for other jobs. A little preparation beforehand would make it easier for them to identify jobs for which they are suited and reduce all the stress of being turned down.

Activity: Researching different jobs

Use the Internet to research opportunities within the business administration job sector. Try to find ten jobs and get an idea of what they involve.

After carrying out your research, choose three of the jobs and create realistic job advertisements for them.

To help you, have a look at the diagram below which contains a number of job titles.

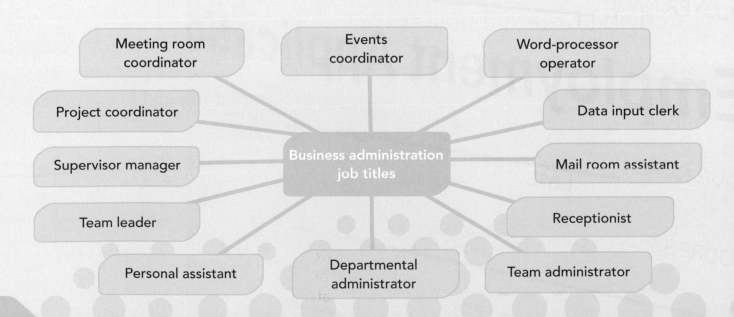

Functional areas

The phrase 'functional area' simply means 'department'. In order to run a large business successfully, it is important to have specialist staff who can deal with the tasks that need to be done.

In smaller businesses you may find that one person does all the tasks or the work is spread among a small number of people. Large businesses are made up of several main functional areas which will usually include:

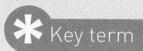

Key term

Functional areas
Different parts or departments of a business that focus on a limited range of important tasks.

Production

Facilities Management

Finance

Research and Development

Functional areas of a business

IT Support

Customer Service

Marketing and Sales

Human Resources

Activity: Research functional areas

Work in pairs and carry out research into functional areas. You need to do this in the following way:

- Choose one functional area and research the job roles that exist within it
- Find out what a company structure chart is
- Research what is meant by 'chain of command' and 'span of control'.

Activity: Create a poster

Create a poster which indicates all the job roles included in the functional area you have investigated.

To make your poster professional you are to draw your job roles on a company structure chart.

Present your poster to the rest of your group.

Check

- It is important to get a full picture of what a job involves and the skills and qualifications needed to fulfil a post before you apply. A little research early on will reduce the frustration later.

L02 Terms and conditions of employment

Work patterns

In today's business world, organisations cannot afford to close for long periods of time between working days.

Many businesses, particularly those involved in the production sector, stay open for 24 hours a day, 7 days a week, 365 days a year. It is therefore important to know the different terms that describe work patterns. The term 'work pattern' simply means the way a person's working hours are organised.

The table below explains a range of typical work patterns you will come across when researching jobs.

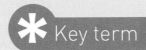 Key term

Work pattern
The way a person's working hours are organised, for example times, days of the week.

Work pattern	Explanation
Shift work	When an employee usually works different hours on different weeks. Usually, shift work is used when a business needs to stay open all the time. Examples include factories and 24-hour supermarkets. Normally shift work will follow a two or three week pattern. For example, during the first week, an employee may work 6 a.m. to 2 p.m. and 2 p.m. to 10 p.m. If it is a three shift pattern (sometimes known as a 'continental' style system) they will work the two shifts plus a third shift from 10 p.m. to 6 a.m.
Early starts	An early start shift pattern is one which starts early in the morning, for example, 4 a.m. An example would be a milkman.
Late finishes	A late finish shift pattern usually refers to working hours which finish after 10 p.m. An example would be a doctor working in a hospital.
Night work	Night work, as the title suggests, is when a person works through the night, maybe starting at 10 p.m. and finishing at 6 a.m. An example would be a nurse.
Weekend work	Weekend work is a popular shift pattern for students. Again, as the name suggests, the working hours are throughout a weekend. A person may work one or both weekend days. An example would be a student working in a DIY store.
Bank holiday work	Bank holiday work is work that is undertaken on national bank holiday weekends. Such hours may be part of a person's contract of employment or additional. An example would be a vehicle repair and rescue worker.
Flexitime	Flexitime is a type of work where a person has core hours of work. A person has to attend work between, for example, the hours of 10 a.m. and 3 p.m. A person must work their normal working week (normally 37.5 hours). However, they can make up their hours at whichever time they choose outside the core hours. An example would be an office worker.

Work pattern	Explanation
Irregular work pattern	An irregular work pattern is one which does not follow the same working hours week after week. An example would be a salesman.
Days off during the week	Traditionally shopkeepers used to close for one day a week to make up for working weekends. However, in most businesses this is not the case. A person would take a day off in the week to make sure that they did not work more than their full-time working hours. This might be the case if the job they did involved working weekends. An example would be a full-time shop assistant in a department store.
Annual leave	Annual leave is the time each employee is allowed to take off as holiday. Annual leave for a typical full-time job in the UK is 28 days. However, this can increase depending on how long you have worked for the company.

Activity: Different work patterns

Carry out research into the ten work patterns shown in the table.

Choose one job type for each work pattern (it should be different from the example given in the table).

Put together a presentation for your tutor or group.

Check

- Different types of jobs need employees to work different work patterns. For example, teachers work different hours from nurses.

- If you are asked to work irregular hours you may be paid an extra amount of money on top of your normal hourly rate.

L02 Pay and benefits

Pay

Getting paid is the reason most people work. However, enjoying the job you do and feeling valued are also important factors – especially for your self-esteem.

It is important to know that there are different ways in which people are paid. Nowadays, most employed staff are paid monthly straight into their bank account. In many jobs there are also opportunities to increase your wage by getting promotion or taking on more responsibility. This will usually involve moving up a salary scale. A salary scale is a document which highlights how much people should be paid at different levels in an organisation.

The diagram below provides information about **pay**.

Hourly
Paid a set amount for every hour worked.

Example job: Shop Assistant.

Monthly
Paid a set amount on a specific day of the month

Example job: Teacher.

Salary Scales
A document which sets out how much employees are paid taking into account their position in the business.

Example job: Banker.

Increments
A term used to explain by how much a person's wage will increase by if, for example, they have gained promotion.

> **✳ Key term**
>
> **Pay**
> The amount of money received in return for working.

◎ Activity: How much are people paid?

Research how much people get paid for five different jobs. You could do this by visiting a job centre or by researching job sites on the Internet.

After you have carried out your research, create a poster which shows, for each job:

- the responsibilities
- the pay and benefits.

Benefits

Along with pay, many jobs also provide extra **benefits** to employees. These can come in many forms. The reason a business may decide to give these is simple – to **motivate** the people who work for a business. Benefits can also make people think twice about leaving a company to look for another job if the benefits they receive are particularly good.

Examples of benefits which businesses may offer employees are shown below.

Activity: Know your perks

Pick one of the terms listed in the diagram above and research what it means for the employee.

Try to find three examples of different businesses that give their employees this benefit.

Now present your findings back to the group.

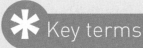

Key terms

Benefits
Extra 'perks' received by employees to encourage loyalty and motivation.

Motivation
Motivation is how much you want to do something. If you are highly motivated, it is likely that you enjoy your job and your work is of a high quality.

Check

- The way in which you are paid may depend on the type of job that you do. For example, some employees are paid an hourly rate while others will be paid an annual salary.

- Often jobs offer other benefits apart from pay. These may include private health care or a company pension.

(L03) Qualifications

When you apply for a job, your qualifications and grades are often the first thing a potential employer will look at. In order to present yourself in the best possible way, you need to know:

* What qualifications you have got

* What grades you have achieved

* The type of qualification such as vocational (BTEC, NVQ, etc.) or academic (GCSE).

You also need to know the difference between 'essential' and 'desirable' qualifications. This will help you understand what you need to have in order to apply for a job.

Essential qualifications

Essential qualifications are the ones you need in order to start work in certain jobs or professions. For example, a person cannot work as a qualified accountant until they have passed the relevant professional examinations.

Anyone applying for the job must have these essential qualifications before the business will think about employing them.

Desirable qualifications

Desirable qualifications are different from essential qualifications because you do not necessarily need them to enter a job or profession.

However, employers like job applicants to have other qualifications in addition to essential ones. This shows a wider knowledge and range of skills which the person can offer. For example, this might include qualifications in the skills of word-processing, keyboarding, audio transcription and shorthand.

Practical qualifications

As well as, or instead of, academic or vocational qualifications, employers like job applicants to have practical qualifications. These can include subjects like first aid and lifting and carrying.

As with desirable qualifications, practical qualifications show that the person has a wider range of skills.

Activity: What are my qualifications worth?

Individually, research a range of qualifications which are relevant to business and administration.

You must complete a table like the example below by writing the full name of the qualification, whether the qualification is vocational or academic and the grade value of the qualification.

Try to research at least ten different qualifications. Your tutor will be able to help you with this task.

Full name of qualification	Academic/Vocational	Grade value
E.g. NVQ Business and Administration	Vocational	Level 1

Check

- It is important to understand fully the type and value of a course you are studying.

- Courses vary a lot so it is important you choose the correct one from the outset.

L03 Skills and qualities

When you apply for a job, as well as looking at your qualifications, a potential employer will look at the skills and qualities you will bring to the organisation. Employers look at skills and qualities for three main reasons:

1. To see if you have the skills to do the job you have applied for.

2. To make sure your skills fit in with the business's needs and that no crossover of skills exists with current employees.

3. Employers will want to get an idea of how you will fit into the business as a team member and make sure that you would work well with their other employees.

An employer is likely to look for:

- Personal qualities including:

  o Ability to organise yourself

  o Ability to work well with others

- Work-related skills including:

  o Self-organisation

  o Team working

  o Problem solving

  o Self-management

- A level of fitness that means:

  o Ability to carry out tasks

  o Good attendance at work.

Planning

You should now be in a position to start planning to find a job.

However, an important question you must ask yourself is 'What can I offer an employer?' It can be difficult to think of what you have to offer off the top of your head. That is why it is best to use a 'skills scan'. A skills scan is simply a way of assessing your own skills, qualities and qualifications.

Activity: My skills scan

This is an individual task. You need to be totally honest about yourself.

The list below provides the questions you need to ask yourself when checking your skills, along with some sample ideas for responses. It is important that you answer honestly or the whole process will not work.

You need to put your own answers to the questions into a table using a professional looking format.

My skills scan

- **What personal qualities do I possess?**
  - Self-organiser
  - Good communicator
  - Work well with others

- **What work-related skills do I possess?**
  - Good communicator
  - Teamwork
  - Problem solving
  - Good level of fitness to work

- **What skills and abilities do I possess?**
  - Good with ICT
  - Good at maths
  - Deal well with complex problems
  - Good at working under pressure

- **What interests do I have?**
  - Sport
  - Music
  - Nature
  - Cooking

- **What are my values?**
  - Hardworking
  - Honesty

- **What are my personal qualities?**
  - Supportive
  - Caring
  - Can easily adapt to new situations

- **Lifestyle constraints**
  - Want to work in home town
  - Only want to work part-time so I can attend college

Check

- To improve your chance of success when entering the job market, it is important that you plan what you are doing. This will help you know the skills and qualifications needed to be successful in your chosen career.

- It is important to make plans so that you know what you need to do to move to the next stage of your educational or working career.

L04 Finding out about jobs

It is important that you know about different jobs, and routes into jobs, as the employment market is more competitive than ever. Nowadays it is expected that the average person will have between 5 and 15 jobs in a working lifetime.

Many jobs these days ask for experience and this can be difficult if you are looking for a first job. The problem is you cannot get experience because you cannot get a job.

Don't worry – these days many people volunteer in order to get experience. Internships are also becoming more common in the UK. An internship is unpaid employment offered by an organisation. When thinking about these options you must always take a long-term view and remember that a short period of unpaid work could lead to a satisfying lifelong career.

Below are some practical examples of where you can get guidance and help.

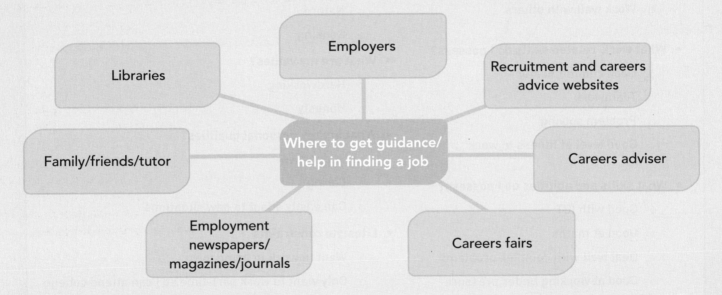

Goals

Before starting to look for a job, you must plan out what you are going to do. The key to planning is to have SMART targets which allow you to focus on what you have to do and by when.

Specific	Goals should be well defined and clear
Measurable	There must be a way of measuring whether a goal has been completed or how far away it is from completion
Achievable	The goal must be attainable (it must be possible to reach the goal)
Realistic	The goal must be something that can be achieved with the available resources, knowledge and time
Timed	There needs to be enough time to complete the goal and there should be a time frame for when the goal should be completed

Activity: Making plans

Create an action plan like the one below. An example of how it needs to be completed is given.

Your action plan should clearly show your short, medium and long term goals. You should also include the steps you have to take to achieve them and a timescale.

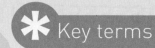

Action Plan		
Name:		Date:
Steps I need to take?	By when?	How will I know I have been successful?
	Short term targets:	
E.g. Pass BTEC Course	July 2011	Written confirmation that I have passed the course
	Medium term targets:	
	Long term targets:	

Key terms

Short term goals
Those which typically take up to 12 months to achieve. An example of a short term goal would be to achieve a qualification which will allow you to access a particular job or course of study.

Medium term goals
Those which typically take between one and three years to complete. An example of a medium term goal would be to gain work experience in a company that will allow you to get a full-time position or a higher level course of study.

Long term goals
Those which typically take between three and five years to complete. An example of a long term goal could include an ambition to work in a management position within five years.

Check

- Different types of jobs will be advertised in different places. When searching for a job remember to look at a range of sources.

- It is important to set goals for yourself so that you have something to aim for. Goals give you direction and help you to achieve your ambitions.

ASSESSMENT OVERVIEW

While working through this unit, you will have prepared for completing the following assessment tasks:

○	1.1	Identify jobs in different sectors of business administration	Page 142
○	1.2	Describe the job roles in one functional area of business administration	Page 143
○	2.1	Describe the terms and conditions of employment within business administration	Pages 144–147
○	3.1	Present information about the qualifications and skills required for selected jobs in business administration	Pages 148–151
○	4.1	Produce a plan to start work within business administration	Pages 152–153

Assignment tips

- You need to identify three different jobs within business administration. You need to give details about the skills, qualities and qualifications required to work in *each* different job role. Since jobs adverts will also include the terms and conditions of the employment, you should also explain what the terms and conditions for each job mean.

- Your career plan should identify one long-term goal and two short-term goals. You should think of short term as within the next 12 to 18 months. A long-term goal could be anything beyond 18 months.

Key terms

Abbreviate – To make a word shorter, either by taking out letters (e.g. 'tomorrow' becomes 'tmro') or by cutting the word short (e.g. 'Saturday' becomes 'Sat').

Accurate – Free from errors. To make sure documents are accurate, you need to check them carefully.

Acronym – Shortening a long name by using the initial letters of each word. For example, the BBC is an acronym for the British Broadcasting Corporation.

Agenda – An agenda is a document that is sent to attendees before a meeting to let them know what is going to be discussed.

Benefits – Extra 'perks' received by employees to encourage loyalty and motivation.

Business documents – Documents either in paper or electronic form which are used in business for a number of different purposes. For the document to be useful, it must be completed with accuracy.

Business goal – A business goal is what the business is aiming to do – this might be as simple as make a profit.

Cash flow – Money flowing in and out of a business in the form of payments and receipts.

Collate – To mix copies of different documents together to give information in a specific order.

Colleague – Someone from the same organisation as you. They could be more junior than you, someone at the same level as you (sometimes called a 'peer'), or someone at a more senior level than you.

Communication skills – The ability to talk and listen to others with a high degree of accuracy.

Comply – To act by the guidelines or rules set out in a law, such as the Data Protection Act. It is a business's legal duty to comply with these laws.

Confidential – Information that should not be shared, such as salary details, company strategies, customer contact details, etc.

Confirm – To check that something is right. For example, if you have missed anything, your tutor should be able to tell you what else you need to do.

Consistent – If something is consistent, it remains the same or largely unchanged.

Correspondence – A broad term for any form of written communication. This could include letters, emails, faxes, text messages, etc.

Customer – Someone to whom you provide a service. This might be someone from a different organisation, or it could be someone who works for the same business as you.

Customer needs – The needs of customers that a business must consider when developing a product.

Cybercrime – A type of crime that uses computers. This can include identity theft, stealing from online bank accounts, stealing information, etc. You have to be very careful with information you give away online to avoid cybercrime.

Data Protection Act – A law which protects the general public from having their personal data misused.

Dealing with mail – A very important operation within a business as many customers still use mail as a way of doing business. Efficient mail delivery ensures that mail does not go missing and customers receive good levels of customer service.

Delegate – Someone attending a meeting. This person may represent another business, and so will want to give a positive impression of their organisation.

Delegate pack – Information given to delegates which is designed to support the meeting.

Email etiquette – Good practice guidelines. These are things to consider when sending emails, and can help avoid embarrassing cases of misunderstanding.

Etiquette – Good manners and thinking about other people. It is good etiquette to refill the photocopier because it would be irritating to have to fill it with paper before you wanted to use it each time.

Feasible – Possible and practical to do. If a business idea is feasible, research will show that there are enough people who will want to buy the service or product.

Feedback – Constructive and helpful comments that will help you to identify what you have done well and what you can improve.

Financial documents – Specific documents that are used to record the buying and selling of goods.

Flow chart – A list of tasks or stages that need to be completed, linked together in a specific order. Some tasks will need to be completed before others can be started. For example, you would need to type the letter in word-processing software before spell checking it.

Flow of mail – The process which mail goes through from when it is sent until it arrives at its destination.

Formal communication – Communication which uses professional language, and a record of what has been communicated is kept on record for future reference.

Formal meeting – A meeting between senior staff or a business and their suppliers or customers. Records are always kept.

Formal quote – This is when a business puts together a set of costs for a customer. For example, if you wanted to buy a computer, you might ask for a quote for a particular model. This would tell you how much you would pay if you decided to buy the computer.

Franking – The process of passing mail through a machine which franks a stamp on to it. The purpose of franking is to save time.

Functional areas – Different parts or departments of a business that focus on a limited range of important tasks.

Graphical communication – The use of visual images such as diagrams, illustrations or designs to convey meaning.

Health issue – A potential problem in the workplace that may affect a person's health.

Impression – The image of a person that someone is left with after talking to or dealing with another person.

Informal communication – Communication which uses 'everyday' language and is not kept on record for future reference.

Informal meetings – Often a meeting between colleagues. Records are rarely kept.

Instant Messaging (IM) – An instant text messaging service that happens in 'real time'.

Investment risk – a risk in business is often based on how likely it is that a business or investors will lose money.

Investors – People or businesses that give a business money. They invest in the business because they expect to receive some of the profits.

Invoice – A document sent to customers requesting payment for the supply of goods or services.

Leaked data – Information that is made available to the public when a business or individual wants to keep the information to themselves.

Legal duty – Something a business has got to do. If a business does not do their legal duty, they could be acting illegally.

Long term goals – Those which typically take between three and five years to complete. An example of a long-term goal could include an ambition to work in a management position within five years.

Manufacturing sector – This includes businesses that focus on making a product.

Medium term goals – Those which typically take between one and three years to complete. An example of a medium-term goal would be to gain work experience in a company that will allow you to get a full-time position or a higher level course of study.

Minutes – Minutes are a formal record of a meeting which highlight what has been agreed and who is taking responsibility for completing a particular task.

Motivation – Motivation is how much you want to do something. If you are highly motivated, it is likely that you enjoy your job and your work is of a high quality.

Multimedia Message Service (MMS) – Allows you to send and receive not only text but also sound, images and video.

Negative impression – When a customer receives poor service and bases their future opinions of the business on that view.

Open questions – Questions that require a longer answer – not just 'yes' or 'no'.

Pay – The amount of money received in return for working.

Policy – A principle or course of action adopted by an organisation or individual.

Poor posture – Positioning of the body which could cause long-term damage while working. Always try to adopt the correct posture.

Postal services – The term given to a range of different mail delivery companies.

Primary research – Original research carried out by you, for example a questionnaire.

Prioritise – Decide on the order for dealing with a number of tasks according to their relative importance.

Problem solving – The process of developing creative and flexible solutions to problems that may arise.

Procedure – A process for doing something, such as welcoming visitors or ordering stationery, that is set by the organisation.

Production costs – Any costs that are involved in the production of a product or the provision of a service.

Professional behaviour – Acting in a business-like manner. When receiving visitors, answering the telephone, etc., you are the public face of your employer. First impressions of an organisation are as important as first impressions of a person.

Professional demeanour – This is how someone appears in a first impression. If you are dressed smartly, are polite and helpful, and address the visitor's needs effectively, you are likely to be thought of as having a professional demeanour.

Profit – Money left over when all costs have been taken out of the turnover. In order to make the pie, Mulkern's Foods needs to spend a total of £1.50 on ingredients, making the pie and cooking the pie. The difference between what Mulkern's Foods spends to make the pie and the amount the customer pays for the pie is its profit.

Profit margin – The amount of profit expressed as a proportion of the turnover. So if a customer buys an item for £2, which costs £1.50 to produce, the profit margin is $33\frac{1}{3}$ per cent.

Promotion – When your employer rewards you by giving you a more important job. It often means earning more money.

Purpose of document – Each type of document performs a specific function. It is important that the correct document is used for the correct function if an administrative system is to work efficiently.

Recipient – Someone who receives something. In this case, someone who receives an email.

Responsibility – When you are responsible for a task, it is your duty to complete the task on time and follow any instructions you have been given.

Risk – A risk is the chance that something might happen. For example, if wires are trailing across a corridor there is a risk someone could trip over them.

Secondary research – Research carried out by another person which you have used in your work, for example a quotation from a book.

Self-management – The process of organising your time and your work in order to successfully complete tasks.

Selling costs – All the costs that are involved in selling a product.

Service sector – The service sector includes industries that provide a service such as banking and insurance.

Setting up a room – The process of making sure that rooms are set up and fit for the purpose of the meeting.

Short Message Service (SMS) – Allows you to send and receive text messages only up to 160 characters in length.

Short term goals – Those which typically take up to 12 months to achieve. An example of a short-term goal would be to achieve a qualification which will allow you to access a particular job or course of study.

Sorting – The process of putting mail into different piles so it can be distributed to the correct department.

Sources of information – Places where information can be found, to provide a realistic idea of the potential success of a business idea.

Stakeholder – Anybody with some form of interest in a business who stands to lose if it is run badly.

Targets – Things you want to achieve, also known as objectives. These are usually goals you want to complete in the next 6 or 12 months in order to improve your performance at work.

Tone – The way in which one person speaks to another person.

Transaction – The process of paying or receiving money for goods that have been bought or sold.

Turnover – Money coming into a business from customers. For example, if a customer buys a pie from Mulkern's shop for £2, this money counts towards the business's turnover.

Verbal communication – Talking to someone – or a group of people – to give them information.

Visitor's badge – A badge or security pass, identifying the visitor.

Work pattern – The way a person's working hours are organised, for example times, days of the week.

Index

THE SMITH COLLEGE MUSEUM OF ART

EUROPEAN AND AMERICAN PAINTING AND SCULPTURE

1760–1960

THE SMITH COLLEGE MUSEUM OF ART

European and American Painting and Sculpture 1760–1960

JOHN DAVIS AND JAROSLAW LESHKO

Introduction by Suzannah J. Fabing

HUDSON HILLS PRESS

NEW YORK

In Association with the Smith College Museum of Art, Northampton, Massachusetts

First Edition

© 2000 by the Smith College Museum of Art.

Published in the United States by Hudson Hills Press, Inc., 1133 Broadway, Suite 1301, New York, NY 10010-8001.

Distributed in the United States, its territories and possessions, and Canada by National Book Network.

Editor and Publisher: Paul Anbinder

Proofreader: Fronia W. Simpson

Indexer: Karla J. Knight

Designer: Martin Lubin

Composition: Angela Taormina

Manufactured in Japan by Toppan Printing Company.

Library of Congress Cataloguing-in-Publication Data

Smith College. Museum of Art.

Smith College Museum of Art: European and American painting and sculpture, 1760–1960 / John Davis and Jaroslaw Leshko; introduction by Suzannah J. Fabing. — 1st ed.

    p.   cm.

"In association with the Smith College Museum of Art, Northampton, Massachusetts."

Includes bibliographical references and index.

ISBN: 1-55595-194-5 (cloth: alk. paper)

1. Art, European — Catalogues. 2. Art, American — Catalogues. 3. Art — Massachusetts — Northampton — Catalogues. 4. Smith College. Museum of Art — Catalogues. I. Davis, John, 1961– II. Leshko, Jaroslaw, 1939– III. Title.

N6750 .S67 2000

7098.4807474423 — dc21   00-40936

CONTENTS

American Painting and Sculpture

10 cents
EACH

THE SMITH COLLEGE MUSEUM OF ART
EUROPEAN AND AMERICAN PAINTING AND SCULPTURE
1760–1960

ACKNOWLEDGMENTS

Our foremost debt is to Suzannah Fabing, who first conceived of this volume and graciously invited us to become its authors. She then took on the task of editing the book, which she performed superbly. Suzannah's tenure as director of the Smith College Museum of Art has been marked by a series of fruitful collaborations between the museum and the art department. The benefits of this teamwork are manifold, and her efforts have had the virtue of returning the museum to its historical mission as a rich and rewarding teaching collection, as she outlines in her introduction. In this spirit, we are delighted to have been able to play a role in making one of Smith's greatest resources even more widely known to the larger public.

The museum's staff, in addition to its director, has facilitated our work by answering questions, making curatorial records available, and responding to repeated requests to view works in storage. Here David Dempsey, Stefne Lynch, and Linda Muehlig were notably generous with their time, and Michael Goodison deserves particular thanks. Michael capably managed all the details of this project from its inception, and in addition, he stepped in to type the European half of the manuscript. Nancy Noble, as well, performed a great service by compiling most of the bibliographies for the European section from which the selections were made. Daniel Bridgman was generous with his time and patience solving a vexing photograph problem.

The administration of Smith College, through the offices of the president, the provost, and the dean for academic development, has contributed to this project through the welcome gift of time; both authors were granted Harnish Fellowships from the college to lighten their teaching loads.

Although we had already come to know and love many of the works in this volume through our regular teaching, we are mindful of the students, colleagues, and friends who have previously conducted research on this collection and, in some cases, published their findings. We have greatly benefited from the intellectual labor of these scholars, especially Cynda Benson, Ann Boutelle, Walter Denny, Elizabeth Evans-Iliesiu, Amanda Glesmann, Caroline Jennings, Betsy Jones, Patricia Junker, Amy Kurtz, Megan McIntyre, Linda Merrill, Linda Muehlig, Margaret Oppenheimer, and Giovanna Sabatini.

Finally, John Davis would like to express his thanks to his partner, Jason Heffner, who among his other good deeds willingly put home life on hold when the deadline loomed. Jaroslaw Leshko wishes to thank his wife, Alla, and their daughter, Adriana, for their insight, patience, and loving support.

J.D. AND **J.L.**

11

INTRODUCTION

This book presents one hundred of the most admired paintings and sculptures belonging to the Smith College Museum of Art, which is widely acknowledged to have one of the most important art collections at an American liberal arts college. The authors are professors in Smith's art department who have thought about and taught from these works for years, and they here share their reflections with readers who may not have had the good fortune to sit in their classrooms. John Davis, whose field is American art and architecture, came to Smith from the National Gallery of Art in 1992, and Jaroslaw Leshko, whose specialty is nineteenth- and twentieth-century European art, has taught at Smith for more than thirty years, having begun his career at the college in 1968. Professor Davis has written the essays on fifty American works for this book, and Professor Leshko has written on fifty by European artists.

Choosing what to include in this publication was not easy, because the collection contains many memorable works of art. After considerable thought, we decided to focus on European and American works of the period 1760–1960, recognizing that the modern era has historically been the area of greatest strength in the museum's holdings. Smith is fortunate to have extensive collections of drawings, prints, and photographs from this period, but with reluctance we decided to concentrate on paintings and sculpture only. Had we not, the pain of narrowing the list to one hundred works would have been even more acute.[1]

How did a small liberal arts college come to have a collection of this importance? The answer is that it began early, acted adventurously, and from the outset established a focus for its activity. Its founders conceived of Smith College as a school that would have an academic rigor equivalent to the men's colleges of its day but that would differ in giving the arts equal emphasis with other disciplines. In 1872 a prospectus for the new college explained,

More time will be devoted than in other colleges to aesthetical study, to the principles on which the fine arts are founded, to the art of drawing and the science of perspective, to the examination of the great models of painting and statuary, to a familiar acquaintance with the works of the great musical composers, and the acquisition of musical skill.

In his inaugural address in 1875 the first president, Laurenus Clark Seelye, elaborated further:

In the fine arts, as in literature and science, the College should simply aim to give that broad and thorough acquaintance with mind which is in itself the best preparation for special work in any calling. If this be its aim, however, it cannot be true to its character and ignore art. Too many of the grandest creations of the human intellect are embodied in the fine arts to remain unnoticed by an institution which seeks the highest mental culture.... [The College] should have its gallery of art, where the student may be made directly familiar with the famous masterpieces....

To that end, Seelye saw to it that College Hall, the new school's first building, included an art gallery. Initially, as was customary in schools and even in America's few city museums of this era, the contents of the gallery were largely plaster casts of famous antique sculptures and engravings or photographs reproducing well-known paintings. Art students were typically trained by copying such models, and early photographs of Smith students at work in College Hall show that they, too, followed this practice. Seelye made it clear, however, that the arts should not be "mere accomplishments" for Smith students, "but ... serious pursuits which demand strenuous intellectual work in order to prosecute them successfully."

With this in mind, President Seelye also believed that it was important for Smith students to become familiar with the work being made in America by artists of their own time. As early as 1879 he set about building a collection of contemporary paintings, often by buying work directly from the artists in their studios. Thomas Eakins's *In Grandmother's Time* (pp. 148–49) is one of the earliest of Seelye's purchases. By the end of 1879 the *Springfield Republican* wrote enthusiastically of the twenty-seven paintings that had been hung in the college art gallery, "It may well be doubted if there is as good a collection of the works of American artists to be found anywhere among the same number of paintings.... For the artists are for the most part representative men, and the pictures are representative paintings, as good as any they have produced." Seelye was advised in his buying initially by J. Wells Champney, a noted artist whom he had hired to teach drawing at Smith in the early years, and later by the tonalist landscape painter Dwight W. Tryon (see pp. 230–33), who joined the faculty in 1886 and remained until his retirement in 1923.

Tryon proved to be pivotal in the collection's development in more ways than one. As Henry White observed in a memorial tribute in 1924, "It was the good fortune of the College that, through Mr. Tryon's early association with most of the artists, in some cases before they had achieved success, he was able to acquire works for the College that are now beyond the reach of most of our museums and collectors." Tryon limited his buying to American paintings of the last quarter of the nine-teenth century, explaining that "the best examples of other art are usually out of our reach financially, and as I do not believe in adding any but the best it leaves us little scope." Whistler (pp. 234–35), Hunt, Chase (pp. 138–39), Kent (pp. 188–89), Blakelock, Dewing (pp. 144–45), Thayer, and Wyant were among the painters whose work he was influential in acquiring for Smith. Saint-Gaudens's *Diana of the Tower* (pp. 216–17) was an audacious early entry into sculpture collecting.

The college was remarkable in dedicating substan-tial funds to building its art program in its early years. Already in 1877 a trustee had offered a $2,000 gift for an art collection, with the proviso that the trustees appro-priate a matching sum. Not only was that challenge met, but an additional $3,000 was raised by subscription, yielding $7,000 — roughly the equivalent of $350,000 today. This money was largely used to purchase plaster casts of famous Greek and Roman sculptures and a series of autotypes by the photographer Adolphe Braun — reproductions of drawings and paintings in many of the great museums of Europe — for the art gallery in College Hall.

In 1881 a retired Northampton businessman named Winthrop Hillyer, who had previously indicated no par-ticular interest in Smith or in art, came forward with an offer of $25,000 to construct an art building — if the col-lege would commit $8,000 to increasing the art collec-tion. Again, the college complied, and Hillyer Art Gallery was completed in 1882. The following year Hillyer died, having indicated his intent to give an addi-tional $50,000 for increasing the art collection and maintaining the building. In 1887 his brother and sister fulfilled his intended bequest and also contributed $10,000 for an addition to Hillyer Art Gallery, and his sister established a $15,000 trust to fund the collection.

With a dedicated building for the study of art, plus not inconsequential funds with which to shape a collec-tion, Smith had already differentiated itself from many of the other liberal arts colleges of its day. Often, the art collections at such colleges began as a hodgepodge of random gifts from alumni, curiosities picked up by trav-eling faculty or missionary graduates, and portraits of college worthies. At Smith, the collections were pur-posefully shaped from the college's inception, with its educational aims firmly guiding the choices made.

Alfred Vance Churchill played an important role in this shaping process. Churchill was hired in 1905 as the first incumbent of a chair of History and Interpretation of Art and given charge of the growing art collection. It was under his leadership that the first loan exhibition took place, a show of old master etchings held in 1911 for the benefit of students in Professor Churchill's Art 14, "History of Painting." Inspired by this show, student members of the Studio Club and their friends got together and bought a fine impression of Rembrandt's

Three Crosses, the first European work — and the first print — to enter the collection. In 1914 Churchill affirmed the expansion of the museum's collecting hori-zons with the purchase of a Rodin bronze, *Children with Lizard*, and finally in 1919 — the year Churchill was named director of the Smith College Museum of Art and the collections were first formally so designated — he embarked on the purchase of European paintings, beginning with Georges Michel's *Landscape*.[2]

When they named him director, the college's trustees asked Churchill to articulate a collecting plan for the newly formalized Museum of Art. He termed his response a "Concentration Plan" and recommended the radical course of centering the collection on modern European and American art. In reflecting back at the end of his directorship, Churchill described his thought process in these terms:

No one engaged like myself in teaching the history of art could have failed to be impressed with the total inade-quacy of a collection limited to American works. What, I reflected, would a professor of literature think if he had nothing for his students to read but American authors of the fourth quarter of the 19th century? A college museum of art ought surely to aim at representing the art of the world, not that of a single nation or period.

Yet selection and concentration imposed themselves inex-orably. But what field ought we to choose? What nations and periods were of first importance?

It seemed to me that attention must be devoted, first of all, to the cultures from which our own is derived and on which it rests, — Egypt, Greece, Rome, and the rest, down through the Renaissance. We must follow the main stream of west-ern civilization. The arts of Europe may not be more important in themselves than those of the Orient. They are more important *to us*.

But even this area was impossibly vast. While its chief phases might eventually be illustrated with a few examples we could never do justice to all. The only practicable plan was to do what we could for the great historic periods, and to choose a limited field for more adequate representation. The educated man has been defined as one who knows "everything of something and something of everything." So a college museum might hope to acquire "something" of every period, and richer and fuller illustrations (if not "everything") of one of them. . . .

The next step was the choice of a special field for concentra-tion — a difficult choice. My proposal was this: Let us select, not a nation or school but a *topic* — the Development of Modern Art. . . . Where does modern art begin? . . . Let us assume that modern art begins with the period of the French Revolution. At that period ancient beliefs, tradi-tions and practices were ruptured and new ones started in every realm of thought including art. The break with the past has never been more complete.

The solution was novel and radical. No college had empha-sized the modern period. Too often the interests of educa-tional institutions had been "one with Nineveh and Tyre," and still are, as far as art is concerned. Yet the modern period is one of great richness and significance, and very close to our sympathies. . . .

The other key plank in Churchill's platform was quality:

for our purpose quality had to be the first consideration. A weak or inferior work could only be misleading to the student. Everything in the collection must show the imaginative conception of the master who made it, must reveal something of his suppleness, strength, and beauty. And it must show his "handwriting": it must be "signed all over" with the characters that he and he alone has given the world or could give.

Unlike the best museums of Europe, however, he observed:

I was willing to acquire a *fragment* where they would not, for even a fragment may reveal the master. I would take an *unfinished work* where they would not, for such a work may convey quite as much as a finished one.

(While he recognized that European museums might acquire fragmentary or damaged works of antiquity or the Renaissance, Churchill saw his uniqueness in adopting this policy for "modern" art.) Among Churchill's acquisitions, Courbet's *Preparation of the Dead Girl* (pp. 38–39) and Cézanne's *Turn in the Road at La Roche-Guyon* (pp. 32–33) — both unfinished paintings by artists he considered "indispensable" to the collection — hold pride of place alongside Eakins's brilliant *Edith Mahon* (pp. 150–51).

Thus, Churchill set himself a dual mission: a "distribution project" involving collecting individual strong examples to establish a broad representation of the chief phases of Western civilization, and a "concentration project" covering modern art. The selections in this book, which very closely match the period of his "concentration project," are testimony that the museum's greatest strengths today lie in what Churchill defined as the modern era.

As the museum grew, its quarters in Hillyer Art Gallery became increasingly inadequate. Having long hoped to do so, in 1924 Dwight Tryon and his wife, Alice, pledged $100,000 to build a new, dedicated museum building. Tryon did not live to see his building realized; he died in July 1925, shortly after the groundbreaking. His will included a handsome endowment of $300,000 for maintenance of the new Tryon Gallery, adding to the art collection, and supporting the college's teaching in the field.

It was Churchill's successor as director, Jere Abbott, who turned the museum's acquisition funds to brilliant use. Abbott had been associate director of the Museum of Modern Art in New York during its initial years, immediately before he came to Smith in 1932. He arrived in Northampton armed with knowledge about the avant-garde art of Europe, acquaintance with many of the important taste-makers of the day, a discriminating eye, and President William Allan Neilson's mandate to run a professional museum at Smith. His early purchases,

including Picasso's cubist *Table, Guitar, and Bottle* (pp. 96–97), shocked many. "A geometrical nightmare," thundered the *Worcester Sunday Telegram* in 1938. Abbott bought boldly; many of the works that are today considered masterworks of the collection were purchased within a year or two of their creation. The Calder mobile (pp. 136–37) and Sheeler's *Rolling Power* (pp. 220–21) come readily to mind. He was instrumental in the college's decision in 1943 to commission a mural for the Hillyer Art Library from the Mexican artist Rufino Tamayo, who was little known in this country at the time. The resulting work, *Nature and the Artist: The Work of Art and the Observer*, was the artist's first American fresco. Important paintings and sculptures by Degas (pp. 42–49), Monet (pp. 82–87), Manet (pp. 78–79), Seurat (pp. 118–19), Vuillard (pp. 120–23), and many other artists entered the collection during Abbott's tenure.

Abbott left the directorship in 1946, to be succeeded for a year by Frederick Hartt, who was brought to Smith as acting director and as a visiting lecturer in the art department. With the concurrence of the art department, the president, and the trustees of the college, Hartt carried out a spate of deaccessioning of works considered to be of little use in teaching. Many of the American paintings acquired in the early years of the college were sold, for the most part at nominal prices, since these works were out of artistic fashion at the time. Some now grace the walls of other distinguished museums: Thayer's *Winged Figure* is at the Art Institute of Chicago, for example, and Dewing's *Lady with a Lute* can be seen at the National Gallery of Art in Washington. Others, such as two rare garden still lifes by Maria Oakey Dewing, cannot be traced. This regrettable chapter in the museum's history constitutes an object lesson in the vagaries of taste and the need for caution in "pruning" collections that should be heeded by museum directors everywhere.

The noted architectural historian Henry-Russell Hitchcock served as director from 1949 through 1955. He bought both American (pp. 168–69 and 222–23) and European (pp. 74–75, 88–89, 92–93, and 124–25) works, with a particular emphasis on strengthening the English holdings.

Robert Owen Parks succeeded Hitchcock and served as director until 1961. His wide-ranging acquisitions include Kirchner's *Dodo and Her Brother* (pp. 72–73) and Stuart's *Henrietta Elizabeth Frederica Vane* (pp. 228–29). He was followed in the directorship by Charles Chetham, during whose lengthy tenure (1962–88) the collection more than tripled in size. Chetham made a particular effort to build the museum's holdings of contemporary art and photography. Among his purchases were the Barye *Theseus Slaying the Centaur Bienor* (pp. 22–23), the Carpeaux *Bust of a Chinese Man* (pp. 30–31), Degas's *Dancer Moving Forward* (pp. 48–49), the Fantin-Latour *Mr. Becker* (pp. 52–53), the untitled canvas by Joan Mitchell (pp. 198–99), two Rodin sculptures, *Man with the Broken Nose* (pp. 112 13) and *The Walking Man* (pp. 114–15), and John Singer Sargent's *My Dining Room* (pp. 218–19).

By the 1960s the popularity of art courses with students and the growth of the museum's collections again put pressure on the physical facilities, and planning for a new building began. Hillyer, Tryon, and Graham (an auditorium wing that had been added to Hillyer in 1910) were razed and replaced in 1972 by a new Fine Arts Center incorporating buildings that retained these three names, arranged around a central courtyard. Tryon Hall, the new home of the Smith College Museum, was four times the size of the former Tryon Art Gallery. It afforded space to show much more of the collection and state-of-the-art facilities for making those works not on display readily available on request to visitors and students.

Chetham's successors, Edward Nygren (director 1988–91), Charles Parkhurst (acting director 1991–92), and I, have faced a different challenge. While the most recent purchases to appear in this volume, Boilly's *Young Painter and His Model* (pp. 26–27) — executed on the eve of the French Revolution — and Guérin's *Clytemnestra Hesitating before Stabbing the Sleeping Agamemnon* (pp. 64–65), fall squarely within Churchill's "concentration" and would, I like to think, have met fully with his approval, it is no longer quite so straightforward to conclude, at the outset of the new millennium in America, that we must follow only the "main stream of western civilization." Today the art historical canon is being challenged and stretched in many directions. The curriculum addresses not only the Western tradition but the equally rich traditions of Africa, Asia, Islam, the Native American and pre-Columbian cultures, and the multiethnic strands, drawing on all of the above, that constitute the complex American cultural fabric. The historical roles of women and other formerly ignored groups are being reexamined. Contemporary art speaks not with a single voice, or even with two in opposition as in earlier times. It is a babble of many competing voices, delivered not only in conventional formats but also as installation and performance work and in forms incorporating video, film, sound, light, and computer imagery.

Our challenge, as a teaching museum that supports Smith's instructional mission, is to redefine the "distribution project" on which Churchill embarked and to realize it, while at the same time maintaining and building on our historic strength, already achieved by his farsighted "concentration project." It is a daunting challenge indeed. As we proceed, his exhortation to quality must remain ever in the forefront.

This is no longer a solitary effort, however. For the first seventy-five years of Smith's existence, the collections were shaped largely through purchases made by the key individuals discussed above. By the 1950s the few purchases the museum could make each year — usually no more than two or three paintings and sculptures were already easily outnumbered by gifts. Increasingly as the second half of the century wore on, gifts became the primary means of building the collection. The body of alumnae who had learned to love art at Smith continued to swell. Some became collectors and remembered their alma mater; others worked in the arts or volunteered their talents there and used their connections to help the museum. Alumnae unable to contribute art to the museum themselves sometimes turned their friends' or families' munificence toward the college. Others with no connection to the college have supported the museum because of the high standard it upholds and because they recognize the importance of its mission. Without these donors, the museum's collection would be a much more modest affair, particularly as rising prices in the art market have diminished the power of the museum's acquisition funds. The generosity of alumnae and friends of the college has been remarkable, and their adherence to the standard of quality put forward by Churchill equally so.

Among the many donors to the museum, those associated with works in this book deserve special mention here. They include Jere Abbott; Mr. and Mrs. Duncan Boeckman (Elizabeth Mayer, class of 1954); Joseph Brummer; Mrs. Charles W. Carl (Marie Schuster, class of 1917); Jane Chace Carroll, class of 1953; Beatrice Oenslager Chace, class of 1928; the Chace Foundation, Inc.; Annie Swan Coburn (Mrs. Lewis Larned Coburn); Mr. and Mrs. Ralph F. Colin (I. Georgia Talmey, class of 1928); Eleanor Lamont Cunningham, class of 1932; Mrs. Henry T. Curtiss (Mina Kirstein, class of 1918); Mrs. John Stewart Dalrymple (Bernice Barber, class of 1910); the Dedalus Foundation; E. Porter Dickinson; Louise Ines Doyle, class of 1934; Mr. and Mrs. Allan D. Emil; Alice Rutherford Erving, class of 1929; Dr. and Mrs. Joel E. Goldthwait (Jessie Rand, class of 1890); Frank L. Harrington; Mr. and Mrs. Harold D. Hodgkinson (Laura White Cabot, class of 1922); Mrs. Charles Inslee (Marguerite Tuthill, class of 1915); Anne Holden Kieckhefer, class of 1952; Mrs. Sigmund W. Kunstadter (Maxine Weil, class of 1924); Anne Morrow Lindbergh, class of 1928; Mrs. Charles MacArthur (Helen Hayes, LHD 1940); Nanette Harrison Meech, class of 1938; Constance Morrow Morgan, class of 1935; Dwight W. Morrow, Jr.; Roy R. Neuberger; Louise Nevelson, DFA 1973; Eliot Chace Nolen, class of 1954; Mrs. John W. O'Boyle (Nancy Millar, class of 1952); Helen Haseltine Plowden; Mrs. Winthrop Merton Rice (Helen Swift Jones, class of 1910); Paul Rosenberg and Company; Madeleine H. Russell, class of 1937; Mrs. Otto Seiffert (Marjorie S. Allen, class of 1906); Ettie Stettheimer; Mrs. Robert S. Tangeman (E. Clementine Miller, class of 1927); Mrs. Charles Lincoln Taylor (Margaret Rand Goldthwait, class of 1921); Bernice Hirschman Tumen, class of 1923; the Honorable and Mrs. Irwin Untermyer; the Carey Walker Foundation; Adeline F. Wing, class of 1898; Caroline R. Wing, class of 1896; and the Robert R. Young Foundation. Donors who have established endowment funds for the purchase of works of art are equally important. Our thanks go to Beatrice Oenslager Chace, class of 1928; donors to the Acquisition Fund in honor of Charles Chetham; Mr. and Mrs. Charles C. Cunningham (Eleanor Lamont, class of 1932); Elizabeth Halsey Dock, class of 1933; Mr. and Mrs. Richard Evans (Rebecca Morris, class of 1932); Rita Rich Fraad, class of 1937; Drayton Hillyer; Winthrop Hillyer; Janet Wright Ketcham, class of 1953; Sarah J. Mather; Eva W. Nair, class of 1928; Diane Allen Nixon, class of 1957; Janice Carlson Oresman, class of 1955; Katherine S. Pearce, class of 1915; Madeleine Haas Russell, class of 1937; Kathleen Compton Sherrerd, class of 1954; Josephine A. Stein, class of 1927; Dwight W. Tryon; donors to the Class of 1990 Art Fund; and donors to the Museum Acquisition Fund with gifts in honor of Marjorie Resnikoff Botwinik, class of 1937, Caroline Newburger Berkowitz, class of 1921, and Barbara Petchesky Jakobson, class of 1954.

Finally, I would like to thank the many people who have made this book possible. When the idea for such a volume first arose, it was the wholehearted enthusiasm of the museum's Visiting Committee and Tryon Associates that moved the project swiftly from dream to reality. Dr. and Mrs. Julius H. Jacobson II (Joan Leiman, class of 1947) immediately stepped forward with a generous gift to begin work, and the Tryon Associates, the Friends of the Museum, and the Kunstadter Fund have supported its continuation.

My colleagues in the art department, John Davis and Jaroslaw Leshko, also eagerly volunteered for the all-important task of writing the text. Although they may since have had second thoughts, they have graciously not voiced them as they have labored mightily to condense their insights into no more than six hundred words per object. It has been a genuine pleasure to work closely with them on this undertaking, one that will doubtless bear further fruit as they teach from the collection in the future. Paul Anbinder of Hudson Hills Press has been enormously helpful — and patient — throughout, and has given us a handsome volume. Fronia Wissman Simpson, class of 1974, was our admirable copy-editor. Stephen Petegorsky deserves kudos for the new transparencies used in production of the book. Many members of the museum staff have also been essential contributors to the effort. They are thanked in the authors' acknowledgments, and I heartily second those accolades.

Once again, the Smith College Museum of Art and the art department have outgrown their quarters. Before this book sees publication, the Fine Arts Center will have been emptied and a major renovation and expansion, designed by the Polshek Partnership, will have begun. The jewels of the collection — many of the works in this volume and others — will travel across the country in two separate exhibitions during the years 2000–2002, while building work proceeds. *American Spectrum*, featuring seventy-five of our most important American paintings and sculptures, will be shown at the Faulconer Gallery, Grinnell College, Grinnell, Iowa; National Academy of Design, New York, New York; Norton Museum of Art, West Palm Beach, Florida; Museum of Fine Arts, Houston, Texas; Pennsylvania Academy of the Fine Arts, Philadelphia, Pennsylvania; Memorial Art Gallery, Rochester, New York; and Tucson Museum of Art, Arizona. *Corot to Picasso*, fifty-seven European works bracketed by these artists, will be seen at the Indianapolis Museum of Art, Indiana; Faulconer Gallery, Grinnell College, Grinnell, Iowa; Cummer Museum and Gardens, Jacksonville, Florida; John and Mable Ringling Museum of Art, Sarasota, Florida; Iris and B. Gerald Cantor Center for Visual Arts of Stanford University, Stanford, California; Marion Koogler McNay Art Museum, San Antonio, Texas; and the Phillips Collection, Washington, D.C. A third exhibition, *Master Drawings from the Smith College Museum of Art*, will tour as well. Much as we deplore the necessity of depriving Smith students of these works for two years, we welcome the opportunity to share them with audiences across the country that might otherwise not come to know them. We hope that this volume will help accomplish that same goal.

Suzannah J. Fabing
Director and Chief Curator
September 1999

Notes

1 Some of the most significant drawings appear in *Master Drawings from the Smith College Museum of Art*, edited by Ann H. Sievers (New York: Hudson Hills Press, 2000). The two catalogues of the Selma Erving Collection, produced by the museum in 1977 and 1985, present the extraordinary *livres d'artiste* and prints of the late nineteenth and early twentieth century that came to the museum through this alumna's generosity. For a further representation of the museum's holdings, the reader is referred to our World Wide Web site or, preferably, encouraged to visit after the museum reopens in 2003, following extensive renovations and expansion.

2 Ironically, it was Dwight Tryon's most important patron, Charles Lang Freer, who had been responsible for the first non-American paintings entering the collection. Freer, a Detroit industrialist, had built a superb collection of Asian and American art that he later gave to establish the Freer Gallery, part of the Smithsonian Institution in Washington, D.C. Through his friendship with Tryon, one of a handful of American painters whose work he collected, Freer kept abreast of the burgeoning collection at Smith. In 1917 he presented the college with a modest group of Chinese and Japanese paintings, along with some Asian ceramics and bronzes, thereby single-handedly extending the painting collection's reach far beyond the American field.

European Painting
and Sculpture

Hans (Jean) Arp

Strassburg, Germany (now Strasbourg, France) 1886–1966 Basel, Switzerland

Torso, 1953

Marble
31¼ × 14½ × 13⅜ in. (79.4 × 36.8 × 34 cm)
Not signed or dated
Gift of Mr. and Mrs. Ralph F. Colin (I. Georgia Talmey, class of 1928)
1956:13
© 2000 Artists Rights Society (ARS), New York/VG Bild-Kunst, Bonn

Jean Arp's *Torso* was conceived as a small-scale plaster in 1930, at a time when the artist turned his attention to three-dimensional biomorphic forms he called concretions. *Torso* was transformed into a large, pristine marble in 1953, after Curt Valentin, Arp's friend and prominent art dealer, noticed the small plaster in the studio and asked him to create a more monumental version. According to Arp, the request came at a time when his own intent was to reintroduce human form into his art. Arp commented on the *Torso:* "I believe that this sculpture represents the realization of a basic shape of the female torso and that it is a descendant from the torsos and dolls appearing on reliefs and collages of the Dada period." Just how this graceful image could have been born out of Dada, the anti-art movement that plunged art into nihilistic spasms after World War I, becomes clear in the context of Arp's unique contributions to the movement. While he was philosophically positioned against rationalism and celebrated nonsense with wit and irony, he never lost sight of the aesthetic component of art. This was most consistently manifest in his use of the curving line closing in on itself to create biomorphic shapes. A form like the navel, which came into being during the Dada period and was often used in a humorous context with forks, anchors, bottles, and so forth, became a recurrent motif for Arp. Its centrality to life's processes and its oval, biomorphic shape established an early connection between organic forms and the creative process.

Arp experimented with automatism in a series of drawings made about 1916. His process, in which conscious will was suspended and the creative act was processed through the unconscious, was important for his later work in which images evolve organically and spontaneously, motivated not by a predetermined idea but by the inner necessity of the creative act. Throughout his long career he would explore countless permutations of the organic shape in all media.

Torso is a brilliant manifestation of Arp's lifelong researches, and it addresses important touchstones in his art. At the time he created the small plaster version of *Torso* he visited Constantin Brancusi, whose radically simplified forms encouraged Arp to turn to sculpture. In 1952, a year before executing the large marble version of the work, Arp traveled to Rome and Greece, reestablishing contact with classical thought and art. The classical world provided him with a vast array of formal and expressive possibilities—from the austere grace of the archaic Kouros figures to the writhing forms of the Laocoön group. Exposure to antiquity also reinforced his decision to use bronze and marble in his later work. The fragmented state of much of classical statuary, with missing heads and limbs, validated those omissions in his own work, which he also knew from Auguste Rodin's partial figures. Yet *Torso* differs in that it is interpreted as a cohesive organic entity—complete in its omissions.

Torso also differs from Brancusi's universal, iconic shapes on special pedestals set before the viewer for contemplation. Arp's work suggests an inner energy through the rhythm of swelling forms, evocative of fertility and organic growth. It provokes the viewer to move around it in a process of discovery and revelation. Art for Arp is a process of growth and is profoundly connected with nature's regenerative essence. He wrote in his diary, "Art is a fruit that grows in man, like a fruit on a plant, or a child in a mother's womb." *Torso* exemplifies this sentiment, for it is as much about art as it is about life.

Further Reading

Hancock, Jane, et al. *Arp, 1886–1966.* Cambridge: Cambridge University Press, 1987.

Soby, James Thrall, ed. *Arp.* New York: The Museum of Modern Art, 1958.

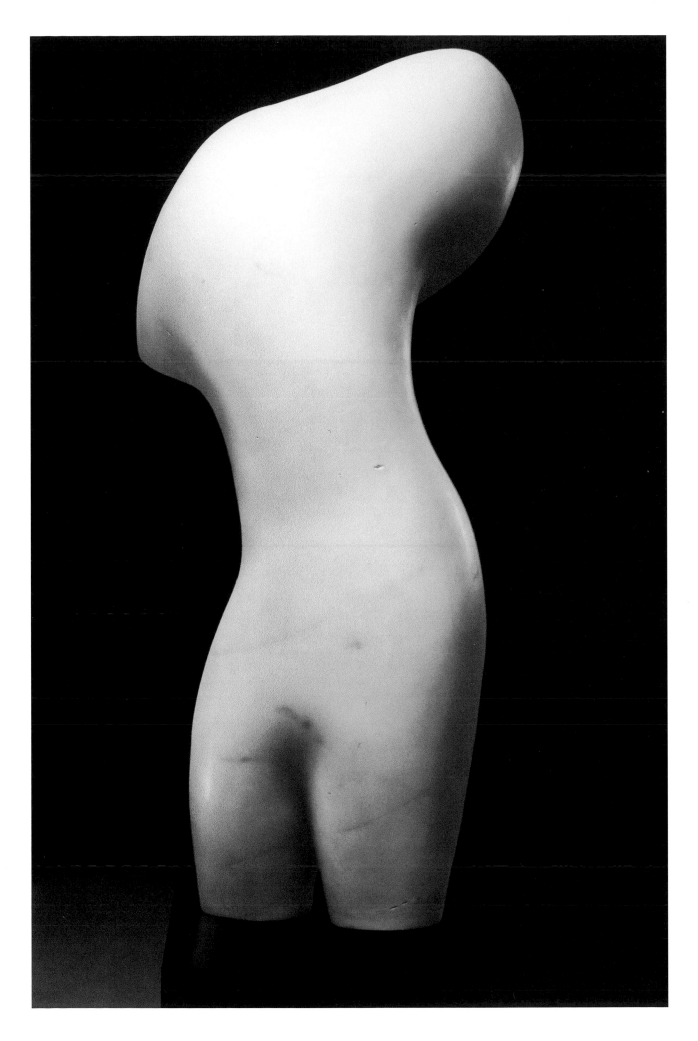

Antoine-Louis Barye

Paris, France 1796–1875 Paris, France

Theseus Slaying the Centaur Bienor,

modeled 1849–50

Bronze on self-base

21½ × 19 × 5 in. (54.6 × 48.2 × 12.7 cm)

Incised signature on rock, below proper left hind leg of centaur:
A. L. Barye

Foundry mark on rock, below proper right hind leg:
F. BARBEDIENNE Fondeur

Purchased

1973:4

Antoine-Louis Barye's sculptural career, which spanned nearly six decades, began in 1816 when Neoclassicism was the prevailing style with only early stirrings of Romanticism. The dominant sculptor was Antonio Canova, whose influence was universal. During the 1860s, toward the end of Barye's career, he taught the young Auguste Rodin. Barye's place in the historical span between these two major sculptors is important and indispensable.

Barye's ascendancy among the leaders of the romantic movement was assured by his immensely successful entry in the Salon of 1833, *Lion Crushing a Serpent* (Musée du Louvre, Paris), for which he received the cross of the Legion of Honor. For many viewers at the time, the image embodied the ideals of the July Revolution of 1830. By giving import to an animal conflict, Barye challenged the prevailing hierarchy of elevated subjects. He and Eugène Delacroix, the preeminent romantic painter, spent long hours in the Jardin des Plantes in Paris, sketching animals and studying their anatomy. Beyond their love of animals, Romanticism's major metaphor, Barye shared with Delacroix and other romantic artists a fascination with themes of cruelty and conflict. Barye's exploration of the animal initiated a school of sculptors known as the *animaliers*. Yet no other sculptor possessed Barye's capacity to marshal raw animal violence into a controlled coil of energy. The critic Théophile Gautier, after viewing Barye's *Jaguar Devouring a Hare* at the Salon of 1850 (Musée du Louvre, Paris), referred to the artist as the "Michelangelo of the menagerie."

Barye's other entry in the Salon of 1850 was *Theseus Slaying the Centaur Bienor*, based on a scene from Ovid's *Metamorphoses*. The complex composition is predicated on his 1840 sketch, *Lapith Combating a Centaur* (Walters Art Gallery, Baltimore), a conflict immortalized by Phidias in the metopes of the Parthenon. The

legend focuses on the intrusion of the centaurs into the wedding of Peirithous, king of Lapithae, and Deïdameïa. Theseus helped the king defeat the centaurs in their attempt to carry off the bride. While the Theseus group shares with many of Barye's animal groups the act of conflict, here the visceral life/death struggle of the animals is transformed into a confrontation whose outcome is preordained by the literary sources from which the themes are drawn. This sense of inevitability is most evident in the serene countenance of the hero, whose idealized features, based on classical prototypes, betray mere concentration on the coup de grâce he is about to inflict on the anguished, disheveled head of the centaur. Humanity will conquer barbarism, the rational will prevail over the irrational.

To give majesty to this noble theme, Barye invents one of his most ambitious and resolved compositions — a charged pyramid of rippling energy in which man, nature, and mythological beast — half man, half horse — participate in a struggle for primacy. The swelling rock and jagged plant atop it form a stark and precarious base on which the dramatic conflict is played out. In a brilliant conceit, Barye places Theseus in a posture of conquest atop the horse half of the centaur, transforming the beautifully articulated, tensed animal into an appropriate platform for his heroic deeds.

Romantic sculptors preferred the tactile, painterly quality of patinated bronze, whereas the neoclassicists gravitated toward highly polished marble. Barye's bronzes were made in editions of numerous casts — much like an edition of a print. Unlike a print, the sculpture could also be produced in various sizes. Barye offered the Theseus group, for example, in sizes up to fifty inches in height. Foundries like Barbedienne continued to produce high-quality casts of his work in different sizes. The Smith cast is a Barbedienne foundry reduction. There are many issues that Barye had to confront in dealing with edition sculptures, including those of uniqueness and quality of casts. Yet in establishing the viability of multiple casts in different sizes, Barye was instrumental in making sculpture accessible to a wide and receptive audience.

Further Reading

Benge, Glenn F. *Antoine-Louis Barye, Sculptor of Romantic Realism*. University Park: Pennsylvania State University Press, 1984.

Pivar, Stuart. *The Barye Bronzes*. Woodbridge, England: Antique Collectors' Club, 1974.

Vanessa Bell

London, England 1879–1961 Charleston, Firle, Sussex, England

Landscape with Haystack, Asheham, 1912

Oil on board

23¾ × 25⅞ in. (60.3 × 65.7 cm)

Not signed or dated

Purchased with funds given by Anne Holden Kieckhefer, class of 1952, in honor of Ruth Chandler Holden, class of 1926

1989:23

© 1961 Estate of Vanessa Bell, courtesy Henrietta Garnett

"You're doing splendid things, damn you, and mine will always be makeshift." This generous assessment of Vanessa Bell's art by Roger Fry, England's preeminent critic, at the expense of his own artistic effort, demonstrates her esteemed position among the members of the Bloomsbury Group. The artists and writers belonging to this unique assembly were bonded by friendship and a desire to bring modernism to England. The exhibitions of post-impressionist art organized by Fry in London in 1910 and 1912 caused a sensation and unnerved the conservative English public. In 1913 an even more advanced brand of European avant-garde was brought to New York in the notorious Armory Show, to a scandalized reception. With these events, the English-speaking art world was jolted into the twentieth century. Bell's *Landscape with Haystack, Asheham* was likely painted in the fall of 1912, on the eve of the second post-impressionist exhibition. In it she depicts the landscape around Asheham House (seen here partially behind the haystack), near Beddingham in Sussex Downs, which she and her sister Virginia had leased that year.

Virginia, who became one of the major literary figures of the century, married Leonard Woolf in the summer of 1912, and Asheham became their country home. It was an important gathering place for the members of the Bloomsbury Group. Vanessa and her husband, Clive Bell, the writer and critic whom she had married in 1907, frequently resided in the house.

Bell's artistic development was rich and prescient. Between 1901 and 1904 she studied with John Singer Sargent at the London Academy of Art, and then for a brief period at the Slade School of Art. By 1905 she had journeyed to Paris, where she saw the work of the post-impressionists and was especially taken with the works of Paul Cézanne.

Here Bell includes the house, underscoring her penchant for subjects with close personal resonance. Yet in focusing on the haystack, the artist is also referring to Claude Monet's famous series of grainstacks of the 1890s, painted at various times of day and in different seasons. Bell's painting is fundamentally about structure. There is no hot sun here, dissolving form and defining a moment, as in Monet. Bell has consciously gone beyond Impressionism toward Post-Impressionism. A black outline delineates the bold geometry of the haystack as in a cloissonist painting by Paul Gauguin. But her major inspiration is Cézanne. The color scheme of greens, browns, and blues, with hints of gray and mauve, approximates Cézanne's palette. The repetitive, regularized brushstrokes of the sky at the upper right and in the foreground area resemble Cézanne's constructivist brushstrokes, which give texture to the painted surface and structure to the composition. The form of the haystack establishes reciprocal relationships with the large house and two small ones to its right and with the dark shape of foliage to its left. The massing of large forms in the middle and background is contrasted with the relative emptiness of the foreground, into which we are introduced by a sweeping curve demarcated by the delicate, rhythmically cadenced posts. The central haystack stabilizes the composition by unifying foreground and background, left and right sides into a cohesive structural whole.

Structural design was, for her mentor Fry, the universalizing principle in all great painting, a lesson Bell took to heart. To create a landscape based on the laws of art and not of nature, in which the interplay of forms and the juxtaposition of colors dominate and unify the image, was for Bell the ultimate expression of freedom. In *Landscape with Haystack, Asheham,* she has indeed done "splendid things."

Further Reading

Shone, Richard, et al. *The Art of Bloomsbury: Roger Fry, Vanessa Bell and Duncan Grant.* London: Tate Gallery, 1999.

Spalding, Frances. *Vanessa Bell.* New Haven, Conn.: Ticknor & Fields, 1983.

Vanessa Bell, 1879–1961. Poughkeepsie, N.Y.: Vassar College Art Gallery, 1984.

Louis-Léopold Boilly

La Bassée (near Lille), France 1761–1845 Paris, France

A Young Painter and His Model, c. 1788–92

Oil on canvas

18⅛ × 14⅞ in. (46 × 37.8 cm)

Signed in black paint, lower left (on the verso of the outermost of the stacked canvases): L Boilly ft

Purchased with the Beatrice Oenslager Chace, class of 1928, Art Acquisition Fund, the Madeleine H. Russell, class of 1937, Fund and the Hillyer, Mather, Tryon Fund

1996:21

Few artists chronicled the mores and societal changes of late-eighteenth- and early-nineteenth-century France with the acuity and sophistication of Louis-Léopold Boilly. The layered act of being, viewing, and chronicling events of the Revolutionary period and the Napoleonic era in France lies at the core of Boilly's art.

Soon after the artist arrived in Paris in 1785, his early work focused on gallant imagery — most often subjects of amorous dalliances still closely tethered to rococo sensibility. These small paintings, with their high finish and focus on rich interior settings, are reminiscent of seventeenth-century Dutch and Flemish cabinet pictures by such artists as Gabriel Metsu and Gerrit Dou. The active market for such old master paintings at the time also created a demand for Boilly's work.

A Young Painter and His Model belongs to this early period. In it we are privy to a flirtation in progress. A young artist is making his case to a seemingly engaged participant. He hovers over her shoulder and points to a canvas at the right, which depicts a sleeping bare-breasted woman being fondled by a leering older man. The woman of the artist's desires tilts her head in the direction of the painting; her self-conscious smile, outstretched neck, and revealing décolletage suggest acquiescence.

The flirtation is taking place in a studio context, identifying the male figure as the artist and the female as a possible model. The artist's studio became a prominent and frequent theme in Boilly's art. Invariably the contents of a studio provide an introduction to the artist himself, defining his predisposition and erudition. The reference to the arts is here all-encompassing. In addition to the painting-within-the-painting at the right, to the left of the pair are two sculptures by Etienne-Maurice Falconet, the *Sleeping Bacchante* on the table in the foreground, *The Bather* in the background. Between them is a folio — likely of drawings and prints. A domed rotunda on Ionic columns looms in the background, loosely referencing both the Pantheon in Rome and the dome of the church of Ste. Geneviève in Paris, which was being built at the time. The table is covered by a beautiful Turkish carpet, likely from Ushak, and on it are books — one of which the woman holds in her hand. At the extreme left is a barely visible stringed instrument. Thus literature, music, and all of the visual arts are brilliantly woven into the fabric of this work.

A pink ribbon, which cascades from the folio down the side of the table, visually links the two sculptures and by extension the woman around whose torso the ribbon was tied just moments ago. The woman is flanked by works of art — a sculpture and a painting — in which the image of sleeping women perpetuates the idea of male gaze and desire. Yet the different presentation of the two reflects the painting's complexity. The sleeping woman in the painting adds an element of vulnerability to the narrative of violation. The *Sleeping Bacchante* sculpture is admired as both an image of a nude and an exquisitely resolved work of art.

To the eighteenth-century viewer, books would have been seen as objects of a woman's temptation and fall, often identified with specific texts of illicit liaisons, such as the popular medieval love story of Héloise and Abelard. Boilly's painting is less specific in its protagonists and less explicit in its narrative, deliberately remaining an image of flirtation, perhaps to appeal to a wider audience. Yet Boilly convincingly orchestrates an arsenal of keenly observed elements that enhance the content and meaning of the work. He takes us beyond the realm of gallant imagery into a discourse about the meaning of art and its capacity to enrich and persuade.

Further Reading

Rand, Richard, et al. *Intimate Encounters: Love and Domesticity in Eighteenth-Century France.* Hanover, N.H.: Hood Museum of Art, Dartmouth College; Princeton, N.J.: Princeton University Press, 1997.

Siegfried, Susan L. *The Art of Louis-Léopold Boilly: Modern Life in Napoleonic France.* New Haven, Conn.: Yale University Press, 1995.

Pierre Bonnard

Fontenay-aux-Roses (near Paris), France 1867–1947 Le Cannet, France

---

Landscape in Normandy (formerly *Landscape in the Midi*), 1920 (completed later)

Oil on canvas
24⅝ × 32 in. (62.5 × 81.3 cm)
Signed in thinned black paint, lower left of center: Bonnard
Purchased, Drayton Hillyer Fund
1937:8

Landscape in Normandy exemplifies the uniqueness of Bonnard's artistic vision and his singular place in twentieth-century modernism. He recognized that his approach to nature was out of line with the dramatic "isms" that defined art in the first decades of the century. "The march of progress is rapid, and the world was ready to welcome Cubism and Surrealism before we had achieved what we had set out to do. We felt ourselves suspended in mid-air," he wrote.

This most private of artists initiated his dialogue with modernism as a member of the Nabis (Hebrew for "prophet"), a group of artists, including Maurice Denis and Edouard Vuillard, who defined issues of Symbolism during the 1890s. He was first exposed to Paul Gauguin's theories of expressive use of color, and only thereafter did he explore Impressionism. This reversal of historical sequence led him to transform Impressionism into an expressive idiom. "When my friends and I sought to pursue the investigation of Impressionists and develop them further, we wanted to go beyond the naturalistic impression of color. Art is not nature," he explained. After the initial contact with the motif, "I leave [it], control it, come back to it and then return to it after a while. That way I don't allow [myself] to be absorbed by the object itself." To that end, he worked exclusively in his studio, where, "before I start painting, I reflect, I dream."

In *Landscape in Normandy* the evocation of an image rather than the image itself is the determining norm. As our eye scans the colorful speckled sky or moves across the diagonal path from lower right toward the house at left, it always comes back to the exuberant cluster of trees in the middle. Varied in size, shape, and vegetation, they create a dazzling silhouette that is generously diffused into the surrounds. Combinations of color add to the richness. The dark green of the path is juxtaposed above with a stretch of yellow-gold and below with the lighter green of the tree. The dark green and yellow-gold are further linked with black vertical forms arranged in a rhythmic pattern, which could be interpreted as people walking down the path. The triangular shape of the green tree at center left both stabilizes the composition and releases an explosion of nature's fireworks, in which trees, sky, and ground are subsumed in a luxuriant display. It is here that we perceive not only the artist's sensitive and restless eye but his whole being immersed in the joy of color, the drama of form created by an extensive array of marks moving across the canvas boldly or tentatively but insistently, to soothe, to startle, to bring sensual joy. We are awed by the inspiring spectacle of nature's beauty and the artist's ability to release it from his imaginings.

The colors in *Landscape in Normandy* are so lush and saturated with nature's warmth that for years the painting was thought to have been done in the Midi, the southern region of France, which has inspired brilliant celebratory landscapes by Henri Matisse, André Derain, and others. The present title was given to the Smith painting only after an affinity was noted with Bonnard's *Landscape in Normandy* of 1920 (Musée d'Unterlinden, Colmar), which depicts the same trees and house. In his confession that "Personally, I am very weak. It is difficult for me to control myself in front of an object," Bonnard, in fact, defines his strength. It is precisely that passionate intensity through which he transforms nature into art.

Further Reading

Hyman, Timothy. *Bonnard.* New York: Thames and Hudson, 1998.

Newman, Sasha M., ed. *Bonnard: The Late Paintings.* New York: Thames and Hudson, 1984.

Whitfield, Sarah, and John Elderfield. *Bonnard.* New York: Harry N. Abrams, 1998.

Jean-Baptiste Carpeaux

Valenciennes, France 1827–1875 Courbevoie, France

Bust of a Chinese Man (Le Chinois),

modeled 1868; cast c. 1872–74

Bronze

26½ × 20½ × 13⅝ in. (67.3 × 52.1 × 34.6 cm)

Signature incised under proper right shoulder termination: Carpeaux

Stamped twice inside the base: Propriété Carpeaux

Purchased

1970:4

Jean-Baptiste Carpeaux's career, often viewed as a manifestation of the effusive elegance of the Second Empire, is also a brilliant coda to Romanticism. Carpeaux entered the Ecole des Beaux-Arts in 1844 as a student of François Rude, an influential romantic sculptor best known for his monumental stone relief, *Departure of the Volunteers*, for Paris's Arc de Triomphe. Carpeaux admired Rude's artistic discipline, and his own *Fisherboy Listening to a Seashell* of 1857 (plaster, Musée du Louvre, Paris) is an homage to the naturalism of his mentor's *Neapolitan Fisherboy* of 1833 (marble, Musée du Louvre, Paris). Rude's uncompromising republican politics limited his official acceptance, so Carpeaux, in a desire to enhance his career, soon left his studio for that of Francisque Duret, a less talented but less controversial artist than Rude.

In 1854, after years of trying, Carpeaux won the Prix de Rome, but an illness postponed his departure until 1856. A trip to Florence in August 1858 galvanized his interest in Michelangelo, under whose influence he sculpted *Ugolino and His Sons* of 1860 (marble version of 1867, The Metropolitan Museum of Art). Based on the story of Count Ugolino in Dante's *Inferno*, canto 33, the large, chillingly powerful group established Carpeaux's career as a sculptor of monumental works. The figures of the sons writhe around the anguished Ugolino, creating a dynamic circular pattern that Carpeaux employed in a number of his public monuments. The exuberant *Dance* of 1866–69 on the façade of Charles Garnier's Opéra (removed to Musée d'Orsay, Paris), Carpeaux's most popular and resolved work, is a brilliant example of such centrifugal energy.

Circular movement also dominates his last monumental project, *Four Parts of the World*, commissioned by the architect Gabriel Jean-Antoine Davioud in 1867 as the culminating group of the Fontaine de l'Observatoire in the Luxembourg Gardens in Paris. The monument, which was unveiled in 1874, depicts four large female nudes representing Africa, America, Asia, and Europe, holding up a sphere whose shape reiterates their circular, animated motion. *Le Chinois* is a more finished variant of an earlier sketch for the figure of Asia. Because Carpeaux could not find a Chinese woman to model, he had a man pose for him. He then grafted the male features onto a female body for the monument. *Le Chinois* is typical of Carpeaux's practice of casting individual figures or groups from his most famous public monuments. Yet Carpeaux transformed *Le Chinois* significantly enough to consider it an independent work—at once a portrait and a representation of a racial type.

The power of the image derives from its dynamic torque, an expression in a single figure of the concern with movement found in his monumental, multifigural works. From the frontal upper torso, the neck and head turn sharply to the right, riveted there by the intense gaze. The viewer is compelled to move around the work, and each new vantage point is a discovery. From the right, the intensity and integrity of the character reveal themselves in the full face of the model. In the back, a serpentine braid snakes as an independent force from the back of the head at left to the lower right, a brilliant reiteration of the work's pattern of movement.

One of Carpeaux's frustrations with the monument for the fountain was that it was not polychromed. Carpeaux was keenly aware of the expressive power of color in sculpture, an important trend among nineteenth-century sculptors. Smith's cast of *Le Chinois* is especially fine, its expressiveness reinforced by the different patination of the face, hair, and garment of the model. The reflected light from the rippling surface enhances the colors and adds further vibrancy to the whole. In this compelling image of *Le Chinois*, the elements that most fully define Carpeaux's art coalesce—movement, light, color, and psychological insight.

Further Reading

Lovett, Jennifer Gordon. *A Romance with Realism: The Art of Jean-Baptiste Carpeaux*. Williamstown, Mass.: Sterling and Francine Clark Art Institute, 1989.

Wagner, Anne Middleton. *Jean-Baptiste Carpeaux: Sculptor of the Second Empire*. New Haven, Conn.: Yale University Press, 1986.

Paul Cézanne

Aix-en-Provence, France 1839–1906 Aix-en-Provence, France

A Turn in the Road at La Roche-Guyon (La Route tournante à La Roche-Guyon), c. 1885

Oil on canvas

25¼ × 31½ in. (64.1 × 80 cm)

Not signed or dated

Purchased

1932:2

Cézanne painted this work during a summer spent with his friend Pierre-Auguste Renoir in the village of La Roche-Guyon, northwest of Paris along the Seine. Camille Pissarro, the dean of the impressionists and Cézanne's early mentor, had already explored numerous views of the region in the 1870s.

In *A Turn in the Road at La Roche-Guyon* the image reveals itself grudgingly and profoundly. The lower left quadrant depicts the turning road, which disappears behind the building at the left as abruptly as it appears. The road consists largely of unpainted canvas, which dramatically reiterates its two-dimensionality and deliberately limits the viewer's movement into the painting. Cézanne creates a physical and psychological barrier and thus redirects our involvement with the painting to the visual and analytical realm, that is, to painting as process. His colors are limited to beiges, ochers, greens and light blues, and the brushstroke, rather than serving as surrogate for nature's furtiveness, becomes a building block by which the painting is constructed. Cézanne, who could spend hours, days, weeks in front of a motif extracting its essential characteristics, involves us here deeply in the art of seeing. The unfinished state of the painting, with areas of raw canvas, pencil markings, passages partially resolved with halting strokes, aids in our discovery by exposing stages of Cézanne's working process. Here the act of painting unfolds over time and reveals layers of reality in direct contrast to the specificity of time and space in an impressionist painting.

A Turn in the Road at La Roche-Guyon has become an important work in Cézanne's historiography since the publication of John Rewald's site photograph showing the mountain range as much smaller and more distant than in the painting. Erle Loran in *Cézanne's Composition* concludes that Cézanne radically collapsed the space in the painting by moving the range closer to the foreground and upward, thus making it larger. Conversely, others have since demonstrated that by placing the camera farther to the right and aligning the intersections to correspond with those in the painting, a photograph would show the mountain range adhering closely to that in the painting.

Of course no mechanical process that arrests a single moment and place can replicate Cézanne's probing, thinking eye assessing a motif from a variety of positions over a period of time. As an example, the chalk cliff at left center, which in site photographs is at an oblique angle, in the painting appears parallel to the picture plane, thus demonstrating the principle of multiple vantage points. The chalk cliff's undulating outline, seen to its best advantage frontally, echoes that of the building in the left foreground. The cluster of houses, simplified geometric volumes at the epicenter of the composition, defined by lines of varied dimensions and energies, color and tonal contrasts, is set off by a backdrop silhouette of foliage whose gentle curves move around the houses to the right and reappear with frenetic force in the right foreground. The density of the expressive brushstrokes creates a counterpoint to the compact geometry of overlapping houses, and both are directed and contained by the dynamic arc of the road, the dominant element in the painting. It compresses the busy middle of the painting between the powerful empty space of the road and the looming mountain range in which the curve of the road is reiterated in the slope of the mountain at upper right. Such counterpoints and reciprocities imbue the painting with vitality and tension.

What Cézanne makes manifest in this work is his intense, probing, sustained effort in distilling from nature a radically new pictorial order that is his lasting legacy.

Further Reading

Machotka, Pavel. *Cézanne: Landscape into Art.* New Haven, Conn.: Yale University Press, 1996.

Rewald, John. *Cézanne: A Biography.* New York: Harry N. Abrams, 1986.

Schapiro, Meyer. *Paul Cézanne.* New York: Harry N. Abrams, 1952.

Jean-Baptiste-Camille Corot

Paris, France 1796–1875 Paris, France

The Fair Maid of Gascony
(*La Blonde Gasconne*), c. 1850

Oil on canvas
15¾ × 11⅞ in. (40 × 30.2 cm)
Sale stamp in red paint, lower left: VENTE COROT [Lugt 461]
Purchased, Drayton Hillyer Fund
1934:7

Camille Corot's gentle nature and the charm of his paintings make him one of the beloved artists of the nineteenth century. Yet his immense popularity too often obscures his true historical achievements. As artists in England and Germany were establishing a rich landscape tradition in the early decades of the nineteenth century, French artists concerned themselves mainly with subjects taken from history, allegory, and the like, which advanced figural imagery. It was Corot who more than any other artist established the integrity of French landscape painting, paving the way for the Barbizon artists, many of whom were his friends, and later the impressionists. His early landscapes of the 1820s and 1830s, especially of Italy, are among his most compelling works, transforming well-known sites into masterpieces through the poetry of light and form. His late landscapes, especially those of the 1860s — dreamy evocations of sylvan nature — are among his most popular works.

Corot's figural paintings are less well known and constitute a smaller portion of his oeuvre. They are, nonetheless, a pivotal and integral component of his art. Corot's interest in the figure can be traced to the 1830s, but the largest number and most important of his figural works date from the late phase of his career, especially the 1860s. The emphasis on the human form in these late works can be seen on one level as a counterpoint to the ephemerality of his late landscapes.

The generally accepted date of about 1850 for *La Blonde Gasconne* lies on the threshold of Corot's late achievement as a figure painter. The magnetic power of the painting rests primarily in its restraint and discipline and in the imposing presence of the sitter, whose identity we do not know. The viewer is forced to address the image on its own terms. It is as if Corot grasped the extraordinary physical and psychological power of the sitter and subordinated all else to her. Elements that tend to delight in so many of his canvases are here suppressed. Vestiges of a tree, Corot's beloved motif, which originally formed part of an extensive background, can still be discerned beneath the overpaint to the right of the sitter. What remains is an insistently reductive setting consisting of a blue sky layered by gray-brown clouds, a small triangle at the lower right that likely represents water, and a stone block at the lower left placed parallel to the picture plane.

Presiding majestically over the scene is a young woman whose direct pose and simplicity of dress are a perfect complement to the unadorned setting. The separate, distinctive features in the work galvanize around the figure, who at once dominates the scene and is of the scene. Her arms help define the placement of the figure's volume in a spatial context as they move across her torso in a seamless curve and meet in the gently touching hands that serve as the unifying metaphor for the whole work. Subtle passages like the space between her neck and the wisp of hair gently cascading onto her shoulders, or the space between her left arm and torso, further integrate the figure into the surrounding space. Serenity and dignity emanate from the ample features of her face, whose arched brows and large eyes reiterate the exquisite oval of the head. The simple formality of pose and setting are rooted in the classical tradition of Western art — in the serene quietude of the *Aldobrandini Wedding* (Vatican Museums, Rome), the perfectible beauty of Renaissance portraiture, and the magisterial figures of Nicolas Poussin.

La Blonde Gasconne remained in the artist's possession until his death in 1875. Its seminal role in Corot's oeuvre is underscored by its prominent inclusion in the two most resolved of six versions of his *Artist's Studio* of 1865–70 (National Gallery of Art, Washington, D.C., and Musée du Louvre, Paris). In these paintings, a woman sits before an easel reflecting on the artist's recently completed landscape. By placing *La Blonde Gasconne* on the wall immediately above the landscape painting on the easel, Corot comments on his dual passions. Here *La Blonde Gasconne* underscores his overarching interest in the human figure.

Further Reading

Hours, Madeleine. *Jean-Baptiste-Camille Corot.* New York: Harry N. Abrams, 1984.

Tinterow, Gary, et al. *Corot.* New York: The Metropolitan Museum of Art, 1996.

Jean-Baptiste-Camille Corot

Paris, France 1796–1875 Paris, France

Dubuisson's Grove at Brunoy, 1868

Oil on canvas
18 × 21½ in. (45.7 × 54.6 cm)
Signed in black paint, lower left: COROT
Purchased with funds given by Louise Ines Doyle, class of 1934
1952:116

Louis-Désiré Dubuisson and his family were friends of Corot and collected his work. When the artist visited one day he found no one at home; while waiting he made sketches of the grove that he later translated in his studio into *Dubuisson's Grove at Brunoy*. The landscape is an example of Corot's lyrical late style of feathery brushstrokes and sylvan green-gray foliage tonally arranged in a rhythmic light-dark pattern across the canvas. A field of grass and flowers in the foreground invites the viewer into the grove. A path at the right leads to distant sheds. The willowy trees on either side of the path create a perspectival funnel. The paired trees respond to a swaying rhythm as if engaged in a flirtatious dance. The trees left of center are dispersed more uniformly across the meadow, like markers defining space. Two of the foreground trees bracket the woman with a child, and to either side two girls bend in unison to pick flowers. The figures add a splash of bright color to the work. A thin dark tree appears to emanate from the back of the girl at right and then dissolves into the foliage above—an apt metaphor for the light, lyrical quality of the whole.

Commentary on Corot's late works often focuses on his *souvenir* paintings, evocations of suffused nature recalling places Corot had visited earlier or mere inventions painted from his imagination. Nymphs and other creatures only add to the flight of fancy in these Arcadian settings. In fact, the preponderance of Corot's late landscapes represent specific sites like *Dubuisson's Grove at Brunoy*. In both cases, however, Corot's late landscapes are a vehicle for emotional escapism, a salve for an aging artist who can still delight countless followers with his visual poems.

By 1868, the year of the Smith painting, Corot was a revered elder statesman among landscapists—a clear indication that his moment had passed. Even as he was being remembered for giving impetus to French landscape painting earlier in the century, a new vision of nature was being formulated by the young impressionists. Thus while his role as the precursor to Impressionism was well established, he was personally wary of many of its members, and the vision of his late landscapes did not accord with theirs.

The dilemma even for his admirers is tellingly expressed by Emile Zola: "If M. Corot agreed to kill off, once and for all, the nymphs with which he populated his works and replace them with peasant women I would like him beyond measure." *Dubuisson's Grove at Brunoy*, with its simply clad figures in the field, shifts the discourse only in degree and not in kind. Dubuisson's grove is less frenetic without nymphs dancing across it, and our reverie focuses more on nature's allure. Zola concludes, "I prefer a thousand times a study, a sketch made by him right out in the fields, face to face with powerful reality." In this statement Zola clearly aligns himself with the impressionist future while acknowledging Corot's mastery at painting a sketch "right out in the fields." *Dubuisson's Grove at Brunoy* may have evolved from such a sketch. Yet Corot was always a poet of nature. As he sketched in Dubuisson's grove, he was constructing in his mind a poetic tribute to his friend's environs. For him the feeling of nature had become more important than its actuality.

Further Reading

Clarke, Michael. *Corot and the Art of Landscape*. New York: Cross River Press, 1991.

Tinterow, Gary, et al. *Corot*. New York: The Metropolitan Museum of Art, 1996.

Gustave Courbet

Ornans, Franche-Comté, France 1819–1877 La Tour-de-Peilz (near Vevey), Switzerland

The Preparation of the Dead Girl (La Toilette de la morte), **formerly called** ***The Preparation of the Bride (La Toilette de la mariée),*** c. 1850–55

Oil on canvas
74 × 99 in. (188 × 251.5 cm)
Not signed or dated
Purchased, Drayton Hillyer Fund
1929:1

Gustave Courbet's *Preparation of the Dead Girl* demonstrates that works of art in museums are constantly open to scholarly reinterpretation. Most often, labels change in museums because of reattributions. A painting that is by Rembrandt one day may not be the next. In the case of this painting, it is not the authorship but the subject that was reappraised during research for a major Courbet retrospective exhibition in 1977–78. The painting had remained in Courbet's possession until his death in 1877, when it passed to his sister, Juliette. It was then bequeathed to Mmes de Tastes and La Pierre, who auctioned it in 1919 as *The Preparation of the Bride.* The painting entered the Smith College Museum of Art in 1929 with that title, which was unchallenged until 1977. In working on the catalogue for the Courbet exhibition of 1977–78, the researchers, unable to find evidence that Courbet had ever painted a work titled *The Preparation of the Bride,* concluded that this canvas must instead be the documented but lost *Preparation of the Dead Girl.*

X-radiographs of the painting taken in 1960 reveal that the central seated figure was originally nude, her head slumped and her left land lying across her lap. The painting was apparently deliberately overpainted in critical areas, probably to make it more marketable around the time of the 1919 sale, when it also acquired its new title. An unknown hand painted in the dress, lifted the head, raised the left hand, and placed a mirror in it, thus transforming a corpse into a bride looking into a mirror as she prepares for her wedding. The awkward overpainting was generally overlooked, partly because of the overall unfinished state of the painting.

The funereal theme is reinforced by many passages in the painting. The women hovering around the seated corpse are preparing it for the funeral—the tub at her feet is there to wash the body. The two women at left are spreading a winding sheet over the bed, which is being readied for the corpse. The table at right is being prepared for the wake, and the group of women at its far end are probably reciting prayers for the dead from their prayer books. The dark areas of the canopied bed, the open door and stairway above the central group, as well as the open window at right all add to the somber mood and may also allude to the passage to the hereafter.

The ambitious scale of *The Preparation of a Dead Girl,* its probable date of execution in the early 1850s, and especially its theme align it with Courbet's masterpiece, *A Burial at Ornans* of 1849 (Musée d'Orsay, Paris). The latter became a clarion call for a new generation of realist artists of whom Courbet was the leader. In these works of the 1850s Courbet was seeking artistic truths predicated not on elevated subjects of history, allegory, or religion, but on depicting the lives and rituals of everyday people.

In *A Burial at Ornans,* as in *The Preparation of the Dead Girl,* Courbet depicts the death of ordinary individuals whose identities we do not know, thus defying the convention of celebrating the heroic deaths of famous people. *The Preparation of the Dead Girl* captures a moment prior to the burial—the preparation for the funeral and wake that takes place in the home. The two paintings complement each other and underscore Courbet's commitment to record and commemorate local customs, which were being eroded by societal change.

Further Reading

Faunce, Sarah. *Gustave Courbet.* New York: Harry N. Abrams, 1993.

Toussaint, Hélène, and Marie Thérèse de Forges. *Gustave Courbet, 1819–1877.* Translated by P. S. Falla. London: Arts Council of Great Britain, 1978.

Gustave Courbet

Ornans, Franche-Comté, France 1819–1877 La Tour-de-Peilz (near Vevey), Switzerland

Monsieur Nodler the Elder at Trouville, 1865

Oil on canvas

36¼ × 28¾ in. (92.1 × 73 cm)

Signed and dated in reddish orange paint, lower left: 66/G.Courbet

Purchased, Winthrop Hillyer Fund

1935:3

The Courbet who painted *Monsieur Nodler the Elder* in 1865 is a significantly different artist from the firebrand of the 1850s whose treatment of contemporary life transformed the subject matter of art (see pp. 38–39). By the 1860s Courbet had turned his attention away from genre painting and focused on landscape and portraiture.

In the late summer of 1865 Courbet arrived at Trouville, a bustling seaside resort town on the English Channel made prominent a decade earlier by the duc de Morny and rendered accessible to the Parisian leisure class by the railroad. Courbet's notoriety and his larger-than-life persona as much as his immeasurable talent assured him of commissions for portraits and seascapes. Courbet in the 1850s would have focused his attention on the fishermen of the region who were being displaced by the vacationers. Now he was content to establish himself among these well-to-do clients.

During this time Courbet befriended Claude Monet, whom he observed struggling with his large figural work, *Women in the Garden* of 1866–67 (Musée d'Orsay, Paris). In trying to capture on canvas nature's changeable moods, Monet often had to wait long periods for proper weather conditions. Courbet's sense of reality was too robust and concrete for such an approach. In this and several other portraits painted at Trouville, Courbet used the coastal setting as a backdrop to contextualize the image, rendering the figure and the landscape as two distinct, interdependent components.

In *Monsieur Nodler the Elder*, Courbet defines the leisure class. A handsome young man of means is being painted by a prominent artist. There is an inherent discreet formality to the relationship that is evidenced in the erect pose of the sitter, whose pyramidal structure can be traced back to Renaissance portraiture. This somewhat formal presentation of leisure is apparent in Nodler's accoutrements — his dress, appropriate for leisure activities, the simple ladder-back chair on which he sits slightly turned to one side, and the cane or riding crop in his hand. The coastal setting creates a luminous background that underscores the place and time of leisure.

In November 1865 Courbet wrote to his parents: "Besides the portraits of women, I have done two men and many seascapes." There is ample other documentation identifying the two male sitters as the Nodler brothers. It is a happy coincidence that these two portraits are today in museums only twenty miles apart, the elder brother at Smith and *Monsieur Nodler the Younger* at the Museum of Fine Arts, Springfield, Massachusetts. Despite their execution in 1865, Courbet deliberately dated both works 1866 to make them seem more current when he included them in his solo exhibition at the Pavillon de l'Alma in 1867.

The familial resemblance between the two sitters can be seen in the structure of their faces, and both hold the same riding crop or cane. Yet the two are very different images. The younger brother is painted against a neutral, dark background and presented in three-quarter view. Wearing a robe and a loose bow tie, hair flowing over his forehead, he is an archetypal romantic figure. In contrast, a formal grace characterizes the portrait of the older brother. The artist seems to project aspects of his own identity onto his subjects. The romantic spirit of the young Nodler brother evokes Courbet's youthful self-portraits, which had been done in a self-consciously romantic style. But the elder Nodler in many respects reflects the current self-image of Courbet, the handsome, prosperous, self-assured artist who hobnobs with the aristocracy and moneyed clients.

Further Reading

Faunce, Sarah, and Linda Nochlin. *Courbet Reconsidered*. Brooklyn: The Brooklyn Museum, 1988.

Toussaint, Hélène, and Marie Thérèse de Forges. *Gustave Courbet, 1819–1877*. Translated by P. S. Falla. London: Arts Council of Great Britain, 1978.

41

Edgar Degas

Paris, France 1834–1917 Paris, France

René de Gas (1845–1926), 1855

Oil on canvas
36¼ × 29½ in. (92.1 × 74.9 cm)
Not signed or dated
Purchased, Drayton Hillyer Fund
1935:12

Edgar Degas's early career is often viewed as a preamble to his later achievements—a period when he searched for his artistic voice by studying the old masters at the Louvre, during his stay in Italy, and briefly as a student at the Ecole des Beaux-Arts. Yet during this same early phase Degas produced some of his most memorable portraits, mainly of family members, among them the monumental *Bellelli Family* of 1858–67 (Musée d'Orsay, Paris) and the arresting double portrait of his sister Thérèse and her husband, *M. and Mme Edmondo Morbilli*, of 1865 (Museum of Fine Arts, Boston).

Degas's portrait of his younger brother, René de Gas, painted in the spring of 1855, is among his earliest essays in portraiture, and in it are distilled both the tentativeness of a youthful work and the promise of genius. The portrait captures an exquisite moment in their relationship—a passage in their nascent growth. The image is at once formal and intimate, and both artist and model are caught up in the serious act of making art. René, who at age ten posed for Degas after school in his student uniform, exhibits a near-reverential respect toward his older brother and his capacity to breathe life onto a canvas. Edgar in turn brings to the process the solemnity of serious effort evident in the formal stillness of the pose, the somber palette, and a conscious affirmation of a tradition of portraiture that began with the Renaissance masters and continued up to the brilliant portraits of Ingres. The latter's sumptuous, elaborate portraits of women as well as his more austere male portraits, which often have a simple, dark background, set the tone for a whole generation of younger artists.

Degas arranges the various aspects of the work into a cohesive visual and iconographic whole, giving it its psychological acuity. The still life to the left of René comprises a thick book, notebooks, inkwell, and pen. These attributes of a young student form a second nexus in the painting and establish an interactive reciprocity with the sitter. Degas positions René's right hand, holding a cap, close to the still life, reinforcing the bond between the student and his tools. Furthermore, the face of René, his shirt and red bow tie, and the elements of the still life are the only vividly colored passages in the composition. The portrait is among the first in which Degas contextualizes the sitter by introducing a significant supportive element in the form of a still life. He would later often explore this idea in inventive ways, as he did, for example, in *Woman Seated beside a Vase of Flowers* of 1865 (The Metropolitan Museum of Art).

Here, as often in his later works, Degas energizes the periphery of the painting as a critical compositional construct. The dark backdrop, which isolates and highlights René, does not reach the outer edges of the painting, leaving vividly rendered strips on either side. The subtle drama of the hands also guides the viewer toward the outer edge. The right hand moves toward the still life, while the left disappears into the trouser pocket at lower right—a casual, even irreverent gesture shared between brothers. Ultimately it is in the image of René that the psychological power of the painting resides. The deep bond between the artist and his youthful brother, evident in every aspect of René's demeanor, is palpable and memorable. Degas's greatest gift as a portraitist is already apparent here: his ability to insinuate himself as an integral force into the interiority of his sitter.

Further Reading

Baumann, Felix, and Marianne Karabelnik, eds. *Degas Portraits*. London: Merrell Holberton, 1994.

Boggs, Jean Sutherland, et al. *Degas*. New York: The Metropolitan Museum of Art, Ottawa: National Gallery of Canada, 1988.

43

Edgar Degas

Paris, France 1834–1917 Paris, France

The Daughter of Jephthah, 1859–60

Oil on canvas

77 × 117½ in. (195.6 × 298.5 cm)

Sale stamp in reddish orange paint, lower left: Degas [Lugt 658]

Purchased, Drayton Hillyer Fund

1933:9

Degas began this painting soon after returning to Paris from a three-year sojourn in Italy. Its extraordinary scale and ambition are in large measure the result of that interlude, during which Degas was exposed to Italian art and antiquity. While there he also befriended Gustave Moreau, who became a mentor and introduced him to the work of Eugène Delacroix. *The Daughter of Jephthah* reflects the influence both of the Italian masters, especially those of the early Renaissance, and of Delacroix. The matte finish and suffused, muted colors relate to fresco cycles by quattrocento masters such as Piero della Francesca, while the intense, brilliant coloristic accents can be directly related to passages in Delacroix's works, some of which Degas refers to specifically in his letters. The large scale of the painting and its religious subject reflect the frescoes, but also Delacroix's grand compositions depicting historical, religious, and literary subjects.

The biblical theme of the painting derives from the Book of Judges. Jephthah the Gileadite is recalled from exile by the Israelites to do battle with the Ammonites. To assure victory, Jephthah vows to God to sacrifice on his return "whatsoever cometh forth of the doors of my house to meet me." Tragically his daughter and only child is the first to greet him. His moment of greatest triumph turns into one of deepest despair. Degas depicts the piercing instant of recognition and awareness and orchestrates all the elements in the painting to heighten the drama. The horse comes to an abrupt halt, and Jephthah raises his arm—too late to shield himself from the horrific inevitability of the unfolding events. Degas's choice of the story of Jephthah was especially popular among nineteenth-century writers, and his interpretation of the scene, which focuses attention on the daughter's fate, has been linked to Alfred de Vigny's dramatic poem "La Fille de Jephté" of 1820. Degas's choice may also reflect his concern for the fate of Italy and the role of Napoleon III in its political events.

The achievement of *The Daughter of Jephthah* must ultimately be judged by the integrity of its pictorial experiments and the degree to which these point to Degas's subsequent development. The many human figures in a variety of poses and groupings underscore the artist's fascination with human form as the pivotal instrument of his artistic investigation. Many of the figures derive from identifiable Renaissance sources; the cluster of women in the background, for example, is taken from Andrea Mantegna's *Crucifixion* (Musée du Louvre, Paris), of which Degas made a loose copy in 1861 (Musée des Beaux-Arts, Tours). Degas saw copying from old masters as necessary and sustaining for his artistic growth. The reductively simple landscape is the product of numerous studies, influences, and radical changes—an early indicator of the seriousness with which Degas would explore the landscape tradition. The aggressively tilted vista without a horizon, which serves as an arena for the unfolding events, also prefigures the stage sets of Degas's later ballet paintings. A dramatic tension leaps across this space, from Jephthah in the center to his daughter in the background group, reinforced by the poses and gestures of others. The tension of figures relating across a void would become one of Degas's most successful compositional devices; in his ballet rehearsals it is evident in the relationship between the ballet master and the ballerinas.

Degas eventually left the oversized canvas unfinished and kept it until his death. Of his early historical paintings, it remains the most problematical and challenging. Its scale, incipient drama, and sheer bravura, declare it as a very early landmark in the artist's development, and its lessons for him were numerous and profound.

Further Reading

Reff, Theodore. *Degas: The Artist's Mind.* Cambridge, Mass.: Belknap Press of Harvard University Press, 1987.

Sutton, Denys. *Edgar Degas: Life and Work.* New York: Rizzoli, 1986.

Edgar Degas

Paris, France 1834–1917 Paris, France

Dancer on the Stage, c. 1877–80

Oil on canvas
36 × 46½ in. (91.4 × 118.1 cm)
Sale stamp in reddish orange paint, lower left: Degas [Lugt 658]
Gift of Paul Rosenberg and Company
1955:14

Few artists have assimilated another art form as part of their own identity as completely as Degas has the ballet. From his first essays on the theme in 1867, he became increasingly interested in the ballet world, attending rehearsals and performances to observe his "rats," as the young dancers were called, and to learn about the ballet with them. Their animated poses and groupings on stage or in rehearsal halls became the vehicle for his own "performances," as he transformed their balletic rituals into some of the most compelling paintings of the century. In some of the works Degas comments obliquely but powerfully on the existing social conditions of the ballet world, which had declined in public esteem. In such works we discover the young age of the dancers and learn of their modest background—initially from the lower classes, later from families of Opéra staff members, musicians, and others. We learn how the socially powerful members of the Jockey Club interacted behind the scenes with the ballerinas, whose performance for them did not end on the stage. We also meet the dance masters, musicians, and ambitious backstage mothers. Degas's panoply of images traces these sobering and exhilarating realities—from arduous rehearsals to graceful bows at the end of performances. We view these scenes from exciting, unusual vantage points—from the wings, from rows near the orchestra pit, from the loge where the emperor would have viewed them, and from backstage, where the dancers relaxed, adjusted their costumes, and even arranged liaisons with Jockey Club members.

Dancer on the Stage depicts a ballerina in a gauzy light blue-green costume whose sparkling accessories suggest an orientalizing motif. Her long black hair and full chin have been likened to those of the prominent Spanish ballerina Rosita Mauri, who made her debut in Paris in 1878. While not all have accepted this intriguing identification, it is evident that this lone dancer on stage in midperformance is an *étoile*—a principal dancer, literally a star. Scenes of individual performers are rarer in Degas's oeuvre than those of ensemble performances, rehearsals, or dancers at rest. The positioning of the ballerina at extreme right reflects the artist's assimilation of the compositional devices of Japanese prints, a prevalent influence at the time. The atypical vantage point from which we usually view Degas's ballet scenes is absent here. Unable to discern our locus, we are thrust into close proximity to the action, as if on stage—only a sliver of dark at the lower right provides a degree of separation. The precise moment depicted seems to be when the ballerina enters the stage from the right. Her graceful pose extends her presence in all directions as she balances her forward movement with outstretched arms and contrapuntal leg extended back. The dancer and the loosely painted background, evocative of foliage, establish a dual focus that holds the composition in taut balance.

In *Dancer on the Stage* the ballerina's expansive yet purposeful, animated pose is controlled by the decorum of her discipline. In contrast, Degas gives his brush free rein in treating the background—an exuberant, swirling array of gestural strokes—generating a kind of abstract, expressive force that encompasses the dancer and shares the stage with her. *Dancer on the Stage* is foremost a compelling depiction of a ballet scene by Degas, but it is also an intriguing commentary on the complex interaction between the art of ballet and the art of painting.

Further Reading

Muehlig, Linda D. *Degas and the Dance.* Northampton, Mass.: Smith College Museum of Art, 1979.

Shackelford, George T. M. *Degas: The Dancers.* Washington, D.C.: National Gallery of Art, 1984.

Edgar Degas

Paris, France 1834–1917 Paris, France

Dancer Moving Forward, Arms Raised, Right Leg Forward, modeled 1882–95 (cast posthumously)

Bronze

25 × 12⅝ × 8¼ in. (63.5 × 32.1 × 21 cm)

Incised signature, cast number, and founder's mark on proper left foot: Degas/72/E/CIRE PERDUE A.A. HEBRARD

Purchased

1965:29

After Degas's death in 1917, his dealer Durand-Ruel discovered in his studio approximately 150 pieces of sculpture, some whole, others as fragments, made mainly of wax but also of plastiline and plaster. Seventy-four of these were cast in bronze, in an edition of twenty-two plus a master set, by the foundry of A.-A. Hébrard under the supervision of its master founder, Albino Palazzolo. *Dancer Moving Forward* is among the works that was thus preserved for posterity. Today many of these works grace private collections and museums and have contributed to Degas's reputation as the greatest painter-sculptor of the nineteenth century. Yet during his lifetime the public knew Degas as sculptor by the single work he exhibited. *Little Dancer Aged Fourteen*, which caused a sensation at the 1881 impressionist exhibition, has since become one of the best-known and most beloved sculptures of the century. It marked a pivotal moment in Degas's development as a sculptor. During the 1860s and 1870s he painted scenes of race horses and the ballet, but his early sculptures were exclusively of racehorses. *Little Dancer Aged Fourteen* was his first sculpture of a ballet dancer and, indeed, his first human figure. At the same time, it is atypical in the use of real accessories like the gauze skirt, silk bodice, and ribbon. It is also unique in Degas's oeuvre in its high level of finish, the penetrating psychological insight into the young dancer, and its coiled tautness.

With the exception of a few portrait heads, most of Degas's surviving sculptures, like *Dancer Moving Forward*, are studies of form in motion, as if fulfilling the potential of *Little Dancer Aged Fourteen*. Degas's sculptures, with their textured surfaces reflecting light, come closer to Impressionism than do his paintings, which fre-quently depict figures in interiors that are artificially lit. Of the pieces that were cast, *Dancer Moving Forward*, while among the least well preserved, is most revealing of Degas's working practices. The artist's legendary inability to let go of a work of art, always reworking it over extended periods, applies equally to his sculptures. Half the sculptures found in his studio could not be cast at all, having deteriorated in part because of Degas's repeated experimenting with them over time. His obliviousness to accepted sculpture practices is evident in *Dancer Moving Forward*. The missing right forearm reveals a flimsy armature, and the lower legs are fragmentary. Degas's lack of formal training in sculpture was a contributory factor, but so were the nature and purpose of these works, which he viewed as "exercises to get me going: documentary, preparatory notions, nothing more. None of this was intended for sale." These private exercises were also varied. Some relate directly to his paintings, pastels, and drawings, while others exist as independent works. In the case of *Dancer Moving Forward*, its graceful pose with upraised arms, right foot forward, basic to ballet, recurs often in his works and thus does not relate to a specific image.

Degas's reliance on sculpture increased as his eyesight deteriorated, and late in his career it became a substitute for painting. Yet his interest in sculpture goes back to the early years of his career. His artistic genius lies in his ability to draw on the expressive aspect of each medium to enhance the others. Of his sculptures, he said, "the only reason that I made wax figures of animals and humans was . . . to give my paintings and drawings greater expression, greater ardour, and more life." Yet sculptures such as *Dancer Moving Forward* possess these traits because they are informed by an artistic intelligence that has probed the same ideas in other media.

Further Reading

Kendall, Richard, et al. *Degas and the Little Dancer.* New Haven, Conn.: Yale University Press; Omaha: The Joslyn Art Museum, 1998.

Millard, Charles W. *The Sculpture of Edgar Degas.* Princeton, N.J.: Princeton University Press, 1976.

Narcisse Virgile Diaz de la Peña

Bordeaux, France 1807–1876 Menton, France

Forest Pool, Barbizon, 1862

Oil on canvas

30¼ × 38¾ in. (76.7 × 98.4 cm)

Signed and dated in black paint, lower right: N. Diaz. 1862.

Gift of Mrs. Otto H. Seiffert (Marjorie S. Allen, class of 1906)

1950:57

The truism that it is impossible to separate the artist from the person is especially valid in the case of Narcisse Diaz de la Peña. Born in Bordeaux in 1807 to a Spanish emigrant family, he was by age ten an orphan wandering the streets of Paris. He also lost a leg in an accident as a youth. Despite or perhaps because of such misfortunes, Diaz became a genuinely positive individual—a wit, a charmer, an effervescent presence at all occasions. A telling example of his character was his response to the peg leg he was forced to wear. Diaz's *pilon* became part of his persona and a source of endless stories.

He began his career as a porcelain painter, not unlike Pierre-Auguste Renoir and other artists, including Jules Dupré, who worked with Diaz in the Sèvres factory and became a fellow Barbizoner. Diaz had little formal training, and his early work of the 1830s and 1840s consists largely of charming Venuses, cupids, gypsies, and so on—themes evocative of eighteenth-century imagery, which had an important revival at the time. To accommodate public taste for soft, charming images, his figures reflected the influence of artists like Correggio, Leonardo da Vinci, and Pierre-Paul Prud'hon. His popular and highly saleable works made him quite well off.

Diaz was rescued from his popularity only by his talent. He was interested in landscape from the beginning of his career. While the sources for his genre pictures were eclectic, his master in landscape was primarily Théodore Rousseau, who was central to all issues dealing with French landscape at the time. From the outset Diaz admired his works and wanted to learn his secrets. He studied his compositions assiduously, and it was Rousseau who unlocked the mystery of the forest and its surrounds for him. When Diaz had earned enough money, he moved to Barbizon to be closer to his master and to explore the Fontainebleau forest. Diaz's artistic temperament differed significantly, however, from Rousseau's deeply emotional, moralizing outlook. Diaz's evolution as a landscapist, which blossomed to maturity after 1850, reflected that difference. He would entice the viewer with his virtuoso technique and his willingness to people his forest scenes with the Venuses, cupids, and sundry characters of his earlier period.

Forest Pool is an excellent example of Diaz's mature style, in which he explores one of his most important motifs—the forest interior. The darkness of the scene is pried open with a sliver of blue sky at the upper left—a passage for light to enter and enliven the grottolike interior of the forest with a rhythmic cadence of flecks of brilliant light on the tree trunks and their gnarled branches. The pool of water, which partly receives the light and reflects the trees, is a calming, life-sustaining oasis deep in the heart of the forest. A lone faggot-gatherer, left of center, is a picturesque and poignant presence in the scene.

Diaz establishes here a compelling duality. His free, gestural strokes of bright color are light's surrogates, penetrating the forest. They also exist as a material presence vibrantly animating the canvas surface. The twentieth century has for too long turned a blind eye to the Barbizon artists, celebrating instead the revolutionaries they helped to spawn, the impressionists. Only in recent decades has interest rekindled in the work of the earlier artists. An image like Diaz's *Forest Pool*, evoking nature's unspoiled glory, has deep emotional resonance, and in its vigorous, assertive, gestural style of painting it is also a precursor to similar tendencies in twentieth-century art.

Further Reading

Adams, Steven. *The Barbizon School and the Origins of Impressionism.* London: Phaidon Press, 1994.

Herbert, Robert L. *Barbizon Revisited.* New York: Clarke & Way, 1962.

Henri Fantin-Latour

Grenoble, France 1836–1904 Buré, Orne, France

Mr. Becker, 1886

Oil on canvas
40 × 32½ in. (101.6 × 82.5 cm)
Signed and dated in brown paint, upper left: Fantin. 86
Purchased
1964:33

Henri Fantin-Latour counted among his closest friends artists who changed the face of nineteenth-century painting. Although he was witness to the impressionist revolution, he was not a participant. His vision of art was predicated on different principles. For example, in an impressionist painting sunlight as a specific source often permeates a scene, eliminating tonal distinctions. In Fantin's work, light is primarily a function of modeling — it need not have a specific source, and its main purpose is to articulate the form's light and dark passages to give an object a palpable three-dimensional reality. His refined technique, seen to great advantage in *Mr. Becker,* quite literally layers on paint like a membrane, giving the flesh luminescence.

Other than the fact that he was an American in Paris, we know little about Mr. Becker — not even his first name. He accompanied a mysterious woman to Fantin's studio. She gave her name as Mme Leroy, but Fantin thought it to be fictitious. She was eager to have her portrait painted, for which she paid in advance. When Fantin completed the portrait, she took it away in a cab, never to be seen again. At the time, Mr. Becker decided to have his portrait painted by the artist as well. The only further hint of his identity comes from an American artist living in Paris, Frank Boggs, who saw the portrait at the dealer Hector Brame's and proclaimed it to represent his uncle.

Mr. Becker has all the traits of a classic Fantin male portrait — reserved and formal, respectful of the sitter and of the decorum of portraiture. It recalls most closely seventeenth-century Dutch male portraits, where dark-clothed men in formal dress, with a white accent of a ruffled collar, are usually arranged against a dark background. In this work Fantin shows his mastery of the genre. Faced with enlivening the large dark area of

Mr. Becker's suit, he arranges the hands and the white shirt as accents at intervals that animate the lower, middle, and upper part of the suit. The Kazak prayer rug adds vibrant touches of color at the lower left. The composition culminates near the top with the thoughtful, graying and balding head of the sitter.

The most distinctive aspect of the pose is Mr. Becker's right hand, partly tucked between the buttons of the suit — a gesture made prominent by Napoleon and immortalized in numerous images, most notably in Jacques-Louis David's evocative *Napoleon in His Study* of 1812 (National Gallery of Art, Washington, D.C.). Fantin's direct source for this gesture, however, even to the upturned thumb, is Edouard Manet's *Portrait of Zacharie Astruc* of 1866 (Kunsthalle, Bremen).

Fantin was keenly aware of Manet's portrait of Astruc. One of Fantin's most celebrated group portraits is *L'Atelier des Batignolles* of 1870 (Musée d'Orsay, Paris) — an homage to his friend Manet, who is depicted seated before an easel surrounded by other artists and writers. Manet is shown painting the very same Astruc, seated in the foreground next to him. Indeed, Fantin's arrangement of the composition into a dense, dark area of figures at right and a lighter, more open area at left reflects in general Manet's bifurcated *Portrait of Zacharie Astruc.* Thus the source of Mr. Becker's gesture is irrefutable, but why Fantin turned to the earlier image is open to interpretation. Manet's death in 1883 may have been a motivation. Mr. Becker was, after all, a stranger to Fantin. Fantin, a very private person happiest in the company of family and friends, has personalized the commission by assimilating into *Mr. Becker* a pose from a portrait by a departed friend, whose creation he documented in *L'Atelier des Batignolles.*

Further Reading

Druick, Douglas W., and Michel Hoog. *Fantin-Latour.* Ottawa: National Gallery of Canada, National Museums of Canada, 1983.

Henri Fantin-Latour, 1836–1904. Northampton, Mass.: Smith College Museum of Art, 1966.

Lucie-Smith, Edward. *Henri Fantin-Latour.* New York: Rizzoli, 1977.

Unknown French Artist

(possibly Anne-Louis Girodet-Trioson)

Portrait of a Youth, possibly c. 1795

Oil on canvas
18⅜ × 15 in. (46.7 × 38.1 cm)
Not signed or dated
Purchased, Drayton Hillyer Fund
1931:6

When this *Portrait of a Youth* entered the collection in 1931, it was generally accepted as a work of Théodore Gericault, the progenitor of the romantic movement in France. Some considered it to be one of the lost portraits of the insane that Gericault painted in 1822 for his friend Dr. Etienne Giorget, who was engaged in pioneering work on mental illness. Only five portraits survive from this series of at least ten. Most modern scholars have rejected the Gericault attribution, yet the high quality of the painting is so evident that this orphaned youth has nearly always graced the walls of the museum.

Over the years there have been numerous unconvincing attempts at attribution. It is therefore a happy coincidence that as the present volume is to be published, a plausible attribution of the painting to Anne-Louis Girodet-Trioson has been put forth by Margaret Oppenheimer, an independent art historian. She bases her thesis on careful comparison of *Portrait of a Youth* with other Girodet male portraits, such as *Portrait of Jacques Cathelineau (1759–1793)*, known as the "Saint of Anjou," of 1824 (Musée d'Art et d'Histoire, Cholet). This full-length portrait was done some thirty years after Cathelineau's death, so it was of necessity idealized since no other image of him exists. In most respects the head of Cathelineau is very close to *Portrait of a Youth*. They share a near identical turn and tilt of the head. The eyes, glancing sideways and upward, bear the same relationship to the nose and lips. Oppenheimer postu-

lates a date in the mid-1790s for Smith's portrait, on the basis of the sitter's hairstyle—long in front and short in back, exposing the neck in defiant reference to the ubiquitous guillotine. It is possible that this early work, or one like it, served as a prototype for Girodet's idealized interpretation of Cathelineau some thirty years later.

A contemporary document citing a half-length life-size study of a youth with arms crossed and head turned in three-quarter view may refer to Smith's *Portrait of a Youth*. It records dimensions of 67.5 × 41.6 cm, larger than the Smith portrait, but a conservation examination reveals that the Smith canvas has been cut down. The treatment of the shoulders—somewhat slumped and pulled forward, much as they would be if the arms were crossed, suggests that the portrait may indeed originally have been a half-length.

The strength of the image lies in its physicality and directness of presentation. We confront the simply dressed youth on his own terms and are impressed by his bearing—self-possessed and conscious of things around him. His romantic appearance—tousled hair, upturned collar, and engaged, gleaming eyes—speaks to his youth. Girodet's male sitters are often prominent, recognized individuals more formally dressed. Yet they generally share with *Portrait of a Youth* a romantic air, enhanced by an absorbed gaze. If *Portrait of a Youth* is an early Girodet, it will complement the museum's other impressive Girodet portrait of approximately a decade later (see pp. 60–61).

Further Reading

French Painting, 1774–1830: The Age of Revolution. Detroit: The Detroit Institute of Arts; New York: The Metropolitan Museum of Art, 1975.

Wintermute, Alan, ed. *1789: French Art during the Revolution.* New York: Colnaghi, 1989.

Paul Gauguin

Paris, France 1848–1903 Atuona, Marquesas Islands

The Market Gardens of Vaugirard, 1879

Oil on canvas
26 × 39½ in. (66 × 100.3 cm)
Signed and dated in blue paint, lower left: P. Gauguin 79
Purchased
1953:55

By 1879, the year Gauguin painted *The Market Gardens of Vaugirard*, his relationship to Impressionism and to the impressionists themselves had evolved in important ways. The young financier/banker-turned-artist, who as early as 1876 had exhibited in the official Salon, had only a few years later become a significant collector of the impressionists, specifically Camille Pissarro. In fact, he lent two paintings and a fan decoration by Pissarro to the fourth impressionist exhibition of 1879, to which he also contributed a portrait bust of his older child, Emil.

The following year, Gauguin contributed seven paintings and a portrait bust of his wife, Mette Sophie (Courtauld Gallery, London), to the fifth impressionist exhibition. Among these was *The Market Gardens of Vaugirard*, a painting heavily indebted to Pissarro, who had become his mentor, but also to Paul Cézanne. Mark Roskill argues convincingly that the short, even brushstrokes in this work come from Cézanne's *Harvest* of about 1876 (private collection), which Gauguin probably owned by this time and which he also used as a source for a fan and a pot. It has also been observed that the horizontal planes in this work derive from similarly arranged village scenes by Cézanne and Pissarro.

Gauguin lavished great attention on *The Market Gardens of Vaugirard*. It depicts the neighborhood south of the Seine in Paris where the artist lived with his wife and two children. In positioning himself on the upper story of his house to paint the scene, Gauguin conforms to one of the impressionists' most compelling innovations: defining the energy of their city motifs from a high vantage point. From this position Gauguin depicts in slightly angled parallel passages the garden, a long wall beyond which is a street lined with trees, and atop this a line of houses that define and animate the horizon line. This, too, is a convention favored by the impressionists, especially Pissarro, who frequently depicted an interestingly arranged expanse of open space in the foreground, culminating in a horizontal strip of buildings. The chimney of Gauguin's house, in the left foreground, initiates a vertical counterpoint to the prevalent horizontality. A house above the chimney in the middle part of the composition helps unify the foreground with the houses in the background.

While *The Market Gardens of Vaugirard* underscores Gauguin's connection to Impressionism, it also strongly hints at his later development. The repoussoir tree at the lower left, a conventional device that here establishes the foreground-background axis, will eventually evolve into a significant pictorial element in such seminal works as *A Vision after the Sermon: Jacob Wrestling with the Angel* of 1888 (National Gallery of Scotland, Edinburgh).

In a rather surprising gesture for a young artist trying to emulate his impressionist mentors, Gauguin fills the sky with clouds, depriving the scene of the sparkle of sunlight. The lack of sunlight prevents the diffusion of form and thus allows the tightly arranged brushstrokes to define clear, broad areas of color, for example in the garden area and the wall, prefiguring Gauguin's later synthetist style.

Further Reading

Goldwater, Robert. *Paul Gauguin.* New York: Harry N. Abrams, 1957.

Roskill, Mark. *Van Gogh, Gauguin, and the Impressionist Circle.* Greenwich, Conn.: New York Graphic Society, 1970.

Thomson, Belinda. *Gauguin.* New York: Thames and Hudson, 1987.

Anne-Louis Girodet-Trioson

Montargis, Loiret, France 1767–1824 Paris, France

Madame Benoit-François Trioson (?), 1804

Oil on canvas

25½ × 21⅜ in. (64.8 × 54.3 cm)

Signed with the artist's monogram and dated in brown paint, lower right: GRT/1804

Purchased with the assistance of the Eleanor Lamont Cunningham, class of 1932, Fund

1956:19

On the face of it, the career of Anne-Louis Girodet-Trioson followed the course of other successful neo-classical artists who were trained in the studio of Jacques-Louis David. David considered Girodet among his most talented students, and in 1789, the year of the Revolution, Girodet won the Prix de Rome. He departed for Rome a year later and stayed for five years. While there he produced his most important work, *The Sleep of Endymion* (Musée du Louvre, Paris), which was a success at the Salon of 1793. In this highly personal interpretation of the scene, Girodet depicts the sleeping youth in a languorous recumbent pose, visited by the goddess Diana in the form of a moonbeam. The dreamy, suffused quality of the painting, evocative of Correggio and Leonardo, presented a challenge to David's Neo-classicism. Girodet tried consciously, even willfully, to distinguish himself in this work from his master and to manifest his originality. In his quest to be original and in the visionary imagery of this and other works, Girodet prefigures the romantic movement.

This romantic tendency is also seen in his portraiture, but Girodet's *Madame Benoit-François Trioson* (?) of 1804 emphasizes that classicism remained for him a viable and important avenue of self-expression. It embodies a tradition of portraiture prevalent in the first decade of the nineteenth century, as evidenced by the distinctive coiffure that many portraits of the period share. The fashion is Empire, as indicated by the high waistline of the dress, and the image is at once elegant and discreet, formal and accessible.

Issues of light were always of paramount importance to Girodet. Here the sitter emerges from a dark green background as a pristine, exquisitely modeled form. The source of light is direct, just to the viewer's left, and the play of light and shade is subtle and sustained. The shaded part of the face is outlined by a thin string of light, which at once helps define the form of the head and establishes distance from the background. The braid, tightly arranged across the sitter's meticulously coiffed head, initiates a cascade of curls encircling the forehead. Rather than being flattened against the forehead as in Ingres's *Mme Philibert Rivière* (Musée du Louvre, Paris), here the curls, illuminated from the front, animate space around the head by casting shadows on the forehead. The calligraphy of the curls and their shadows is the most exuberant passage in the painting. It initiates a process that is echoed in the border of the elaborately articulated shawl and in the delicate outline of the dress, whose waistline is braided, much like the hair, thus completing the cycle. Within this refined, exquisitely detailed image, Girodet achieves a degree of intimacy and openness through the engaged gaze of the sitter's large oval eyes and his choice of subtly modulated warm colors, ranging from soft white to beiges and pinks.

When the painting entered the collection in 1956, George Levetine published it as *Madame Benoit-François Trioson*. He based his conclusion on a document referring to a portrait of Mme Trioson dated 1804. Believing the Smith painting to be Girodet's only extant portrait of a woman dated 1804, he concluded that it must be that of Mme Trioson, the young wife of Dr. Benoit-François Trioson, Girodet's guardian, who would adopt the artist in 1806 and who was probably his natural father. This deductive identification has been challenged by subsequent scholars, notably Stephanie Nevison-Brown, who has discovered other portraits by Girodet also dated 1804, among them one of Mme Merlin, which in many respects is similar to the Smith portrait. Levetine's identification of the sitter therefore awaits further documentary confirmation.

Further Reading

Honour, Hugh. *Neo-classicism*. Harmondsworth, England: Penguin Books, 1991.

French Painting, 1774–1830: The Age of Revolution. Detroit: The Detroit Institute of Arts; New York: The Metropolitan Museum of Art, 1975.

Juan Gris

Madrid, Spain 1887–1927 Boulogne-sur-Seine, France

Fruit Dish, Glass, and Newspaper, 1916

Oil on canvas

13 × 18¼ in. (33 × 46.4 cm)

Signed and dated in brown paint, lower left: Juan Gris 1916

Gift of Joseph Brummer

1923:2-1

© 2000 Artists Rights Society (ARS), New York/ADAGP, Paris

Juan Gris is well established as one of the four great masters in the history of Cubism, the others being Georges Braque and Pablo Picasso, the founders of the movement, and Fernand Léger. Gris began his career in his native Spain, in provincial Madrid rather than advanced Barcelona. When he arrived in Paris in 1906 and searched out his compatriots at the Bateau Lavoir (Laundry Boat), a complex of artists' studios in Montmartre, Gris could not have known that he had positioned himself at the epicenter of artistic innovation. He worked as a graphic artist for a newspaper but kept a watchful and respectful eye on the Bateau Lavoir's most famous tenant, Picasso. By 1910, when Braque's and Picasso's Cubism had reached its analytic phase, Gris made the fateful decision to devote himself to art and to the new visual language of Cubism.

Gris's art is closely aligned thematically with that of Braque and Picasso, deriving its subjects from the studio and the café world. Yet his interpretation of these themes was from the outset distinctly his own. Braque's and Picasso's cubist paintings are intuited from facet to facet, while Gris establishes an a priori gridlike structure onto which he arranges the various elements of a composition. He articulates his vision with clarity and precision—a by-product of an analytic temperament, but also the result of having been emboldened by the pioneering work of his predecessors.

Gris's most prolific subject is the still life. Gertrude Stein observed that for Gris, "still life was a religion," underscoring the single mindedness of his commitment. Stein's words also allude to a spirituality and a contemplative stillness that has been likened to the still lifes of the seventeenth-century Spanish master Francisco de Zurbarán. The early gray still lifes of 1911–12 correspond to Braque's and Picasso's brown-ocher monochrome analytic cubist works, but in 1913 Gris introduced exuberant colors, reflecting the influence of Robert Delaunay's Orphism, in which the cubist facet and vibrant color are merged.

Fruit Dish, Glass, and Newspaper belongs to a larger group of oil paintings of 1916, arranged with similar elements. In this work a host of important influences coalesce. As in other paintings of that year, its color scheme is more subdued—limited to brown, beige, violet, greens, and one or two other colors. Gris focuses on the textural materiality of objects, in which we can discern the pervasive influence of collage. This is evident in the reference to the newspaper, in the wood graining of the table, and in the white cloth at the lower center, whose thickly built-up crosshatched strokes approximate the texture of rough cloth. Gris was very conscious of the tradition of super-real imagery in Spanish art.

In this and other still lifes done in 1916, the fruit dish dominates the composition. It derives from one of Paul Cézanne's most significant works, Still Life with Compotier, of about 1879–80 (The Museum of Modern Art, New York). Gris repeats the asymmetry of Cézanne's compotier, as well as the dual vantage point—seeing both the side and the top simultaneously—one of Cézanne's key contributions to Cubism. "Cézanne turns a bottle into a cylinder. . . . I make a bottle, a particular bottle, out of a cylinder," he commented, distinguishing his more conceptualized approach to art from Cézanne's emphasis on extracting form from observable reality.

Fruit Dish, Glass, and Newspaper brings together all that was artistically current at the time, yet Gris transforms the momentary aspect of the work into a meditation on and elucidation of pictorial issues.

Further Reading

Green, Christopher, et al. Juan Gris. London: Whitechapel Art Gallery; New Haven, Conn.: Yale University Press, 1992.

Kahnweiler, Daniel-Henry. Juan Gris: His Life and Work. Translated by Douglas Cooper. New York: Harry N. Abrams, 1969.

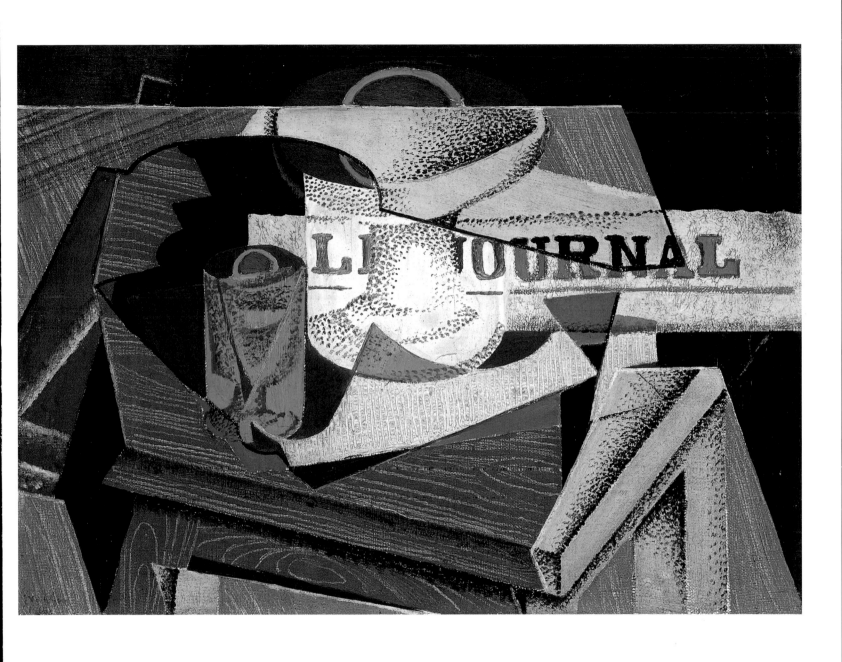

Pierre-Narcisse Guérin

Paris, France 1774–1833 Rome, Italy

Clytemnestra Hesitating before Stabbing the Sleeping Agamemnon, c. 1817

Oil on canvas

30 × 33½ in. (76.2 × 85.1 cm)

Signed with the artist's monogram in black paint, lower left (base of column): PG

Purchased with the Hillyer, Mather, Tryon Fund and with funds realized from the sale of works given by Caroline R. Wing, class of 1896, Adeline F. Wing, class of 1898, and Mr. and Mrs. Allan D. Emil

1999:24

Baron Pierre-Narcisse Guérin is one of the most celebrated and accomplished neoclassical artists, bridging the late eighteenth and early nineteenth centuries. He was born on the threshold of the neoclassical movement and died at the height of Romanticism; in different ways he contributed to both. Guérin had a deep appreciation of the historical sweep of the French classical tradition, with its roots in the works of Nicolas Poussin. Although never a student of Jacques-Louis David, he was nonetheless strongly influenced by him.

Guérin's career began early and progressed rapidly. His most influential early teacher was Jean-Baptiste Regnault. During the 1790s Guérin was at the Académie, and in 1797 he won the coveted Prix de Rome for his interpretation of the Death of Cato (Ecole Nationale Supérieure des Beaux-Arts, Paris). Poor health limited Guérin's productivity, and in his later years he focused on teaching. Among his students were many celebrated artists of the romantic movement, including Théodore Gericault, Eugène Delacroix, and Ary Scheffer.

Smith's canvas is a smaller replica of Guérin's 1817 painting in the Louvre. It is an image of betrayal, revenge, love, lust, and murder—all intertwined in the convoluted story of Agamemnon, King of Mycenae, and his wife, Clytemnestra. As the leader of the Greeks during the Trojan wars, he beseeched the goddess Artemis for aid, appeasing her by sacrificing their daughter Iphigenia—an act that Clytemnestra could not comprehend or forgive. Meanwhile, in Agamemnon's absence at war, Clytemnestra betrayed him with her lover Aegisthus. In Homer's account, she and her paramour threw a banquet for Agamemnon upon his return, during which he was killed. Aeschylus places the murderous deed in the king's chamber while he bathed. Guérin, in contrast, depicts the king asleep in his chamber, as Aegisthus urges the hesitant Clytemnestra to kill him.

Guérin takes care to represent a scene of archaeological verisimilitude—from the dress of the figures to Agamemnon's military hardware to the building at upper right, which evokes the palace of Argos. What keeps the image from spilling over into melodrama, more than the archaeological references, is the discipline of its pictorial structure. The background divides and distinctly defines space for each of the three protagonists—an idea already brilliantly resolved by Jacques-Louis David in his highly ordered *Oath of the Horatii* of 1784 (Musée du Louvre, Paris). Guérin's debt to David is also evident in the figure of the sleeping Agamemnon, with his military garb and weapons, reminiscent of David's dead Hector in *Andromache Mourning Hector* of 1783 (Musée du Louvre, Paris).

The dramatic poses and gestures in this work evoke artists such as Henry Fuseli, but even more importantly they underscore Guérin's lifelong love of the theater. The story unfolds here like a stage play. The dramatically colored tripartite division of the backdrop is pregnant with symbolic meaning. The scene at left is cast in darkness, which is linked with death as it envelops the urn with Iphigenia's ashes at extreme left, and with guilt as it highlights the leaning figure of the duplicitous Aegisthus. Thus the two conflicting yet intertwined impulses for Clytemnestra's act emanate from this dark passage. At right, the pose of the sleeping Agamemnon, illuminated with an eerie pink glow, links the notion of sleep with his impending death. In the center, the lantern glows through the curtain, and light becomes heat as the lurid red-orange engulfs Clytemnestra's tense, anguished silhouette, revealing and intensifying her conflicted passions. As she stands at the precipice—hesitant, determined, resigned—about to plunge the knife into her husband—she is the embodiment of the complex nature of human actions. This painting demonstrates how Guérin continued to be nourished by his neoclassical roots, even as he responded to the new romantic artistic and cultural currents.

Further Reading

French Painting, 1774–1830: The Age of Revolution. Detroit: The Detroit Institute of Arts; New York: The Metropolitan Museum of Art, 1975.

Rosenblum, Robert. *Transformations in Late Eighteenth Century Art.* Princeton, N.J.: Princeton University Press, 1969.

Jean-Antoine Houdon

Versailles, France 1741–1828 Paris, France

Bust of the Abbé Barthélemy (1716–1795),

1793/94–before 1802

Marble

20½ × 11⅞ × 11¼ in. (52.1 × 30.2 × 28.6 cm)

Not signed or dated

Purchased with the Hillyer, Mather, Tryon Fund

1989:22

Jean-Antoine Houdon, the Enlightenment's most brilliant portraitist, studied with some of the best sculptors of the period, including René-Michel Slodtz, Jean-Baptiste Lemoyne, and Jean-Baptiste Pigalle. He won the Prix de Rome in 1761 at the age of twenty. After three years at the Ecole des Elèves Protégés, he traveled to Rome in 1764 and stayed for four years. His most important sculpture from this period was *Saint Bruno* for the church of Santa Maria degli Angeli, Rome.

Houdon established himself as a portraitist with the bust of Denis Diderot of 1771 (painted plaster, Yale University Art Gallery, New Haven), the most successful image of the great encyclopedist. It was at once an excellent likeness and a penetrating, insightful formulation of Diderot's physical and intellectual vibrancy. It set the tone for portraits of other men of the Enlightenment, especially his full-length image of the seated, elderly Voltaire of 1778–80 (terra cotta, Musée Fabre, Montpellier, France). He is best known in America for his busts of Benjamin Franklin (marble, The Metropolitan Museum of Art) and Thomas Jefferson of 1789 (marble, Museum of Fine Arts, Boston). One of his most successful statues was a full-length, life-size marble portrait of George Washington (1786–96) for the State Capitol in Richmond, Virginia.

Houdon's activity waned soon after the French Revolution, in part because Jacques-Louis David, the dominant artist of the period, actively disliked him and limited his access to commissions. *Abbé Barthélemy* was the sculptor's only entry in the Salon of 1795. It must have been a source of some pleasure and solace for Houdon to work on the portrait of an individual who so clearly embodied the ideals of the Enlightenment. Jean-Jacques Barthélemy, known as Abbé, was for many years the curator of the Cabinet des Médailles de la Bibliothèque du Roi. Yet his reputation rests on his immensely successful book, *Voyage du jeune Anacharsis en Grèce*, published in 1788, which helped rekindle interest in Greek culture. He uses the literary device of a Greek traveler in the fourth century B.C. who details the history, customs, philosophy, and art of ancient Greece, intertwining them with moving human stories. Its compendium of factual information was a great resource for artists.

Houdon's portrait of Abbé Barthélemy reflects the sensibility of his Enlightenment portraits of the 1770s and 1780s. This is an old, wizened head — thoughtful, reflective, unself-conscious. The subtle smile and insightful eyes are at once the instruments of his wisdom and the defining features of his gentle character. The keenly observed details of Barthélemy's physiognomy reflect the artist's method of taking precise measurements of the sitter's features, often even making a life mask. Yet the resulting portrait goes far beyond the factual data. Houdon's rich, complex character study rests on his willingness to sublimate his artistic temperament to the character of the sitter and on his ability to inculcate the image with the defining ideas of the Enlightenment. In choosing to depict Barthélemy on a herm base, the artist alludes to the sitter's knowledge of the ancient world.

The Smith marble portrait was originally given by Houdon to the medallist Jean-Pierre Droz, after a break in the neck made further work on it impractical. When the Smith portrait is compared with a completed marble of Barthélemy, it is clear that the break occurred well into the process, for only the degree of finish separates the two. The main difference is in the eyes. In the completed version the pupils are carved deeply so that Barthélemy's glance to the side is directed and alert. In the Smith portrait the pupils are left blank, making the image more frontal and pensive in demeanor.

Further Reading

Arnason, H. H. *The Sculptures of Houdon.* New York: Oxford University Press, 1975.

Levey, Michael. *Painting and Sculpture in France, 1700–1789.* New Haven, Conn.: Yale University Press, 1993.

Jean-Auguste-Dominique Ingres

Montauban, France 1780–1867 Paris, France

The Death of Leonardo da Vinci, c. 1851

Oil on canvas
16¼ × 19¼ in. (41.3 × 48.9 cm)
Not signed or dated
Purchased
1950:98

This canvas is a later variant of a painting done in 1818 for the comte de Blacas, a prominent statesman who was the French ambassador to Naples and then Rome. *The Death of Leonardo da Vinci* belongs to a group of paintings executed in the troubadour style between 1814 and 1825: Ingres's troubadour paintings, usually small in scale, are rich in narrative and detail, vibrant in color, and eloquent in their manipulation of line. In these, he adopts a style for each painting that corresponds to the historical period depicted. Among them are such prominent works as *Raphael and the Fornarina* of 1814 (Harvard University Art Museums, Cambridge, Massachusetts) and *Paolo and Francesca* of 1818 (Musée des Beaux-Arts, Angers), both of which likewise exist in multiple versions.

The Death of Leonardo da Vinci, like *Raphael and the Fornarina*, focuses on the life of a famous artist, an immensely popular theme. The death of Leonardo had been a subject for paintings from the late seventeenth century onward, most famously in François-Guillaume Menageot's version shown in the Salon of 1781 (Musée de l'Hôtel-de-Ville, Amboise). Ingres depicts a story taken from Vasari's *Vite* of 1551, which relates that Francis I arrived at the last moment to catch the expiring genius in his arms.

Leonardo died on May 2, 1519, at the château du Clos-Lucé, near Amboise. While it is documented that Francis I wept on hearing of Leonardo's death, there is no proof that he was present at the event.

Ingres, like his hero Nicolas Poussin in the seventeenth century, had spent much of his career in Italy and drew heavily on Italian sources. (Indeed, his head of Francis I here is based on a portrait by Titian [Musée du Louvre, Paris]). He thus embodied the synergy between France and Italy and made it an important subtext of the work. Francis I, who had lured Leonardo to France,

was instrumental in the development of French art and architecture. Implicit in depicting Leonardo in his arms is the transfer of artistic hegemony from Italy to France. With this gesture, Francis I also shows his deep humanity and elevates the stature of the artist in society.

Recent scholarship has argued for a date of about 1851 for the Smith work, since it depicts the *Mona Lisa* in the background. This relates it to the Etienne-Achille Réveil print of 1851, which, unlike other variants, includes the Leonardo masterpiece. In comparing the Smith version with the 1818 painting (Petit Palais, Paris), we see differences both obvious and discreet. The Smith variant reverses the original and has a simpler, more summary treatment of the figures and of such elements as the chair and bed canopy. The elaborate incised treatment of the floor suggests that Ingres may have intended to carry the Smith painting further.

There are enough subtle but important differences between the original and the Smith version to suggest a fundamental rethinking of the narrative by Ingres. Three key figures carry the emotional message of the painting: Francis I, Leonardo, and the figure standing behind the chair, who may represent Leonardo's friend Melzi. In the 1818 version he serves as an interlocutor, gesturing with both arms toward the deathbed scene, where the heads of Francis I and Leonardo are closely bonded, both physically and emotionally. Although this version was generally well received, critics pointed out that Francis I appeared to be suffocating Leonardo. In the Smith version, the two heads are held apart and the emotional burden has been transferred to the figure behind the chair, who is shown despairing and wringing his hands. It would appear that Ingres remembered the criticism of the original in working on the later version and decided to reorder a major dynamic in the painting.

Further Reading

Condon, Patricia, et al. *Ingres, In Pursuit of Perfection: The Art of J.-A.-D. Ingres*. Edited by Debra Edelstein. Louisville, Ky.: The J. B. Speed Art Museum; Bloomington: Indiana University Press, 1983.

Rosenblum, Robert. *Jean-Auguste-Dominique Ingres*. London: Thames and Hudson, 1990.

Wassily Kandinsky

Moscow, Russia 1866–1944 Neuilly-sur-Seine, France

Autumn Impression, 1908

Oil on paperboard
13 × 17½ in. (33 × 44.5 cm)
Signed in red paint, lower right: KANDINSKY
Bequest of Mrs. Robert S. Tangeman (E. Clementine Miller, class of 1927)
1996:24-1
© 2000 Artists Rights Society (ARS), New York/ADAGP, Paris

Autumn Impression was painted in 1908, probably in late September, in the small Bavarian town of Murnau, nestled in the foothills of the Alps south of Munich. Between 1907 and 1914 Kandinsky stayed there for extended periods with his companion, the artist Gabriele Münter. His investigation of form and color achieved a new intensity during this period, manifested most fully in his landscapes. A few years earlier, in Paris, Kandinsky had exhibited at the historic Salon d'Automne of 1905. There he was exposed to the startling coloristic experiments of the Fauves, led by Henri Matisse.

This important contact with the French avant-garde partly explains the sonorous, rich color rhythms of Kandinsky's work. The fauves validated his own experiments on the properties of color. Yet for Kandinsky color has an interactive synesthetic connection to sound and music, serving as predicate to art's spiritual essence: "The word is an inner sound. It springs partly, perhaps principally, from the object denoted. Thus green, yellow or red trees in a meadow are accidental realizations of the concept 'tree' which we formed upon hearing the word."

Autumn Impression, a celebratory view of nature, seems to embody Kandinsky's words. In it, he creates a rich array of brightly colored and varied shapes, evoking trees and other natural forms and dominated by a blue and white church and steeple. These move horizontally in a rhythmic pattern across a field locked between the snowcapped deep blue mountain range in the distance and the green meadow in the foreground.

The astonishingly liberated treatment of the middle passage allows for multiple interpretations. The brown-red mosaicked shape that moves up the mountain at the left next to the green tree, for example, may be read

as a running horse. The horse was pivotal for Kandinsky from the outset of his career. In 1911 Kandinsky and Franz Marc named their historic movement Der Blaue Reiter (The Blue Rider), emphasizing the significance for both of the horse-and-rider motif.

Kandinsky's artistic evolution reflected both his Russian origins and his exposure to Western art. His refined sensibility resulted from the interaction of a keen intellect and deep spirituality, and he absorbed impulses from varied, often surprising sources. In *Autumn Impression* we discern lessons learned from the Fauves and their predecessors, Paul Gauguin and Vincent van Gogh. The rich traditions of Russian fairy tales and folk art are also evident here, as is the luminosity of Bavarian reverse glass painting, to which the artist was introduced by Münter at about this time.

Early in his career Kandinsky became aware of art's abstract potential. At an impressionist exhibition in Moscow in 1896, just a month before he moved to Munich, Kandinsky reportedly stood transfixed before a painting of a grainstack by Claude Monet, unable to recognize the subject of the work immediately, responding instead to its bold forms and vivid colors. In his seminal treatise *Concerning the Spiritual in Art,* written in 1910 and published in 1912, still a few years before his own paintings became fully abstract, Kandinsky invests color with meaning derived from other references: "color directly influences the soul, color is the keyboard, the eyes are the hammer, the soul is the piano with many strings." In *Autumn Impression,* colors and forms cascade across the surface like so many musical sounds, creating a richly resonant, suggestive vision of nature. Shortly thereafter, this vision would be transformed into one of art's earliest and most compelling experiments in abstraction.

Further Reading

Grohmann, Will. *Wassily Kandinsky: Life and Work.* New York: Harry N. Abrams, 1958.

Kandinsky in Munich: 1896–1914. New York: Solomon R. Guggenheim Foundation, 1982.

Weiss, Peg. *Kandinsky in Munich: The Formative Jugendstil Years.* Princeton, N.J.: Princeton University Press, 1979.

Ernst Ludwig Kirchner

Aschaffenburg, Germany 1880–1938 Frauenkirch, Switzerland

Dodo and Her Brother, 1908/20

Oil on canvas
67⅛ × 37⁷⁄₁₆ in. (170.5 × 95.1 cm)
Signed in black paint, lower left: E.L. Kirchner
Purchased
1955:59

Kirchner painted *Dodo and Her Brother* in late 1908 and retouched it about 1920, when he was systematically repainting earlier canvases. The painting comes at an important moment in Kirchner's early development. Three years earlier, in 1905, he and three other architecture students in Dresden—Fritz Bleyl, Erich Heckel, and Karl Schmidt-Rottluff—had formed an artist group called Die Brücke (The Bridge). It was the earliest twentieth-century manifestation of a cohesive modern artistic program north of the Alps. From the outset, Kirchner was the group's leader and its most talented artist. The Fauves, founded in France that same year under Henri Matisse's leadership, would especially influence Die Brücke artists in the use of an intensified color palette.

Dodo was Kirchner's friend and most important model during this period. She is depicted with her brother in a frontal pose, completely filling the narrow canvas and shallow space so that our confrontation with them is total and inevitable. They are posed and dressed formally. Shattering the decorum are the high-pitched, dissonant colors, aggressively applied.

At this critical juncture, where form and content intersect, the influence of Vincent van Gogh, Paul Gauguin, and Edvard Munch becomes apparent. Kirchner strongly responded to their expressive palette and to the emotional and psychological acuity of their art. In the bold blue outlining of the man's suit and the sinuous line of the woman's bright yellow dress he evokes the expressive use of the curvilinear by these artists. The intense green and red backdrop defining the shallow space, especially behind the brother, is a device they often used. In numerous self-portraits these artists used red, alone or in combination with other colors, to enhance the psychological impact. Indeed, Kirchner could have taken Van Gogh's description of his *Night*

Café (Yale University Art Gallery, New Haven, Conn.) as the credo for his painting: "I have tried to express in this picture the terrible passions of humanity by means of red and green." Munch shared Van Gogh's concern for existential issues. He often framed them in the context of city dwellers, and this had special resonance for Kirchner. *Dodo and Her Brother* is an extension of themes that Kirchner addresses in his early masterpiece *The Street* (The Museum of Modern Art, New York), also painted in 1908, which depends extensively on Munch's powerful and haunting *Evening on Karl Johann Strasse* (Rasmus Meyers Samlinger, Bergen, Norway) of 1889. Kirchner's use of color is bolder than Munch's, evoking the legacy of Van Gogh and Gauguin but also of the fauves. Unlike the fauves, however, Kirchner here uses color as a vehicle for content. It becomes the language in which he articulates the unspeakable anxiety of modern society, whose identity was being challenged on every front.

The male-female context, a critical subject for Kirchner that taps into one of Munch's central themes, is explicit in this painting. Despite their familial ties, the tension between the two is palpable. She dominates the composition as he recedes, wedged into a space that barely contains him. His strutting pose, the exaggerated moustache on his lime green face, and his red ears render him at once startling and comical. Dodo's larger physical presence is enhanced by the exuberance of her costume, topped off by an enormous, vibrantly colored hat. Her sexuality is underscored by the outline of her legs beneath the dress, her black gloved arms linked at her midriff, and the open fan she holds over her genital area. The cigar that her brother holds in a pink hand furthers the painting's sexual interplay, as does the suggestive pink stroke between his legs.

In this unnerving, powerful work Kirchner explores some of his major themes, creating an archetype of twentieth-century humanity.

Further Reading

Gordon, Donald E. *Ernst Ludwig Kirchner: A Retrospective Exhibition.* Boston: Museum of Fine Arts, 1968.

Gordon, Donald E. *Ernst Ludwig Kirchner.* Cambridge, Mass.: Harvard University Press, 1968.

Fernand Léger

Argentan, Orne, France 1881–1955 Gif-sur-Yvette, Seine-et-Oise, France

Mechanical Element I, 1924

Oil on canvas
25½ × 20 in. (64.8 × 50.8 cm)
Signed and dated in gray paint, lower right: F. Leger. 24
Purchased, Joseph Brummer Fund
1954:75
© 2000 Artists Rights Society (ARS), New York/ADAGP, Paris

Mechanical Element I is a defining statement of Léger's impassioned belief in modernism as codified by the machine age. At the outset of the 1920s the machine became a focus of attention for many artists. Léger's evolution toward this historic moment began when he was a soldier in World War I, when for the first time he found himself in surroundings outside the art world. Previously he had evolved his own distinctive brand of Cubism, more robust and concrete than Georges Braque's and Pablo Picasso's. His tubular forms, depicted at times in mechanized motion, had clearly defined and interlocked shapes, differing from the penetrating planes of Analytic Cubism.

Léger was prepared for his conversion when it came: "I was dazzled by the breech of a 75-millimeter gun that was standing uncovered in the sunlight: the magic of light on white metal. This was enough to make me forget the abstract art of 1912–13. A complete revelation to me — both as a man and as a painter." This experience made Léger a champion of everyman — the engineer, the artisan, the soldier — seeing in their contributions acts more worthy and profound than those of the aesthetes of the art world, and it reiterated the centrality of the machine for his artistic vision.

The early 1920s were immensely productive for Léger. His experiment with cinema culminated in *Ballet Mécanique* of 1924, in which he explored the action and interaction of fragmented mechanical and human forms. In his important *Grand Déjeuner* of 1921 (The Museum of Modern Art, New York), three tubular female nudes inhabit a room with corresponding furnishings, anticipating by two years Le Corbusier's famous dictum, "a house is a machine for living." In its formality and clarity this painting also reflects the larger revival of classicism at the time and posits Léger among such distinguished French classicists as Nicolas Poussin and Jacques-Louis David. For Léger, clarity and order were manifest in the machine, a view also shared by Purism.

In *Mechanical Element I* Léger clarifies and reconciles the relationship between machine and art. In a lecture at the Collège de France in 1923, he explained: "I never played around by copying machinery. I invent machines as others invent landscapes." He assimilates into his art the principle of the machine — its precision, the logic and clarity of its formal arrangement — and then invents forms that suggest machine parts.

The iconic force of *Mechanical Element* is in its directness. Three small black circles vertically arranged at the left and four horizontal ones at the upper right bolt the structure of interlocking forms to the canvas. The straight strip of ocher-red, which moves diagonally through the middle from top to bottom where it jigs to the left, is the main color accent in a painting in which blacks, grays, and whites prevail, accented in places by yellows and reds. A white semicircle overlaps the diagonal. Its pristine curving body, modeled from light to dark like glistening metal, is the most assertively three-dimensional form in the painting, propelling the whole image forward. Tension between flat and three-dimensional forms, color and non-color, curvilinear and rectilinear shapes — all arranged along a diagonal axis — infuses the work with dynamic energy.

Some of the forms in *Mechanical Element I* recur in other paintings by Léger, much as machine parts are used interchangeably. Ultimately, Léger's forms function in this painting primarily as an art machine, recalling Charles Baudelaire's commentary on the Salon of 1846, "A picture is a machine the systems of which are intelligible to the practiced eye."

Further Reading

De Francia, Peter. *Fernand Léger*. New Haven, Conn.: Yale University Press, 1983.

Kosinski, Dorothy, ed. *Fernand Léger 1911–1924: The Rhythm of Modern Life*. Munich: Prestel-Verlag, 1994.

Lanchner, Carolyn, et al. *Fernand Léger*. New York: The Museum of Modern Art, 1998.

Wilhelm Lehmbruck

Duisburg-Meiderich, Germany 1881–1919 Berlin, Germany

Torso of the Pensive Woman, 1913–14

Cast concrete on self-base, reworked
50⅞ × 18 × 13⅛ in. (129.2 × 45.7 × 33.3 cm)
Not signed or dated
Purchased, Winthrop Hillyer Fund
1922:19

Wilhelm Lehmbruck, a miner's son, underwent rigorous academic training at the Kunstakademie in Düsseldorf under Karl Janssen. An artist of extraordinary sensibility and emotional depth, he searched for universal verities through the vehicle of the human form. His first major influence was Auguste Rodin, from whom he learned the expressive potential of the body as carrier of psychological import. By 1910 Lehmbruck had moved to Paris, where he became acquainted with Aristide Maillol, whose work embodies the classical Mediterranean tradition. He also responded to the classicism of the German painter Hans von Marees, his native Gothic past, and imagery of the Belgian symbolist sculptor George Minne.

Lehmbruck's artistic ascendancy occurred at the time when young German artists were in the throes of a revolution. German Expressionism, led by the Brücke (Bridge) group and later by Der Blaue Reiter (The Blue Rider), as well as by a number of independent artists, reached its apex in the first two decades of the twentieth century. Lehmbruck and Ernst Barlach were its major sculptors. Lehmbruck's relationship to German Expressionism is predicated on common goals of expressing through art a heightened emotional and psychological state. His articulation of this state necessitated a resolution or rather a reconciliation of all the impulses that helped define his vision. The tension between the classical and northern traditions as they are filtered through a sensitive, introspective temperament lies at the core of Lehmbruck's art. This tension is defined in a sculpture like *Torso of the Pensive Woman*, which is a truncated variant of a larger work, *Pensive Woman* (family of the artist, on loan to the Nationalgalerie, Berlin) of the same date, 1913–14.

In *Pensive Woman* Lehmbruck tempers the northern impulse and adds an emotional expressiveness to his classical idiom. He reconciles the Gothic imagery and gaunt, elongated forms of his famous *Kneeling Woman* of 1911 (The Museum of Modern Art, New York) with the Maillol-inspired classicism of works like *Standing Woman* of 1910 (National Gallery of Art, Washington, D.C.) to produce a synthesis. The full figure of *Pensive Woman*, with her left leg bearing weight and her right leg slightly forward and bent at the knee, evokes a classic contrapposto stance. In a gesture of self-absorption, her left arm is entwined behind the lower back as her left hand grasps her right arm, which hangs by her side. Her eyes glance downward, and her tilted head on an elongated neck further adds to the reflective mood.

The relationship between *Pensive Woman* and Smith's *Torso of the Pensive Woman* is both evident and intriguing. In *Torso of the Pensive Woman* Lehmbruck omits the head, cuts the arms cleanly above the biceps, and shows only the upper legs. In doing so, he eliminates those aspects of the full figure that carry its introspective, lyrical quality. *Torso of the Pensive Woman* is, instead, an erect, alert form throbbing with controlled intensity—at once elegant, assertive, and vulnerable.

As one moves around the torso to the back view, a rough area along the lower back and down the right hip indicates where the arms of *Pensive Woman* were located. The variants of *Torso of the Pensive Woman* that exist today are in bronze and cast concrete, the marble having been destroyed. Cast concrete, the material of the Smith torso, was used as an inexpensive substitute for bronze. Yet its matte, granular texture gives a physicality to the form that is absent in the dissolved, reflective surface of the bronze.

Just how much passion courses through Lehmbruck's work is indicated by his tragic suicide in 1919, a product of his irreconcilable revulsion to World War I. In *Torso of the Pensive Woman* that passion is manifest in an extraordinarily disciplined, nuanced interpretation of one of Western art's enduring motifs.

Further Reading

Heller, Reinhold. *The Art of Wilhelm Lehmbruck*. Washington, D.C.: National Gallery of Art, 1972.

Hoff, August. *Wilhelm Lehmbruck: Life and Work*. New York: Praeger, 1969.

Hofmann, Werner. *Wilhelm Lehmbruck*. New York: Universe Books, 1959.

Edouard Manet

Paris, France 1832–1883 Paris, France

Marguérite de Conflans, 1873

Oil on canvas
21 × 17½ in. (53.3 × 44.5 cm)
Signed and dated in black paint, lower left: Manet/1873
Purchased, Drayton Hillyer Fund
1945:6

The accessibility of this portrait results from its forthright informality. The brilliant painting technique of animated, varied strokes arranges Marguérite's negligee and her loose, cascading hair. The spontaneous, quick execution is the perfect vehicle to reinforce the casual nature of the portrait, established by the sitter's pose and demeanor. She is shown at half length, close to the viewer, enveloped by a green sofa, her elbow resting on its arm (where Manet signs and dates the work). Her head, while more tightly painted, is filled with vibrant passages. The thick black eyebrows arch above white and brown markings that create the eyes' sparkle, and smudged red paint forms an uneven outline of the upturned mouth. Her tilted head is propped up by fingers whose malleable curves are defined by strokes of color. As Paul Mantz has written of another Manet portrait, "the head and hands are in a merely indicated, unexecuted state."

Manet, who was a close friend of Marguérite's family, painted her five times. Her father was related to the Guillemardet family, which owned works by Francisco Goya that Manet was able to study in the 1860s. Given that Marguérite was only seventeen when this work was done, Adolphe Tabarant suggests that she must have posed for the portrait at home, a more appropriate venue than the artist's studio. Anne Coffin Hanson identified a photograph of Marguérite in a similar pose in Manet's family album (Bibliothèque Nationale, Paris). After exploring the possibility that Manet used the photograph for the painting, she concluded that the affinity may also be coincidental.

Marguérite's casual attitude and state of dress, mirrored in the loose, painterly brushwork, challenge the convention of portraiture as a lasting formal record of an individual. The contrast with one of Ingres's elaborate, tightly painted female portraits is dramatic, the two styles articulating profoundly different visions of portraiture.

Manet insists on presenting the work primarily as a portrait. The image of woman *en déshabillé,* as Marguérite is here, has a long tradition going back to antiquity and had an especially delicious moment during the rococo period. In the nineteenth century, Gustave Courbet's *Portrait of Jo, the Beautiful Irish Girl* of 1865 (The Metropolitan Museum of Art) is an important antecedent. Courbet's sitter is an identifiable individual, James McNeill Whistler's mistress, but she is shown looking in a mirror and running her fingers through her hair in a self-absorbed private moment, which allows for casualness more akin to genre painting than to portraiture. Manet's Marguérite is similarly casual but clearly posing for her portrait.

The issue of Manet's intent in this work comes into play because of his consistent ability to shock and to dislodge the operative norm. Such is the case with his two most scandalous works—*Olympia* and *Luncheon on the Grass* (both 1863, Musée d'Orsay, Paris). In both, a nude woman confronts us directly. One is a prostitute, the other is picnicking in the company of dressed men and a semiclad companion. It is in this context that we dare wonder whether Manet has here transformed the seventeen-year-old daughter of a friend into a *demi-mondaine.* The question is unanswerable. Yet in its astonishing matter-of-factness, Manet's *Marguérite de Conflans* provokes speculation and challenges the decorum of portrait conventions.

Further Reading

Fried, Michael. *Manet's Modernism, or, the Face of Painting in the 1860s.* Chicago: University of Chicago Press, 1996.

Hanson, Anne Coffin. *Edouard Manet: 1832–1883.* Philadelphia: Philadelphia Museum of Art; Chicago: The Art Institute of Chicago, 1966.

Tabarant, Adolphe. *Manet et ses oeuvres.* Paris: Gallimard, 1947.

Jean-François Millet

Gruchy, near Gréville, France 1814–1875 Barbizon, France

Farm at Gruchy, 1854

Oil on canvas
21¼ × 28⅝ in. (54 × 72.7 cm)
Sale stamp in red paint, lower left: J. F. Millet [Lugt 1415]
Purchased, Tryon Fund
1931:10

Farm at Gruchy was painted during the epochal period of Millet's most famous works, *The Sower* of 1850 (Museum of Fine Arts, Boston) and *The Gleaners* of 1857 (Musée d'Orsay, Paris). He defines in them, more powerfully than any other artist, the epic drama of the peasants and the land they work. These paintings secured the artist's stature as a seminal figure in the realist movement and exposed for the disquieted public the brutal reality of the working classes.

Farm at Gruchy depicts an area of Millet's native coastal hamlet near Gréville, not far from Cherbourg. His early years in the region, often doing farm chores as the son of prosperous peasants, would have a lasting impact. In 1849 he abandoned Paris after four years' stay and chose the village of Barbizon on the edge of the Fontainebleau forest, where he could again observe the arduous ritual of peasant life that would inspire his many paintings. In *The Sower*, his most important work, the heroic figure strides across the hilly landscape of Millet's native region.

The artist and his family returned to Gruchy for the summer of 1854 after a long absence, although he had visited the village briefly in 1853 for the funeral of his mother. When he had initially left Gruchy in 1844, Millet was ten years younger and a vastly different artist, painting mainly portraits and pastoral scenes. During his summer stay he reconnected with the region of his youth by painting and drawing its environs. In the interim, his style and vision had been profoundly transformed by the social upheavals of 1848 and the concomitant revolution in art toward naturalism.

Farm at Gruchy also addresses the larger question of Millet as landscapist. His closest friend at Barbizon was Théodore Rousseau, who, along with Camille Corot, was the most important landscapist of the generation. Yet for Millet pure landscape held little interest, and only toward the end of his career did he turn to it in a more sustained way. Landscape mattered to him mainly as a way to elucidate the drama of his heroic peasants. When he painted landscapes, he invariably depicted land that had been worked by human hands.

In *Farm at Gruchy*, verdant nature subsumes the landscape thickly painted in broad, soft strokes of contrasting light-and-dark patterns, which enhance the gentle undulating rhythm of the rolling meadows and trees. In the background, along with the trees, are houses that announce the village. We stand with our back to the precipitous drop of the rocky seashore. The middle is dominated by a stone wall, which at once protects from the strong sea winds and divides and orders the land into discrete parcels. The sun illuminates the wall's left side, where a dark shaft indicates an entrance. The light dances along the top of the middle wall and highlights a crumbled portion indicative of time's ravages. The dominant horizontal wall, cast in shadow, engulfs a peasant shouldering a tool as he strides from right to left. His daily ritual is reminiscent of the equally small image of the country priest engaged in his daily routine in Rousseau's famous *Under the Birches, Evening* of 1842–43 (The Toledo Museum of Art, Ohio). Significantly, in Rousseau's work majestic birches tower over the priest on horseback, whereas in Millet's painting the man-made wall encases the peasant. By diminishing the scale of the peasant, Millet here consciously emphasizes the landscape, but one in which man's physical effort is an indispensable component.

Further Reading

Herbert, Robert L. *Jean-François Millet*. London: Arts Council of Great Britain, 1976.

Murphy, Alexandra R. *Jean-François Millet*. Boston: Museum of Fine Arts, 1984.

Claude Monet

Paris, France 1840–1926 Giverny, France

The Seine at Bougival, Evening, 1869

Oil on canvas
23⅝ × 28⅞ in. (60 × 73.3 cm)
Signed in reddish orange paint, lower right: Claude Monet
Purchased
1946:4

Monet's *Seine at Bougival, Evening* represents a pivotal time and place in the early years of Impressionism. During that moment, three practitioners of the evolving movement, Monet, Pierre-Auguste Renoir, and Camille Pissarro, interacted for the first time; they exchanged ideas about the nature of plein-air painting and created works that expanded their artistic vocabulary—still years away from being derisively labeled Impressionism. Monet and Renoir initiated the habit of working together on the same motif. During the summer the two painted nearly identical views of La Grenouillère, a popular resort featuring a round island called "Camembert." Their vibrant interpretation of a place where people engaged in such leisure activities as dining, boating, and swimming defined a carefree era. Years later, Renoir said nostalgically of this lost moment, "The world knew how to laugh in those days."

The village of Bougival had come into its own during the reign of Louis XIV, who built a château in nearby Marly as a retreat from Versailles. His successors continued to enjoy the region, and the châteaux that grace the landscape date from the pre-Revolutionary period. By the mid-nineteenth century, Bougival had become a popular retreat for the prosperous and for prominent artists and writers as well as pleasure-seekers. Seventeen kilometers northwest of Paris, easily accessible by railroad from the Gare Saint-Lazare, it sits on the banks of the Seine surrounded by gently rolling hills. Bougival's natural beauty and its artistic milieu distinguished it from other places in the region.

The Seine at Bougival, Evening is Monet's first painting at Bougival. He chose a picturesque motif that includes the houses across the river, the Croissy Island wedged into the right foreground, and, on the horizon, the dramatic silhouette of an aqueduct between Bougival

and Port-Marly, built during the reign of Louis XIV. A modern bridge below the aqueduct is barely visible. All is subsumed in the awesome beauty of a sunset. Monet here creates a work apart from his more prevalent images bathed in high sun. The focus on an emblazoned sky at the end of the day gives the work an emotional intensity that is more melancholy than joyous. A restless, vigorous brushstroke evident in the dramatic sky, in the lush green of the island, and in the fluidity of the river creates a scene of flux for which the boat with two figures at the left serves as a metaphor.

The insistent romantic mood of the painting is tied to the sensibility of the Barbizon artists, who, in reviving a tradition of French landscape painting at midcentury, paved the way for the impressionists. Specifically, Monet turns here to the work of Charles-François Daubigny, an artist he greatly admired and toward whose work the term *impression* was first applied critically. Daubigny was a preeminent essayist of river views, especially of his beloved Oise. One of the pioneering artists to paint *en plein air*, he traversed the river on a studio boat he had built, from which he painted motifs—an idea Monet would later emulate. Eugène Boudin, another pioneer who became Monet's major mentor, taught him to paint directly from nature along his native northwest coast, in places like Trouville and Saint-Adresse.

Monet's vaulting ambition and exceptional talent transcended both Daubigny and Boudin, as his exploration of nature transformed the history of art. *The Seine at Bougival, Evening* is a reminder of Monet's awareness of the earlier landscape tradition, even as the vigorous energy coursing through the canvas already indicates a pictorial investigation of a different order.

Further Reading

Champa, Kermit Swiler. *Studies in Early Impressionism.* New Haven, Conn.: Yale University Press, 1973.

Champa, Kermit Swiler, and Dianne W. Pitman. *Monet and Bazille: A Collaboration.* Edited by David A. Brenneman. Atlanta: High Museum of Art; New York: Harry N. Abrams, 1999.

Herbert, Robert L. *Impressionism: Art, Leisure, and Parisian Society.* New Haven, Conn.: Yale University Press, 1988.

Claude Monet

Paris, France 1840–1926 Giverny, France

Field of Poppies, 1890

Oil on canvas

23½ × 39½ in. (59.7 × 100.3 cm)

Signed and dated in reddish orange paint, lower right: Claude Monet 90

Gift of the Honorable and Mrs. Irwin Untermyer in honor of their daughter Joan L. Untermyer, class of 1940

1940:10

Field of Poppies of 1890 initiated a decade in Monet's creative life that would establish this preeminent impressionist as the most important artist of his generation. By the 1880s the impressionist revolution had become the inevitable instrument against which the next generation of artists rebelled—led by Georges Seurat's Neo-Impressionism. During that decade Pierre-Auguste Renoir had a crisis of confidence about Impressionism's aims, and Camille Pissarro actually bolted for a time to the neo-impressionist camp. Monet, however, remained committed to the movement. During the 1880s he disengaged from the subject of Paris and its surroundings. He criss-crossed France, searching out its most picturesque motifs from Etretat to Antibes, to reassert the vitality of the movement and establish his own broader authority.

By 1890 Monet had purchased a home in Giverny, where he had been renting since 1883, and settled into a more permanent residency. He turned his attention to painting series of the same motif—the ultimate validation of Impressionism's aims. Nearly all of his major series paintings of the 1890s were done near Giverny. The only exception, the Rouen Cathedral series, was painted a mere sixty kilometers away and finished in Giverny. Works like *Field of Poppies*, along with the closely related group of paintings of the Oat Fields and his famous Grainstacks series, underscore Monet's interest in the agrarian character of the region around Giverny.

Field of Poppies is arranged in horizontal striations: the poppy field, a row of trees, and the sky. Each holds our interest, distributing the visual energy throughout the work. The densely packed field of red poppies interspersed with green establishes a base for the eloquent orchestration of various silhouettes of trees, closely clustered at the left, more sparsely arranged at the right. The artist gives the trees at the right more dramatic, tall silhouettes—as if to compensate for their limited number—and unifies them by the diagonal of the hill of Giverny in the background. All this is under a sky that subsumes more than half the painting.

One telling feature that differentiates the many paintings Renoir and Monet painted side by side is Monet's emphasis on a dynamic horizon. In *Field of Poppies* the horizon, with its strip of trees, dominates and holds our interest more than either the poppy field or the sky. Such intricate horizons give many of Monet's paintings that special visual intelligence about which Paul Cézanne commented, "Monet is just an eye—but what an eye!"

Smith's painting is one of four variants of the same motif likely painted in July 1890, at different times of day. Others belong to the White Fund, Lawrence, Massachusetts (on extended loan to the Museum of Fine Arts, Boston) and the Art Institute of Chicago. The Chicago painting is bathed most directly in sunlight, so that the trees are a yellow-green color. The sky is bright blue, with only a few puffy clouds. In contrast, in the Smith canvas the sky is predominantly filled with clouds, and shadows turn the trees dark violet mottled with intense green. This coloristic intensity carries over to the poppy field.

The Field of Poppies paintings were executed at about the same time as the Grainstacks series but are not usually considered a series. The reason is in part quantitative—there are four Field of Poppies paintings and a great many Grainstacks. Monet's subject—a rather expansive view of the poppy fields in the meadows of Les Essarts—lacks an identifiable focal object such as the grainstacks or a cathedral façade. Otherwise *Field of Poppies* adheres to the same principles as the series paintings—a singular achievement unmatched by any other impressionist.

Further Reading

Monet's Years at Giverny: Beyond Impressionism. New York: The Metropolitan Museum of Art, 1978.

Tucker, Paul Hayes. *Monet in the '90s: The Series Paintings.* Boston: Museum of Fine Arts; New Haven, Conn.: Yale University Press, 1989.

Claude Monet

Paris, France 1840–1926 Giverny, France

Cathedral at Rouen (La Cour d'Albane), 1892–94

Oil on canvas
36½ × 29¹/₁₆ in. (92.7 × 73.8 cm)
Signed and dated in brown paint, lower right: Claude Monet 94
Gift of Adeline F. Wing, class of 1898, and Caroline R. Wing, class of 1896
1956:24

This painting initiates Monet's most celebrated series. He painted some thirty canvases of Rouen cathedral between 1892 and 1894. Twenty were exhibited in 1895 at the Durand-Ruel Gallery in Paris, where they became a focus of serious critical commentary. Georges Clemenceau wrote: "With twenty pictures the painter has given us the feeling that he could have made . . . fifty, one hundred, one thousand, as many as there are seconds in a day."

By reiterating numerous versions of a motif, differing primarily in treatment of light and atmosphere, these works go to the very core of Impressionism's raison d'être. In them, Monet achieves the most comprehensive symbiosis of creative expression with nature's changeable processes. Monet's primary concern is to interpret the unfolding drama of the interplay of light on the intricate lacework of the cathedral's gray stone at various moments of the day.

Like Clemenceau, twentieth-century artists from Kasimir Malevich to Roy Lichtenstein have focused on the formal aspects of the series. Malevich viewed it as a precursor to his suprematist abstractions, noting that the theme of the cathedral "is not so important, with regards to the pictorial relationships and to the changes of colored elements."

To be sure, Monet's own stated indifference to the cathedral as subject contributed to this line of criticism. Yet it is impossible to overlook the significance of the cathedral as subject in Monet's series, much as it is impossible not to consider the profound impact of Russian icons on Malevich's abstract works.

Smith's painting is at once an integral part of the cathedral series and unique in the representation of the motif. It takes as its subject not the façade, the focus of most of the paintings in the series, but the Tour d'Albane as viewed from the courtyard. It is also only one of two paintings in the series that Monet painted out of doors. All of the others, mainly façades, were painted indoors, where Monet was able to narrow his "picture window" and concentrate on the façade to the near exclusion of all else. The result is a series of close-up views of the façade that shimmer with color and light like visions — at once adhering to the principles of Impressionism and reflective of the new tendency toward Symbolism and spirituality in the 1890s.

In contrast, by placing himself outdoors to paint the Tour d'Albane, Monet observed and absorbed into the work a broader context of relationships of the tower to the side of the cathedral seen partially at left, and to the adjoining structures — a haphazard array of secular buildings that cluster around the tower like children clinging to their mother, establishing a bond that references the cathedral's societal and religious functions.

Instead of emphasizing the picturesque silhouette of the cathedral and tower that gives the courtyard its charm, Monet cuts off the top of the tower and focuses on the extraordinary intersection — a juncture between the spiritual and secular, between earth and sky. As such, the artist allows for a reading that addresses both the formal concerns and the relationship of the Gothic cathedral to the people as a transcendent symbol that defines France like no other.

The Rouen Cathedral series is the only one where Monet uses an existing historically and artistically significant monument as a point of departure for his work, thus creating a connectedness that bridges centuries. As stone was transformed by the Gothic mason into a compelling vision of heaven on earth, so Monet's brush, saturating the portals, pinnacles, and in this case the tower and adjoining structures with color and light, imbues the cathedral with the transient beauty of nature. By focusing here on the cathedral's interaction with its secular surroundings, Monet explores yet another layer of meaning in this endlessly revealing series.

Further Reading

Pissarro, Joachim. *Monet's Cathedral: Rouen, 1892–1894*. New York: Alfred A. Knopf, 1990.

Tucker, Paul Hayes. *Monet in the '90s: The Series Paintings*. Boston: Museum of Fine Arts; New Haven, Conn.: Yale University Press, 1989.

Henry Moore

Castleford, England 1898–1986 Perry Green, Much Hadham, England

Working Model for Time-Life Screen, 1952–53

Bronze

14⅞ × 39⅛ × 3 in. (37.8 × 99.4 × 7.6 cm)

Not signed or dated

Purchased from the artist

1953:114

Reproduced by permission of the Henry Moore Foundation

Working Model for Time-Life Screen is a model for Henry Moore's large-scale screen on the Time-Life Building on New Bond Street in London, which was completed in June 1953. The commission came to Moore late in the selection process. After models from four other sculptors were rejected, Barbara Hepworth was asked to work on the project. She responded eagerly to the idea but suddenly withdrew when, it has been suggested, she discovered that Ben Nicholson, from whom she was recently divorced, was working on the murals in the building. Moore, who was already doing a draped reclining female figure for the terrace where the screen would be placed, was then approached and enthusiastically accepted the challenge. Within months he presented four working models to the committee. The Smith sculpture, the last and most resolved of the four, was chosen to be translated into the large Portland stone screen, with some further changes.

Moore's enthusiasm about the project grew from his belief that sculpture and architecture enhance each other:

I think architecture is the poorer for the absence of sculpture and I also think that the sculptor, by not collaborating with the architect misses opportunities of his work being used socially and being seen by a wider public. And it was [the] feeling that the time is coming for architects and sculptors to work together again that brought me to do the double commission for the Time Life building in [New] Bond Street.

The architect, Michael Rosenauer, designed the six-story building with a drop-off to a lower floor on one side to accommodate a screened-off terrace. The screen could have been simply architectural, but, in an act of farsightedness and courage, Rosenauer decided to adorn the International Style structure with a sculpted screen. The horizontal rectilinearity of Moore's screen continues the horizontal bands on the building that visually define the floors. Its division into four panels echoes the cadence of the fenestration. The sculptures within each opening are both organic and abstract. The cartoonist Francis Brennan recalls watching the evolution of the concept:

As we talked Moore pulled down a battered old shoe-box from a shelf. It was brim filled with old bones and weather-worn stones of wondrous shapes and sizes. Picking through them, he'd choose one, hold it up and turn it around in the light, much as a jeweller might show a gemstone. Finally he had a collection of a dozen or so laid out on his drawing board. I began to see his idea for the screen—a quartet of icon-like images, mysteriously ancient in feeling, yet unmistakably modern in execution.

Each of the four sculptures is finished front and back, but their placement within the framed openings limits their functioning in the round. Moore wanted each sculpture to be rotated on its axis at intervals—he suggested once a month or seasonally. He felt this would make the sculptures more interactive with the public, since they would physically hover over the space below, "like some of those half animals that look as if they are escaping through the walls in Romanesque architecture." Due to the heaviness of each piece and the possibility of a mishap, the idea proved unworkable.

The terrace space and the street relate through the perforations in the sculptures themselves and the zones between each frame and sculpture. It is here that the relationship between sculpture and architecture is most fully explored. Each opening is irregularly shaped in response to the format of the sculpture, even as the sculptures in their arrangement respond to the demands of the architecture. The rich promise of collaboration between architecture and sculpture, rarely met in this century, is fulfilled here.

Further Reading

Henry Moore: The Human Dimension. London: HMF Enterprises for the Henry Moore Foundation in association with the British Council, 1991.

McCaughey, Patrick. *Henry Moore and the Heroic: A Centenary Tribute.* New Haven, Conn.: Yale Center for British Art, 1999.

Moore, Henry. *Henry Moore on Sculpture: A Collection of the Sculptor's Writings and Spoken Words.* Edited with an introduction by Philip James. New York. Viking Press, 1971.

89

Berthe Morisot

Bourges, Cher, France 1841–1895 Paris, France

The Mozart Sonata, 1894

Oil on canvas
18⅛ × 21¹⁵⁄₁₆ in. (46 × 55.7 cm)
Sale stamp in blue paint, lower right: Berthe Morisot [Lugt 1826]
Bequest of Mrs. Robert S. Tangeman (E. Clementine Miller, class of 1927)
1996:24-2

Berthe Morisot's upper-middle-class parents considered art a civilizing component of her upbringing from an early age. From her early teacher, Camille Corot, she absorbed the feathery, flickering stroke of his late, lyrical style and his love of nature. She exhibited with some success in the Salon from the mid-1860s into the early 1870s and became a friend of Henri Fantin-Latour and Edouard Manet. Manet painted her handsome dark features many times. In 1874 Morisot married his brother Eugène, who would be a devoted husband, supportive of her artistic activities.

That year Morisot exhibited nine paintings in the first impressionist exhibition, alongside works by Edgar Degas, Pierre-Auguste Renoir, Claude Monet, Camille Pissarro, and Paul Cézanne, among others. Thereafter she abandoned the Salon and took part in all but one of the impressionist shows. She was vilified alongside her male colleagues in Louis Leroy's now famous satirical review of the first impressionist exhibition:

Now take Mlle Morisot! That young lady is not interested in reproducing trifling details. When she has a hand to paint, she makes exactly as many brushstrokes as there are fingers and the business is done. Stupid people who are finicky about the drawing of a hand don't understand a thing about impressionism.

Too often those sympathetic to Impressionism have misunderstood her role in it, and only recently has a more balanced account of her achievement emerged. Neither her historic marginalization by scholars nor the image of her as an intuitive feminine painter naturally suited to the surface superficiality of Impressionism does justice to her important contribution to the movement. For Morisot, the élan of her painterly gesture was hard-won.

Morisot did not exhibit with the impressionists in 1879 because she was recuperating after the birth of her daughter, Julie, in 1878. This was a transforming event that provided one of her main motifs. She documented every phase of Julie's life in her paintings, drawings, and prints, her daughter's growth paralleling her own development as an artist. A shift in her art in the 1890s corresponds to a different artistic climate enunciated by the symbolists, whose main literary force, the poet Stéphane Mallarmé, was one of Morisot's closest friends. Her portraits of Julie from the 1890s are psychologically more probing—pensive, introspective, and sensual. This shift parallels Julie's maturity into young womanhood—a process Morisot explored with fascination and generosity.

The Mozart Sonata, painted a year before Morisot's untimely death in 1895, is a brilliant example of her late work. The calligraphic, airy strokes of her earlier paintings have become thicker, restless gestures densely covering the surface. The impressionist premise of the work is defined by the brilliant light piercing the window at center background. It illuminates the room and announces the proximity of the outdoors, yet it suggests more than defines. The light negates our view through the window and subsumes the forms within. Julie, playing the violin, and her cousin Jeannie Gobillard at the piano are defined by curving strokes that function as a metaphor for the music they play. Their faces and hands have blurred in the sunlight, and their bodies have become dramatic silhouettes. The violin seems to succumb to the force of light, losing its materiality at the point where Julie's bowless right hand comes close to the strings. Mallarmé's proposition, that the essence of a work lies in that which is not expressed, seems to emerge out of this impressionist context.

During the early 1890s Morisot painted a number of portraits of Julie playing the violin. The fact that she could paint as her daughter played, thus documenting their common creative experience, was a source of immense satisfaction for the artist.

Further Reading

Adler, Kathleen, and Tamar Garb. *Berthe Morisot.* Ithaca, N.Y.: Cornell University Press, 1987.

Higonnet, Anne. *Berthe Morisot's Images of Women.* Cambridge, Mass.: Harvard University Press, 1992.

Shennan, Margaret. *Berthe Morisot: The First Lady of Impressionism.* Thrupp, Stroud, Gloucestershire: Sutton Pub., 1996.

Ben Nicholson

Denham, Buckinghamshire, England 1894–1982 London, England

Still Life (West Penwith), 1949

Oil and graphite on canvas
47 × 71¾ in. (119.4 × 182.2 cm)
Signed, dated, and titled in pencil on back, upper left: Ben/
Nicholson/Octo 30/-49/Still/life/(West Penwith)
Purchased, Eleanor Lamont Cunningham, class of 1932, Fund
1955:15
© 2000 Artists Rights Society (ARS), New York/DACS, London

Ben Nicholson was a cultivated artist whose nuanced style belies the expansiveness of his vision and his passionate pursuit of it. His father, Sir William Nicholson (1872–1949), a prominent artist, was a powerful early influence. Nicholson recalled:

I owe a lot to my father, especially to his poetic idea and to his still-life theme . . . not only from what he made as a painter, but from the very beautiful striped and spotted jugs, mugs and goblets, and the octagonal and hexagonal glass objects he collected. Having these things in the house was an unforgettable early experience.

Nicholson's formal training was limited to a few terms at the Slade School of Art during 1910–11. His real education came from his artistic heritage and from his thoughtful, considered analysis of pictorial problems. In that he was aided by his interaction with fellow artists in England, especially the sculptor Barbara Hepworth, who became his second wife and encouraged him to explore nonfigurative work. Visiting the Continent with Hepworth in the early 1930s, he met many artists who came to maturity after World War I, among them Constantin Brancusi, Joan Miró, Jean Arp, and Piet Mondrian. From the mid-1920s Nicholson began to incorporate the principles of Cubism, which would become the most comprehensive and sustaining influence on his work. He especially responded to the still lifes of Georges Braque and Pablo Picasso from the 1920s. One need only compare Still Life (West Penwith) with Picasso's Table, Guitar, and Bottle of 1919 (pp. 96–97) to see the affinity of their pictorial idiom.

The lucidity of this canvas, discreet and unobtrusive despite its large size, belies its complexity. The subtly modulated, thinly applied colors become a perfect receptacle for the elegant calligraphy of drawn shapes. They are either abstract or suggest outlines, mostly partial, of tabletop objects like pitchers, goblets, glasses, and cups. The vessels, stripped of their materiality, integrate seamlessly with the abstract shapes into the larger formal ensemble, which is enframed by a light brown border. The adumbrated passages are toned from light gray to black and are mostly done in graphite. They help define shapes or create independent ones and facilitate the interplay of the thin planar membranes within the shallow space. Their arrangement across the surface of the painting enlivens the composition and creates its own rhythm.

Nicholson defines reality variously. The still life is painted in front of a window in West Penwith, Cornwall, where he and Hepworth moved in 1939. The abstract rectilinear shapes of gray-blue and light blue at upper middle allude to ocean and sky. This poetic evocation of reality is every bit as compelling to him as an outline of a pitcher. In 1921 he recalled viewing an abstracted cubist painting by Picasso from 1915: "And in the center there was an absolutely miraculous green—very deep, very potent and absolutely real . . . it still remains a standard by which I judge any reality in my own work."

When Nicholson was starting his artistic career, his mother, herself a painter whose advice he valued, introduced him to a ritual of scrubbing a table surface clean. This simple act resonated with him both as a tactile, physical act and as an idea of a clean slate. There is something of a scrubbed quality to the thinly painted surface of Still Life (West Penwith). The tabletop on which he posits the various forms and the surface of the painting are an integrated whole. Through his eloquent visual language he transforms and positions the image at a unique intersection of realities, through which he explores the expansive interaction of art and nature.

Further Reading

Lewison, Jeremy. Ben Nicholson. London: Tate Gallery, 1993.
Lynton, Norbert. Ben Nicholson. London: Phaidon Press, 1993.

Pablo Picasso

Málaga, Spain 1881–1973 Mougins, France

Figures by the Sea (Les Misérables au bord de la mer), 1903

Oil on canvas
23½ × 19½ in. (59.7 × 49.5 cm)
Signed in black paint, upper right: Picasso
Gift of Jere Abbott
1965:33
© 2000 Estate of Pablo Picasso/Artists Rights Society (ARS), New York

In the winter of 1901 a blue veil enveloped Picasso's art. The varied themes and eclectic styles of his formative years gave way to a sustained investigation of the dispossessed, the poor, the disadvantaged. Rendered in blue tonality, this body of work from Picasso's Blue Period has a searing poignancy: Lone figures or small groups are isolated against a stark setting, collapsed onto themselves in their misery.

Picasso's decision to explore these themes comprehensively goes to the core of his own vulnerable state and to his overarching ambition as an artist. When he returned to Barcelona from Paris in 1902, he was poor and little known—still some years removed from becoming Paris's leading light. Themes focusing on human misery would seem a natural outgrowth of his state of mind.

In his Blue Period works, Picasso for the first time established a powerful link between the condition of his life and his need to express it through his art. This equation would become a hallmark by which he defined his persona. In putting his own imprimatur on the universal theme of poverty and despair, he established a dialogue with a rich artistic tradition. In 1901 he had seen a retrospective exhibition of the works of Honoré Daumier, whose transient saltimbanque families, moving like apparitions through the streets of Paris, had a great impact on him. In his native Spain a fellow artist, Isidro Nonell y Monturiol, depicted the poor in a manner similar to Picasso's. El Greco's work exposed Picasso to imagery of gaunt, elongated saints that he would apply to his downtrodden. Symbolists in France and the north—England and Norway, among other countries—dealt with similar themes. Picasso's favorite café, El Quatre Gats, the meeting place for all that was stimulating in Barcelona, was referred to as "a Gothic tavern for those in love with the North."

Figures by the Sea (Les Misérables au bord de la mer) depicts a man and woman walking in unison like Adam and Eve after the Fall—their silhouettes joined in misery that each suffers separately. The man extends his arm to a boy in front of him, who reciprocates the gesture of tender union and vulnerability. The man, with a stiff gait, head tilted upward, tethered to the boy, has been described as blind, a type Picasso employed often during the Blue Period. The woman, huddled in a red shawl, holds an infant subsumed in her gaunt silhouette. Her head covering creates a deep shadow around her face, whose lit profile is like a sad quarter moon. A swirling calligraphic stroke animates the bodies, adding expressive intensity to the tragic scene. The Rothko-like bands of sky, sea, and land serve as the backdrop, underscoring the barrenness of the figures' existence.

The theme of humanity at water's edge as an expression of despair can be traced back to Caspar David Friedrich's Monk by the Sea of 1809–10 (Schloss Charlottenburg, Berlin). In this German romantic painting an isolated figure on a barren shore defines for one of the first times the issue of existential aloneness. Picasso assimilated this central theme through the works of Edvard Munch, whose protagonists, often rendered at water's edge, are directly related to Friedrich's. Yet the most compelling prototype for Picasso's work is Pierre Puvis de Chavannes's Poor Fisherman of 1881 (Musée d'Orsay, Paris), in which the despairing family of the fisherman, his daughter and an infant, confront their dilemma in a stark setting of water, land, and sky. In Puvis's poignant, powerful work Picasso found a resonant voice in articulating the universal issues of poverty and deprivation.

Further Reading

Daix, Pierre, and Georges Boudaille. *Picasso: The Blue and Rose Periods, a Catalogue Raisonné of the Paintings, 1900–1906*. Translated by Phoebe Pool. Greenwich, Conn.: New York Graphic Society, 1967.

McCully, Marilyn, ed. *Picasso: The Early Years, 1892–1906*. Washington, D.C.: National Gallery of Art, 1997.

Palau i Fabre, Josep. *Picasso, the Early Years, 1881–1907*. New York: Rizzoli, 1981.

Pablo Picasso

Málaga, Spain 1881–1973 Mougins, France

Table, Guitar, and Bottle (La Table), 1919

Oil on canvas
50 × 29½ in. (127 × 74.9 cm)
Signed in black paint, lower right: *Picasso*
Purchased, Sarah J. Mather Fund
1932:15
© 2000 Estate of Pablo Picasso/Artists Rights Society (ARS), New York

Table, Guitar, and Bottle is among Picasso's most abstract cubist works. Because Picasso's art is wedded to objective reality, the term *abstract* is not, strictly speaking, applicable here. A series of objects—table, guitar, and bottle—are embedded in the complex maze of shapes and colors, yielding their identities grudgingly.

Between 1908 and 1911 Picasso and Georges Braque developed a radically new artistic style that came to be known as Analytical Cubism, in which forms were broken into transparent, interpenetrating facets that dissolved into space. This painting belongs to the subsequent phase known as Synthetic Cubism. Synthetic cubist paintings and collages, dating from 1912 onward, were more colorful, exuberant, even witty, with facets that were larger, flatter, opaque, and interlocking. In the case of collages, varied materials added textural and iconographic interest. Rather than analyzing objects, Picasso was now inventing them. By 1918 a new movement, Purism, predicated on the clarity and precision of the machine aesthetic, began to challenge Cubism. It was at variance with the studio and café subject matter of Cubism and with its formal language, which valued suggestiveness over clarity. *Table, Guitar, and Bottle* is the culminating statement in a series of synthetic cubist works structured in a strictly geometric, planar arrangement. Its sustained intensity may be in part Picasso's response to Purism's challenge. Picasso is here insisting on the seriousness of effort inherent in cubist painting.

The large rectilinear shape defined along the left border of the vertical canvas delineates a table. Yet the gentle S-curve at lower left suggests a leg of a pedestal table whose top could be the white rectangle at the upper left. Many of the smaller rectilinear and curvilinear forms are suggestions of the shape of the bottle. The small circle above the center is the round opening of the guitar. Its bottom is the curved, striated shape to its left, and its top is the angled and curved form jutting out at the right. Musical instruments are common in Picasso's cubist works, and this painting is the perfect analogue for music's abstract language.

It is precisely this aspect of the work that speaks most forcefully. Its imagery is secondary to its formal language. In this sense, Picasso here comes closest to the conceptual vocabulary of Analytic Cubism and to abstraction. The painting is predicated on the interactive resonance of its myriad forms. Curving shapes of all sizes and swellings, massed mainly but not only on the left, serve as counterpoints to the triangular shapes dispersed mostly in the center and at right. This contrapuntal activity is absorbed into and leavened by rectilinear forms of all sizes and shapes that layer the composition from top to bottom. They overlap and wedge into one another—a process reinforced by a series of L and T shapes. The result is an extraordinarily balanced and stable composition cadenced by a series of strong vertical lines.

Picasso employs an array of nuanced colors: shades of gray to black, white into ivory, light and dark browns, rusts and olive greens, light blues, beiges, and yellows. Adding texture to the painting are the striated forms. This effect was achieved by applying corrugated board to wet paint, and then painting in the lines. Both the textural and the coloristic arrangements are an integral part of the painting's subtle interplay.

Table, Guitar, and Bottle is an effort of extraordinary visual thinking. It is for Picasso an act of faith. In this large, ambitious work he reiterates in unequivocal terms the viability and validity of the cubist experiment.

Further Reading

Barr, Alfred H., Jr. *Picasso: Fifty Years of His Art*. New York: The Museum of Modern Art, 1946.

Boggs, Jean Sutherland, et al. *Picasso and Things*. Cleveland: Cleveland Museum of Art, 1992.

Cowling, Elizabeth, and John Golding. *Picasso: Sculptor/Painter*. London: Tate Gallery, 1994.

Pablo Picasso

Málaga, Spain 1881–1973 Mougins, France

Seated Nude, 1922

Oil on canvas

25⅝ × 21³⁄₁₆ in. (65.1 × 53.8 cm)

Signed in brown paint, upper left: Picasso

Gift of the Carey Walker Foundation

1993:19

© 2000 Estate of Pablo Picasso/Artists Rights Society (ARS), New York

From the moment Picasso set pencil to paper as a precocious student in the academies of Madrid and Barcelona, he began to explore the classical world through copying casts. Picasso always saw himself as part of the Mediterranean tradition. Throughout his career the imagery of the classical world would inform his art, and its mythology would charge his fantasy and imagination. Classicism became a foundation that gave Picasso license, even courage, to experiment freely. The sustaining rootedness of the classical world permeated all aspects of his artistic inquiry, allowing Jean Cocteau to comment that "Cubism was Classicism." Picasso would return to the classical ideal at different intervals during his career, interpreting it differently each time. This *Seated Nude* belongs to his most heroic classical period of the early 1920s. That this is also the moment of his greatest synthetic cubist works underscores Picasso's capacity to work concurrently in different styles.

Various influences contributed to Picasso's monumental classicism at this time. In 1917 he visited Italy for two months to work on the curtain design for Cocteau's *Parade*, being performed by Serge Diaghilev's Ballets Russes. While there, he viewed major sites in Rome, Florence, Naples, and also Herculaneum and Pompeii, directly absorbing the experience of antiquity. On a personal level, Picasso's classical periods correspond to times of relative tranquility in his life. The birth of his son Paul in 1921 led to such a moment. It inspired the artist to explore the serenity of the mother and child motif. These images also had a more public meaning, addressing the need for regeneration in postwar France. Viewed in this light, Picasso's classicism reflects a palpable longing among the people for peace and stability after the devastating cataclysm of World War I. The

heavy-limbed monumentality of Picasso's figures has antecedents in his own early work and in the imagery of such artists as Paul Gauguin and Aristide Maillol. But on the most profound level, these works are a reaffirmation of his faith in humanity's enduring strength, which the classical tradition has sustained for millennia.

In this context, *Seated Nude* is an intriguing image. Picasso repeats the figure's pose with slight variations in a number of paintings and drawings, as if working out pictorial and thematic ideas toward a final state. The background in *Seated Nude* is rendered summarily, with vertical and horizontal lines suggesting rather than defining space. The figure is modeled with light flesh-toned colors and outlined with a resolute line. The head is carefully constructed and fully resolved, giving the image as a whole a cognitive presence.

That Picasso was searching for a symbolic figure is convincingly argued by Kenneth Silver. In his book *Esprit de Corps*, he concludes that the artist's *Woman in White* of 1923 (The Metropolitan Museum of Art) is his "greatest postwar meditation on the endurance of culture." Picasso's *Seated Nude* approximates closely the physiognomy and the psychological aspect of *Woman in White*. The two establish an interesting parallel with Pierre Puvis de Chavannes's two versions of *Hope*, one nude (Musée d'Orsay, Paris), one in a white dress (The Walters Art Gallery, Baltimore), painted in 1872 as the embodiment of rebirth after the devastation of the Franco-Prussian War. It may be that Picasso, in searching for the archetype to define a pivotal moment in France's history, explored the possibility of a monumental nude to fill that role before deciding on *Woman in White*, and that Smith's *Seated Nude* is the most complete expression of that image.

Further Reading

Cowling, Elizabeth, and Jennifer Mundy. *On Classic Ground: Picasso, Léger, de Chirico, and the New Classicism, 1910–1930.* London: Tate Gallery, 1990.

Silver, Kenneth E. *Esprit de Corps: The Art of the Parisian Avant-Garde and the First World War, 1914–1925.* Princeton, N.J.: Princeton University Press, 1989.

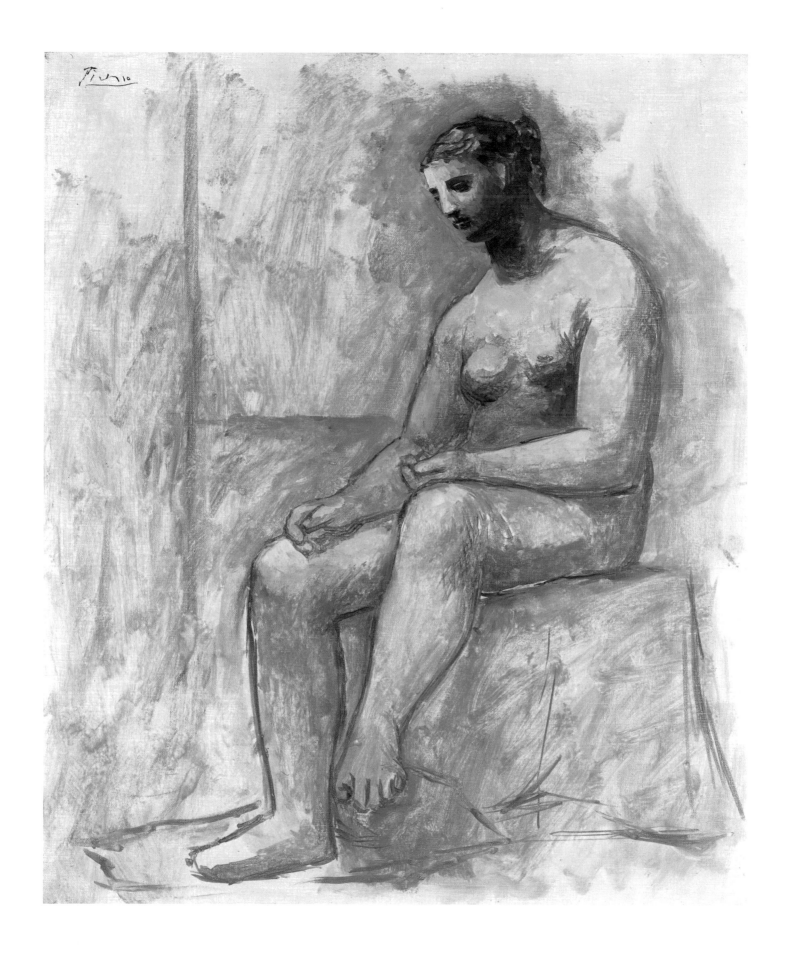

Pierre Puvis de Chavannes

Lyon, France 1824–1898 Paris, France

The Poor Fisherman, c. 1879–81 (possibly 1887)

Oil on canvas
28¾ × 36¼ in. (73 × 92.1 cm)
Not signed or dated
Gift of Mrs. Charles Lincoln Taylor (Margaret Rand Goldthwait, class of 1921) in memory of Dr. Joel E. Goldthwait
1966:10

The Poor Fisherman of 1881 (Musée d'Orsay, Paris) is Puvis's best-known work, rivaled only by his murals of the life of St. Geneviève in the Panthéon in Paris. The large canvas defines his unique artistic vision, which gained him respect from artists representing both the conservative and the avant-garde factions in the French art world of his day. *The Poor Fisherman* has neither the polished finish of an academic work nor the shimmering vibrancy of an impressionist painting. The boat in the foreground is reiterated rather than reflected in the water, whose opaque surface and muted green color are the perfect complement to the isolated pose of the fisherman in establishing the painting's melancholy mood.

Unique, too, is the painting's universalizing theme, differing from the academic hierarchy of subjects and from the impressionists' focus on leisure and nature. The painting has become an important archetype for artists dealing with existential issues of poverty and aloneness. Pablo Picasso's *Figures by the Sea* (pp. 94–95), depicting a poor family at water's edge, is directly related to it. Although the subject of *The Poor Fisherman* is not overtly religious, the fisherman, in his vulnerable pose, has been associated with Christ from the outset. Puvis seems to reinforce this reading by having the sliver of land at the upper left extend across the mast to create a cruciform shape. The pose of the fisherman references numerous examples of the subject in the nineteenth century, including Puvis's own *Ecce Homo* (private collection) of about 1858. Paul Gauguin in *Christ in the Garden of Olives* (Norton Museum of Art, West Palm Beach, Florida) uses the pose of Puvis's fisherman for the prayerful, vulnerable Christ, whom he represents as a self-portrait.

Puvis conceived *The Poor Fisherman* while visiting Honfleur on the northwestern coast of France. Already the fishermen in the coastal towns had been supplanted in importance by vacationing city dwellers, the subjects of numerous impressionist paintings. Puvis tells us that the female figure in the background is the fisherman's daughter and the child's older sister. This fact intensifies the poignancy of the scene and reminds us that the artist had lost his mother in his youth and had been brought up by his older sister.

Smith's painting is a smaller, unfinished version of the original in the Musée d'Orsay. Some scholars have judged Smith's painting to be a contemporary copy, while others have called it a later version, executed by the artist himself. The fact that the painting lacks final definition and is missing the critical detail of the rope connecting the post to the trap would argue for its being by the artist, but set aside before completion. In 1887 *The Poor Fisherman* was selected for the French national collection as representative of Puvis's oeuvre from the collection of Emile Boivin, an astute and important collector. Puvis may have started Smith's painting as a replica to compensate Boivin for his loss. Before completing it, however, he may have decided on a more original variant. Boivin was ultimately presented with a painting of vertical format, in which the child was placed in the boat and the girl was omitted, thus substantively transforming the pictorial and iconographic focus of the original.

Puvis de Chavannes was one of the titans of the art world during his lifetime. In recent decades there has been an extensive reappraisal of his important contributions. In this context, we have gained a deeper appreciation of *The Poor Fisherman* as one of the pivotal canvases of its time.

Further Reading

d'Argencourt, Louise, et al. *Puvis de Chavannes: 1824–1898*. Ottawa: National Gallery of Canada, 1977.

Price, Aimée Brown, et al. *Pierre Puvis de Chavannes*. New York: Rizzoli, 1994.

Wattenmaker, Richard J. *Puvis de Chavannes and the Modern Tradition*. Toronto: Art Gallery of Ontario, 1975.

Odilon Redon

Bordeaux, France 1840–1916 Paris, France

With Closed Eyes (Les Yeux Clos), c. 1895–1905

Oil on canvas

25¾ × 20 in. (65.4 × 50.8 cm)

Signed in red paint, lower right: ODILON/REDON

Gift of Mrs. Charles Inslee (Marguerite Tuthill, class of 1915)

1956:16

Redon's singular vision makes him one of the most distinctive artists of his time. He was of the impressionists' generation, but his art delved into the interior world of dreams rather than celebrating nature's external verities. The search for alternatives to Impressionism began in the 1880s, and by 1890 the symbolist movement, closely aligned to its literary manifestation, coalesced around such artists as Gustave Moreau, Pierre Puvis de Chavannes, and Redon. Of these, Redon belonged to the tradition of artists of fantastic imagery, such as Francisco Goya and Hieronymous Bosch, both of whom he admired.

Moreau's dictum, "I believe only in what I do not see and solely in what I feel," expresses one of Symbolism's key tenets, the primacy of idea over nature. Redon's *Yeux Clos*, depicting a head with closed eyes, would seem to be its visual manifestation. Yet the relationship of art and nature for Redon was more complex. Early in Redon's career, the botanist Armand Clevaud exposed him to all aspects of biological studies including microscopic life. The artist speaks succinctly of his powers of observation and their impact on his art: "After the effort of copying minutely a pebble, a blade of grass, a hand, a face or any other object from the organic or inorganic world, I experience mental elation; I then need to create, to allow myself to move to the representation of the imaginary." The creatures that crawl out of his imagination are that much more compelling because of Redon's deep understanding of nature's processes.

Les Yeux Clos is among Redon's most important images. Conceived in 1889 as a painting, it exists in a number of variants, including a lithograph of 1890. The most resolved and authoritative interpretation is a painting of 1889–90, done soon after the original, which was acquired by the State for the Musée du Luxembourg in 1904 (now Musée d'Orsay, Paris). The work demarcates two distinct, interrelated halves of Redon's oeuvre, being the first significant image in which he introduced color. Previously in his graphic work he had used black and white almost exclusively. Referring to black as "the prince of color," he had extracted from it extraordinarily rich effects in fashioning his world of fantastic images, for example a head depicted as a marsh flower or an eye as a floating balloon.

The head's distinctive features in *Les Yeux Clos* have been related to those of Redon's wife, and the artist himself called it "this androgynous head," alluding to Symbolism's view of androgyny as an ideal human state. In his journal, *A soi-même (To Myself)*, Redon writes of contemplating "the closed eyes of the *Slave*" by Michelangelo in the Louvre. His moving assessment of it could apply to *Les Yeux Clos*: "He sleeps, and the worried dream that crosses the brow of this marble lifts our dreams into a pensive and moving world."

The difference between the earlier versions and the Smith College painting is substantive. In the earlier image Redon uses color tentatively, as he begins to explore its potential, while here he is its master. In the earlier works the locus of the dream is concentrated in the lone head, partly lit but mostly in shadow — an apt metaphor for the introspective state evoked by the closed eyes. In the Smith painting, the head, smaller and less well defined, has been subsumed into a larger ensemble, floating in a sumptuously colored aureole of clouds and flowers. The internalized world behind the closed eyes has been given outward manifestation, and we are witness to a transcendent, otherworldly realm.

Further Reading

Berger, Klaus. *Odilon Redon: Fantasy and Colour.* Translated by Michael Bullock. New York: McGraw-Hill, 1965.

Druick, Douglas W., et al. *Odilon Redon: Prince of Dreams, 1840–1916.* Chicago: The Art Institute of Chicago; Amsterdam: Van Gogh Museum; London: Royal Academy of Arts; New York: Harry N. Abrams, 1994.

Redon, Odilon. *To Myself: Notes on Life, Art, and Artists.* Translated by Mira Jacob and Jeanne L. Wasserman. New York: George Braziller, 1986.

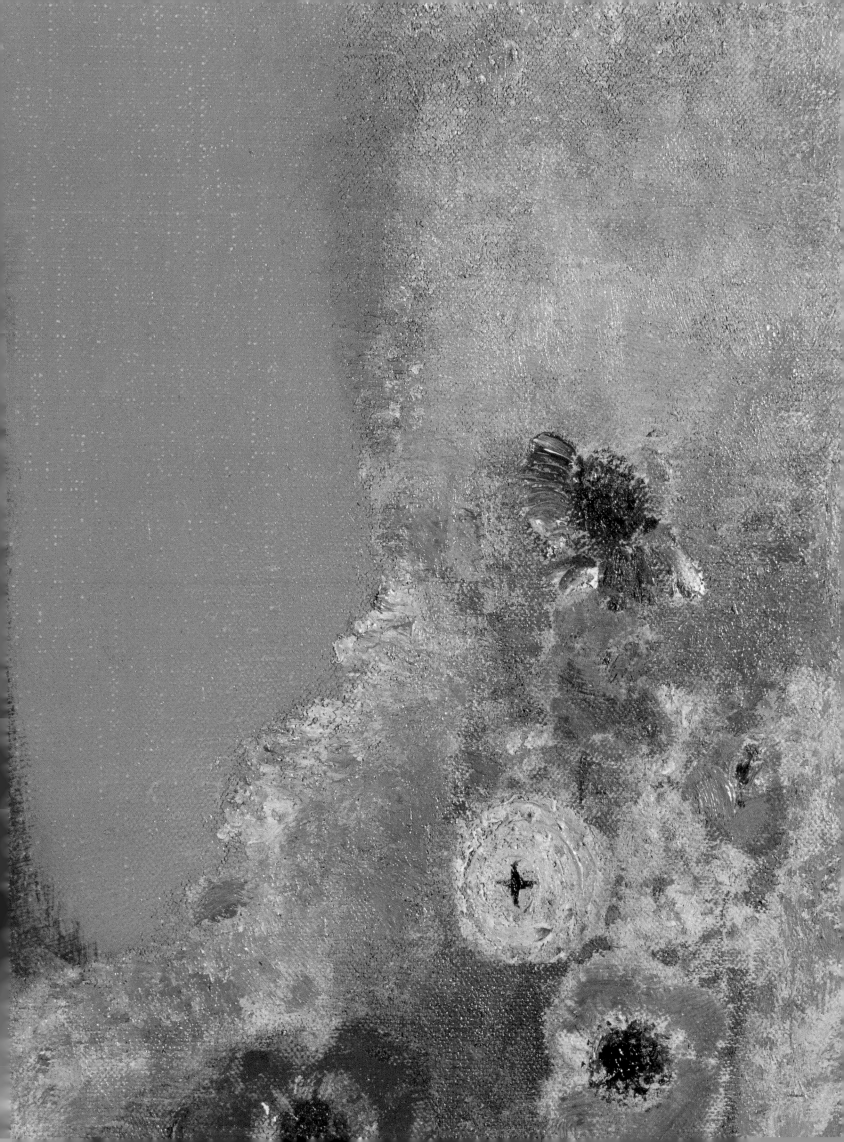

Pierre-Auguste Renoir

Limoges, France 1841–1919 Cagnes-sur-Mer, France

Rapha Maître (Madame Edmond Maître),

c. 1870–71

Oil on canvas
14¾ × 12¾ in. (37.5 × 32.4 cm)
Signed in brown paint, upper left: Renoir
Purchased
1924:16

Renoir's hold on the public imagination as the purveyor of sun-drenched days of leisure — of boating parties, dancing couples, ample nudes at river's edge — is so pervasive that it takes a conscious effort to think of him as a portraitist. Yet his portraits are among his singular achievements. Georges Rivière's comment that "no other artist has looked so deeply into the sitter's soul nor captured its essence with such economy" unnecessarily excludes some artists — Edgar Degas comes to mind — but nonetheless is essentially valid in assessing Renoir's achievements as a portraitist. What Renoir brings to the task is his own generous nature, revealing an artist of deep humanity. Renoir's most penetrating portraits are of people he knew best, so that he could draw on the experience of his interaction with them to forge an image. For example, his portrait of Victor Chocquet (Harvard University Art Museums, Cambridge, Massachusetts), a customs official who on a limited salary helped many young artists by purchasing their works, reveals an individual of uncommon goodness and of disciplined sensibility and refinement.

Rapha Maître of about 1870–71 depicts the lifelong mistress who took the name of her lover, Louis-Edmond Maître, a civil servant devoted to music and art. He was an avid supporter of avant-garde artists, and among his close friends were Frédéric Bazille and Henri Fantin-Latour. Renoir's friendship with Rapha is not well documented, but his three portraits of her, as well as his relationship with the family, are evidence of a close bond. During 1870, just before entering the military, he stayed in their apartment on an irregular basis. An early date of spring of 1870 has plausibly been suggested for the Smith portrait, which was probably painted during one of Renoir's stays with the Maîtres. After having left the military, Renoir painted another portrait of her

(private collection) in April 1871, on which he lavished great attention. In this more formal and expansive work, Rapha is shown in a fashionable floor-length costume, holding a fan and glancing at a birdcage. There is an array of flowers at her feet and a decorative trellis wallpaper as a backdrop. In its opulent display, this second portrait evokes the works of James Tissot and even more those of Alfred Stevens. While it is very much a document of the sitter's station in life, the earlier Smith portrait focuses on her interiority. The fact that the nature of the relationship between sitter and artist is unknown makes the image that much more compelling. The reason for the existence of this work is to record a friendship and to probe its nature.

The large Maître portrait has been interpreted as Renoir's reaffirmation of the joy of painting after the debilitating events of the Commune. It may be that the Smith portrait, painted just months before his conscription into the military, reveals Renoir's desire during those anxious days to record a moment of quiet intimacy with a friend. To achieve this, Renoir renders an image close-up and in a small format. He centers the head so that it becomes the focus of his insight. The white cushion with geometric design behind her head echoes the black, gray, and white checkered costume. Undulating strokes of brown and ocher in the upper background reiterate the sweeping energy of the loosely painted jet black hair. The tilted, frontal head is modeled with a physicality reminiscent of portraits by Gustave Courbet. Rapha looks back with eyes that are reflective and engaged — probing the artist as he investigates her features and records her insight. The formal decorum of portraiture has been discarded in this image of total involvement and unself-consciousness.

Further Reading

Adriani, Götz. *Renoir*. Cologne: DuMont; New Haven, Conn.: Yale University Press, 1999.

Bailey, Colin B., et al. *Renoir's Portraits: Impressions of an Age*. New Haven, Conn.: Yale University Press; Ottawa: National Gallery of Canada, 1997.

Rouart, Denis. *Renoir*. Translated by James Emmons. New York: Skira/Rizzoli, 1985.

107

Joshua Reynolds

Plympton, Devon, England 1723–1792 London, England

Mrs. Nesbitt as Circe, 1781

Oil on canvas
49¼ × 39½ in. (125.1 × 100.3 cm)
Not signed or dated
Gift of Dwight W. Morrow, Jr., Anne Morrow Lindbergh,
class of 1928, and Constance Morrow Morgan, class of 1935
1958:4

Sir Joshua Reynolds, one of England's preeminent artists of the eighteenth century, was determined to elevate English art to the level of art on the Continent. This goal motivated his artistic vision, defined in his famous "Discourses on Art" delivered at the Royal Academy between 1769 and 1790. He believed that art was not mimesis but an expressive force filtered through the intellect, that art should strive for the universal rather than the particular, that history painting is the highest category of art, and, above all, that artists should learn by emulating masters of the past. His role as the first president of the Royal Academy provided him the opportunity to create a climate in England receptive to his ideas and ambition. Reynolds's artistic reputation depends largely on his portraits. These exhibit a breadth of expression and interpretation often based on earlier artists such as Rembrandt van Rijn and Anthony van Dyck; Van Dyck's elegant portraits were especially popular during the second half of the eighteenth century. In 1781, the year Reynolds painted *Mrs. Nesbitt as Circe*, he traveled to Flanders to study the great seventeenth-century masters, especially Peter Paul Rubens and van Dyck.

In *Mrs. Nesbitt as Circe*, Reynolds confronts a fascinating sitter. Her mysterious early years, filled with rumors of an immoral past, would remain part of her allure. She became the mistress of Augustus John Harvey, third earl of Bristol, who was a confidant of George III. Harvey died in 1779, leaving her most of his estate, including a house in Norwood. Her proximity to the monarchy would engage her in affairs of state as a secret agent for the government during the momentous upheavals in Europe. She brought to the task well-honed attributes—especially her facility with men and languages.

Reynolds depicts Mrs. Nesbitt as Circe, daughter of the sun god Helios, who dwelt on the island of Aeaea to which she enticed men with wine and other delights, then turned them into docile animals by the touch of her wand. Reynolds made famous this type of portrait, in which the sitter is imbued with historical, mythological, or allegorical attributes. In this way he elevated portraiture, which was much in demand, close to the level of history painting, for which commissions were fewer. Here he depicts Lady Nesbitt seated in natural surroundings with a dominant tree behind her—a ubiquitous prop in eighteenth-century English portraits. Her simple white dress evokes classicizing drapery and underscores her pale features. Her carefully rendered face, beautiful and intelligent, glances out alertly at the viewer. Her pose and the animals around her define her powers and domain. In the right hand she holds her wand, and her left hand rests near the gilded goblet used for libations for her guests. As she crosses her left leg, she makes explicit the distinction between her space and ours.

The domesticated white cat, its paws in its mistress's lap, is further identified with her because it echoes her dress in color. The monkey, which in the eighteenth century was often associated with licentious behavior, may refer to her allegedly scandalous past. Like Circe on her isle, Mrs. Nesbitt presided over her estate at Norwood, where she charmed and impressed prominent men including the king. The tame leopard at the lower left may refer to this special company of powerful men, over whom she was able to manifest her will. In this extraordinarily erudite and refined portrait, Reynolds achieves his ambition of elevating English art to international stature.

Further Reading

Pointon, Marcia. *Hanging the Head: Portraiture and Social Formation in Eighteenth-Century England.* New Haven, Conn.: Yale University Press, 1993.

Wendorf, Richard. *Sir Joshua Reynolds: The Painter in Society.* Cambridge, Mass.: Harvard University Press, 1996.

Hubert Robert

Paris, France 1733–1808 Paris, France

Pyramids, c. 1760

Oil on panel
24 × 28½ in. (61 × 72.4 cm)
Not signed or dated
Purchased
1950:15

Hubert Robert's reputation rests on his inventive translation of Roman architectural ruins. He began his training in Paris under the sculptor René-Michel (Michel-Ange) Slodtz. He arrived in Rome in 1754 in the entourage of the French ambassador to the Holy See, comte de Stainville. During the next eleven years in Italy, Robert became one of the most popular and accomplished interpreters of Roman architecture. His love of Roman ruins was strongly influenced by Giovanni Paolo Pannini, his teacher and friend, and by Giovanni Battista Piranesi, also a friend. In different ways, these three artists reclaimed for the generation of the Enlightenment the glory of antique architecture.

A number of tendencies intersect in Robert's art. The whimsy and charm of the landscape environs in which he places architectural ruins display a rococo sensibility. His rich and supple handling of surfaces comes close to Fragonard, whom he met in Rome. In his commitment to antiquity he shares a philosophical link with Neoclassicism. And in his dramatic rendering of scenes, touching on the sublime, he is a precursor to Romanticism.

In *Pyramids* of about 1760, Robert transports the viewer through time and space to the Egypt of the pharaohs. A massive partial pyramid, dominated by a diagonal, anchors the scene. The small size of a second pyramid at lower right implies a vast open space between the two structures. At the extreme right stand two obelisks, grand in scale in proportion to the people below but, like all else in the painting, insignificant next to the pyramid. We are convinced, as every eighteenth-century viewer of the painting must have been, that we are in the presence of one of the wonders of the world — permanent, timeless, compelling in the clarity of its idea and purity of its geometry.

Such is Robert's interpretive power that it comes as a surprise to discover that the pyramid in the painting is based on the pyramid of Caius Cestius located outside Rome, which is much smaller and steeper than the pyramids at Giza. In effectively transforming the setting and scale of the Caius Cestius pyramid, Robert retained one important element of that structure, namely its steep angle, which adds significantly to the sense of soaring height.

Other inventive interpretations add to the painting's dramatic effect. The arched openings at the base of the pyramid absorb the diminutive figures in an awesome processional ritual. The clouds, rare in Egypt's dry climate, are more common to Rome's environs, where the motif was conceived. They move across the upper part of the pyramid, emphasizing the immense size of the structure. Only careful scrutiny of the work yields a patch of blue at upper left, indicating the pyramid's downward slope. In focusing on the pyramid and arch, Robert isolates two perfectible forms that feature in contemporary utopian renderings by architects such as Etienne-Louis Boulée and Claude-Nicolas Ledoux.

Ancient Egyptian culture exercised a sustained hold on Robert's imagination from the outset. Public interest in Egyptian motifs intensified greatly toward the end of the eighteenth century as a result of Napoleon's campaign in Egypt. Nearly forty years after executing Smith's canvas, Robert painted *Young Girls Dancing around an Obelisk* (Museum of Fine Arts, Montréal). His investigation and inventive adaptation of Egyptian art, predicated on works brought to Rome from Egypt by ancient Romans, yielded some of his most visionary and compelling images.

Further Reading

Hubert Robert: The Pleasure of Ruins. New York: Wildenstein, 1988.

Radisich, Paula Rea. *Hubert Robert: Painted Spaces of the Enlightenment.* Cambridge: Cambridge University Press, 1998.

French Painting, 1774–1830: The Age of Revolution. Detroit: The Detroit Institute of Arts; New York: The Metropolitan Museum of Art, 1975.

Auguste Rodin

Paris, France 1840–1917 Meudon, France

Man with the Broken Nose, modeled 1863–64; this cast c. 1900

Bronze

12 × 7½ × 6¾ in. (30.5 × 19 × 17.1 cm)

Signature incised at neck termination, proper right: A. Rodin

Stamped inside, in relief, proper left: A. Rodin

Purchased

1963:57

Man with the Broken Nose, one of Rodin's best-known works, was indispensable for the artist's development. Executed in 1863–64, it was among his earliest images. He considered it "the first good piece of modeling I ever did," and the work became his talisman: "I have kept that mask before my mind in everything I have done," he later said.

The reference to it as a mask is telling. The original clay head on which the artist had worked for over a year cracked during extremely cold weather in Rodin's drafty studio, leaving the interior exposed as in a mask. Rodin decided to turn accident into invention. Realizing its expressive potential in its new format, he presented the work to the Salon of 1865, only to be rejected. Despite this setback, Rodin's tendency to take advantage of unforeseen circumstances to explore new creative possibilities would become a hallmark of his artistic process.

The model for the original was a local worker named Bibi who, according to Rodin, had "a fine head . . . no matter if it was brutalized." The broken nose, its most vulnerable feature, introduces the head's other plastic features: the deeply furrowed forehead and blank eyes give the face special poignancy. In the process of manipulating clay to give form to his insights, Rodin understood art's expressive potential. Through a sustained expenditure of effort over a long period, he produced a highly orchestrated image in which each aspect has been worked through for maximum effect. Even the psychological impact of the forward tilt of the head has been considered. The malleable clay, which defines the sitter's features with such intensity, would be handled with greater flexibility and freedom in his maturity. The looser, more abstract surfaces of his later works become expressive passages in themselves and thus help interpret rather than define the image.

Rodin's transcendent realism in *Man with the Broken Nose* imbues the head with noble dignity that reflects his early concentrated study of ancient sculpture in the Louvre. The restrained emotional resonance of the features and the frankness of their interpretation evoke traits in Hellenistic portraiture. Part of a ribbon or fillet can be seen running across the top of the head, an adornment common on classical sculptures. Rodin reworked the sculpture in a plaster in 1872, which was then translated into marble in 1875. He depicted this version as a bust with upper torso and shoulders, much like an antique philosopher portrait, and it was given the title *Portrait of M. B. . . .* (marble, Musée Rodin, Paris). A portrait of Crysippus in the Louvre has been suggested as a possible source. Because of the evident quotation from the antique, the marble was readily accepted for the Salon of 1875.

Due to its popularity, many casts were made of *Man with the Broken Nose*. Smith's cast is said to have been acquired from Rodin by Mrs. Emil Hesslein, sister of the prominent English artist William Rothenstein. The most recent scholarship suggests a date around the turn of the century. Among its distinguishing characteristics is a bit of hair loss at the left center of the forehead, resulting from a casting flaw.

A youthful work transforms many artists' careers. But it is much rarer to come across an early work like *Man with the Broken Nose*, which in its artistic integrity, humanity, and inventiveness establishes itself as a masterpiece and cogently defines the critical issues for the artist's future development.

Further Reading

Elsen, Albert E., ed. *Rodin Rediscovered*. Washington, D.C.: National Gallery of Art, 1981.

Wasserman, Jeanne, ed. *Metamorphoses in Nineteenth-Century Sculpture*. Cambridge, Mass.: Fogg Art Museum, Harvard University, 1975.

Auguste Rodin

Paris, France 1840–1917 Meudon, France

The Walking Man, modeled 1877–78; this cast 1965

Bronze

7½ × 2½ × 5¼ ft. (228.6 × 76.2 × 160 cm)

Signature incised in base: A. Rodin; incised at rear of base:
© by Musée Rodin. 1965; incised at proper right side of base:
Georges Rudier./.Fondeur. Paris.

Purchased

1965:30

The evolution of *The Walking Man* to this monumental scale is an intriguing process that began with a scandal. When in 1877 Rodin exhibited his first freestanding male nude, *Age of Bronze* (The Metropolitan Museum of Art), the realism of the image was so compelling that he was accused of having cast it from life. To answer his critics, he created *St. John the Baptist* in 1878 (Musée Rodin, Paris). The passive, introspective pose of *Age of Bronze* was replaced by a striding figure of such dynamic force, nervous energy, and purpose that it was impossible to accuse the artist of casting it from life. Related to *St. John the Baptist* is a freely executed, vigorous image, *Torso* (Petit Palais, Paris). Balanced on the right leg cut off at the knee, with its other extremities missing, *Torso* is, as well, the starting point for *The Walking Man.*

The heroic demeanor of *Torso* has been compared with fragmented antique torsos and to terra-cotta torsos attributed to Michelangelo, whose influence on Rodin was profound. *Torso*'s violated features also echo imagery from Francisco Goya's *Disasters of War* etchings of 1820–23. In one of these, *Great Deeds against the Dead,* a body without head and arms, bearing an affinity to *Torso,* hangs upside down from a tree branch.

Considering that *St. John the Baptist* became one of Rodin's most popular sculptures, his decision to explore the theme further and in a more radical context is indicative of the constancy and intensity of his search for new expression. *The Walking Man* is more than an amalgam of *Torso* and the powerful striding legs taken from *St. John the Baptist.* As it evolved into the new, highly charged entity, it clearly became more than the sum of its parts.

Judith Cladel, Rodin's companion and confidante, proposed that the torso and legs of *The Walking Man* were brought together only in 1900, a suggestion rein-forced in Ruth Butler's authoritative biography, in which she related the assembling of fragments of sculptures, including the torso and legs, to Rodin's exhibition of 165 works at the 1900 Exposition Universelle.

The gait of *St. John the Baptist,* which has the right shoulder and leg moving forward in unison, is explained by the forward thrust of the saint's gesticulating arm. In the armless *Walking Man,* this unique alignment of leg and shoulder acquires an elemental force that thrusts the figure forward. The torso's bruised passages not only relate to missing appendages but also exist as independent expressive pockets, as for example the gouge on the right side of the back. The legs, pillars of rippling energy, are more finished than the torso. To capture the heroic essence of movement rather than its fleeting actuality, Rodin rivets both feet to the uneven base, which in its sweep helps to propel the back leg forward. By elongating the rear leg he captures the stride at the nascent moment when weight shifts from the back to the front leg. In ignoring anatomical correctness for expressive results, he invokes Masaccio's Adam in the *Expulsion* fresco in the Brancacci Chapel (c. 1427, Santa Maria del Carmine, Florence).

The Walking Man has become one of Rodin's most resonant images, supplanting *St. John the Baptist* as the incarnation of a striding figure. It avoids the symbolic, religious, or historical context that characterizes much nineteenth-century sculpture and thus attains universality. Its radical presentation startles the viewer, posing more questions than it answers. In this sense it is a resoundingly modern work. It at once addresses our fears and our hopes. Its arch dichotomy between torso and legs is resolved in the act of walking. It is a manifestation of indomitable spirit, even as it documents life's vicissitudes.

Further Reading

Butler, Ruth. *Rodin: The Shape of Genius.* New Haven, Conn.: Yale University Press, 1993.

Elsen, Albert. *Rodin.* New York: The Museum of Modern Art, 1963.

Tancock, John L. *The Sculpture of Auguste Rodin: The Collection of the Rodin Museum, Philadelphia.* Boston: David R. Godine; Philadelphia: Philadelphia Museum of Art, 1976.

115

Théodore Rousseau

Paris, France 1812–1867 Barbizon, France

The Bridge at Moret, c. 1828–29

Oil on canvas
10½ × 13¼ in. (26.7 × 33.7 cm)
Stamped in brown paint, lower left: TH.R [Lugt 2436]
Purchased
1957:32

When Rousseau painted *The Bridge at Moret* in 1828–29, he was a sixteen year old on the threshold of an important career as one of France's major landscapists and the leader of the Barbizon school.

French art of the 1820s was dominated by the emergence of Jean-Auguste-Dominique Ingres and Eugène Delacroix. For them, landscape was a component of a larger drama — be it the background of an Ingres portrait or a setting for one of Delacroix's literary or historical paintings. In England, meanwhile, J. M. W. Turner, John Constable, and Richard Parkes Bonington established the primacy of landscape.

The influence of Bonington and Constable was especially significant in France, which was in the process of developing its own landscape tradition during the 1820s. A special category for historical landscape had already been established for the Prix de Rome in 1817, and Achille-Etna Michallon, the mentor of the young Camille Corot, was its first winner. Rousseau and Corot became the preeminent landscapists of their generation. During the 1820s they were already following similar paths. Each painted in the Fontainebleau forest — Corot earlier in the decade, Rousseau toward the end — long before it became the favorite haunt for the Barbizon artists. Both also visited Moret-sur-Loing, a few miles southeast of Fontainebleau, and painted its medieval bridge. By the 1840s they had become close friends.

Rousseau's *Bridge at Moret* is at once formal and picturesque. Slivers of land at the left and right foreground introduce the motif and distance us from it. The bridge's three arches move across the middle of the composition in a paced cadence. The outer interior walls of the left and right arches are rendered as wider than the inner ones, thus positioning the viewer directly on line with the center of the middle arch. This specificity of vantage point and the reflection of the arches in the still water add formal clarity to the work. Corot's freely sketched *Bridge at Moret* of 1822 (private collection) depicts a close-up view of one of the bridge's supporting posts, surrounded by lively water energized by a waterfall. Its palpable immediacy and freshness contrast with Rousseau's measured, comprehensive view of the town's distinctive features, to which land, water, and sky serve as complements.

The picturesque cluster of structures at the right creates a visually alluring passage. The various buildings begin at water's edge, where the top floor of the house overhangs the river in deference to its potential for flooding. The wooden buttresses propping up the house enunciate a series of repetitive rhythmic patterns throughout the work. Above and beyond the house are more substantive buildings, including the tower announcing the bridge, behind it a compact Romanesque chapel, and in the middle of the bridge a millhouse. Passages like the flickering of light across the stone wall atop the bridge, the wedge stones of the bridge's arches, and the subdivision of the house's windows at the right into discrete panes all add visual vibrancy to the painting.

Rousseau's capacity to hold the energy of the smaller details in complementary balance with the dynamic of larger passages proved to be one of his great strengths as an artist. This vivid, richly painted landscape underscores his ability to orchestrate elements of nature and man-made structures into a compelling and appealing whole. In *The Bridge at Moret*, Rousseau moves beyond early promise.

Further Reading

Adams, Steven. *The Barbizon School and the Origins of Impressionism*. London: Phaidon Press, 1994.

Green, Nicholas. *Théodore Rousseau, 1812–1867*. Norwich, England: Sainsbury Centre for the Visual Arts, University of East Anglia, 1982.

Herbert, Robert L. *Barbizon Revisited*. New York: Clarke & Way, 1962.

Georges Seurat

Paris, France 1859–1891 Paris, France

Woman with a Monkey (study for *A Sunday Afternoon on the Island of La Grande Jatte)*,

1884

Oil on wood panel

9¾ × 6¼ in. (24.8 × 15.9 cm)

Not signed or dated

Purchased, Tryon Fund

1934:2-1

Woman with a Monkey, a sketch for Seurat's *Sunday Afternoon on the Island of La Grande Jatte* of 1884–86 (The Art Institute of Chicago), helps to elucidate that painting's role as one of the seminal works of nineteenth-century art.

The year 1886 marked the last group exhibition of the impressionists. Tellingly, the most important canvas exhibited was Seurat's masterpiece, which more than any other image defined the direction of art beyond Impressionism. In presenting an alternative to the impressionists' search for nature's fugitive moments, Seurat extracts nature's order, encased in its immutable laws. Through a system of highly regulated and tightly arranged small strokes, the artist explores the laws of color interaction predicated on the earlier investigations of Eugène Delacroix and the researches of Michel-Eugène Chevreul, Charles Henry, and Ogden Rood. Thematically, he evokes such images of leisure as Jean Antoine Watteau's *Pilgrimage to the Isle of Cythera* (1718, Musée du Louvre, Paris). In his search for more permanent and timeless priorities, he turns to early Renaissance art and to the Persian and Egyptian traditions. In establishing a link with a historical period of great innovation, he refers to the classical world of Phidias's Parthenon frieze: "The Panathenaeans of Phidias formed a procession. I want to make modern people, in their essential traits, move about as they do on those friezes." In addressing the moderns, Seurat's modishly dressed two-dimensional figures reference contemporary advertising practices. Thus *A Sunday Afternoon on the Island of La Grande Jatte* is an amalgam of an extraordinary array of disparate impulses, filtered through Seurat's unique vision to create a document both radical and cohesive.

Woman with a Monkey is one of a large group of small oil sketches executed early in the painting's development. In it, the artist introduces a structural order that points to his distinctive transformation of Impressionism, even as the luminous colors of areas of sunlight remind us of Seurat's roots in that movement. He experiments with color interactions, using an intense mixture of light blue and violet-blue that, like a haze, permeates the foreground, the dark areas between trees, their shadows, and every aspect of the woman's clothing including the parasol, thus interacting with every other color in the sketch. The hatched brushstrokes give the work textural unity, and their sustained pattern carries over to the strict organization of the compositional elements. The diminishing scale of tree trunks and horizontal shadows creates a perspectival grid. The vertical pattern of the cluster of trees at the right is reiterated in the woman, whose front becomes the dominant vertical, unifying top and bottom, foreground and near background. Her curved back with the exaggerated bustle creates a counterpoint to the curves of the tree at the upper left. The undulating silhouette of the monkey and its exuberantly curving tail reiterate the curving patterns in the work, as does the parasol in the upper right.

The monkey, traditionally associated with lust, may also be a mildly ironic commentary on the woman's pretentiousness. Or perhaps Seurat simply endowed the most important figure in his painting with an exotic attribute, making her and her consort appear as royalty among their subjects in the final work.

Many sketches for the painting depict the woman with her top-hatted, dapperly dressed partner. This sketch is unique in presenting the woman alone, in profile, with her monkey. The most critical and compelling passages of the final painting have already coalesced in this intelligent, highly resolved image.

Further Reading

Herbert, Robert L., et al. *Georges Seurat, 1859–1891.* New York: The Metropolitan Museum of Art, 1991.

Homer, William Innes. *Seurat and the Science of Painting.* Cambridge, Mass.: M.I.T. Press, 1964.

Smith, Paul. *Seurat and the Avant-Garde.* New Haven, Conn.: Yale University Press, 1997.

Edouard Vuillard

Cuiseaux, Saône-et-Loire, France 1868–1940 La Baule, near Saint-Nazaire, France

The Suitor (also called *The Workshop*; formerly *Interior at l'Etang-la-Ville*), 1893

Oil on millboard panel

12½ × 14¹⁵⁄₁₆ in. (31.8 × 37.9 cm)

Signed and dated in thinned black paint, lower right: V. 93

Purchased, Drayton Hillyer Fund

1938:15

© 2000 Artists Rights Society (ARS), New York/ADAGP, Paris

For Edouard Vuillard, the interior, especially one peopled by his closest relatives and friends, was a source of comfort, solace, and endless pictorial possibilities. He never tired of revisiting it, and each encounter produced new revelations. The quiet drama of these intimate paintings is dependent on their evocative properties. They suggest much but explain little, echoing the attitude toward poetry of his close friend Stéphane Mallarmé, "To name an object is to do away with three quarters of the enjoyment of the poem . . . to suggest it, to evoke it — that is what charms the imagination."

Vuillard, an intensely private artist, flourished during the 1890s, a decade when introspection was the dominant creative focus. At the core of Vuillard's introspection was the interior space of his everyday experiences, which defined and sustained his emotional life. It is not surprising that among earlier artists he favored the seventeenth-century Dutch masters of genre scenes and Jean Baptiste Siméon Chardin, even as his own interpretation of such spaces would differ markedly from theirs.

In *The Suitor*, Vuillard orchestrates a scene of extraordinary visual complexity and subtlety, surprising in its animated human drama and laced with wit and charm. The protagonists are the artist's mother, a dressmaker; his older sister Marie; and a fellow Nabi artist and close friend, Ker–Xavier Roussel — the suitor of the title — who would marry Marie in the same year. The setting is Madame Vuillard's workroom in the rue St. Honoré. The scene develops from the mundane — Marie, with her back to us, is arranging a blue cloth on a table, while her mother leans out the window holding fabric in her hand as if to air it out. In the center the bearded Roussel appears, partly hidden, from behind a partition and exchanges glances with Marie, an intimate moment enhanced by the mother's obliviousness. It is a spring day, an apt metaphor for the young couple; the open window is dappled with sunshine, nearly obscuring the outline of a flowering tree.

The pictorial drama enhances the human one. The work is divided horizontally just below the middle, producing two distinct yet complementary areas. The bottom is a dazzling array of angled shapes of the floor, shafts of light, stools, table legs, and multicolored cloth, establishing a lively, vibrant pulse for the love dance of the young couple. The upper part physically and metaphorically adds texture to the scene, transforming it into an evocative, magical moment. The decorative floral wallpaper pattern is rendered in patches of paint that animate the surface and, along with the tightly mottled pattern of Marie's dress, become so many pulsating particles, creating a weightless environment of floating forms. At the epicenter the curving black silhouette of Roussel seems to emerge as from a genie's bottle. He not only surprises Marie, he startles the viewer and challenges the viewer's acuity. The charming scene gives up its secrets grudgingly as we only slowly identify a differently patterned rectangle, from behind which Roussel is emerging. Usually termed a screen, it may be a door. Its upper edge is angled as would be an open door, and the square shape to the right of Marie's sleeve corresponds to the position of a plaque for a doorknob and keyhole. The subtle insinuation of the door alerts us to a sequence of other vertical shapes: the open window, the window frame, and the orange armoire at the left, which establish a cadence of shifting forms. Vuillard arranges and orchestrates all these elements to delight the viewer with a moment of joy in the life of those closest to him and in the creative act.

Further Reading

Easton, Elizabeth Wynne. *The Intimate Interiors of Edouard Vuillard.* Houston: The Museum of Fine Arts; Washington, D.C.: Smithsonian Institution Press, 1989.

Thomson, Belinda. *Vuillard.* New York: Abbeville Press, 1988.

Warnod, Jeanine. *E. Vuillard.* New York: Crown Publishers, 1989.

Joseph Wright of Derby

Derby, England 1734–1797 Derby, England

A *Cavern, Evening,* 1774

Oil on canvas

40 × 50 in. (101.6 × 127 cm)

Signed and dated, lower right: J. Wright/1774

Purchased

1950:16

Joseph Wright of Derby remained little known outside England until recent decades. In 1950 the Smith College Museum of Art acquired A *Cavern, Evening,* of 1774, and in 1955 it held the first exhibition in America devoted to the artist, thus contributing to the early interest in his art in this country.

Wright lived contentedly for most of his life in Derby, where he made his livelihood as an established portrait painter. Derby was a vital community, and, while not London, it provided him much intellectual and cultural stimulus. He belonged to the Lunar Society, which met on Mondays closest to the full moon to discuss scientific issues. Among its members were such prominent figures as Josiah Wedgwood and Dr. Erasmus Darwin. The discovery of laws that govern the physical world, the planets, and the stars was a source of great fascination for Wright, a child of the Enlightenment. His two greatest paintings were devoted to scientific experiments. In 1766 he painted A *Philosopher Lecturing on the Orrery* (Derby Museum and Art Gallery)—a model showing the movement of the solar system—and in 1768, *An Experiment on a Bird in the Air Pump* (National Gallery, London). These two works affirm Wright's deep interest in the use of light to affect both the pictorial drama and the meaning of his paintings. Among the artists whose use of light he admired are Caravaggio, Gerrit van Honthorst, and Rembrandt.

Wright's only trip to the Continent was a two-year sojourn in Italy. On a visit to the Kingdom of Naples, he witnessed the erupting Vesuvius in October 1774; it would become his most frequently painted motif. He also visited coastal caverns near Naples, overlooking the Gulf of Salerno on the Mediterranean Sea. He recorded the view from the grottoes in two highly finished drawings and, on returning to Rome, used them as the basis for a pair of large paintings, A *Cavern, Morning* (private collection) and this work, A *Cavern, Evening.* As pendants depicting different times of day, they are important precursors to romantic interpretations of such themes, as in the work of Caspar David Friedrich and J. M. W. Turner.

Rarely has Wright aligned the poetry of art so perfectly with scientific observation as in A *Cavern, Evening.* His geologist friend John Whitehurst from the Lunar Society must have been pleased with the artist's scrupulous recording of the rock's formations.

Wright's brilliant conceit of positioning the viewer on the right ledge inside the cavern and his glorious use of light instill poetry in the scene. The limpid light of an early Mediterranean evening, the sky still vividly blue, insinuates itself into the cavern through the irregular opening and gives form to the surrounding rocks, whose gray-brown surface is interspersed with lively sparkles of white and passages of pinks and ochers. The still water, delineated with thin wavy lines, flows deep into the cavern, and as light reflects on it the whole interior is filled with awesome calm. Outside the cavern, three small sailboats on the horizon catch our eye, yet we remain, transfixed, within, as if held there by an elemental force. It would be over one hundred years before there would be as dramatic a juxtaposition of sky, sea, and rock—in Claude Monet's depictions of La Manneporte in the cliffs at Etretat.

Further Reading

Egerton, Judy, et al. *Wright of Derby.* London: Tate Gallery, 1990.

Nicolson, Benedict. *Joseph Wright of Derby, Painter of Light.* 2 vols. London: Paul Mellon Foundation for British Art, and Routledge and K. Paul; New York: Pantheon Books, 1968.

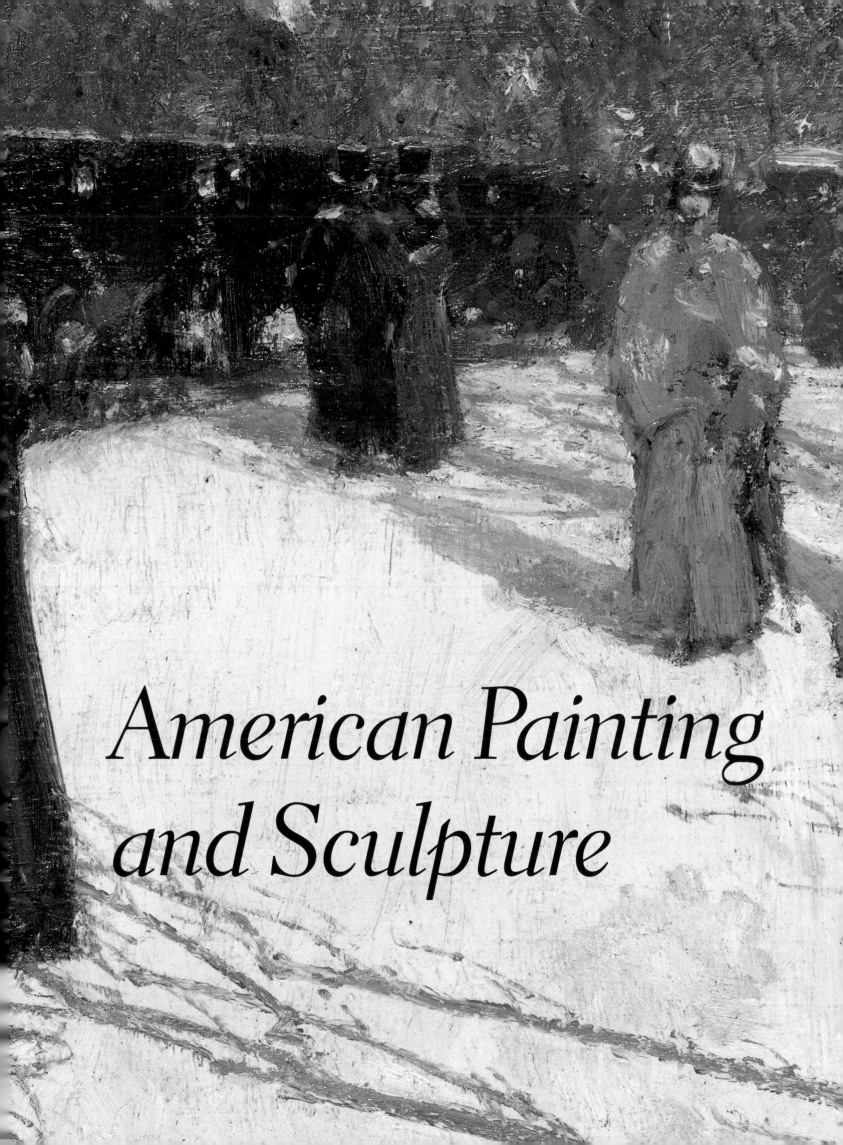

American Painting
and Sculpture

Milton Avery

Sand Bank (now Altmar), New York 1885–1965 New York, New York

---

Surf Fisherman, 1950

Oil on canvas
30 × 42 in. (76.2 × 106.7 cm)
Signed and dated, lower left: Milton Avery 1950
Gift of Roy R. Neuberger
1953:51
© 2000 Milton Avery Trust/Artists Rights Society (ARS), New York

In the decades before his critical "discovery" in the mid-1940s, Milton Avery was known as a painter's painter — appreciated, even revered, by his peers but largely ignored by most writers on art. In particular, several of the group who would later be known as the abstract expressionists — Mark Rothko, Adolph Gottlieb, and Hans Hofmann — found inspiration in his flat, simplified paintings and, even more, in his expressive use of broad areas of color as the principal building blocks of his compositions. *Surf Fisherman* is a classic example of Avery's mature work, not only in its strong, interlocking design, which so appealed to his colleagues, but also in its seaside theme, a perennial subject the artist pursued during many summers spent in Gloucester and Provincetown, Massachusetts, among other northeastern locations.

Against his typical three-banded background (shore, water, sky), Avery has arranged his limited repertoire of forms: three gulls, two fish, and the gravitational center of the image, the heavy-limbed fisherman. That several of the gulls, as well as the fisherman, cross the borders between the horizontal registers only serves to weave together figure and ground, heightening the sense of two-dimensional design. The fuzzy-edged forms appear almost as crudely torn collage elements arranged on a page, awaiting their final placement by the artist. Avery's composition, however, is far from improvisatory. He almost always worked up his oil paintings from preliminary drawings and watercolors, carefully laying in the forms on his canvas with charcoal. Here, he has made use of underpainting and compositional reserve areas, with the several layers of dry color overlapping and meeting along the contours of his forms, a tonal calibration that concerned him greatly and that accounts for the resonant, vaguely vibrational quality of his pure chromatic shapes.

The magic of Avery's painting is his ability, in a severely reduced format, to convey a remarkable range of expressive nuances, without recourse to narrative detail or linear description. Instead, the energetic interaction of color, shape, and space is responsible for communicating the "content" of his work. The close-toned avocado and olive hues, for example, forge a link between man and sea, and the fish on either side of him form a complementary pair of simplified lavender and blue forms (their scaly surfaces indicated by Avery's characteristic scratching into the paint, often using a fork as his tool). Most remarkable is the way that the figure of the man, though greatly pared down and lacking any trace of modeling, nevertheless leaves us with a visceral sense of posture, weight, heft, and balance. In a surprising move, the artist has painted out the taut rod and line initially held in the meaty hands of the sportsman, perhaps concluding that it rendered his work too explicit and illustrative. The result is an even better sense of the tensions and relationships — the abstract balance — between the man and forms that seemingly rotate around him. As usual with Avery, it is the overall unity of the pictorial field, rather than the emphasized part, that leaves a lasting impact.

Further Reading

Haskell, Barbara. *Milton Avery.* New York: Whitney Museum of American Art, 1982.

Hobbs, Robert. *Milton Avery.* New York: Hudson Hills Press, 1990.

Albert Bierstadt

Solingen, Germany 1830–1902 New York, New York

Echo Lake, Franconia Mountains, New Hampshire, 1861

Oil on canvas

25¼ × 39⅛ in. (64.1 × 99.3 cm)

Signed and dated in red paint, lower left, initials conjoined: ABierstadt. /1861.

Purchased with the assistance of funds given by Mrs. John Stewart Dalrymple (Bernice Barber, class of 1910)

1960:37

Although the highly successful landscape painter Albert Bierstadt tends to be associated either with the European subjects that inaugurated his career or the oversized views of the Rocky Mountains that sustained it, he actually had close ties to New England, as his impressive *Echo Lake, Franconia Mountains, New Hampshire* attests. Born in Germany, Bierstadt was brought at age two to New Bedford, Massachusetts, where his father established a barrel-making business. There the young artist began offering instruction in painting as early as 1850; his earliest canvases were exhibited in New Bedford and in Boston. By 1853, however, he had left for Düsseldorf, joining a loosely federated group of international artists and immersing himself in the countryside of Germany and Italy. On his return to the United States, the training of his lengthy European sketching treks prepared him well for the most important trip of his life: his journey westward with the explorer Frederick Lander in 1859. From this and subsequent visits came a steady stream of panoramic "machines" of enormous dimensions—all celebrating the open wilderness as an almost holy field for United States expansion.

During this early period in his career, Bierstadt was nevertheless making regular trips to the highest and most rugged region of New England, the White Mountains of New Hampshire. Often traveling with family members, he is known to have spent several summers sketching among these peaks in the 1850s and early 1860s. By this time, the White Mountains had become a popular tourist destination, and painters by the dozens flocked to their lakes and "notches," where grand hotels offered comfortable lodgings undreamed of by earlier artist-travelers such as Thomas Cole. Although Bierstadt included evidence of human civilization in other New Hampshire landscapes, *Echo Lake, Franconia Mountains* bears no trace of the touristic enterprise that surrounded such pristine sites at the time. Indeed, Cannon Mountain, one of the dark, pine-clad slopes that seem to form a protective wall around this serene and quiet scene, was actually named for the periodic summer practice of firing a cannon over the lake, to induce a thunderous echo and delight hotel guests.

Critics complained of a certain sameness in Bierstadt's works, and this painting was once assumed to depict generic western scenery, a not uncommon element of confusion in his oeuvre. Yet the distinctive profile of Eagle Cliff in the center of the canvas clearly identifies the New Hampshire location, and the painting is now known to have been the sole New England subject sent by the artist to the important National Academy of Design annual exhibition in 1861. Bierstadt has worked with the local topographic features and has skillfully managed his light to avoid another frequently mentioned defect in his compositions: a jarring, abrupt jump from middle ground to distant mountain peaks. In this instance, the double scallop of the shore at left leads the eye gradually and rhythmically to the further reaches of the lake. Periodic bursts of sun manage to pierce the cloud cover and create an incremental progression of highlighted areas, which, following the beautiful column of rising mist, moves into the cradle of blue hills beyond. Bierstadt's celebrated attention to detail (which is often simply the *impression* of detail, applied selectively with a small brush over a loosely painted background) animates the foreground. Thick dollops of green impasto become floating lily pads, and quick hatch marks dance along the surface to form coarse shoots of grass. Perhaps his most affecting touch, however, is the pair of diminutive turtles, one sunning itself on a prominent, lichen-coated rock, the other floating half-submerged in the cool, dark shallows of the undisturbed water.

Further Reading

Campbell, Catherine. "Albert Bierstadt and the White Mountains." *Archives of American Art Journal* 21, no. 3 (1981): 14–23.

Ferber, Linda S., and Nancy K. Anderson. *Albert Bierstadt: Art and Enterprise.* New York: Hudson Hills Press, 1990.

Hendricks, Gordon. *Albert Bierstadt: Painter of the American West.* New York: Harry N. Abrams, 1974.

Joseph Blackburn

Born London, England; active in North America 1754–63

Andrew Faneuil Phillips, 1755

Oil on canvas
50⅜ × 40⅜ in. (128 × 102.5 cm)
Signed and dated in black paint, left, below midline: Jos. Blackburn
Pinxit 1755
Gift of Mrs. Winthrop Merton Rice (Helen Swift Jones, class of 1910)
1973:25

Ann Phillips, 1755

Oil on canvas
50⁷⁄₁₆ × 40⁵⁄₁₆ in. (128.1 × 102.3 cm)
Signed and dated in black paint, left, below midline: I. Blackburn
Pinxit 1755
Gift of Mrs. Winthrop Merton Rice (Helen Swift Jones, class of 1910)
1982:27

Few artists of his era have left less of a paper trail than Joseph Blackburn, whose first name was not even known to modern scholarship until experts in the early twentieth century discovered the faint, wispy signature (unique in his oeuvre) on Smith's portrait of Andrew Phillips. And yet few eighteenth-century Anglo-American artists have left such a clearly marked body of work (some one hundred American portraits), a corpus of images bearing the distinct personality imprint of a gracious painter steeped in the rococo vocabulary of Georgian London. It was this repertoire of refined stylistic effects that made his brief fame in New England, and for about a decade in the late 1750s and early 1760s he reigned supreme as the preeminent portraitist in the region. His influence was felt most notably by the young John Singleton Copley, whose work underwent a sudden shift toward lighter pastel colors, elaborate costumes, and contrived poses in the wake of the older man's arrival in Boston.

Smith College possesses a suite of four Blackburn portraits, still in their original frames, of members of the well-to-do Phillips family: father Gillam, mother Mary Faneuil (sister of the noted merchant Peter Faneuil), and their two children, pictured here, Andrew (1729–1775) and Ann (1736–before 1770), neither of whom lived into old age or appears to have married. The small family was the recipient of substantial inheritances from both the husband's and the wife's lines, and their mercantile standing, along with their loyalist sympathies, made them perfect customers for Blackburn's modish London likenesses. In the son's and the daughter's portraits, we see the standard stylistic "tics" of the artist: high foreheads, flattened facial planes, elongated fingers, lateral glances, and a pursed expression to the lips—what one scholar has dubbed "the Blackburn smirk."

Andrew Phillips appears in a lilac or dove-colored outer coat and breeches, his icy blue waistcoat—fashionably flared, most likely, with the aid of inserted wires at the bottom edges—encrusted with silver gilt. The fingers of his right hand fan out impossibly, their slightly queasy curves serving as a prominent marker of the sitter's exaggerated elegance. Above, all is prim and composed: a tightly knotted neckcloth, a powdered wig with carefully curled side rolls, and the dark bow of his queue falling lightly down his back. His cool, even delicate, composure provides a dramatic contrast to the darkly mysterious landscape setting, with skeletal branches reaching in from the left and a shaggy, beetling cliff forming a more unrestrained backdrop for his head.

Andrew's sister Ann finds herself in a more protected interior space, complete with a marble-topped table and paired swags enframing her upper body. The paint on her sack-type dress is applied thickly, with a roseate hue worked over an underlayer of white to approximate the ever-changing reflective qualities of silk. A much finer brush was employed for the sumptuous lace collar and sleeve attachments (or *engageants*). Here, Blackburn has attended with great care to the complex pattern of different-sized flowers, leaves, and geometric borders of the lace; he was especially known for his ability to render this important sign of economic status. Elsewhere, his invented accessories appear more fantastic, particularly the glassy roped pearls and pendant festooned across the bodice, the multiple hair ornaments, and the flyaway shawl. Most striking of all, however, is the Chinese vase with its costly tulips, which Ann holds protectively. These objects of the transatlantic luxury trade would have served as a reminder of the source of her family's unusual wealth.

Further Reading

Bolton, Theodore, and Harry Lorin Binsse. "An American Artist of Formula: Joseph Blackburn." *Antiquarian* 15 (November 1930): 50–53, 88, 90, 92.

Morgan, John Hill. "Further Notes on Blackburn." *Brooklyn Museum Quarterly* 7 (July 1919): 147–55.

Park, Lawrence. "Joseph Blackburn: Portrait Painter." *Proceedings of the American Antiquarian Society* n.s. 32 (1923): 271–79, 308–10.

Lee Bontecou

Providence, Rhode Island 1931

Untitled, 1959

Canvas and metal

20½ × 20¹³⁄₁₆ × 7¼ in. (52.1 × 52.8 × 18.4 cm)

Signed and dated, lower right: BONTECOU 59

Purchased with a gift from the Chace Foundation, Inc.

1960:14

When Lee Bontecou had her first one-person show in 1959 at the age of twenty-eight, her canvas wall constructions—linear welded metal armatures with planes of salvaged canvas stretched between the ribs and secured with tiny twisted wires—caused something of a sensation in the New York art world, even if subsequent critical opinion has often failed to understand her achievement as anything but a brief, isolated event. Difficult to classify (are they paintings or sculptures? abstract expressionist or neo-surrealist?), Bontecou's reliefs were hailed on the one hand as an important feminist statement in their evocation of traditional patchwork fabric assemblage, and on the other as a groundbreaking development in a new sculptural vocabulary.

Smith's wall relief is an early example of the type, rather pure in its exclusive use of found canvas, unlike her later, larger works which came to include saw blades, zippers, or other metal objects. These reliefs from the 1960s are often characterized as menacing, aggressive, and sinister, but in Bontecou's early sculptures, such as this one, the mysterious plastic effects are somewhat less heightened, more subtle and evocative. The imagery is at once topographic and biomorphic, with the forms—sometimes sharply faceted and angled, sometimes nestled in telescoping, concentric arcs—pushing forward as if subject to pressure from within.

Evocative of both a vast terraced landscape and a small barnacle or crustacean, the tentlike shapes appear to mutate and develop asymmetrically as we watch. The surface cells vary considerably. Some swatches of canvas are bleached white, others bear random smudge marks; some are finely woven, others have the alligatored texture of fire hoses. The puckering, fraying, and wrinkling of the cloth further differentiates these random patches of "skin." Though segmented, the relief is a single, unified form, with a seemingly organic visual momentum building up to the central crater. Thus, the ribs approaching the hole are set closer and closer together, and the antlike wire "sutures" increase in number. This busyness of line results in a bristling, intensified texture toward the center, a charged spikiness that ultimately gives way to the embrace of the velvet-lined, angled cavity, the focal point of almost every Bontecou relief.

Further Reading

Field, Richard S. *Prints and Drawings by Lee Bontecou.* Middletown, Conn.: Wesleyan University, 1975.

Smith, Elizabeth A. T. *Lee Bontecou: Sculpture and Drawings of the 1960s.* Los Angeles: Museum of Contemporary Art, 1993.

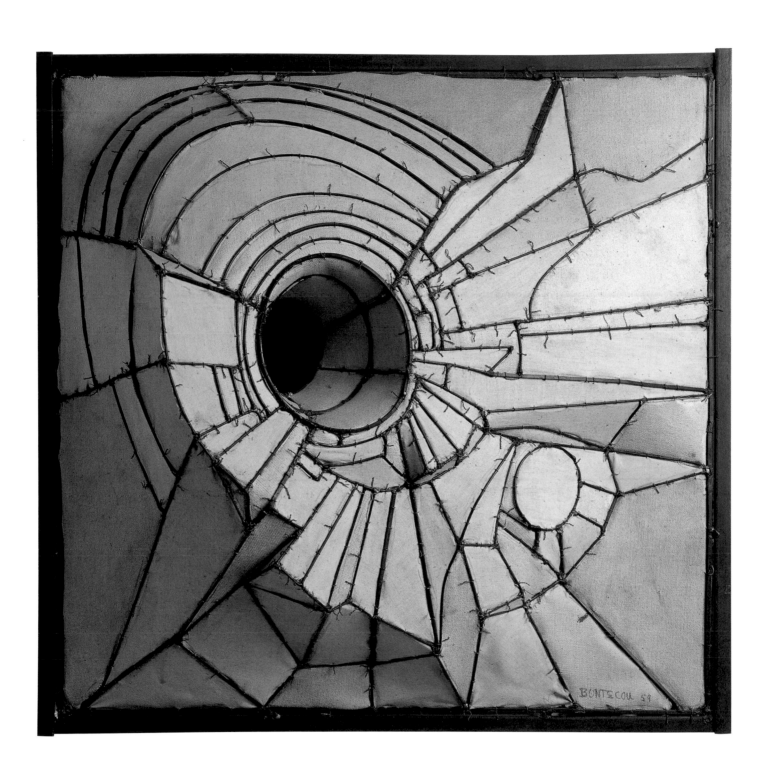

Alexander Calder

Philadelphia, Pennsylvania 1898–1976 New York, New York

Mobile, 1934

Nickel-plated wood, wire, and steel
42½ × 11⅞ in. (107.9 × 30.2 cm); base diameter 11⅞ in. (30.2 cm)
Not signed or dated
Purchased, Director's Purchase Fund
1935:11
© 2000 Estate of Alexander Calder/Artists Rights Society (ARS),
New York

It is a rare distinction to have invented an art form as ubiquitous as the mobile is in contemporary culture, but until Alexander Calder began his exploration of gravity-defying objects hanging from nested, cantilevered arms, there was simply nothing like these delicate composi-tions of shape, color, motion, balance, and counterbal-ance. With a degree in engineering, Calder was perhaps predisposed toward an interest in mechanics and kinet-ics. Still, the fertile artistic environment of Paris in the late 1920s and early 1930s — in which he was immersed to an extent unusual for an American — also had a telling impact on the sculptor's researches. It was one of his French colleagues, Marcel Duchamp, in fact, who is credited with coining the term *mobile*.

His earliest such creations, of which this is an impor-tant example, seem related to the floating, biomorphic forms of the surrealist paintings of Joan Miró, or the sculptures of Jean Arp. The latter connection is particu-larly apt here, for unlike the thin, flattened, sail-like shapes of the later mobiles, the hanging objects in Calder's first kinetic compositions were usually more substantial, solid forms of carved wood, as is the case with the Smith work. The artist was also greatly interested in modern astronomical knowledge (Pluto had been recently discovered in 1930), and planetary metaphors pervade his art during this era. Here, the five distinctive shapes (some, such as the flattened double cone, appear-

ing regularly in his work) approximate stars, asteroids, and other galaxial matter: each one spinning slowly on its own, yet also bound to a common network of larger orbits, much like the constituent elements of a discrete solar system.

More than most Calder works, this mobile almost playfully invokes the sometimes naïve, early imagery of science fiction — an association stemming largely from the sleek, machinelike simplicity of the steel ring and rod and the metallic polished surfaces of the dangling objects, so different from the primary colors often favored by the artist. This treatment is unique to the Smith College mobile, and it results from an interesting New York episode shortly after Calder created the work. Asked by the Art Deco artist Donald Deskey to borrow a sculpture for a design exhibition, Calder lent this mobile. Deskey, however, proceeded to nickel-plate the work without the sculptor's collaboration (and ironically, he ultimately chose not to use it in his show). The plat-ing certainly changed the character of the mobile's parts, yet it does not completely obscure the pock marks, scratches, and dents that betray the hand of the carver. Moreover, the reflective surfaces of the abstract objects, sparkling brightly as they twirl, nicely accentuate the effects of randomness that concerned the artist through-out his career. Calder's knowledge of and reaction to this alteration of his work are unknown, but we can assume that he accepted it artistically, for he allowed the mobile to be shown a year later at the Pierre Matisse Gallery, where it was purchased by Smith College in 1935.

Further Reading

Marter, Joan M. *Alexander Calder.* New York: Cambridge University Press, 1991.

Prather, Marla, Alexander S. C. Rower, and Arnauld Pierre. *Alexander Calder: 1898–1976.* Washington, D.C.: National Gallery of Art, 1998.

William Merritt Chase

Franklin, Indiana 1849–1916 New York, New York

Woman in Black, c. 1890

Oil on wood panel

15⁵⁄₁₆ × 10 in. (38.9 × 25.4 cm)

Signed in brown paint, lower left: Wm. M. Chase

Purchased

1900:16

Woman in Black, a relatively small, unassuming panel painting by William Merritt Chase, nevertheless exhibits many of the pictorial features that marked his more ambitious compositions and led to his reputation as a skilled technician, powerful designer, and judicious assimilator of a range of stylistic influences. From his earliest days as a student in the Munich Royal Academy, he was drawn to the dark tonalities and virtuosic brushwork of the seventeenth-century Dutch old masters. His subsequent meeting with the by-then famous James McNeill Whistler in 1885 introduced him to the flattened spaces and reductive compositions of that artist. *Woman in Black* demonstrates the best of this mix, with its sure paint application, avoidance of overly detailed preliminary drawing, constant attention to values, and simplified, abstractive composition.

Chase's picture is a marvel of restraint, minimally composed of three interlocking shapes: the textured backdrop of drapery flecked with touches of red and green; the flat, unmodulated ground plane seemingly tipped down to further reduce the spatial depth; and the quiet, contained form of the young woman, set slightly to one side but balanced by her lateral gaze in the opposite direction. She is a thoughtful, stable figure, her clasped hands emerging from her three-quarter sleeves to reinforce the lines of her bodice and provide a visual foundation for the only other high-value note, her graceful neck and head. Here as well, the form is accented and warmed by judicious strokes of red at the throat, ear, and mouth. The result is a highly aesthetic essay in browns and blacks shot through with a subtle coloristic surface animation.

The pert, finely drawn profile of the model also serves to enliven the painting, and her distinctive features have allowed her to be identified as Marietta Benedict Cotton (1868–1947), one of Chase's many female students who would later follow a career as a portraitist. When the nineteen-year-old pupil first entered his studio, Chase immediately felt a desire to paint her. "Such a model," he later wrote about her, "is a treasure-find. It is the personality that inspires, and which you depict on canvas." *Woman in Black* was probably purchased directly from Chase by Smith President L. Clark Seelye, and though her identity likely remained unknown to the early generations of Smith students who studied this work, Cotton would have been an appropriate role model for the independent and successful graduates the college was just then sending out into the budding twentieth century.

Further Reading

Gallati, Barbara Dayer. *William Merritt Chase.* New York: Harry N. Abrams, 1995.

Pisano, Ronald G. *A Leading Spirit in American Art: William Merritt Chase, 1849–1916.* Seattle: Henry Art Gallery, 1983.

139

Thomas Cole

Bolton-le-Moor, Lancashire, England 1801–1848 Catskill, New York

Compositional study for *The Voyage of Life: Manhood,* c. 1840

Oil on academy board
12¼ × 17³⁄₁₆ in. (31.1 × 43.7 cm)
Not signed or dated
Purchased
1950:13

More than most artists of his generation, Thomas Cole believed devoutly in the moral mission of landscape painting. Though he painted a good many transcriptive "views" of recognizable passages of American scenery, he reserved his greatest efforts for several ambitious multicanvas series: ideal, allegorical works—a "higher style of landscape" in his own words—that would elevate and instruct the large crowds that flocked to see them. The most popular of these narrative groups was his four-part *Voyage of Life*, an easily understood metaphor of the course of human life played out by a lone male protagonist navigating a sometimes dangerous river in a small boat. Along the way, Cole's Everyman encounters a guardian angel, demonic spirits, and a variety of emblematic landscape features that give shape to the aspirations and challenges that mark the stages of his earthly pilgrimage. In the end, as an old man, the voyager in his battered boat finally reaches the open ocean, where beams of radiant light welcome him to his final, heavenly rest.

The path to this deliverance from worldly cares is not an easy one, and in the third canvas, *Manhood*, for which the museum's menacing sketch is a preparatory study, Cole depicts the darkest, most precarious moment of the cycle. At the time that he was working out the iconography and composition of this scene, the middle-aged artist was wracked with his own doubts and worries: He was struggling financially, the generous patron who had commissioned *The Voyage of Life* had died unex-

pectedly, and the future of the series, not to mention his career, seemed shrouded in uncertainty. "Trouble is characteristic of the period of Manhood," wrote Cole in his descriptive key to the paintings, and his own despair and pessimism appear to have marked this image to a degree that is unusual, even in his highly personalized oeuvre.

While the voyager and his boat (as well as the benevolent and evil spirits who will watch him from above in the final version) do not appear in this study, the terrifying forms of the landscape are more than enough to convey the dangers of his watery path. Moving in from the left, the river suddenly plunges into a narrow cleft in the fantastic rocks; furious rapids and half-submerged boulders are glimpsed throughout the serpentine descent of the stream. The arch of dark cloud forms and the dramatic "keyhole" view to the distance create the impression of a swirling vortex of destructive energy, with only the yellow and pink glow of the faraway ocean sky offering a ray of hope. The *Manhood* composition gave Cole the greatest trouble of the four, and his artistic struggle is evident in the inchoate shapes of the jagged rocks and the single skeletal tree at right. It is as though the entire landscape has been spun out of some kind of organic primal matter, still in the process of formation. This fury of creation, vigorously conveyed by Cole's loaded brush and glistening, oil-rich paint, contributes to the surprising visual power of the small study.

Further Reading

Parry, Ellwood C., III. *The Art of Thomas Cole: Ambition and Imagination.* Newark: University of Delaware Press, 1988.

Schweizer, Paul D., Ellwood C. Parry III, and Dan A. Kushel. *The Voyage of Life by Thomas Cole: Paintings, Drawings, and Prints.* Utica, N.Y.: Munson-Williams-Proctor Institute, 1985.

Truettner, William H., and Alan Wallach, eds. *Thomas Cole: Landscape into History.* New Haven, Conn.: Yale University Press, 1994.

John Singleton Copley

Boston, Massachusetts 1737–1815 London, England

The Honorable John Erving, c. 1772

Oil on canvas

50½ × 40½ in. (128.3 × 102.9 cm)

Not signed or dated

Bequest of Alice Rutherford Erving, class of 1929

1975:52-1

One of the marvels of the career of John Singleton Copley is the astonishing speed with which he essentially taught himself to seize the likeness of his sitter, infuse it with a profound depth of character, and present it in a carefully calibrated environment of dress, posture, and attributes—a "portrait" that went beyond mere physiognomy to telegraph important clues of social and economic status to his audience. Copley had more or less mastered this subtle process by the end of his teenage years, but he continued to develop throughout his time in the colonies. In the several years prior to his departure for Europe in 1774, he painted a series of rich, sober portraits in which he pushed the effects of his normally deep chiaroscuro to a new level of psychological focus and intensity. His portrait of John Erving (1693–1786), a wealthy, Scottish-born merchant who had originally come to Boston as a common sailor, is a particularly successful example of the type.

Erving looms large in the picture's narrow slice of space; his piercing gaze—emanating from hard, glassy irises that all but subsume the whites of his eyes—creates a sense of almost overwhelming immediacy. Color is dense and highly saturated, particularly in the regal drapery swag and table covering at left. The depth of this hue nicely sets off the radiant still life, the silver inkwells sparkling with fluid touches of white and the bright letter—addressed to the sitter—floating in a sea of royal blue. The viewer's attention nevertheless focuses on Erving's face and hands, his bronzed skin warmed by contrast with the white neckcloth, wig, and sleeve ruffles. The merchant's seemingly resolute nature is conveyed by his tightly set mouth, although the high forehead rising above his bushy brows is surprisingly serene and uncreased. There is a liveliness to his visage, but signs of age appear in the loose skin under the chin and, more dramatically, on his left hand. This is a location of suppressed formal tension in the painting, for upon close observation, the powerful grip of the right hand appears to wring the left mercilessly. A link is formed that closes the circular sweep of Erving's arms, and here again, there is a kind of elastic force to the pose as he hooks his elbow over the ear of the Chippendale chair and leans his weight in the opposite direction.

The large head and firmly set hands convey the image of a man of thought and action, but it is in his costume that eighteenth-century viewers would have read further details of personality. The plum-colored suit is striking in color, but the material is of practical wool, the simple buttons are cloth-covered, and there is a complete absence of any gilt trim or fancy work. The unbuttoned opening in his vest and the dusting of wig powder on his right shoulder further inject a certain ease and informality that accord well with his casual pose. One is left with an impression of confidence, moderation, and even conservatism, for by the 1770s a suit with each of the components—coat, vest, and breeches—made of the same material was decidedly old-fashioned. Similarly, Erving's frizzed "physical" wig, as it was termed, was more voluminous and wider in silhouette than was currently the mode for younger men, many of whom had given up wigs altogether. In the end, Copley and Erving appear to have contrived a judicious image that underscores the sitter's acumen, probity, and traditional values—perfect attributes of the successful man of business.

Further Reading

Prown, Jules David. *John Singleton Copley.* 2 vols. Cambridge, Mass.: Harvard University Press, 1966.

Rebora, Carrie, et al. *John Singleton Copley in America.* New York: The Metropolitan Museum of Art, 1995.

Thomas Wilmer Dewing

Boston, Massachusetts 1851–1938 New York, New York

Lady with Cello, before 1920

Oil on canvas
20⅛ × 16⅟₁₆ in. (51.1 × 40.8 cm)
Signed in brown paint, lower right: T. W. Dewing
Bequest of Annie Swan Coburn (Mrs. Lewis Larned Coburn)
1934:3-4

Perhaps no American painter of the late nineteenth century so successfully created a distinctive body of work—utterly unlike that of his many professional peers—as Thomas Wilmer Dewing, who engaged in a lifelong exploration of elegant, enigmatic female figures in spare interiors and absorptive landscapes. In their technique, his paintings have little to do with the prevailing impressionist mode of his day, and though his women are usually constructed on the canvas with an underlying armature of immaculate academic draftsmanship (the fruit of his student years in Paris in the late 1870s), they have none of the hardened didacticism of standard atelier training. Instead, Dewing's work can most fittingly be associated with the small, rarefied strain of American painting known as Tonalism, a movement primarily concerned with landscape that boasted as one of its principal exponents longtime Smith College art professor Dwight Tryon. Like the work of his friend Tryon, Dewing's canvases are close-keyed, sometimes hazy explorations of mood and memory, often restricted to a single pastel hue that is nevertheless tremulous and unstable. Dewing, however, is unique in his pursuit of the tonalist idiom in the realm of figure painting rather than pure landscape.

His *Lady with Cello* is suffused in a burnished, green-gold tonality (with undercurrents of mauve and dun) that is evocative of gilded surfaces bearing the tarnished patina of age. It is a composition of distilled essences: a reduced interior, a single figure clad in a rich gown, the darkly iconic cello, the curiously undersized and spindly bench, and the flat, abstractive painting—a crucial self-referential pictorial element easily recognized as an example of Dewing's own treatment of the idealized landscapes inhabited by his women in reverie. Each element is tugged slightly askew—the frame to the right, the bench and its cushion away from the wall and to the left—provoking in the viewer a sense of spatial tension, a mildly charged feeling of unease experienced as a pregnant, suspended moment in time.

The binding element of the image seems to be the soothing retreat into the imaginative world of aesthetic contemplation suggested by both the solo melody of the cello and the diaphanous dreamscape of the framed work of art. Indeed, the tilt of the cello and the angle of the impossibly delicate bow accord with the sloping lines of the painting on the wall, rather than the chilly rectilinear space in which the woman sits. Dewing's love of music is well known, so it is not surprising to find this connection between his ethereal compositions and the insubstantial art of sound. His cellist, uncharacteristically modern with her bobbed haircut, seems visually defined by her music making. While the lower half of her body remains a wonderfully nebulous cascade of scumbled drapery, her figure immediately seizes into form above the bow, as though this focusing activity has willed her into consciousness. Still, she inhabits her own world, her eyes closed and her head delicately shrouded in a pointillist aura of moist pastel tones. It is as though the misty forms of the painting have gravitated toward the figure, enveloping and transporting her to what Dewing termed "the poetic and imaginative world where a few choice spirits live."

Further Reading

Hobbs, Susan A., and Barbara Dayer Gallati. *The Art of Thomas Wilmer Dewing: Beauty Reconfigured.* Washington, D.C.: Smithsonian Institution Press, 1996.

Pyne, Kathleen. "Evolutionary Typology and the American Woman in the Work of Thomas Dewing." *American Art* 7 (Fall 1993): 13–29.

Asher Brown Durand

Jefferson Village (now Maplewood), New Jersey 1796–1886 New York, New York

---

Woodland Interior, c. 1854

Oil on canvas
23¹¹⁄₁₆ × 16¹³⁄₁₆ in. (60.2 × 42.7 cm)
Signed in black paint, lower right: A. B. Durand
Purchased
1952:107

Few American artists did more to establish and popularize the practice of painting out of doors—*en plein air*—than Asher B. Durand. His widely read "Letters on Landscape Painting," published just a year or so after he executed *Woodland Interior*, codified a kind of apprenticeship to nature to which the aspiring painter should willingly commit. There was, he felt, a degree of moral cultivation necessary for a proper appreciation of God's lessons in nature, but Durand placed even more stress on actually observing and copying raw botanical and geological minutiae. He believed, along with the influential English writer John Ruskin, that intimate familiarity with the basic components of a landscape composition could only come from prolonged exposure to the unedited complexity of the natural world. Each leaf or stone had a role to play in the painter's education, and Durand was firm in his conviction that painting in oil colors out of doors should not begin until these basic forms had been mastered with the pencil, no matter how long and no matter how many sketching trips it took.

Once an acceptable degree of proficiency had been reached, however, the student of nature was encouraged to sketch in oils out of doors, a practice made considerably easier by the invention of the collapsible tin paint tube in the early 1840s. In his approach to the oil sketch, Durand differed from many of his colleagues in his belief that broad, summary studies were of little use. If one was to go to the trouble of plein-air study, he maintained, the result should ideally be a fully realized painting, even if its execution was rapid. Thus *Woodland Interior*—part, if not all of which was almost certainly painted out of doors—is nevertheless a highly finished composition, with particular attention paid to the mossy, mottled textures of the foreground trees and the effect of filtered light piercing the lacy screen of foliage. Durand often kept such studies as studio aide-mémoire, but unusually for his time, he also exhibited and sold them, just as he would his larger, final compositions.

In this case, the study, *Woodland Interior*, served as the preliminary version of Durand's grand watershed work, *In the Woods* (1855, The Metropolitan Museum of Art). When that painting was exhibited at the National Academy of Design, it was praised extensively by critics, who perceived it as inaugurating a new taste for highly naturalistic effects in landscape art, essentially bringing the era of Thomas Cole's allegorical narratives (exemplified by Smith's *Voyage of Life* study, pp. 140–41) to a close. Yet in both *Woodland Interior* and its nearly identical progeny, *In the Woods*, nineteenth-century viewers would have still found some measure of moral inspiration in its quiet forest clearing, for the arcing tree limbs and diffused effects of light of Durand's vertical compositions were often likened to the interior of a Gothic cathedral—an untouched, virginal setting appropriate for the nature worship so dear to mid-nineteenth-century painters and poets.

Further Reading

Harvey, Eleanor Jones. *The Painted Sketch: American Impressions from Nature, 1830–1880.* Dallas: Dallas Museum of Art, 1998.

Lawall, David. *A. B. Durand, 1796–1886.* Newark, N.J.: Montclair Art Museum, 1971.

Novak, Barbara. *American Painting of the Nineteenth Century: Realism, Idealism, and the American Experience.* New York: Praeger, 1969.

Thomas Eakins

Philadelphia, Pennsylvania 1844–1916 Philadelphia, Pennsylvania

In Grandmother's Time, 1876

Oil on canvas
16 × 12 in (40.6 × 30.5 cm)
Signed and dated on spinning wheel: Eakins 76
Purchased from the artist
1879:1

Traditionally regarded as the first work of art acquired by Smith President L. Clark Seelye, Thomas Eakins's *In Grandmother's Time* can rightly be considered the foundation of the Museum of Art's strong holdings in American art. Seelye apparently first saw the small canvas in the inaugural exhibition of the renegade Society of American Artists in New York, out of which he eventually purchased several paintings by various artists. At the time it bore the title *Spinning* and was advertised for sale at $200. Some months later, Eakins exhibited it, this time under its present title, at the Utica (New York) Art Association for the reduced price of $150. A canceled check in the Smith archives indicates that in the end Seelye paid Eakins only $100 for the work, which was nevertheless a good price for the artist at the time. The purchase by Smith of a work by this then "undiscovered" master was extraordinarily prescient; Eakins would see only one other painting bought by a public collection in his lifetime, and he would have to wait nearly two decades for that honor.

In Grandmother's Time is the first in an extensive series of over two dozen works by Eakins exploring historic American handicraft activities: spinning, sewing, and knitting. Beginning in 1876, when he likely witnessed a spinning-wheel display in the re-created "New England Log House" at the Centennial Exposition in Philadelphia, he devoted himself for some seven years to colonial revival themes in oils, watercolors, and sculpted reliefs. (Coincidentally, the recently opened Smith College was also a presence at the fair in 1876, displaying campus plans and photographs and distribut-

ing five hundred copies of a flyer explaining its new curriculum.) His elderly model, clothed in a nostalgic gown and mob cap, was a family relative known as "Aunt Sallie" King. She posed for the artist on several occasions during this period.

The painting exhibits several standard features of Eakins's early interior scenes. The warm rag carpet—its intense red hue a favorite of the artist at the time—establishes a forceful ground plane, with the figure and accessories rising with carefully plotted, geometric specificity from the floor. Color is otherwise restrained and sober, and the soupy background gives little indication of the exact nature of the room. The reduced illumination accents the downturned head (particularly the wonderful highlight on the satin ribbon) and the almost exaggerated hands—together hinting at the intellectual concentration and dexterous precision required by her task. The woman sits erect, making no use of the chair back to rest. Instead, she moves close to her machine, her foot working the pedal and her fingers twisting the fibers in a way that joins worker and tool in unified rhythm and action, as the busy whir of the wheel attests. Indeed, this animated, long-legged spinning wheel almost seems to lean into *her*, much like an affectionate pet eager to please. The overall tone of the work, however, is one of earnestness and calm. In fact, Eakins nicely underscores the peaceful, steadfast nature of this elderly person's work by contrasting her with the youthful, neglected toys in the shadows, somewhat innocently turned away from the central scene of labor.

Further Reading

Homer, William Innes. *Thomas Eakins: His Life and Art.* New York: Abbeville Press, 1992.

Sewell, Darrel. *Thomas Eakins: Artist of Philadelphia.* Philadelphia: Philadelphia Museum of Art, 1982.

Wilmerding, John, ed. *Thomas Eakins.* Washington, D.C.: Smithsonian Institution Press, 1993.

149

Thomas Eakins

Philadelphia, Pennsylvania 1844–1916 Philadelphia, Pennsylvania

Edith Mahon, 1904

Oil on canvas
20 × 16 in. (50.8 × 40.6 cm)
Inscribed on back of canvas: To My Friend Edith Mahon/
Thomas Eakins 1904
Purchased, Drayton Hillyer Fund
1931:2

Near the end of his life, the distinguished art historian Meyer Schapiro observed that when portraits are classed as that rarest of categories, the masterpiece, "they are always based on empathy and sympathy, depicting—in addition to a semblance—an interior life, a soul." This is certainly true of Thomas Eakins's portrait of the pianist Edith Mahon (1863–1923), long recognized as one of the artist's most powerful efforts and, indeed, thought by many to be among the greatest American portraits ever painted. Mahon's almost palpable interior life, to say nothing of her soul, has nevertheless seemed elusive to generations of viewers. Eakins has managed to peel away the protective Victorian veneer of detached composure and emotional constraint to reveal in his sitter the often hidden surfaces of deep psychological pain and weariness. Yet the nature and source of her anguished reverie seem to resist definition, even as it wells up so devastatingly from within.

One of the most affecting paradoxes of the painting lies in the fact that though Eakins's portrayal convinces us that we know this woman so well that we share her suffering (and that she forgets herself in our presence), there are, in fact, few clues as to the events of her life during the time that the painter knew her. Born in London, she went to Philadelphia about 1897, where she supported herself as a teacher and accompanist. She played often in the Eakins household, and the artist indicates a degree of familiarity in his inscription on the back of the canvas, "To My Friend Edith Mahon." In 1931 Eakins's wife wrote cryptically that Mahon "had suf-fered from great unkindness," and census records indicate that she was divorced and that at least one of her three children had predeceased her. Even the painterly "facts" of this portrait, the most tangible remaining incident of her life, have been called into question. While the closely cropped space and the immediacy of her image leave an impression of a strong woman of significant stature, a friend described her as "small and rather frail looking." Mahon herself is reported to have disliked the portrait, accepting it as a gift out of politeness. Six years after Eakins's death, she sold it before returning to England.

Eakins depicts his friend in a formal dress, seated in a favorite studio chair, its baroque crest familiar from other portraits. These loosely brushed elements, however, recede before the overwhelming presence of Mahon's fatigued countenance. Her head, leaning back somewhat resignedly against the chair back, seems heavy, her shoulders burdened, and her features drawn. The wisps of hair over her brow are dry and frayed, her neck is creased, and her thin lips appear tightened and resolute. Most telling are her eyes, which focus inward rather than outward, effectively guarding her thoughts from the viewer. The light of the portrait is somewhat harsh—throwing her features into relief and accentuating the underlying skeletal mask. The touches of red at her eyes, mouth, and nose do not so much warm the image as leave an impression of a worn, haggard surface, as though the visual penetration of her psyche has been achieved with the use of a pumice stone. The effect produced by the image, no matter how many times it is experienced, is profound and exhausting. In the particular features of his friend, Eakins has uncovered an emotional touchstone that seems to resonate as powerfully in the viewer as it does in the breast of Edith Mahon.

Further Reading

Wilmerding, John, ed. *Thomas Eakins.* Washington, D.C.: Smithsonian Institution Press, 1993.

Edwin Romanzo Elmer

Ashfield, Massachusetts 1850–1923 Ashfield, Massachusetts

Mourning Picture, 1890

Oil on canvas
27¹⁵⁄₁₆ × 36 in. (70.9 × 91.4 cm)
Not signed or dated
Purchased
1953:129

Edwin Romanzo Elmer's eerie and affecting *Mourning Picture* has fascinated several generations of museum-goers, and the facts behind the painting are no less intriguing than the arresting visionary qualities of the image. Elmer, the last of twelve children born to a poor farming family in the hills of western Massachusetts, spent most of his life in an isolated area twenty miles north of Northampton. As a young man, however, he traveled to Cleveland, Ohio, where he successfully entered the silk thread business. On returning to Massachusetts about 1875, Elmer and his brother Samuel built (with their own hands) the imposing Italianate house seen in the painting. Its urban stylistic vocabulary served to announce the newfound prosperity of the Elmer clan, and the brothers and their families invited their parents to join them in their new mansion.

Within a few years, however, the others had moved away, leaving the artist, his wife, and their only child, Effie, as the sole residents of the large structure. Tragedy then struck in 1890, when the nine-year-old child died of appendicitis. Elmer's wife, Mary, was stricken with grief and could no longer bear to stay in the home they had shared with their daughter. The couple boxed up Effie's possessions and gave away her pets, but before leaving the house forever, Elmer painted this remembrance of their lives together. The parents, in mourning dress, are shown near the house seated on parlor furniture: Their hands are occupied with the standard domestic attributes of newspaper and knitting, but their faces are remote and impassive, blankly staring as though still stunned by their loss. To the left, dramatically silhouetted against the landscape, Effie stands with her pet lamb, her toys, and her nimble-footed kitten marching in from one side. They make a poignant group, their meticulous rendering and looming placement in the foreground leaving the impression that they are more alive, more "real" than the desolate, passive adults.

Nothing in Elmer's career prepares one for this powerful masterpiece produced by a forty-year-old artist with no known formal instruction in painting. The textured carpet of flowers at Effie's feet might indicate knowledge of similar symbolic flora in early quattrocento altar-pieces, and the concentrated attention given to each butterfly, blade of grass, and distant leaf—as well as the sharp, fresh green hue used throughout—argues for some exposure to Pre-Raphaelitism. The emotional power and vital energy of the work, however, seem to stem more directly from the tragic circumstances it commemorates. The vibrant colors of the doll carriage, the exquisite curls of red ribbon on the grass, Effie's virtually tangible lace collar and strand of pearls: It is as though Elmer has willed his grief into a tight focus on the compacted matter of his daughter's world. The intensity pushes this quiet, crystalline scene nearly to the breaking point; indeed, as the painting has aged, the sky and clouds have developed a prominent craque-lure that seems almost to result from the considerable repressed tension below. The effect is one of time arrested, and though her parents appear left behind, tied to a more prosaic realm, Effie herself seems strangely at home in this heightened, charged landscape.

Further Reading

Jones, Betsy B. *Edwin Romanzo Elmer, 1850–1923.* Northampton, Mass.: Smith College Museum of Art, 1983.

Edwin Romanzo Elmer

Ashfield, Massachusetts 1850–1923 Ashfield, Massachusetts

***A Lady of Baptist Corner, Ashfield, Massachusetts* (the artist's wife),** 1892

Oil on canvas
32¹⁵⁄₁₆ × 24¹³⁄₁₆ in. (83.7 × 63 cm)
Signed and dated in brownish black paint, lower left: E. R. Elmer/1892
Gift of E. Porter Dickinson
1979:47

Just a year or so after he painted Smith College's *Mourning Picture* (pp. 152–55), Edwin Elmer executed *A Lady of Baptist Corner*, another highly personal and idiosyncratic canvas, this time featuring his wife alone. (The title was given the work in the twentieth century; it derives from the name of the village in Ashfield, Massachusetts, where Mary Ware Elmer [1860–1927] was born.) Here, as in the *Mourning Picture*, Elmer weaves together a record of his family and his mechanical accomplishments, depicting his sober wife—still dressed in mourning garb—at work before his whipsnap machine, one of several labor-saving devices invented by the artist. His machine was used to braid the silk threads that formed the ends of horsewhips, a regional cottage industry that brought extra money into many western Massachusetts households at the time. Mary Elmer, perhaps shown in their upstairs apartment in Shelburne Falls, Massachusetts, is said to have maintained a personal bank account for her earnings from this homework.

Elmer's striking image has something in common with the many late-nineteenth-century genre paintings that took as their subject a single, contemplative (often elderly) woman engaged in some sort of productive handiwork in a domestic interior. Yet the industrial emphasis of the whipsnap machine, with the unromantic, repetitive piecework it produced, is unusual and would seem to puncture the nostalgia and sentimentality normally associated with the theme. The view out the window, another standard iconographic element in such images of feminine solitude, is here bleak and barren. This dry, wintery landscape, moreover, is largely blocked by the unrelieved, flat surface of the machine. Indeed, the unmodulated planes of the device, the cool gray wall, and the central, compositionally complex passage of intertwined cranks and rods leave an overall impression of a cold, metallic starkness, in keeping with the austere demeanor of the mother who has so recently lost her only child. Perhaps the only touch of whimsy lies in the colorful, richly patterned carpet with its fantastic pavilions, bouquets, and foliate scrolls. This floor, tilting precipitously, almost seems subject to different physical laws than the squared-off pair of machine and worker above. Even the industrial-sized spools in the foreground hover dangerously at the lower edge of the pictorial space.

Yet despite this singular environment, the viewer's gaze ultimately rests on the calm, focused figure of Mary Elmer as she leans into the machine slightly and wraps her hands firmly around its metal handles. Her lowered eyes and her thin arms joining those of her husband's invention indicate a firmness of purpose and a resolute concentration brought to the task. But it is the almost religious quality of light, seemingly emanating from within the machine, that most noticeably marks her. Cascading down her snowy apron and creating a warm halolike glow around her head, it appears to separate her quietly from the spinning walls around her, providing a luminous moment of solace, perhaps, as she loses herself in the specialized work so associated with the ingenuity of her husband.

Further Reading

Jones, Betsy B. *Edwin Romanzo Elmer, 1850–1923.* Northampton, Mass.: Smith College Museum of Art, 1983.

Thomas Charles Farrer

London, England 1839–1891 London, England

View of Northampton from the Dome of the Hospital, 1865

Oil on canvas
28⅛ × 36 in. (71.4 × 91.4 cm)
Monogrammed and dated in red paint, lower right, initials conjoined: TCF 65
Purchased
1953:96

Though Northampton played host to the young artist Thomas Farrer for only a few months in the late summer of 1865, the fruit of that brief sojourn, his *View of Northampton*, is now acknowledged as the masterwork of his small oeuvre, as well as the most important nineteenth-century view of the town. This painting, the largest extant work he executed, can be seen as a hopeful "policy statement" for the Association for the Advancement of Truth in Art, a group of zealous young artists imbued with the precepts of John Ruskin and intent on overhauling what they perceived to be the lax and misguided methods of American landscape painting.

Farrer had arrived in the United States in the late 1850s, fresh from his training at London's Working Men's College, where the uncompromising Ruskinian philosophy of "selecting nothing and rejecting nothing" held sway. A dynamic teacher, he soon gathered around him a group of like-minded men who not only formed their small association during a meeting in Farrer's studio in 1863, but also founded an energetic periodical entitled *The New Path*. It was in these pages that they launched their attack on the status quo, indicting even the most prominent American landscape painters as insufficiently attentive to the minutiae of nature. In contrast, Farrer's "Pre-Raphaelites," as they were styled, became known for unusually meticulous and time-consuming studies of such humble subjects as patches of weeds and grass. Difficulty arose, however, when they tried to translate the results of their highly finished drawings—with dimensions measured in inches—into much larger paintings several feet in width. Members of the association had encouraged Farrer to make the attempt, and when he arrived in the congenial setting of Northampton, he evidently discovered a subject to his liking.

His panoramic view is from the hill where a state hospital for the insane had recently been constructed, and the spectator looks down on Paradise Pond, the adjoining area (which would become the campus of Smith College), the town center, and the Connecticut River valley in the distance. True to the Pre-Raphaelite philosophy, Farrer has taken great care in describing the topographical elements, particularly the tiny, cubical buildings huddled under the carefully delineated trees lining Northampton's thoroughfares. The trees are often discernible by type, such as the tall elms along Elm Street at left (they tower over a structure recognizable as the idiosyncratic residence designed by William Fenno Pratt and known as Hopkins House, one of the few buildings visible that remains on the Smith campus today).

The surface of the painting seems slightly matte and chalky, particularly in the distance, yet this in no way diminishes its intensity of vision. There is a glassy, unruffled stillness to the scene, a beguiling suspension of time that seems almost vacuum-sealed. It was this slightly clinical quality, however, that troubled the New York critics, who found much to criticize in the detailed view. Farrer had painted the Northampton of the surveyor and the real estate agent, one wrote; it was "the prose, not the poetry, of landscape." "Crude," "bald," "faulty," and "unbeautiful" were other words used, and though the painting had been praised enthusiastically while on view in Northampton, Farrer's experiment was dubbed a failure in New York. Shortly thereafter, his association ceased activity, and by 1872 Farrer had returned to England.

Further Reading

Ferber, Linda S., et al. *The New Path: Ruskin and the American Pre-Raphaelites.* Brooklyn: The Brooklyn Museum, 1985.

Lyonel Feininger

New York, New York 1871–1956 New York, New York

Gables I, Lüneburg, 1925

Oil on canvas

37¾ × 28½ in. (95.9 × 72.4 cm)

Signed and dated in green paint, upper right: Feininger/25; inscribed on stretcher in artist's hand: Lyonel Feininger/"Old Gables" (Lüneburg)

Gift of Nanette Harrison Meech (Mrs. Charles B. Meech), class of 1938, in honor of Julia Meech, class of 1963

1985:20

© 2000 Artists Rights Society (ARS), New York/ VG Bild-Kunst, Bonn

Although Lyonel Feininger was fifty years old when he first sought out the medieval brick buildings of the small north German town of Lüneburg, he had been intrigued by the expressive power of architectural forms his entire life. Born into a German immigrant family, he spent much of his childhood in Manhattan, where, at age fifteen, he took a job as a Wall Street messenger, delighting in his work among the earliest New York skyscrapers. As a young artist in Europe, where he lived for some five decades before fleeing Nazism in 1937, he had repeatedly expressed his wonder at what he termed "the quaint old houses" of Brussels, or the tall, rickety Parisian buildings he enjoyed sketching on the rue St. Jacques. Indeed, it was while living in Paris in 1906 that he took on the commission of drawing two serialized cartoons for the *Chicago Tribune*, "The Kin-der-Kids" and "Wee Willie Winkie," which were groundbreaking in their fantastic visual worlds of exaggerated, jagged architectural forms populated by angular, elongated inhabitants.

So it is not surprising that after a difficult year teaching at the famous Bauhaus school in Weimar, he and his wife set out in 1921 on a restorative tour of several towns, including Lüneburg, which featured the regional medieval style known as *Backsteingotik*. There, he made a number of drawings as he walked the streets and marveled at the patchwork series of Gothic and baroque façades — the former narrow and bristling with their towering stepped gables organized by prominent grids of brick moldings, the latter less busy, characterized by swooping rooflines and broader planes. It was, in fact, this intriguing juxtaposition of forms that he explored in a charcoal drawing a few years later and then chose as the central motif of *Gables I, Lüneburg*.

Feininger's street view is, in some respects, dependent on early explorations of cubist space by Braque and Picasso, whose paintings had profoundly impressed him when he saw them in Paris in 1911. His shimmering forms are built up from intersecting shards of space and matter; his paint surface is rather dry and mottled, with subtly valued, individual touches of the same hue defining the planes; and his objects are viewed simultaneously from two vantage points, with the main façade of the orange baroque building, for example, seen in perspective while its crown and volutes remain parallel to the picture plane. Yet Feininger rightfully distinguished his style from Cubism, suggesting at one point that his manner be dubbed "Prism-ism" for its refractive, gemlike effects of light. His buildings do seem internally lit and unusually vibrant in their coloring, giving off energized lines of force that rake the sky. Still, the street scene has not been so transmuted as to lose its spatial legibility. Thus, the foreground human figures loom larger than those nearer the buildings, and the slanting ground plane, though tipped up, lends a sense of momentum to the paths they thread through the small town. Lüneburg's historic architecture and modern residents are, at least at this point in Feininger's decades-long exploration of its urban character, compellingly bound together by this interpenetrating network of faceted modules of space.

Further Reading

Hess, Hans. *Lyonel Feininger*. New York: Harry N. Abrams, 1961.

Luckhardt, Ulrich. *Lyonel Feininger*. Munich: Prestel, 1989.

Ness, June L., ed. *Lyonel Feininger*. New York: Praeger, 1974.

Erastus Salisbury Field

Leverett, Massachusetts 1805–1900 Leverett, Massachusetts

Bethiah Smith Bassett, c. 1836

Oil on canvas
35 × 28⅞ in. (88.9 × 73.3 cm)
Not signed or dated
Purchased
1985:29–2

In the early nineteenth century, the region of western Massachusetts did not possess sufficient economic inducement for urban-trained painters of the first order to consider settling along the Connecticut River or among the Berkshire Hills to ply their trade. The extended families spread over this rural area, whose patriarchs and matriarchs were often the original founders of their small towns and who commanded a good deal of local respect, were nevertheless hungry for portrait likenesses to commemorate their accomplishments and preserve the record of their clan. Erastus Salisbury Field, a fascinating figure who spent most of his ninety-five years in the tiny villages of Leverett and Sunderland, worked for several decades in his early career to answer this local need. With a minimum of stylistic and iconographic devices, he often succeeded in isolating what appear to be singular strengths of character in his sitters, rendering them in crisp, unflinchingly spare presentations that rarely fail to confer dignity.

During the summer of 1836, Field left the Connecticut River valley and made an extended visit to the Berkshire region, spending several months in Great Barrington, Egremont, and Lee. In the last town, he had the good fortune to attract the business of the prosperous Bassett family, who commissioned at least eight portraits (for which he likely charged about $4 each). In 1783 Nathaniel Bassett, a blacksmith and Revolutionary War veteran, had moved with his wife, Bethiah (1761–1849), from their Cape Cod birthplace to Lee, just five years after that town's incorporation. They were considered among the most important of Lee's founding families, and Bethiah, depicted here in her seventy-fifth year, presided over a large kinship network of nine children, several branches of in-laws, and many grandchildren.

Bethiah Smith Bassett exhibits all the hallmarks of a standard Field portrait: the bright highlight of the red chair at the sitter's shoulder, the cloudlike gray "halo" that seems to radiate from her head and upper body, and the quick (even sloppy) brushwork as glimpsed in the ends of the bonnet ribbons and the blocky, flattened fingers. More distinctive still is the flat, decorative patterning of the body, with the freely painted foliate motif of the silk shawl laid over the pyramidal silhouette of the bodice and exaggerated leg-o'-mutton sleeves. The tapering ends of the shawl meet where the hands cross, drawing attention to her worn book, a visual marker of intellect.

It is with some force that Bassett's solidly rendered head punctures this cool arrangement of two-dimensional shapes, seemingly occupying a more proximate order of space. Enframed by the whimsical, dotted ruffle of the bonnet, its ribbons almost gushing forward from her chin, the face of this septuagenarian is lively, despite the resolute cast of her features. Her eyes are shaded, but her brows are lifted with a hint of skepticism, an expression that opens her countenance considerably and forms a striking range of wrinkles on the forehead. Below, there is a firm matter-of-factness to the set of her mouth and jaw, a plainly rendered characterization that does not shrink from attending carefully to her moustache and double chin.

Further Reading

Black, Mary. *Erastus Salisbury Field: 1805–1900.* Springfield, Mass.: Museum of Fine Arts, 1984.

Daniel Chester French

Exeter, New Hampshire 1850–1931 Stockbridge, Massachusetts

The May Queen, 1875

Marble

16 × 14 × 7½ in. (40.7 × 35.6 × 19.1 cm)

Signed, dated, and inscribed on base: D.C.FRENCH./SCULP./Florence, 1875

Gift of Dr. and Mrs. Joel E. Goldthwait (Jessie Rand, class of 1890)

1915:8

When Daniel Chester French's *May Queen* entered the Smith collection in 1915 as an early alumna gift, the art professor Alfred Vance Churchill noted in a letter to then President Marion Burton that it was Smith's first example of marble sculpture and that it would be "valuable as an example to classes of marble and marble technique." It is, indeed, a pristine embodiment of the waning neoclassical mode in sculpture, which had largely governed American expatriate production during the middle decades of the nineteenth century. Though he would later practice a more "modern" style, characterized by greater naturalism and drama and less sentiment and delicacy, French here demonstrates his mastery of the prevailing sculptural vocabulary of his teachers, especially his fellow New Englander Thomas Ball, in whose Florentine studio he first modeled this bust in clay.

French's early career is a wonderful story of innate talent and curiosity, for he was able to achieve a remarkable competence in his art—most notably in his famous *Minute Man* (1871–74) for the town of Concord, Massachusetts—with only minimal instruction. Still, the limited facilities of the United States made it imperative for any serious sculptor to spend time in Europe, and in 1874, largely because of his friendship with Preston Powers, son of the famous artist Hiram, French decided to move to Florence, where the Powers family had long presided over a flourishing expatriate community of sculptors. On his way to Italy, French was

tempted to stay in Paris, but he wrote that he found the artists there too "realistic" and "opposed to idealization of any kind." Yet when it came time to produce a domestic-scale allegorical figure for one of his Boston financial backers, he seemed curiously unengaged by his youthful subject, which just a few years later he admitted was "rather foolishly called 'The May Queen.'" Even before the clay original had been translated into marble by Italian carvers, French wrote breezily to his brother about "The bust 'May Queen' or something," remarking, "The marble work is beautifully done, but I have outgrown the model and cease to have much regard for it."

The artist's ambivalence can largely be attributed to his realization that the late-nineteenth-century art world was beginning to dismiss works such as *The May Queen* as artificial and overly sweet, but this in no way detracts from his accomplishment in this early bust. Throughout his career, French was known for his attention to detail and finish, refining and polishing his marble surfaces once the hired carvers had completed their task. This care is evident in *The May Queen,* particularly in the delightfully active crimping of the neckline of the girl's classical chiton and the carefully delineated textures of the hawthorn leaves and buds threaded through her hair and spilling over the base. Despite his own doubts as to the wisdom of the enterprise, he has successfully melded the real and the ideal in his model, with the blank, undrilled eyes and the impossible sparkle of her polished white Carrara forehead giving way to the more intimate suggestion of a slight pudginess and trace of girlish baby fat in the cheeks and under her chin.

Further Reading

Cresson, Margaret French. *Journey into Fame: The Life of Daniel Chester French.* Cambridge, Mass.: Harvard University Press, 1947.

Richman, Michael. *Daniel Chester French: An American Sculptor.* Washington, D.C.: Preservation Press, 1983.

Robert Swain Gifford

Naushon Island, Massachusetts 1840–1905 New York, New York

An Old Orchard near the Sea, Massachusetts,

1877

Oil on canvas

22⅛ × 40¼ in. (56.2 × 102.2 cm)

Signed and dated, lower left: R. Swain Gifford 1877

Purchased

1916:6-1

When Smith President L. Clark Seelye traveled to New York and visited the inaugural exhibition of the Society of American Artists in 1878, he was attending the most progressive display of American art assembled anywhere in the nation. That he eventually purchased at least three paintings from this show, including R. Swain Gifford's *Old Orchard near the Sea*, briefly made Smith College the foremost institutional patron of the new American avant-garde. Gifford was slightly older than many of the relatively unknown artists who took part in that event, and his reputation had recently been established as a moody painter of the barren, rugged shore of his native Massachusetts. Reviewers thus took note of his "strong, poetic" contribution, calling it "massively painted" and elevating it above most of the other landscapes. Gifford seems to have agreed; he reproduced his composition in an etching of 1877, and in March 1879 it represented him as an illustration in an important article on contemporary artistic trends in *Harper's New Monthly Magazine*. With its unusually high price of $900, this work signaled a new ambition for Gifford (even though Seelye, ever in search of a good deal for the college, eventually paid only $450).

An Old Orchard near the Sea is typical of the artist in its simplified composition and asymmetrical clumping of the wizened apple trees—their scraggly, unpruned branches testifying to years of neglect and abandonment. The sky is clotted and brooding, with a hint of heavier weather moving in from the left. Aside from the rude shack, stranded wagon, and anonymous seated figures, there is little to note beyond the active, open brushwork itself; broad, dense, and layered, it is built up in the rutted foreground with pointillist dabs of dry color and a scrubbing in of thicker, silvery paint. During this period of the budding colonial revival, Gifford's audience responded vigorously to the poignant, sober air of melancholic retrospection in his work. Reading in the gnarled trees, spiky stubble, and bleak, hooded atmosphere a laudable, virile expression of the hardscrabble Puritan existence that had come to be romantically associated with this terrain, they indulged in a wash of aching nostalgia before his sterile moorland.

The critic Susan Carter, in a notably extended commentary on the painting, wonderfully epitomized this response:

> We can all of us, who are used to New England, recall such places as this is, and know the feeling and the look of the grass that yet grows up, and keeps partially green, out of dry earth that the sun bakes into a hard crust.... The picture is a poem in paint, full of the meat of thought, and palpable to the senses, till we smell the dry, warm air, and crunch the coarse grass beneath our tread; and the objects in the picture cluster about themselves a vast crowd of unseen associations of the near farm, the open, moaning sea, and through the pleasant summer weather blows a whiff from the winter days which scarred these trees so, and blew up the white sand to trench upon the fertile fields. Mr. Gifford's beautiful, rich colour and his firm use of his brush have long been admired; but in this fresh story-picture it is not till after we have appreciated the thoughts it awakens that we notice how rich and how fine are the browns, the purples, the blues, and the grey tones, so completely is the manner lost in the matter of this fine work.

Further Reading

Carter, S. N. "First Exhibition of the American Art Association." *Art Journal* 4 (April 1878): 124–26.

Hall, Elton W. *R. Swain Gifford, 1840–1905*. New Bedford, Mass.: Old Dartmouth Historical Society, 1974.

Marsden Hartley

Lewiston, Maine 1877–1943 Ellsworth, Maine

Sea Window — Tinker Mackerel, 1942

Oil on Masonite

40 × 30 in. (101.6 × 76.2 cm)

Signed and dated in black paint, lower right: MH/42; inscribed on back: Sea Window—Tinker Mackerel

Purchased, Sarah J. Mather Fund

1947:8-1

Sea Window — Tinker Mackerel was painted in the last year of Marsden Hartley's life, during a period of mixed personal fortunes. After a decade or more of financial difficulties and perceived neglect from critics, the artist was finally enjoying renewed fame and sales. Yet at the same time his health was declining precipitously, and his enthusiasm for his work was tempered by his increasing physical debility. The situation seems to have prompted him to adhere with even greater conviction to his self-identified role as the preeminent native-born painter of Maine, territory he had deliberately laid claim to when he first revisited his home state in 1937 after a relatively long absence. It was no doubt with a sense of solace and security that the artist returned to Maine subjects and, in particular, to his favored window view, which had preoccupied him during difficult periods in his career for some twenty-five years. In works like *Sea Window — Tinker Mackerel,* he was able to combine his love of still life and seascape, while also continuing his exploration of the symbolic, even religious significance of his humble iconography.

Hartley invested the lives of the New England fisherfolk he so admired with mystical import. In his search for a congenial location in which to paint, the stalwart simplicity of the local inhabitants was as crucial to him as the strong scenery that would inspire his paintings. In the small village of Corea, Maine, he felt that he had found all the necessary components for his art, including a generous host family, Forest and Katie Young and their children, who solicitously cared for the elderly artist. It was there that he painted *Sea Window — Tinker Mackerel,* with its affecting arrangement of glistening blue-gray fish arranged in the foreground like an offering before his view of faraway islands.

The vaguely Christian symbolism of Hartley's fish had been established in earlier works such as *Give Us This Day* (1938, private collection), but here they also function formally as an enlivening element in his conceptual, abstractive composition of overlapping planes and expressionistically worked areas of color. Their reflective, silvery tonality and the quivering lines of motion that surround them give this "school" of fish the appearance of swimming on the tipped-up, blood red tabletop, as though they have just been scooped out of the distant ocean. Other biomorphic forms, such as the floating clouds and the maroon blotches on the walls framing the window, further punctuate the rectilinear fields, yet with very different spatial results. The clouds diminish in size in the distance in much the same way that the animated brushwork in the water grows calm at the horizon. Hartley thus achieves a telescoping impression of depth, without resorting to conventional perspectival means. The darkened interior space of the viewer, in contrast, remains flat and compressed. Its somber tonality, coupled with the longing gaze across the sunlit sea, creates a balanced mood and a powerfully suggestive arrangement of interlocking parts.

Further Reading

Haskell, Barbara. *Marsden Hartley.* New York: Whitney Museum of American Art, 1980.

Robertson, Bruce. *Marsden Hartley.* New York: Harry N. Abrams, 1995.

Scott, Gail R. *Marsden Hartley.* New York: Abbeville Press, 1988.

William Stanley Haseltine

Philadelphia, Pennsylvania 1835–1900 Rome, Italy

Natural Arch, Capri, c. 1855–76

Oil on canvas
15¹⁄₁₆ × 23¹⁵⁄₁₆ in. (38.3 × 60.8 cm)
Not signed or dated
Gift of Helen Haseltine Plowden (Mrs. Roger H. Plowden)
1952:4

William Haseltine's "rock-portraits," to use a term coined by the contemporary critic Henry Tuckerman, are utterly distinctive in their pronounced attention to the weathered, faceted textures of the cliffs towering dramatically above limpid seas. A graduate of Harvard in 1854, Haseltine no doubt became attracted to the pictorial possibilities of coastal geology while a member of the university's Natural History Society. Traveling within the influential orbit of the Harvard naturalist Louis Agassiz, the young painter, who once said that "every real artist is also a scientist," came to study the massive, slablike forms of the rocks that rise from the ocean at Nahant, Massachusetts. This resort was a primary inspiration for Agassiz's theory of a pervasive ice age, and Haseltine's petrologically precise drawings and paintings were seen as remarkably expressive of the telltale natural evidence of the glacial formation of the earth's topography. Indeed, after returning from a period of study in Düsseldorf, he became well known in his early career for these evocative compositions of water, sky, and rock — in all their elemental purity.

In 1866, however, Haseltine left his New York home and settled with his family in Europe, participating in the general American thirst for travel and change in the wake of the debilitating Civil War. Although he made frequent trips back to the United States, the remainder of his career was centered in Italy, where he exhibited rarely and became much less involved in the American art scene. Possessed of independent means, Haseltine did not suffer from his diminished public reputation. Living extremely comfortably in large apartments in Rome's Palazzo Altieri, he regularly sold his paintings to visiting American tourists, whose constant demand for a limited range of Italian subjects meant that the artist's work changed little over the years.

One such site, which Haseltine first visited as a student in 1858 and returned to at least four times, was the craggy island of Capri, in the Bay of Naples. The artist repeatedly explored its precipitous limestone cliffs, which plunge almost vertically into the sapphire depths of the Mediterranean; a Caprese landscape subject was almost always among the groups of paintings he occasionally sent to represent him at international exhibitions. The Centennial Exposition in Philadelphia, for example, included a painting of the famous Arco Naturale of Capri, although not, in all likelihood, the Smith canvas. Still, this moderately ambitious study of clear, bright sun breaking across the chiseled heights of the island is entirely typical of Haseltine's restrained tonal style. The cool blues of the sky and water, lending a pastel tinge to the flattened promontory in the distance, are very thinly painted. At left, the highly tactile forms of the rocks are constructed with more opaque paint, but the pictorial surface is still relatively sheer, with careful networks of olive green and blue veining shot through in a liquid medium. Light — indicated by cream-colored touches of slight impasto — edges the sharpest corners of the forms, but the most dramatic contrast comes from the "keyhole" view through the natural arch and its toothy, jagged upper contour silhouetted asymmetrically against the sky. Here, in the quiet play of these abstracted natural formations, Haseltine hints at the majestic force that underlies their genesis in the distant past.

Further Reading

Plowden, Helen Haseltine. *William Stanley Haseltine: Sea and Landscape Painter (1835–1900).* London: Frederick Muller Ltd., 1947.

Simpson, Marc, et al. *Expressions of Place: The Art of William Stanley Haseltine.* San Francisco: The Fine Arts Museums of San Francisco, 1992.

Childe Hassam

Dorchester, Massachusetts 1859–1935 East Hampton, New York

Cab Stand at Night, Madison Square, 1891

Oil on wood panel
8¹⁵⁄₁₆ × 14⅜ in. (irregular) (22.7 × 36.4 cm)
Signed and dated in blue paint, lower left: Childe/Hassam/1891;
inscribed on back of panel, upside down, in pencil, across entire
height and width of panel: Electric Light [illegible]
Bequest of Annie Swan Coburn (Mrs. Lewis Larned Coburn)
1934:3-2

No American impressionist was more devoted to the exciting visual spectacle of urban life than Childe Hassam, an artist who first explored the pictorial possibilities of Boston's parks and avenues in the mid-1880s, discovered the even grander boulevards of Paris while a student in the late 1880s, and later became the premier painter of his adopted city of New York, where he moved in 1889. Upon arriving, Hassam and his wife took a studio apartment on the second floor of a building at the corner of Fifth Avenue and Seventeenth Street, a perfect location for observing the bustle and flux of the heavy pedestrian, cab, and omnibus traffic concentrated in this developing commercial and entertainment district. He completed more than fifty New York paintings during the decade of the 1890s, and most of them depict scenes in the ten-block area surrounding his initial home, bounded by the famous parks of Union and Madison Squares.

In an interview Hassam gave just a year after completing *Cab Stand at Night, Madison Square,* he reflected on his attraction to street scenes: "There is nothing so interesting to me as people. I am never tired of observing them in every-day life, as they hurry through the streets on business or saunter down the promenade on pleasure. Humanity in motion is a continual study to me." In his pursuit of the momentary and the fleeting, he often had recourse to hiring a relatively new form of urban transportation, the one-horse hansom cab. Hassam would sit in the cab, stationary by the curb, and sketch his impressions of the crowds who streamed past his window. In the process, he became aware of the picturesque effects of his professional drivers. "There is no end of material in the cabbies," he explained. "Their backs are quite as expressive as their faces. They live so much in their clothes that they get to be like thin shells, and take on every angle and curve of their tempers as well as their forms. They interest one immensely."

In this small panel, Hassam turns the backs of his cabbies to the viewer as they huddle together for conversation and warmth while awaiting their fares. The street curves into the distance, with its lineup of lantern-lit cabs at the ready. The peach-colored twinkle of lights and the suggestion of a buzzing mass of people in the background perhaps signal the end of a performance, with the audience spilling onto the sidewalk in search of a way home. The warm glow of the throng, however, has not yet reached the small group of cabbies in the foreground. They stand alone in the bare, metallic glare of the high electric lamps that had been introduced along this stretch of Broadway several years earlier. While newspaper accounts of the time worried about the harsh effects of this new form of illumination — "dismal and depressing in comparison with the deep and agreeable yellow of the gas jets," according to the *New York Times* — Hassam embraces this resolutely modern scene, delighting in the artificial shift in tints of his nocturnal palette and the haunting quality of the saplings' shadows, reaching across the snowy pavement and up the cabbies' greatcoats like spidery blue veins filled with ice water. It is a daring pictorial statement that would have been inconceivable even a decade earlier, one that revels in the new possibilities of vision in the modern era.

Further Reading

Fort, Ilene Susan. *Childe Hassam's New York.* San Francisco: Pomegranate Art Books, 1993.

Ives, A. E. "Talks with Artists." *Art Amateur* 27 (October 1892): 116–17.

Hiesinger, Ulrich W. *Childe Hassam: American Impressionist.* New York: Jordan-Volpe Gallery, 1994.

Childe Hassam

Dorchester, Massachusetts 1859–1935 East Hampton, New York

Union Square in Spring, 1896

Oil on canvas
21½ × 21 in. (54.5 × 53.3 cm)
Signed and dated, lower right: Childe Hassam 1896
Purchased
1905:3-1

Union Square in Spring, painted seven years after Childe Hassam returned from a student sojourn in Paris, marks a decided leap in his work toward greater abstraction and more radical compositional strategies. The artist had long since assimilated the broken impressionist brushwork and the penchant for transient, blurred effects of movement and atmosphere that he had first explored tentatively in Paris, but with the elevated point of view and the unconventional square format of this painting, he moved further toward an authoritative and personal embrace of the sprawling visual energies of New York, the city he championed as the greatest metropolis the world had known. His French predecessors, such as Claude Monet and Pierre-Auguste Renoir, were pioneers in the investigation of the novel, glancing perspectives on urban life achieved through a raised vantage point, notably in a pair of views of the Pont Neuf they painted in Paris in the 1870s. The advent of the skyscraper, however, allowed Hassam to push such effects far beyond these more gentle antecedents.

Union Square had been opened and developed in the early nineteenth century as a privileged residential enclave, surrounded by three- and four-story row houses inhabited by such prominent New Yorkers as the mining and railroad magnate Anson G. Phelps and the lawyer Samuel G. Ruggles. Yet few of these quiet structures remained by the time Hassam arrived on the scene, for the neighborhood had gone through several periods of comprehensive redevelopment and transition to retail and entertainment uses. As the southern anchor of the stretch of Broadway known as "Ladies Mile," the park had become bordered by vast cast-iron department stores, and other specialized "industries" — such as hotels, theaters, and piano showrooms — had also flocked to the neighborhood.

Hassam's view of this busy crossroads was likely taken from a perch atop the seven-story Century Building at the north end of the park, a structure housing a publishing company for which he had done some illustration work. Scanning from the left, he captures the blunt, protruding form of the Empire-style Union Square Hotel at the edge of his composition, the multibuilding complex of the Morton House Hotel and Union Square Theatre at center, and the giant double colonnade of the Domestic Sewing Machine Company at right. In the distance, the parallel thoroughfares of Fourth Avenue and Broadway extend the perspective to the hazy lower reaches of Manhattan, the prominent steeple of Grace Episcopal Church breaking the horizon just right of center. At the bottom of the composition, the humble roof of a public "comfort station" provides a more intimate bridge into the pictorial space.

With some background knowledge, these structures can be readily identified, but Hassam by no means paints an exacting architectural "portrait" of the square (indeed, several scholars have mistakenly assumed that his view faces north, rather than south). What seems to interest him are the contrasts inherent in this telescopic slice of urban topography: the twisting paths and relaxed islands of grass versus the rigidity of the densely built-up grid beyond, and the fresh colors of the budding leaves versus the smoky haze of the background. While the park might be seen as a refuge, it nevertheless possesses a sharp, acidic edge, with the close tones of Hassam's lichenous greens and pale yellows giving rise to scintillating optical vibrations. His paint fairly sizzles on the surface of the canvas, capturing the seasonal urban excitement the artist once referred to as "this Spring festival of life."

Further Reading

Fort, Ilene Susan. *Childe Hassam's New York.* San Francisco: Pomegranate Art Books, 1993.

Gerdts, William H. *Impressionist New York.* New York: Abbeville Press, 1994.

Hiesinger, Ulrich W. *Childe Hassam: American Impressionist.* New York: Jordan-Volpe Gallery, 1994.

Childe Hassam

Dorchester, Massachusetts 1859–1935 East Hampton, New York

White Island Light, Isles of Shoals, at Sundown,
1899

Oil on canvas

27 × 27 in. (68.6 × 68.6 cm)

Signed and dated in maroon, purple, and black paint, lower right:
Childe Hassam/1899; inscribed on back of canvas in brown paint
over pencil, upper right: White Island Light Isles of Shoals/at
Sundown./[initials in a circle, probably C.H.]/1899

Gift of Mr. and Mrs. Harold D. Hodgkinson (Laura White Cabot,
class of 1922)

1973:51

Childe Hassam's views of New York constitute a remarkable artistic achievement, but his extremely productive
career went far beyond the single category of "urban
impressionist." Indeed, to judge by the numbers alone,
the windswept Isles of Shoals, a cluster of bare granite
outcroppings that rise from the sea ten miles off the
coast of New Hampshire, became the artist's primary
geographic touchstone; he is estimated to have executed
some four hundred images of the islands during the
three decades he visited them habitually. Individually
and as a group, they are among the most luminous and
brilliantly colored works of his oeuvre.

Hassam owed his experience of the Isles of Shoals to
the poet and gardener Celia Thaxter, who had spent
part of her childhood on White Island when her father
served as keeper of the lighthouse, the same structure
that is visible on the horizon in the Smith College painting. Her father later purchased several of the islands
and developed them as warm-weather resorts, and as an
adult she came to preside over a small artistic community that gathered each summer around her cottage on
Appledore Island. Thaxter was renowned for her expansive beds of perennials, which she used largely as a cutting garden to provide a constant supply of flowers for
her famed parlor, where Hassam was a regular guest.
The two became devoted friends, and the artist began to
work in a private studio nearby to enable him to paint
the clouds of color that seemed to drift daily from her
garden into her airy home. In 1894, however, Hassam lost
his supportive friend to heart disease, and for the next
five years he did not visit the island. When he returned
in 1899, the year *White Island Light, Isles of Shoals* was
painted, he began a new series of images that he would
pursue for well over a decade.

With Thaxter gone, Hassam turned to the sea and
began an extended exploration of the elemental confrontation of water and stone. Appledore was celebrated
for its stark, vertiginous cliffs and its deeply cut fjords,
such as South Gorge, the rugged inlet depicted here.
Hassam takes full advantage of this dramatic topography, creating a shifting, almost galloping perspective
with sudden visual plunges and abrupt leaps between
two- and three-dimensional spaces. His brushwork is
unusually assertive, with dry, bristling hatch marks
swarming over his forms—the saturated cobalt blue, in
particular, hovering insistently on the surface. These
uniformly short strokes appear to arrange themselves
like boldly colored iron filings, manipulated by some
unseen magnet underneath the canvas. Yet the direc-
tionality of his brushwork also serves as the primary
indicator of the varying textures described in the view:
scratchy foliage bursting outward and spreading indis-
criminately in the foreground, knobby protuberances
swelling slightly in the rocks, and parallel ripples in the
water creating a calmer impression of regularity and
flow. It is resolutely conceptual in its construction, and
in the end, we identify as much with the painterly act
of dragging the loaded brush across bare canvas as with
the affecting scene itself.

Further Reading

Curry, David Park. *Childe Hassam: An Island Garden
Revisited.* Denver: Denver Art Museum, 1990.

Hiesinger, Ulrich W. *Childe Hassam: American Impressionist.*
New York: Jordan-Volpe Gallery, 1994.

Martin Johnson Heade

Lumberville, Pennsylvania 1819–1904 Saint Augustine, Florida

New Jersey Meadows, c. 1871–75

Oil on canvas
15⅛ × 30⅛ in. (38.4 × 76.5 cm)
Signed in black paint, lower left: M. J. Heade
Purchased
1951:298

The life of Martin Johnson Heade was filled with contradictions. One of the most widely traveled nineteenth-century American artists, he nevertheless maintained a distinctly low profile in the cosmopolitan art capital of New York City. Socially and professionally unconnected, he was refused membership in the prestigious Century Association and National Academy of Design; one of his only artist friends was Frederic Edwin Church, whose grand, global landscape vision was the antithesis of Heade's small, intimate views of undramatic terrain. Though he sold hundreds of paintings, he went relatively unmentioned in the contemporary review literature. The critic James Jackson Jarves's tepid characterization of Heade's landscapes as "wearisome" in their "horizontal lines and perspective" was a typical comment. In this light, Heade's favorite subject of flat salt marshes seems appropriate to the man: ubiquitous and unremarkable, but also odd and lonely, even poignant in their celebration of the banal places bound by inland hills and the ocean shore.

Heade's marshes are actually fascinating "in-between" landscapes, flourishing environments for hardy strains of grasses that grow wild but were nevertheless harvested for a brief cutting season in late summer or early autumn—an unusual combination of the savage and the pastoral. Rutted and spongy, with snaking canals meandering into the distance, his resolutely horizontal landscapes seem to offer little to the eye accustomed to crashing waves or towering mountain ranges. Indeed, Heade's banded compositions seem to laugh in the face of received aesthetic theory regarding the picturesque and the sublime. Among the only notable pictorial elements are the huge haystacks—some in the nineteenth century rising to heights of twenty feet—which kept the salt grasses elevated and dry as they awaited use as fodder and packing. Perhaps their only visual comparison in American art is found in views of the western plains, where grazing buffalo dotting the prairie have a similar monumental presence.

New Jersey Meadows (the title was given the work in the twentieth century) may well depict the marshes near Hoboken, close to Heade's Manhattan home during the late 1860s and 1870s, but it could also refer to the Massachusetts marshes near Newburyport, where he first pursued this landscape subject. The tiny brown cow, in fact, with its curving back reiterating the lazy bend of the nearby canal, comes from a drawing in one of Heade's Massachusetts sketchbooks dated to 1862. The painting's proportions are normal for the artist: twice as wide as it is high, with nearly two-thirds of the canvas area devoted to the sky. Here, the changing effects of light and weather constitute the principal interest. A storm passes to the right, its screenlike sheet of dark rain giving way to blue sky and fluffier white cumulus clouds at the left. Bright sunlight breaks across the plain, setting the texture of its many-colored stipple strokes into relief. The absence of conventional framing motifs adds to the sense of movement and mutability. Heade's compositional elements—the clouds, the rutted ditches, the switchback canal, and the succession of haystacks receding infinitely into the distance—all induce a lateral rocking motion, a sweeping, panning vision that moves us naturally, not forcibly, through space. In the end, the artist takes advantage of his unpromising subject to connect the viewer with surprising effectiveness to the slow rhythms of the landscape.

Further Reading

Frazier, Nancy. "Mute Gospel: The Salt Marshes of Martin Johnson Heade." *Prospects: An Annual of American Cultural Studies* 23 (1998): 193–207.

Novak, Barbara, and Timothy A. Eaton. *Martin Johnson Heade: A Survey, 1840–1900.* West Palm Beach, Fla.: Eaton Fine Art, 1996.

Stebbins, Theodore E., Jr. with the assistance of Janet L. Comey and Karen E. Quinn. *The Life and Work of Martin Johnson Heade: A Critical Analysis and Catalogue Raisonné.* New Haven, Conn.: Yale University Press, 2000.

Winslow Homer

Boston, Massachusetts 1836–1910 Prout's Neck, Maine

Shipyard at Gloucester, 1871

Oil on canvas
13½ × 19¾ in. (34.3 × 50.2 cm)
Signed and dated in reddish brown paint, lower left: HOMER '71
Purchased
1950:99

With the end of the Civil War in 1865 and the completion of his first trip to Europe in 1867, Winslow Homer found himself free, in the late 1860s and early 1870s, to explore a range of new subjects—quite a few of them stemming from his experiences of the varied activities and terrain of the Atlantic seacoast. Whereas earlier he had evinced a mild interest in the touristic, leisured environment of Long Branch, a bathing place on the New Jersey shore, Homer was attracted instead to the traditional maritime trades of fishing and boat-building in Gloucester, Massachusetts (much like his predecessor Fitz Hugh Lane, the painter most associated with the site). The idle summer visitors who had been flocking to the Cape Ann port for several decades make no appearance in the Gloucester works that occupied Homer off and on throughout the 1870s.

Shipyard at Gloucester, a broadly brushed but careful study, is an important foundation work for this series. For some time, however, its title and identification have been disputed by scholars. According to the written record, Homer's earliest documented trip to Gloucester took place in 1873, thus the date of 1871, clearly painted by the artist in the lower left corner, suggested to many authorities that the location depicted in this work was necessarily another seaport, perhaps nearby Essex. Comparison with a securely documented contemporary photograph of the David A. Story shipyard in Gloucester Harbor, however, has affirmed the title. Homer clearly visited the port of Gloucester prior to the trip of 1873; the architectural details at left and right are unmistakably local. Though it is difficult to believe that there could still be lacunae in the biography of this much-studied artist, the Smith painting nevertheless stands as the only trace of Homer's initial visit to the harbor.

Beyond the realm of art history, the painting provides valuable information to naval historians regarding the construction of the typical Gloucester fishing schooner, or "clipper." Well over a dozen workers surround the hull, busily drilling, hammering, and planing. The distinctive outline of the local type of ship, with its sharply pointed ends, wide beam, and flattened bottom (so as better to navigate the shallow harbor of Gloucester), is readily apparent, as are the traditional methods of craftsmanship in use before the advent of power tools. Though anonymous, the shipbuilders are presented as a team, their black silhouettes nicely punctuating the solid, planar form of the hull. There is something heroic about the sleek vessel elevated on a kind of pedestal. Dwarfing its makers, it is lifted suggestively at the bow, as if already mounting a heaving Atlantic wave.

This effect is heightened by the dramatic perspectival rush of the foreground, with the thick oak slabs fanning out laterally and leading the viewer's eye to the gangboard and scaffolding. Homer accentuates the raw, solid qualities of these materials—still bearing the imprint of nature in their organic profiles and bark-lined edges. With the visually cacophonous pile of squared-off beams added at the left and the pervasive textures and warm tones of sawdust and wood shavings throughout, we are left to wonder at the ability of these workers to transform such rude building blocks into an object of such calculated refinement. Two years later, when Homer used this composition as the background for an engraving depicting several Gloucester boys intently building their own toy boats, the generational nature of this craft tradition, passed from fathers to sons, was also underscored.

Further Reading

Atkinson, D. Scott, and Jochen Wierich. *Winslow Homer in Gloucester*. Chicago: Terra Museum of American Art, 1990.

Hendricks, Gordon. *The Life and Work of Winslow Homer*. New York: Harry N. Abrams, 1979.

Ronnberg, Erik A. R., Jr. "Vincent's Cove in the 1870s: A Pictorial Record of Gloucester Shipbuilding." *Nautical Research Journal* 41 (December 1996): 209–18.

Edward Hopper

Nyack, New York 1882–1967 New York, New York

Pretty Penny, 1939

Oil on canvas

29 × 40 in. (73.6 × 101.6 cm)

Signed in green paint, lower right: EDWARD HOPPER

Gift of Mrs. Charles MacArthur (Helen Hayes, LHD, class of 1940)

1965:4

Edward Hopper's *Pretty Penny* is, on the one hand, closely linked to the formative years of the artist and to his lifelong pursuit of American architectural subjects; on the other hand, it stands as a complete (and even painful) anomaly in his career, a work he likely would have preferred never to have executed. The house depicted stands just down the road from Hopper's boyhood home in Nyack, some forty miles north of New York City. The Hopper home, built by the artist's maternal grandfather, was modest in comparison with its twenty-room neighbor, but its bracketed, clapboard exterior was of the mid-nineteenth-century vernacular tradition Hopper grew to love, memorably describing it as "our native architecture with its hideous beauty, its fantastic roofs, pseudo-Gothic, French Mansard, Colonial, mongrel or what not."

By the late 1930s, Hopper had become celebrated for his moody, haunting evocations of neglected revival-style homes, often bordering railyards or otherwise relegated to the dusty margins of formerly thriving towns. It was knowledge of this predilection that prompted the actress Helen Hayes and her playwright husband, Charles MacArthur, to attempt to commission the artist to paint a "portrait" of their large home in Nyack, which they had purchased in 1930, renamed Pretty Penny, and restored with great effort. The combination of Hopper's status as a neighborhood boy made good and the busy, eclectic exterior of their home — which they considered a sympathetic example of the typical Hopperesque architectural mode — no doubt seemed like the perfect match of artist and subject.

Hopper, however, unaccustomed to accepting commissions of any type, chafed at the imposition of a subject not of his choosing. After grudgingly making a trip to Nyack to scout the site, he pronounced the house unpaintable. "There's no light and there's no air that I can find for that house," Hayes remembered him complaining. Mindful of the celebrity of the patron and the generous fee of $2,500 that was offered, Hopper's wife, Jo, and his dealer, Frank Rehn, worked hard to convince the artist to reconsider. In the end, he rode the bus up from New York on two subsequent November days. Avoiding contact with Hayes as much as possible, he sat alone in the cold, making a series of careful drawings of the house. Jo Hopper's diary records his attempts to find the right angle that would allow him to simplify the façade — clarifying the lines, making it less fussy, and countering the homey, sweet appearance that Hayes and MacArthur had spent so much time achieving.

The chilly winter sunlight Hopper encountered helped to deaden the cheery mood of the house, and the bristly textures of the long, curving evergreen boughs, seemingly raking the picture surface from the upper left corner, effectively keep the assertive, sculptural details of the house in check, somewhat collapsing the three-dimensional qualities of the image. The angular, slanting shapes of the low shrubs are worked with a rougher style of brushwork than the house, imparting a sense of visual movement that also counteracts its more regular geometries. Though it must have been galling for Hopper to paint each of the individual brackets and clapboards of the house, they are treated, in their shadows, with a cool blue tonality not out of keeping with the artist's normal aesthetic. The warm light and glimpses of furniture in the windows, however, give Pretty Penny an open and friendly air, in contrast to the charged, anguished qualities of so many of his other domestic subjects.

Using a squared-off grid to transfer the composition from his drawing, Hopper actually completed the painting in relatively short order just before Christmas 1939. Fending off a last-minute request from Hayes to include her daughter, Mary, and her pet poodle, Camille, in the composition, Hopper must have been relieved to turn the finished composition over to his dealer. He never again accepted a commission.

Further Reading

Goodrich, Lloyd, et al. "Six Who Knew Edward Hopper." *Art Journal* 41 (Summer 1981): 125–35.

Hobbs, Robert. *Edward Hopper.* New York: Harry N. Abrams, 1987.

Levin, Gail. *Edward Hopper: An Intimate Biography.* New York: Alfred A. Knopf, 1995.

George Inness

Newburgh, New York 1825–1894 Bridge-of-Allan, Scotland

Landscape, 1877

Oil on canvas
25⅝ × 38½ in. (65.1 × 97.8 cm)
Signed and dated in black paint, lower right: G. Inness 1877
Bequest of Frank L. Harrington in honor of Louise Cronin
Harrington, class of 1926
1989:6

Almost single-handedly, George Inness can be credited with effecting a sea change in that most important category of mid-nineteenth-century American art, landscape painting. Although he began his career in the mid-1840s at the same time as such luminaries of the Hudson River School as Frederic Edwin Church and Jasper Cropsey, within little more than a decade Inness had largely abandoned their careful approach to botanical and geological detail, as well as their grandiose, panoramic embrace of more terrain than the eye and brain can easily comprehend. Profoundly affected by the looser, more subdued style of the French Barbizon painters (whose work he studied during several European sojourns), Inness gradually moved toward a ruminant, painterly means of expression, one richly imbued with undertones of nostalgia, quietism, and mysticism. By the time of his death, he had become lionized as a poetic seer whose landscape vision had surpassed that of every other artist in the nation.

Part of Inness's innovative approach was a retreat from geographically specific scene painting; thus his Landscape, an important example of his mature style of the late 1870s, cannot be definitively associated with a particular place. After returning from his third European trip in 1875, he lived in Medfield, Massachusetts, near Boston, for two years and then moved to the New York area, painting in northern New Jersey and settling definitively in Montclair in 1878. This composition might be derived from any of these places, or from another loca-tion visited by the artist in earlier years; the "facts," Inness would have argued, are unimportant, as is the social utility or "message" that critics of painting often searched for at the time. Just a year after finishing Landscape, Inness made one of the many aesthetic pronouncements to which he was prone: "A work of art does not appeal to the intellect," he wrote. "It does not appeal to the moral sense. Its aim is not to instruct, not to edify, but to awaken an emotion."

The emotions awakened by Landscape necessarily depend on the individual viewer, but its general themes are favorites to which Inness returned again and again: a lone "peasant" figure moving slowly through the middle ground, a settled landscape with farm structures dotting the terrain, and a pronounced pictorial focus on a single tree — in this case forming the compositional crux around which his several, partially obscured vignettes seem to pivot. The brushwork of the painting is not at all consistent, as though the artist changed stroke with each passing mood. Thus the bright field at left is a boldly applied, uninterrupted streak of rich yellow paint, while the surrounding foliage is composed of his more characteristic dabbing. At times his brush is quite dry, used to indicate scratchy, tentative branches against the sky or the broken textures of the darkened foreground. Scale (among the figure, the log, the fence, and the nearby cottage) also appears unresolved, but overall, a soft, billowing impression and a certain sobriety of tone bring these elements into accord. Time seems heavy, and Inness leaves the viewer, as in all of his most successful canvases, with a suggestive, wistful distillation of memory and mood.

Further Reading

Cikovsky, Nicolai, Jr., and Michael Quick. George Inness. Los Angeles: Los Angeles County Museum of Art, 1985.

Gerdts, William H., et al. George Inness: Presence of the Unseen. Montclair, N.J.: Montclair Art Museum, 1994.

Rockwell Kent

Tarrytown, New York 1882–1971 Au Sable Forks, New York

Dublin Pond, 1903

Oil on canvas
28 × 30 in. (71.1 × 76.2 cm)
Signed and dated in blue paint, lower right: Rockwell Kent 1903
Purchased, Winthrop Hillyer Fund
1904:2-1

Dublin Pond was Rockwell Kent's first professional success, a work that exhibits the influence of his powerful mentor, Abbott Thayer, but also shows a more modern exploration of abstraction and compositional simplicity. Although he had studied briefly with William Merritt Chase as a teenager, the young Kent was still very much a student when he arrived in Dublin, New Hampshire, in the summer of 1903. Thanks to an introduction from his aunt, an amateur painter who had formerly studied with Thayer, the older artist had invited Kent to serve as his assistant, participating in the unusual studio practice he devised to safeguard his paintings against his own unstable nature and unpredictable experimentation in brushwork. Once he had worked a painting to a certain degree of finish, Thayer had it copied by one of his students and then worked further on the copy to push forward his conception, only returning to the original when it was clear that he had not ruined the initial motif.

As it turned out, Thayer had little need of an assistant that summer, and, impressed by Kent's ability, he encouraged him to paint on his own. The degree to which anyone in the tightly knit Thayer ménage could do that, however, is questionable. Highly idiosyncratic and domineering, the older artist demanded near-worship from his family and students. All were forced to bow to his odd notions of rustic living, and his own version of transcendental mysticism was the local gospel. This included an awed reverence for the blunt, hulking form of nearby Mount Monadnock and the quiet calm of Dublin Pond. Thayer's repeated exploration of these subjects usually took the form of somewhat top-heavy compositions with the central motif of the pine-clad mountain arcing gently against a narrow band of sky and trailing off to unfinished empty space below. This, not surprisingly, became the conceptual template for Kent as well.

Still, *Dublin Pond* is no slavish copy of Thayer's obsessive image. Its slablike, squarish arrangement of forms is much more elemental, even brutal, than his teacher's work. At the same time it is also contrived and consciously aesthetic in its reduced, close-keyed palette and its Asian-inspired asymmetry and subordination of the parts to the whole. The reflective surface has the quality of baked enamel, yet close examination reveals a textural relief of many layers of impastoed application. The eye is drawn to the borders of the interlocking parts: the irreal glow of the mint green sky meeting the blue-black mountain and, below, its darkened, ragged-edged reflection stitched together with the luminous water by Kent's splintered brushstrokes. With these extremes of contrast, one has to look hard to discern the delicate, thin forms of the evergreen trees and architectural structures along the water line. These subtle details nicely complicate the first impression of the painting as monolithic and starkly iconic. All told, it was a rather audacious decision by L. Clark Seelye to acquire *Dublin Pond* out of the Society of American Artists exhibition of 1904; it became the first public purchase for the little-known artist.

Further Reading

A Circle of Friends: Art Colonies of Cornish and Dublin. Durham, N.H.: University Art Galleries, 1985.

Kent, Rockwell. *It's Me, O Lord.* New York: Dodd, Mead & Co., 1955.

West, Richard V., et al. *"An Enkindled Eye": The Paintings of Rockwell Kent.* Santa Barbara, Calif.: Santa Barbara Museum of Art, 1985.

Franz Kline

Wilkes-Barre, Pennsylvania 1910–1962 New York, New York

Rose, Purple and Black, 1958

Oil on canvas
45 × 36⅛ in. (114.3 × 91.8 cm)
Signed and dated on back: Franz Kline 1958
Gift of Mrs. Sigmund W. Kunstadter (Maxine Weil, class of 1924)
1965:27
© 2000 The Franz Kline Estate/Artists Rights Society (ARS), New York

Although Franz Kline had been painting in New York in a variety of styles for over a decade, it was not until his one-person exhibition at the Charles Egan Gallery in 1950 that he burst into the critical limelight and popular consciousness. There he showed eleven large abstract canvases in what would become his signature mode of expression: stark arrangements of thick black bars seemingly moving through a worked white environment with the force of pile drivers. While only two of the paintings found buyers (they were priced at about $700 each), Kline's breakthrough style became seared into the minds of the writers, collectors, and artists who followed Abstract Expressionism. He would continue this path of exploration fruitfully for the rest of his comparatively short career.

Rose, Purple and Black, as the title implies, comes from the last period of Kline's work, when he allowed color to become more of an integral compositional agent than it had been in the "classic" black-and-white images of the early 1950s. Still, the complex, layered surface of the painting, along with the additive working method of the artist, ensures that viewers must become intimately acquainted with his active brushwork in order to discern its surprising chromatic range. Indeed, this invitation to "watch it happen" as his stratified relief of strokes takes shape constitutes one of the thrills of studying a Kline, a close-up pleasure in the fullness of his paint that is completely different from the experience of viewing his powerful, outsize compositions from a distance. Despite the slapdash appearance of his works (especially apparent in the splinterlike drips of black paint at the bottom in *Rose, Purple and Black*), Kline usually planned his paintings carefully, often working from smaller ink or oil-on-paper sketches. It was not uncommon for the thick black forms to be laid down over time with small brushes, and the major compositional elements were continuously tested, shifted, and painted over in an attempt to work out the optimal dynamic balance of weight, value, and hue.

In *Rose, Purple and Black*, this process is conspicuous in the disparity between the upper and lower forms. While the horizontal bar at the top is painted vigorously over lighter paint, the white and pink below are pulled back over the black in ragged, broken strokes, intensifying the sense of a void or recess. (Kline insisted, "I paint the white as well as the black, and the white is just as important.") The jumble of dragged, slashing strokes often allows fleeting glimpses through several layers to areas of colorful paint far more varied than the title would suggest. A deep red ground can be seen at the edges, for example, and in the mix of wet-into-wet touches throughout the work, shades of orange, brown, gray, silver, and light blue can be distinguished. In this respect, the blunt, near-monolithic, trapezoidal image and its dense envelope of creamy white can be understood as a pictorial result built on a process of gradual concealment. As Kline was once reported to say approvingly about the surfaces of the works of Albert Pinkham Ryder, "There are seven or eight others underneath it you can't tell about."

Further Reading

Anfam, David. *Franz Kline: Black and White, 1950–1961*. Houston: The Menil Collection, 1994.

Gaugh, Harry F. *The Vital Gesture: Franz Kline*. New York: Abbeville Press, 1985.

Paul Manship

Saint Paul, Minnesota 1885–1966 New York, New York

Centaur and Dryad, 1913, cast 1915

Bronze (edition 4/5)

28 × 18½ × 11½ in. (71.1 × 47 × 29.2 cm)

Signed and dated on ground on which figures stand: PAUL MANSHIP © 1913; inscribed on base edge, front left corner, below frieze: ROMAN BRONZE WORKS-N-Y-

Purchased from the artist

1915:14-1

Paul Manship's mature career began with a stunning, overnight success in 1913. Returning from a three-year fellowship at the American Academy in Rome, the sculptor showed ten small works at the Architectural League in New York. Sales were immediate, and the glowing reviews created a sensation. Of the exhibited sculptures, *Centaur and Dryad* received the most attention. Awarded the Barnett Prize by the National Academy of Design, it became even further distinguished when the Metropolitan Museum of Art purchased a cast of it in 1914. A year later, Smith College also bought a cast of *Centaur and Dryad*, making it the fourth acquisition from the artist in a matter of months and establishing the college as one of his strongest institutional supporters. Manship, clearly pleased with Smith's latest purchase, wrote art professor Alfred Vance Churchill in March 1915, "The 'Centaur and Dryad' is the piece, of all my small bronzes, on which I have expended the greatest effort; in fact, it was in the process of making, from the time that I began it until the day of its completion, for four years. I have always considered it, therefore, to be the best . . . of the small bronzes."

The long gestation period for *Centaur and Dryad* is closely tied to Manship's time in Rome, where his art underwent an evolution from a dramatic, tactile expressionism to a more taut, distilled stylization. His residency in Italy—far from the more popular and cosmopolitan Paris, where Auguste Rodin's tremulous, impressionistic surfaces were still the dominant mode—placed a lifelong aesthetic stamp on his oeuvre, but more important still was his six-week trip to Greece in 1912, where he discovered the streamlined, pure expression of preclassical, archaic sculpture. As Manship wrote of this then-underappreciated period, "We feel the power of design, the feeling for structure in line, the harmony in the division of spaces and masses—the simplicity of the flesh admirably contrasted by rich drapery, every line of which is drawn with precision."

Centaur and Dryad is a remarkable melding of the archaic love of etched pattern, smooth surfaces, and sin-

uous line with a modern predilection toward abstraction and a surprisingly intense evocation of passion and desire. The aggressive mood of the struggle between centaur and nymph is set by Manship's complex pedestal, with its bacchic grapevines snaking over the cushioned base, its exaggerated depictions of bawdy satyrs and maenads in low relief, and its inventive lower frieze of running animals (a fox catching a rabbit, a lion attacking a gazelle, rams butting heads, and so forth). Above, the meaty right arm of the centaur encircles the fleeing dryad as he rears back on his hind legs. Her garment, fanning out behind in a rhythmic series of radiating swallowtail folds, is secured only by a single band below her breasts, thus revealing her naked, open body for display. A study of dynamic torsion, she turns her head sharply away from the hot breath of the centaur, who pulls her shoulder toward him in the opposite direction. Her knee, still seemingly moving forward, cuts through space like the prow of a ship, while his tail answers with a downward, slicing curve like a scimitar. Although the schematized composition favors the frontal view, the frenzied conflict is even more apparent from the back, where the centaur's face is completely hidden as he burrows into her neck, their hair writhing and intertwining like a nest of twisting snakes. While this elevated level of emotion might seem a surprising addition to the collection of a women's college in 1915, President L. Clark Seelye nevertheless rationalized its presence on campus. Commenting shortly after its acquisition, he described Manship's theme as "the struggle of the beastly with the womanly," dryly concluding, "Smith is a most appropriate place for it."

Further Reading

Paul Manship: Changing Taste in America. Saint Paul: Minnesota Museum of Art, 1985.

Rand, Harry. *Paul Manship.* Washington, D.C.: Smithsonian Institution Press, 1989.

Rather, Susan. *Archaism, Modernism, and the Art of Paul Manship.* Austin: University of Texas Press, 1993.

193

Alfred Henry Maurer

New York, New York 1868–1932 New York, New York

Le Bal Bullier, c. 1900–1901

Oil on canvas
28¹³⁄₁₆ × 36⁵⁄₁₆ in. (73.2 × 92.3 cm)
Signed in black paint, lower right: Alfred H. Maurer
Purchased
1951:283

As one of the earliest "finds" of the avant-garde dealer Alfred Stieglitz, A. H. Maurer is most often remembered as a pioneering twentieth-century American modernist whose still lifes and figure studies bear the imprint of Cubism and, especially, Henri Matisse's Fauvism. This abstractive work was never greatly appreciated in its day, and Maurer, who committed suicide after several decades of professional disappointment, is generally viewed as a casualty of the American public's refusal to support the progressive formal explorations of European-influenced artists between the world wars. Before he moved away from a more naturalistic mode, however, Maurer had achieved a relatively impressive record of success, winning the lucrative Carnegie Prize in 1901 for his Whistlerian *Arrangement* of an anonymous female model in aesthetic dress amid Asian studio props (Whitney Museum of American Art, New York).

In retrospect, the late 1890s and the first few years of the new century can be seen as the most engaged and fulfilling of Maurer's career. An expatriate living on the Left Bank of Paris, he threw himself into the lively bohemian community of young artists. Known for his love of cafés and dance halls, he cut a dandified figure in cape, spats, and felt hat. Although he was somewhat older than many of his friends, he nevertheless played an important social role in the Montparnasse community, which included Robert Henri, Mahonri Young, and George Luks, among others. It was during these years, about 1900–1904, that he painted a series of dark interiors of Parisian amusement palaces. Combining the impressionist love of the fragmented, charged spaces of the public *café-concert* with the somber palette and direct application of paint of the Ashcan school, these works (many of which were lost in the aftermath of World War I) speak movingly of Maurer's identification with and sensitivity to the hard-worn working-class crowds who populated large emporia such as the Bal Bullier, a huge enclosed garden–dance hall popular at the time with students, clerks, and servants.

To judge from the number of times Maurer sent it to exhibitions, *Le Bal Bullier* was a painting of which he was particularly proud. In it he managed to capture both the unusual scale of the establishment—the cavernous dining area illuminated by electric lights and extending ambiguously into the distance—and the poignant loneliness of the edge of the dance gallery, where a few remaining clients take their last spin on the floor or simply pause and watch on their way out, holding their wraps. There is a suggestion of desperation in the manner in which the faceless dancers—heavy-footed, shadowy men embracing bony, teetering women—clutch their partners and lurch about the empty space. At the left, a trio of angular, slouching women, each one clad in a dingy shirtwaist and made up so as to exaggerate her coarse, blasé features, deflects attention toward the picture's edge, where a cut-off figure in a Spanish skirt hints at still another spectacle. Rising above it all is the presiding, ominous silhouette of a top-hatted man, whose isolation, anonymity, and elevated position of surveillance suggest connections to the viewer, or to the artist himself.

Further Reading

Madormo, Nick. "The Early Career of Alfred Maurer: Paintings of Popular Entertainments." *American Art Journal* 15 (Winter 1983): 4–34.

McCausland, Elizabeth. *A. H. Maurer.* New York: A. A. Wyn, 1951.

Reich, Sheldon. *Alfred H. Maurer, 1868–1932.* Washington, D.C.: National Collection of Fine Arts, 1973.

Willard Leroy Metcalf

Lowell, Massachusetts 1858–1925 New York, New York

Willows in March, 1911

Oil on canvas

26 × 29 1/16 in. (66 × 73.8 cm)

Signed in gray paint, lower left: W. L. METCALF

Gift of Mrs. Charles W. Carl (Marie Schuster, class of 1917)

1955:7

Although Willard Metcalf began his career as a student of painting at the age of seventeen, he would have to wait until he was nearly fifty before achieving unqualified professional success. Throughout his student years in France and during most of his early maturity, his Barbizon-inspired work was generally well regarded, but financial stability was elusive, and a penchant for hard living at the edges of social propriety in New York took its toll on his personal life. It was in a moment of crisis and near-breakdown in 1904 that Metcalf, penniless, left the city and traveled to Maine to spend almost a year with his elderly parents. There he found spiritual and professional revitalization in the surrounding landscape. The confident, more resolutely impressionist canvases with which he returned in 1905 were immediately acclaimed as a stylistic breakthrough. Metcalf had found his principal subject matter in the New England terrain, and, fueled by increased sales and enthusiastic criticism, he flourished in his pursuit of the gentle, seasonal qualities of a region that, more than any other, had taken on tones of mythic nostalgia for Americans.

Willows in March is one of an important group of meditative winter scenes executed during yet another period of renewal and growth in the spare landscape of northern New England. Rebounding from an embarrassing divorce after his first wife left him for another painter, Metcalf somewhat impetuously asked Henriette McCrea, a woman nearly three decades his junior, to marry him. This they did in January 1911, spending the first few months of their married life in the quietly off-season art colony of Cornish, New Hampshire. In a sustained burst of exploration and creativity, Metcalf embarked on what historians now see as his single most successful year of painting. In particular, he tackled the pastel nuances of winter snowscapes, actually taking his easel outdoors and painting full-scale canvases in freezing temperatures.

Metcalf moved often in his work between a softly ruminant Tonalism and a more vigorously textured Impressionism, but in his winter scenes, the close-keyed, shrouded environments prompted some of his purest explorations of the former mode. Of these, *Willows in March* is pushed to an unusually abstractive extreme, with its shallow, tipped-up space, its meandering lines of scalloping hills, and its wispy screen of shrubs and saplings — the feathered tips of their branches seemingly hovering like tinted aureoles. The areas of snow are formed by a thick, relatively smooth blanket of pastelike paint, while the more tentative lines of the lavender-gray twigs are dragged fleetingly over this surface with a thin, dry brush. Metcalf uses a white glaze to unify the color scheme further — diminishing value contrasts, eradicating deep shadows, and lessening any remaining effect of depth. A silvery ether seems to cling to the painting's forms, and its texture and light leave an impression of insubstantiality akin to a translucent, tissue-paper collage. These subtleties were noted by quite a few reviewers, and the artist evidently thought it an important work as well: Within two years of its execution, he had included it in six important exhibitions before it was purchased by a Boston patron.

Further Reading

De Veer, Elizabeth, and Richard J. Boyle. *Sunlight and Shadow: The Life and Art of Willard L. Metcalf.* New York: Abbeville Press, 1987.

MacAdam, Barbara J. *Winter's Promise: Willard Metcalf in Cornish, New Hampshire, 1909–1920.* Hanover, N.H.: Hood Museum of Art, 1999.

Joan Mitchell

Chicago, Illinois 1926–1992 Paris, France

Untitled, c. 1960

Oil on canvas
50 × 38 in. (127 × 96.5 cm)
Signed in brown paint, lower right: J. Mitchell
Purchased with funds given by Mrs. John W. O'Boyle (Nancy Millar, class of 1952)
1981:30

Though her time in Northampton does not seem to have had any lasting effect on her work, Joan Mitchell holds the distinction of being the only abstract expressionist to have attended Smith College. She spent two years there beginning in 1942, later finished her undergraduate training at the Art Institute of Chicago, and subsequently passed a seminal fellowship year in France in 1948–49. She then returned to New York City, immediately immersing herself in the exciting downtown community of painters whose joint exploration of "heroic" subjects and grandly scaled nonrepresentational spaces had already crystallized into the loose movement now known as Abstract Expressionism. Greatly affected by the works of Arshile Gorky, Franz Kline, and Willem de Kooning, Mitchell adopted the strong gestural language of these painters; she soon became one of the few women accepted into their "club" as a peer.

With a tenacious philosophical consistency, Mitchell would remain devoted to this revelatory means of expression for over four decades. Disproving the thesis that "action painting" was inextricably linked to New York, she worked for most of this long period in France, where she moved in 1955 for part of each year, residing there more or less permanently as of 1960. Though her work went through a number of transformations during her career, her particular brand of Abstract Expressionism is notable for its richly varied spectrum of bright colors and its dependence on landscape imagery, which Mitchell claimed she never painted directly but rather experienced through emotion-tinged memories.

Smith College's untitled canvas was likely painted in 1960, during the last summer that Mitchell worked in the United States, when she visited East Hampton, New York, with her partner and fellow artist, Jean-Paul Riopelle, and his children. The temporary studio conditions of that visit might have led to the unfortunate flattening of the thickest areas of impasto (the still-tacky work was evidently stacked with another canvas, which has left the imprint of its weave in a number of areas of raised paint), but in every other respect it is a powerful example of what Mitchell would later describe as the "very violent and angry paintings" of the early 1960s.

The composition is anchored by several jostling horizontal bars of dark paint that serve as a kind of foundation for the explosion of crisscrossing strokes above. Mitchell's palette is unusual, with almost all the colors consisting of secondary or tertiary hues—violet, mustard yellow, brick red, evergreen, turquoise, and earthen brown. The individual touches throb in intensity against the painted white ground (an important formal component in all the work of her early maturity), but the coloristic mix nevertheless remains a bit muddy and confused. The tangled, chaotic brushwork is also a factor, with squarish, wet-into-wet strokes of a housepainter's brush, thick with viscous pigment, contrasting with liquid spatters and gravity-induced dripping patterns. An unresolved, dynamic tension results, in keeping with Mitchell's abhorrence of images that seemed overly pat and considered in their composition. It is all a bit off-putting, encouraging viewers who might otherwise linger too close to step back and take in the burgeoning painting from the greater visual distance generally preferred by the artist.

Further Reading

Bernstock, Judith E. *Joan Mitchell.* New York: Hudson Hills Press, 1988.

Kertess, Klaus. *Joan Mitchell.* New York: Harry N. Abrams, 1997.

Robert Motherwell

Aberdeen, Washington 1915–1991 Provincetown, Massachusetts

La Danse, 1952

Oil on canvas
30 × 38 in. (76.2 × 96.5 cm)
Not signed or dated
Purchased with the gift of Jane Chace Carroll, class of 1953, and Eliot Chace Nolen, class of 1954, and gift of the Dedalus Foundation
1995:7-1
© Dedalus Foundation, Inc./Licensed by VAGA, New York, NY

In 1948 Robert Motherwell almost casually created the compositional motif that would become his signature theme, sustaining him in a variety of media and scales for over four decades. Faced with the task of providing a visual accompaniment to a poem by the critic Harold Rosenberg, he filled half a sheet of rag paper with a shoulder-to-shoulder arrangement of heavy rectangular and rounded shapes brushed in rich, black india ink. This asymmetrical, rhythmic lineup of resolute bars and trembling ovals became *Elegy to the Spanish Republic No. 1*, the first of a remarkable series that "used black massively as a color form rather than an absence of color," as the artist later characterized it. Black became an assertive "protagonist" in Motherwell's work, a color he associated with Spain and all things Spanish. Profoundly affected by an early visit to Mexico in 1941, he similarly adopted ocher (reminiscent of traditional adobe walls) and deep red (blood and wine) as particularly meaningful and personally expressive hues.

All of this is evident in *La Danse*, where the A-b-A-b-A sequence of biomorphic black shapes relaxes somewhat from the percussive force of the *Elegy* forms but nonetheless retains a powerful iconic presence against the nested rectangles of thinly brushed sienna and more saturated orange-red. There is more than a little whimsy in this painting, where the quivering "figures" seem almost to breathe—expanding and contracting—as they shimmy to the left like an amoeboid conga line viewed through a microscope (though they also hold their own on a much larger scale, as evidenced by *La Danse II*

[1952, The Metropolitan Museum of Art], a version of the composition four times the size of the Smith painting). The black forms float in a kind of dimensionless environment, an arrangement that does not quite read as a figure-ground spatial relationship but that nevertheless sets up an opposition of organic and geometric shapes—another constant concern in Motherwell's oeuvre.

One other important development in the artist's early career was his discovery of his love of collage, which he first began using in 1943. The flat, additive qualities of that medium are defining characteristics of *La Danse*, but the torn, ragged edges usually found in Motherwell's collages are here replaced by precise, cut-out silhouettes, a slight stylistic anomaly usually attributed to the influence of Henri Matisse's *Jazz* series of *papiers découpés* of 1947 or, less directly, to the abstractions of Joan Miró. This has led some critics to complain of the pronounced decorative qualities of this and other Motherwell paintings of the early 1950s, finding them too calculated and pat, lacking in the artist's usual brushy experimentation. Indeed, Motherwell wrote often of the pleasure of the touch, of feeling his hand at work, of weighing the physical act of each stroke. In fact, close examination of the apparently seamless edges of his black forms reveals a good deal of adjustment and play, with late touches of the brush extending or reducing the borders of his fields of color. *La Danse*, in any event, seems to have pleased the artist, for though he subsequently destroyed much of his work from this period, Motherwell kept this painting for the rest of his life, moving it from studio to studio for nearly forty years.

Further Reading

Arnason, H. H. *Robert Motherwell*. New York: Harry N. Abrams, 1982.

Ashton, Dore, and Jack D. Flam. *Robert Motherwell*. New York: Abbeville Press, 1983.

Motherwell. Barcelona: Fundació Antoni Tàpies, 1996.

Elie Nadelman

Warsaw, Poland 1882–1946 New York, New York

Resting Stag, c. 1915

Gold-leafed bronze on wood-veneered base
14⅜ × 20½ × 10 in. (36.5 × 52 × 25.4 cm)
Not signed or dated
Purchased with income from the Hillyer, Tryon, and Mather Funds and funds given by Bernice Hirschman Tumen, class of 1923, in honor of the class of 1923
1983:24

Around 1915, when Elie Nadelman briefly turned from his better-known human subjects to a series of related fawn and stag statuettes, he was still enjoying what would be the apogee of his international reputation. Born into a cultured, liberal family in czarist Poland, he had studied at the Warsaw Art Academy before fleeing its conservative atmosphere for the more progressive climate of Munich in 1904. This too proved something of a disappointment, and six months later Nadelman left for Paris, where he would remain until World War I. After working for several years in a consciously reductive style at odds with the prevailing expressionistic virtuosity of Auguste Rodin, he became an overnight artistic celebrity when his solo exhibition of 1909 produced a storm of excited and favorable criticism. Though the fluent, classically inspired work he exhibited seems, in hindsight, relatively tame, it was received as a significant revelation, and at least one of his more innovative heads is thought to have served as a catalyst for Picasso's cubist pursuits. Almost immediately there were complaints of a lack of "depth" in Nadelman's sometimes decorative work (a charge that would plague him for the rest of his life), but for a period of about a decade his work was seen as defining an important new direction in modern sculpture.

It was thus as a notable figure of the avant-garde that Nadelman was received in New York when he arrived in 1914; his first American exhibition was staged by Alfred Stieglitz at his progressive 291 gallery a year later. During this period the artist always exhibited his drawings alongside his works of sculpture, and it is clear that the supple balance of swelling volumes in works like *Resting Stag* derives from the formal researches of these drawings, with their swinging lines of mounting curves and their suppression of anecdotal detail in favor of what Nadelman described as pure "plasticity." This he defined as an elemental internal life force or "will of matter," which he felt existed independently of an image's actual representational qualities. "The subject of any work of art is for me nothing but a pretext for creating significant form," he famously wrote in 1910.

A sense of this formal vitality so important to Nadelman is evident in the series of effortless arcing and scalloping curves that develop through the low-slung belly, powerful haunches, and elongated neck of *Resting Stag*. In the delicate act of licking its hind leg, the almost pneumatic body of the animal folds in on itself with affecting grace and equilibrium. The pleasing amplitude of the torso is nicely set off by the piquant sharpness of the rhythmically attenuated legs and the knobby antlers, which seem drawn in space with a whimsical, nervous hand. The weathered patina of the work—mottled, matte, and naturally blotchy where the gold leaf has been rubbed away to expose darker green and brown patches—also adds to the intimate, artisan-like finish of Nadelman's sculpture, a quality it shares with American folk art, of which he was a pioneering and passionate collector.

Further Reading

Baur, John I. H. *The Sculpture and Drawings of Elie Nadelman.* New York: Whitney Museum of American Art, 1975.

Kirstein, Lincoln. *Elie Nadelman.* New York: Eakins Press, 1973.

Louise Nevelson

Near Kiev, Ukraine 1899–1988 New York, New York

Moving-Static-Moving, 1955

Terra cotta

21 pieces of various sizes

Not signed or dated

Gift of the artist

1973:27-3

© 2000 Estate of Louise Nevelson/Artists Rights Society (ARS), New York

Even those who think they know Louise Nevelson's work well might be surprised by *Moving-Static-Moving,* a group of twenty-one abstract shapes in fired clay. Nevelson is known for her personal attention to room-sized installations and for the tight coherence of her found-wood assemblages, with each element carefully fixed in place by a battery of nails. In *Moving-Static-Moving,* however, the sculptor relinquishes that control, there being no prescribed manner in which the component parts should be arranged. What links these elements to her more famous work is the familiar matte black paint that became the artist's signature in the 1950s. "One of the reasons I originally started with black was to see the forms more clearly," she once explained. "Black seemed the strongest and clearest."

Before she developed her interest in large-scale wood constructions, Nevelson had worked prolifically in terra cotta, especially during the years following the death of her dealer, Karl Nierendorf, in 1948, a personal setback that prompted a retreat from public exhibitions for several years. Always obsessed with quantity, Nevelson and her assistants produced hundreds and hundreds of blunt terra-cotta pieces during this time, with the artist roughly shaping or cutting them from huge slabs of clay and an assistant later hollowing them out once they had hardened. Their worn, pitted surfaces and fragmentary nature have been connected to Nevelson's fascination with Aztec and Mayan ruins in Mexico and to what she saw as an elemental, "primitive" expression. (Some critics, however, found them derivative of earlier work by Robert Laurent and Constantin Brancusi.)

Visitors to Nevelson's four-story house on East Thirtieth Street in Manhattan remember huge piles of the forms lying about. Numbers of them were grouped into compact arrangements that the artist called "Gifts of the Sea" in her well-received installation, *Royal Voyage,* at the Grand Central Moderns Gallery in 1956. "She had lots of anthropomorphic pieces painted black that previously hadn't found their way to any given sculpture," remembered the director of the gallery. "They were interesting forms in themselves and she simply placed them on the floor, in a random happening." A similar expediency probably led Nevelson to give *Moving-Static-Moving* to Smith on the occasion of her honorary degree in 1973. Though the work bears the date of 1955, some of the pieces were likely fashioned during earlier years. The title is also recycled, having been given previously to a group of similar terra-cotta slabs stacked on metal dowel rods, the parts capable of being rotated in space (*Moving-Static-Moving Figures,* c. 1945–48, Whitney Museum of American Art, New York).

Whatever the genesis of the work, it has proven a boon to the teaching mission of the museum. With no installation instructions from the artist beyond the suggestion of an asymmetrical, multitiered pedestal, groups of students over the years have repeatedly explored the sculptural elements of shape, mass, texture, and silhouette as they arrange the forms in different configurations—sometimes dense and closely interlocked, sometimes scattered and open, but always revealing of the tactile and visual richness of pure spatial relationships.

Further Reading

Glimcher, Arnold B. *Louise Nevelson.* New York: Praeger, 1972.

Lipman, Jean. *Nevelson's World.* New York: Hudson Hills Press, 1983.

Lisle, Laurie. *Louise Nevelson: A Passionate Life.* New York: Summit, 1990.

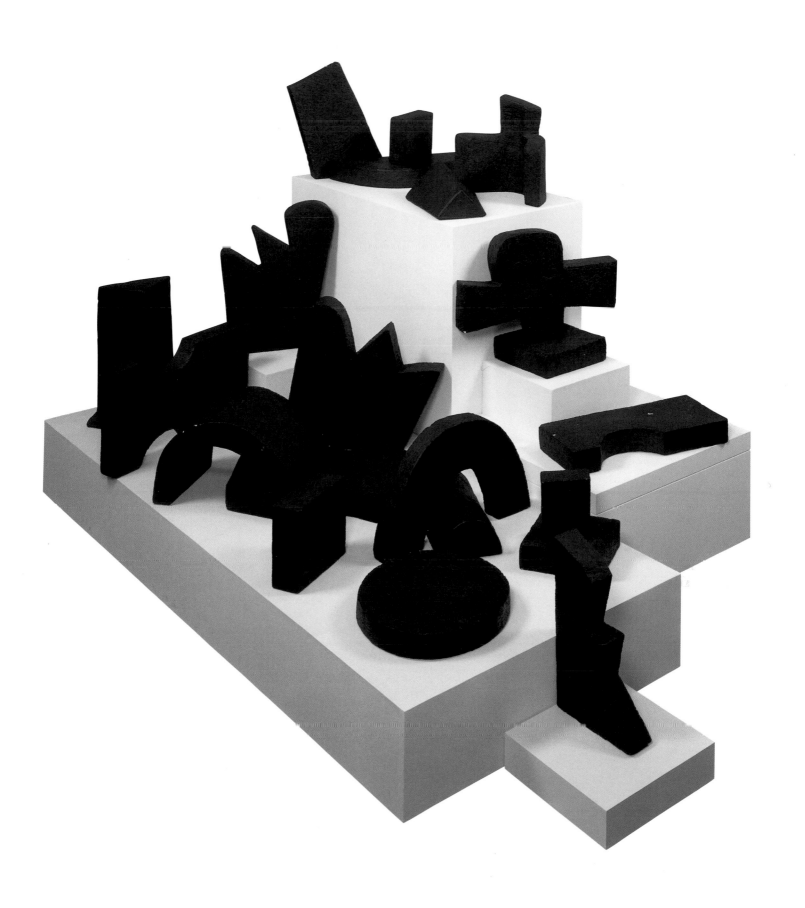

Georgia O'Keeffe

Sun Prairie, Wisconsin 1887–1986 Santa Fe, New Mexico

Grey Tree, Fall, 1948

Oil on canvas

39⅞ × 29⅞ in. (101.3 × 75.9 cm)

Not signed or dated; inscribed in artist's hand in pencil on stretcher, at bottom under canvas tacking edge: 2 Glue size 10/25/47; at top under canvas tacking edge: Turpentine & Little Linseed Oil 5/28/48 Dutch Boy zinc white

Gift of the Robert R. Young Foundation in memory of the family of Robert R. Young

1987:13

© 2000 The Georgia O'Keeffe Foundation/Artists Rights Society (ARS), New York

From the earliest years of Georgia O'Keeffe's career, trees had occupied an important place in her personal iconography. She and her husband, Alfred Stieglitz, were greatly attached to certain magisterial chestnuts and birches at the Stieglitz family summer home at Lake George, New York, and she was also known to paint an occasional "arboreal portrait," letting a distinctive tree—the associative qualities of which reminded her of a friend or acquaintance—stand in for that person. Once she began to spend time in her beloved New Mexico, however, the lush greenery of Lake George seemed oppressive to her, overwhelming in its contrasts with the hot, bare desert she had adopted as her natural "place."

Still, trees—usually desiccated skeletal remains—sometimes figured in the desert landscapes she painted at her small house on the remote property called Ghost Ranch (north of Santa Fe). However, it was not until her purchase in 1945 of a more historic adobe structure at the nearby Hispano-Indian village of Abiquiu that she pursued the subject in earnest. Her new home looked down on the Chama River, a tributary of the Rio Grande, and its banks were lined with impressive ranks of cottonwood trees, a species of poplar. She often walked by the river, forming a collection of perfectly rounded rocks from its bed, and she had large windows cut in the walls of her new home to enable her to study the trees in all seasons. The cottonwood paintings, which she pursued for about a decade beginning in the mid-1940s, constitute one of her least-known series, perhaps because their soft, billowing forms seem unusually amorphous next to her typically hard-edged compositions (the famous Pelvis and Patio Door series, for example, are contemporaneous with the cottonwood paintings).

O'Keeffe painted *Grey Tree, Fall* during a difficult period following the death of Stieglitz in 1946. For the next three years, the settling of his complicated estate frequently required her presence in New York, cutting significantly into her time in New Mexico, and into her painting. It must have been with some relief that she arrived in Abiquiu in October 1948 and immediately set to work on *Grey Tree, Fall*, a canvas she described in a letter at the end of that month: "My first painting—a dead tree surrounded by the autumn is very gentle and pleasant and high in key but it holds its place on the wall alone more than forty feet away." The cottonwood is a burgeoning grey presence at the center, as much a network of rivers or arteries as it is solid branches and twigs. It reads as a fluttering efflorescence of dark-edged, folded planes, as vibrating envelopment rather than firm stability. Most remarkable are the radiant colors that form a kind of pulsating aura around the tree. The liveliness of these hues, along with their names—citron, peach, melon—seem to act synesthetically on the palate as well as the eye, reminding us of O'Keeffe's own visceral response to pure color, memorably revealed in her confession late in life of often feeling the urge "to eat a fine pile of paint just squeezed out of the tube."

Further Reading

Cowart, Jack, and Juan Hamilton. *Georgia O'Keeffe: Art and Letters.* Washington, D.C.: National Gallery of Art, 1987.

Eldredge, Charles C. *Georgia O'Keeffe: American and Modern.* New Haven, Conn.: Yale University Press, 1993.

Lisle, Laurie. *Portrait of an Artist: A Biography of Georgia O'Keeffe.* New York: Seaview Books, 1980.

209

Charles Sprague Pearce

Boston, Massachusetts 1851–1914 Auvers-sur-Oise, France

A Cup of Tea, 1883

Oil on canvas
27 × 22½ in. (68.6 × 57.1 cm)
Signed, lower left: Charles Sprague Pearce — Paris —
Bequest of Annie Swan Coburn (Mrs. Lewis Larned Coburn)
1934:3-6

Mary Cassatt may now be the best-known American expatriate painter to have taken up residence in France in the late nineteenth century, but in her embrace of the radical impressionists she was anything but typical. Far more numerous were artists such as Charles Sprague Pearce, who happily apprenticed themselves to the more conservative masters then dominating the crowded ateliers that made Paris the most vibrant and cosmopolitan city of the international art world. Pearce — who after arriving in France at the age of twenty-two would never again reside in the United States — eventually married a French artist and purchased a small country estate outside Paris. He threw himself into all the expected channels of success for an aspiring, versatile academic painter: study under the famous Léon Bonnat, exhibitions and medals at the Salon, portrait commissions from titled grandees, and frequent trips to the French provinces, Spain, and North Africa to search for "exotic" subjects.

In an effort to establish a reputation during the early part of his career, Pearce pursued a number of more or less "orientalist" themes — Arab genre studies, ancient Egyptian biblical reconstructions, Greek mythological scenes — that demanded a high degree of archaeological and ethnographic detail. For a brief period in 1883, the year in which he first achieved a measure of professional renown, he added Japanese subjects to his arsenal. Thus he joined the extremely diverse group of Western artists who sought aesthetic renewal in the spare forms, nuanced color, and suspended quietude of the Asian art then making its way to Europe and America. A Cup of Tea revels in its careful description of Eastern fabrics and ceramics, but, in the best academic tradition, it remains a pastiche — a careful arrangement of model and studio bibelots designed chiefly to showcase the artist's taste and compositional prowess.

Above all, the painting demonstrates the exquisite technique for which Pearce was celebrated. The face and hands of the woman appear flawless, rendered softly and with utmost control, as though viewed through a silken veil. Critics often faulted him for this smooth academic emphasis, noting a lack of emotional sympathy — a coolness and austerity that seemed almost clinical. Indeed, one Boston reviewer of A Cup of Tea, wearied by Pearce's "too placid sweetness," found in "the beautiful vase at her back" and "the delicately-finished teacup" held by the model, "as much expressive value as the woman" herself. Still, by this point in his career the artist was experimenting with bolder, fresher brushwork, as evidenced in the activated textural effects of the bare walls and the rich impasto highlight on the shoulder of the vase. His freest indulgence, though, is found in the floral imagery, both in the dance of the brush that creates a shower of colorful blossoms seemingly scattered across the blue-gray silk of the model's kimono and in the actual spring blooms that frame her on either side. The rendering of the billowing, complex textures of the mass of pink peonies is remarkable, but in his quick evocation of the spiky irises — each petal a single, unblended stroke of creamy white and lavender — he makes his most forceful and eloquent reply to his critics.

Further Reading

Lublin, Mary. A Rare Elegance: The Paintings of Charles Sprague Pearce (1851–1914). New York: Jordan-Volpe Gallery, 1993.

John Frederick Peto

Philadelphia, Pennsylvania 1854–1907 New York, New York

Discarded Treasures, c. 1904

Oil on canvas

22 × 40 in. (55.9 × 101.6 cm)

Signed with forged signature in black paint, lower right: WMH[in monogram]ARNETT

Purchased, Drayton Hillyer Fund

1939:4

Along with his friend and idol, William Harnett, John F. Peto occupies an important place in the tradition of trompe-l'oeil still-life painting that developed in Philadelphia in the late nineteenth century. Although both spent much of their careers toiling well outside the limelight of cosmopolitan art circles, Harnett's precise, even magical arrangements of perfectly rendered objects—antiques, musical instruments, game— attracted a certain notoriety shortly before his death in 1892, prompting a significant rise in his prices. Peto, on the other hand, working quietly in his softer, more generalized style in the small resort community of Island Heights, New Jersey, was almost completely erased from the documentary record.

This disparity in name recognition resulted in the epidemic of false Harnett signatures that were later added to Peto paintings by unscrupulous dealers. Indeed, when Harnett's reputation was resuscitated in 1939 by a revelatory exhibition entitled *Nature Vivre*, some of the works included—such as the show's centerpiece, *Discarded Treasures*—were actually Petos masquerading as Harnetts, and it was as a masterwork of the latter artist that Smith College made its much-heralded purchase of this brooding, precarious pile of worn volumes. A decade later, when the meticulous research of the art critic Alfred Frankenstein proved conclusively that Peto's oeuvre had been wrongly sublimated into Harnett's, Smith College once again moved quickly, issuing a dramatic press release reattributing the painting to Peto, thus providing an institutional imprimatur for Frankenstein's revelations.

Painted near the end of his life, when the artist was suffering from Bright's disease, *Discarded Treasures* is imbued with an unmistakable air of resignation and a haunting evocation of time's inevitable ravages, but its doleful mood can also be linked to the general fin-de-siècle anxiety about change and the abandonment of more traditional ways of life. In the case of books, long considered a precious repository of a culture's most important values, narratives, and lessons, the modern technology of Peto's day produced industrial machines capable of churning out thousands of cheaply bound copies per hour. The hand-crafted leather volume—and the culture that surrounded it—seemed endangered, if not wholly eradicated. In *Discarded Treasures*, the character of the books on the junk-shop table is indeterminate; the hand-rubbed spines announce no titles or authors, and the few visible pages of type are illegible— a decaying heap reminiscent of indecipherable ruins. These incommunicative volumes, though they bear visible signs of use indicating once-cherished ownership, are now reduced for quick sale, available for "10 cents each."

Peto's dramatic illumination, chaotic composition, and rich use of paint amplify considerably these themes of neglect and nostalgia. An intense beam of light, as though from a small window, breaks across the jumbled, teetering mass, accentuating the protruding edges of some books and casting others into a thick shroud of darkness almost unbelievable in its enveloping pitch. The volumes are scattered in a manner suggestive of violence, their pages and backs forced into unnatural and damaging configurations. The entire composition is a movement-filled web of slashing lines and angles replete with formal interest. But perhaps the most distinctive quality of the painting is the artist's use of color: oddly radiant pinks, teals, and rusts composed of dense, matte paint that seems at once chalky and claylike in texture. It is this plangent sense of touch that gives Peto's anonymous shapes—his cubic slabs of dusty, velvety color—the elemental abstractive quality that found such favor with the devotees of modern art who enthusiastically greeted this painting at the time of its rediscovery in 1939.

Further Reading

Frankenstein, Alfred. *After the Hunt: William Harnett and Other American Still Life Painters, 1870–1900*. Berkeley: University of California Press, 1969.

Wilmerding, John. *Important Information Inside: The Art of John F. Peto and the Idea of Still-Life Painting in Nineteenth-Century America*. Washington, D.C.: National Gallery of Art, 1983.

Albert Pinkham Ryder

New Bedford, Massachusetts 1847–1917 Elmhurst, New York

Perrette, c. 1885–90

Oil on canvas mounted on paper composition board
12¹³⁄₁₆ × 7¹¹⁄₁₆ in. (32.5 × 19.5 cm)
Signed in red paint, lower left: A. P. Ryder
Purchased, probably from the artist, Winthrop Hillyer Fund
1893:1

Of all the early purchases of American art made under Smith's first president, L. Clark Seelye, *Perrette,* by Albert Pinkham Ryder, is certainly one of the boldest. In his mid-forties at the time he painted it, the romantic, childish painter had already started to withdraw into his dark and cluttered boardinghouse rooms, exhibiting infrequently and laboring slowly over his small, ruminative paintings, some of them receiving years and years — and layers and layers — of his idiosyncratic attentions. His public was not large, but from the start his supporters recognized something rare and poetic in his jewellike, almost enameled images (and they frequently congratulated themselves on their skills of discernment, using the acquired taste for Ryder's art as the dividing line between cognoscente and philistine). Smith College thus placed itself at the forefront of the aesthetic and intellectual elite when in 1893 *Perrette* became the first painting by the artist to enter a public collection.

It is one of several small works from the late 1880s and early 1890s taking as their subject a poor, guileless young woman in a pastoral setting. In this case the source is a fable by Jean de La Fontaine that explores the dreams of profit and wealth of a young farm wife as she carries her milk to market, only to see these hopes dashed when, her head in the clouds, she trips and spills the milk. The Perrette fable had been represented a number of times in the eighteenth century (notably by Jean-Honoré Fragonard), but in Ryder's day the subject was quite esoteric. Typically, he selected the earlier moment of the milkmaid's dreamy state, rather than the disastrous pratfall that had more commonly been figured by artists. As though a sympathetic emanation of her distracted thoughts, the landscape tips up dramatically to form a series of sinuous, two-dimensional shapes that rhyme pleasingly with the forms of her body — the tree, in particular, twisting in space as if hoisting up its own pail of milk. The intertwined pair of cows also forms a lighthearted S-curve; a flowing line moves from the spinal ridge of the ponderous foreground animal up to the rolling back and whiplike tail of its companion, who appears to use the slender tree trunk for a teasing game of hide-and-seek.

Ryder's unstable methods and materials caused his paintings to darken and change almost immediately (the artist once used the verb "ripen" in discussing his work). At times, the pernicious, fluidic underlayers of bitumen he used resulted in paintings literally melting before the eyes of their owners, who often resorted to drastic procedures to "restore" the images. *Perrette,* because of its early entrance into a controlled and documented museum collection, is thus valued by Ryder scholars as an unadulterated example of his work. As early as 1931, when viewers were already scratching their heads at the rhapsodic turn-of-the-century descriptions of the artist's color, the cultural critic Lewis Mumford pointed to *Perrette* as one of the few paintings that still hinted at its former beauty. Since then, the Smith canvas, like all Ryders, has further deteriorated, with wide drying cracks and black, open seams appearing in a number of areas. Yet even if the famed chromatic sparkle of a century ago has somewhat lessened under his resinous blanket of thickened medium, the burnished, old masterish patina Ryder sought — with its mellow, green-gold tonality secured by countless glazes — can still be readily appreciated.

Further Reading

Broun, Elizabeth, et al. *Albert Pinkham Ryder.* Washington, D.C.: Smithsonian Institution Press, 1990.

Homer, William Innes, and Lloyd Goodrich. *Albert Pinkham Ryder: Painter of Dreams.* New York: Harry N. Abrams, 1989.

Augustus Saint-Gaudens

Dublin, Ireland 1848–1907 Cornish, New Hampshire

Diana of the Tower, 1899

Bronze on self-base

36 × 14¼ × 11 in. (91.4 × 36.2 × 27.9 cm)

Inscribed on front face of tripod base: DIANA/OF THE/TOWER; signed and dated on top of base platform, proper right rear: AUGUSTUS/SAINT-GAUDENS/MDCCCXCIX; bronze or copper circular inset stamped on top of base platform, front, proper left: COPYRIGHT/BY AUGUSTUS/SAINT-GAUDENS/M/DCCCXC/IX; inscribed on top of base platform, proper left rear: AUBRY BROS/FOUNDERS. N.Y.

Purchased, Winthrop Hillyer Fund

1900:22-1

The decades-long collaboration between the architect Stanford White and the sculptor Augustus Saint-Gaudens is one of the most fruitful in the history of American art. Saint-Gaudens's first great public triumph, his *Farragut Memorial,* owed a great deal to the sensitive bluestone pedestal designed by White, and when the bronze statue was unveiled to a stunned audience in New York's Madison Square in 1881, it was heralded as the beginning of a new era in public sculpture. A decade later, the two friends returned to the northeast corner of the same park. There, several hundred feet away from the Farragut statue, White was completing his Madison Square Garden, the famous sports and pleasure palace with its signature tower modeled after the Giralda spire of Seville, Spain. At White's invitation, Saint-Gaudens conceived of a culminating "weathervane" for the tower, an 18-foot, 1,800-pound figure of Diana at the hunt.

This project was a labor of love for the two men, with White paying the costs of fabrication and Saint-Gaudens undertaking the statue without a fee. For the sculptor, the project allowed him to pursue a purely ideal figure—a welcome break from his customary work in portraiture. The *Diana* statue thus became his first and only fully finished nude. From the moment of the unveiling, however, White and Saint-Gaudens were dissatisfied with the work. Though placed at an elevation of 347 feet (the highest object in New York City at the time), *Diana* appeared oversized and heavy from the park below. An elaborate whirl of drapery conceived by the sculptor as a wind rudder ballooning from her shoulder was also deemed unsuccessful. In an admirable display of humility and perfectionism, they committed to

considerable extra time and money, and Saint-Gaudens fashioned a new *Diana,* this time only thirteen feet tall. In this second version, the drapery was diminished and the figure's proportions were attenuated significantly: The face was thinner, the limbs longer, and the torso less cylindrical and barrel-chested. From the second unveiling of 1894 until the destruction of Madison Square Garden in 1925, Diana's sprightly, easily legible silhouette pirouetted in the sky above the prizefights and circuses taking place in the great auditorium below.

Although there were scattered objections to the statue's nudity, *Diana* quickly became a much-loved landmark in New York. Perhaps seeking to forestall unauthorized copies, Saint-Gaudens copyrighted the second version of the work and began to produce reduced-scale replicas (often including slight variations in the pedestal and proportions). The Smith *Diana* is one of at least a dozen of the smaller-sized reductions, which Saint-Gaudens periodically sold to private patrons, yielding him a profit of about $100 with each sale. It is unique among the many copies, however, in its ability to turn on its three-sided pedestal—a feature made possible by a bronze knob and gear-driven apparatus built into the base. Indeed, the sensitive design of the pedestal contributes greatly to the impression of lightness and motion of the statue above. The sphere appears intriguingly precarious as it balances on the heavier podium, and because of the tripartite configuration of the latter, the body of Diana never seems to lock into a specific plane, to resolve into a stable rectilinear relationship with the viewer. Always alert and rotating, her flexed, elastic figure remains breathless in its anticipation of the moment of release when bow, arrow, and hunter will all snap from their perfectly calibrated balance of dynamic forces.

Further Reading

Dryfhout, John H. *The Work of Augustus Saint-Gaudens.* Hanover, N.H.: University Press of New England, 1982.

Greenthal, Kathryn. *Augustus Saint-Gaudens: Master Sculptor.* New York: The Metropolitan Museum of Art, 1985.

Wilkinson, Burke. *Uncommon Clay: The Life and Works of Augustus Saint Gaudens.* New York: Harcourt Brace Jovanovich, 1985.

John Singer Sargent

Florence, Italy 1856–1925 London, England

My Dining Room, c. 1883–86

Oil on canvas
29 × 23¾ in. (73.7 × 60.3 cm)
Not signed or dated
Purchased with funds given by Mrs. Henry T. Curtiss (Mina Kirstein, class of 1918) in memory of William Allan Neilson
1968:10

Born to expatriate American parents, John Singer Sargent spent his peripatetic youth traveling between European spas and resorts. His first real measure of stability and identification with a single place of residence came in 1874, when he moved to Paris and became the prized pupil of Charles-Emile-Auguste Durand (Carolus-Duran), a swashbuckling painter of dramatic society portraits. To some critics, Sargent quickly became the equal of his master, and after a series of enthusiastic reviews of his submissions to the Salons of 1882 and 1883, the young painter had every reason to consider himself at the beginning of a lifetime of success in the international art world of Paris. In an act of exuberant self-confidence, Sargent abandoned his walk-up studio in the bohemian Montparnasse district and rented a small, purpose-built house at 41, boulevard Berthier, locating himself in a high-culture, wealthy neighborhood of the Right Bank. With a private rose garden, a large second-floor studio decorated in aesthetic fabrics and papers, and a modest suite of private, public, and staff rooms on the ground floor, this artist's residence became the first true home Sargent had known. It would seem to have been with some measure of pride that he painted one of these rooms and pointedly titled it *My Dining Room.*

In this work Sargent successfully blends the lessons of his teacher, Carolus-Duran, with the avant-garde currents of Impressionism, a style that attracted him without ever winning him over completely. Carolus-Duran preached direct painting, wet into wet, and he placed the greatest stress on a correct sequence of values, a principle of pictorial organization far more important than color in his view. Sargent's somber palette of grays and duns bespeaks this influence — a range of middle hues that is neither cool nor warm, from which he works up and down to the blazing whites of the tablecloth and the deepest browns of the shadowy sideboard. The blurred brushwork, however, moves beyond Carolus-Duran's academic manner. The highlights on the bottles at left, for example, are small globs of pure white seemingly flicked onto the surface, and the amorphous linens and china on the table are formed by smooth, buttery paint that appears effortlessly stroked on the canvas, as if with a feather. A sense of palpable atmosphere swirls and eddies amid these objects awaiting removal after a meal.

The foreground chair is pushed back as if its occupant has just left the table, and one feels the warmth and lingering conversation of a space recently inhabited by such animated visitors as Oscar Wilde, whom Sargent entertained here on at least one occasion. Another touch of the personal is found in the tripartite horizontal frame hanging low on the wall above a background table; it featured three informal sketches of the artist Paul Helleu, a close friend from Sargent's student days. During the period of the mid-1880s, Sargent painted a small series of dining-table scenes, and each one conveys a certain quiet attachment to the intimate detritus of the repast, along with a moving connection to the friends and relatives he encountered in these private places. It is a sentiment somewhat at odds with the usual description of Sargent as detached and uninterested in conversational small talk. In the case of *My Dining Room,* there may also be a certain wistfulness associated with the scene for the artist; in 1886, impoverished by the scandal that developed around his daring *Madame X* (1884, The Metropolitan Museum of Art), he was forced to give up his home and decamp for England, where he resided for the rest of his life.

Further Reading

Fairbrother, Trevor. *John Singer Sargent.* New York: Harry N. Abrams, 1994.

Kilmurray, Elaine, and Richard Ormond, eds. *John Singer Sargent.* Princeton, N.J.: Princeton University Press, 1998.

Olson, Stanley. *John Singer Sargent: His Portrait.* New York: St. Martin's Press, 1986.

Charles Sheeler

Philadelphia, Pennsylvania 1883–1965 Dobbs Ferry, New York

Rolling Power, 1939

Oil on canvas
15 × 30 in. (38.1 × 76.2 cm)
Signed and dated in black paint, lower right: Sheeler-1939
Purchased, Drayton Hillyer Fund
1940:18

In 1938 Charles Sheeler received perhaps the most generous commission of his career, one wonderfully adapted to the themes and aesthetic concerns that had crystallized in his work during the previous decade. *Fortune*, the glossy magazine that chronicled and celebrated the modern marriage of business and industry, engaged the artist to execute a series of paintings on the theme of "Power" (Sheeler eventually painted six works). The patron made no other demands of subject, the paintings would remain the property of the artist, and he was free to exhibit them as he pleased. *Fortune* asked only for the right of first publication. Knowing that Smith College was interested in purchasing a Sheeler, the artist's dealer, Edith Halpert, offered the museum a preview of the series. Much to Sheeler's delight, *Rolling Power*, a close-up view of the drive wheels of the famous Twentieth Century Limited steam engine, was purchased before the exhibition at Halpert's Downtown Gallery closed. Since then, it has become a well-known icon of the period's reverence for the machine. A dense image packed with tactile values and visual information, it effectively transmutes the compressed, charged volumes of its machinery into a pristine relief of overwhelming purity and otherworldly plasticity.

The seemingly narrow range of hues chosen by Sheeler was ideally suited for *Fortune*'s commercial reproduction needs, but his carefully nuanced blend of color only becomes apparent when the original painting is studied closely. With controlled subtlety bordering on the sensual, he works through infinitesimal gradations of gray, blue, rose, eggshell, and lavender, with a tawny reddish-brown tonality reserved for the shadowed recesses that throw the myriad bolts and rods into sharp relief. The result is an uncanny, almost brittle oscillation between the flawless, pearlescent surface planes and the bristling accumulation of layered contours and edges, the artist's exacting armature of pencil lines still very visible.

Though the low point of view forces viewers into a kneeling posture before the powerful wheels and pistons (*Fortune*'s explanatory captions were rich in religious imagery), it is actually quite difficult to come to an understanding of scale and context in the work. From several feet away, the moderate-size canvas looks like a small slotted opening exposing the impossibly complex workings of a Swiss watch, while at close range, the wall of silent technology described by Sheeler might as well be a sheer stone cliff carved with indecipherable geometric hieroglyphs. Only the irregular beat of the ends of the railroad ties hints at the landscape through which the streamlined engine moved at speeds of up to one hundred miles an hour.

This denial of context is a hallmark of Sheeler's work, and at the time of the exhibition, he was criticized by at least one writer for his interest in power's "static shell" as opposed to its "throbbing internal life." That the artist aestheticized the machine and scoured it of any trace of grease or rust is undeniable. Similarly, the accusation that he discounted, even ignored, the contributions of human labor in the creation and servicing of his noble industrial forms seems relevant here, as it is throughout his oeuvre. Yet the intensity of Sheeler's formal means nevertheless argues for a visceral connection to this wondrous assemblage of linked components. His own personal identification with his immaculate mechanical world is perhaps conveyed by the only passage of the painting where the geometric rigor is relaxed: the single plume of smoke at lower right seemingly emanating from Sheeler's tiny signature like a cartoonish dialogue balloon. Though the mammoth Twentieth Century Limited might be momentarily stilled, the artist, an inveterate cigarette smoker, is nevertheless present and actively puffing away.

Further Reading

Fillin-Yeh, Susan. "Charles Sheeler's *Rolling Power*." In *The Railroad in American Art: Representations of Technological Change*, edited by Susan Danly and Leo Marx. Cambridge, Mass.: MIT Press, 1988, 147–64.

Lucic, Karen. *Charles Sheeler and the Cult of the Machine.* Cambridge, Mass.: Harvard University Press, 1991.

Troyen, Carol, and Erica E. Hirshler. *Charles Sheeler: Paintings and Drawings.* Boston: Little, Brown, 1987.

Lilly Martin Spencer

Exeter, England 1822–1902 New York, New York

Reading the Legend, 1852

Oil on canvas
50⅜ × 38 in. (127.9 × 96.5 cm)
Signed and dated, lower left: Lilly M. Spencer/Artist/1852
Gift of Adeline F. Wing, class of 1898, and Caroline R. Wing, class of 1896
1954:69

The extraordinary career of Lilly Martin Spencer stands alone in the middle decades of the nineteenth century. An indefatigable worker, she painted actively for over sixty years and, in her heyday, was virtually the only woman to achieve viability as a professional easel painter in the art capital of New York. Indeed, Spencer was the primary means of support for her family of eight children; her husband, Benjamin, an unsuccessful artist, served as her occasional assistant. Her pathbreaking achievements may be best understood against the background of her unusual upbringing in Ohio by French émigré parents deeply involved in the reform movements of communitarianism, abolitionism, and women's suffrage. Their proto-feminism was demonstrated early in Spencer's life when her emerging talent became evident; the household was broken up, and the father accompanied his teenage daughter to Cincinnati, where she began her professional career.

Life, though, was never easy for Spencer, and from the moment she moved to New York in 1849, she was forced to struggle for sales and recognition in an art world unaccustomed to the presence of a professional woman. She had high hopes of establishing herself as a history and literary painter, but like many American artists, she found the market unreceptive. In her case, critics made it clear that they preferred her still lifes and humorous domestic scenes — subjects thought to be more in keeping with her gender. A further blow came in 1851, when the American Art-Union, an art lottery that had consistently supported her, was declared illegal. In this climate, *Reading the Legend*, a romantic view of a young couple contemplating the picturesque ruins of Ireland's Blarney Castle, became one of her last attempts to work in a more elevated style. When the painting was shown at the National Academy of Design's annual exhibition of 1853, however, it was ignored by critics, and its subsequent appearance at art auctions in 1856 and 1860 indicates a similar lack of appreciation among collectors.

This public disinterest notwithstanding, *Reading the Legend* clearly demonstrates Spencer's mastery of the brush and the precepts of academic figure painting. The modeling of the couple and their dog is solid and complex, and throughout the composition the artist is attentive to surface textures — especially in the brilliantly rendered floral shawl, the slight impasto of the dotted lace fichu, and the way in which the silk dress and butternut coat wrinkle and stretch in response to the actions of the bodies beneath them. Light and dark values are kept in a state of dynamic balance, and the various levels of space are carved dramatically out of the rich, complementary chiaroscuro of the upper and lower halves.

Spencer builds a natural upward momentum into the composition, linking the shadowed ground plane with the soaring tower — blind and toothless — that rises like a dream from the dense undergrowth attempting to reclaim it. This line of visual narrative is anchored by the self-possessed dog, his sober expression and proprietary command of the cane and hat humorously suggesting a more gentlemanly demeanor than that of his nearby master, sprawled informally on the ground. Highlights then lead diagonally to the reflective woman, who functions as the crux of the composition. Unconsciously fingering the ribbons of her bonnet as it falls over her knee, she deflects attention through her uplifted gaze back to the castle itself, visualizing the story read aloud by her anonymous partner and thoughtfully mediating between text and image. By depicting the man with his back to the viewer, Spencer subtly constructs a painting embodying the woman's experience of the tale, creating a rare nineteenth-century alternative to the more typical masculine point of view.

Further Reading

Bolton-Smith, Robin, and William H. Truettner. *Lilly Martin Spencer, 1822–1902: The Joys of Sentiment.* Washington, D.C.: National Collection of Fine Arts, 1973.

Lubin, David M. *Picturing a Nation: Art and Social Change in Nineteenth-Century America.* New Haven, Conn.: Yale University Press, 1994.

223

Florine Stettheimer

Rochester, New York 1871–1944 New York, New York

Henry McBride, Art Critic, 1922

Oil on canvas

30 × 26 in. (76.2 × 66 cm)

Inscribed in green paint, within composition, middle left: B/HENRY H/McBRIDE Mc/Stetthei [obscured] Florine S; signed and dated in black paint on stretcher: By Florine Stettheimer 1922

Gift of Ettie Stettheimer, the artist's sister

1951:198

The art of Florine Stettheimer inhabits two overlapping worlds. One is highly personal and rarefied, intelligible only to the select group of friends and family privy to the visual puns and coy in-jokes seeded throughout her paintings. The other is more philosophically grounded in early-twentieth-century modernism, concerned with nonlinear theories of time, the flux of memory and intuition, and the exploration of phenomenological, flowing space. These worlds come together arrestingly in the series of what her fellow artist Marsden Hartley called "her fragrant portraits, . . . penetrations in the mind and spirit of these highly accentuated types." Her sisters and her mother—with whom she lived most of her life cocooned in the privileges of wealth—as well as a charming group of artists, writers, and dancers who flocked to the Stettheimer salon, all found themselves, along with their accomplishments and foibles, spread on the painter's canvases like pastel cake frosting. This highly original blend of sweetness and light, however, almost always carries multilayered associative meanings that season and transform the rococo prettiness for which her art has sometimes been dismissed.

The playful qualities of *Henry McBride, Art Critic* document a friendship that developed between artist and writer in their later careers; the portrait was executed when both were in their fifties. After a lackluster early career teaching art, McBride had begun writing criticism for the *New York Sun* in 1913. Gradually, he became an important advocate and interpreter of the advanced European art, notably Cubism, then making its way to America's shores. At the same time, he wrote sympathetically about the American avant-garde, furthering the careers of Georgia O'Keeffe and John Marin, among others. McBride appears to have first noticed Stettheimer's work in 1918, at an exhibition in New York. He continued to review her work enthusiastically for several years before making her acquaintance. By 1922, the year of the portrait, they had become good friends,

and McBride was a frequent guest that summer at the artist's vacation home in Sea Bright, New Jersey.

Stettheimer includes McBride's likeness five times in her painting—once at the center, where he looms in a grandmotherly way on a dowdy, triple-overstuffed rocking chair–throne, and four times in the portrait's quadrants, where his tiny, dapper figure locates itself in a series of fantastic scenes alluding to his hobbies and activities as a critic. A devotee of tennis, McBride clutches a scorecard for the Sea Bright International Tennis Tournament, which he followed with great interest that summer. Glancing to the lower left quadrant, he sees a smaller, identically dressed version of himself presiding as a line judge on the courts, the players—weightless sprites in white—pirouetting gaily on the lawns. To the right, McBride is pictured in a less formal moment, painting a winding picket fence reminiscent of one he had recently erected around his small farmhouse in Pennsylvania—a Tom Sawyerish project he complained of repeatedly in letters to the artist.

Above, two more renditions of the critic stand gazing into dreamy landscapes symbolizing the best of nineteenth- and twentieth-century American art. At right, three witty quotations from Winslow Homer's sea paintings of the 1880s and 1890s allude to McBride's interest in restoring the reputation of that painter (he launched a similar crusade on behalf of Thomas Eakins). And at left, in the most brilliant passage of the work, Marin-like skyscrapers tower above works representative of other contemporary painters he championed—a self-referential bouquet of flowers for Stettheimer and the famous *Standing Woman* of Gaston Lachaise, for example. Despite this service to his native culture, McBride was often criticized for elevating French art above that produced in New York. By choosing only American works of art for his portrait, Stettheimer might have been gently tweaking her friend for his Continental sympathies, literally waving the flag of patriotism above his demure, slightly dazed countenance.

Further Reading

Bloemink, Barbara J. *The Life and Art of Florine Stettheimer.* New Haven, Conn.: Yale University Press, 1995.

McBride, Henry. *Florine Stettheimer.* New York: The Museum of Modern Art, 1946.

Sussman, Elisabeth, et al. *Florine Stettheimer: Manhattan Fantastica.* New York: Whitney Museum of American Art, 1995.

John Storrs

Chicago, Illinois 1885–1956 Mer, Loir-et-Cher, France

Auto Tower, Industrial Forms, c. 1922

Painted plaster

12⅞ × 3¼ × 2⅞ in. (32.7 × 8.3 × 7.3 cm)

Inscribed in plaster on rear above base: JS [conjoined initials, S reversed] 2550

Purchased with funds given by Mr. and Mrs. Duncan Boeckman (Elizabeth Mayer, class of 1954)

1989:1

Among the small group of American sculptors working in the early twentieth century to incorporate the lessons of Cubism and Futurism into a professional practice still dominated by waning Beaux-Arts precepts, John Storrs is not as well known as might be expected. Storrs's inventive work forged a unity of expression between the plastic media of sculpture and architecture. In addition, his spiritual investment in the spare simplicity of distilled geometric form gave a weightier philosophical cast to the sometimes surface-oriented effects of the style that came to be known as Art Deco. Personal circumstances, however, forced him to divide his time between the Loire Valley in France and his hometown of Chicago, a frustrating situation for the artist, which prevented him from becoming fully integrated into the larger art centers of New York and Paris.

As a young student in his early twenties, Storrs searched restlessly for the right teachers and material examples of art that would speak to his developing aesthetic sense, and during a seven-year period he must have come close to setting a record in studying at no fewer than ten art academies in Hamburg, Paris, Chicago, Boston, and Philadelphia. The strong angularity of the Vienna Secession movement appealed to him, but perhaps his most profound influence in this early period was the powerful personality of the aged Auguste Rodin, whose palpable, quavering style would nevertheless have little to do with Storrs's mature, architectonic

work. By the time of his first one-person show in 1920, he had produced a number of cubist figural sculptures, the faceted planes of his blocky forms often strengthened and defined in space by selective surface painting. His primary experimental idiom, however, would become single, rectilinear towers—sleek and evocative in their suggestion of soaring skyscrapers, but self-contained sculptural statements, nonetheless, in their investigation of purely abstract volumes.

Auto Tower, Industrial Forms, while representative of these compositional essays in three-dimensional space, is somewhat anomalous in its specific iconography and witty transformative instability between architectural totem and upended automobile. Although not overly devoted to the cult of the machine, Storrs admired American technical ingenuity, and he was particularly fond of the stylish roadsters just then being introduced to the market. Through a complex series of flared curves, parallel incisions in the plaster, and judicious accents in black paint, he suggests the streamlined, speeding form of an open-topped auto, seemingly taking off like a rocket, its wheels spinning. The lower half of the work, in contrast, appears more sober in its thoughtful exploration of planar edges, deeply channeled voids, uncut surfaces, serrated textures, and mosaic patterns. These stark effects do not distance the work from the viewer, however, for far from being cold and clinical in its outward appearance, *Auto Tower, Industrial Forms* bears traces of the hand of its carver—scratches, smudges, and less-than-straight lines that humanize the sculpture and tell the tale of the playful fiddling with form that underlies its conception.

Further Reading

Frackman, Noel. *John Storrs.* New York: Whitney Museum of American Art, 1987.

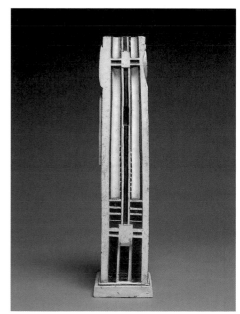

227

Gilbert Stuart

North Kingston, Rhode Island 1755–1828 Boston, Massachusetts

Henrietta Elizabeth Frederica Vane, 1783

Oil on canvas

65⅞ × 38⅝ in. (167.3 × 98.1 cm)

Not signed or dated

Gift in memory of Jessie Rand Goldthwait, class of 1890, by her husband, Dr. Joel E. Goldthwait, and daughter, Mrs. Charles Lincoln Taylor (Margaret Rand Goldthwait, class of 1921)

1957:39

Gilbert Stuart's portrait of the ten-year-old Henrietta Elizabeth Frederica Vane — a rarity in his oeuvre in that he did few full-length canvases and even fewer of children — came at a propitious moment in his early career. The young colonial had attempted to establish himself in London in 1775, but after a year or so of penury and near-starvation, he had somewhat sheepishly become a student and assistant of his compatriot, Benjamin West, whose success in England inspired many a late-eighteenth-century American artist. Stuart chafed under the less talented West, but his deliverance came in 1782, when his novel portrait of William Grant (*The Skater,* National Gallery of Art, Washington, D.C.) became a sensation after it was unveiled at the Royal Academy annual exhibition. This was the recognition he needed to enable him to move out on his own into the competitive London portrait trade, and soon thereafter the parents of Henrietta Vane, a Norfolk branch of a family studded with noble titles, commissioned this portrait of their only daughter and heiress.

Stuart places his well-dressed sitter in a generalized outdoor setting in keeping with the standards of British portraiture of the era. Her childish figure is made to seem grander and more imposing through the device of the heavy cloak that engulfs her and passes over her extended arm. This upward-reaching gesture provides some focus to her pose, as she delicately grasps the trailing vine of a trumpet honeysuckle plant. The meandering sprig appears to wind down to meet her light-tipped fingers, and her touch almost seems to pull it into a more tangible, concrete existence, at odds with the translucent, generalized dabs of foliage surrounding it. Below, for example, a basket of flowers already gathered is treated in a most summary fashion, as though it were being glimpsed through shifting, shadowed waters.

In this confident pictorial statement, the twenty-eight-year-old artist announces his mastery of the free, painterly style and radiant, silvery illumination that were the hallmarks of the aristocratic English likeness. The sky is vigorous and brushy, with rich yellow paint casually scribbled into the blue surrounding her head, the clouds retreating in this area so as to form a kind of azure halo. Her dress is resplendently luminous, the long, looping strokes of white melting into the transparent gray underlayer. Throughout, there is a pleasing fullness to Stuart's paint, nowhere more so than in the rich bronze-colored fabric accents to her costume — the oversize bows and, in particular, the dramatic hat, its floral sunburst built up as if with gesso. The blend of color on her face is, appropriately, more modulated and smooth, with the slight plumpness in the cheeks contrasting nicely with the delicate point of her chin, a feature that has prompted some viewers to discern a slightly impish quality in this otherwise poised and self-possessed youngster.

Further Reading

Evans, Dorinda. *The Genius of Gilbert Stuart.* Princeton, N.J.: Princeton University Press, 1999.

McLanathan, Richard. *Gilbert Stuart.* New York: Harry N. Abrams, 1986.

Dwight William Tryon

Hartford, Connecticut 1849–1925 South Dartmouth, Massachusetts

The First Leaves, 1889

Oil on wood panel
32 × 40 in. (81.3 × 101.6 cm)
Signed in blue-green paint, lower right: D. W. TRYON
Purchased from the artist
1889:6-1

The artist most closely linked to Smith College is surely Dwight Tryon. A professor at the college for some four decades (during which time he was a prominent figure in New York art circles), he brought a level of professional renown to Smith that few educational institutions could match. Though Tryon only visited the campus every three weeks to offer criticism to students, he worked hard on Smith's behalf, playing a significant role in expanding the college's collections through his many donations as well as his encouragement of other strategic gifts and purchases. On his retirement, he and his wife gave the funds to construct Smith's first freestanding art museum, the Tryon Gallery.

Tryon studied in France for nearly five years, and when he sailed back to New York in 1881, he bore the distinct imprint of the Barbizon tradition, a plaintive, summary style that he had imbibed through contact with such older artists as Charles-François Daubigny. In this he was not alone, and during the early years of his career his broad, solidly composed landscapes had little to distinguish them from many others then being produced by young painters returning from extended periods of European study. In May 1889, however, several years after joining the Smith faculty, Tryon was taking one of his habitual walks through the countryside surrounding his summer home in South Dartmouth, Massachusetts, when he was seized by the arresting motif of a line of slender birches, just beginning to leaf out, at the edge of a field. This became The First Leaves, a turning point in his life that stands as the template for nearly all that followed in his lengthy career.

The formula Tryon hit on consists of three rigorously parallel bands: meadow, trees, and sky — with the tips of the diaphanous branches forming a continuous, slightly humpy rhythm of two-dimensional "hillocks"

traced against the creamy sky. The architecture of the composition is simple and clear, but this reduced, distilled quality in no way precludes the creation of the rich, poetic effects for which Tryon became famous — particularly his stylistic hallmark, the shimmering, feathery brushwork. His application of paint here is rapid and discontinuous. The foreground area consists of a web of impasto strokes smeared onto the panel, with the reddish color of the wood support occasionally remaining visible. Tryon's dabbing brush moves in many different directions, but his active surface nevertheless leaves a quiet, peaceful impression — the fresh, mossy green of new spring growth lingering like a mist among the yellowed, winter-desiccated weeds. The middle zone is even more variegated in tone, with a mosaic of mustard, brown, chestnut, and lavender strokes giving a sense of spatial depth to the distant hills.

The manner in which this bewildering mix of pastel hues holds together and coalesces into a logical, if abstractive, whole was something new in American art, and The First Leaves accordingly won the Webb Prize of the Society of American Artists for the most promising landscape by an American artist under forty. Critics were favorably impressed by the painting's originality, with the New York Sun dubbing it "perhaps the finest landscape of the year." Although his style is today known as Tonalism, reviewers in 1889 were hard-pressed to define Tryon's "new look." The Magazine of Art observed that its "effect of delicate iridescence of color" had "something of the quality of a Sisley," and the New York Times likewise found the color scheme suggestive of "the extreme impressionism of France." In time, Tryon's style would seem less radical, but even those who found this early painting unsuccessful, like the critic for the New York Tribune, had to admit that it definitely revealed "new lines of progress" for the future.

Further Reading

Merrill, Linda. An Ideal Country: Paintings by Dwight William Tryon in the Freer Gallery of Art. Washington, D.C.: Freer Gallery of Art, 1990.

White, Henry C. The Life and Art of Dwight William Tryon. Boston: Houghton Mifflin Co., 1930.

James McNeill Whistler

Lowell, Massachusetts 1834–1903 London, England

Mrs. Lewis Jarvis (Ada Maud Vesey-Dawson Jarvis), 1879

Oil on canvas
25 × 16 in. (63.5 × 40.7 cm)
Not signed or dated
Purchased, Winthrop Hillyer Fund
1908:2-1

Whistler's portrait of the Irish wife of his friend and supporter, a Bedfordshire gentleman brewer with artistic pretensions, was executed during one of the most difficult moments in the painter's career, and the rushed sitting and uncharacteristic bust format he was forced to employ for the sake of expediency left him dissatisfied with the result. Still, in its wistful, subdued range of dim pastels and its demure, ghostlike quality, *Mrs. Lewis Jarvis* stands as a fully representative example of the highly aesthetic, consciously distilled art of Whistler, which during the decade of the 1870s more than any other was greatly concerned with portraiture.

In the months leading up to the Jarvis likeness, the artist had suffered a very public humiliation when his libel suit against the imperious, conservative critic John Ruskin netted him a paltry farthing in damages. Whistler had spent a great deal in court costs, and at the same time, his relationships with formerly supportive patrons and creditors, such as Frederick Leyland, were faltering. Forced into bankruptcy in the spring of 1879, Whistler reluctantly put his beloved "White House" in London up for sale, made plans for an auction of his possessions, and prepared to depart for Venice, where he would spend more than a year recuperating from these setbacks. In this darkest hour, Whistler's friend, Lewis Jarvis, lent him fifty pounds, though he himself could ill afford it and had no hope of ever seeing it repaid. In thanks, the artist agreed to paint a portrait of Lewis's wife, Ada. She traveled to London for a sitting in mid-August, even as her host was packing for his departure.

Whistler's canvas is rough and irregular in its weave, creating a constant underlying texture, which his evanescent image never fully covers. As a result, Lewis's faint visage seems thin and hovering, stained onto the fabric rather than painted—absorbed into its thirsty fibers. The hues are low in tone, the dress a light coppery green, the background the palest of lavender-grays, and her hair a slightly richer auburn, a soft patch of ambient color that gives no real sense of local texture. Her eyes are hazel and seem somewhat small and intense set within her fine, carefully modeled face (traces of delicate drawing are visible at the chin, nose, and ears). All in all, her calm, retreating, but nevertheless iconic form seems to repel both the bright light of the modern gallery and the probing gaze of the interested viewer. This effect is accentuated by Whistler's reeded, burnished gold-leaf frame, which further quiets the wan image within.

Further Reading

Houfe, Simon. "Whistler in the Country: His Unrecorded Friendship with Lewis Jarvis." *Apollo* 98 (October 1973): 282–85.

Young, Andrew McLaren, et al. *The Paintings of James McNeill Whistler*. 2 vols. New Haven, Conn.: Yale University Press, 1980.

INDEX